U.S. Aerial Armament in World War II Vol. 2

U.S. Aerial Armament in World War II

The Ultimate Look:

Vol. 2: Bombs, Bombsights, and Bombing

William Wolf

Schiffer Military History
Atglen, PA

Book Design by Ian Robertson and Stephanie Daugherty.

Library of Congress Control Number: 2009925581

Printed in China.
ISBN: 978-0-7643-3524-2

We are interested in hearing from authors with book ideas on related topics.

Published by Schiffer Publishing Ltd.
4880 Lower Valley Road
Atglen, PA 19310
Phone: (610) 593-1777
FAX: (610) 593-2002
E-mail: Info@schifferbooks.com.
Visit our web site at: www.schifferbooks.com
Please write for a free catalog.
This book may be purchased from the publisher.
Please include $5.00 postage.
Try your bookstore first.

In Europe, Schiffer books are distributed by:
Bushwood Books
6 Marksbury Avenue
Kew Gardens
Surrey TW9 4JF, England
Phone: 44 (0) 20 8392-8585
FAX: 44 (0) 20 8392-9876
E-mail: Info@bushwoodbooks.co.uk.
Visit our website at: www.bushwoodbooks.co.uk
Free postage in the UK. Europe: air mail at cost.
Try your bookstore first.

Contents

Preface

While researching and writing my "Ultimate Look" series of bomber books, including the B-29, B-32, B-18, and B-25, I realized two things. One, that there was no definitive book available regarding American World War II aerial armament and ordnance. Two, I had a large source of technical manuals, microfilm, books, and magazines in my library on the various aspects of the subject on which I had to spend hours and hours digging out research material for these Ultimate Look bomber books. It was not long into my gathering of data that I realized that the massive subject would have to be divided into two books: Volume 1 on Guns, Ammunition, and Turrets (which is available) and a second volume on U.S. Air-Dropped Weapons. Then, while I was gathering material for Volume 2 I found it also would have to be divided into two volumes: this volume on Bombs, Bombsights, and Bombing; and Volume 3 on Air-Dropped, Air-Launched, and Secret Weapons. I hope this volume will serve as an easy to reference and definitive work on the subject for WWII aviation historians, modelers, and enthusiasts.

Acknowledgments

My lifelong hobby has been WWII aerial combat, and over the past 35 years I have collected over 16,000 books and magazines, along with over a thousand reels of microfilm on the subject. I probably have nearly every book written on WWII aviation and complete collections of every combat aviation magazine published since 1939. Also included in my collection are hundreds of aviation unit histories; intelligence reports; pilot, crew, flight, and training manuals; and technical, structural, and maintenance manuals for aircraft ordnance, armament, engines, and equipment. My microfilm collection includes vintage intelligence reports; hundreds of USAF, USN, and USMC group and squadron histories and After Combat Reports; complete Japanese Monograph series; and complete U.S. Strategic Bombing Surveys, as well as complete USAF Historical Studies. Over the years I have been fortunate to meet many fighter aces, other pilots, and fellow aviation buffs who have shared stories, material, and photographs with me (I have over 5,000 photos of fighter aces alone). I have made numerous multi-day expeditions to various military libraries, museums, and photo depositories with my copy machine and camera, accumulating literally reams of information and 1,000s of photographs. Also, in particular, I wish to thank George Eaton, ASC Command Historian at the Rock Island Arsenal, for his invaluable help in securing access to several Bombing Technical Manuals.

Over the past decade I have completed ten books on WWII aviation that included many hundreds of photos and drawings, many in color. Most of the photos gathered for this volume and the others were from the WWII era and before, and over the years were not well cared for and showed their age. As described above, almost all were copies or copies of copies were made before the Digital/Photoshop Age by a standard film 35mm camera on a copy stand; many hundreds at a time over several days while visiting various facilities. At one time I had a photo darkroom where I developed 1,000s of rare photos from microfilm negatives which were not of the best quality. Many photos were copied from printed dot-type photos from contemporary World War II publications. The reproductions of the many technical drawings were made by my non-digital drum copy machine 20 years ago or more from yellowed manuals that originally were poorly printed on poor quality wartime paper. So I apologize in advance for the quality of some photos and drawings in this book (despite being photo-shopped), but I feel photos of marginal quality are better than no photos in describing topics in this book.

The author wishes that every person who contributed photos and materials to my collection over the past 35 years could be specifically mentioned. Over the years the origin of some of the 1,000s of photos I have been lent to copy or have copied and collected have become obscured. Most are from military and government sources, but many are from private individuals, so I also apologize if some of the photos are wrongly credited.

And last but not least, for the tenth time thanks go to my persevering wife, Nancy, who allows me to spend many hours researching and writing, and patiently (mostly) waits while I browse bookstores and visit air museums in search of new material and photos. Also, I thank her because her car sits out in the hot Arizona sun as my WWII library luxuriates in the remodeled, air-conditioned three-car garage.

1

The Development of Bombs and Bombing Theory and Strategy

Pre-1900

On 4 June 1783, the Montgolfier brothers, Joseph and Jacques, demonstrated a tethered-lined silk balloon in the marketplace at Annonay, France. Soon after, on 15 October 1783, Pilatre de Rozier and Marquis d'Arlandes became the first human passengers on a Montgolfier free flight balloon. Once manned flights occurred dire predictions arose of cities being destroyed from the sky. But it was evident that the hot air and hydrogen balloons which appeared simultaneously would not be a suitable platform for aerial bombardment, as they were dependent on the caprice of the shifting winds. The only use which the military could find for them was to tether them to the ground and use them for observation posts. To be of any real use for reconnaissance or as a carrier of bombs the balloon had to be able to move and be steered. As early as 1785 French military engineer Jean-Baptiste-Marie Meusnier designed an ellipsoidal steerable balloon; however, it lacked a viable powering unit. It would not be until September 1852 when Henri Giffard developed a hydrogen-filled elongated envelope that was moved by a three horse power steam engine fueled with 500 pounds of coke. The first powered and navigated flight in history took place when Giffard took off from the Paris Hippodrome, sailed 17 miles at six mph over the city and suburbs, and landed at Trappe. The curiosity gave the military the future promise of being able not only to perform a reconnaissance role, but also to drop bombs on a selected target.

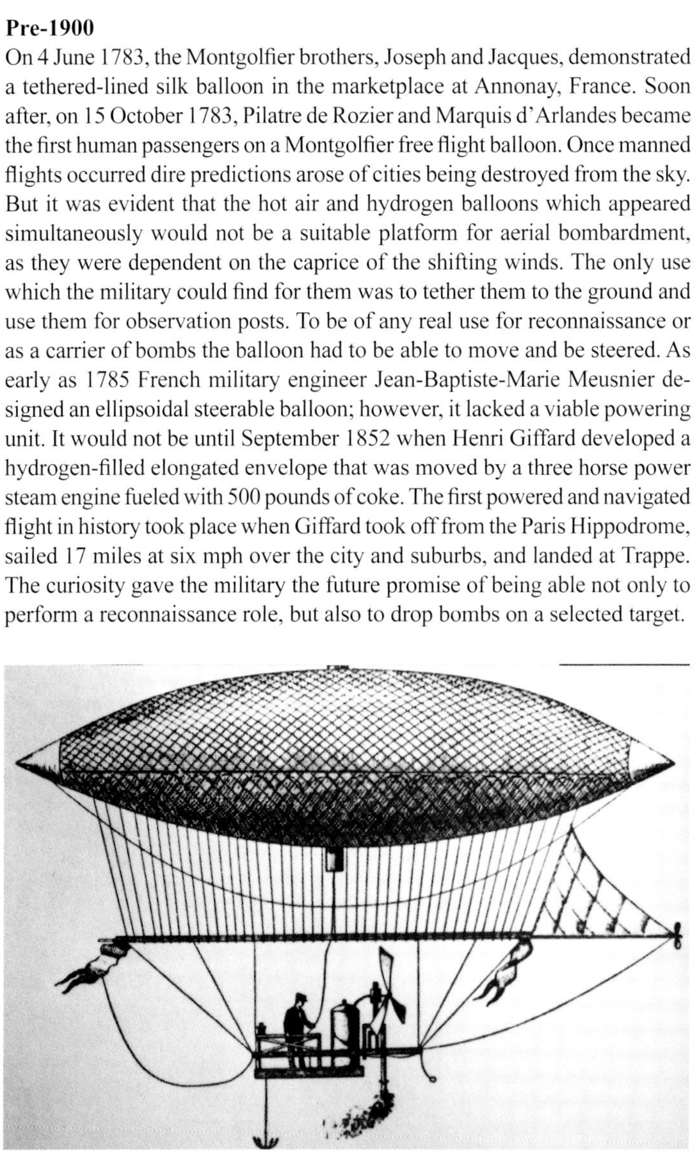

The first powered and navigated flight in history took place when **Henri Giffard** took off in a dirigible from the Paris Hippodrome when he sailed 17 miles at six mph over the city. (Author/AFHRC)

In 1848 the European revolutions had spread to Venice, which declared itself a republic free of Austrian rule. By the next year the city was surrounded by Austrian troops commanded by the acclaimed Field Marshall Joseph Radetzky, but on the Adriatic Sea side of the city the naval blockade had been ineffective due to the weakness of the Austrian fleet. To break the impasse Radetzky considered the suggestion of bombing Venice from the air using hot balloons carrying explosive devices. Brothers Franz and Josef Uchatius, *Artillerie-Oberleutnants*, developed a cast iron pear-shaped bomb called a "luft torpedo" that was to be suspended below an unmanned 18.67 foot diameter spherical paper hot air balloon capable of lifting about 66 pounds. The 48 pound bomb was attached below the fire pan by a lanyard with a suspension ring at the top and a percussion fuse striker protruding from the bottom to ignite its black powder charge. The balloons were released from a naval vessel in a favorable wind, to rise and float over the city where a time fuse would sever the lanyard and the bomb would fall, and the striker would be compressed on contact, causing the bomb to explode. Due to the fickle winds many of the launched balloons dropped their bombs in the sea or the lagoon. However, a few bombs actually dropped on Venice, and on 15 July one struck the Lido and another hit the ground in the public gardens, causing little physical damage, but they did instigate some panic and intimidation of the population. The Uchatius brother's luft torpedo was the archetype of the aerial bomb, a pear-shaped missile with tail fins and a nose percussion cap.

Giffard's airship was the forerunner of airships which progressively increased in size and power as the end of the nineteenth century neared. Airships were slow, subject to the vagaries of the weather, required large ground crews and hydrogen making equipment, and large sheds in which to house them. At the turn of the century Germany would dominate the air with her large Zeppelin and Schutte-Lanz airships and the smaller Parsevals. It was not long before the German military saw the Zeppelin's potential and conducted some early bomb dropping experiments from them.

French inventor and engineer Clement Ader was credited with the first self-propelled flight in history when his steam-powered aircraft, the *Eole*, took off and flew approximately 150 feet on 9 October 1890. Ader's work attracted the interest of Charles de Freycinet, the French minister of war, who contracted Ader in February 1892 to develop and construct the world's first military aircraft, the *Avion III*, which was to carry 150 pounds of bombs in place of the observer. The bat-like bomber had a wingspan of 48 feet and was powered by two steam engines. There are conflicting reports concerning its initial flight on 14 October 1897, with some spectators verifying that the aircraft got off the ground and flew 900 feet, while

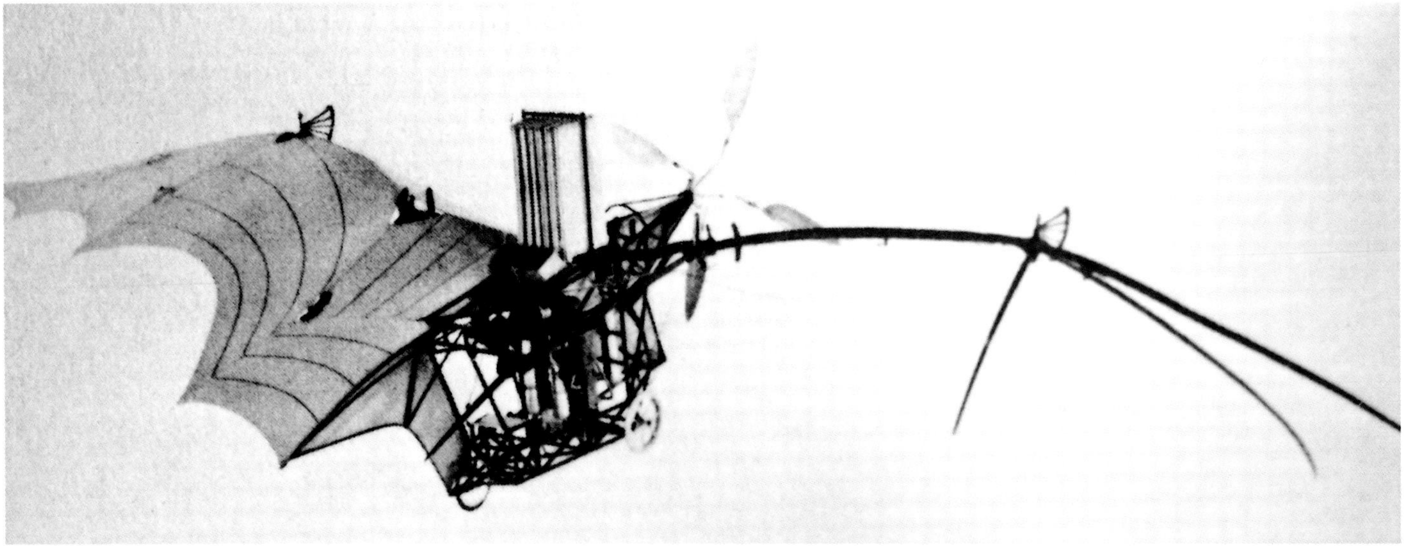

Ader's steam-powered bat-like aircraft, the ***Eole***, took off and flew approximately 150 feet on 9 October 1890. (Author)

others stated the *Avion* crashed before takeoff. Perhaps the latter report is correct, as Ader's funding was withdrawn, but six years later, when the Wright Brothers made their successful flight, the French suddenly released reports stating that Ader's flights were successful.

Pre-World War I

In 1909 Clement Ader published his very popular book, *L'Aviation Militaire*, in which he promoted his vision of the airplane for use as a weapon in war and discussed the use and organization of a military air service. Ader submitted a precise description of the concept of the modern aircraft carrier and allocated a large portion of his book to the types of "missiles" (bombs) to be used and the methods of aiming them. The French military maneuvers of 1910 used the airplane for the first time, and it was so successful in its role that by 1912 the French air wing, the *Avaition Militiare*, had 234 aircraft in its inventory.

During the Italian-Turkish War of 1911-12 the Italians sent an ultimatum to Turkey to relinquish Tripoli and Cyrenaica (Libya) on the North African Mediterranean coast. In mid-October 1911 Italy sent the *Flottiglia Aeroplani*, consisting of nine aircraft and 11 pilots under the command of Capt. Carlo Piazza, to Libya. The first ever wartime flight was made on 23 October 1911 by Capt. Piazza on a reconnaissance flight in a Blériot XI over Aziza. Three days later Piazza and Capt. Ricardo Moizo directed Italian naval gunfire on Turkish forces. But it was not until 1 November that Lt. Giulio Gavotti, flying a Taube monoplane, dropped the first bombs in wartime. Gavotti carried four 4.5 pound grenade-type Cipelli bombs in a leather bag with the detonators in his pocket. He flew 60 miles to a Turkish camp in the town of Ain Zara, where he assembled the bombs on his lap and dropped them individually on four passes over the target. While the damage done was insignificant, Gavotti was celebrated by the Italian Press as the first aviator to drop bombs in wartime.

French inventor and engineer **Clement Ader** has often been credited with the first self-propelled flight in history. (Author/AFHRC)

Pre-World War I America

In the years before the start of the World War I, the military leaders of all nations showed little interest in the use of airships or aircraft as offensive weapons, and only thought of them in an observation/reconnaissance role at best. The U.S. Army was not unlike its European counterparts, and probably was even more conservative in regard to the use of the military aircraft. The first American military aircraft was a Wright Flyer purchased in 1909 by the Signal Corps for trials and was followed by the purchase of a Curtiss pusher. In early 1910, to promote his aircraft Glenn Curtiss dropped dummy bombs on a target on the waters of Lake Keuka, in upper New York State. Then, in July Curtiss dropped three oranges onto the deck of a yacht which was standing in for a warship during exercises off Atlantic City, NJ.

Left: In 1910 American aviation pioneer and manufacturer **Glenn Curtiss** promoted his aircraft's military potential by dropping dummy bombs on a target on Lake Keuka, NY, and then dropping three oranges onto the deck of a yacht that was standing in for a warship during exercises off Atlantic City, NJ. (Author)

Right: On 19 January 1910 **1Lt. Paul Beck** conducted a rudimentary bombing test demonstration at the large international 1910 Los Angeles Air Meet, dropping inert bombs of varying weights. (Author)

Famous English aviator **Claude Grahame-White** appeared at the Harvard-Boston flying meet held on 3-13 September 1910 and won most monetary prizes, including a "bombing contest," scoring the most hits with Plaster of Paris bombs on a mock warship. (Author)

At the Harvard-Boston meet American **Arthur Johnson** finished second in the bombing contest flying a Wright biplane. (Author)

The War Department delegated 1Lt. Paul Beck of the U.S. Infantry to act as its representative at the large international 1910 Los Angeles Air Meet. Beck was commissioned as a 2Lt. in the U.S. Army in September 1899 and went on to graduate from the Infantry School and Cavalry School. He was then assigned to the Signal Corps in 1907 and was selected to attend the first aviation school in San Diego, CA, where he was taught by Glenn Curtiss. On 19 January 1910 Beck, together with Phillip Paulham, conducted a rudimentary bombing test demonstration, dropping inert bombs of varying weights to determine the bomb's effect on the aircraft's equilibrium and also to find whether or not they could hit a target on the ground. They dropped bombs of up to 15 pounds with reasonable accuracy and without affecting equilibrium. However, the basic bombing tables Beck calculated were found to be inaccurate and unusable.

In 1910 the Harvard Aeronautical Society offered the then princely sum of $50,000 to the famed English aviator, Claude Grahame-White, to appear in the Harvard-Boston flying meet held on 3-13 September. No aviation meet up to that time had such a representative list of American and international aviators, and included 17 aviators flying 11 types of aircraft competing for the $40,000 in prize money in a dozen events. Grahame-White opened the first flying school in Britain in 1909, and then was the first English pilot to carry mail and the first to fly by night. He flew the *Daily Mail's* air race in 1910 and the Gordon Bennett Race in the U.S. the same year, winning the latter.

Although Grahame-White was the major attraction of the meet, he was to compete in various flying contests against such American aviation notables as Glenn Curtiss, Walter Brookins, Charles Willard, and international fliers such as A.V. Roe and Didier Masson. Observers in the crowd for the first major air show on the East Coast included President William Howard Taft and an upcoming New York politician named Franklin Roosevelt. Grahame-White flew passengers for $500 and then proceeded to pick up another $22,000 in flying contest prize money. He won first prizes for speed, landing accuracy, and shortest takeoff (27 feet), and collected $10,000 for making two over water round trips to the Boston Light and back. Grahame-White, flying a Farman, also won a "bombing contest," scoring the most hits with plaster of Paris bombs on a mock warship set up in a field. American Arthur Johnson finished second flying a Wright biplane.

During the 7 January 1911 air meet at Tanforan, an empty area adjacent to Selfridge Field, near San Francisco, 1Lt. Myron Crissy of the Coastal Artillery demonstrated his 12 inch long, 36 pound, finless, pear-shaped bomb with a cast iron nose and a conical sheet iron body. Crissy also devised a bomb release apparatus and a set of tables which enabled him to determine mathematically with substantial accuracy where the bombs would strike the ground from varying altitudes. These experiments were successful, showing conclusively that a weight up to 36 pounds could be dropped within 20 feet of the target from an altitude of 1,500 feet, and Crissy became the first man to drop a live bomb from an aircraft.

1Lt. Riley E. Scott of the Coast Artillery was convinced that with the correct utilization of scientific principles bombs could be dropped accurately. On 10 October 1911 he demonstrated his bomb sighting mechanism/release gear at the U.S. Signals Corps Aviation summer base at College Park, MD, from a Wright Model B piloted by Lt. Thomas DeWitt Milling.

During the 7 January 1911 air meet at Tanforan, near San Francisco, **1Lt. Myron Crissy** (right) of the Coastal Artillery demonstrated his 12 inch long, 36 pound, finless, pear-shaped bomb with a cast iron nose and a conical sheet iron body. (Author)

The apparatus weighed 64 pounds, but if constructed of light metals and simplified Scott thought he could reduce the weight to approximately 40 pounds. A small viewing tube telescope, pivoting on a quadrant in a front to rear direction, served first for determining the actual speed over the ground of the aircraft in flight by solving a right angle triangle with two known sides, height above the ground from an altimeter reading and a stop-watch reading upon passing over a previously observed ground position. Tables were prepared for reference so there would be no necessity of making computations in flight. Scott lay prone on the lower wing with the device immediately in front of the wing.

Scott's two 18 pound practice bombs were streamlined with tail fins attached to a tubular extension and were suspended from the aircraft horizontally. Both were to be released at the same time so the balance of the sighting would not be disrupted. The tables were prepared for 400 feet altitude; consequently, the trial flights were made from the altitude, although Scott realized that 3,000 feet was probably the safe minimum altitude in combat. On the first trial, with Lt. Milling as the pilot of the Wright B biplane, Scott missed the target by 62 feet; the second time, the bombs fell about 32 feet to the right of the target. On Scott's final try both bombs landed within 10 feet of the 4x5 foot target. In an effort to determine what an inexperienced bombardier could do, Sgt. Idzorek of the Signal Corps replaced Scott on one flight. Sgt. Idzorek missed the target by only 11 inches, demonstrating that the apparatus was dependable, even when operated by an inexperienced bombardier. After these Scott wanted to conduct further tests from 3,000 feet, but he was committed to a bomb dropping competition in France.

Scott resigned his commission to take part in the Concourse de l'Aero-Cible Michelin held at Chalons Camp, France, in the first half of 1912. The competition, offering generous prizes, was sponsored by the Michelin brothers, and a large 50,000 Franc prize was offered the best performance in dropping 15 regulation missiles of six inches in diameter and weighing 15 pounds from a height of 200 m (660 ft.) or more into a circle of 10 m (33 ft.) radius. Another prize of 25,000 Francs was offered for the greatest number of projectiles placed within a rectangular target representing the shed of a dirigible balloon, 40x120 m (132x396 ft.), from a height of 800 m (2,640 ft.). In addition, there was a special, prize of 10,000 Francs for the most scientific and practical apparatus entered, whether the winner of a prize or not. The first trials were held in July, and of the 10 competitors only Scott was not French. To qualify Scott built a new version of his 1910 bomb dropping apparatus and sight in France and installed it in an Astra-

In August 1912 **Riley Scott** (left), formerly of the Coast Artillery, took part in the French Michelin-sponsored air meet, which offered a large prize for the best performance in dropping 15 regulation missiles of six inches in diameter and weighing 15 pounds from a height of 600 feet or more into a circle of 30 foot radius. (Author)

Scott's bombs were streamlined with tail fins attached to a tubular extension and were suspended from the aircraft horizontally, and enabled him to win the contest over the conventional spherical bombs of the time. (Author)

built Wright airplane. Since Scott was not a pilot he engaged a Frenchman named Lt. Gaubert. All the other competitors flew Farman aircraft and used the standard spherical projectiles stipulated for the competition, and generally their dropping and sighting mechanisms were rudimentary. Scott was able to get his own specially-shaped bombs accepted by the competition organizers as the actual shape of the missiles was not specified, only their weight and volume. On 16 August 1912, the final day of the competition, in poor weather, Scott and Gaubert won the competition by landing 12 of 15 bombs in the ten meter circle from 200 m and eight of 15 from 800 m, easily beating the second place finisher. Scott's performance was so outstanding that he won all the prizes offered at the competition, but his win was not popular with the other competitors, who complained that he did not use the spherical competition bombs and his bomb dropper, although manufactured in France, was designed in America. Scott had satisfied the competition committee before the contest began, and the judges realized that his streamlined bombs were more practical than the spherical bombs, and that the use of a streamlined bomb designed by Scott with a guiding set of tail fins would be the bomb design of the future; so much so that both Germany and France adopted his bombsight (dropper).

In 1910 Didier Masson was a mechanic for French aviator Louis Paulhan, who was flying an American exhibition tour, and after the tour Masson decided to remain in the U.S. to barnstorm on his own. In early 1913, while in Los Angeles, Masson was recruited by Mexican rebels who offered him $300 a month base pay, plus $50 for each reconnaissance flight, and $250 for every bombing run. He was equipped with a 75 hp Martin pusher biplane that could fly 100 miles carrying a passenger and 150 pounds of bombs. The aircraft, named the *Sonora*, was smuggled by truck across the Arizona/Mexican border and on to Hermosillo, where rebel railway workers converted the Martin into a bomber by adding a bombardier's seat, an ingenious bombsight, and a bomb rack. Masson's mechanic, Thomas Dean, fabricated 30 pound bombs from 18 inch sections of iron pipe, packing each bomb with sticks of dynamite and steel rivets and screwing a cap on each end. A detonator rod protruded from the nose cap with a safety clip keeping the rod from moving until just before the bomb was dropped. At the rear end of the bomb another rod held the directional fins. The bombardier pulled a cord, which withdrew the safety clip and simultaneously released the bomb from the rack slung under the bomber. A basic bombsight was fashioned from a square with cross wires attached to a pivoting rod fastened to the bombardier's seat. Through trial and error, the bombardier could adjust the angle of the sight to the best position for bombing at a given speed and altitude. On 30 May 1913, Masson and his Mexican bombardier-observer, Capt. Joaquin Alcalde, took off on the world's first aerial bombing of a warship. Flying into a fusillade of return fire the *Sonora*, flying at an altitude of 2,500 feet, dropped their bombs on the Mexican government gunboat *General Guerrero* but made no hits. The next day the two airmen attacked the *Guerrero* again with the same negative results. After making a number of adjustments to the bomb's fins and the sight Masson again failed to score a hit on his third attempt, and on his fourth he crashed on takeoff and had to wait four weeks while replacement parts were smuggled from America. Once the *Sonora* was repaired Masson resumed his attacks on the gunboats with Thomas Dean as bombardier. After failing on the next two attacks, on the third attack the *Sonora's* Curtiss engine was hit by gunfire and stopped, but Masson was able to glide into friendly territory and land safely with minor damage. The next day, Masson and Dean took off and soon the engine failed, and after struggling back to base the two aviators resigned. Masson remained in America, and during World War I he flew with the Americans in the *Lafayette Escadrille*.

Didier Masson (left) and Thomas Dean in the Martin pusher *Sonora* prior to a bombing mission for Rebel forces on government gunboats during the 1913 Mexican Revolution. (Author)

American soldier of fortune **Leonard Bonney** flew a Moisant pusher biplane for the Mexican government during the Civil War of 1913-15 against revolutionaries In dive bombing attacks Bonney threw small bombs from his aircraft armed with shotgun shell detonators. (Author)

The first use of dive-bombing should probably be credited to Leonard Warden Bonney, an American soldier of fortune who was taught to fly by the Wright Brothers. Bonney was paid to fly a Moisant pusher biplane for Gen. Venustiano Carranza's Mexican government during the Civil War of 1913-15 against revolutionaries in Tampico and Vera Cruz. During 1913 Bonney threw small bombs from his aircraft armed with shotgun shell detonators that had been developed by Mexican mining engineers. Bonney put his aircraft in a shallow diving attack from about 1,500 feet, aiming his aircraft directly at the target without using any sighting device, dropping the bombs just as he pulled out of his dive. Bonney claimed to hit his target about half the time, but his aircraft was hit by numerous bullets from the ground. During WWI Bonney became a USN flight instructor and an early proponent of dive-bombing in that service.

World War I

In the several years before World War I, the attitude of the future major combatants toward the military airplane was that it was to be primarily used as a reconnaissance instrument. They felt that the addition of guns and bombs would only detract from the efficiency of the small number of reconnaissance aircraft that would be required. The few concerned aerial warfare tacticians determined that bombing problems could be separated into three elements: the bomb, the method by which it could be carried and released, and the aiming of the bomb. The first two problems were uncomplicated and a mechanical solution could be provided, but the third problem, aiming the bomb so that it would hit a selected target, was the most difficult to solve.

At the start of the war none of the major powers had a functional bomb or a bomb aiming sight in their inventory. Those bombs and sights that were available were simple devices which could not function in the crude, drafty, rolling, and vibrating contraptions that passed for aircraft in 1914. Combatants on both sides used early air-dropped gravity weapons called Flechettes (French for "dart" or "little arrow"), which were pointed steel projectiles four inches long and weighing a several ounces, fitted with a vaned tail for stable flight. These weapons were dropped from aircraft or Zeppelins over enemy trenches or airfields and were capable of penetrating a helmet and the wearer's skull.

In 1912 the Germans developed the APK (Artillery Test Commission) bomb, which was the first bomb specifically intended for aircraft use. It was a spherical cast iron shell filled with high explosive and detonated by an impact fuse, and was produced in five kg and 10 kg sizes, but was found to be too light for effective aerial use and did not see combat. A similar type of bomb was designed by F. Martin Hale in 1913 for the Royal Navy Air Service which pioneered British bombing. The first Hale bomb was a 20 pound version, but by early 1915 10 and 100 pound types were being manufactured.

By 1915 the French, since they considered bombing as a logical extension of artillery, adapted crude bombs from artillery shells fitted with tail fins and equipped their day bombing air units with them. The most commonly used shells were 75, 90, and 155 mm caliber. The modified 75 mm artillery shell became the most widely used and successful of the French bombs throughout the war. Because the French were much less interested in strategic bombing than the Allies they had no need of large bombs, although later in the war the French developed more conventional bombs, such as the 22, 55, and 110 pound Gros-Andreau types.

As the war progressed, a considerable range of bombs and other missiles was produced to meet the specific needs of the two British air services, the Royal Naval Air Service (RNAS) and the Royal Flying Corps (RFC). Some were designed by private venture, but the majority were designed

The majority of British bombs were designed and produced by the Royal Laboratory and the Royal Aircraft Factory, with the RNAS generally preferring the former manufacturer and the RFC the latter. Pictured are 1,100 and 550 pound bombs used in the last year of the war by large Handley-Page bombers. (Author/AFHRC)

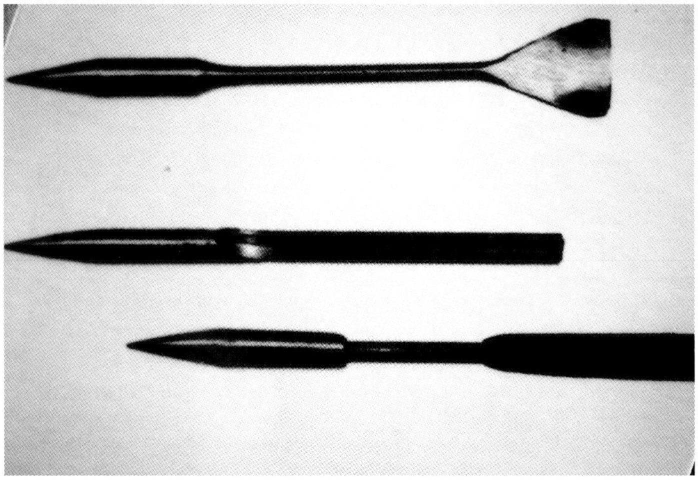

During early World War I combatants on both sides air-dropped pointed steel projectiles called **Flechettes** from aircraft or Zeppelins over enemy trenches that were capable of penetrating a helmet and the wearer's skull. (AAF)

Until under wing or fuselage bomb racks were introduced bombs were launched by hand. (Author/AFHRC)

A **FE-2b** Pusher being armed with 112 pound RL Mk VI of VII bombs. (Author/AFHRC)

and produced by the Royal Laboratory and the Royal Aircraft Factory, with the RNAS generally preferring the former manufacturer and the RFC the latter. From late 1914, the Royal Laboratory at Woolwich began designing a series of bombs, ranging in size from 16 to 550 pounds, while during 1915-1916 the Royal Aircraft Factory also developed a range of bombs up to 585 pounds intended for the larger aircraft then coming into use. By August 1916 there were over 20 main types of bombs in the British arsenal, and in an effort towards standardization the number was reduced to approximately 10 by May 1917, and by the end of the war four main bomb types had become standard. These were the small 20 pound heavy case Cooper bomb, the medium 50 pound heavy case RL MkIV, the large 112 pound heavy case RL Mks VI and VII, and the large 230 pound light case RFC. Heavier bombs, such as the 550 pound heavy case RL Mk I/N, were occasionally used during the last year of the war, and a special series of heavy SN bombs was developed for the large Handley-Page bombers, ranging from 1,100 to 1,800, and finally to 3,360 pound types.

From the German experiments with the APK the more advanced Karbonit series of bombs was developed, ranging in size from 4.5 kg to 20 kg, and were widely used by the Germans until late 1915. The German Artillerieprufungs Kommission, in collaboration with the Karbonit AG firm, replaced the Luft Torpedo with the new pear-shaped Karbonitbombe. This bomb was produced in sizes varying in weight from 10 to 44 pounds and was used until the end of 1915.

In 1915 the Prifanstalt und Werft der Fliegertruppe (Test Establishment and Workshop of the Air Service) co-operated with the Goerz Company to develop the new P.u.W bomb, which had a streamlined torpedo shape to give it better aerodynamic performance and has been considered as the true prototype of the modern aircraft bomb. The first P.u.W. bombs arrived at the Front in 1916 in 27.6, 110, 220, 661, and 2,205 pound sizes. It was made of high-grade steel rather than cast iron, which gave it superior penetration power. But of more significance were the slanting fins fitted to the tail, which gave a rotary motion to the bomb as it fell. In this way the fuses could be armed by centrifugal force in a similar fashion to artillery fuses instead of using propeller devices. Unlike most Allied bombs at that time, which were carried vertically in racks either under the wing or fuselage by British aircraft or on the fuselage sides by the French, the P.u.W bombs could be suspended initially horizontally in racks under the wing or fuselage and later in bomb bays inside the aircraft, lessening wind resistance.

During World War I the organization, the technology, and the operational doctrine of the various flying services made remarkable progress. Reconnaissance, fighter, bomber, and ground attack aircraft were developed to meet and then influence events on the battlefield. During the war the armament, ordnance, and equipment carried by bombers continually developed. A large variety of bombs was developed to fulfill different purposes and could be dropped from both high and low altitudes with increasing effectiveness.

While limitations of contemporary aircraft payload and bombing accuracy restricted aerial bombardment in World War I, the use of airpower in this age of trench warfare did have some advantages. The static character of the front required that supplies and reinforcing troops be assembled in large quantities in the rear beyond the range of artillery. Aerial reconnaissance and bombardment was the only means of observing and interdicting enemy logistical movement. When defending units were confined within salients, as the French were at Verdun and the Germans at St. Mihiel and Chateau-Thierry, there was a restriction of transportation and communication lines that rendered these positions especially vulnerable to interdictional bombardment. Consequently, resupply of both German and Allied front lines was nocturnal due to the risk of aerial observation and aerial and artillery bombardment. Given time, improved bombsights and the introduction of larger bomb-carrying aircraft could have had a dramatic influence upon trench warfare on the Western Front, as it would have greatly increased the problems of reinforcement and supply and compelled the evacuation of salient positions.

After the end of the war a limited American strategic bombing survey was conducted, showing that most American bombardment targets were interdictional—railroad stations and yards, troop concentrations, and bridges—all of which were within 65 miles of the principal bases located first at Amanty and later at Maulan. Generally, the American strategic bombardment effort was also interdictional, concentrating on the same targets but conducted at greater distances. The American survey team also investigated British bombing efforts, which were more extensive and destructive. The survey found that the Allied bombing campaign had no predetermined agenda to destroy the industries that were most essential to maintaining German armies in the field. Attacks were directed at strategic towns, rather than the military objectives within those areas. Bombing was extremely inaccurate. Bombing for morale effect alone was not a productive use of airpower. Failure to bomb a target continuously permitted quicker repair of the destroyed facility and also failed to destroy the target permanently. Importantly, the American survey team staunchly supported a unified theater command and added that there should be no separate or independent bombing force; an admonition that would affect Air Force autonomy for decades to come.

The *Bolling Mission* and the Initial Failure of American Airpower

In July 1917, after America entered World War I, Congress authorized $640 million to build the world's premier and largest air force from a current inventory of just 224 aircraft. A group of veteran army aviators under Gen. Benjamin Foulois prepared a production plan stipulating the construction of 22,625 aircraft, including trainers, concurrently with 45,250 engines, although the actual aircraft types were not decided. Beleaguered Britain and France looked to America's manpower and industrial might to tip the scales in the stalemate of bitter trench warfare, particularly with the use of aircraft.

On 17 June 1917, a fact-finding mission was dispatched to Europe led by Col. R.C. Bolling, including Army, Navy, and civilian aeronautical experts whose expertise embraced metallurgy, engines, production, and finance. Ninety-three experienced personnel from American industry were also sent to examine European aircraft production techniques. The main charge of the "*Bolling Mission*" was to investigate Allied aircraft designs and make recommendations on the ones to accept. By 15 August the *Mission* returned home, and Bolling stated it would require up to nine months before reaching full production, and after crating and shipping, the first American aircraft would not arrive in Europe until July 1918. Also, American-built *Liberty* engines were to be used in American-built aircraft, as Allied engine production was hard-pressed to meet their own needs. The *Bolling Mission* selected aircraft which were just

In June 1917 **Col. R.C. Bolling** led a fact-finding mission including Army, Navy, and 93 civilian aeronautical experts whose expertise embraced metallurgy, engines, production, and finance. The *Bolling Mission* was to examine European aircraft production techniques and make recommendations on the ones to accept for American combat use. (AAF)

about to enter production in Europe and whose design seemed likely to remain viable for some time. These aircraft included:

DH-4 equipped with a U.S. *Liberty* engine
SPAD XIII with either a 200 hp Hispano-Suiza or a U.S. *Liberty* engine
SPAD XV (monocoque) with a 150 hp *Gnome* engine
Martinsyde F-3 with a U.S. *Liberty* engine
Handley-Page bomber with two U.S. *Liberty* engines
Caproni bomber with three U.S. *Liberty* engines

But by the Armistice on 11 November 1918, there were only 196 American-built aircraft in combat units on the Western Front (33 had been lost), with 270 more in training units, 323 in supply depots, 415 in transit, and more than 2,000 pending shipment overseas. An additional 1,400 pursuit aircraft had been purchased from European nations and about 6,000 trainers had been built; all of which still added up to a considerable deficit towards the anticipated 22,000 combat aircraft. Before the war was over four independent investigations of the American aircraft program were underway and found several major problems that prevented the fulfillment of the ambitious production plan.

The blueprints for the Allied aircraft had to be redrawn for U.S. mass production, and those for the French and Italian designs also had to be converted from metric measurements. The prototype of the American DH-4 version first flew after the two heavy bombers, the Handley-Page and the Caproni, which were not considered part of the immediate production program, and the monocoque SPAD and the Martinsyde did not meet their expected potential and were discontinued. The Bristol Scout and SE-S were selected, not for combat, but as advanced trainers. The Army then decided that the single-seat fighter was about to become obsolete and the Bristol Fighter was adopted instead.

However, the biggest impediment to the introduction of American aircraft into combat was the German advance during March 1918 that caused a change in priorities and a virtual embargo on the shipment of anything but infantry personnel and machine guns for several months to stem the German threat. It would not be until 2 August that the first squadron of American-built aircraft, powered by American engines and flown by American crews, flew a combat mission.

Mass production can only work effectively when a product is standardized, but it was found that detail changes inherent in aircraft production could not be introduced without significant disruption in production. In American Henry Ford-type mass production unskilled workers were to assemble the entire aircraft, but it was determined that final fit and finish needed to be completed by fully skilled craftsmen, and until this problem was solved mass production was hindered.

From its beginning, the entire American aircraft program depended on the availability of suitable engines in sufficient numbers to meet airframe production. The British and French had both experienced a shortfall in their engine production so the U.S. Standardized Aero Engine, called the *Liberty*, was to be used in American-built airframes. It was specifically designed for mass production based upon an existing Packard design, but it proved to be too big and heavy for the Bristol Fighter and production of this design was canceled after only 27 had been built. However, in the DH-4, and later in other designs of similar configuration, the *Liberty* more than proved its worth and could have been manufactured in great numbers given sufficient time. If the bloodletting on the Western Front would have continued into 1919, American airframe and engine production problems would have been solved, and large air armadas of American-built aircraft would have appeared in combat.

Inter-War Years

After the carnage and regrets of the Great War the climate of public opinion militated against all forms of armament. Governments expected that

The British **DH-4** equipped with a U.S. *Liberty* engine was selected as the primary U.S. produced aircraft. It first flew on 29 October 1917, and the first production models were completed in February 1918, but the first DH-4s did not reach France even in limited numbers until 11 May 1918. (Author/AFHRC)

Twin-engined **Keystone LB-5** bombers, one of the AAC's two major bombardment aircraft in the mid-1920s. (Author/AFHRC)

they would have five to 10 years of lead time to react to any future threat and, consequently, little funding for armament research and development was made available. This situation continued mostly unchanged until the great rearmament drive in the mid-1930s, which ended this period of forced stagnation. In the inter-war years the British conducted a number of minor "policing" skirmishes to maintain order in the Empire using bombs of First World War vintage which were sometimes updated with minor modifications.

Virtually every bombing technique employed by the AAF during World War II owed its existence to the training and the maneuvers conducted in the pre-war. Bridge-busting was a technique that was refined during tests conducted by the Air Corps in December 1927 using twin-engined Keystone LB-5 bombers, one of the AAC's two major bombardment aircraft at the time. The bombers, stationed at Pope Field, near Fort Bragg, NC, attacked the condemned Pee Dee River Bridge. The Keystones made attacks singly, in formation, at varying altitudes, and with different size bombs and achieved excellent accuracy during various bombing runs. Later trials during the 1930s using the various Norden Bombsight models will be described in the bombsight section.

Three years after the interdiction strike tests against the Pee Dee River Bridge, the AAC conducted a series of experiments to improve its offensive capabilities against an enemy air force. Airfield attacks were carried out in World War I, but not with the aim of gaining air superiority by destroying the enemy on the ground. On 3 November 1930, Camp Stanley, TX, was lined with obsolete DH-4 bombers as if they were operational. AAC attack and light bombers flew simulated low altitude "surprise attacks" in several waves, destroying the "enemy" DH-4s. The lessons learned from these simulated combat attacks had a profound influence on AAF attack aviation during World War II when light and medium bombers, flying on deck, devastated the enemy with the tactical advantages of speed and surprise. These experiments also determined the most effective bomb sizes and types for destroying enemy aircraft caught in exposed positions. Bomb weights ranged from 17 pounds upward and Fragmentation, General Purpose, and other types were employed. The Fragmentation Bomb, descending slowly by parachute and exploding at ground height, was found to be very effective.

On 3 November 1930, Camp Stanley, TX, was lined with obsolete DH-4 bombers as if they were operational. AAC attack and light bombers flew simulated low altitude "surprise attacks" in several waves, destroying the "enemy" DH-4s. The lessons learned from these simulated combat attacks had a profound influence on AAF attack aviation during World War II. (AAF)

Keystone bombers stationed at Pope Field, near Fort Bragg, NC, attacked the condemned Pee Dee River Bridge during bombing tests in December 1927. (AAF)

Airpower Pioneers

Early in World War I most military officers considered the airplane as a useful device to supplement the traditional forms and manner of warfare, and so they employed it for observation, reconnaissance, and aiming of artillery. Soon aircraft were found to be effective in attacking in close support of the infantry or at targets a short distance in the enemy rear. Aircraft were then used for more strategic targeting to attack vital centers, such as headquarters, supply depots, railheads, troops moving to the front, and similar military targets. However, there were a few early airpower theorists who saw more imaginative possibilities. These men envisioned aircraft operations that would be independent of armies or navies, and that the objective of warfare was not the attrition of surface forces but the destruction of essential aspects of the enemy's capability to wage war. While the role of aircraft in World War I was insignificant, the potential of airpower thereafter was momentous. Seven men emerged from World War I as advocates of airpower as the key to victory in future wars and would have a profound influence on American bombing theory and the development of bombardment and pursuit aircraft.

Gen. Giulio Douhet

Giulio Douhet's *The Command of the Air*, first published in 1921, was the first detailed appraisal of the offensive and defensive use of aircraft in warfare. Douhet's work was subsequently translated into English, French, German, and Russian, influencing the air warfare doctrines of those countries prior to World War II.

Born in 1869, Douhet served many years as a career officer in the Italian Army before World War I, being assigned to the aviation branch in 1911. In the four years before Italy entered the war he had contemplated the use of airpower in warfare and blatantly criticized Italian military leaders during the war, stating that they lacked the innovative thinking which could reduce casualties and shorten the war. His criticisms resulted in a court martial and he was sentenced to a year in prison. After the Italian Air Force suffered a defeat by the Austrian Air Force at Caporetto Douhet was recalled to active duty during the last year of the war.

Douhet was promoted to Brigadier General in 1921, the same year that the Ministry of War published the first edition of *The Command of the Air*. After Mussolini ascended to power in 1922 Douhet served as Commissioner of Aviation, but soon resigned and committed his full time to developing and disseminating his airpower philosophy until his death in 1930. The 1927 edition of *The Command of the Air* elucidated Douhet's basic concepts about military aviation.

Douhet's basic premise was that the airplane could revolutionize warfare. World War I, which had been a long war of attrition, convinced Douhet that land warfare was primarily a defensive struggle in which a decisive outcome over an enemy's ground armies would require a prolonged and costly effort in men and equipment. Douhet proclaimed that the airplane, with "complete freedom of action and direction," provided the means to achieve a swift victory without first defeating enemy ground armies.

Giulio Douhet's *The Command of the Air*, first published in 1921, was the first detailed appraisal of the offensive and defensive use of aircraft in warfare. Douhet's basic premise was that the airplane could revolutionize warfare. (Author)

Douhet believed that aircraft were "instruments of incomparable offensive potential," being "the offensive weapon par excellence," capable of making devastating mass attacks nearly anywhere. Command of the air was essential to attaining victory in war, as with "one's own air force is free to operate whenever and wherever it desires, while the enemy's air arm is rendered permanently helpless. The enemy then has no effective defense against the ensuing air attacks." All future conflicts would be uninhibited, total wars. There was no longer to be a distinction between the military and civilians, as when a nation was at war every person in that nation was considered to be involved. A war could be won more easily, quickly, economically, and with fewer casualties by attacking a nation's vulnerabilities: its cities, industries, and civilian morale. Douhet also realized that "There is no practical way to prevent the enemy from attacking us with his air force except to destroy his airpower before he has a chance to strike us.... We must therefore resign ourselves to the offensives the enemy inflicts upon us, while striving to use all our resources to inflict even heavier ones upon him."

As stated, Douhet believed that the first priority in air operations was to achieve command of the air, which would make all other tenants possible. This objective was accomplished by destroying the enemy air force on the ground by attacking his airfields and aircraft industries with an armed and armored bomber that would be able to fight its way to and from the target. The attacking bomber force was expected to suffer losses, but by employing surprise and flying in formation these losses were predicted not be too costly. The bombers were to hit hard and often until command of the air was achieved. And once achieved, the bombers were to destroy the enemy's resolve and capacity to resist by bombing his cities. When an enemy population experienced this ruthless aerial battering it would suffer a total breakdown of morale and social structure and demand an end to the war.

Douhet felt that no effective air defense was possible because only the attacking force knew what the target was to be. To stop an attacker, the defenders would need as many fighters covering every possible target as the attacker had aircraft in the attacking force, even if the entire attack was against only one target. For example, if there were 100 attacking aircraft and 100 potential targets, the defenders would require an enormous and too costly force of 10,000 intercepting fighters. Far too numerous antiaircraft guns, which were considered to be generally ineffective, would also have to be dispersed to cover the multitude of potential targets. Douhet felt that since there was no effective air defense possible against bombers, the attacking nation was to expend no resources on fighters and antiaircraft guns to defend itself, and all funds were to be directed toward building the largest possible bomber force to attack the enemy. He felt this end could be more easily achieved because armies and navies lacked the ability to carry out rapid and decisive offensive operations and would be needed only as a small defensive force.

Douhet firmly believed that strategic airpower was an instrument capable of delivering quick victory, and his *The Command of the Air* convinced other nations of the viability of his idea. In the United States the book reinforced the views of Air Corps officers who had come independently to the same conclusion. While Douhet's hypotheses had a great effect on airpower development in the first four decades of the 20th century, after World War II it was criticized for overestimating the impact of airpower, especially his supposition that airpower alone could cause the enemy to surrender.

Sir Hugh Trenchard

Sir Hugh Trenchard was an airpower advocate who emerged during World War I as Britain's first air commander and helped to lay the foundations of the future British air tactics and operations. Trenchard was born in 1873 and entered the British army, serving in Africa before the turn of the century.

Sir Hugh Trenchard was an airpower advocate who emerged during World War I as Britain's first air commander, and his influence on British airpower was immense, as he established its initial institutions and doctrine and helped to lay the foundations of the future British air tactics and operations. (Author)

He learned to fly in 1912 at the relatively old age of 40, and when war was declared Trenchard was named the head of the embryonic Royal Flying Corps (RFC), which was a branch of the Army. In January 1918 he was Knighted and appointed Chief of Air Staff, but resigned that same year. He was re-appointed Chief of Air Staff 1919, and after the war was involved in training colleges for air cadets and formulated bombing concepts from his experience in the Great War. He remained as Chief of Air Staff until 1927 and was made the first Marshal of the RAF in that year. He retired two years later to become the Commissioner of the London Metropolitan Police, serving until 1935, when he was made a Viscount and entered private business until he died in 1956 at 83.

Trenchard's influence on British airpower was immense, as he established its initial institutions and doctrine. Originally Trenchard, a former infantry man, was opposed to the creation of a single air arm for tactical and strategic bombing because the British Expeditionary Force in France was vital for Britain to win the war, and therefore, the RFC's priority was support of the BEF.

However, after the war Trenchard increasingly argued that the role of army and navy forces in future warfare would be secondary, and that strategic rather than tactical air attack would have the principal role. He believed in the offensive function of airpower and was convinced that the primary mission of airpower was to destroy the enemy through aerial bombardment. Therefore, he fervently advocated the need to allocate maximum resources to the development of airpower. He argued that an enemy would be forced to surrender by conducting a devastating strategic bombing campaign against him and by denying him the capability to do likewise. However, he did not advocate attacking the civilian population directly to affect morale. He was committed to establishing air control so that armies and especially navies would not become vulnerable to enemy airpower. During his tenure as Air Staff Chief, he was able to counteract the impact of meager government funding while deflecting Royal Army and Navy attempts to abolish the independent RAF.

As the Chief of Staff of the world's first independent air force, Trenchard's philosophy was to have a major impact on the RAF's organization and performance during World War II, and also influenced the thinking of American airpower advocates. Trenchard helped to kindle the U.S. Army Air Service and the Air Corps' commitment to strategic bombardment and gave reinforcement to the arguments for an independent American Air Force. Trenchard's insistence on combining British Army and Navy aircraft into the RAF proved to be deleterious to the Royal Navy, and the USN used this fact to retain naval aviation within the Navy.

Gen. William "Billy" Mitchell

William "Billy" Mitchell was born on 28 December 1879, the son of a wealthy Wisconsin Senator, and enlisted as a Private in the Army at 18 during the Spanish American War. At 32 he was assigned to the General Staff as its youngest member, but became interested in flying and was assigned to the Aeronautical Division of the Signal Corps, the precursor of the Army Air Service. Once America entered World War I Lt.Col. Mitchell was immediately deployed to France, where he studied British and French air strategies and aircraft. Using this knowledge, Mitchell was awarded the rank of Brigadier General and commanded all American air combat units in France. In September 1918 he planned and led nearly 1,500 British, French, and Italian aircraft in the air phase of the Battle of Saint-Mihiel, one of the first coordinated air/ground offensives in history. With his success he expected to receive the post-war assignment of Director of Air Service after returning to the United States in early 1919. However, the outspoken and flamboyant Mitchell alienated most of his superiors and was appointed the Deputy Director of the Air Service and retained his one star rank. Gen. Pershing chose a classmate, Maj.Gen. Charles Menoher, an infantryman, to the Director post in order to maintain operational control of aviation by Army ground forces. Meanwhile, Mitchell's post-war associations continued to disintegrate as he publicly criticized both the War and Navy Departments and his superiors for being shortsighted regarding the potential of airpower and used every means of publicity to promote aviation and airpower.

During tests during the summer of 1921 **Gen. William "Billy" Mitchell** demonstrated the future of airpower by sinking the ex-German WWI battleship *Ostfriesland*, which the Navy considered unsinkable. The demonstration led to his court-martial in 1925, where he was found guilty of insubordination and suspended from active duty for five years without pay. (AAF)

Mitchell alleged that the building of battleships was taking defense funding from military aviation. To defend America's coastline Mitchell believed that a force of anti-shipping aircraft was more economical than a combination of coastal guns and warships, maintaining that a 1,000 bombers could be built at the same cost as one battleship and then could sink that battleship. Mitchell incensed the Navy by claiming he could sink ships "under war conditions" and could substantiate his assertion if he were permitted to bomb captured German battleships in a demonstration.

To offset Mitchell's allegations, Navy aircraft attacked the old battleship *Indiana* (BB-1) near Tangier Island, MD, on 1 November 1920. Secretary of the Navy Josephus Daniels released a report on the results written by Capt. William Leahy, stating: "The entire experiment pointed to the improbability of a modern battleship being either destroyed or completely put out of action by aerial bombs." However, the *New York Tribune* revealed that the tests were done using inert sand bombs and that the ship was actually sunk by coastal guns off Pensacola on 22 November, and Congress introduced two resolutions urging new tests.

In February 1921, Mitchell was anxious to test his theories on the destruction of ships by aerial bombing and Secretary of War Newton Baker and Secretary of the Navy Josephus Daniels agreed to a series of joint Army-Navy exercises, known as *Project B*. There was to be a news blackout until all data had been analyzed, at which time only the official news report would be released by the Navy. Mitchell publicly stated that the Navy couldn't be trusted to analyze the results. Mitchell's allegations embarrassed the Chief of the Air Corps, who attempted to have Mitchell dismissed a week before the tests began, but the new Secretary of War John Weeks relented when it became apparent that Mitchell had widespread public and media support.

On 1 May 1921, Mitchell marshaled the 1st Provisional Air Brigade composed of 125 aircraft and 1,000 men based at Langley, VA. Six squadrons tested bombs, fuses, and other equipment at Aberdeen Proving Ground. He began training the Brigade in anti-ship bombing techniques and confirmed that near miss bombs would produce more damage than direct hits by causing an underwater concussive effect against the hull.

As the stated purpose of the tests was to determine how much damage the ships could withstand, Gen. John J. Pershing allowed the Navy to establish the rules and conditions of the tests, which improved the survivability of the targets. The Navy chose an area 50 miles off the mouth of Chesapeake Bay rather than either of two possible closer areas, which reduced the effective time the Army's bombers would have over the target. The bombers were prohibited from using aerial torpedoes and would be permitted only two hits on the battleship using their heaviest bombs, and then would have to stop between hits so that a Navy damage assessment party could go aboard. Smaller ships could not be attacked with bombs larger than 600 pounds and also were subject to the same inspection interruptions in attacks.

Mitchell abided with the Navy's restrictions for the tests of 21 June, 13 July, and 18 July 1921, and successfully sank an ex-German destroyer and the ex-German light cruiser *Frankfurt*. On 20 July the ex-German WWI battleship *Ostfriesland*, considered unsinkable, was scheduled to be attacked with 230, 550, and 600 pound bombs dropped by Marine, Navy, and Army aircraft. The *Ostfriesland* was hit and settled three feet by the stern with a 5° list to port and was taking on water. Further bombing was delayed for a day, as the Navy claimed that rough seas prevented their observers from going aboard. Mitchell responded publicly that this extensive damage was accomplished despite as the Army bombers approached they were ordered not to attack for 47 minutes, using fuel, and therefore were able to drop only half their bombs and none of their large bombs.

One of five Martin MB-2 bombers carrying two 1,100 pound bombs on its way to bomb the *Ostfriesland* on 21 July. (AAF)

A 1,100 pound bomb hauled on a trolley into a shallow pit to be slung on steel cables on a Martin MB-2 bomber that was to take part in the Mitchell bombing demonstration. (AAF)

On the morning of 21 July, five Army bombers each dropped a single 1,100 pound bomb, scoring three direct hits, and the Navy again stopped further drops to assess damage, although the Army bombers had nine bombs remaining. At this point 2,000 pound bombs were loaded and a flight of eight bombers was dispatched and dropped six bombs in quick succession, aiming for the water near the ship. There were no direct hits, but three of the bombs landed close enough to rip hull plates open, as well as cause the ship to roll over and sink. Mitchell publicly used the sinking to tout airpower, though his results were downplayed in public by Gen. Pershing, who hoped to smooth ever-strained Army/Navy relations. Nevertheless, the test was highly influential at the time, causing budgets to be redrawn for further air development and forcing the Navy to look more closely at the possibilities of naval airpower. Mitchell asserted that "sea craft of all kinds, up to and including the most modern battleships, can be destroyed easily by bombs dropped from aircraft, and further, that the most effective means of destruction are bombs. (They) demonstrated beyond a doubt that, given sufficient bombing planes, in short an adequate air force, aircraft constitute a positive defense of our country against hostile invasion." Mitchell went on to repeat successful results twice in tests conducted on obsolete U.S. battleship *Alabama* in September 1921, and the battleships *Virginia* and *New Jersey* in September 1923.

On a trip to Europe in 1922, Mitchell met the Italian airpower theorist Giulio Douhet, who had similar ideas on airpower and soon an excerpted translation of *Douhet's The Command of the Air* began to circulate in the Air Service. In 1924, Mitchell's superiors transferred him to Hawaii, then Asia, to get him away from the eager American media. While he was away Mitchell wrote a 324 page report which was published in 1925 as the book *Winged Defense* that predicted future war with Japan, including the attack on Pearl Harbor, and predicted the future of airpower:

> "Those interested in the future of the country, not only from a national defense standpoint but from a civil, commercial and economic one as well, should study this matter carefully, because airpower has not only come to stay but is, and will be, a dominating factor in the world's development."

Mitchell continued to rankle his superiors, Major Generals Charles Menoher and later Mason Patrick, and when he appeared before the Lampert Committee of the U.S. House of Representatives, where he stridently chastised Army and Navy leadership. Mitchell was further incensed when the War Department sanctioned a proposal to establish a General Headquarters Air Force as a means for modernization and expansion of the Air Service, but then rescinded its approval when the Navy objected.

In March 1925 he reverted to his permanent rank of Colonel and was assigned to San Antonio as air officer to a ground forces corps, a posting with no political influence. Although such demotions were not unusual at the time, the move was nonetheless widely seen as punishment and exile, since Mitchell had petitioned to remain as Assistant Director of the Air Service when his term expired.

When the Navy dirigible *Shenandoah* crashed in a storm, killing 14 of the crew, Mitchell issued a statement accusing senior leaders in the Army and Navy of incompetence and "almost treasonable administration of the national defense." In 1925 he was court-martialed at the direct order of President Calvin Coolidge, found guilty of insubordination, and suspended from active duty for five years without pay. Mitchell resigned instead, as of 1 February 1926, and spent the next decade writing and preaching airpower to all who would listen. However, his departure from the military greatly reduced his ability to influence either policy or public opinion.

The Presidential election of Franklin Roosevelt, a former Navy man, was seen as beneficial for airpower, and Mitchell believed the new President might even appoint him as Assistant Secretary of War for Air, or perhaps even Secretary of Defense in a new and unified military organization. Without seeing his aspiration materialize Mitchell died on 19 February 1936.

After the celebrated Billy Mitchell bombing demonstration against captured German warships in 1921 America did very little on ordnance development. In general, due to the insufficiency of funds, and in some cases a lack of motivation, the future Allies made little progress in developing improved navigational and bombing equipment and techniques. Unfortunately, many of the lessons learned during World War I were all too quickly forgotten or ignored, and the Allies' total inter-war experience fell far short of that gained by the Luftwaffe during the Spanish Civil War.

However, the inter-war experience did produce a number of capable leaders of middle rank in both America (Arnold, Eaker, and Spaatz) and Britain (Portal, Slessor, and Harris). These future and prominent leaders not only influenced the build up of their air forces in the mid and late 1930s, they also dominated air force philosophy and operations during World War II. It is widely believed that when bombing inadequacies became evident in the early days of World War II it was the consequence of these air leaders of the 1930s lacking foresight. But in reality they were acutely conscious that tactical and strategic bombers were likely to play a major role in any future wars, and these men lobbied for new bomb designs and aircraft to carry them.

Mitchell went on to repeat successful warship bombing results twice in tests conducted on obsolete USN battleship *Alabama* in September 1921. (USN)

Col. Edgar Gorrell

The achievements of the colorful William "Billy" Mitchell and Benjamin "Benny" Foulois have caused the accomplishments of Col. Edgar S. Gorrell of the U.S. Air Service to be overlooked as an influential personality in shaping American airpower. Gorrell was not entirely innovative in his thinking about airpower theory, but his approach was very pragmatic, and formed the basis for American airpower, and as such he has never been duly recognized.

Col. Edgar Gorrell of the U.S. Air Service has been overlooked as an influential personality and very pragmatic thinker in shaping American airpower. (AAF)

Gorrell was born in Baltimore in 1891, graduated from West Point in 1912, and was a qualified military aviator when America entered the war in April 1917. Gorrell deployed with the advance group of the American Expeditionary Forces (AEF) on 16 June and arrived in France in July 1917 as part of the Bolling Mission. He served as the head of the U.S. Air Service Technical Section and was responsible for investigating requirements and implementing policy and programs to initiate the emerging American bombing program. In this pursuit Gorrell was greatly influenced by French and British air officers, especially Maj.Gen. Hugh Trenchard, head of the RFC/RAF, and Trenchard's liaison British officer, Maj. Lord Tiverton.

In September 1917 Tiverton, as part of the British Air Commission in Paris, prepared a comprehensive four part plan for the aerial bombardment of Germany and submitted it to the Air Board of the British Admiralty. By October, Gorrell also developed a plan and presented it to the AEF commanders in late November 1917. The "New American Plan," as the paper was later known, drew heavily upon Tiverton's plan and utilized all of its four main concepts, duplicating Tiverton's sequence of paragraphs, transposing exact phrases and terminology, and accepting his logical arguments and conclusions, nearly word for word. Gorrell's proposal was for a massive Allied bombardment campaign against German troop concentrations, dockyards, industrial areas, and major population centers deep inside Germany. The first of the Gorrell/Tiverton concepts was the determination of bombing targets, distances, enemy offensive and defensive capabilities around them, projected casualties figures, and weather patterns around the selected target zone. Next was the evaluation of American and Allied air resources and capabilities assigned to the determined objective. This was followed by logistical studies and the planning of implementation means. Last, Gorrell encouraged commanders to plan their assaults on areas where the impact of saturation heavy bombing would cause the greatest effect to German civilian morale, which was the plan's original combat target. Gorrell's plan was acclaimed as original and inspired but was not implemented, and he wrote a second paper in early 1918, entitled "The Future Role of American Bombardment Aviation," repeating Tiverton's doctrine and adding Trenchard's views on bombing's morale effect on the enemy civilian population.

At the time, however, Gorrell's visionary plan was overshadowed in part by the February 1918 debut of the first fully trained combat American Air Service units on the Western Front, which required his full attention. The other problem was lack of aircraft production, as American airmen in France had few U.S.-built airplanes and had to depend on England and France for the production of their Spads, Breguets, and de Havillands. Soon Gorrell was transferred to other duties for the Air Service, and by the time the paper was ready for serious consideration the Armistice was signed and Gorrell's paper was relegated to obscure long term planning divisions. Although postwar demobilization and lack of funding was preeminent, surprisingly the two papers were not forgotten, and in fact during the inter-war years many of Gorrell's ideas were implemented in the Army Air Corps Tactical Manual, which were forming the basis of the U.S. air effort little more than twenty years later.

In October 1918, at the age of 27, the hardworking Gorrell was promoted to Colonel, and he wanted a wide-ranging analysis of the extensive American air operations in 1918, plus those of the Allies, which would lay the basis for future planning and appropriations as airpower expanded within the U.S. Army. At the time the AEF was writing a full war history under Brig. Gen. Fox Conner. During early 1919, Gorrell's researchers gathered thousands of pages of information resulting in more than 280 detailed volumes, with many photographs, describing everyday operations and the longer-term vision of the Air Service. "Gorrell's History" was the main source for the Air Service's final report and for subsequent World War I Air Service histories.

Gorrell comprehensively examined "strategical" bombing, as it was then called. The Air Intelligence Section produced a strategic bombing assessment of both U.S. and Allied efforts using a combination of target photographs, interviews, and estimations of financial impact on bombed factories, towns, and railroads. The result was a detailed compendium of material damage recorded in 66 of 140 bombed cities that the team visited. The survey recorded casualties, took photographs, and tabulated damage costs in German marks, which provided an idea of how sustained bombing might alter future air warfare. The report also examined the costs of protection against air raids, such as the manufacturing and operational costs for providing anti-aircraft guns and dedicated pursuit aircraft. It concluded that the results of Allied night bombing more than justified the cost. Gorrell's survey cautioned that the effects of bombing on civilian morale and fighting forces were not to be overestimated. Targets, in order, should be war industries, railroad lines, and enemy troops in the field. Above all, the report recommended: "The operations of bombardment aviation must be an integral part of the mission of the entire air force and consequently of the ground forces and the army as a whole." The suggestions for future campaigns were outlined directly, and were the main issues that would emerge 20 years later in World War II.

Gorrell resigned his commission in 1920 and continued on as a successful executive in the automotive and aviation industries. Seeing the rise of the Luftwaffe and Japan launch its invasion of China, Gorrell cautioned about the lack of U.S. war preparedness. In 1940, Gorrell unhappily pointed out that his history was "languishing in the vaults of the War Department in Washington, some of the pages torn, some yellowing." But after a decade his systematic analysis and research in gathering information to come to conclusions on strategy, tactics, training, basing, and production had been rediscovered. Gorrell died in 1945, but the influence of his work is seen in Air War Planning Document 1, prepared by the Air Corps' Tactical School. In 1941, AWPD-1 called for more than 100,000 aircraft and two million airmen to defeat the Axis.

Maj.Gen. Benjamin Foulois

Benjamin Foulois was born in Connecticut on 9 December 1879. He was commissioned as an Army 2nd Lieutenant in 1901 and served in the Philippines from 1903-1905. Foulois attended the Infantry-Cavalry School at Fort Leavenworth, KS, where his final thesis was "The Tactical and Strategical Value of Dirigible Balloons and Aerodynamical Flying Machines." Included in this thesis was the following: "In all future warfare, we can expect to see engagements in the air between hostile aerial fleets. The struggle for supremacy in the air will undoubtedly take place while the opposing armies are maneuvering for position." He also forecast the replacement of the horse by the airplane in reconnaissance and the use of wireless air-to-ground communications. In 1908 Foulois was assigned to the Signal Corps' Aeronautical Division, where he commanded the first U.S. dirigible, and after a year advised the Army General Staff that there was no military potential for lighter-than-air aircraft; the first of many disagreements he was to have with the military establishment.

After having taken a few hours of basic flights with the Wright Brothers, Lt. Foulois was the only active pilot in the U.S. Army from 1909 until 1911. While at San Antonio, TX, Foulois flew the Army's only aircraft, Signal Aeroplane No. 1, which he taught himself to fly by trial and error. In 1914, Capt. Foulois organized and took command of the First Aero Squadron, which later redeployed to Fort Sam Houston, TX, in what was the first cross-country flight by a flying unit. The squadron took part in the Mexican Punitive Expedition from March to August 1916 flying Curtiss JN-2 biplanes under the command of Gen. John J. Pershing. While this air expedition was generally considered a failure, Foulois gained experience in operational planning and logistics.

At the start of World War I Maj. Foulois, as the Chief Signal Officer, headed the Joint Army and Navy Technical Committee, where he not only had to cope with ingrained Army-Navy animosities, but also with the Army and Navy senior leadership's adversity to any change in the status quo. In the end Foulois was instrumental in formulating a detailed proposal that led to the rapid Congressional approval of the unprecedented $640 million funding bill for aviation as America entered World War I. During the war, with increasing responsibilities, Foulois received a temporary promotion to Brigadier General and served in a variety of aviation positions in Europe, beginning as the Chief of Air Service, American Expeditionary Forces, and ending as the Assistant Chief of the Air Service, Service of Supply.

In November 1917 he was named Chief of Air Service, American Expeditionary Forces, and assumed additional responsibilities as a member of the Joint Army and Navy Aircraft Committee in France; representative of the Commander in Chief, American Expeditionary Forces on the Inter-Allied Expert Committee on Aviation of the Supreme War Council; and commandant of the Army Aeronautical Schools. The arrival of Foulois with a staff of inexperienced and recently commissioned non-flying officers brought about a certain confrontation between Foulois and Brig.Gen. William "Billy" Mitchell, who commanded the Air Service Zone of Advance. Over the years the ambitious, strong-willed, free-thinking Mitchell and Foulois would engage each other in acrimonious disagreements, and both would play an important part in the development of the independent Air Force. The more flamboyant Mitchell worked toward that end by swaying public opinion, while Foulois favored direct testimony to Congress, often with controversial attacks against the military establishment.

In May 1918, Foulois recommended to Gen. Pershing that he replace Mitchell as Chief of Air Service because of his overt insubordination and inability to follow the chain of command in giving orders. Pershing appointed Foulois as Chief of Air Service, First Army, with Mitchell as Chief of First Corps. The acrimony between the combat savvy Mitchell and the bureaucratic Foulois continued. In August 1918, a major breakdown of organization between offensive units and replacement units occurred due to Foulois and Pershing reinstated Mitchell to his previous command as Chief of Air Service, while Foulois was designated as Assistant Chief of the Air Service, Zone of the Advance.

After the Armistice, just as quickly as he had been promoted from Major to Brigadier General, Foulois was reduced in rank to permanent Captain in the Infantry and temporary rank of Major in the Air Service. Foulois served with the Chief of the Air Service on the Supreme War Council, drafting the air clauses of the Treaty of Versailles. Upon his return to the U.S. in July 1919, Foulois was assigned to the Office of the Director of Air Service at Washington, D.C., in charge of the Air Service Liquidation Division, and was responsible for the settlement of war claims against America.

In October 1919, Foulois was called before the Senate Military Affairs Subcommittee, and testified very negatively against the Army General Staff and Franklin D. Roosevelt, the Assistant Secretary of the Navy. Foulois' testimony did not sit well in Washington and he was exiled as the American Air Attaché to several European countries. Lt.Col. Foulois returned to the U.S. and attended the Army Command and General Staff School at Fort Leavenworth. In 1925 Foulois served a brief stint as Commander of Mitchel Field, NY. The same year Billy Mitchell was court-martialed, which resulted in his resignation in February 1926 and opened the door for Foulois to further his career. In 1927 Foulois was appointed Assistant Chief of the Air Corps and promoted to Brigadier General. In December 1927, Foulois was appointed Assistant Chief of the Air Corps, and in June 1929 Chief of the Materiel Division at Wright Field, Dayton, Ohio. He was then reassigned to the Office of the Chief of Air Corps, Washington, D.C., in July 1930.

In May 1931 Foulois commanded the Air Corps Coast Defense Exercises that included 672 aircraft, coast-to-coast defense flights, and combat competition. The success of these trials earned him the Mackay Trophy, and on 19 December 1931 he was designated Chief of the Air Corps, and promoted to Major General. He then held the distinction of being the first Chief of the Air Corps who was actually a military aviator.

As Chief of the Air Corps, Foulois was instrumental in helping to alleviate the constant dispute between the Army and Navy regarding coastal defenses. A compromise was reached between the Chief of Naval Operations and Gen. Douglas MacArthur in December 1931 that gave the Army land-based air arm the mission of defending the coasts (i.e. the land), while the Navy was to defend the fleet (i.e. the sea). In exercises the new long range Martin B-10 bombers appeared to be invincible against the slower Boeing P-12 pursuit aircraft, which led Foulois and the AAC leadership to begin the development of long-range bombers in 1933. Without Foulois' forethought the development of the B-17 and B-24 would not have occurred.

During his career **Gen. Benjamin Foulois** was instrumental in the development of long-range bombers in 1933, and due to his foresight the development of the B-17 and B-24 would not have occurred. (AAF)

During the next four years, a time when economic hardships were forcing severe budget cuts, Foulois was in constant contact with Congress, stressing the importance of the Air Corps in the future. Within the ACC Foulois pushed for more sound doctrinal studies and assigned Brig.Gen. Oscar Westover to expand the curriculum at the Air Corps Tactical School and plan for the establishment of an independent operational organization that later became the General Headquarters Air Force. Foulois advocated dedicated research and development programs for aircraft and weapons.

General Foulois was Chief of the Air Corps during the so-called "Air Mail Fiasco" of 1934. At the time, commercial air carriers were basically subsidized and kept in business by carrying the mail. There were charges of a conspiracy to defraud the government in these contracts which resulted in the transfer of all air mail delivery to the Air Corps, beginning on 19 February 1934 and continuing for three months. Inexperience and poorly equipped AAC pilots flew 1.5 million miles, resulting in numerous fatal crashes. Foulois became the middleman in a political battle between commercial aviation, the Congress, and the AAC. The 1934 Rogers Subcommittee investigated the alleged improper contracting and procurement of Air Mail awards and called for Foulois' resignation. Although he carried his fight to the public through the media, Foulois was virtually forced to retire from active duty 31 December 1935, after 37 years of service without any of the typical rituals of a retirement of a Major General. However, a result of the "Fiasco" was that it identified the requirements of the peacetime Air Corps and the Baker Board's recommendation for a GHQ Air Force, which was implemented in March 1935.

After retirement Foulois correctly warned of the buildup of German airpower and the need to build a strong air force and to take defensive measures to protect the East Coast. He declined a summons to return to active duty in 1942 but continued to write and speak for U.S. airpower until he died on 25 April 1967, following a heart attack at age 87.

Gen. Henry "Hap" Arnold was responsible for the expansion of the AAC into the world's largest air force, and developed a war plan for fighting both Germany and Japan. (AAF)

Gen. H.H. "Hap" Arnold

Henry Harley "Hap" Arnold was born on 25 June 1886 near Philadelphia. After graduating from West Point in 1907 he spent several years in the infantry mapping remote areas in the Philippines and then eagerly volunteered for the newly established Aeronautical Division of the Signal Corps. In 1911 he received his pilot's wings at the Wright Brothers flying school in Dayton, obtaining Federation Aeronautique Internationale (FAI) pilot certificate No. 29 worldwide and Military Aviator Certificate No. 2 in America a year later. As a young Lieutenant, Arnold became one of the Army's first pilot instructors at the newly established College Park, MD, aviation school. He was involved in early experiments concerning the uses for military aircraft, set a number of early altitude records, and used radios to communicate from aircraft to the infantry below. He organized the first deployment of an American aerial unit when the aviation school moved south to Georgia in search of better flying weather. In September 1911 Arnold became the first U.S. pilot to carry mail, flying letters five miles on Long Island, NY. On 9 October 1912 Arnold flew a "Most Meritorious Flight" in a reconnaissance competition over Virginia to win the first MacKay Trophy ever awarded. After a near fatal flying accident later that year Arnold developed a fear of flying and grounded himself, and did not fly again until late in 1916.

On 5 August 1917 Arnold was promoted again and became the youngest full Colonel in the Army, and ten days later was named Executive Officer of the Aviation Section. Arnold would not see combat in World War I, as during the next year he tried to implement a large military aviation appropriations bill despite the opposition of the Army General Staff. Arnold secured adequate funding and also gained considerable experience in aircraft production and procurement, the construction of airfields and air training schools, and the recruitment and training of large numbers of personnel, as well as becoming educated in the Washington political wrangling, all of which would be of great help 25 years later.

After the war, in December 1918 Arnold was sent to Rockwell Field to supervise the demobilization of 8,000 airmen and surplus aircraft. After demobilization Rockwell became a remote outpost, but Arnold continued to promote military aviation with air shows and publicity stunts. At Rockwell, Arnold established associations with his Executive Officer, Capt. Carl Spaatz, and his adjutant, 1Lt. Ira Eaker; officers who would become important aides in the future. During this time the three men embraced and supported the views on airpower of Brig.Gen. William Mitchell. Arnold was given the permanent rank of Major on 1 July 1920, but also suffered several serious illnesses and accidents requiring hospitalization at Rockwell.

In August 1924, Arnold was finally freed from the isolation of Rockwell and assigned to attend the Army Industrial College. After completing the course he was reassigned to duty as Chief of Air Service Information in January 1925, under Brig.Gen. Mitchell. During Mitchell's court martial Arnold, Spaatz, and Eaker all supported him despite jeopardizing their careers. After Mitchell was convicted on 17 December 1925, Arnold used his post in the Information Office to supply propaganda to airpower-friendly journalists despite orders from the Army General Staff. In February 1926 Secretary of War Dwight Davis ordered Maj.Gen. Patrick, who had no fondness for Arnold, to discipline him for his disobedience. Arnold was given the choice of resignation from the Army or a General Court Martial. Arnold chose the latter, and the Army decided it did not want another public Mitchell-type debacle and transferred Arnold to command the 16th Observation Squadron at Fort Riley, KS, a forlorn cavalry post.

While in virtual exile at Fort Riley Arnold participated in war games at Fort Sam Houston, TX, in May 1927, where he met Maj.Gen. James Fechet,

Ira Eaker (left) and **Carl "Toohey" Spaatz** were early associates of Arnold in embracing Billy Mitchell's doctrine of airpower and would become important air leaders in the ETO. (AAF)

who had succeeded Patrick as head of the newly designated U.S. Army Air Corps. Fechet intervened with Army Chief of Staff Gen. Charles Summerall to have Arnold assigned to the Army's Command and General Staff School at Fort Leavenworth. Despite not agreeing with the airpower doctrine that was taught at the school Arnold graduated with high grades in June 1929 and was assigned as Commander of Fairfield Air Service Depot, OH. In 1930 he became the Executive Officer of the Air Materiel Division and was promoted to Lieutenant Colonel on 1 February 1931. On 27 November 1931 he became Commander of March Field, CA, where his role was to convert a primary flying school into two operational units; one bomber and the other fighter. Arnold realized that despite the financial constraints of the Depression there were significant technological developments in aviation that needed to be implemented. Monoplanes with retractable landing gear and all-metal construction were the wave of the future for military aircraft. More powerful engines and more efficient propellers were being developed and enclosed cockpits were introduced. At March Field he was instrumental in the development of a strategic and tactical air defense doctrine which, while continually modified, was never abandoned through World War II. His championed airpower concepts would emphasize long-range bombers and massed airpower, the development of new fighter tactics, strategic bombing, and cargo transport.

In 1934, Arnold commanded the Western Division of the three military zones during the Air Mail Scandal, but his reputation was relatively unaffected. Later that year he won his second Mackay Trophy when he led ten of the new Martin B-10 bombers on a 16,600 mile round trip flight from Washington to Fairbanks, AK. The flight demonstrated that bombers could be flown in a large formation over vast distances and the publicity began to restore public confidence in the Air Corps.

On 9 March 1935, the General Headquarters Air Force (GHQ) was created to take control of all flying units of the AAC. Its first commander, Maj.Gen. Frank Andrews, appointed Arnold to command its First Wing, headquartered at March Field, and was also given an increase of two grades to Brigadier General. He commanded three fighter squadrons and three bomber groups, and conducted intensive simulated combat exercises. Arnold advocated maneuvers and exercises with bombers and fighters to be held in various parts of the country to gain experience in supply, operations, and command, and to publicize American airpower to the nation and the world.

On 28 December 1935, Army Chief of Staff Gen. Malin Craig appointed Arnold as Assistant Chief of the Air Corps under its new Chief, Maj.Gen. Oscar Westover. When Westover was killed in an air crash in September 1938 Arnold became Chief of the Air Corps, with an immediate promotion to Major General on 22 September. While this promotion did not return Arnold to the operational Air Force, it allowed him to promote and plan for expansion of the Air Corps into a branch of the Army that was equal to the ground forces. Arnold made dozens of speeches and wrote many articles showing the need for the expansion of the Army Air Corps to respond to the growth of the German Luftwaffe. But in the Depression of the mid-1930s the penurious Congress did not award funds for the military.

Finally, in fall 1938, with a war looming in Europe, President Roosevelt called for the production of 10,000 planes in 1940 and 20,000 the year after, which at last was a directive for Arnold to expand the Army Air Corps. Hap Arnold's Army Air Forces would grow exponentially from a small force of about 22,000 officers and 3,900 aircraft in 1938 to 2.5 million men and 75,000 aircraft by the end of the war. The division of authority between the AAC and the GHQ Air Force was finally removed with a revision of Army Regulation 95-5 that created the United Stated Army Air Forces on 20 June 1941. Arnold was made Chief of the Army Air Forces and acting Deputy Chief of Staff for Air with command authority over both the Air Corps and the Air Force Combat Command, which was the successor to GHQ Air Force. The new AAF was thus provided with its own staff, was under the command of one General (Arnold), and had near autonomy. But the price the AAF paid was that it would not become independent as an equal with the Army and Navy until after the war and remained subordinate to the Army Ground Forces.

The first responsibility Arnold and his new Air Staff undertook was to develop a war plan for fighting both Germany and Japan. The result was AWPD-1; the basis for air strategy during the war. Arnold, a strong supporter of strategic bombing, closely watched over the creation of the Eighth Air Force in England; limited the diversion of Army bombers to anti-submarine patrol and to the Pacific Theater; and blocked British lobbying to have U.S. bombers sent as individual replacements for the RAF. After Pearl Harbor, on 15 December 1941 Arnold was promoted to Lieutenant General. On 9 March 1942, War Department Circular 59 granted the USAAF full autonomy, equal to and entirely separate from the Army Ground Forces and Services of Supply. The office of the Chief of the Air Corps and the Air Forces Combat Command were eliminated and Arnold became Commanding General of the USAAF, and a member of both the Joint Chiefs of Staff and the Combined Chief of Staff. In August 1942 President Roosevelt directed Arnold to have the Air War Plans Division revise its war estimates and AWPD-42 was issued, calling for 75,000 aircraft and 2.7 million men. (Note: AWPD-1 and -2 are discussed in detail next.) Thus, Arnold was granted the men, weapons, and directives to conduct his "Global Mission," which was the title of his 1949 autobiography.

During his lifetime Arnold had survived at least five heart attacks, but his heart finally quit on 15 January 1950 at his ranch near Sonoma, CA. He was 63 years old and had served his country for 42 of those years. Arnold never fired a gun or dropped a bomb in combat, but he was responsible for the development and employment of the world's largest air force.

Adm. William Moffett

William A. Moffett was born on 31 October 1869; graduated from the Naval Academy in 1890; and received the Medal of Honor for his actions as the captain of the *USS Chester* in 1914 during the invasion of Veracruz, Mexico. During World War I he commanded the Great Lakes Naval Training Center and there established an aviator training program. After the war he commanded the battleship *Mississippi* (1918–1921) and created a scout plane unit on the ship and used aerial spotters.

After the war Congress drastically cut defense funding and naval aviation had a low priority. There were no aviators among the ranking naval officers. The few naval aviators were too junior to influence policy, and as line

Adm. William Moffett is remembered as the Father of Naval Aviation, who brought the Navy into the modern era through his ability to understand the technical and tactical aspects of the weapons he advocated, especially the few aircraft carriers America had on hand at the start of the war. (USN)

officers they had to spend two years at sea before they could be promoted, which lowered their flying proficiency. There were no aircraft carriers and no aircraft capable of landing on ships. Moffett pushed for a Naval air arm similar to that of the Marine Corps or Army and the establishment of an air bureau similar to the BuOrd. Fortunately, Moffett had the support for an air bureau from the Secretary of the Navy, Josephus Daniels, and Moffett spoke before Congress, specifying the need for a central agency to coordinate air affairs. At the same time Brig.Gen. Billy Mitchell supported the idea of an independent Air Force, but Moffett wanted the Navy Air Wing as part of the Navy. President Harding authorized a subcommittee to recommend legislation on both civil and military aviation, and he and Congress approved air bureaus for the Navy and Commerce Departments.

On 25 July 1921, President Warren G. Harding appointed Moffett as the first chief of the newly created Bureau of Aeronautics, and he was promoted to the rank of Rear Admiral. For an unprecedented 12 years, from 1921 until 1933, he conducted a sustained campaign against Navy establishment that was entrenched in surface warship tradition of the value of airpower. As Chief of the Bureau of Aeronautics Moffett controlled the activities of the Naval Air Force; became the major advisor to the Chief of Naval Operation's overseeing the development of tactics for naval aircraft; and controlled purchasing, and supervised the construction, design, and installation of equipment provided by other bureaus.

The Washington Conference of November 1921 through February 1922 affected the new Bureau of Aeronautics profoundly in Moffet's quest for aircraft carriers that could serve as advanced bases. There was to be a ten year ban on the construction of capital ships under the Five Power Naval Disarmament Treaty, but some ships that were laid down and partly built as battlecruisers could be converted to aircraft carriers while under construction. Two fleet carriers, the *Lexington* and the *Saratoga*, were converted, and with these two carriers, five aircraft tenders, and an airship tender, Moffett felt that the Navy could support a Pacific war and then initiated a five year/thousand planes construction program. As BuAer Chief, Moffett ordered improvements in both the liquid-cooled and radial engines and switched from the use of wood, wire, and fabric to metal for aircraft manufacture; USN aircraft would hold 22 of 42 world records. He supported the fledgling American aircraft industry by purchasing new equipment on the open market. Moffett's carriers and their aircraft performed superbly during fleet exercises and proved the importance of naval aviation in warfare.

In 1929 President Hoover appointed Moffett to an unprecedented third term as Chief of Aeronautics, and Moffett continued to campaign for more funding from Congress at a time when Hoover wanted to reduce naval power. Moffet's other interest was in dirigibles, and he obtained funding for two large rigid aircraft, the *Akron* and the *Macon*. On 4 April 1933 he went up in the *Akron* and was killed when it was caught in air currents off the coast of New Jersey. So today Moffett is remembered as the Father of Naval Aviation who brought the Navy into the modern era. He had the ability to understand the technical and tactical aspects of the weapons he advocated; the personal charisma and political power; and awareness of what he could accomplish and what he could not to convince Congress to fund his projects. The few carriers that the U.S. Navy possessed when it entered World War II had excellently trained carrier and aircrew personnel and more than held the line after America's battleships were sunk at Pearl Harbor.

U.S. Bomber Procurement and Development

Role of the Air Materiel Command in Bomber Procurement and Development

The Air Materiel Command, headquartered at Wright Field, Dayton, OH, was an important factor in bomber development programs. For mostly good and sometimes bad it acted as a liaison between the taxpayer, government, Army Air Corps, and the aircraft industry in formulating military aircraft designs, developing those designs, purchasing the completed design, and placing it into production as soon as possible. The Air Materiel Command did not design aircraft, but after receiving a list of requirements from the Air Staff it formulated performance—but not dimensional—specifications for the requisite aircraft. The Command's Procurement Division then sent out requests to aircraft manufacturers to draw up and tender designs for the specified aircraft. Air Materiel Command engineers considered the submitted designs and consulted with the designers to determine if the design met specifications, was workable, and if the manufacturer was capable of producing the specified aircraft. If these criteria were met then the manufacturer was contracted to build mockups and conduct wind tunnel tests, followed by contracts to build one or more experimental models. Finally, if the experimental model met specifications better than other contracted designs, the manufacturer was issued a contract to build combat aircraft and service test them.

The Air Materiel Command merged with the Air Service Command in 1944 to become the Air Technical Service Command (ATSC). The ATSC was made up of six divisions: Engineering, Procurement, Supply, Maintenance, Personnel, and Base Services. Of the six ATSC Divisions, the Engineering and Procurement Divisions had a direct affect on aircraft development and manufacture.

The function of the Engineering Division's ten extensively equipped laboratories was to research, develop, test, and evaluate every aspect of aircraft design, including those of the enemy. It had separate sections, such as Armament, Power Plant and Propeller, Aero-Medical, Radio and Electronics, etc. to study, test, develop, and approve equipment and systems in these sections. The Procurement Division evaluated design proposals, let contracts, and then followed up on the terms of the contract. At one time this division had 40,000 contracts with over 26,000 individual contractors comprising 400,000 plus items. The Production Section of the Procurement Division was responsible for the correct and timely supply of raw materials to over 15,000 manufacturers. It guaranteed the steady supply of combat-worthy aircraft into battle by providing for the expansion or construction of manufacturing facilities, dispersing government-furnished equipment (GFE) and parts, and obtaining and supervising subcontractors. Another responsibility of this division, which was to greatly affect bomber development programs, was its function to prescribe changes to aircraft and equipment as determined by fight testing and combat experience and then incorporate them into the production line. Another Procurement section was the Quality Control Section, which employed thousands of officers and civilians to inspect and accept all aircraft, aircraft accessories, and equipment for the AAF. The inspection ran the gamut from raw materials to the finished article. Larger manufacturing plants often had a resident representative who supervised inspection personnel who had been trained by the Division. There was a chronic shortage of ATSC Quality Control personnel to staff the thousands of factories doing defense work, and the factories also provided quality control that could range from meticulous to negligent.

Martin B-10: "Airpower Wonder of its Day."
In December 1929 the Air Materiel Command requested proposals for a revolutionary new bomber, and Glenn Martin's engineering staff produced two unimaginative designs that were not even contemporary, much less avant-garde. The AAC offered to help Martin secure a contract if it would privately develop a creative new all-metal monocoque design at its own expense but with no promise of a production contract. After six months of work Martin's design offering, the Martin 123, still fell short of expectations, and Wright Field made suggestions for improvement. The problems were thought to be solved, but on its first flight on 26 February 1932 the prototype performed very poorly and the project was threatened with cancellation.

At this point talented Wright Field engineers took over the project, virtually relegating Martin to a subcontractor status. The aircraft was thoroughly reevaluated and sent back to the factory with numerous recommendations for changes. Without the B-10 contract the Martin Company would go into bankruptcy, and the company readily acquiesced to the seeming endless number of subsequent changes ordered by the Air Materiel Command. The improved aircraft was finally ready for retesting on 7 October 1932 at Wright Field and was awarded the 1932 Collier Trophy for the number of innovations it displayed. The all-metal B-10 monoplane bomber (Martin 139) looked sleek for its time with its enclosed nose turret and cockpit enclosures for its three man crew. The wing had a span of 70 feet, 6 inches and an area of 678 square feet; the fuselage length was 44 feet, 8.6 inches, and its height was 15 feet 5 inches. It was a stable aircraft for bombing, and its two 675hp Wright R-1820 *Cyclones* made it faster at 207mph than any contemporary fighter. It was the first American bomber to have internal bomb stowage and retractable landing gear. A total of 154 were built: 121 as B-10 and B-10Bs and later 32 as B-12s and one XB-14; keeping Martin production lines busy for three years. The B-10B was the most produced type and was powered by a 790hp Wright R-1820-33 engine. The bomber served with 28 squadrons over seven years of operational duty. After its introduction Hap Arnold described the B-10 as "the airpower wonder of its day." The B-10 led to the B-12, which was to be overshadowed by the B-18 and then the redoubtable B-17.

Medium Bomber Procurement and Development
On 16 December 1937, the Air Corps issued Specification Circular AC 98-102 that provided detailed specifications for a light, three to four-place (pilot, bombardier, and one or two gunners), twin-engine attack bomber. The new bomber was to replace the single-engine types currently in service, which were too slow and could not carry sufficient firepower and bombs to be effective against well-defended targets. AC 98-102 stated the new bomber's mission was "to form close-in responsive support of the ground forces, by the attack and destruction by bombs of ground or naval personnel and light material targets." The Circular went on to state that the aircraft would also "be capable of laying smoke and chemicals and carrying out both precision and area bombing missions." The general performance requirements were that the candidates carry a payload of 1,200 pounds internally over 1,200 miles at over 200mph (at 5,000 feet). A minimum top speed was set at 250mph (at 5,000 feet), but optimally at 280mph, while a minimum service ceiling of 20,000 feet was set but 25,000 feet was favored. The armament was specified as six .30 caliber M-2 Browning machine guns; four of which were to be forward firing (two in each wing), preferably fixed, which were to be fired by the pilot. One of the other two guns was to be defensive, protecting against "an attack from any direction as measured on a sphere of 100 yard radius, having its center in the pilot's cockpit." The pilot was to control the release of bombs less than 30 pounds (e.g. fragmentation), while the bomber, as the bombardier was designated at the time, would control the release of larger bombs.

The **Martin B-10** was the first U.S. modern monoplane bomber, and was described by Hap Arnold as "the airpower wonder of its day." (AAF)

On 18 January 1938 the Air Corps issued Circular Proposal 38-385 that directed that any sealed bid proposals for the new attack bomber be submitted for opening and review 14 months later on 17 March 1939. The unstated reason for the long development period was that a prototype was to be constructed at the bidder's expense for a fly-off competition. The Air Materiel Command requested that interested companies submit data on their proposals, particularly concerning the power plants and propellers, and to project a unit cost at various production numbers. Five firms submitted proposals: Bell (Model 9), Boeing-Stearman (Model X-100), Douglas (Model 7B), Martin (Model 139), and North American (NA-40), with each company submitting several engine/prop combination proposals. North American submitted seven combinations: three using the P&W R-1830, one using the P&W R-2180, and three using the Wright R-2600. Boeing Stearman also submitted seven combinations: four using the R-2180, one the R-1830, one the R-2600, and the last using the new P&W R-2800. Douglas submitted five R-1830, R-2600, and R-2800 combinations. Martin submitted four combinations, all using the R-1830. There is no record of a Bell proposal, but it appears that it was to be powered by two liquid cooled Allison inline engines; however, the company withdrew from the competition before it submitted any data. After reviewing the submissions it appears that the Air Corps assigned each company specific engine/propeller combinations to incorporate in their prototype.

AC 39-640 Proposal for a Medium Bomber
Toward the end of the 1930s it became evident that America would eventually be at war, and that new designs were needed to match those of the Luftwaffe as reported by Charles Lindbergh after his pre-war visits to Nazi Germany. On 11 March 1939 the Air Corps issued AC 39-640, calling for a new medium bomber with a crew of five that would have a maximum speed in excess of 300mph, with 350mph desired; carrying a bomb load of 3,000 pounds over 2,000 miles; and was to be armed with four .30 caliber machine guns. It was to operate at altitudes between 8,000 and 14,000 feet with a service ceiling of 20,000 feet while acting primarily to support ground units, but also to be able to operate in a tactical role. The engine specifications called for the P&W R-2800, the Wright R-2600, or the new Wright R-3350. The bidding companies could submit any number of proposals offering design options, mainly engine/propeller combinations but also airframe, armament, and other redesigns. This procedure offered the Air Corps an a la carte selection of designs, saving the bidding companies the cost of building a prototype that was expensive and, more important with war looming, time consuming and usually requiring extensive modifications. The reward

for the winning design was an order for 385 aircraft. Seven companies submitted designs. Consolidated, Vought-Sikorsky, and Burnelli submitted bids but quickly dropped out of the contest. Martin (Model 179), Douglas (B-23), Stearman (XA-21), and NAA (NA-62) were the only companies to remain in contention to meet the 10 September deadline.

The AAC Decision on the AC 39-640 Proposal

The AAC sent a bulletin entitled "The Method of Evaluation" to each bidder that described how the competing designs were to be evaluated and a winner selected. A number of weighted design characteristics were listed with speed being the most important. Each aircraft design would receive a total numerical score consisting of numerical values given to each design characteristics with 1,000 being the highest theoretical score.

The Air Corps studied and evaluated each of the proposals with the North American and Martin proposals being "off the drawing board" with no experimental XB-25s or 26s or service test YB-25s or 26s. The Douglas and Stearman proposals were partially garnered from "hard copies." The results were: Martin Model 179 scored 813.6 points; North American's NA-62 trailed by a sizeable 140.2 points at a distant 673.4 points; while surprisingly the Douglas B-23 was not too far behind the NA-62 at 610.3 points; and the Boeing-Stearman XA-21 was a non-contender at a lowly 442.7 points. Both Martin and NAA were requested to submit per unit cost bids. Martin quoted $7,868.15 for its Model 179 and NAA quoted $6,397.28 for the NA-62, which was a significant 19% under the Martin bid.

On 10 August, Secretary of War Harry Woodring approved the AAC order for 201 Model 179s, designated as the B-26, from Martin at $15,815,000, with the contract approved on 19 August. The Martin contract was for 201 aircraft instead of the 385 promised, as Martin was unable to provide that many B-26s. Martin was too committed in building the Model 167s as the Maryland (309 total) for the French and as the more powerful Model 187 Baltimore (1,575 total) for the British. In addition, the company was about to go into production of its PBM Mariner for the Navy. On 4 September 1939, in anticipation of receiving the contract, Martin had begun expansion of its Middle River Plant in Maryland to produce the B-26. On 20 September 1939, the Secretary of War Woodring contracted the remaining 184 medium bombers of AC 39-640 as the B-25 (plus one test airframe) to NAA under contract #AC-13258 for $11,771,000. Thus, the B-25 and B-26 went on to become the best medium bombers of World War II.

Attack Bomber Procurement and Development

In 1938, while the bidding companies were working toward the March 1939 fly-off, world military aviation was changing, and it became evident that the specifications of AC 98-102 were no longer adequate to produce an attack bomber with performance to meet anticipated combat requirements. On 10 September 1939 the Air Corps issued new specifications designated as C-103 that requested the development of an experimental attack bomber design and the fabrication of a prototype much as was outlined by AC 98-102. On 15 October 1938 the AAC issued a data request to accompany C-103 which asked for engine/propeller combinations and cost estimates. Unlike AC 98-103, C-103 specified new and increased requirements in maximum speed that was to be increased by 100mph to at least 350 mph, and the optimal operating altitude increased from 5,000 feet to a range falling between 14,000 to 20,000 feet. The bomb load remained at 1,200 pounds, and the range continued at 1,200 miles. The crew number was reduced to three.

On 12 January 1939, President Roosevelt asked Congress for an immediate appropriation of an unprecedented $525 million for defense improvements, including $300 million for the purchase of aircraft. Congress earmarked $210 million for Fiscal Year 1939, ending June 1939. On 13 December 1938, C-103A was issued as part of an "Emergency Procurement Program." On 17 January 1939, days after Roosevelt's request, a

On 17 January 1939 Circular 39-460 outlined a manufacturer's bid process for the light attack bomber, and Douglas began work on the DB-7, which would culminate in the **A-20 Havoc** with 7,380 of all variants being built. (AAF)

On 11 March 1939 the Air Corps issued AC 39-640, calling for a new medium bomber, with the North American and Martin proposals being "off the drawing board" with no experimental XB-25s or 26s or service test YB-25s or 26s. As a result of the tests 201 B-26s and 184 B-25s were contracted, and the two went on to become the best medium bombers of World War II. (AAF)

manufacturer's bid process for the light attack bomber was outlined in Circular 39-460, and on 18 February 1939 the AAC requested that the first three aircraft off the production line be used for testing. With this impetus the Douglas Company diverted resources from the Model 7B and began work on a more promising C-103A attack bomber proposal designated as the DB-7, which would culminate in the A-20 Havoc, with 7,380 of all variants being built.

Heavy Bomber Procurement and Development

The Air Materiel Command and the Long-Range Bomber Requirements

In the early 1930s the Army Air Corps realized they needed a bomber with both speed and range. However, range was contingent on aircraft size; the more fuel carried for longer range meant a bigger aircraft with a larger wing to carry the increased fuel supply. Large aircraft were dependent on the availability of a sufficient power plant(s). In 1933 the requirements of a long-range bomber were discussed at Wright Field by chief engineer James Howard, his assistant Al Lyons, aircraft branch chief James Taylor, Hugh Kneer of the field service section, and Leonard "Jake" Harman, the Air Materiel Command representative. The group decided to categorize the future bomber types that would be required:

Wingspan, 75 feet; gross weight 15,000 pounds (that was already contemporary in the B-9 and B-10)

100 feet span; 40,000 pounds gross weight
150 feet span; 60,000 pounds gross weight
200 feet span; 150,000 pounds gross weight
250 feet span; 200,000 pounds gross weight
Etc.

In the fall of 1933 it was decided to disregard the No.2 category and category No.3 was considered as a feasible choice, and it was to be identified as "Project A." Jake Harman drew up the requirement and Gen. Conger Pratt of the Air Materiel Command authorized the money for engineering designs and sent the request to Washington for approval. At the time strategic airpower had few advocates, but long-range defensive patrol aircraft did have their proponents in Air Chief Benjamin Foulois and the Army General Staff. In 1933 Foulois directed his assistant, Brig.Gen. Oscar Westover, to fly missions testing the defense of the West Coast. Westover's report to the General Staff found the observation and patrol aircraft that flew these missions to be "woefully obsolete." But he suggested that modern bombers flying in formation with increased speed and range could frustrate any "known agency." Pratt was able to sell the idea of the "5,000 mile bomber," as it could protect Alaska and Hawaii, and this was a step in establishing a mobile GHQ Air Force.

Baker Board and the GHQ Air Force

In the early 1930s there was a dichotomy in the War Department. The conflict engaged the traditionalists, led by Army Chief of Staff Gen, John J. Pershing, who believed that the infantry ruled the battlefield, while the Army Air Arm, led by the defrocked Gen. Billy Mitchell, espoused the future role of airpower in warfare. The government organized a number of boards and committees to study air doctrine and its role in future warfare. The most influential of these groups was the Baker Board, and its report of July 1934 that recommended America's national defense policy was to be based on the defense of America and its overseas possessions with the Army air forces fending off any invader until ground armed units and civilian forces could be mobilized. While seeming to advocate airpower, there was no mention of the use of the air force in any aggressive or strategic manner, and the air force was relegated to a supporting role to ground forces by the Baker Board:

"The idea that aviation can replace any of the other elements of our armed forces is found on analysis, to be erroneous. Since ground forces alone are capable of occupying territory, the Army with its own air forces remains the ultimate decisive factor in war."

Baker Board member Jimmy Doolittle voiced the minority dissent supporting the separation of the Army and its air forces and advocating the development of an air doctrine for its employment.

Although the Baker Board rejected an independent strategic air force, it did support the creation in March 1935 of a General Headquarters Air Force (GHQAF) that would be under the control of the Army commander in the field. However, there were conflicting opinions of the role of the GHQAF. One was that it would be allocated and attached to field armies and utilized under their direct control. Another view had the GHQAF engaged as an integrated force acting to further the mission of the Army. The view held by most airmen was to have it act as a unified force not only to support the Army, but also to act beyond the realm of the Army, flying missions of its own. Maj.Gen. Frank Andrews was the CO of the GHQAF and forcefully advocated the airmen's point of view.

The formation of GHQ Air Force in the Regular Army on 1 March 1935 caused a revolutionary alteration in U.S. Army aviation organization. The new GHQAF, now under one air commander, organized active combat units so that they could be quickly mobilized in case of war. Previously, in peacetime, these units had been dispersed among various corps for administration and training. Thus, for the first time, the peacetime organization of the Army air arm paralleled that for war. Further reorganization in 1936 transferred GHQ Air Force bases, which had previously been under the control of Corps commanders, to the Air Force. Divisions, corps, and field armies continued to have observation aviation assigned to them and under their control but lost the pursuit and attack aviation that once had been part of a field army's air force. With this change all bombardment, attack, and pursuit aviation, plus some observation aviation for reconnaissance, became part of GHQ Air Force.

In organizing the GHQ the War Department placed it under the control of the War Department Chief of Staff in peacetime and under the Commander in Chief in the field in wartime. Also under the Chief of Staff, the Chief of the Air Corps retained responsibility for personnel and materiel for the Army's air arm, including the Air Force. This plan caused problems for both parties. The subordination of the Air Force Commanding General to the Chief of the Air Corps was tried in 1939, but failed to produce a satisfactory solution. GHQ Air Force was a great letdown for some air officers, as it did not result in the independence they had sought for many years. But still it was an immense improvement and was hoped to be a step toward the creation of a separate and independent air force, which it eventually would prove to be. The leaders of the GHQAF used it to build the dominant long-range bombing force for the strategic air operations they foresaw as a decisive factor in

Maj.Gen. Frank Andrews was the first CO of the GHQAF, formed on 1 March 1935. The GHQAF, now led by one air commander, organized active combat units so that they could be quickly mobilized in case of war. (AAF)

an inevitable future war. The building of this air force was a frustrating undertaking until international military developments in the late 1930s affected funds and airpower attitudes.

The Development of the American Heavy Bomber

In a memorandum of 14 July 1934, the Air Materiel Command had changed its thinking and decided that a second bomber that was not as grand as the Project A bomber could more easily be realized and put into production. The new AAC bomber was to have the same 2,000 pound bomb load, but its speed was to be 200mph and its range was to be at least 1,020 miles, but 2,200 miles was much preferred. The AAC proposal was for "multi-engines," which to the AAC meant two, but to Boeing it meant four. On 26 September 1934, the board of directors of the newly independent Boeing Airplane Company met for the first time after parent United Aircraft & Transport was finally dissolved. The new board bravely voted $275,000 to design and build a bomber to meet the new AAC specification and to start to work on the Model 299 that had been unofficially designated as the "XB-17" by Boeing before it had been approved by the AAC. The bomber was to be a low-wing monoplane that would have four engines to power it, and was essentially an upscaled version of Boeing's streamlined Model 247 twin-engine airliner that had been first flown in February 1934. The Model 299 made its first flight on 28 July 1935, and the media was impressed by its size and dubbed it the "Flying Fortress." On 20 August, project test pilot Leslie "Les" Tower flew it cross-country 2,100 miles to Wright Field for evaluation at an average speed of 232mph.

During testing at Wright Field the four-engine Boeing Model 299 was to challenge Douglas Aircraft's twin-engine DB-1 bomber, the XB-18 that had been developed from the company's successful DC-3 airliner design. From August and into October the AAC examined both bombers, and the Boeing's better range and reliability earned it the lead in gaining a contract. On 30 October 1935, Boeing test pilot Les Tower, AAC pilot Maj. P.P. "Pete" Hill, and the test crew took off in the Model 299. But once it became airborne the bomber became uncontrollable, and as it passed over the end of the runway it crashed in a nearby pasture. Hill was killed on impact, but Tower survived with horrible burns but died 20 days later. Investigation showed that the ground crew had not unlocked the tail control surfaces, causing the crash that would put the Boeing program in jeopardy.

The crash of the Boeing Model 299 certainly had a devastating effect on Congressional thinking and the ACC's procurement decision that led to the contracting of 133 Douglas B-18s and only 13 Boeing YB-17s. The 13 aircraft order kept Boeing financially viable, as its losses on the Model 299 after insurance reimbursement was $500,000; a great amount of money for that time. Manufacture would at least keep Boeing employees busy on a project that the company firmly believed would be very successful. With the AAC's decision the B-18 was to be put into immediate production with minor modifications and then to be put into squadron service as soon as possible. Compared to the four engine YB-17, the B-18 was much smaller and lighter, and its performance was slower, its range shorter, ceiling lower, and it carried a smaller bomb load and was considered to be a medium bomber. The XB-17 had more range, more speed, more bomb carrying capacity, more defensive firepower, and had the potential for far greater design modification. In June 1936, Congress authorized an increase of serviceable aircraft from the 1,800 funded by the 1926 Air Corps Act to 2,320 recommended by the Baker Board. The mid-1930s was a time when American air policy emphasized hemispheric defense. The GHQ Air Force and the AAC wanted more four engine bombers to use to implement its defense objectives: long range aerial reconnaissance and to reinforce and supply Hawaii, the Panama Canal, and Alaska in case of an emergency. However, the General Staff considered four engine bombers as offensive weapons, and it was the Navy's responsibility for the long range defense of coastal America. The medium bombers were considered more desirable, as they could be more easily adapted to the Army's intention to use them in support of the ground army. More medium bombers could be purchased for the same money as a lesser number of heavy bombers, and the goal of 2,320 aircraft could be fulfilled and replacements would cost less. On 17 January 1936 the AAC ordered an initial 133 B-18s that were followed by an order for 217 B-18Bs. The first B-18 was sent to Wright Field in the fall of 1936 and then to Langley for testing. By mid-1937 the Bolo was released for unit use, and personnel liked the aircraft better than the Martin B-10s and B-12s it replaced. The B-18 became known as the "budget bomber," a decision that would have consequences in coming years.

B-17

However, the upper echelons of AAC favored the Model 299/YB-17 despite the devastating effect of the 30 October crash of the prototype. The Air Ma-

After the disastrous 30 October 1935 crash of the prototype Model 299, on 17 January 1936 the Army General Staff decided to order 13 of the promising Model 299s, now designated the **YB-17**. (AAF)

Although the B-17 was a success, Gen. Arnold was concerned that if war came Boeing would be unable to build sufficient numbers of the bomber and issued Specification C-212 for a bomber with a 3,000 mile range, 35,000 foot ceiling, a maximum speed of 300 mph, and a bomb load of 8,000 pounds. On 21 February 1939 the AAC stated that Consolidated was the only company that had a C-212 contender and on 30 March awarded Consolidated a contract for a single **XB-24** prototype. (AAF)

teriel Command felt that the problem laid in the need "to develop the most advanced types too rapidly" (e.g. the crash of the ground-breaking Model 299), and it would be better to settle on a more conservative proposal that could be produced without fear of crashes (i.e. B-18) and not meeting specifications (i.e. B-10). With the conservative B-18 design the AAC would be assured of equipping its squadrons with a dependable and less costly, albeit mediocre, bomber. It was ironic that before the war was over the Douglas Long Beach facility would assemble over 3,000 Boeing B-17s!

Nonetheless, also on 17 January 1936 the Army General Staff decided to order 13 of the Model 299s now designated the YB-17 (the "Y" meant that the aircraft was not experimental but a "service test" model that could, or not, precede production aircraft). Boeing put the now designated Y1B-17 (the 1 because they were purchased out of F-1 fiscal year supplementary funds) into production. The first Y1B-17 rolled off the Seattle line on 2 December 1936 and the last of the 13 was finished on 5 August 1937. One Y1B-17 was sent to Wright for testing and the other 12 were assigned to the Second Bombardment Group at Langley Field, VA, under Lt.Col. Robert Olds.

In late 1937 the Air Corps ordered ten more aircraft, designated B-17B and, soon after, another 29. Improved with larger flaps, rudder, and a Plexiglas nose, the B-17Bs were delivered between July 1939 and March 1940. They equipped two bombardment groups, one on each U.S. coast. Prior to the attack on Pearl Harbor fewer than 200 B-17s were in service with the Army, but production quickly accelerated, and the B-17 became the first truly mass-produced large aircraft. The aircraft went on to serve in every World War II combat zone, and by the time production ended in May 1945, 12,731 aircraft had been built by Boeing, Douglas, and Vega (a subsidiary of Lockheed).

B-24

By the autumn of 1938, Gen. H.H. Arnold, the recently appointed Chief of the Air Corps, while confident the B-17 was a qualified success, was concerned that if war came Boeing would be unable to build sufficient numbers of the bomber. Arnold considered the possibility that Consolidated should manufacture the B-17 under license, and in December Consolidated representatives went to Seattle to discuss licensing with Boeing. They found that Boeing did not have enough work at that time to share orders, and moreover the B-17 design was already four years old in an evolution of rapidly changing aircraft designs. The Air Corps had recently issued Type Specification C-212 for a bomber with a 3,000 mile range, 35,000 foot ceiling, a maximum speed of 300 mph and a bomb load of 8,000 pounds. The Consolidated engineering staff was confident that they could design a new bomber that would be able to carry the same bomb load as the B-17 but at higher speeds and longer range. Consolidated had experimented with the Davis Wing on its Model 31 deep-hulled twin engine flying boat and found the wing to improve performance by 20%. By the end of January 1939 Consolidated met with Wright Field with specifications and primary data for the proposed Model 32 bomber (B-24). The Air Corps had made inquiries of Sikorsky and Martin, asking if they had any designs that could meet the C-212 Specifications, and neither had anything on the drawing board, as they had only three weeks to respond to C-212. However, Consolidated had a wooden mock-up ready for AAF assessment on 1 February 1939. On 21 February the Air Corps declared that Consolidated was the only company that had a C-212 contender, and on 30 March awarded Consolidated a contract for a single XB-24 prototype (USAAC s/n 39-556) with a completion date of 30 December 1939. Since the world situation was deteriorating in early 1939, seven YB-24 service test aircraft with spare parts for $2.88 million were contracted in April and 38 B-24As were added in August. On 29 December 1939 the XB-24 prototype piloted by William Wheatley and George Newman flew from Lindbergh Field on a 17 minute test flight. Early test flights proved the Davis wing to be everything that its designers had hoped for, and by the end of the war 18,481 B-24s and variants had been built, the largest production run for any American bomber.

Long-Range Bomber Procurement and Development

Kilner Board Recommendation of 1939

In late 1938, Maj.Gen. Arnold called a secret meeting of AAC officers and aviation experts to discuss the future of the AAC and the bomber predicament. Charles Lindbergh had visited Hitler's Germany and was impressed and alarmed over the emphasis that the Luftwaffe had put on bombardment aircraft. Arnold asked Lindbergh to serve on a board headed by Brig.Gen. Walter Kilner and assisted by Col. Carl Spaatz, Col. Earl Naiden, and Maj. Alfred Lyon. The Kilner Board issued its report in June 1939, and members of the group thought that in a European war Germany would not only overrun the Continent but also conquer Great Britain and then Africa, and perhaps establish bases in South America. If the Japanese began a war in the Pacific it would have to be fought over long expanses of ocean extending from Alaska to Hawaii to the Philippines to as far as Australia. In this scenario the B-17 would surely be inadequate, and the super bomber notion was revived. The role of the super bomber was no longer thought to be as a strategic bomber, but was to be a defensive bomber able to fly long distances to strike an enemy advancing on the American continents. The Board proposed a five-year research and development program for new engines and aircraft. Engine development was to be liquid-cooled and range in horsepower from 1,500 to 2,400, and eventually to 3,000hp. A 2,000 mile four-engine heavy bomber was to be developed along with another heavy bomber with a large fuselage that could carry bombs and/or enough fuel to give it a range of 5,000 miles. From the former specification the B-17 and B-24 were in the process of completing development, and to the latter specification the B-29 and ill-fated B-32 would eventually be developed "for hemispheric defense." The Board recommended that two-engine light and medium bombers be developed, with the B-18 being the only contemporary type available and with the B-25 and B-26 available in the near future. Although the Kilner recommendation was accepted by the AAC, unfortunately it was at the time that there was an isolationist sentiment in America, and the AAC could do nothing until Congress appropriated funds.

Chief of Staff Malin Craig established an Air Board to conduct a study of hemisphere defense and ordered it to make its report before his term expired on 1 September 1939, the day George C. Marshall would start his six-year reign as Chief of Staff. The Air Board report was issued on that day and found that U.S. naval forces and coastal defenses were insufficient to protect America. The report pointed out that contemporary bombers made America vulnerable to aerial attack, and the only answer was a flexible, Long-Range air fleet. When Boeing designer Edward Wells visited Dayton in late 1939, Col. Oliver Echols, head of the Air Materiel Command, encouraged Boeing to continue work on the superbomber by telling Wells that there would be a new bomber requirement soon.

RB-40-B Contracts

Due to an energetic campaign by Maj.Gen. Henry Arnold in November 1939 Congress approved funding, and Arnold was authorized by Gen. George Marshall to let R-40-B study contracts (R-40-B translates to Requirement number 40, Bomber) for the very Long-Range heavy bomber. Capt. Donald Putt of the Air Materiel Command at Wright Field established a statement of the military characteristics of the new bomber. The bomber was to have a range of 5,333 miles and be able to carry a bomb load of a ton over half that distance and have a speed of 400mph. In early 1940, after the experience of five months of war in Europe, the AAF saw that there were limitations in its earlier requirements and issued another specification to succeed its R-40-B specs. The AAF then restructured its heavy bomber requirements, requesting self-sealing fuel tanks, increased armor protection, and multiple turrets with heavier caliber machine guns and cannons. On 29 January 1940 the AAC sent the Request for Data R-40-B and Spec XC-218 to a number of

Boeing had experience building heavy bombers on the B-17 program, and also was working on the Model 341 and Model 345. So on 27 June 1940, when the AAC issued contracts for preliminary engineering data for the new "superbomber" to four manufacturers, Boeing had a head start and on 24 August 1940, the AAC ordered two prototypes under the designation **XB-29**. (AAF)

As insurance against the possible failure of the favored Boeing XB-29 the AAC also ordered two **XB-32** prototypes from Consolidated. With the eventual success and investment in the B-29 only 118 B-3s were built, and those were of the non-pressurized, conventional heavy bomber variety. (AAF)

aircraft companies that designed heavy bombers. The request was sent via the mail marked as "Urgent" from Washington D.C. The companies were given 30 days to submit design proposals and then were expected to finish a full-scale engineering mockup by 5 August 1940; the first completed aircraft was to be ready by 1 July 1941 and subsequent aircraft one month later. Four West Coast companies would submit designs: Lockheed and Consolidated of San Diego, Douglas of Los Angeles, and Boeing of Seattle. Again, none of the companies was motivated to submit far-reaching designs. Whatever resources they had available were being invested in expanding their factories and work force to build established but mediocre contemporary aircraft for the three American military services and foreign air forces that were at war and in dire need of anything that would fly.

It was not until 5 February 1940 that Boeing President Philip Johnson received the Data R-40B and Spec XC-218 specs. Boeing had previous experience in heavy bomber design, and since 1938 had engaged a few of their best young designers on working on the super bomber concept. By the late 1930s Boeing finances were finally recovering, but the Boeing engineering department was stretched thin, as the Boeing B-17 venture was ready for mass production and the AAC was about to place an order for 250 B-17Es. Boeing had a head start on the VLR program, as in August 1939 Boeing had started work on the Model 341 project, but in order to meet the requirements of Data R-40B it was reworked into the Model 345. The Model 345 design was submitted to the AAC on 11 May 1940 and the AAC awarded Boeing additional funds to continue the project. On 27 June 1940, the AAC issued contracts for preliminary engineering data for the new "superbomber" to four manufacturers, but on 24 August 1940 the AAC ordered two prototypes from Boeing under the designation XB-29 and two XB-32 prototypes were ordered from Consolidated as insurance against the failure of the favored Boeing XB-29.

With the increasing probability of war the B-29 project became more critical, and 14 service-test aircraft were ordered under the designation YB-29. On 17 May 1941, the AAC ordered 250 B-29s to be built in a new government-owned Boeing plant at Wichita, KS, and by the end of the war 1,620 B-29s were built there, along with 536 by Martin at its Omaha, NE, plant and 357 by Bell at its plant in Marietta, GA. Boeing-Renton, WA, exclusively built 1,119 B-29As, while the Bell-Marietta factory exclusively built 311 B-29Bs for a total of 3,943 of all types.

Development of World War II Bombing Strategy

AWPD-1

In the early1930s there was a dichotomy in the War Department. The conflict engaged the traditionalists, led by Army Chief of Staff Gen. John J. Pershing, who believed that the infantry ruled the battlefield, while the Army Air Arm, led by the defrocked Gen. Billy Mitchell, espoused the future role of airpower in warfare. The government organized a number of board and committees to study air doctrine and its role in future warfare. The most influential of these groups was the Baker Board Report of July 1934 that recommended America's national defense policy was not based on aggression and its purpose was to defend the homeland and overseas possessions, with the Army fending off any invader until civilian forces could be mobilized. The Report stated, "The idea that aviation can replace any of the other elements of our armed forces is found on analysis, to be erroneous. Since ground forces alone are capable of occupying territory, the Army with its own air forces remains the ultimate decisive factor in war." Baker Board member Jimmy Doolittle voiced the minority dissent, supported the separation of the Army and its air forces, and advocated the development of air doctrine for its employment.

Although the Baker Board rejected an independent strategic air force, it did support the creation in March 1935 of a General Headquarters Air Force that would be under the control of the Army commander in the field. However, there were conflicting opinions of the role of the GHQ Air Force. One was that it would be apportioned and attached to field armies and utilized under their direct control. Another view had the GHQ AF engaged as an integrated force acting to further the mission of the Army. The view held by most airmen was to have it act as a unified force not to support the Army, but also to act beyond the realm of the Army with missions of its own. Maj.Gen. Frank Andrews was the CO of the GHQ AF and forcefully advocated the airmen's point of view. As the possibility of a war in Europe approached the War Department was in a state of flux, and the GHQ AF and its concepts were replaced by ideas formulated by the Joint Army-Navy Board that culminated in the First Strategic Air Plan (AWPD-1).

On 20 June 1941 President Roosevelt signed the War Powers Act of 1941 that authorized the creation of the U.S. Army Air Forces (USAAF), which in effect merged the Army Air Corps and the General Headquarters, Air Force into a solitary self-governed entity with its own Air Staff that was no longer answerable to the Army General Staff. Although the USAAF was not entirely independent of the Army or War Department, it could operate autonomously and was able to administer its own training, procurement, and operations. By the end of the year Arnold, the head of the new USAAF, would also be, for all intents and purposes, a member of the Joint Chiefs of Staff.

The urgency of rearmament increased on 22 June 1941 when the German armies invaded Russia. On 9 July 1941, President Roosevelt sent a letter to the Secretaries of War and Navy asking them to prepare "an estimate of overall production requirements required to defeat our potential enemies." To forestall the War Plans Division from preparing a plan that would relegate the Army Air Force into a supporting role to the Army, Arnold's Air Chief of Staff, Brig.Gen. Carl "Toohey" Spaatz, a member of the 1939 Kilner Board, formed the Air War Plans Division (AWPD). The AWPD was to be headed by Lt.Col. Harold George, CO of the Second Bombardment Group, and newly appointed Chief of the War Plans Division, Lt. Colonels; Kenneth Walker, Chief of the War Plans Group; Haywood Hansell, Chief of the European section of the War Plans Group; Lawrence Kuter, G-3 from the General Staff; and Orvil Anderson and Howard Craig. The responsibility of the AWPD was to formulate a general plan for the employment of airpower to defeat the Axis that would utilize airpower to its fullest capability. The AWPD was to determine the size of the air forces required to defeat Germany first and then defeat Japan. Their plan, called AWPD-1, was submitted in nine days to the Army General Staff War Plans Division on 12 August 1941. Generally, it called for 24,500 combat aircraft, of which approximately 10,000 were to be four and six engine bombers. On 11 September 1941 Gen. Marshall accepted AWPD-1, and the B-29 and B-32 were an important element in the plan. In the 1939 Kilner Board recommendation the future B-29 and B-32 were to be hemispheric bombers to operate from American bases, but by early 1941 Britain appeared to be safe from German invasion. If the United States entered the war English and American planners envisioned the Very Long-Range (VLR) Bomber to operate from bases in England and the Mediterranean to bomb Germany. In those dark days AWPD-1 projected that by summer 1944 24 B-29 and 24 B-32 groups would be sent to bomb Germany from England and Egypt as part of the "48 Very Heavy Group Program." As part of this plan, several B-24 groups in the MTO would initially transition to B-32s and B-29s as soon as the bombers' service tests were completed. Then the remaining Eighth and Fifteenth Air Force B-17 and B-24 groups in the MTO and ETO would transition to the two new longer range bombers. Gen. Spaatz also saw the bomber as a weapon against Japan in a future war in the Pacific that seemed to be inevitable, so also embodied in AWPD-1 was the provision for two B-29 and B-32 groups to be available to bomb Japan from Luzon if the Japanese entered the war. This was the beginning of the "Europe first" strategy, in which the Anglo-Americans concentrated their efforts against Germany. Until Germany was defeated Japan would be contained in a defensive battle in which naval forces would predominate.

AWPD-1 was the blueprint for the creation of the Army Air Forces and the conduct of the air war.

AWPD-42

In August 1942 FDR again asked for an estimate of the number of military aircraft that needed to be produced in 1943 to attain air supremacy, and a new air plan designated as AWPD-42 was prepared. AWPD-1 had been created in September 1941, as a contingency plan in case America became involved in the war. AWPD-42 was essentially a requirements plan specifying the aircraft (including those of U.S. allies), munitions, and bases to accomplish an agreed strategy. AWPD-42 retained the basic structure of AWPD-1, as the defeat of Germany remained the first priority and the air offensive against Japan continued to be deferred. Also unchanged was the primary strategic principle of undermining and destroying the capability and will of Germany to wage war by destroying the enemy's war industries and economic systems upon which the military and political economy depended.

The bombing objectives were classified as primary and intermediate, with principal priority given to the intermediate targets:

Fighter aircraft assembly plants
Bomber aircraft assembly plants
Aero engine assembly plants

The primary targets were:

U-Boat manufacture
Transportation targets (rail and canal in Germany)
Electric power system
Synthetic oil plants
Aluminum plants
Synthetic rubber plants

As for the air offensive against Japan, it was too early to give anything more than general guidance in terms of objectives and targets. Nevertheless, AWPD-42 recognized that the strategic air offensive against Japan would follow the defeat of Germany. Once launched, the strategic air offensive against Japan would be similar to that for Germany. It would seek to undermine and destroy the capability and will of the Japanese people to wage war by destroying the industries and systems upon which the war industries and the civilian economy relied.

By mid-1942 it became impossible to maintain the maximum possible air strength directed toward the primary strategic air offensive against Germany as directed by AWPD-1. Campaigns in North Africa, the Middle East, and Far East were absorbing air resources to support land operations there. However, strategic bombing of Germany had not even begun in any meaningful sense and would be further delayed if these diversions of airpower continued to expand.

Combined Bomber Offensive (CBO): The Casablanca Directive

The Casablanca Conference of January 1943 produced the third important air directive of World War II; the Casablanca Directive for the prosecution of the Combined Bomber Offensive (CBO). This document was crafted by Air Vice Marshal Sir John Slessor and Gen. Ira Eaker. During the joint American-British Conference (ABC-1) in February 1941, Slessor pressed for a sustained air offensive against Germany as the key element in Allied air strategy. Slessor completely understood AWPD-1 and AWPD-42 and the objectives expressed in both American plans, and was thoroughly familiar with the target systems of each, the tactics proposed, and results expected.

The CBO plan differed from AWPD-1 and AWPD-42 in that the former were "Requirement Plans," designed to prescribe what should be accomplished and what was needed, while the plan for the CBO was a "Capability Plan." Its purpose was to prescribe what should be done to achieve an objective with forces already committed to production.

The Casablanca Directive specified the "vigorous prosecution by both British and American air forces toward a common grand strategic objective, optimizing the special strength and capabilities of each air force toward that common goal." The ultimate objective of British and American strategic air forces was: "The progressive destruction and dislocation of the German military, industrial and economic system, and the undermining of the morale of the German people to a point where their capacity for armed resistance is fatally weakened." Pending preparation and approval of a plan for the Combined Bomber Offensive, the Casablanca Directive called for destruction or neutralization of German targets taken directly from AWPD-1 and AWPD-42:

1) U-Boat construction yards
2) Aircraft industry
3) Transportation
4) Oil plants
5) Other targets of war industry

The directive sanctioned both American and British grand strategy for airpower, and recognized both RAF doctrine and experience and American tactical doctrine. The Eighth Air Force and RAF Bomber Command would be able to operate independently. RAF Bomber Command was allowed to continue its chosen air strategy of bomber stream nighttime area bombing, while the Eighth Air Force was free to continue to follow its doctrine of the destruction of selective targets by daylight bombing escorted by fighters. This combined bombing offensive would result in the agreed grand objective, the "fatal weakening of Nazi Germany," and was approved by Roosevelt, Churchill, and the Combined Chiefs.

By November 1943 the question of grand Pacific strategy had not been clearly determined, and both the MacArthur SWPA/Philippines and Nimitz Central Pacific surface strategies were endorsed. Air strategists were ambivalent concerning the air offensive against Japan, but Gen. Arnold was determined to employ the B-29s against the Japanese homeland. B-29s were beginning to come off the production line, and the logistical nightmare of basing them out of India as outlined by the *Matterhorn* plan caused the Chief of Staffs to finally decide on the capture of the Marianas

The **Casablanca Conference** of January 1943 produced the third important air directive of World War II; the Casablanca Directive for the prosecution of the Combined Bomber Offensive (CBO). Attending the Conference were Chiang Kai-Shek (L), FDR (C), and Churchill (R). (AFHRC)

for air bases for B-29 operations in their air offensive against the Japanese home islands.

Field Manual 100-20, Command and Employment of Airpower

In June 1943 Gen. Arnold announced: "The Tactical Air Force, as the Air Force to work on a coequal basis with the Ground Forces in the battle has been accepted by the War Department and is now being prepared in Field Service Regulation form."

A slim booklet was published by the War Department on 21 July 1943, entitled *Field Manual 100-20, Command and Employment of Airpower*, which laid the foundation for American tactical airpower at a time when it had only limited battle experience in North Africa, no training scheme, inadequate fighter-bomber aircraft, and few experienced pilots for such an undertaking. The authors of *FM 100-20* were academics who formulated three priorities for waging tactical warfare and affirmed airpower to be an equal and independent entity commanded by a senior air commander who was to be responsible only to the theater commander. Throughout the war USAAF leadership was committed to maximum autonomy in the War Department with the intention of gaining post war independence, but had to settle for the autonomy given to them by *FM 100-20*. Nonetheless, it was the Emancipation Proclamation for airpower.

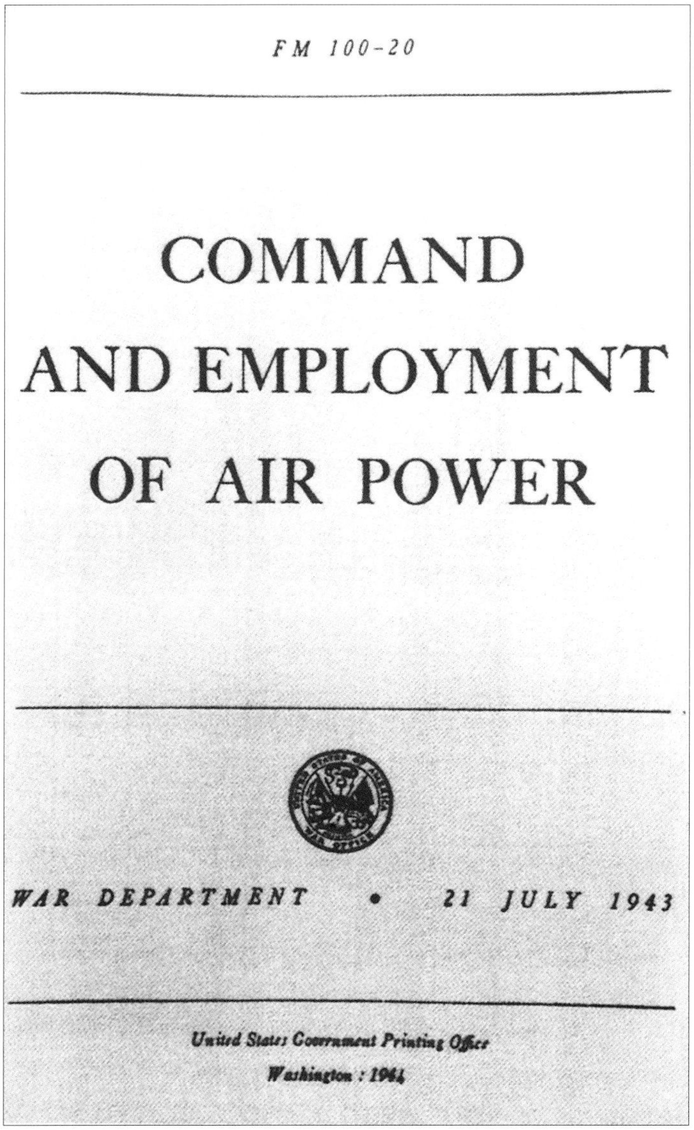

FM 100-20

COMMAND AND EMPLOYMENT OF AIR POWER

WAR DEPARTMENT • 21 JULY 1943

United States Government Printing Office
Washington : 1944

Field Manual 100-20, Command and Employment of Airpower was a slim booklet published by the War Department on 21 July 1943 that laid the foundation for American tactical airpower. *FM 100-20* formulated three priorities for waging tactical warfare and affirmed airpower to be an equal and independent entity commanded by a senior air commander who was to be responsible only to the theater commander. (Author)

Much of this doctrine was taken from the British experience in North Africa. Parts of *FM 100-20* were based on a pamphlet written by Gen. Montgomery in January 1943 entitled *Some Notes on High Command in War*. Vice Air Marshall Sir Arthur Coningham, whose air units supported Montgomery in North Africa, influenced Montgomery's thinking on the application of tactical airpower. In *Ideas, Concepts, Doctrine: A History of Basic Thinking in the United States Air Force, 1907-1964* (Air University, AL, 1974), Robert Futrell quoted Gen. Robert Candee as saying the Air Force "had swallowed the RAF solution of a local situation in Africa hook, line and sinker, without analyzing it or report it in 'Americanese' instead of British speech."

As the Allies took the offensive in the air and on the ground in the ETO and MTO in 1943, *FM 100-20* prioritized an air plan in which to conduct the war. Their first priority was to win air superiority: "The primary aim of the tactical air force is to obtain and maintain air superiority in the theater....Without this air supremacy the initiative passes to the enemy. Air supremacy is best obtained by attack on hostile airdromes, the destruction of aircraft at rest and by fighter action in the air. This is much more effective than any attempt to furnish an umbrella of fighter aviation over our troops. At most an air umbrella is prohibitively expensive and could be provided over a small area for a brief period of time."

The second priority was: "The disruption of hostile lines of communication, the destruction of supply dumps, installations and the attack on hostile troop concentrations in rear areas will cause the enemy great damage and may decide the battle. This accomplishes 'isolation of the battlefield.' If the hostile force is denied food, ammunition and reinforcements, aggressive action on the part of our ground forces will cause him to retire and the immediate objective will be gained. Massed air action on those targets should turn the retirement into a rout." In general, the second priority could be summed up as "behind the lines attacks."

The third priority was: "The destruction of selected objectives in the battle area in furtherance of the combined air-ground effort....Teamwork, mutual understanding and cooperation are essential for this success of the combined effort in the battle area. In order to obtain the necessary teamwork, the command posts of the Tactical Air Force and of the ground force concerned should be adjacent or common, at least during this phase of operations. Air and ground commanders profit greatly from the other's successes. Airplanes destroyed on an enemy airdrome and in the air can never attack our troops. The advance of ground troops often makes available new airdromes needed by the air force. Massed air action on the immediate front will pave the way for an advance. However, in the zone of contact, missions against hostile units are difficult to control, are most expensive and are, in general, least effective. Targets are small, well dispersed and difficult to locate. In addition, there is always a considerable chance of striking friendly forces, due to errors in target designation, errors in navigation, or to the fluidity of the situation. Such missions must be controlled by phase lines, or bomb safety lines, which are set up and rigidly adhered to by both ground and air units. Only at critical times are contact zone missions profitable." The third priority then was "battle front attack/close support."

At the end of the war the air campaign had demonstrated that ground direction of fighter-bombers to targets was very effective and did not cause loss of Air Force control or flexibility. Attacks on Second and Third Priority targets were most effective when the objective and method of the attack was jointly selected and planned by both air and ground staffs.

2

Conventional Bombs

Bomb Components and Accessories

Complete Round

A complete round consisted of all the components and accessories necessary for the ammunition to function as intended. Generally a bomb was shipped including the following assemblies: Bomb Body, Trunnion Band, Fin Assembly, Arming Wire Assembly, and Fuses. The explosive charge was added to the bomb case.

Bomb Body

Components

The bomb body consisted of a steel case which contained the explosive charge and auxiliary boosters. The case was closed at the nose by the fuse seat liner and at the tail by a base plug containing an adapter booster.

Case

The bomb case was a metal container that held explosive, chemical, or inert fillers, and could consist of a single piece of metal, or several pieces welded or otherwise joined together. The bomb case was usually a streamlined steel cylinder that was manufactured by the forging and machining of steel ingots; shaping steel tubing; by forming and welding sheet metal or plate; or by building up rings or bar stock. Suspension lugs were usually welded to the case, but some bombs (Navy AP and depth bombs) had drilled and tapped holes for the attachment of suspension lugs by machine screws. Lugs for double hook racks were located in line with the axis of the bomb, 14 inches apart for bombs up to 1,000 pounds and 30 inches apart for bombs 2,000 pounds and more. This interlug distance provided a convenient reference scale for bomb recognition (except for the 1,600 pound AP bomb that had provisions for attachment of suspension lug and both 14 and 30 inch spacing). The lug for single hook suspension was located diametrically opposite the double lugs in line with the center of gravity of the bomb. The forward end of the case was sized and threaded for the fuse seat liner, nose fuse, or shipping plug. The rear was threaded to receive the base plug.

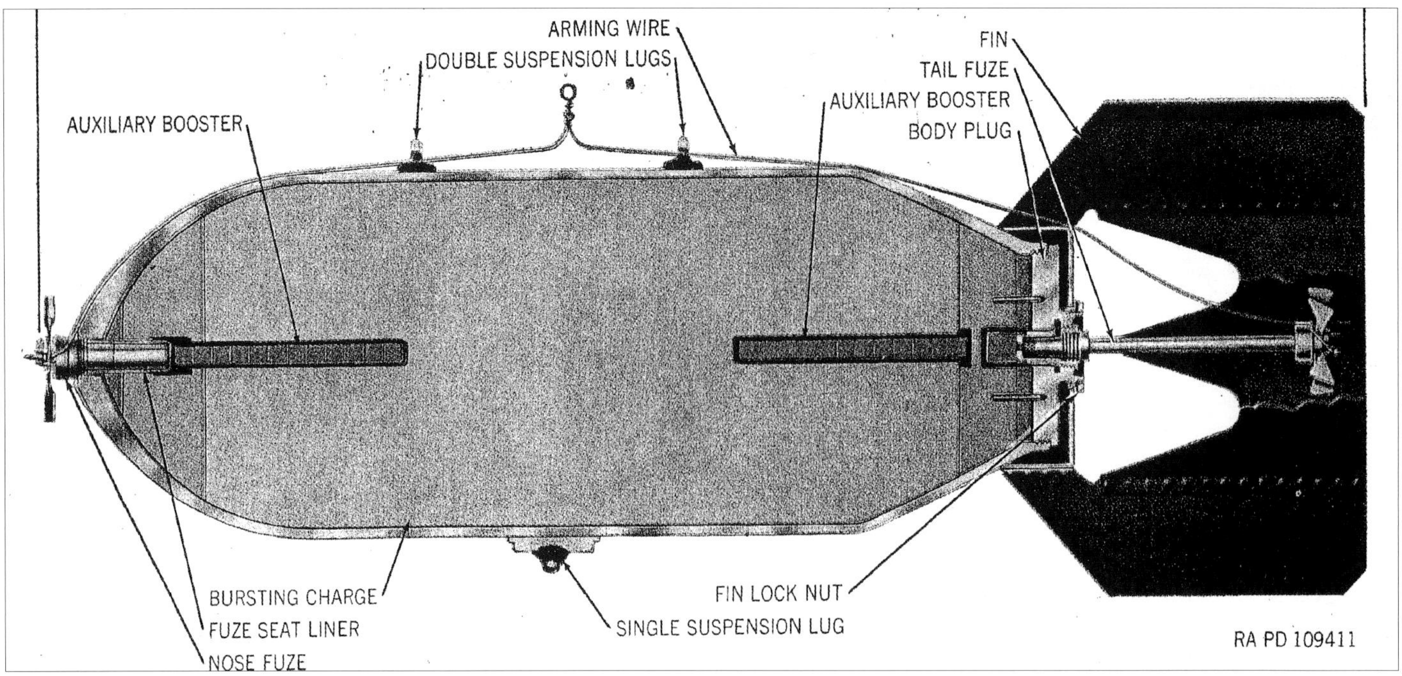

A **complete round** consisted of all the components and accessories necessary for the ammunition to function as intended. (TM 9-1980)

Left: The **bomb case** was a metal container that held explosive, chemical, or inert fillers and could consist of a single piece of metal, or several pieces welded or otherwise joined together. (Author/CAF-AZ)

Right: **Suspension lugs** were usually welded to the case, but some bombs (Navy AP and depth bombs) had drilled and tapped holes for the attachment of suspension lugs by machine screws. Lugs for double hook racks were located in line with the axis of the bomb, 14 inches apart for bombs up to 1,000 pounds and 30 inches apart for bombs 2,000 pounds and more. (Author/CAF-AZ)

Moisture Protection

The explosive charge in General Purpose and Fragmentation Bombs was usually cast, and was uniform throughout unless the explosive was Amatol or Composition B, in which case the nose and tail portions were pure TNT "booster surrounds," which provided protection from moisture. In some bombs, thin pads of inert wax in the nose and tail cavities protected the explosive from moisture and also prevented the entrance of the explosive into thread crevices. These bombs were identified by the marking "with pad."

Closing Plug

Metal closing plugs were used to protect the fuse seat cavity and threads from damage during shipping and stowage. They were removed only for inspection or for fusing the bomb. If a bomb was returned to stowage after being prepared for use, the fuses were removed and the closing plugs replaced. Low-drag GP bombs were equipped with steel nose and tail plugs. When these bombs were to be used with mechanical fuses, the plugs were removed and discarded prior to the insertion of adapter-boosters.

Base Plug

The base plug closed the filling hole in the end of the bomb body. The tail fuse adapter-booster was screwed in the base plug. An extension of the plug to the rear was threaded to provide for attachment of the fin assembly by the fin locknut. For shipping, the fin lock nut was covered by a fiber protector and was wired in place. In later bombs (the A1 modification of GP bombs) the base plug had studs extending into the explosive charge to prevent the removal of the plug. The plug was threaded to receive an adapter-booster and had a circular groove which received the adapter-booster lock pin.

Explosive Charge

The bomb case was completely filled with explosive. In some bombs, thin pads of inert wax in the nose and tail cavities protected the explosive from moisture and also prevented the entrance of the explosive into thread crevices, which was dangerous in the event of mishandling. These bombs were identified by the marking "with pad." The type of explosive depended upon the prospective use of the bomb. Types of explosive charges are described in depth later.

Adapter-Booster

The adapter-booster, as the name implied, was the assembly of the booster to the adapter. An adapter was a bushing threaded on the outside for assembly to the bomb body and on the inside for assembly of the fuse. Tail adapter-boosters, normally assembled to High Explosive and Chemical Bombs as issued, were drilled for the insertion of lock pins to prevent their removal when anti-withdrawal-type fuses were to be assembled to the bomb. Since General Purpose Bombs were usually adapted for large diameter nose fuses, a nose adapter-booster was issued separately to adapt these bombs for use with small diameter fuses. Large bombs were adapted for large diameter nose fuses; an adapter-booster which was externally threaded to fit the large fuse seat and internally to receive the smaller fuse necessary in order to use smaller special purpose fuses with the bombs.

Auxiliary Booster

When the type of explosive charge made it necessary or desirable, an auxiliary booster—a column of Tetryl pellets in a suitable container—was

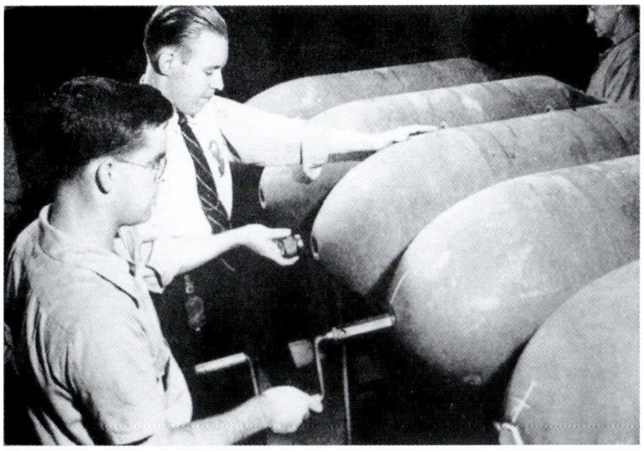

Left: Metal **closing plugs** were used to protect the fuse seat cavity and threads from damage during shipping and stowage. (Author/CAF-AZ)

Middle: **Closing plugs** being screwed in (left) and tightened (right) during the final factory inspection. (AAF)

Right: The **base plug** closed the filling hole in the end of the bomb body. The tail fuse adapter-booster was screwed in the base plug. An extension of the plug to the rear was threaded to provide for attachment of the fin assembly by the fin locknut. (Author/CAF-AZ)

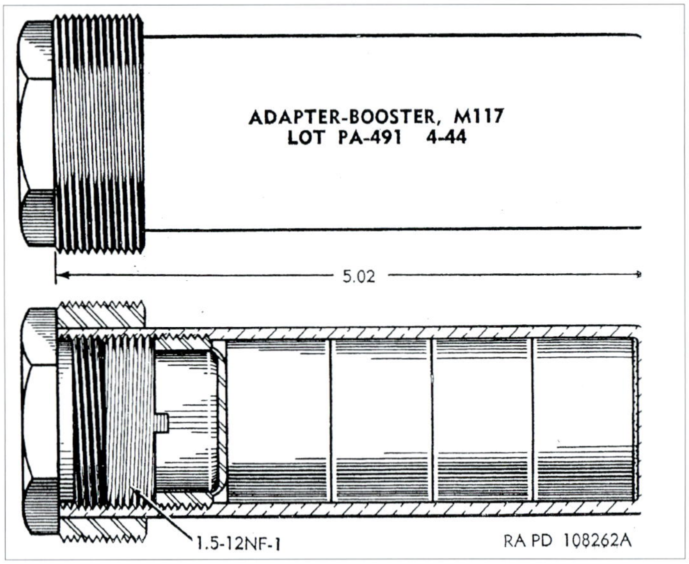

The **adapter-booster**, as the name implied, was the assembly of the booster to the adapter. An adapter was a bushing threaded on the outside for assembly to the bomb body and on the inside for assembly of the fuse. (TM 9-1980)

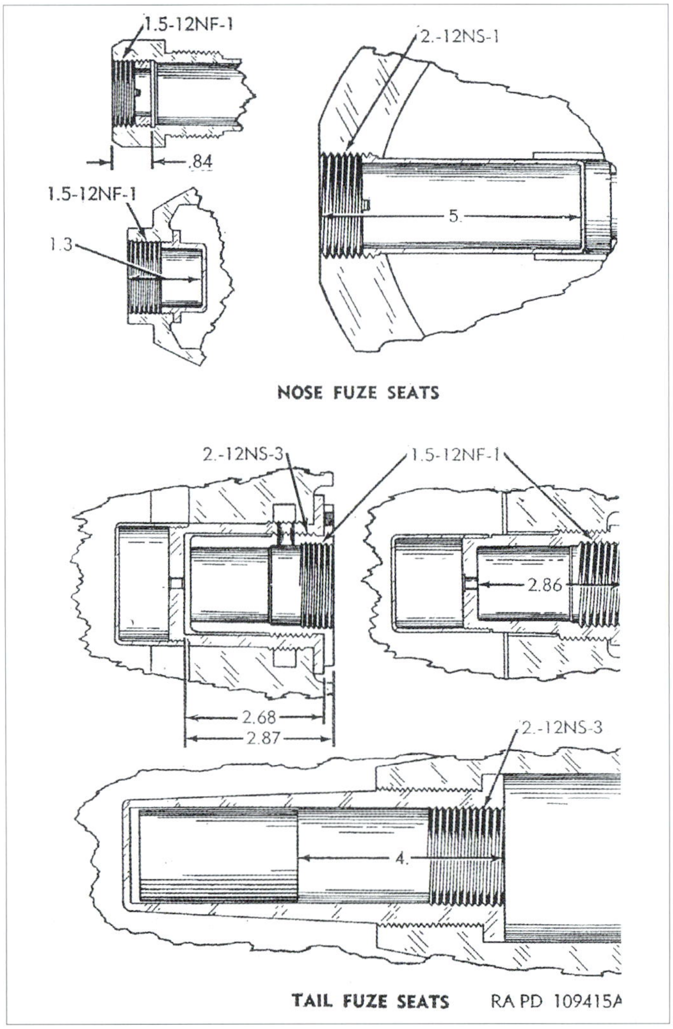

Fuse seats were usually machined in the bomb case and, in order to provide for maximum flexibility, their dimensions (thread size and depth of seat) were standardized as much as practicable. (TM 9-1980)

cast within the charge adjacent to the fuse seat liner, adapter-booster, or both. It also could be issued separately for installation in a fuse seat liner. The function of the auxiliary booster was to relay and amplify detonation waves to insure the explosion of the main charge.

Fuse Seats

Nose Fuse Seats

Seats for nose fuses were usually machined in the bomb case and, in order to provide for maximum flexibility, their dimensions (thread size and depth of

Nose Seat (Author/CAF-AZ)

Tail Seat (Author/CAF-AZ)

seat) were standardized as much as practicable. Large bombs had the C-type fuse seat, which had a two inch thread diameter and was five inches deep. Smaller bombs had the fragmentation-type fuse seat, which was 1.5 inches in thread diameter by 1.3 inches deep. Flares, photo-flash bombs, and clusters had a flare-type fuse seat which was 1.5 inches in thread diameter by 0.84 inches deep. To permit the use of small fragmentation-type fuses in large bombs the M117 adapter-booster was supplied. Adapter boosters were also used to provide fuse seats. Its external contour fit the GP-type fuse seat; its internal contour corresponded to the fragmentation-type seat, and the space between was filled with Tetryl to serve as an auxiliary booster.

Tail Fuse Seats

Tail fuse seats for GP, SAP, Chemical, Incendiary, and Fragmentation Bombs were provided by two models of adapter-boosters, the M102A1 and the M115A1. The Adapter-booster M102A1 was 1.5 inches in thread diameter by 2.86 inches deep. This model was used on all GP bombs of early manufacture and on later models up to 250 pounds. Adapter-booster M116A1 was two inches in thread diameter by 2.68 inches deep, but it also included a fuse adapter which fit this seat and provided a fuse seat similar to that of the M102A1. Both of these models were drilled for the insertion of a lock pin that locked the adapter-booster in the base plug (base plug of the A1 modified GP bombs) while the fuse was in place. The earlier M102 and M115 models did not have this locking device. Tail fuse seats for AP and depth bombs were provided by machining the tail fuse seat liners and were two inches in thread diameter by four inches deep.

Fuse Seat Liner

The fuse seat liner was a metal cup secured inside the nose of the bomb to keep a cavity clear for assembling the nose fuse and auxiliary booster.

Suspension Band

Metal suspension bands provided 14 inch suspension for bombs already equipped with suspension lugs placed 30 inches apart (e.g. 2,000 pound GP bombs).

Shipping Bands

Shipping bands were attached to the bomb to protect the suspension lugs and were not to be removed until the bomb was ready for use. They could be made of compressed paper with a recess for the lug or of metal in the shape of a U-shaped channel.

Trunnion Bands

Trunnion mountings were used for dive bombing, with the trunnions mounted on a steel band which was bolted to the bomb body. The single suspension lug indicated the proper location of the trunnion band. AP and depth bombs were drilled and threaded so that the trunnions could be screwed into the bomb body.

Fin Assembly

Construction

The fin assembly provided stability for the bomb in flight. Smaller bombs (usually 100 pounds and under) had the fin assembled to the bomb body before shipment; some 100 pound GP bombs and all larger bombs were shipped with unassembled fins and shipped separately packed in a metal crate. The fin assembly generally used with bombs up to 4,000 pounds consisted of a fin sleeve that fit over the tail of the bomb (held in place by the fin lock nut) and sheet metal fin blades which were riveted or spot-welded to the fin sleeve and to each other to form a square box-like assembly. Early fin assemblies were made of light gauge metal (0.047 inch). However, increased bomb ceilings required the use of a heavier gauge metal (0.06 to 0.075 inch) to insure more reliable ballistics. Due to increased speeds of aircraft, it was also required that fin assemblies be strengthened even though originally constructed from heavier gauge metal; this was required especially when bombs were carried in exterior suspension. Fin assemblies M123 and M124 were examples of the strengthened type. The *Tallboy* series of GP bombs (12,000 pound and heavier) utilized a fin assembly consisting of an elongated fin cone (fin sleeve) and four streamlined blades assembled perpendicularly to the cone.

Types

There were two types of fin assemblies: the box-type assembly and the conical assembly.

Box-Type Fin Assembly

The box-type fin assembly, generally used with larger bombs, consisted of a fin sleeve that fit over the tail of the bomb and was held in place by a

Left: **Shipping bands** were attached to the bomb to protect the suspension lugs and were not to be removed until the bomb was ready for use. **Trunnion bands** (mountings) were used for dive bombing, with the trunnions mounted on a steel band that was bolted to the bomb body. (TM 9-1980)

Right: **Shipping bands** being attached to 500 pound bombs at the ordnance factory. (AAF)

Left: The **box-type fin** assembly, generally used with larger bombs, consisted of a fin sleeve that fit over the tail of the bomb and was held in place by a thin locknut. Sheet metal fin blades were attached to the fin sleeve and to each other by supports to form a square box-like assembly. (Author/CAF-AZ)

Above: **Conical fins** were designed for use on cylindrical case GP and Fragmentation bombs to provide for better aerodynamic performance and greater ballistic accuracy of these bombs when carried externally on high speed aircraft (500 pound incendiary cluster shown). (AAF)

thin locknut. Sheet metal fin blades were attached to the fin sleeve and to each other by supports to form a square box- like assembly.

Some fin assemblies (earlier than the M118) were made of a light gauge metal, but increased bombing ceilings required the use of heavier metals to insure more reliable ballistics. Only those box-type fin assemblies lower than M118, designated by either A or M-A1, were made of a light gauge metal. All model designations higher than M118 were made of the heavier gauge metal.

Conical Fin Assembly

Conical fins were designed for use on cylindrical case GP and Fragmentation Bombs to provide for better aerodynamic performance and greater ballistic accuracy of these bombs when carried externally on high speed aircraft. The fin assemblies consisted of four quarter sections of sheet steel welded together, with four integral fin blades. The fin assembly was secured to the bomb by a coupling tube, a metal locking web, and a special fin locknut. Each coupling tube had three equally spaced set screws for locking the tube to the base plug of the bomb. The fin assembly was placed over the coupling tube and was secured by the locking web and fin locknut. Since these fin assemblies were longer than the box-type they required longer tail fuses and longer arming-wire assemblies.

Models

The fin assembly M118A2 and fin assemblies designated M-A1 (lower than M118) were made of the heavier gauge steel. Some heavy gauge assemblies issued prior to the assignment of "M" designations were marked with the letter "A" to indicate the heavier metal. Otherwise, the basic model designations M118 and lower (except for the M118A1, which also were constructed from lighter gauge metal) indicate the use of lighter gauge metal. Model designations higher than M118 were being assigned to newly standardized fin assemblies and were not affected by the abovementioned.

Precautions in Assembling Fins to Bombs

When assembling fins to bombs, care had to be taken to insure that all threads and seating surfaces of the bomb, fin assembly, and fin lock nut were clean. The fin blade had to be aligned with the suspension lugs for internal suspension (in the bomb bay) and 45° for external under wing or fuselage suspension. Models Ml to M3 were provided with a set screw for locking purposes. Any bent fin blades were to be straightened. If the fin assembly was loose and turned on the bomb it was to be tightened, as it would pull the arming wire from the tail fuse, allowing it to arm.

Fin Locknuts

The fin locknut was a bushing which was threaded onto a base plug or a coupling tube to secure the fin assembly to the bomb. There were three types of locknuts: Ordinary or Regular Type, New Type Locknut, Conical Fin Locknut, and Locking Web.

1) Ordinary or Regular Type

This type of locknut was assembled to the base plug of a bomb as shipped and was used on bombs assembled in the field with box-type fin assemblies.

When assembling fins to bombs, care had to be taken to insure that all threads and seating surfaces of the bomb, fin assembly, and fin lock nut were clean. The fin blade had to be aligned with the suspension lugs for internal suspension (in the bomb bay) and 45° for external under wing or fuselage suspension. (AAF)

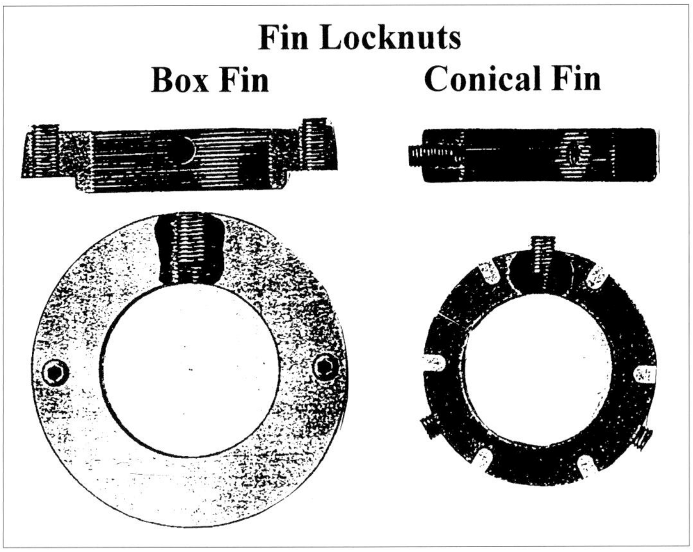

The **fin locknut** was a bushing that was threaded onto a base plug or a coupling tube to secure the fin assembly to the bomb. There were three types of locknuts: Ordinary or Regular Type, New Type Locknut, and Conical Fin Locknut and Locking Web. (TM 9-1980)

During assembly the locknut was removed, the fin assembly was placed over the tail of the bomb, and the locknut was then screwed onto the base plug and tightened with a wrench. The ordinary locknut provided no other means for attachment in the base plug; therefore, it was not normally used when bombs were to be carried externally on aircraft expected to exceed 350 mph, or in bomb bays subject to excessive air currents.

2) New Type Locknut
The new type locknuts differed from the regular locknuts in that they did incorporate a means of locking themselves to the base plug by set screws. These fin locknuts were intended for general use, and were to be installed when bombs with box-type fin assemblies were carried externally on aircraft expected to exceed 350 mph, or were carried in bomb bays subject to air currents that could cause rotation of fins held with the regular locknut. When the new type locknuts were not available the regular type could be used.

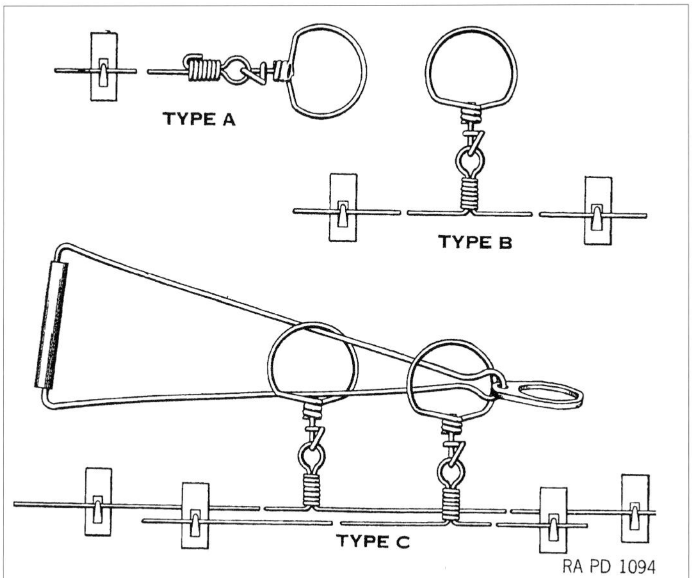

Figure 30. Arming wire assemblies.

3) Conical Fin Locknut and Locking Web
The conical fin locknut and locking web were used to secure the conical fin assembly to the coupling tube.

Parachute Unit
For low altitude bombing, some bombs were equipped with parachute units to retard the fall of the bomb and delay impact until the dropping aircraft cleared the area where it could be in danger from its own bomb's blast. The parachute unit was attached to the bomb in place of the fin assembly. The unit consisted of a closed metal case containing the parachute and its attachment. The cover was removed by withdrawing the arming wire, or by a hang wire when the bomb was released. Since the parachute was compressed in packing, the spring of the cloth forced the parachute from the case when the cover was removed. When the bomb was adapted for tail fusing a fuse adapter and a modified tail fuse were necessary. A kit containing the parachute unit, fuse adapter, and modified tail fuse was designated as the "Anti-Ricochet Device." (The parachute unit is described in detail with fragmentation bombs).

Arming Wire Assembly
Arming wires were used to lock the fuse arming mechanism in the unarmed position. Generally they consisted of either one or two strands of WIRE, arming, low brass, 0.064 inch diameter (or 0.036 inch diameter) for some fuses attached to a swivel assembly loop. When intended for use with only one fuse, the swivel loop was attached at one end of the wire; when furnished for use with two fuses, the loop attached toward the middle of the wire in such position that the two branches of wire were of the correct length. Fahnestock safety clips (two for each end of wire) were attached to the ends of the wires after the installation of the fuses in the bomb, which prevented the accidental withdrawal of the wires when the aircraft was in flight.

The standard arming wire assemblies could be used on any bomb up to and including one of 2,000 pounds (for larger bombs an extension cable was used). Arming wire assemblies were to be free of twists, kinks, and burs, and the wire was to protrude approximately 2.5 inches, but not less than two inches or more than three inches beyond the fuse or fuses when the bomb was installed in the rack or shackle. Excess wire could be cut off when the arming wire was installed. If complete arming wire assemblies were not available they could be made.

When a bomb was to be released as ARMED from the rack the wire was pulled from the fuse head, allowing the fuse vanes to rotate and arm the

Left: **Arming wires** were used to lock the fuse arming mechanism in the unarmed position. (TM 9-1980)

Above: **Arming wire** being threaded through two tail fuses of a 500 pound cluster. (AAF)

HOW THE ARMING WIRE WORKS

(Shown with an arming-vane type fuze. Principle is the same with arming-pin type fuze.)

Figure 3 ① Bomb hanging from its shackle in the bomb bay. Fuzes in nose and tail are "safe" until their propeller-like vanes are spun by the air as the bomb falls, disengaging the safety devices of the fuze. Here, they cannot spin because they are kept from turning by ends of the arming wire. Notice that the arming wire is gripped at its mid-point by a pawl in the shackle.

② Now the bomb has been released with controls in the "armed" position. The pawl holds onto the arming wire; jerks it clear of the vanes; the vanes begin to turn; when they have disengaged the safety devices, the fuzes will be armed. If the controls had been at "safe" the pawl would have let go of the arming wire, which would have stayed with its bomb as it fell, kept the vanes from turning and prevented the fuzes from arming.

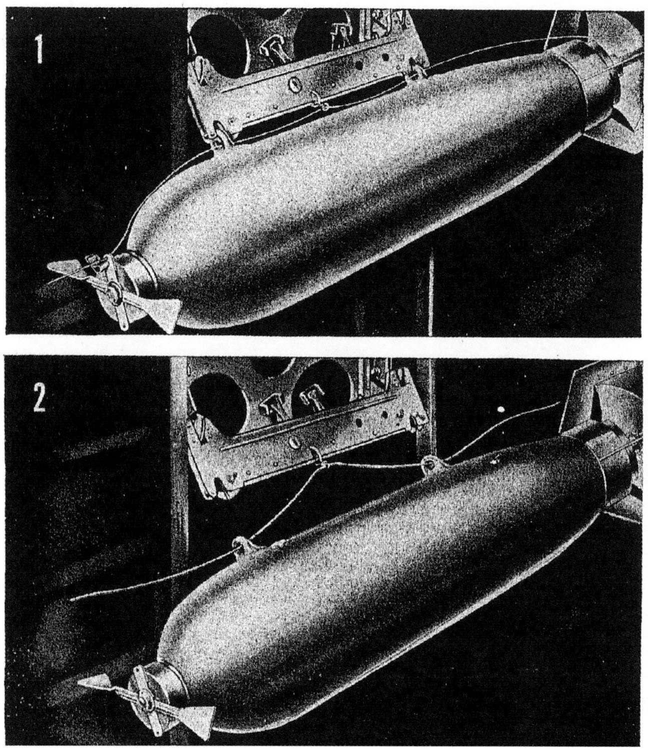

(BIF)

fuse. When the bomb was to be released as SAFE, the arming wire was not separated from the fuse head. Arming wires were subject to considerable wear caused by vibration, and a metal tubular protector was used with the arming wire bracket to prevent chafing of the wire by the fuse vane. If an arming wire was reused it required inspection before the next flight.

Arming wires were usually packed in metal containers holding 50 or 100 assemblies along with the safety clips. Fragmentation Bomb clusters, however, were supplied with their own arming wire assemblies installed.

Bomb Fuses

Background

During World War I Germany and Britain did most of the research and development of bomb fuses. During the war bombs generally contained three different types of explosive. The main bursting charge was some safe and insensitive explosive, such as Amatol or TNT. Amatol was the most commonly used in the early stages of the war, but thereafter, bomb fillings followed the development of explosives in general. The bursting charge could only be detonated by a violent explosion and required an exploder, usually Tetryl, which was similar to TNT but was more sensitive. The exploder was set off by a detonator containing fulminate of mercury. The exploder and detonator were fitted into the bomb before loading it into an aircraft. When the bomb hit the ground the detonator was hit by a striking pin, igniting the exploder which, in turn, exploded the bursting charge.

The fusing mechanism of the early German Karbonit and British Hale bombs was armed by a small propeller mounted in the tail which unwound a spindle inside the bomb during flight and allowed the striker to come into contact with the detonator on impact with the ground. In later, more advanced bombs, arming occurred when the airscrew had turned a certain number of times equaling a predetermined distance. A clip was attached as a safety device to prevent the arming propeller from turning while inside the aircraft and had to be removed before release. This was done by hand on early bombs, which were stored loose on the floor of the cockpit and were dropped over the side. But these loose bombs had a tendency to get in the way and interfere with the controls, so two bombs, each attached to either end of a length of rope, were slung over the fuselage in front of the cockpit, and the pilot released them by simply cutting the rope with a knife. When special bomb release gear was developed for carrying bombs in racks, at first externally and later in bomb bays inside the aircraft, safety devices could either be removed by the automatic trigger mechanism on release or retained if the bombs had to be jettisoned without exploding.

Two main classes of fuse were developed and used depending on the type of target being attacked. The nose fuse had the arming propeller in the nose of the bomb and, since the striker spindle was the first part of the bomb to hit the ground, the explosion was instantaneous on impact. The bomb did not enter the ground and only a shallow crater was formed, while fragments of the bomb case were scattered over a wide area. So, nose fuses were used with thick case bombs where the weight of the case was three or four times the weight of the explosive it carried. The nose fuse was used to attack personnel and light targets such as road transport, aircraft on the ground, and military equipment.

Since the tail fuse was some distance from the exploder the delay was at least 0.4 seconds, but could be set to as long as 15 seconds. Even the shortest delay caused tail fuse bombs to bury themselves in the ground before exploding, producing a large crater but spewing few fragments. This type of bomb, therefore, was used with a light case, where the weight of the explosive carried could be up to 50% more than the weight of the case. The tail fuse was used where violent local destruction was needed, in attacking railways or buildings for instance.

It was not unusual for bombs to fail to explode because of a faulty fuse mechanism. Also, there was a shortage of steel and bombs were instead manufactured of cast iron, which was prone to break up on impact with hard surfaces before the tail fuse could function. Consequently, many bombs, particularly British, were equipped with both nose and tail fuses so that at least some result would be obtained if one failed to operate.

General Description

A fuse is a device which is utilized to initiate the detonation or dispersion of the filling of a bomb under desired conditions. Interchangeable arming vanes may be used on some fuses. These vanes differed in degree of pitch, shape, and length of blade, as it was necessary to control the arming distance of the fuses when used with different types of bombs.

Fuses were classified according to position as nose, tail, and body, and according to function: time, impact, VT, and hydrostatic. Time fuses functioned a predetermined number of seconds after the arming pin was released; impact fuses functioned when the bomb struck a resistant material; hydrostatic fuses functioned by water pressure; and VT fuses were operated electrically on the approach to the target. Impact fuses were classified as delay when they were designed to have a definite time-lag between the instant of impact and explosion of the bomb, and as instantaneous (nose) or non-delay (tail) when there was no delay factor integrated. Instantaneous fuses functioned when the striker or firing pin struck the target. For non-delay fuses to function the entire bomb had to be retarded sufficiently to force the inertia plunger to strike the primer. Hence, the delay for instantaneous fuses was about 0.0005 second, and about 0.0025 seconds for non-delay fuses.

Arming
Artillery shells had to be safe to be transported and handled, then had to survive the shock of discharge from a gun without premature detonation, and finally be able to function on impact. The advantage of the artillery shell was that the large translational and rotational forces arising on discharge could be used to arm the fuse. These forces were so large that fuses could be designed without any detachable safety devices, but aerial bombs were not subjected to such forces on their release and another method had to be found to arm their fuses.

The fuse was considered armed when "the next normal expected event will initiate functioning of the fuse;" the event may be impact (impact fuses), time train running to completion (mechanical time fuses), or approach to the target (VT fuse). Fuses were constructed so that while they were unarmed they could not function, and as shipped the fuses were in a safe (unarmed) condition. A fuse was considered "detonator-safe" when the detonator held out of line with the firing pin and booster lead until the fuse armed.

General Fuse Classification
There were a number of methods of classifying fuses:

Position
Fuses were classified according to the position in which they were assembled to the bomb as nose, tail, and transverse.

Arming
Fuses were classified according to method of arming as pin type and vane type. These were further classified as:

1) Direct arming when the fuse became armed immediately on ejection of the arming pin or by direct unscrewing of the arming stem by the vane.
2) Delayed arming when the ejection of the arming pin initiated a powder train or clockwise mechanism which armed the fuse after a predetermined time, or when the arming vane was connected to the arming stem by a reduction gear assembly.
Action
Fuses were classified according to action as time, impact, and hydrostatic:

1) Time fuses functioned to explode the bomb a specific number of seconds after release; acting like an ordinary alarm clock. A notched disk was rotated by the clock mechanism under a trigger. When the time set elapsed, the notch had turned so as to be under the trigger, which dropped into the notch and released a spring-loaded firing pin. Although the fuse was generally set for the time desired when the complete round was assembled, the time setting could be changed at any time up to release, provided the fuse was accessible.
2) Impact fuses began to function when the bomb struck a resistant material. Fuses classed as superquick (instantaneous) or non-delay acted to explode the bomb immediately; those classed as delay incorporated a component which delayed the explosion of the bomb until a definite time had elapsed and allowed the bomb enough time to penetrate the target or give the low altitude bomber time to clear the danger area before the bomb exploded.
3) Hydrostatic fuses acted under the influence of water pressure to explode the bomb a predetermined depth below the surface. (Hydrostatic fuses are described in detail in Volume 3/Depth Charges)

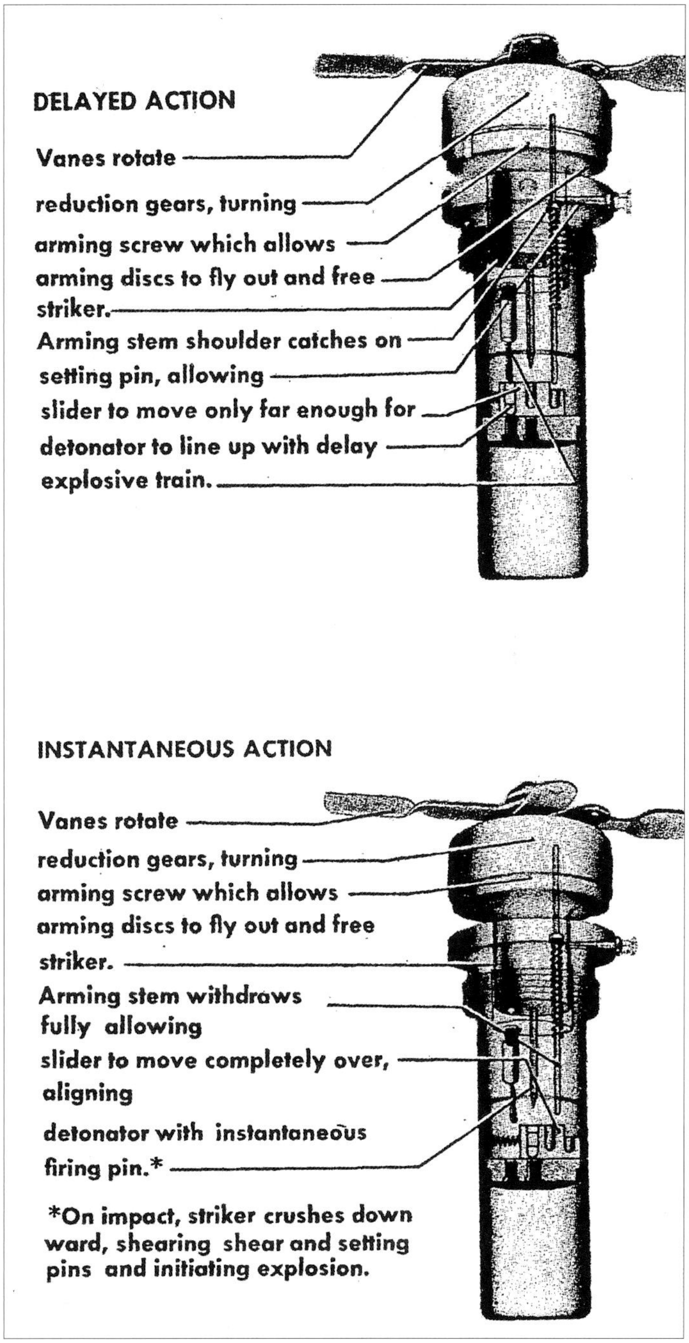

Delayed and Instantaneous Action (TM 9-1980)

Components
Nose fuses
The essential parts of a nose fuse were a striker head, firing pin, safety block, arming mechanism, primer, detonator, and usually a delay element and booster, all assembled in a fuse body. In the arming pin type a spring-loaded arming pin, which passed through the fuse body and firing pin, was held in place by the arming wire. The wire also restrained a plate which held the safety blocks in place. In the arming vane type the striker was restrained by a safety block or a ring of safety disks which were released by the action of the arming vane. The arming vane was kept from rotating

Pin-Type Fuse Gallery

Pin Fuse Nose (TM 9-1980)

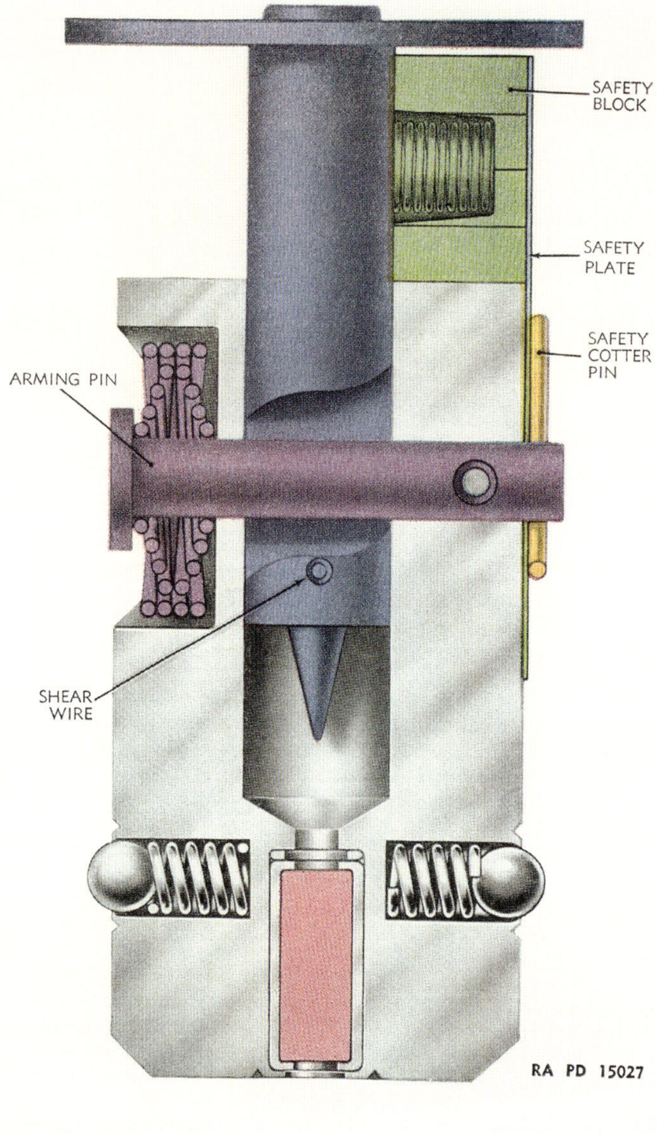

Pin Fuse Tail (TM 9-1980)

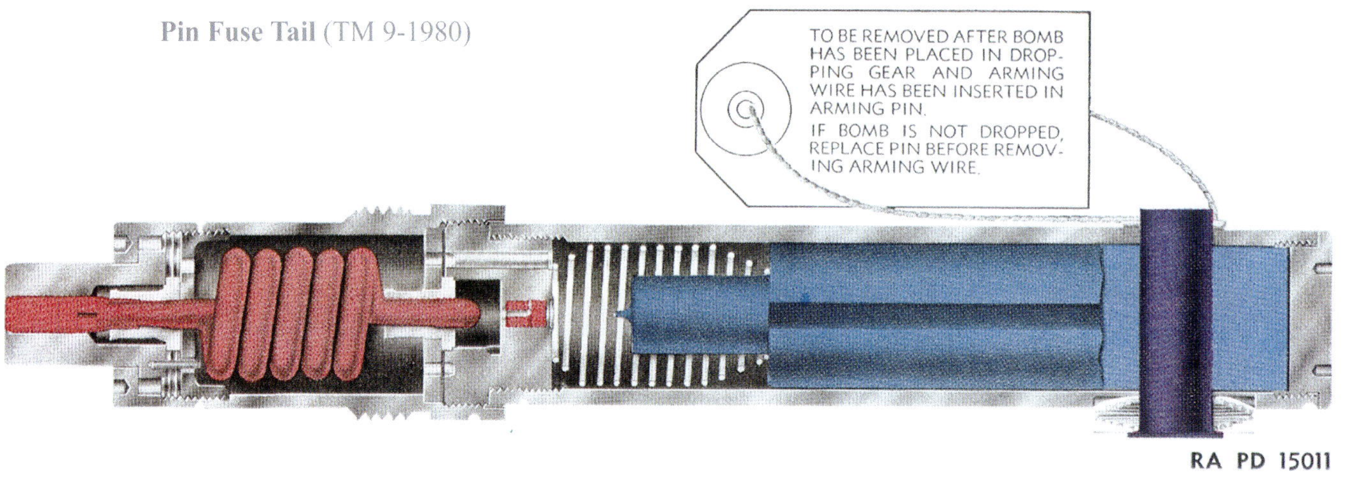

Vane Fuse Nose (TM 9-1980)

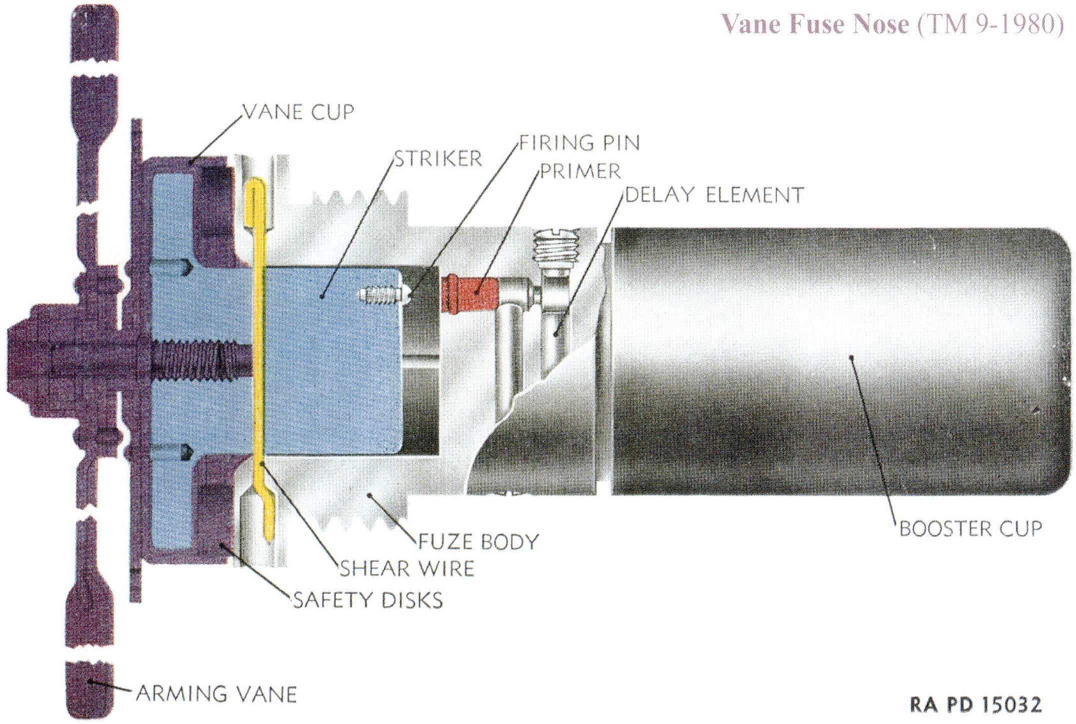

Vane Fuse Tail (TM 9-1980)

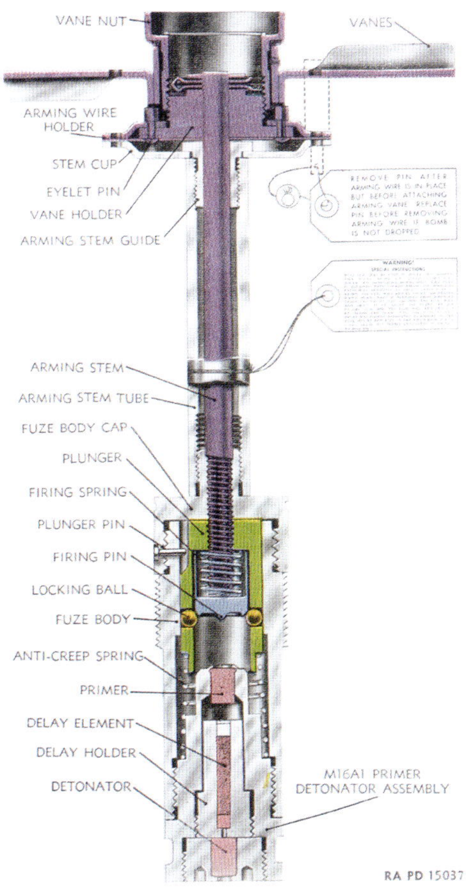

Vane-Type Fuse Gallery

prematurely by the arming wire. In both types the striker was held in place after arming by a sheaf wire.

Tail fuses
The essential parts of a tail fuse were the primer detonator, an inertia type firing pin, and arming mechanism, all assembled in the fuse body. In the arming pin type the arming pin passed through the fuse body and the firing pin. In the vane type, an arming stem was screwed into the firing pin to keep it from striking the primer until the action of the vane unscrewed the arming pin. In both types the firing pin was held in place while the bomb was in flight by a light creep spring. Dependent upon the required degree of sensitivity to impact, the firing pin could be of the simple inertia type or of the cocked type.

Hydrostatic fuses
This fuse worked on the principle of a bellows or diaphragm working against a spring of fixed strength. When the external pressure overcame the resistance of the spring the firing pin was released and driven against the primer by spring action. In some hydrostatic fuses an external lever adjusted a mechanism controlling the compression of the diaphragm spring. In other fuses adjustment was made by interchanging the springs.

Types of Fuses
Impact Nose
These fuses were vane operated and delay armed. Their action was instantaneous or delayed by the setting of the selective setting of a control pin.

Mechanical Time Fuse
These fuses were armed by mechanical and time mechanisms. The time of detonation after release could be preset for a predetermined time. If the time setting was greater than the time of flight impact would cause the fuse to function.

Impact Tail Fuse
Fuses of this type were vane armed and inertia fired. The arming was mechanically delayed by reduction gearing. Fuses of this type were used in GP, Armor Piercing Bombs, and practice bombs.

Long Delay Tail Fuse
These fuses required less than 100 feet of air travel to initiate the delayed action. Any attempt to remove these fuses after installation resulted in the functioning of the anti-withdrawal mechanism, followed by instantaneous detonation.

Hydrostatic Tail Fuse
The hydrostatic fuses were vane operated and required 400 to 500 feet of air travel to arm. Water pressure then operated the hydrostatic mechanism that detonated the fuse. The depth at which detonation occurred could be set.

Side Fuse
These fuses were only used with Fragmentation Bombs. They were armed by the "butterfly wings" of the bomb and were preset to detonate in the air or on impact, either delayed (subject to handling, shock, or vibration) or instantaneous.

Multi-Position Fuse
The inertia firing, impact, and multi-position fuses were fully armed by anemometer type vanes after completing their air travel. Once the fuses were armed, impact forces from any direction would cause instantaneous detonation. These fuses were principally installed in conjunction with igniters or bursters in incendiary bombs.

VT Fuse
VT (proximity) fuses were basically radio transmitting and receiving units that functioned automatically on approaching or passing any material object, causing an air burst at an effective height or distance.

Identification
Fuses were identified by the information marked on their containers and stamped on the fuse body. The bodystamp included on four lines:

Bomb Nose/Tail Fuse
Type/Designation
Lot Number
Loader/Date

They could be identified by inspection, with the detailed differences being: Rapid arming fuses were distinguished from slow arming types by the rod that extended from the arming head forward along the arming stem for approximately 1.5 inches. This rod was present on the slower arming types and absent from the rapid type. Fuses of one series (e.g. fuses with the same mechanism or action, but designed for bombs of different sizes) were distinguished among themselves by the length of the arming stem. Special purpose fuses, such as hydrostatic, had a distinctive appearance and method of operation.

Precautions in Packing and Handling
1) Fuses were packed in sealed moisture proof containers and were not to be unsealed until required for use; fuses unpacked for use and not used were to be resealed and returned to their original packing, which were to be sealed with tape.
2) Fuses were to be protected against excessive heat.
3) Fuses were to be handled with care at all times. Boxes were not to be dropped, tumbled, dragged, or thrown; nor were they to be struck with a hammer or similar tool either to open the box or align in a stack.

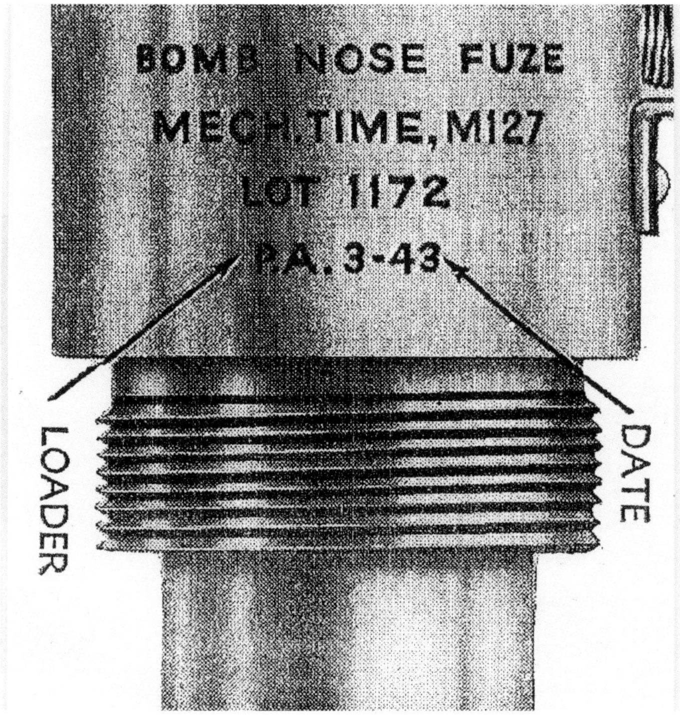

Fuses were identified by the information stamped on the fuse body; included on four lines: Bomb Nose/Tail Fuse, Type/Designation, Lot Number, and Loader/Date. (TM 9-1980)

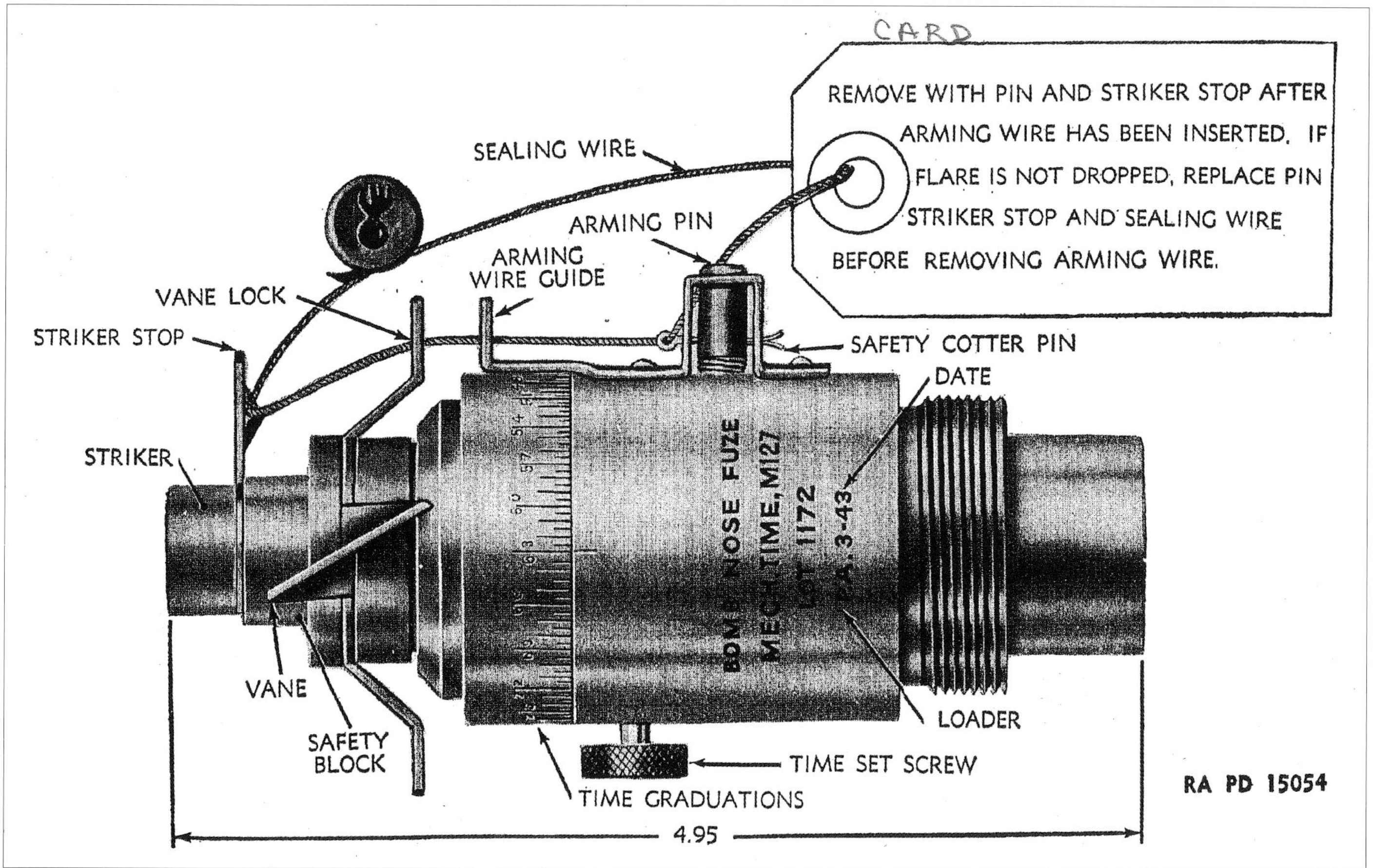

Fuses were shipped with a **sealing wire** that was threaded through the striker stop, vane lock, arming wire guide, and arming pin. The ends of the sealing wire were attached together by a button. A card paper instruction tag for the removal of the sealing wire was attached through the sealing wire. (TM 9-1980)

4) Fuses were not to be unpacked or packed within 100 feet of a magazine containing explosives.
5) When the fuse was unpacked, it was to be examined to insure that shipping seals were intact, that safety blocks or arming pin were in place, or that the arming stem was not unscrewed.
6) Safety cotter pins, shipping wires, and seals were to be left in place until the arming wire was assembled to the fuse.
7) Care was to be exercised not to bend or distort vane assemblies.
8) Only primer detonators authorized for use with a particular fuse were to be used.
9) When an authorized alteration was made to a fuse, the fuse was to be so marked as to clearly indicate the nature of the modification (For example, when the depth setting of a hydrostatic fuse was changed the new depth setting was stenciled on the pistol head.) If the fuse was repacked after alteration the container was also to be so marked.
10) Fuses were not to be disassembled further than authorized without prior approval of the Chief of Ordnance.

Fuse Safety Features

Many fuses incorporated the following special safety features.

Detonator Safe

Fuses that were detonator safe had the elements of their firing train firmly fixed out of alignment in the fuse body while the fuse was unarmed. This increased safety during shipping, stowage, and handling. The arming action of the fuse aligned the firing train.

Shear Safe

A shear safe fuse would not become armed if its arming mechanism was damaged or completely severed from the fuse body. Shear safe fuses afforded additional security for externally mounted bombs, especially for bombs used in carrier operations.

Delay Arming

This feature, mechanically or electrically, slowed the arming of the fuse and kept it in the safe condition until the bomb had fallen a sufficient distance away from the dropping aircraft to minimize the effects of a premature explosion. Delayed arming helped to make dive bombing and carrier operations safer, as bombs accidentally released on takeoff and landing would not ordinarily have sufficient air travel to arm the fuse.

Sealing Wires

Fuses were shipped with a sealing wire which was threaded through the striker stop, vane lock, arming wire guide, and arming pin. The ends of the sealing wire were attached together by a button. A card paper instruction tag for the removal of the sealing wire was attached through the sealing wire.

Fuse Installation

Preparation for Use

When removed from the packing container the fuse was ready for use, except for assembly of the arming vane and for a possible change of the primer-detonator. When it was necessary to change the primer-detonator to provide a different delay the old primer-detonator was unscrewed from the fuse body. The correct M14 primer-detonator was then removed from its packing, in-

Fuse Installation

Nose Fuze

1. Remove nose plug and carefully wipe fuze cavity. Make sure no grit or dirt remains in threads.
2. Remove fuze from container and inspect it.
3. Insert fuze into cavity and screw in hand tight. Don't bump detonator against side of cavity.
4. Cut and remove seal wire.
5. Pass arming wire through eyelets of vane stop.
6. Slip Fahnstock clip over end of arming wire and place flush with vane stop.
7. Hold arming vane by hub, press it into position.
8. Snip off arming wire 2½ inches beyond clip.

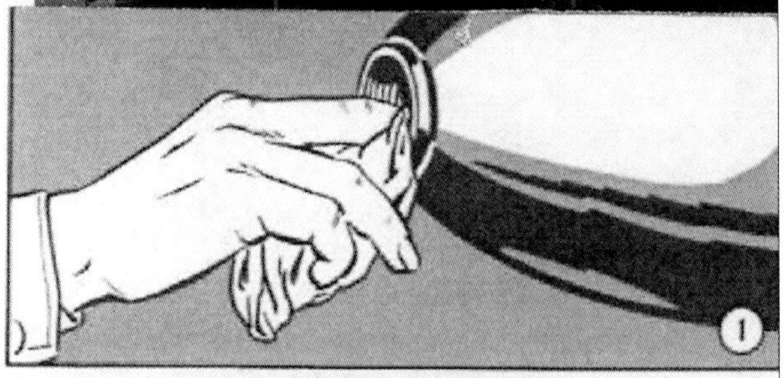

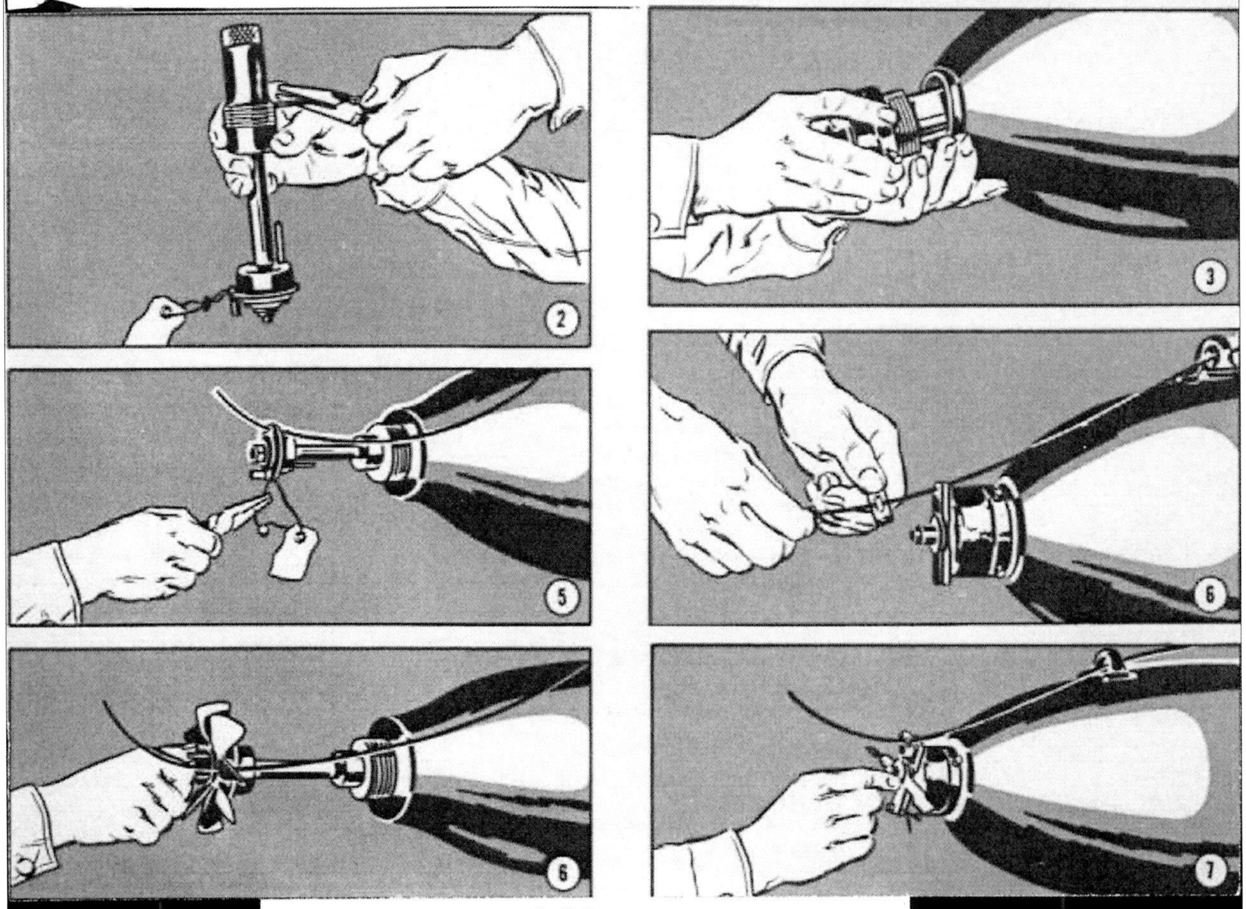

Tail Fuze

1. Remove tail plug; carefully wipe fuze cavity.
2. Remove fuze from container, inspect it, and withdraw safety cotter pin.
3. Insert fuze into cavity and screw in hand tight.
4. Pass arming wire through eyelets of arming wire holder. The fins must now be on the bomb.
5. Cut and remove seal wire.
6. Press vane into position and screw on vane nut.
7. Slip Fahnstock clip over end of arming wire and place flush with vane nut.
8. Snip off arming wire 2½ inches beyond clip.

(TM 9-1980)

Fuse Installation Gallery

Nose Fuse Installation (AAF)

Incendiary Bomb Fuse Installation (AAF)

Tail Fuse Installation (AAF)

Factory Fuse Installation on a 4,000 Pound Bomb (AAF)

spected, and assembled to the fuse body, screwing it until hand tight. The old primer-detonator was removed from the fuse and placed in the packing of the substitute, and marked to indicate the delay. If the plunger spring or spring washer fell out of the fuse when the primer-detonator was removed they were to be replaced before the new primer-detonator was assembled.

Tail Fuse
1) Remove tail plug and carefully wipe the fuse cavity.
2) Unseal the storage container and remove the fuse from its packing and inspect it for serviceability and withdraw the safety cotter pin.
3) Insert the fuse into the cavity and screw it in hand tight.
4) Pass the arming wire through the eyelets of the arming wire holder, removing all kinks and burs.
5) Install the fins on the bomb.
6) Cut and remove the seal wire.
7) Press the vane into position and screw on the vane nut.
8) Slip the Fahenstock Clip* over the end of the arming wire and place it flush with the vane nut.
9) Snip off the arming wire 2.5 inches beyond the clip.
* The Fahenstock Clip was a mechanical electrical terminal consisting of a single piece of flexible metal with a rectangle punched out of one end and a loop punched out of the other. The clip was bent over itself so that the loop could be pushed through the rectangular opening. A wire could be inserted through the loop that was through the cut out, and the spring force of the clip pulling up made an electrically reliable mechanical connection.

Nose Fuse
1) Remove the nose plug and carefully wipe the fuse cavity, making sure no grit or dirt remained in the threads.
2) Remove the fuse from the sealed container and inspect it for serviceability.
3) Insert the fuse into the cavity and screw it in hand tight. Don't bump detonator against side of cavity.
4) Cut and remove the seal wire.
5) Pass arming wire through eyelets of vane stop, removing all kinks and burs.
6) Slip the Fahenstock Clip over the end of the arming wire and place it flush with the vane stop.
7) Hold the arming vane by hub and press it into position.
8) Cut off the arming wire 2.5 inches beyond the clip.

Defusing
If the bomb was not dropped, it was to be defused and the fuse returned to its original condition and packing as follows:

Fuse Mechanisms Nose

The fuse contains four interrelated systems: Arming (purple), Delay Selecting (green), Firing (blue), and the Explosive Train (red). (TM 9-1980)

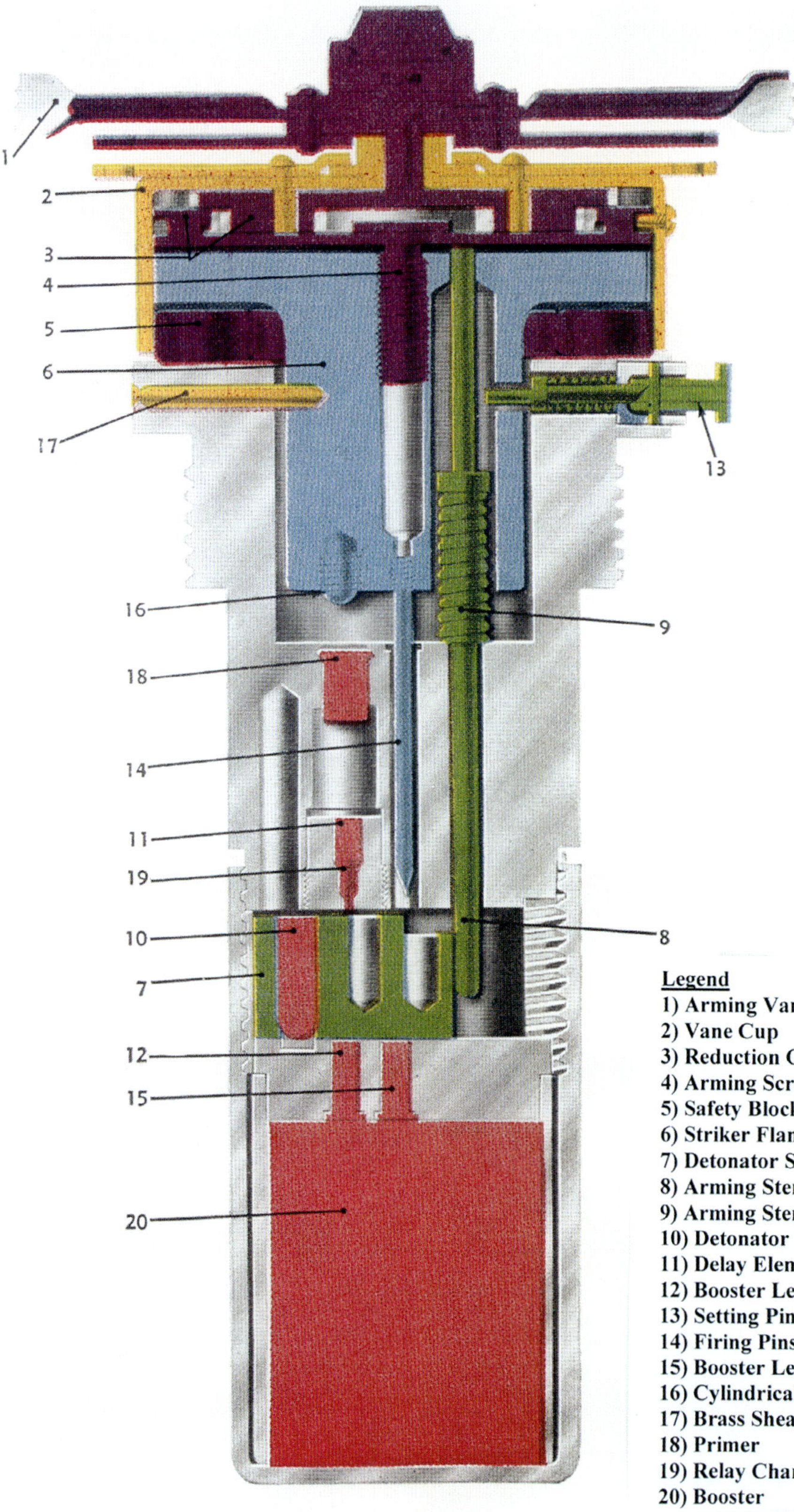

Legend
1) Arming Vane
2) Vane Cup
3) Reduction Gears
4) Arming Screw
5) Safety Blocks
6) Striker Flange
7) Detonator Slider
8) Arming Stem
9) Arming Stem Spring
10) Detonator
11) Delay Element
12) Booster Lead
13) Setting Pin
14) Firing Pins
15) Booster Lead
16) Cylindrical Striker
17) Brass Shear Pin
18) Primer
19) Relay Charge
20) Booster

Figure 48. FUZE, bomb, AN–M103 (nose) unarmed.

Fuse Mechanisms Tail

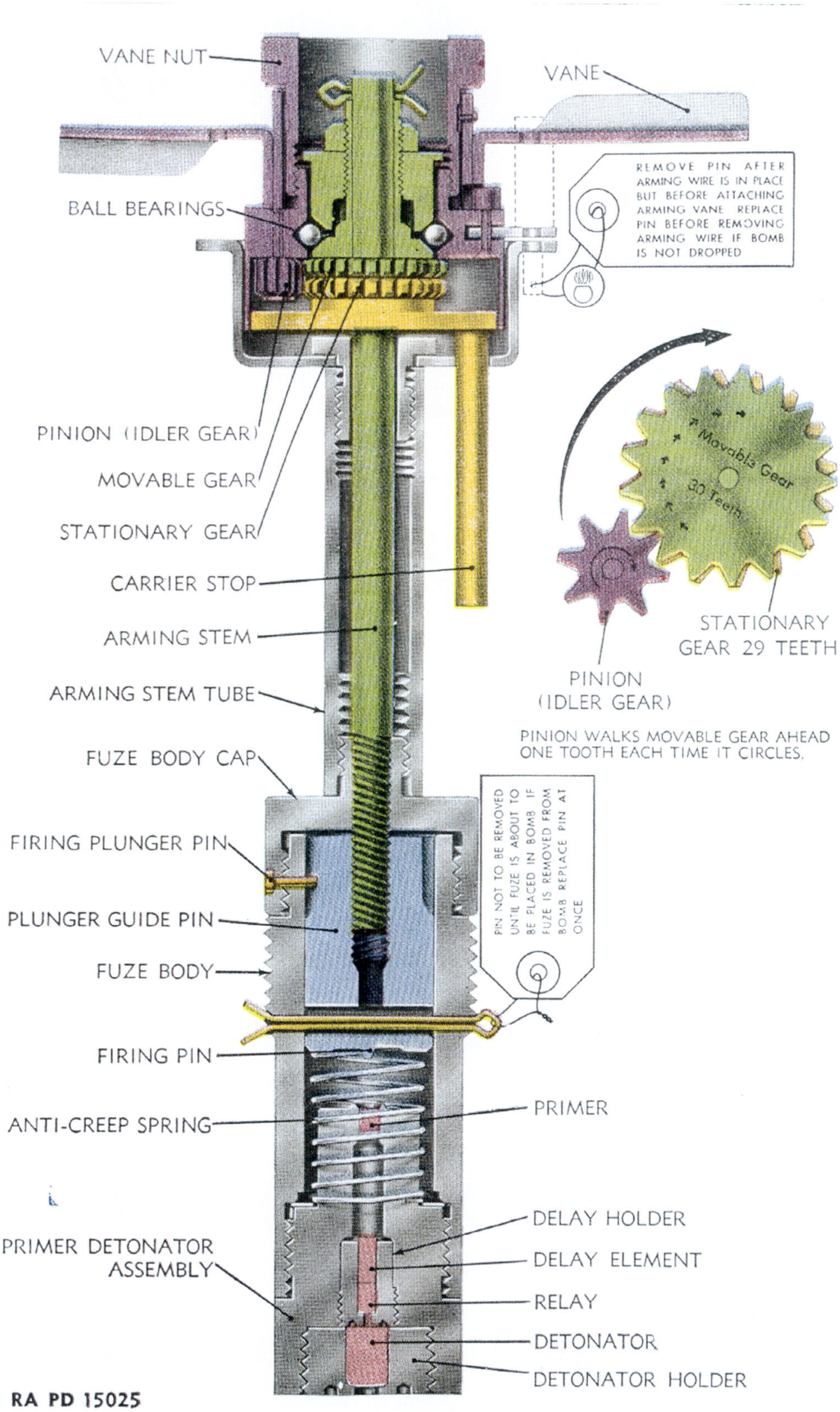

Figure 76. FUZE, bomb, AN–M100A2.

The fuse contains four interrelated systems: Arming (purple), Delay Selecting (green), Firing (blue), and the Explosive Train (red). (TM 9-1980)

1) Remove the safety clips and arming vane from the fuse.
2) Place the safety pin in the unoccupied vane stop eyelet. Secure the safety pin in place with seal wire.
3) Remove the arming wire and repack it and the safe clips.
4) Unscrew the fuse from the bomb and insert the cotter pin in the fuse body, spreading the legs of the cotter pin to prevent its slipping out.
5) Repack the fuse in its container and seal the container with adhesive tape, then replace the containers and arming vanes in their packing box.

How a Fuse Works

The fuse contains four interrelated systems: Arming (purple), Delay Selecting (green), Firing (blue), and the Explosive Train (red). (Nose Fuse AN-M103 is the example in the illustration)

1) The arming system consisted of the arming vane #1 (90° out of position in illustration), vane cup #2, reduction gears #3, arming screw #4, and safety blocks #5. The arming vane, reduction gears, and arming screw were assembled in one unit with the vane cup; the safety blocks were held between the flange of the striker #6 and the fuse body by the vane cup. When the arming vane was rotated by the air stream the arming screw unscrewed from the striker body, carrying the vane, gears, and vane cup with it. When the vane cup moved 0.25 inches the safety blocks were released. Positive ejection was insured by a flat spring assembled within the circle of blocks. The arming vane continued to rotate until the arming screw moved 0.5 inches. Then the entire assembly disengaged from the fuse and fell free.

2) The delay selecting system consisted of the detonator slider #7, which was held in place against spring action by the arming stem #8, which in turn was held in place by the arming assembly. As the arming screw advanced the arming stem followed, driven by its spring #9. When the stem moved 0.25 inch it cleared the first step of the detonator slider, which moved to line up the detonator #10 with the delay element #11 and booster lead #12 of the explosive train. If the setting pin #13 was in the delay position it restrained the arming stem from moving further, and on impact the fuse functioned with 0.1 second delay. If the pin was set for superquick action, the arming stem continued to move until the end of the stem cleared the second step of the detonator slider and the slider moved to line up the detonator with the superquick firing pin #14 and booster lead #15. Upon impact, the fuse functioned immediately. The detonator was out of line with the other explosive elements until the fuse armed; the fuse was detonator safe. (*Note:* Once the fuse armed, detonator slider could not return to its original position.)

3) The firing system consisted of a cylindrical striker #16 and two firing pins, one for the delay train and the other for the superquick train. A flange at the outer end of the striker formed, with the fuse body, a groove which contained the safety blocks. The striker was held in place after arming by a brass shear pin #17 and the setting pin #13, which acted as an additional shear pin. Upon impact, after arming, the striker was driven inward, shearing the pins and driving both firing pins with it.

4) The explosive train consisted of a primer #18 delay element #11, relay charge #19, detonator, booster leads, and booster #20. The primer, delay element, and relay charge were housed in the fuse body in position to be initiated by impact of the delay firing pin. The detonator was assembled in the detonator slider, and the booster was assembled to the inner end of the fuse. When the slider was set for superquick action the superquick firing pin was driven directly into the detonator, which served as its own primer, and the primer, delay charge, and relay charge, although they were fired by the delay firing pin, were bypassed, and the booster was detonated immediately.

Nose Fuses

Types of Nose Fuses

Since many of these fuses were similar only a few of the major types will be described in detail.

Fuse, Bomb, AN-M103 (Nose)

Fuse, Bomb, AN-M103 (Nose) was cylindrical in shape, being 7.1 inches in length overall and weighed 3.7 pounds. The inner portion which assembled inside the fuse seat in the bomb was 5 inches in length and 1.25 inches in diameter, while the outer portion was 1.25 inches long and 2.5 inches in diameter. The arming vane had two blades, with the arming vane hub projecting 0.75 inches from the outer end. A vane stop consisting of two straps attached to the vane hub and fuse top, respectively, was fastened during shipping and handling by a safety cotter pin and a sealed shipping wire. On the side of the fuse were two diametrically opposed lugs which served to prevent the armorer's hand from slipping when fusing or defusing the bomb. The setting pin was located on the circumference midway between the lugs. On the setting pin there was a cross member which formed a key and rested in one of two slots in the pin seat. When the key was in the deep slot the fuse was set for delay, and when the key was in the shallow slot the fuse was set for superquick action.

The AN-M103 was a detonator-safe, arming vane-type nose fuse which required 230 revolutions of the vane to arm for delay action and 345 revolutions to arm for instantaneous action. It was designed to detonate the bomb on impact, either instantaneously or with 0.1 second delay, depending upon the setting of a delay pin. It was authorized for use in all GP demolition, and SAP bombs when the tail fuse used had a delay of 0.1 seconds or less. It could also be used in depth bombs (except AN-Mk 17) and GP bombs with hydrostatic fuses, but only if selective arming racks were available. The M103 fuse was an earlier model which differed from the AN-M103 in requiring 785 revolutions of the vane to arm the fuse, but in all respects the AN-M103 was the same as the M103.

Fuse, Bomb, AN-M104, (Nose)

Fuse, Bomb, AN-M104, (Nose) was cylindrical in shape and tapered to a narrow end 4.4 inches in length and 2.25 in diameter, weighed 1.15 pounds, and was threaded for a 1.5 inch adapter. A mushroom-shaped striker protruded from the narrow head, the arming pin projected from both sides of the cylinder, and the booster cup was attached to the base. There were three plugs in the side of the fuse: one, near the arming pin, a small slotted screw plug which covered the detonator slide lock; a large slotted screw plug covered the detonator slider assembly; and a small smooth delayed arming plug, opposite the detonator slider plug.

The AN-M104 was a detonator-safe, arming pin-type, nose fuse authorized for use with parachute type Fragmentation Bombs. It was armed by the action of a powder train delay element 2.5 seconds after the bomb parachute opened. It was extremely sensitive and, once armed, a slight blow to the striker in any direction would operate the fuse, which detonated the bomb immediately on impact.

Fuse, Bomb, AN-M108 (Nose)

Fuse, Bomb, AN-M108 (Nose) was an arming pin-type nose fuse which was authorized for use on the 100 pound practice smoke bomb. It armed immediately upon withdrawal of the arming wire and acted to detonate the bomb immediately on impact.

Fuse, Bomb, AN-M110A1 (Nose)

Fuse, Bomb, AN-M110A1 (Nose) was an arming vane-type nose fuse that was authorized for use with the 115 pound, M7 gas bomb, with fin stabilized Fragmentation Bombs, and the corresponding practice type. It armed after 325 revolutions of the arming vane and detonated the bomb on impact. It was 3.7 inches long,

BOMB FUZES

CLASSIFICATION		ARMING	FUNCTIONING	BOMBS USED WITH:
AN-M103	NOSE FUZE	VANE	Selective: instantaneous or .1 sec. delay	All GP, light case, and depth bombs
M108		PIN	Instantaneous	100-lb. M47A2 chemical bomb
AN-M110A1		VANE	Instantaneous	20-lb. FRAG. bomb and 115-lb. M70 gas bomb
M111A2		VANE	5-93 sec. mechanical delay	M46 flare bomb
M118		VANE	4-5 sec. delay	All GP bombs
M119		VANE	8-11 sec. delay	All GP and depth bombs
AN-M120A1		PIN	Instantaneous	23-lb. AN-M40 and 23-lb. M72A1 FRAG. bombs
AN-M126A1		VANE	Instantaneous	100-lb. M47A2 gas bomb
AN-Mk219		VANE	Instantaneous	All depth bombs
AN-M100A2	TAIL FUZE	VANE	Interchangeable primer detonators for non-delay, .01 sec., .025 sec., or .10 sec. delay	100-lb. and 250-lb. GP bombs
AN-M101A2		VANE		500-lb. GP and SAP bombs
AN-M102A2		VANE		1000-lb. GP and SAP, 2000-lb. GP, 4000-lb. light case bombs
M112A1		VANE	Interchangeable primer detonators for 8-11 sec. or 4-5 sec. delay	100-lb. and 250-lb. GP bombs
M113A1		VANE		500-lb. GP and SAP bombs
M114A1		VANE		1000-lb. GP and SAP bombs, 2000-lb. GP bombs
M115A1		VANE	Interchangeable primer detonators for 8-11 sec. or 4-5 sec. delay	100-lb. and 250-lb. GP bombs
M116A1		VANE		500-lb. GP and SAP bombs
M117A1		VANE		1000-lb. GP and SAP, 2000-lb. GP bombs
M123A1		VANE	Marked for delay action of 1, 2, 6, 12, 24, 36, 72 or 144 hours	100-lb. and 250-lb. GP bombs
M124A1		VANE		500-lb. GP and SAP bombs
M125A1		VANE		1000-lb. GP and SAP, 2000-lb. GP bombs
AN-Mk228		VANE	.08 sec. delay	1000-lb., 1600-lb. AP bombs
AN-Mk229		VANE	Hydrostatic; selective depth setting of 25, 50, 75, 100, or 125 ft.	500-lb., 1000-lb. GP; light case, and 650-lb. depth bombs
AN-Mk230		VANE		500-lb., 1000-lb., and 2000-lb. GP bombs
M1A1		PIN	Instantaneous	100-lb. M38A2 practice bomb
AN-Mk224	LATERAL		Hydrostatic; interchangeable firing pin springs *See below	All depth bombs
AN-Mk234				

*For depths of 25 (yellow), 50 (black),75 (black and green), 100 (yellow and red), and 125 (black and red) feet.

1.75 inches in diameter, and weighed 1.04 pounds. This fuse was a cylindrical, with the arming vane hub and firing pin protruding from the head and the booster cup protruding from the base. This fuse differed from Fuse, bomb, M110 (nose) in that the latter required 455 revolutions of the vane to arm.

Fuse, Flare, Mechanical Time, M111A2 (Nose)
Fuse, Flare, Mechanical Time, M111A2 (Nose) was cylindrical in shape, with the arming vane hub and striker protruding from the front end and the booster cap protruding from the base. It was a combination type, as it was both time and impact fused. The time function began upon ejection of the arming pin; the safety block was ejected, arming the fuse, after approximately 325 revolutions of the arming vane. The fuse functioned after a predetermined number of seconds, from 5 to 93, after the arming wire was withdrawn, provided that the fuse had armed and also that it had not previously functioned on impact. The fuse was 4.5 inches long, 1.75 inches in diameter, and weighed 1.4 pounds, and was authorized for use with Bomb, photoflash, M46, and Flare, aircraft, parachute, AN-M26, and delayed opening clusters. The booster element of the fuse was loaded with black powder and could not be used with HE bombs.

Fuse, Bomb, AN-M120 (Nose)
Fuse, Bomb, AN-M120 (Nose) was roughly cylindrical in shape, with a mushroom-shaped striker protruding from the head and the booster cup assembled to the base, and with a striker assembly protruding from the head. The arming pin housing protruded from both sides of the fuse body. It was a detonator safe, arming pin-type nose fuse which armed, by mechanical time action, 2.5 seconds after ejection of the arming pin and detonated the bomb instantaneously on impact. This fuse was authorized for use with parachute type Fragmentation Bomb. The fuse was 4.6 inches in length and 2.3 inches in diameter.

Fuse, Bomb, AN-M126A1 (Nose)
Fuse, Bomb, AN-M126A1 (Nose) was the same as Fuse, Bomb, AN-M110A1 (Nose), except that the booster element was replaced by a metal detonator holder. These fuses were authorized for use with modified 100 pound gas, smoke, and incendiary bombs.

Fuse, Bomb, Mechanical Time, M127 (Nose)
This fuse was similar to Fuse, Flare, Mechanical Time, M111A2, except that a Tetryl booster was used instead of the black powder booster of the flare fuse.

Fuse, Bomb, Mechanical Time, M138 (Nose)
Fuse, Bomb, Mechanical Time, M138 (Nose) was the same as the M127, except that the booster charge was reduced by replacing half of the Tetryl with a clay pellet. This fuse was authorized for use with aimable clusters.

Fuse, Bomb, Mechanical Time, M139 (Nose)
Fuse, Bomb, Mechanical Time, M139 (Nose) was a selective SQ-0.01 second delay impact fuse. Except for the delay time and the marking, this fuse was identical with the Fuse, Bomb, AN-M103 (nose). A segment of 1/8th of the head (vane cup) of this fuse was painted black to indicate the delay.

Fuse, Bomb, M140 (Nose)
This fuse was a selective SQ-0.025 second delay impact fuse. Except for the delay time and the marking, this fuse was identical with Fuse, Bomb, AN-M103 (nose). A segment of 1/4th of the head (vane cup) of this fuse was painted black to indicate the delay.

Fuse, Bomb, AN-Mk 219 (Nose)
This fuse was a detonator-safe arming vane-type nose fuse which required 175 revolutions of the vane to arm and detonated the bomb immediately upon impact. This fuse was authorized for use with depth bombs, but only when it was intended to use the bomb for surface demolition effect. The fuse was 5.5 inches long, 2.3 inches in diameter, and weighed four pounds. The fuse was cylindrical with a flat conical head. The fuse body was a cylindrical cup containing the booster and booster lead. The rest of the fuse mechanism, assembled on a central shaft, consisted of an arming nut, detonator holder, firing pin holder, striker, vane carrier with reduction gears, and head. Aft of the head, which did not rotate, were the ring-shaped vane carrier, the flange of the striker, the outer sleeve, and the fuse body.

Impact Tail Fuses: Short and Medium Delay
General
When a bomb struck a target, its impact caused these fuses to function and detonate the bomb immediately or within a short time thereafter, dependent upon the length of delay of the primer-detonator used. All impact tail fuses were of the arming vane type, which was separated from the fuse body by a long arming stem. Fuses of one series (i.e. fuses with the same mechanism and action, but designed for bombs of different sizes) were distinguished among themselves by length of arming stem. The body of the fuse was threaded for an adapter or fuse seat with a diameter of 1.6 inches. The rapid arming impact tail fuses were distinguished from the slow arming types by the rod which extended from the arming head along the arming stem for approximately 1.5 inches. This rod was present on the slower arming types and absent from the rapid type. Since many of these fuses were similar only the AN-M100A2 will be described in detail.

Primer-Detonator
Primer-detonators were interchangeable units that provided a variation of delayed action in tail fuses, but some units were non-delay. Each unit contained a primer, a delay charge (if required), a relay, and a detonator. When the firing pin of a fuse was driven by its spring into the primer, the flame from the primer ignited the delay element. After the correct time interval had elapsed the relay ignited and exploded the detonator. Upon severe impact the plunger was arrested by the shoulder of the primer-detonator so that the blow on the primer had only the force of the firing pin spring, thus avoiding malfunction due to a pierced primer. Since a primer-detonator could be assigned one of a number of different delay periods, the units were stamped and painted to indicate the length of delay. Primer-detonators of different model numbers varied in the pitch of their threads and were not interchangeable, and care had to be taken to install only the proper model primer-detonator in a fuse in order to avoid damage to the threads of both the fuse and the primer-detonator.

Types of Tail Fuses: Short and Medium Delay
Fuse, Bomb, Tail, AN-M100A2, with Primer-Detonator M14
The AN-M100A2 was a vane-type tail fuse which armed after 158 revolutions of the arming vane. As issued, this fuse could be fitted with either the Primer-Detonator M14 non-delay or the Primer-Detonator M14 0.025 second delay. These could be replaced in the field by the M14 primer-detonator of 0.1 second, 0.01 second, or 0.24 second delay. The fuse was approximately nine inches long and weighed 2.7 pounds. It was authorized for use in GP and Fragmentation Bombs of 100 to 300 pounds. Earlier models differed: the fuse, bomb, tail, M100A1 required 675 revolutions of the arming vane to arm the fuse. All earlier models had an eight-bladed vane. The M100A2C tail fuse was designed to provide longer arming time by using finer threads and a longer threaded portion on the arming stem.

Description
This fuse consisted of a stem and arming head; the cylindrical body was threaded to properly engage the adapter of the bomb. A M14 primer-detonator of desired delay was screwed into the end of the fuse body entered

the adapter at the arming stem and was assembled on the opposite end. The body contained an inertia type fin pin and its restraining anti-creep spring. A cotter pin was placed through the body and plunger for safety during shipment. The arming stem tube connected the body and arm head cup. The inner end of the arming stem was screwed through the body into the plunger; the arming mechanism was attached to the outer end by means of a cotter pin. The arming head contained the arming vane assembly reduction gear train. A stop rod (carrier stop) passed through the cup and extended toward the body, parallel to the stem. The 4-blade arming vane was not assembled to the fuse during shipment. A safety pin was sealed into a vane stop eyelet for safety in handling.

Function

When the arming wire was withdrawn the air stream turned the arming vane, which turned the bearing cup assembly. A pinion, mounted on the bearing cup, was in mesh with a 29-tooth stationary gear and a 30-tooth movable gear. A stationary gear was prevented from rotating by the carrier passing through the stem cup. Each revolution of the pin forced the movable gear to advance one tooth (1/3 revolution) ahead of the fixed gear. The fixed gear was connected to the arming stem by a cotter pin passing through the gear carrier and the arming stem. As the arming stem rotated it unscrewed from the plunger. After 6.7 revolutions of the arming stem (approximately 158 revolutions of the vane) the stem cleared the plunger and the fuse was armed. The vane assembly was still attached to the fuse. After about 200 or more revolutions of the vane the stem unscrewed from the fuse body, and the vane arming head and stem were carried clear of the fuse by the air stream. Upon impact, the plunger was driven forward with the firing pin striking the primer. The flame from the exploding primer ignited the delay charge, which burned the required time and ignited the relay charge, thus exploding the detonator.

Preparation for Use

When removed from the packing container the fuse was ready for use, except for assembly of the arming vane and for a possible change of the primer-detonator. When it was necessary to change the primer-detonator to provide a different delay the old primer-detonator was unscrewed from the fuse body. The correct M14 primer-detonator was then removed from its packing, inspected, and assembled to the fuse body, screwing it until hand tight. The old primer-detonator was removed from the fuse and placed in the packing of the substitute, and marked to indicate the delay. If the plunger spring or spring washer fell out of the fuse when the primer-detonator was removed they were to be replaced before the new primer-detonator was assembled.

Marking

The fuse had its type, model, and lot number stamped in the body. The sealing wire of the safety pin carried a tag which read: "Remove pin after wire is in place but before attaching the arming vane. Replace the safety pin before removing the arming vane if bomb is not dropped." The primer-detonator was marked to indicate the amount of delay.

Packing

This fuse was packed without its vane assembly, one per container, with 25 containers and 25 vane assemblies placed on spindle in a wooden box.

Fuse, Bomb, Tail, AN-M101A2

The Fuse, Bomb, Tail, AN-M101A2 was an arming vane-type tail fuse which, except for the length of the stem and the corresponding differences in overall length (12 inches), weight (2.9 pounds), and bombs authorized (GP, SAP, and Chemical Bombs of 500 to 600 pounds), was identical to the Fuse, Bomb, Tail, AN-M100A2. The fuse was designed to provide longer arming time by using finer threads and greater length of threaded portion on the arming stem. It armed after 168 revolutions of the arming vane and detonated the bomb upon impact with a delay determined by the primer-detonator inserted: M14, 0.25-second delay or non-delay, which could be replaced in the field by an M14 primer-detonator of 0.1 second delay, 0.01 second delay, or 0.24 second delay.

Fuse, Bomb, Tail, AN-M102A2

Fuse, Bomb, Tail, AN-M102A2 was an arming vane-type fuse which, except for the length of the stem and the corresponding differences in overall length (16 inches), weight (8.2 pounds), and bombs authorized (all GP and SAP bombs of 1,000 pounds and larger, with the 4,000-pound LC bomb and with 1,000 pound Chemical Bombs non-delay only) was identical to the Fuse, Bomb, Tail, AN-M100A2. This fuse armed after 158 revolutions of the arming vane and detonated the bomb upon impact with a delay determined by the primer-detonator inserted. As issued, either the Primer-Detonator, 0.25 second delay, or non-delay was assembled to the fuse. These could be replaced in the field by a M14 primer-detonator of 0.1 second, 0.01 second, or 0.24 second delay. This fuse was designed to provide longer arming time by means of finer threads and greater length of threaded portion on the arming stem.

Fuse, Bomb, Tail, M112A1

The Fuse, Bomb, Tail, M112A1 was 9.6 inches long and weighed 2.3 pounds, and was authorized for use with 100 to 300 pound GP bombs. It was an arming vane-type tail fuse that armed after 18 revolutions of the arming vane and detonated the bomb eight to 15 seconds or four to five seconds after impact, depending upon the primer-detonator used. The fuse was issued with either the Primer-Detonator, M16A1, 4-5 second delay, or an 8-15 second delay, with these primer-detonators being interchangeable. The fuse was equipped with a cocked-type firing pin which, once the fuse was armed, was extremely sensitive. The M112A1 differed from M112, the issued M16, which had a shoulder to act as plunger stop.

When the arming wire was withdrawn the air stream rotated the arming vane, unscrewing the arming stem from the firing plunger and fuse body. After approximately 18 revolutions the stem was unscrewed from the plunger and the fuse was armed. After 18 more revolutions of the vane the arming stem unscrewed from the fuse body and the vane and stem assembly were carried free from the fuse. Upon impact—even a graze impact—the plunger was carried forward by its inertia, the locking balls were released, and the firing pin was driven by its spring into the primer. The flame from the primer ignited the delay element, which burned eight to 16 seconds (or four to five seconds, depending upon the primer-detonator assembled to the fuse) before igniting the relay, which exploded the detonator. Upon severe impact the plunger was arrested by the shoulder of the primer-detonator so that the blow on the primer has only the force of the firing pin spring, thus avoiding malfunction due to a pierced primer.

Fuse, Bomb, Tail, M113A1

The Fuse, Bomb, Tail, M113A1, except for the length of the stem and the corresponding differences in length (12 inches), weight (2.5 pounds), and bombs authorized (GP and SAP bombs of 500 to 600 pounds) was identical with M112A1. It was an arming vane-type tail fuse which armed after 18 revolutions of the arming vane. Upon impact, it acted to detonate the bomb with a delay of eight to 15 or four to five seconds, dependent upon the particular delay of primer-detonator M16A1 used.

Fuse, Bomb,Tail, M114A

Except for the length of the vane stem and the corresponding differences in overall length, weight, and bombs authorized (all GP and SAP bombs of 1,000 pounds and over, and in all M-Series AP bombs); this fuse was identical with Fuse, Bomb, Tail, M112A1.

Fuse, Bomb, Tail, M115

The M115 was similar to the AN-M100A2, except that the body contained the cocked type firing pin similar to that in the M112A1. The fuse was 9.6 inches long and weighed 2.7 pounds, and was authorized for use with GP bombs of 100 to 300 pounds. It was an arming vane-type fuse which armed after 175 revolutions of the arming vane with a cocked firing pin that was extremely sensitive when the fuse was armed. It detonated the bomb eight to 15 seconds or four to six seconds after impact, dependent upon the primer detonator used.

Fuse, Bomb, Tail, M116

Except for the length of the vane stem and the corresponding differences in overall length (12.5 inches), weight (2.9 pounds), and bombs authorized (all GP and SAP bombs of 500 to 600 pounds), this fuse was identical with Fuse, Bomb, Tail, M112A1.

Fuse, Bomb, Tail, M117

Except for the length of the vane stem and the corresponding differences in overall length (16 inches), weight (3.2 pounds), and bombs authorized (all GP and SAP bombs of 1,000 pounds and over), this fuse was identical with Fuse, Bomb, Tail, M115.

Fuse, Bomb, Tail, M160

This fuse was a vane-type for use in GP and Fragmentation Bombs of 100 to 300 pounds. It required a long travel through the air to arm, which permitted the bombs to be dropped great distances from the aircraft before arming. This type fuse was designed to decrease the possibility of bombs which might bump into each other when dropped in salvo from detonating too close to the aircraft. The first of these slower arming tail fuses was produced as the Fuse, Bomb, Tail, M100A2C, which was later developed into the M160 and was similar in all respects except marking, nomenclature, and construction of arming stem or arming screw. Except for the marking stamped in the fuse body, the M160 was externally identical to the AN-M100A2. A yellow band was painted around the arming stem tube of M160 to differentiate between it and the AN-M100A2 (the color yellow as employed on bomb fuse generally indicated slower arming fuses). The arming stem of the M160 had finer thread, and consequently engaged the firing pin plunger for a greater length of time, requiring greater air travel to arm. For example, the AN-M100A2 assembled to the 250 pound AN-M57A1 bomb, and dropped from a bomber traveling 200 mph would arm after 485 feet of air travel or a vertical drop of 44 feet, while under the same conditions the M160 would arm after 1,900 feet of air travel or a vertical drop of 635 feet.

Fuse, Bomb, Tail, M161

This fuse was of the same type as the M160 and also corresponded to the Fuse, Bomb, Tail, AN-M101A2 in all respects except marking, nomenclature, and required length of air travel to arm. The M161, as the M160, had a yellow band painted around the arming stem tube.

Fuse, Bomb, Tail, M162

This fuse was of the same type as the M160 and also corresponded to the Fuse, Bomb, Tail, AN-M101A2 in all respects except marking, nomenclature, and required length of air travel to arm. The M161, as the M160, had a yellow band painted around the arming stem tube.

Fuse, Bomb, Tail, M167 (T75E2)

This fuse was a modified arming vane-type tail fuse and used an arming device fitted with an anemometer wind vane. The fuse body was similar to the fuse body employed in the AN-M100A2 tail fuse and used the Primer-Detonator, M14, 0.025 second delay. The fuse body was 4.2 inches long and weighed 1.6 pounds. The arming device assembly was 8.7 inches long and weighed 1.3 pounds. The fuse armed after 1,360 revolutions of the anemometer wind vane. The tail fuse, M167 (T75E2) was for use on the 1,000-pound VB-1 AZON Bomb.

The M167 (T75E2) tail fuse consisted of an arming device located at a right angle to the fuse body. The arming device and fuse body were connected by means of a flexible bronze shaft. One end of the fuse safety stem contained two transverse pins to fit in the coupling which joined the flexible shaft and the fuse body. A spacer ring between the fin sleeve and tail unit of the bomb was used to provide the required space and support for the tail fuse. When a bomb equipped with this fuse was released armed the arming wire was withdrawn from the spring-loaded safety pin. The safety pin was ejected from the arming device, leaving the anemometer wind vane free to rotate in the air stream. This rotation was transmitted through a reduction gear train to a flexible shaft, which in turn withdrew the safety stem from the firing pin. When the safety stem cleared the firing pin, the firing pin was free to function upon impact.

Fuse, Bomb, Tail, M169 (T708)

This brass fuse was a simple impact mechanism used with the Primer-Detonator, M40 and Adapter Booster, M118. It measured approximately two inches in diameter at its widest point and 3.98 inches long, and consisted of a cylindrical brass body with a central longitudinal hole and a 1.375 inch diameter thread on the outside. Due to the danger of non-functioning when the bomb was dropped from low altitudes, the use of bombs fitted with the M169 fuse was restricted to high altitudes. The M169 was used with the 12,000 and 22,000 pound GP very heavy bombs. Three fuses M169 and three M40 primer-detonators of desired delay were required to fuse these large bombs. Upon release of the bomb the arming wire was withdrawn from the fuse, leaving the striker supports only by the tabs of the striker support. On impact, the inertia of the striker bent the tabs, thus allowing the striker to move forward and pierce the detonator.

Fuse, Bomb, Tail, AN-Mk 228

The bottle-shaped AN-Mk 228, formerly designated the Mk 28 or Mk XXVIII, was 16.7 inches long and weighed 10.5 pounds, and was authorized for use in 1,000 and 1,600 pound AP bombs of the AN-Mk series. It was a detonator-safe, vane-type tail fuse with a 16-blade arming vane attached to the outer end and a cylindrical extension containing the booster projecting from the base. When the bomb was released the air stream rotated the arming vane, and this rotation was transmitted through a reduction gear train to a central shaft that moved the striker into functioning position. When the striker moved out toward the vane the shaft locked, and the striker began rotation and lined up the firing pins, delay elements, detonators, and booster leads. When the firing elements were in line they locked in the armed position and the vane stopped. The fuse was armed after 160 revolutions of the arming vane, and upon impact inertia caused the striker to shear a pin in the shaft and move forward, driving the firing pins into their respective detonators and acting through two independent firing trains with 0.08 second delay to detonate the bomb.

Long Delay Impact Tail Fuses

Fuse, Bomb, Tail, M123A1, All Delays

This fuse was a vane operated type fuse which had to be regarded as armed at all times. It acted to detonate the bomb after a delay of one hour to six days from the time of release, or immediately upon any attempt to unscrew the fuse from the bomb. The M123A1 was designed to provide a specific delay for an individual fuse, with the amount of delay being 1, 2, 6, 12, 24, 36, 72, or 144 hours specified in the nomenclature and stamped on the fuse body. This type fuse was particularly responsive to heat and cold; high temperatures accelerated its action, while low temperatures slowed it. The amount or delay desired was obtained by choosing the fuse of that particular

The **M123A1 Delay Tail Fuse** was designed to provide a specific delay period of one hour to six days from the time of release or immediately upon any attempt to unscrew the fuse from the bomb. (Author's Collection)

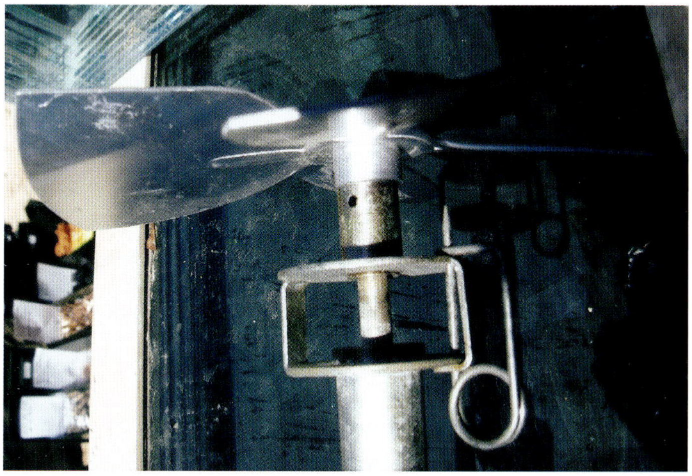

M123A1 Arming Pin in place to prevent the vanes from spinning and arming the bomb by crushing the ampoule. (Author's Collection)

delay and taking into consideration the effect of temperature upon the delay action. After withdrawal of the arming wire a short air travel initiated the delay action. As little as a 1/4 turn in unscrewing the fuse from the bomb caused the fuse body to separate from the fuse extension, which caused the operation of the anti-removal device and detonation of the bomb.

Note: Fuse Extension: The most efficient use of fragmentation and Chemical Bombs required that they detonate at or slightly above the surface of the ground. The nose fuse extension consisted of a steel tube filled with Tetryol, adapted to receive the fuse and screw into the fuse seat of the bomb.

The M123A1 fuse was approximately 9.3 inches long and was authorized for use in GP and demolition bombs of 100 to 300 pounds. This fuse consisted of an eight-bladed arming vane which acted directly (not through the gear train) to rotate the arming stem and armed the fuse. The M123A1 differed from tail fuses previously described in that the vane and direct arming head acted to screw the arming stem into the fuse. The body assembly consisted of two parts: the fuse, body, and fuse body extension. The fuse body contained the firing pin and sleeve assembly, and a glass ampoule filled with solvent. The firing pin was held in place against the action of a compressed firing pin spring by the firing pin balls, which in turn were held in place under the firing pin screw by a celluloid delay collar.

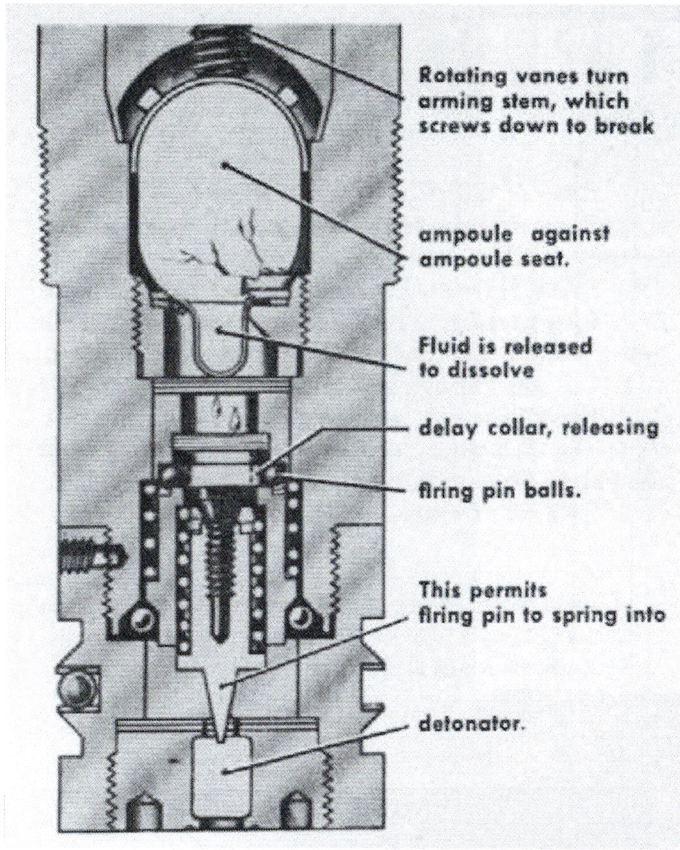

Delay Mechanism Ampoule (TM 9-1980)

This assembly was mounted in a sleeve which was held in place, against the action of a compressed sleeve spring, by steel balls (sleeve balls) bearing on the sleeve shoulder and held in place by the lip of the fuse body.

Delay Mechanism

When the bomb was released, the arming wire was withdrawn and the vane rotated in the air stream, and was transmitted directly to the arming stem, causing the stem to screw into the fuse body. After a short air travel time the stem, moving into the body, crushed the ampoule and freed the solvent. After further air travel the stem progressed far enough to force the stem collar against the retainer locking nut, sealing the outer end of the fuse body and preventing escape of solvent or entry of moisture. Meanwhile, the solvent filtered through the delay wad and started to dissolve the celluloid delay collar, which dissolved sufficiently to release the firing pin balls in approximately the specific time. When released, the balls were forced outward and the firing pin spring drove the firing pin into the detonator.

Anti-Withdrawal Mechanism

The ball groove on the body extension was machined eccentrically, forcing the locking ball outward when the fuse was turned counterclockwise and wedging the ball between the adapter-booster wire and fuse body extension, locking the extension in place. Any further counterclockwise rotation unscrewed the fuse body from the extension. When the body was separated from the extension by 3/64 inch the sleeve balls were released and moved outward. The sleeve and firing pin assembly was driven forward by the sleeve spring, causing the firing pin to strike the detonator. As further insurance against withdrawal the adapter-booster was drilled for insertion of a metal locking pin. When this pin was in place, the adapter-booster was locked to the base plug of the bomb, preventing removal of the fuse by unscrewing the adapter-booster.

Fuse, Bomb, Tail, M123, All Delays
This fuse was an earlier model of the M123A1 and differed principally in that it used an arming head and a reduction gear train similar to the M100 series fuses. The 9.6 inch, four-bladed arming vane required from 80 to 100 feet of air travel to arm.

Fuse, Bomb, Tail, M124A1, All Delays
Except for differences in length (12.3 inches) of stem and corresponding differences in length, weight, and bombs authorized, this fuse was identical to the M123A1. The M124A1 was authorized for use in demolition, GP, and SAP bombs of 500 to 600 pounds.

Fuse, Bomb, Tail, M124, All Delays
Except for differences in length of stem and the corresponding differences in length, weight, and bombs authorized, the M124 was identical to the M123. The M124 was 12.63 inches in length; weighed 3.1 pounds; and was authorized for use in demolition, GP, and SAP bombs of 500 to 600 pounds.

Fuse, Bomb, Tail, M125AI, All Delays
Except for differences in length of stem and the corresponding differences in length, weight, and bombs authorized, the M125AI was identical to the M123A1. The M125A1 was approximately 16.3 inches in length and was authorized for use in all demolition, GP, and SAP bombs of 1,000 pounds and over.

Fuse, Bomb, Tail, M125, All Delays
Except for differences in length of stem and the corresponding differences in length, weight, and bombs authorized, the M125 was identical to the M123. The M125 was 16.63 inches in length; it weighed 3.4 pounds; and was authorized for use in all demolition, GP, and SAP bombs of 1,000 pounds and over.

Fuse, Bomb, Tail, M132
The M132 was a vane type long delay tail fuse that acted to detonate the bomb with delay depending upon the temperature, or upon an attempt to remove the fuse from the bomb. The 9.57 inch long fuse was authorized for use with 100 to 300 pound demolition and GP bombs. The vane reduction gears and arming vane of this fuse were the same as tail fuses M123, M124, and M125, and the general overall appearance was somewhat similar to these fuses. However, the M132 series fuses could be readily differentiated from the M123 series fuses by the reduction of the diameter of the head beyond the lock nut in the M132 series. The time delay mechanism of these fuses was somewhat different from that used in the M123 and M123A1. This mechanism had a metal bellows containing a red-colored solvent which was released at the time of arming the fuse. The anti-withdrawal device was the same as used in the M123 and M123A1.

When the bomb was released the arming wire was withdrawn and the vane was free to rotate. At approximately 100 feet air travel, the metal bellows was punctured and the solvent was forced onto the celluloid cylinder, initiating the softening action of the celluloid, and after the indicated delay the softened celluloid allowed the spring-loaded firing pin to move forward and pierce the detonator, exploding the bomb.

Fuse, Bomb, Tail, M133
The M133 was the same as the M132, except that a larger stem increased the overall length of the fuse to 12.57 inches. The M132 was authorized for use on 500 to 600 pound bombs.

Fuse, Bomb, Tail, M134
The M134 was the same as the M132, except that a larger stem increased the overall length of the fuse 16.57 inches. The M134 was authorized for use in bombs of 1,000 pounds and over.

Fuses with Anti-ricochet M16 and M17 Parachute Devices Types

Fuse, Bomb, Tail, M151, and the Device, Anti-ricochet, M16 and M17
The Fuse, Bomb, Tail, M151 body was the same type of body as utilized in the tail fuse M112A1, except that in the M151 the arming stem was perpendicular to, rather than parallel to, the axis of the body. The fuse was 5.6 inches long and weighed 2.1 pounds. This fuse and anti-ricochet device was used with 100 and 250 pound GP bombs when dropped from low-flying aircraft to break rapid descent of the bomb. Bombs fitted with this device were not to be dropped from aircraft at speeds greater than 350 miles per hour or from altitudes less than 50 feet. The M151 fuse consisted of the M16A1 Primer-detonator, four to five second delay or eight to 15 second delay; the fuse body; a body cap; and an anemometer wind vane. It was a modified arming vane-type tail fuse that armed after 26 revolutions of an anemometer wind vane. It was authorized for use only with the Device, Anti-ricochet, M16 and M17, which were assemblies of a parachute unit, fuse adapter, arming vane (anemometer type), and fuse, used in lieu of fin assemblies with 250 and 500 pound GP bombs. The Device, Anti-ricochet, M17 was essentially the same as the M16, except that it was larger and employed the Parachute Unit, M6 and Adapter and Fuse M202. The M16/17 device was used with 600 pound GP bombs. The M16/17 device consisted of:

1) Fuse, Bomb, Tail, with primer-detonator, M16A1, four to five second delay or eight to 15 second delay.
2) Parachute Unit, M7, which consisted of a parachute housed in a cylindrical metal container closed at one end by a cover assembly and at the other end by a disk; a threaded collar was assembled to this disk for assembly to the fuse adapter.
3) Adapter, Fuse M202 (T3), with vane assembly. This adapter contained a large internal threaded opening which fit the tail threads of the bomb. The other end contained smaller diameter external threads for assembly to the parachute unit. A sleeve, which projected from the side of the adapter, housed the anemometer wind vane shaft and acted as a bearing for the shaft that passed through the sleeve to engage the arming stem in the fuse.
4) Arming Wire Assembly, which consisted of three wires (0.064 diameter): one short and two long wires assembled to one swivel loop.

Functioning
As soon as the armed bomb was dropped, the arming wire was immediately withdrawn from the anemometer wind vane and from the parachute container latch assemblies that opened the parachute container. The air stream turned the anemometer wind vane that turned the safety stem, and after 26 revolutions of the anemometer wind vane, the safety stem cleared the plunger stem and the fuse was armed. Upon impact the plunger was driven forward, causing the firing pin to strike the primer in the primer-detonator.

Marking
This fuse had the model designation, the number, and the date loaded stamped in the metal of the bottom. The sealing wire of the safety stem and retainer pin carried a tag which read: "Remove wire and unthreaded pin when fuse is placed in the bomb. If fuse is to be removed from bomb replace at once."

Packing
The M151 fuse was packed with the vane assembly in a hermetically sealed can, 15 per wooden box. The Parachute Unit M6 was packed one per metal drum with its arming wire assembly, while the Unit M7 was packed two per metal drum with two arming wire assemblies, or one per carton and two cartons with two arming wire assemblies in individual envelopes per wooden box. The Adapter, Fuse, M200 was packed two per carton, with two vanes per

separate carton all contained in a wooden box. The Adapter, Fuse M202 was packed two per carton with two vanes per separate carton, and in quantities of two cartons of each (four adapters and four vanes) per wooden box.

Miscellaneous Fuses

Fuse, Bomb, M129

The M129 was a body-type fuse assembled to the four pound Fragmentation Bomb M83 transversely to the bomb's longitudinal axis. It was designed to give an air or ground (impact) burst dependent upon the setting (only those set for ground burst were used by the Navy). When the bomb M83 was released from its cluster, the "butterfly" wings snapped open and rode to the top of the cable attached to the arming stem of the M129 fuse. The rotation of the wings in this position caused the cable to turn and unscrew the arming stem far enough to initiate the fuse's arming mechanism.

The M129 was comprised of three main assemblies held together by three studs. The cap assembly consisted of the cap marked "air" and "ground," which contained the arming stem, the setting plug, and the setting pin with spring. The movement assembly consisted of the arming mechanism, the firing pin assembly, and primer. The arming mechanism included the segment gear (regulated by gear train or movement assembly), segment gear stop, segment gear cam shaft, and the safety pellet assembly (including the pellet, shell, and spring). The booster assembly consisted of a Tetryl-loaded aluminum cup and a detonator assembly. The cup was screwed into the booster cup retainer, which was assembled to the movement assembly.

This fuse was designed for air or ground burst, and was ordinarily set for ground burst at the time of manufacture. Air burst occurred if the setting plug was turned so that its indicator pointed to the word "AIR" embossed on the outside of the cap; for ground burst, the indicator pointed to the word "GROUND."

Air Burst Functioning

If the setting plug was turned to indicate AIR, the setting pin was forced downward and depressed the safety pellet assembly. This action permitted the segment gear stop, when driven by the segment gear, to pass over the top of the safety pellet. When the arming stem was withdrawn, the firing pin was forced by its spring to act against the segment gear cam, causing the cam and segment gear to rotate. The rotation of the segment gear was retarded by the movement assembly (consisting of the balance, escape wheel, and first wheel or pinion). When the segment gear completed its travel toward the gear stop, the cam had rotated until the half round notch cut in the cam aligned with the firing pin, which permitted the firing pin spring to force the firing pin into the primer, thus detonating the bomb. It required 2.5 to three seconds from the time the arming stem was withdrawn until detonation.

Ground Burst Functioning

If the setting plug was turned to indicate GROUND the setting pin was retracted into the cap. In this case, the segment gear stop was restrained by the tip on the safety pellet that projected through the safety pellet shell. Upon withdrawal of the arming stem, the segment gear rotated until it contacted the gear stop. In this position the firing pin was still restrained from forward action by the cam. Upon impact with the ground, the complete safety pellet assembly was depressed due to inertia, and almost simultaneously with that action the gear stop with segment gear passed over the safety pellet assembly, the cam was further rotated, and the bomb detonated.

Fuse, Bomb, M130 (T48)

The M130 was externally very similar to the M129, consisting of three parts: 1) the cap assembly, which contained the arming stem; 2) the body assembly, which contained the fuse mechanism, firing pin assembly, and primer; and 3) the booster assembly consisted of a Tetryl-loaded aluminum cup and detonator assembly. In this fuse, the booster was screwed directly to the base of the fuse body. It was a mechanically operated, delayed action, body-type fuse also used with the four pound M83 Fragmentation Bomb. It was designed to detonate the bomb at intervals of 10, 20, 30, 40, 50, or 60 minutes, depending upon its setting at time of manufacture. When the arming stem was withdrawn by the action of the butterfly wings the escapement release arm (arming lever) rotated a few degrees, unlocking the escapement wheel and initiating arming action.

Proximity (VT) Fuse

Development and History

For years the military had desired a fuse that could sense the presence of a target and detonate automatically at the optimum effective range, causing an air burst close to the target, rather than on impact. The VT fuse would not only significantly simplify the three-dimensional difficulty of hitting rapidly moving aircraft, but also would alleviate the problems and inaccuracies of the time fuse when placing an air burst over an enemy ground target. The development of the proximity fuse during World War II ranked only second to the development of the atomic bomb in terms of organization and investment, as well as science and engineering. It utilized a large percentage of American electronics and plastics capacity in its production.

The proximity, or VT (Variable Time) fuse, was a very small but extremely sturdy radio transmitter and receiver, and when installed in an aerial bomb or artillery shell sent out high frequency radio waves that caused the detonation of the explosive charge at the optimum point when they bounced back from an enemy aircraft, ground target, or the earth itself. There were two types of fuses. The Navy was assigned the task of developing the rotating type fuse for use in large guns of both services, while the Army had the responsibility for the development and procurement of the non-rotating type fuse for use in rockets and aerial bombs. The Army engaged civilian scientists at a civilian agency to work in close cooperation with industry and academia, while the Navy funded work by the Johns Hopkins Applied Physics Laboratory. After Pearl Harbor the Navy had committed $80 million to its proximity fuse program, and during the last year of the war $450 million was being spent on the production of 40,000 VTs per day.

The Army proximity fuse for bombs, 4.5 inch rockets, and mortars was developed by Division 4 of the National Defense Research Committee (NDRC), Office of Scientific Research and Development (OSRC), headed by Dr. Alexander Ellett. The nucleus of the Central Laboratory of Division 4 was at the National Bureau of Standards (NBS) led by Harry Diamond, who was assisted by Allen Astin, Cledo Brunetti, Wilbur Hinman, and Jacob Rabinow. Diamond and his group, later known as the Ordnance Development Division, had previously completed ground-breaking work at the NBS in the field of radio, developing radiosondes and automatic weather stations, as well as instrument landing systems for aircraft. The Navy and Johns Hopkins were challenged by a separate and possibly more difficult task in developing the VT fuse for spinning shells shot at high velocities and pressures out of rifled naval guns. The ultimate problem with the VT fuse was not in the theory, but in determining the mechanical design detail and developing the small but strong electrical and mechanical components, and also in coordinating the industrial facilities, management, and personnel to manufacture the fuses in large quantities.

In the function of proximity fuse, the development of the rugged gas-filled tube which acted as the vital high energy electrical switch was essential. Beginning in September 1940, a number of miniature radios and hearing aides were tested in centrifuges, fired from 37mm artillery, and unscientifically dropped on concrete. Western Electric, Raytheon, Hytron, Erwood, and Parker-Majestic worked on the development of the thyratron triode, which was finally perfected and manufactured by Sylvania, Raytheon, and Hytron.

In mid-1940, the Navy and NDRC subsidized work at Carnegie Institute's Department of Terrestrial Magnetism (DTM) under **Dr. Merle Tuve**, who soon began investigating acoustic, photoelectric, and radio fuses, and initiated the testing of electronic tubes under extreme conditions for the development of the proximity fuse. (AFHRC)

In mid-1940, the Navy and NDRC subsidized work at Carnegie Institute's Department of Terrestrial Magnetism (DTM) under Dr. Merle Tuve. (Note: after the war Tuve was one of America's preeminent scientists, serving for 20 years as the director of the Carnegie Institution of Washington's Department of Terrestrial Magnetism, where he made significant contributions to experimental seismology, radio astronomy, and optical astronomy.) In September 1940 Dr. John Cockcroft, as part of the British scientific advisory Tizard Mission to Washington, briefed the Navy and Tuve on British photo-electric and radar proximity fuses under development, which he summarized as not being "probable" in the near future. Undeterred, Tuve's staff at DTM was soon investigating acoustic, photoelectric, and radio fuses, and initiated the testing of electronic tubes under extreme conditions. In November, University of Iowa professor Dr. Alexander Ellett arrived in Washington to work with Dr. Tuve. Several weeks later the two started work at the NBS on proximity fuses for bombs and rockets. In December 1940, Drs. Diamond and Hinman of the Radio Section at NBS joined the team and immediately recognized that a fuse utilizing the Doppler effect of reflected radio waves had the most potential, and they designed a diode detector array that operated when the amplitude of the reflected signals exceeded a predetermined value. The efficacy of the Doppler principal was confirmed using a rudimentary model in field tests and was followed in April and May 1941 by successful bomb drops. The next stage was developing and refining electronic circuits, mechanical switches, and safety mechanisms, and in improving the durability of the components and mountings. The VT fuse was a five tube transmitting and receiving set that had to not only be small and rugged but also relatively inexpensive, adaptable to mass-production, unaffected by counter-measures, safe in use, operable in any weather, and most importantly had to detonate the bomb or projectile at the exact moment when the shell or bomb fragments would envelop the target. A tall order at best.

In the meantime, Tuve and his staff at DTM were pressed by the Navy to focus more on development of the radio fuse for shells, and in July 1941 the NDRC moved the DTM photoelectric bomb fuse group over to the NBS, where another group was already actively working on the problem. By November, work had progressed so that the Navy decided to prepare for full-scale production. Early in 1942 the Tuve group was placed directly under the OSRD, and Johns Hopkins replaced the Carnegie Institution as the prime contractor.

The Ellett contingent continued its work at NBS as Section E of Division A of the NDRC, with Diamond and Hinman operating as the central laboratory for the group. In December 1942 NDRC was reorganized, and Section E became Division 4, with Ellett as its head and primary liaison between NDRC and NBS. Concurrently, the Diamond/Hinman central laboratory was reorganized and enlarged as the Ordnance Development Division, with a staff of 200 assigned (increased to 400 by the end of the war) to developing a proximity fuse for rockets and bombs. During this time the Navy remained dedicated in its interest and support for the shell fuse, while Army's commitment for bomb and rocket fuses was not nearly as strong.

In May 1942 the Army issued its first urgent requirements for a specific fuse, which was a VT fuse for the new 4.5 inch rocket to be used against German bomber formations, and Diamond and Hinman completed a design in two days. NBS and Westinghouse produced the preliminary model lots on small-scale production lines, and 55 fuses were tested at Fort Fisher, NC, in June. About 400,000 were manufactured during 1943, but none were used in combat as intended, as Allied air superiority had decimated Luftwaffe bomber formations. Diamond and his NBS group had developed an excellent fuse but had no target to use it on. Production was tapered off during 1943, and the photoelectric project was suspended all together.

Division 4 and the Ordnance Development Division then concentrated on an enlarged program of bomb fuse development. Several engineering problems were encountered and needed to be solved. The fuses had to perform reliably when cooled to the very low temperatures encountered by high altitude bombers. A dry battery proved to be ineffective, as it supplied inadequate voltage for the few seconds it had to function in the extreme cold of high altitudes at which bombers flew. The limited shelf-life of the batteries was another concern, as they soon lost strength in warm climates. Under Signal Corps supervision, a development program was established at the NBS to perfect a generator to replace the batteries. A model was completed in late 1943 utilizing a propeller in the nose of the projectile as a windmill to drive a tiny generator. Whirling at a rate of 100,000 revolutions per minute, 50 times faster than the spin of an airplane propeller, the windmill supplied sufficient power to the generator to create a continuous radiation of radio waves from the bomb or projectile.

To prevent the proximity fuse from detonating its explosive upon receipt of wave echoes from the aircraft which launched it or from other nearby planes, the connection between the fuse and the detonator was left open until after the projectile was launched. The first few spins of the windmill turned on a worm gear that closed the connection and completed the arming of the projectile.

In July 1943 Army and Navy specified the types of bombs for which fuses were required, and the War Department authorized limited procurement in the fall of 1943, even before testing was complete. NBS began small-scale production of models in April 1943 and, in May, NDRC contracted with the Zell Corporation of Baltimore to establish a pilot production line. With preparations for the invasion of France in 1944 the interest in the fuse increased, but the Joint Chiefs of Staff prohibited its use of the fuse over land until October 1944, fearing its capture and duplication by the enemy.

In Spring 1944 the final developmental testing in bombs at Eglin Field, FL, was not entirely satisfactory, causing the AAF to state that the high percentage of early fuse bursts negated any alleged superiority of proximity fused bombs over conventionally fused clusters. Ellett thought that the test procedure was at fault for the poor results and demanded new tests at Eglin in the fall of 1944. These tests irrefutably demonstrated the great advantage of the air burst, but the earlier mediocre report had received wide distribution, and cautious commanders in the ETO were reluctant in using the fuse operationally.

In late 1944, VT bomb fuse advocate E.L. Bowles was sent by the Secretary of War to the Pacific to explain and tout the desirability of the new VT fuse. Following the Bowles tour, the Fifth and Seventh Air Forces requested trial lots of the fuse to be shipped by air, together with technicians to direct its use and handling. Approximately 3,000 arrived, and a successful demonstration was held at Saipan on 22 January 1944 for officials of the 7th Air Force and its various bomber groups. In February the 7th Air Force dropped proximity-fused 500 pound GP bombs and 260 pound Fragmentation Bombs in the pre-invasion bombardment of anti-aircraft defenses and radio and radar installations on Iwo Jima. The initial results were very encouraging, and orders were placed for large quantities, which unfortunately were shipped by sea and did not arrive until just before V-J Day. Meanwhile, the 7th Air Force successfully employed the small remaining quantities of fuses shipped by air in its bombing campaigns against Palau, Marcus Island, Okinawa, and the Japanese mainland. In the final attacks on the Japanese mainland during July and August 1945, about one-third of all bombs dropped by Navy carrier-based aircraft were proximity fused general-purpose, fragmentation, and incendiary devices.

Once the VT bomb fuse went into mass production the Navy requested adaptation of the fuse for use with its 5 inch Aircraft Rocket (AR) and the High-Velocity Aircraft Rocket (HVAR). Production of both air-to-ground and air-to-air versions began in December 1944 and reached a peak just before the surrender of Japan in September 1945.

There were five major contractors for the fuse: Crosley (for 5.21 million fuses), Eastman-Kodak (2.44 million), McQuay-Norris (2.86 million), RCA Camden (2.35 million) and RCA Bloomington (3.53 million), and Sylvania (5.68 million), all of which were supplied by over 100 major subcontractors. The first fuses were produced for $732 per item in 1942, but by the end of the war the per item cost was reduced to only $18. Twenty-two million VT fuses of all types were produced during the war, costing about a billion dollars, or the equivalent of three days of the total U.S. war costs. Of these 22 million fuses over 20 million were unused, as the war ended, and 388,000 were utilized in research and development, and only 1.5 million were fired in combat because, for security reasons, their use over enemy territory was prohibited. The principal trend in ordnance expenditure once the VT fuse was available was the shift from 100 pound and 250 pound GP bombs to the 260 pound fragmentation bomb with the new VT fusing, which were used by all types of aircraft against such primary targets as grounded aircraft and AA guns.

VT Fuse Described

General

VT (proximity) fuses have also been called Influence, Special Buck Rogers, Pozit, and Bonzo fuses. Basically, VT fuses were automatic time fuses which, without setting or adjustment, detonated the bomb as it approached the target at the most effective point on its trajectory. Among various possible types of radio proximity fuses, an active-type fuse operating on the Doppler Effect was selected as being the most promising method.

Essentially VT fuses were radio transmitting and receiving units which in flight broadcast a continuous radio signal. In a Doppler-type fuse, the actuating signal was produced by the wave reflected from a target moving with respect to the fuse. When this signal was reflected from any object to the armed fuse it interacted with the transmitted wave to produce interference in ripples or beats with the transmitter, which resulted in a low frequency beat caused by the combination of the transmitted and the reflected frequencies. When the beat reached a predetermined intensity it tripped an electronic switch (the thyratron) which permitted an electric charge to flow through an electric detonator, exploding the bomb.

VT fuses were used in any operation in which air bursts at heights between 10 and 250 feet increased the effectiveness of the bomb in which it was used. VT fuses were physically interchangeable, but were not tactically interchangeable, in that they functioned before impact. They were similar to time fuses in the production of an air burst, but the time fuse was governed by distance from its origin and the VT fuse by its proximity to the target.

External Description

There were two types of VT fuses, the bar-type AN-M166 and the ring-type AN-M168. The bar-type fuse could be used effectively in *any* bomb with a fuse well that accommodated the M163 type nose fuse, while the ring-type, although it fit the same fuse well, could only be used in the bomb sizes for which it was specified. In both types, the external part of the fuse body was a cylinder three to four inches in diameter and five inches long, with a vane at the nose. The ring-type had a metal ring surrounding the vane with a vane stop pin sealed in the ring. The bar-type had two four inch metal bars extending radially from the head, and a vane stop arm mounted on a bracket on the side. In both types, the part of the body which was installed within the bomb conformed in size and shape to the M163 type nose fuse, except that there was a safety pin clipped around the base and extending into the end of the fuse.

Functioning

The arming vane drove a high speed coupling shaft and then through a reduction gear train connected to a slow speed shaft. An electric generator was mounted on the high speed shaft and furnished power to charge a firing capacitor, and to operate the transmitting and receiving unit that controlled the electronic switch between the firing capacitor and electric detonator. The vane had to rotate at high speed, 2,000 rpm or more, to drive the generator at sufficient speed to charge the firing capacitor and furnish power to operate the transmitting and receiving unit. The vane had to rotate a substantial number of times to turn the detonator rotor a sufficient amount to bring the detonator into line in the explosive train and to bring the electric leads of the detonator into contact with the firing circuit. The number of revolutions ranged from 1,550 for 2,000 feet MinSAT (Minimum Safe Air Travel) to 3,500 for 3,000 feet MinSAT. The detonator rotor was keyed to the slow speed shaft by a spring-loaded pin. The rotor controlled both mechanical and electrical arming, and as it turned to the armed position, the outer end of the key pin was driven by its spring into a recess in the

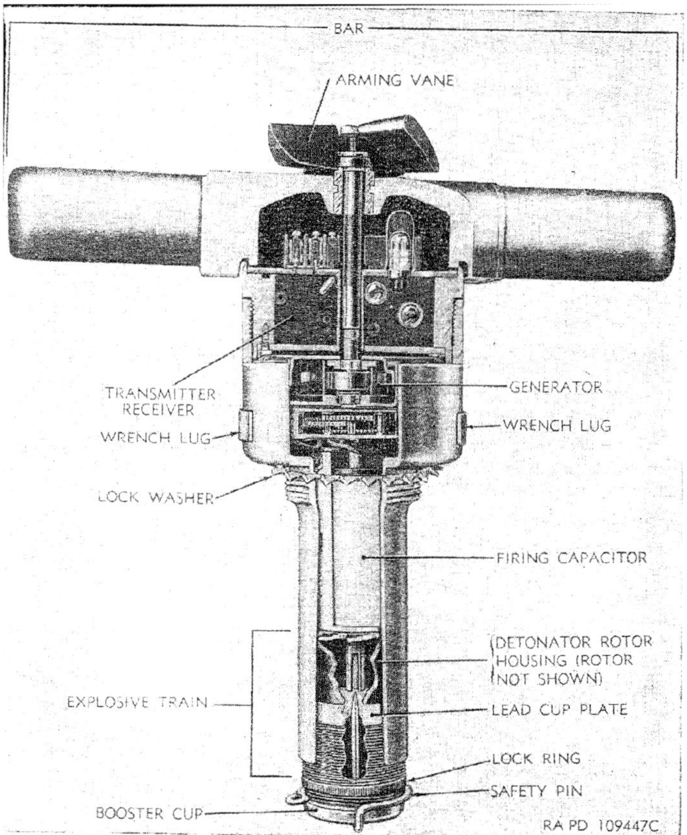

Figure 55. Fuze, bomb, nose, VT, AN-M166—sectioned.

Proximity Fuse (TM 9-1980)

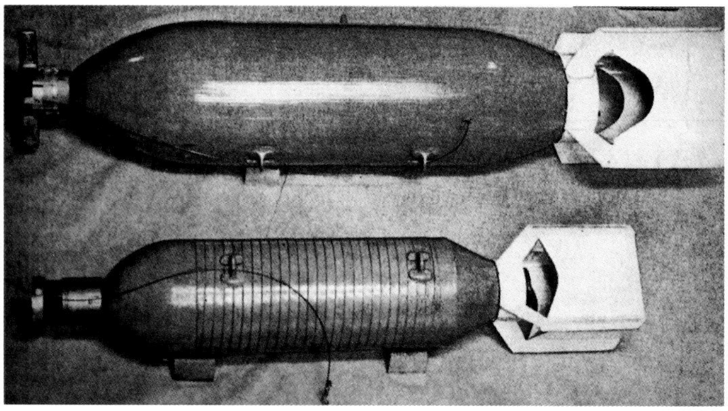

Above: There were two types of VT fuses, the **bar-type AN-M166** (top on 500 pound GP bomb) and the **ring-type AN-M168** (bottom on 200 pound fragmentation bomb). The bar-type fuse could be used effectively in *any* bomb with a fuse well that accommodated the M163 type nose fuse, while the ring-type, although it fit the same fuse well, could only be used in the bomb sizes for which it was specified. (AFHRC)

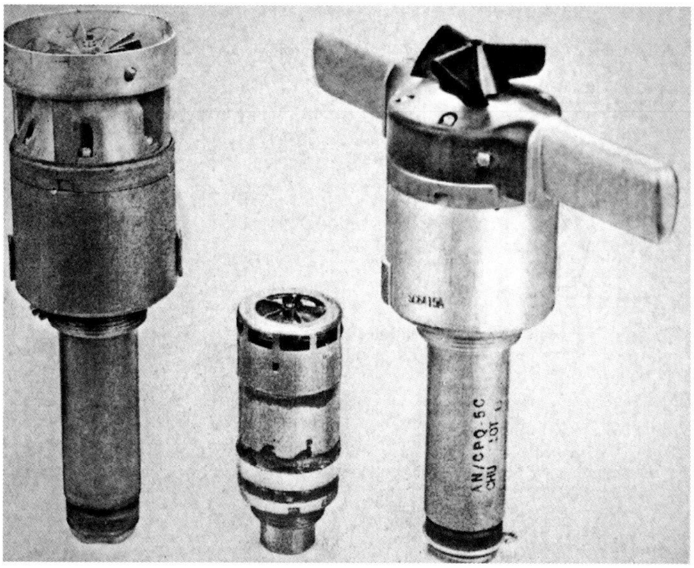

Right: Proximity Ring Fuse for bomb (left) and mortar (center), and Bar Fuse for bomb (right). (AFHRC)

rotor housing while the inner end withdrew the keyway in the shaft. When a material object entered the zone of influence of the fuse, the reflected wave caused the firing switch to operate, passing the charge of the firing capacitor through the electric detonator, thus initiating the explosive train. Since these fuses operated on any object, airborne or grounded, that came within their radius of influence, the MinSAT was carefully calibrated for the protection of friendly aircraft. The MinSAT was measured for representative samples of each lot of VT fuses and was marked on every fuse of the lot. Mechanical arming delay devices were furnished by which the MinSAT could be increased by as much as 20,000 feet.

Fusing

VT fuses were issued completely assembled and ready for installation on removal from their packing. Field assembly consisted of removing the safety pin from the fuse, screwing the fuse into the bomb, installing the arming wire and, if required, the arming delay. If possible, fusing was to be done after the bombs were loaded into the bomb bay.

Characteristics

General

VT fuses functioned automatically on approach to or passing any material target, causing an air burst at an effective height or distance.

Height of Burst

Ring-type fuses produced approximate heights of burst from 10 to 250 feet depending on the size of bomb, nature of target, altitude, and speed of aircraft at release. Bar-type fuses gave average heights of burst of approximately 25 to 125 feet depending on size of bomb and nature of target, the performance being comparatively independent of altitude and speed of release. Various factors affected the height of burst:

1) Effect of target: Functioning (e.g. height of burst) of all types of VT fuses was influenced by the nature of the target, such as over water; over dry or wet earth, or earth containing significant amounts of metal (up to 100% higher); or over dry sand (up to 50% lower). Dispersed vehicles or aircraft did not affect the height of burst, but the approach to high structures or dense foliage could increase the height of the burst.
2) Effect of altitude and speed at release: Ring-type fuses were affected by the striking angle of the bomb, which depended on altitude and true air speed at release. This dependence of height of burst on release conditions could be used to advantage, since it provided a means of control of burst height in the field. Bar-type fuses were generally not affected striking angles and only slightly affected by release angles.
3) Effect of the bomb: The size and shape of the bomb affected the burst height of all types of VT fuses.
4) Dispersion: Variation and tolerance in the manufacture of fuses and components led to variation in height of burst of fuses of any one type, under conditions which were otherwise identical.

Reliability

By the end of the war VT fuses had reached the point where 85% normal functioning was attained. About 3% were duds due to unknown reasons and about 12% were "Earlies" (i.e. they functioned early at some point between the MinSAT and the point of normal functioning above the target) due to faulty operation caused by either previous damage in manufacture, shipment, or handling, or by their improper installation into the bomb.

Heavy rain, snow, and hail were liable to cause an excessive number of early functions; however light rain, haze, sunlight, and darkness did not affect fuse operation. Warm, humid conditions could cause rapid deterioration of exposed VT fuses, so the sealed metal packing containers were not to be opened until the fuses were required for the mission. Normal safety and operating characteristics were not adversely affected when the fuses were used or stored within the temperature range of -60° to 140° F.

Excessive vibration of any component of the complete round during flight caused an increase in the number of early malfunctions. The principal causes of excessive vibration were fin assemblies that were bent, loose, improperly seated, or poorly fabricated; and from fuses which had damaged vanes, or were loose in the fuse seat; or not properly tightened, or from excessive bearing wear due to release at high altitudes without an arming delay.

Train Spacing

Since VT fuses were designed to respond to a sudden change in their surroundings, the detonation of a nearby bomb could cause an armed fuse to function. This restricted the minimum train spacing that could be used with "Armed Salvo" and "Minimum Train" releases, resulting in an increase in early functions. An Intervalometer spacing of 50 feet or more for 100 to 260 pound high explosive bombs or 100 feet for 500 pound GP bombs was satisfactory.

Duds
A VT dud fuse could be armed and charged, and so was prone to fire on any disturbance or on approach of personnel or materiel. A sufficient time, usually 24 hours, had to be allowed for the firing charge to dissipate, after which the VT bomb fuse dud could be handled with comparative safety if the vane was locked, since they contained no impact firing elements.

Air Travel Arming Delay Mechanisms
The arming delay consisted of a wind vane, a reduction gear train, a setting dial, and a lock to attach it to the ring or bracket of the fuse. The arming delay device was attached to the fuse to delay the start of fuse arming until a preset amount of travel had been covered. The arming delay device was attached to the fuse to hold the vane lock in position. When the desired air travel was completed, the arming delay released itself and was forced away from the fuse, and the spring of the vane lock was ejected, thus permitting the fuse to begin to arm. The Arming Delay, Air Travel M1 had a setting dial mounted on one end of a gear shaft which was held in engagement with the gear train by a spring. The opposite end of the shaft protruded through a slot in the housing and formed a stud which was depressed to disengage the shaft and permit rotation of the setting dial.

Optical Proximity Fuses
Early attempts to develop optical fuses were for use with five inch shells and had to be able to withstand great G and centrifugal forces caused by the rotation of the projectile when it was fired from a rifled barrel. Later fuses were developed for use on rockets, which did not rotate like a shell.
The Optical Proximity Fuse was a device which operated on the light signal produced by the target as the projectile approached it. There were three basic parts of the Optical Proximity Fuse: a toroidal lens, a photocell, and an amplifier. The lens was part of the conical nose of the rocket and was arranged to collect light from all directions during its line of flight, and to focus it upon the photocell tube. The photo-sensitive cell then would transform the light into electrical energy which was then sent to an amplifier.

There was no amplifier output until there was a sudden change in the amount of light entering the lens. This change was produced when the rocket approached the target and the light available to the photocell increased. The amplifier output developed a voltage that would then trigger a thyratron tube which, in turn, caused detonation of an explosive charge in the rocket. To operate the fuse, the change in the amount of light entering the lens needed to be just a small percentage of the total light regardless of the ambient light level from dawn to dusk.

The fuse was also provided with a way to prevent the amplifier from operating and a firing pulse from being generated until after the rocket had been fired and was heading towards the target. The fuse was equipped with safety features designed to prevent premature operation should the rocket be accidentally dropped prior to firing. Another innovative element was the self-destruct system which, if the projectile missed the target, would explode the rocket before reaching the ground, which was important if the rocket would head toward friendly territory.

In 1942 Dr. Alexander Ellett, Chief of Section E of the National Defense Research Committee (NDRC), delegated Bell Laboratories to develop a working design for an optical fuse to fit on the 4.5 inch rocket for the Army Ordnance Department. These fuses were to be used against aircraft, as well as being installed on rockets fired from aircraft. Bell Laboratories' Apparatus and Transmission Development Departments worked with the engineers of the National Bureau of Standards on the design and development of this fuse. In the development of the photocell, the lens, electronic tubes, and other circuit components the Bell Lab designers had to make these components fit the nose of the rocket; be able to withstand the large forces of acceleration, which were 1,000 times the force of gravity; and be easily mass produced at a low per unit cost.

The toroidal lens was an integral part of the nose piece, the entire part being made of optically clear Lucite or Plexiglas. The curvature of the toroidal lens was designed to transmit only the light which came through a narrow angle throughout its circumferential surface, and to have the focal axis at any point around the lens lie on a conical surface. It was manufactured by injection molding to the final dimensions, and no polishing of the lens surface was required after the molding. The portions of the surfaces that had to be opaque to light were coated with a black finish by spraying. To obtain the desired sensitivity to light when the projectile was in the most effective position with respect to the target, the glass tube portion of the photocell was made opaque to light except for a slit properly located with respect to the lens. With this arrangement the photocell cathode was made to "see" the target at the angle required to place the target in the densest part of the fragmentation pattern when the projectile exploded.

Explosive Charges
Development of Explosives
The "T'hung-lian-kang-mu" is a Chinese journal translated by St. Julian that describes the Mongol siege of the city of Pien-king in 1232 AD. It appeared that the powerful Mongol army was about to overrun the walled city when the Chinese turned to two newly developed secret weapons: the bomb and a large sky rocket. While the rocket caused more anxiety than damage, the bomb was a more serious threat. It was a heavy container containing gunpowder lowered by iron chains from the walls onto the besieging Mongols below, where it exploded with much noise, smoke, and power, forcing the Mongols to retreat. The bomb's explosive component was the first use of gunpowder, which seems to have evolved from "Greek fire," an incendiary mixture consisting of resins, pitch, asphaltum, and other similar flammable substances invented by the early Greeks before it was brought to China. For some unknown reason the Chinese added saltpeter to this mixture, which caused pieces to explode, and the first use of gunpowder was chronicled. The Chinese alchemists experimented with different quantities of saltpeter and nitrate content and eventually produced bombs and grenades. The 14th century text *Huolongjing* described gunpowder formulas using nitrate levels approaching the maximum theoretical composition for explosive force and also mentioned exploding cannonballs.

In the Arab world, gunpowder was probably invented as a potassium nitrate mixture, as was described by Khalid ibn Yazid in the Seventh Century. In the mid-Eighth Century nitric acid mixture was described by Jabir ibn Hayyan. In 1240 Abdallah ibn Bairhar wrote a treatise that described a saltpeter and explosive mixture called "the flower of the stone of Assos" that had its origins in the Far East as "Chinese Snow." The earliest known military applications of these explosive gunpowder compositions were in 1248 in al-Andalus (Spain) and in 1250 by the Mamluks against the Franks led by Louis IX.

The earliest existing written European reference to gunpowder is from Roger Bacon in his *Epistola* in the 1250s, which stated:

> "We can, with saltpeter and other substances, compose artificially a fire that can be launched over long distances... By only using a very small quantity of this material much light can be created accompanied by a horrible fracas. It is possible with it to destroy a town or an army ... In order to produce this artificial lightning and thunder it is necessary to take saltpeter, sulfur, and (a coded ingredient or quantity) Luru Vopo Vir Can Utriet."

In his *Opus Maior* of 1267, Bacon described firecrackers as "a child's toy of sound and fire and explosion made in various parts of the world with powder of saltpeter, sulfur and charcoal of Hazelwood."

In the early 14th Century Marcus Graecus described a collection of incendiary and gunpowder formulas in his *Liber Ignium* (*Book of Fire*). Ingis volatilis ("flying fire") was a mixture of saltpeter, sulfur, and rosin which, when inserted into a reed or hollow wood, "flies away suddenly and burns up everything."

Another formula for "artificial thunder" stipulated a mixture of one pound native sulfur, two pounds linden or willow charcoal, and six pounds of saltpeter.

In 1838 French chemist T. J. Pelouze discovered that cotton could be made explosive by dipping it in concentrated nitric acid to become "guncotton." In 1845 German chemist Christian Schoenbein improved the method for manufacturing this explosive by dipping the innocuous cotton in a mixture of nitric and sulfuric acids and then washing the substance to remove the excess acid. Another nitro-explosive, nitroglycerin, was discovered by Italian chemist Ascanio Sobrero in 1846 while working under Pelouze at the University of Turin. Nitroglycerine was notorious for its extreme instability, and a number of chemists tried to reduce its sensitivity without decreasing its strength. The best manufacturing process was developed by Alfred Nobel in the 1860s after a long period of trial and error, which in 1867 resulted in a liquid combination of nitroglycerin and gunpowder called Dynamite. Despite Nobel's reservations about its use, his creation would become a "peaceful" explosive with little application as a military weapon.

After the process of nitration was discovered chemists systematically tested numerous substances for their explosive qualities after being nitrated. One of the substances tested was a tri-nitrate, picric acid, while another substance tested was a coal-tar, toluene. TNT (tri-nitro-toluene) was found to have all the features the military required of an explosive: easy to manufacture in large quantities; safe to handle; and when made to explode, by the action of a specially constructed fuse, it was a powerful explosive.

Explosive Charge

When the bomb body was filled with an explosive charge, the type of explosive used depended upon the probable use of the bomb. In general, high explosives were compositions and mixtures of ingredients capable of instantaneously releasing large amounts of energy and doing work of various kinds on objects and bodies surrounding them. In some cases the useful work that was done was limited only by the energy content of the explosive composition, while in other cases the transfer of energy from the explosive composition to surrounding bodies was controlled to a large degree by the momentum or impulse released by the detonating explosive. Brisance was the speed at which the explosive developed its maximum pressure or shattering ability.

Loading High Explosives

High explosive charges are loaded into their containers by one of three methods: cast-loaded, pre-loaded, or extrusion. Cast loading is preferred by pouring the substance as a liquid into a container and letting it solidify. Explosives having no liquid form must be press-loaded, or pressed into their container. The combining of certain explosives results in plastic mixtures that can be loaded only by the extrusion method. The extrusion method employs a pressure system for forcing the plastic mixtures into the various types of projectiles and bomb casings.

Explosive Train

An explosive train, also called a triggering sequence, is a sequence of events that terminates in the detonation of explosives. The basic high explosive train consists of the primer, delay, detonator, booster, and bursting charge. For safety reasons, most widely used high explosives are difficult to detonate. A primary explosive of higher sensitivity is used to trigger a uniform and predictable detonation of the main body of the explosive. Although the primary explosive itself is generally a more sensitive and expensive compound, it is only used in small quantities and in relatively safely packaged forms. By design there are low explosives and high explosives made such that the low explosives are highly sensitive and high explosives are comparatively insensitive. This not only affords inherent safety to the usage of explosives during handling and transport, but also necessitates an explosive triggering sequence or explosive train.

Explosives Used In World War II

Name	Composition
Amatol	Ammonium Nitrate (60-20%) and TNT (40-80%)
Composition A	RDX (88-91%) and Plasticizing Oil (8-12%)
Composition B	RDX (59-60%), TNT (39-40%), and Wax (1%)
Composition C	RDX (77%), Tetryl (3%), TNT (4%), Nitrocellulose (1%) MNT (5%) and DNT (10%)
Cyclotol	RDX (70%) and TNT (30%),
DBX	RDX (21%), Aluminum Nitrate (21%), TNT (40%), and Aluminum (18%)

Steel bomb body being filled with TNT at the factory. (AFHRC)

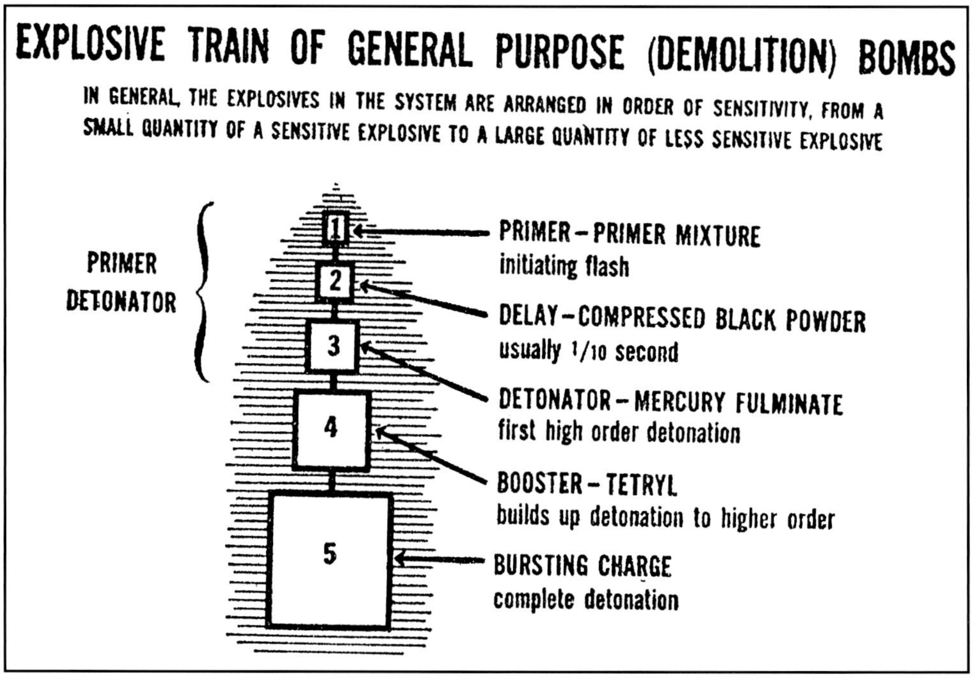

(TM9-1980)

Ednatol	Ethylenedinitramine (57%) and TNT (43%)
HBX	RDX (40%), TNT (38%), Aluminum Powder (17%) and Desensitizer (5%)
Minol	TNT (42%), Ammonium Nitrate (42%), and Powdered Aluminum (10%)
Pentolite	TNT (50%) and PETN (50%)
PEP-3	PETN (86%) and Plasticizer (14%)
PETN	Pure (Pentoerythritol tetranitrate)
Picratrol	Explosive D (52%) and TNT (48%)
PTX-1	RDX (80%), Tetryl (50%), and TNT (20%)
PTX-2	RDX (43%), PETN (28%), and TNT (29%)
RDX	Pure (Cyclomethylenetrinitramine)
Tetryl	Pure (2, 4, 6-trinitrophenyl-N-methylnitramine)
Tetrytol	Tetryl (70%) and TNT (30%)
Torpex	RDX (45%), TNT (37%), and Aluminum Powder (18%)
Tritonal	TNT (80%) and Aluminum Powder (20%)
TNT	Pure (Trinitrotoluene)

Amatol

Amatol was a highly explosive substitute for TNT made from a mixture of ammonium nitrate and TNT; the percentage of ammonium nitrate, depending on the availability of TNT, varied from 40% to 80%. TNT was comparatively expensive and complex to manufacture, and was deficient in oxygen, which was evident from the black smoke residue from a pure TNT explosion. Depending on the ratio of TNT used, Amatol left white or grey smoke after detonation. When compared to TNT, ammonium nitrate had a fairly low detonation velocity and correspondingly low brisance, but was extremely cheap and easy to manufacture; but more importantly, it contained a surplus of oxygen which the TNT content used during detonation. Amatol's power, brisance, and its sensitivity decreased with the increasing percentages of nitrate. Amatol allowed existing supplies of TNT to be considerably diluted with little reduction in the destructive power of the final product as long as the amount of TNT in the mixture did not fall below 60%. Nonetheless, Amatol remained a fairly good high explosive, even when the TNT content was reduced to 20%.

The Amatol production process was very straightforward and inexpensive, which made it a widely used explosive. TNT was gently heated until it melted into a syrupy mass, at which point the correct weight ratio of powdered ammonium nitrate was added and mixed in. While this mixture was still in a molten state, it was poured into empty bomb casings and allowed to cool and set into a solid. Amatol remained soft for long periods of storage and was relatively stable, but could be detonated by severe impact. Amatol had a disadvantage in that it was very hygroscopic (moisture absorbing), which complicated long term storage, and so it was usually protected by pouring pure TNT as a seal. It was not to be stored in copper or brass containers as it could form dangerous compounds.

Primary explosives, such as mercury fulminate, were often used as a detonator in combination with an explosive booster charge such as Tetryl. The velocity of detonation of 50/50 mixture was 19,700 feet per second at a density of 1.54. Its Laboratory Impact Value was 98. Its Bullet Impact Value was about 100. The color of Amatol ranged from off-white to slightly yellow or pinkish brown, depending on the mixture used.

Amatol was used extensively during the World Wars as an explosive in weapons such as aircraft bombs, shells, and naval mines, but was eventually replaced with alternatives, such as Composition B, Torpex, and Tritonal. Due to the shortages of TNT and RDX most World War II mines had had 50/50 ammonium nitrate and TNT (Amatol) warheads. This was a low quality explosive, but was later improved by the addition of about 20% aluminum to produce Minol.

Composition A

Composition A (Comp A) was a coated, granular mixture of 91% RDX and 9% plasticizing oil, which caused it to become semi-plastic. The oil content was sufficient to desensitize the mixture and lubricate it enough to allow it to be pressed into smaller caliber (20mm, 37mm, and 40mm) anti-aircraft shells, which would be its principal use. It was also used for boosters, and could be used in Armor Piercing shells due to its insensitivity and high brisance. Composition A was also used in land mines and 2.75 and 5 inch rockets.

Composition A was a mixture incorporated by rolling, whereas Composition A-2 denoted the same explosive prepared by kettle-drying an unrolled mixture, while Composition A-3 was a mixture prepared by tray-drying an unrolled product. Composition A-3 was granular in form, resembling Tetryl in granulation. It was less sensitive than TNT in both drop and bullet impact tests, and was substantially more brisant and powerful, as was indicated by its velocity of detonation of 27,000 feet per second at a density of 1.62. Its Laboratory Impact Value was 105. Its Bullet Impact Value was over 100. Its color was white or buff, depending on the color of the oil.

Composition B (Cyclotol)

Composition B, occasionally referred to as Cyclotol, was intended to be used as a more powerful replacement for TNT, where an explosive with more power and brisance was of tactical advantage and there was no problem with a slight increase of sensitivity. Composition B was a castable mixture of 59% RDX, 40% TNT, and 1% wax to improve handling qualities, while Composition B-2 was a mixture of 60% RDX and 40% TNT. The TNT reduced the sensitivity of the RDX content to a safe range and lowered the melting point to 178°F, allowing the material to be cast-loaded. It was one of the most powerful explosives, and was less sensitive than Tetryl but more sensitive than TNT. It had extremely high shaped-charge efficiency. Its velocity of detonation was 24,500 feet per second at a density of 1.60. Its total energy of blast in air was about 116% of that of TNT. Its Laboratory Impact Value was 79. Its Bullet Impact Value was 79. Its color was yellow to brown.

Composition B was a very common ingredient in U.S. and other allied nations' munitions, and was the standard explosive filler from early World War II until the early 1990s, when less sensitive explosives began to replace it in many weapons systems. It was an authorized filling for AN (Army-Navy) standard GP bombs and in fragmentation aircraft bombs, mines, and torpedoes, and could be used in boosters for large bombs, demolition charges, and larger-caliber projectiles. It is used as a burster in artillery projectiles, rockets, land mines, and hand grenades. It was also used for the explosive lenses in the first implosion-type nuclear weapons developed by the United States.

Composition C (PE)

Sometimes referred to as PE, Composition C was a plastic explosive containing RDX and an inert plasticizer.

Composition C-2

Compositions C-2 and C-3 were similar, except that an explosive plasticizer was used. Composition C-2 consisted of a mixture of RDX plus nitrocotton and an explosive plasticizer containing no Tetryl. C-2 explosive was easily moldable at most temperatures and withstood water submersion well.

Composition C-3

Composition C-3 consisted of RDX plus nitrocotton and a plasticizer containing Tetryl substituted in part for RDX. It was composed of 77% RDX, 3% Tetryl, 4% TNT, 1% Nitrocellulose, 5% MNT (Mononitrotoluol), and 10% DNT (Dinitrotoluol). The fundamental difference between Composition C-3 and Composition C-2 was the substitution of 3% Tetryl for 3%

RDX, which improved the plastic qualities. The change in ingredients was made in order to obtain a plastic composition that would meet the requirements of an ideal explosive for molded and shaped charges, and that would maintain its plasticity over a wide range of temperatures and not exude oil. At temperatures between 0° and 110°F Composition C-3 was plastic or pliable, closely resembling putty. It was considerably less sensitive than TNT and was detonated by a blasting cap, and had considerably greater brisance (1.35 times more) than TNT and was particularly effective under water. For these reasons it was used principally as a commando and demolition explosive. Its velocity of detonation was 26,000 feet per second at a density of 1.58. The Laboratory Impact Value was 98. Its Bullet Impact Value was over 100. Its color was brown. Composition C-3 was the only one of the Composition C series in production at the end of the war.

DBX

DBX was another aluminized RDX mixture comprised of 21% RDX, 21% Aluminum Nitrate, 40% TNT, and 18% Aluminum. Half of the strategic RDX in Torpex was replaced by Ammonium Nitrate in DBX. DBX, which could be cast, was designed to replace Torpex, which it closely resembled in sensitivity, strength, brisance, and energy of shock in water. Its velocity of detonation was 22,300 feet per second at a density of 1.68. It was 143% as powerful as TNT under water. Its Laboratory Impact Value was not given. Its Bullet Impact Value was 51. Its color was gray.

Ednatol

Ednatol was a mixture of 57% Haleite or Explosive H (ethylenedinitramine) and 43% TNT, and was one of the most powerful explosives of the war. It was developed in 1935 to ease the shortage of RDX, and also was to be loaded as a substitute for Composition B in large GP bombs and Fragmentation Bombs. Ednatol was used for the same purposes as Pentolite in rockets, grenades, and high explosive antitank shells. It was less sensitive than Tetryl, PETN, or RDX, and was the equivalent to Tetryl in brisance. It could be cast in the same manner as Amatol. Ednatol was very stable, non-hygroscopic, and could be stored for long periods. At a density of 1.60, it had a velocity of detonation of 24,300 feet per second. Its Laboratory Impact Value was not given. Its Bullet Impact Value was 83. Its color was yellow.

Explosive D (Ammonium Picratol/Dunnite)

Explosive D, also known as Ammonium Picratol or Dunnite, was developed by Major Dunn in 1906, and was used extensively by the United States Navy during World War I. Explosive D consisted of ammonium picarate powder, which made it an insensitive substance. By 1911 the United States Army had abandoned its use, but the Navy used it in Armor Piercing artillery shells and projectiles, and in coastal defense. During World War II it was brought back into use due to its insensitivity to shock and friction, and for this reason it was used in Armor Piercing Bombs, which had to withstand severe shock and stresses before detonating. Explosive D typically did not detonate when it contacted heavy armor; rather, the hard bomb encasing it would tear the protective armor open and the fuse would then be triggered, producing the detonation.

Haleite

Haleite was a new explosive introduced at the end of the war that was used in combination with other explosives. It was somewhat more powerful than TNT and its sensitivity was about the same as Tetryl. Its rate of detonation was 25,000 feet per second at a density of 1.5. Its Laboratory Impact Value was 46. Its Bullet Impact Value was not available.

HBX

HBX was a chemically stable, non-corrosive high explosive made from RDX (40%), TNT (38%), aluminum powder (17%), and wax desensitizer (5%). HBX was developed during WWII to replace the more shock-sensitive Torpex used in depth bombs and torpedoes. Tests indicated that it was similar to Composition B, about 98% to 100% as powerful as Torpex, that it was definitely less sensitive than Torpex, and was slightly more sensitive than TNT. The warhead for the 2.75-inch "Mighty Mouse" rocket was filled with HBX (40% RDX, 38% TNT, 17% aluminum powder, and 5% desensitizers) or Composition B (59% RDX, 40% TNT, and 1% wax). The major improvement during the war was the Navy's development of HBX type explosives combined with asphaltic, "hot melt" liners for bombs and other munitions. The hot melt liners were developed to coat and eliminate metal-to-metal pinch points. After the Naval Magazine, Port Chicago, CA, accident of 17 July 1944 , HBX and H-6 explosives were developed that incorporated wax and other chemicals to desensitize the explosive, and hot melt liners were introduced for lining bombs and warheads to give some thermal protection and eliminate potential pinch points from cracks or fissures in the bomb or warhead case. The original HBX was superseded by HBX-1 and HBX-3, which provided greater stability and power than HBX and were used as explosive fillers in underwater ordnance. Later, plastic-bonded explosives were developed for increased thermal protection and fragment impact resistance.

Minol

Minol was developed early in World War II to augment stores of TNT and RDX that were in short supply at the time. The aluminum component in Minol significantly prolonged the explosive pulse, making it ideal for use in underwater naval weapons, such as mines, depth charges, and torpedoes, where munitions with a longer explosive pulse were more destructive than those with high brisance. Minol was not to be used in weapons fired from gun barrels (e.g. artillery shells) because of the risk of detonation when subjected to over 250 G's of acceleration. Typically, four different Minol formulas were used:

Minol-1: 48% TNT, 42% ammonium nitrate, and 10% powdered aluminum.
Minol-2: 40% TNT, 40% ammonium nitrate and 20% powdered aluminum.
Minol-3: 42% TNT, 38% ammonium nitrate and 20% powdered aluminum.
Minol-4: 40% TNT, 40% ammonium nitrate & potassium nitrate (90/10) and 20% powdered aluminum.

Pentolite

Pentolite was a mixture of equal parts of TNT and PETN. Its chief uses were in small shell loading, in grenades, and in cast shaped charges where it had very high shaped-charge efficiency. It was not as stable as TNT in stowage, and separation of the PETN component could occur. Efforts were to be made to keep it cool. Its sensitivity was such that it could not be drilled, and the fuse cavities in shells that had to be drilled were poured with a 90/10 mixture. It had about the same sensitivity as Tetryl in drop tests and was more sensitive than Torpex to bullet impact. Its brisance and power were equivalent to Composition B. At a density of 1.65 its rate of detonation was 24,000 feet per second. Its Laboratory Impact Value was 47. Its Bullet Impact Value was 48.

PETN (PEP 2/3)

Although PETN was first synthesized in Germany in 1891, it was a new plastic explosive being tested by the U.S. at the end of the war. It was one of the most powerful explosives at the time, being 1.66 times more effective than TNT, and was one of the ingredients of Semtex plastic explosive. PEP-2 was 86% PETN and 15% oil, but it was a little too soft. PEP-3 was a mixture of 86% PETN and 14% plasticizing oil. It was about 90% as powerful and brisant as Composition C, but its stowage stability and plastic range were much better. Its sensitivity was about the same as Composition C, though it had much less tendency to burn. It was used primarily in booster and bursting charges of small arms and in the detonators of some land mine and shells. Interestingly, PETN was used as a vasodilator in treating heart disease, similar to nitroglycerine.

Picratol

Picratol was a mixture of 52% Explosive D and 48% TNT. The main advantage of Picratol was its insensitivity to shock, and as a result it was used as the main explosive filling in Armor Piercing shells and aerial bombs. It was used in the 2,000 pound SAP M103 Bomb and was considered for other AAF AP and SAP bombs. Picratol's stability was about equal to that of Explosive D and TNT, and had a rate of detonation of 22,875 feet per second at a normal loading density of 1.625. Brisance tests, peak pressure tests, and impulse tests indicated that Picratol's destructive force was somewhat less than that of TNT, but greater than that of Explosive D.

RDX

RDX was also known as Cyclotrimethylenetrinitramine, RDX, cyclonite, hexogen (Germany), and T-4 (Italy). There are many interpretations of its acronym, including Royal Demolition eXplosive, Research Department (composition) X, and Research Department eXplosive. The discovery of RDX as a medicine dates to the 1890s in Germany. Its explosive properties were not discovered until 1920 when RDX was produced by the direct nitration of hexamine. RDX was used by both the Axis and Allies in World War II, often in explosive mixtures with TNT, such as Torpex. RDX formed the base for a number of common military explosives: Composition A (wax-coated, granular explosive consisting of RDX and plasticizing wax), Composition B (castable mixtures of RDX and TNT), Composition C (a plastic demolition explosive consisting of RDX, other explosives, and plasticizers), Composition D, HBX (castable mixtures of RDX, TNT, powdered aluminum, and D-2wax with calcium chloride), H-6, Cyclotol, and C4. Today, RDX is also used as a major component of many plastic bonded explosives; it is also a popular terrorist explosive.

In its pure, synthesized state RDX was a white, crystalline solid that was nitrated from an evaporated aqueous solution of ammonia and formaldehyde. As an explosive it was usually used in mixtures with other explosives and plasticizers or desensitizers. It was stable in storage, and was considered one of the most powerful and brisant of the military high explosives, but was considered much too sensitive to use alone. The British and Canadians solved the sensitivity problem and increased the power as well when they mixed RDX and TNT together and added aluminum to produce Torpex, which had both blast and brisance effect much more than TNT alone. Torpex was too expensive and TNT was not powerful enough.

Werner Bachmann of the University of Michigan was assigned by the OSRD to develop a manufacturing technique to produce RDX cheaply in quantity, and in only three months RDX was being manufactured in huge quantities; later the OSRD estimated that the Bachmann process saved America more than $100 million. After a delay of more than a year American and British scientists convinced the military to use RDX, which was 40% more powerful than TNT. By July 1943 the Kingsport, TN, ordnance plant was producing 170 tons per day, and to forestall the enemy from learning about the new explosive the shipments were labeled as golf balls. The Soviet Union Allies also were not informed of the important new explosive.

Tetryl (Nitramine or Tetralite)

Tetryl (2, 4, 6-trinitrophenyl-methylnitramine) was also known as Nitramine or Tetralite, and was produced by action of a mix of concentrated nitric acid and sulfuric acid on dimethylaniline and can be found naturally in the environment. Tetryl was usually used on its own, though was sometimes found in compositions such as Tetrytol. Because of its combination of high power, brisance, and sensitivity, Tetryl was the standard U.S. booster charge. It was used as a base charge in compound detonators, making it a small booster in intimate contact with the initiating explosive. Tetryl was quite safe to handle and was extremely stable in stowage. Exposed or loose Tetryl was not to be handled without adequate protection as it caused dermatitis. The velocity of detonation was 24,400 feet per second at a density of 1.55. Its color was light yellow, but it was usually gray because of the graphite content. It was more powerful than TNT. Its Laboratory Impact Value was 45. Its Bullet Impact Value was 61.

Tetrytol

Tetrytol was a mixture of 70% Tetryl and 30% TNT. This mixture was slightly less powerful and less sensitive than Tetryl, as Tetryl was significantly more sensitive than TNT and had a slightly higher detonation velocity. Since it formed the main part of the Tetrytol explosive blend, the sensitivity of Tetrytol and its brisance was also high. It was designed to obtain a Tetryl booster that could be cast. Its particular use was in burster tubes for Chemical Bombs, in demolition blocks, and in cast shaped charges, and was approved for use in all other boosters. Its velocity of detonation was 24,000 feet per second at a density of 1.60. Its Laboratory Impact Value was 45. Its Bullet Impact Value was 65. Its color was yellow.

TNT

TNT was a crystalline substance with the chemical names trinitrotoluene and trinitrotol. It is a common misconception that TNT and Dynamite are the same. Though both were high explosives, there was no other similarity between them. Where Dynamite is an absorbent mixture soaked in nitroglycerin, then compacted into a cylindrical shape and wrapped in paper, TNT was a specific chemical compound called trinitrotoluene. TNT was prepared by dripping toluene, a close relative of benzene, into a mixture of fuming sulfuric and nitric acids, then running the resulting exothermic mixture of sulfuric acid, TNT, and by products over a refrigerated surface and scraping off the resulting TNT crystals.

TNT was first prepared in 1863 by German chemist Joseph Wilbrand and was originally used as a yellow dye. Its potential as an explosive was not discovered for several years, mainly because it was so difficult to detonate. TNT could be safely poured as a liquid into shell cases, and was so insensitive that in 1910, it was exempted from the United Kingdom's Explosives Act of 1875 and was not considered an explosive for the purposes of manufacture and storage. The German military adopted it as a filling for artillery shells in 1902. Because of the low sensitivity it was discovered that TNT-filled Armor Piercing shells would explode after they had penetrated the armor, whereas the British Lyddite-filled shells tended to explode upon striking armor, thus expending much of their energy outside the target. So in 1907 the British started replacing Lyddite with TNT. TNT was first used on a wide scale during World War I and II, and the U.S. military stopped production of TNT in the mid-1980s; it is still used for civilian purposes today.

TNT manufacturing yields were high and production relatively economical. TNT was synthesized in a three-step process. First, toluene was nitrated with a mixture of sulfuric and nitric acid to produce mononitrotoluene, or MNT, which was then nitrated to dinitrotoluene (DNT). In the final step, the DNT was nitrated to trinitrotoluene, or TNT. The acids used in the manufacture of TNT were recycled and reused.

TNT was and is one of the most commonly used explosives for military and industrial applications. The importance of TNT as a military explosive was based upon its relative safety in manufacture, loading, transportation, and stowage, and upon its explosive properties. The risk of unexpected detonations was reduced due to its insensitivity to shock and friction. TNT melts at 176 °F, far below the temperature at which it would spontaneously detonate, allowing it to be poured as well as be safely combined with other explosives. TNT neither absorbed nor dissolved in water, which allowed it to be used effectively in wet environments. Additionally, it is comparatively stable when compared to other high explosives.

TNT was classified as a secondary explosive because it was less susceptible to initiation and required a primary or initiating explosive to ignite it. TNT was used as a booster, or as a bursting charge for high explosive shells and bombs. Although blocks of TNT were available alone in various sizes, it was more commonly encountered in synergistic (e.g. two or more discrete agents acting together create an effect greater than that predicted by knowing only the separate effects of the individual agents) explosive blends comprising a variable percentage of TNT plus other ingredients. Examples of explosive blends containing TNT included: Amatol, Ammonal, Composition B, Ednatol, Minol, Pentolite, Picratol, RDX, Tetrytol, Torpex, and Tritonal. TNT was a relatively insensitive high explosive of great stability and was used as the main charge in many GP bombs, but was superseded by more powerful explosives, such as Tritonal.

Torpex

Torpex was a secondary explosive, introduced in late 1942, that was 50% more powerful than TNT by weight. The original Torpex (Torpex 1) was a mixture of 45% RDX, 37% TNT, and 18% Aluminum powder (with 1% wax added), but the more common refined version, Torpex 2, was 42% RDX, 40% TNT, and 18% Aluminum powder (with 1% wax added). The name was short for "Torpedo Explosive." It was originally developed for use in torpedo warheads, mines, and depth bombs, and was particularly effective in underwater munitions because the aluminum component had the effect of making the explosive pulse last longer, which improved the destructive power. Torpex was relatively expensive to produce compared to TNT, and was only used in critical applications, such as submarine launched torpedoes and bombs such as the *Tallboy* and *Aphrodite* B-17 drones.

Torpex was developed at Britain's Royal Gunpowder Factory as a more powerful military alternative to TNT. RDX was developed in 1899, but was too sensitive to shock to be used in military applications. It was discovered that by mixing TNT and RDX the sensitivity could be reduced and the improvement in power retained. Aluminum powder was also added to the mix to further enhance the effect. Beeswax was also added to reduce sensitivity to shock and impact.

Soon after Torpex was introduced an unexplained explosion at the Naval Mine Depot at Alameda, CA, was followed shortly afterward by another explosion at Hawthorn, Nevada. On 16 November 1943, a huge explosion at the Naval Mine Depot at Yorktown, VA, killed four men and injured 25 more. Initially the cause was blamed on careless handling, but further investigation disclosed that Torpex developed highly explosive hydrogen gas. The explosive danger was decreased by merely mixing more beeswax into the Torpex. For a while Torpex manufacturers had priority for all the bees in the country to develop wax for them. In June 1943 Torpex manufacture reached 340 tons a day from one factory alone, and it became apparent that all the bees in America couldn't produce enough wax, so it was replaced with a petroleum based product and calcium carbonate was added as a moisture absorber to reduce the production of hydrogen gas under high humidity.

Torpex was more sensitive than TNT; its bullet impact and drop test sensitivities were of the same order as those of Tetryl. It was quite stable in stowage, though it produced gas, causing pressure in the case. It was insensitive enough to stand all normal handling. Its melting point was low enough for it to be cast-loaded. Its velocity of detonation was 24,000 feet per second at a density of 1.72. It was 141% as powerful as TNT, and under water it was 50% more destructive than TNT, whereas in air the difference was approximately 30%. Its Laboratory Impact Value was 58. Its Bullet Impact Value was 48. Its color was slate gray.

Tritonal

Tritonal was a generic term for explosives containing TNT and aluminum, generally 80% TNT and 20% Aluminum powder. The aluminum powder improved the brisance of the TNT and produced a greater blast effect than TNT, or Composition B. Tritonal was approximately 18% more powerful than TNT alone. It was used in some 4,000 pound Light Case Bombs and in several 500 and 1,000 pound GP bombs, where maximum blast effect was desired. Tritonal was cast, and the segregation of the aluminum was prevented by a pellet loading technique. The Laboratory Impact Value was 89; Bullet Impact Value was 64; and velocity of detonation was 18,000 feet per second at a density of 1.70.

Relative Blast Effect of Various Explosives (TNT = 100)

	Effectiveness	Load-bearing walls	
Explosive	**Peak Pressure**	**Radius**	**Area**
Torpex	**122.5**	**125**	**156**
Minol	**115**	**117.5**	**138**
Tritonal	**112.5**	**117.5**	**138**
RDX	**110**	**110**	**121**
TNT	**100**	**100**	**100**
Picratol	**100**	**100**	**100**
Amatol	**95**	**87.5**	**77**

Explosive Handling and Loading

Millions of pounds of powder and high explosive were safely handled during the war, and in 1944 the explosives industry ranked second in safety only to the women's garment industry. The powder was tested repeatedly by the mills that manufactured it, and then again by the ammunition manufacturers upon receiving it. The ammunition manufacturer divided this tested explosive into six packages which were stored under constant temperature (120°F) and humidity (75-85%). After a week it was retested and compared to the powder from the other packages to determine if the divergence fell within set limits. To test uniformity, samples were taken from six packages and blended and then comparatively test fired with cartridges loaded from each of the six packages. The ballistics department tested the powder once more before it was loaded.

The buildings where explosives were processed and loaded were spaced in accordance to Ordnance Department specifications and were located several miles from the main factory, and even further from residential areas. The building's walls were thick, while the construction of the roofs was flimsy so that in case of an explosion most of the force would be directed upward. Heavy concrete or earth deflectors were located around storage warehouses so that there would be no domino effect in case of an explosion. All employees in danger areas wore special non-conductive shoes that automatically dissipated electrical charges into copper wires embedded in the cement floors. Of course smoking, matches, and lighters were not allowed. In handling and processing explosives the temperature and humidity were closely monitored, and the cleaning of the machinery was given a high priority. Lightning was an uncontrollable threat, and the Department of Commerce set up many specialized weather stations around the country's ammunition plants. When a thunder storm approached the explosive mixing houses were closed and explosive loading was stopped, and the area cleared and cleaned as quickly as possible. Explosive mixtures were transported from the mixing houses to the loading houses in low-slung wooden carts with non-conducting metal frames and rubber tires. The cart's dead man's brake prevented it from moving accidentally, and its low center of gravity made it very difficult to overturn. The explosives were carried in the cart in rubber cups that were cooled and kept moist with ice. Once outside the loading houses the cups were taken from the cart and placed in a compartment with an outer and inner door leading to the inside.

Packing and Shipping

In general bombs were shipped unfused, with the fuse holes closed with metal closing plugs. These plugs were not to be removed except for inspection and for assembly of the complete round. Most bombs were shipped with two paper or metal shipping bands to protect the suspension lugs. The fin assemblies of such bombs were shipped separately in metal crates, while small Fragmentation Bombs were packed in wooden boxes.

Markings and Identification

Bombs and bomb components were identified by standard nomenclature and ammunition lot numbers stamped on all packing, as well as on the item itself.

Mark Numbers

In order to distinguish between different designs of the same type, a MK/Mark number (Navy) or M/Model (AAF) was assigned at the time a design was adopted as a standard item.

Navy

Items of Navy designs were designated by the word Mark or its abbreviation Mk, followed by an Arabic numeral (i.e. Mk2). Modifications of the original design were indicated by the term Mod and an Arabic numeral following the Mark designation (i.e. Mk107 Mod1). An original design included the term Mod0 to distinguish it in later modifications (i.e. Mk107 Mod0).

Army

On items of Army design the Model designation consisted of the letter M followed by an Arabic numeral (i.e. M6). Modification of the original design was indicated by a letter A and the appropriate Arabic numeral added to the model designation (M6A1).

The designation T1, T2, etc., indicated experimental items. While in the developmental stage and when a major change was incorporated the item took a designation, such as T1E1 or T1E2. Such a designation indicated a change affecting military characteristics or installation.

Army-Navy (AN)

Certain items were standardized for use by both the Army and the Navy. The model designation of such an item was prefixed by the letters AN (i.e. AN-Mk107M). When an AN item was de-standardized by either the Army or the Navy, the AN was deleted from the model designation; however, to preclude loss of identity, the AN designation was carried parenthetically in standard nomenclature; for example, M120A1 (AN-M120A1). When an item was classified as AN standard the previous model was carried parenthetically; for example, AN-M146 (M146).

Color Coding

Bombs were painted in various color schemes as a ready means of identification. Colored bands, depending upon their color, size, and location, indicated the type of bomb and the type of explosive used. Identification marking and its color provided further identification of the bomb.

Bomb Markings

GP-TNT: Olive with yellow nose and tail bands. Marked on nose: G.P. 500lb./AN-M64A1/TNT/S1HTA

Shipping Containers for Bombs

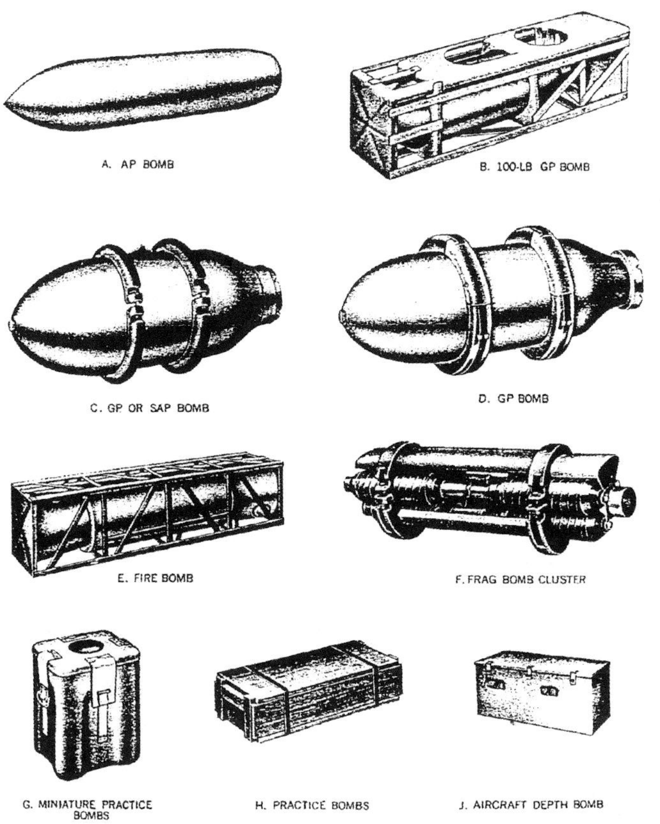

(TM9-1980)

Shipping Containers for Bombs Fins & Arming Wires

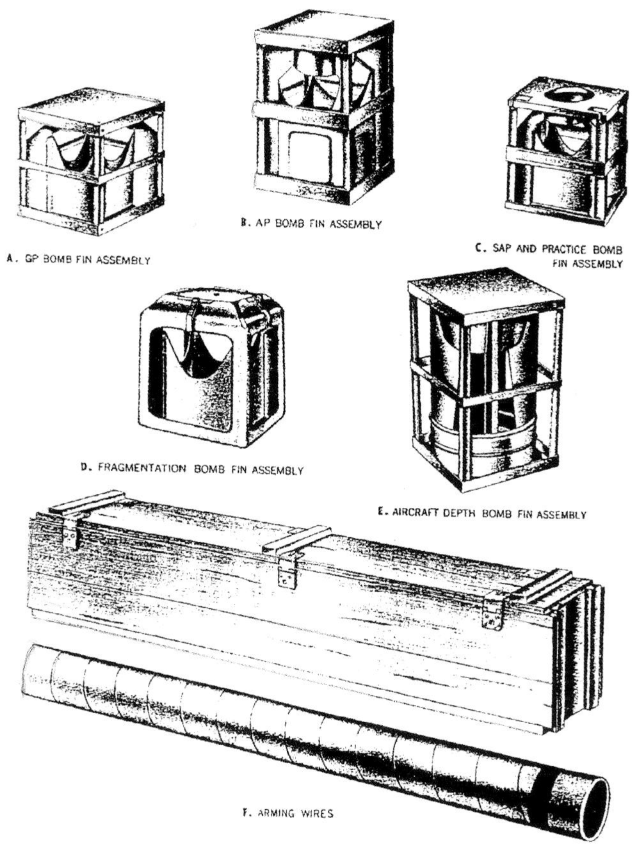

(TM9-1980)

GP-COMP B: Olive with double yellow nose and tail bands with inner bands marked COMP. B: Marked on nose: G.P. /500lb./AN-M64A1/ COMP./ B/S1HWA
GP-TRITONAL: Olive with triple yellow nose and tail bands with inner bands marked TRITONAL: Marked on nose: G.P./500lb./AN-M64A1/ TRITONAL/S1ICA
INCENDIARY: Silver-white with three red bands: top middle and bottom. Marked on nose: INCENDIARY/500lb./AN M 76/PT 4
CHEMICAL: Silver-gray with green band(s):
One green band: non-persistent gas
Two green bands: persistent gas
Marked on nose: C.G. GAS/xxlb./AN M 78
All these bombs had dark lettering and the lot number marked on mid-section, and all but the Chemical Bomb had the arsenal named on the mid-section
LEAFLET: Olive with no stripes. Marked on long axis: BOMB LEAFLET/ xxlbs Size M 105A1/LOT #
23lb.FRAGMENTATION: Olive with yellow bands on the top of the first segment. Marked on first segment: FRAG/AN M 81/Lot #
4lb. FRAGMENTATION: Olive with yellow band on each side. Marked on side M83
PWP SMOKE: Silver-gray with yellow band on middle and bottom section. Marked in yellow lettering: 100lb./M47A4

PAINTING AND MARKING: BOMBS

BOMB	BODY	BANDS	MARKING (letters and figs.)
HIGH EXPLOSIVE: (G.P., Demo., AP., SAP., Frag*)			
Filled with TNT or Amatol	Olive Drab	Nose: One 1″ yellow Tail: One 1″ yellow	Black
Filled with Comp B	Olive Drab	Nose: Two 1″ yellow Tail: Two 1″ yellow	Black "Comp B" stenciled on one nose band and one tail band.
PRACTICE	Light Blue	None	White
DRILL	Olive Drab	Nose: One 1″ black Tail: One 1″ black	Black: Drill (inert)
CHEMICAL			
Nonpersistent gas	Blue-Gray	1 Green, nose, tail, and center	Green
Persistent gas	Blue-Gray	2 Green, nose, tail, and center	Green
Irritant smoke (vomiting gas)	Blue-Gray	1 Red, nose, tail, and center	Red
Screening Smoke	Blue-Gray	1 Yellow, nose, tail and center	Yellow
Incendiary	Olive Drab	1 Purple, nose, tail, and center	Purple

* Small fragmentation bombs: nose and tail painted yellow (no bands), Body—olive drab.

MARKING: FUZES

Fuzes are stenciled or stamped with type and model, lot number, number and length of delay.

PAINTING AND MARKING: PRIMER DETONATORS
(See fig. 42)

Head painted:
All black—0.1 Sec. delay
½ black—0.05 Sec. delay
¼ black—0.025 Sec. delay
⅛ black—0.01 Sec. delay
All white—Nondelay

Types of Conventional Bombs

General Purpose (GP) and Light Case (LC) Bombs

General Purpose (GP)

The General Purpose Bomb was designed to meet the requirements of the great majority of bombing situations, with the various models ranging in weight from 100 to 44,000 pounds. The explosive content of GP and demolition bombs represented approximately 50% of their total weight. The weights and percentages of explosives for the GP, demolition, and LC bombs were based on a Tritonal loading, but these bombs could be loaded with TNT, and some were field-loaded with Comp B or Amatol.

General Purpose Bombs could be used for blast, fragmentation, or mining (deep) effect. They were designed for use with both nose and tail fuses. Bombs larger than the 4,000 pound light case used only the tail fuse. Nose fuses produced more efficient surface effect, while tail fuses produced more efficient mining effect. Both fuses were generally used, with the secondary fuse used as insurance against malfunction. The General Purpose Bomb had a cylindrical body which tapered in an oval to the nose and in a straight cone to the base. It had two suspension lugs for double-hook suspension welded to the case on one side and, diametrically opposite, one lug was welded on for single suspension. Double suspension lugs were spaced 14 inches apart on bombs weighing 1,000 pounds and less, and they were spaced 30 inches apart on bombs weighing 2,000 to 4,000 pounds. Bombs larger than 4,000 pounds had no suspension lugs, but were carried by two chain slings which were a component of the bomb rack. The metal case was strong enough not to rupture on impact with normal soil when released from 8,000 feet, but it would fail on impact with heavy armor or high strength reinforced concrete structures.

Light Case (LC)

Light Case Bombs were designed to carry a maximum charge which represented approximately 70% of their total weight. Since the strength of the case had been sacrificed to obtain maximum charge this type of bomb was not to be used for penetration, since the case was not strong enough to withstand impact. The LC bomb had to be fused to explode before the case broke up on impact, and instantaneous fuses were used with this bomb to provide an above ground burst. In all other respects this type resembled the General Purpose bomb.

Early GP bombs (L-R): 100, 2,000, 1,100, and 600 pound. (AAF)

Cutaway 500 Pound GP Bomb AN-M64

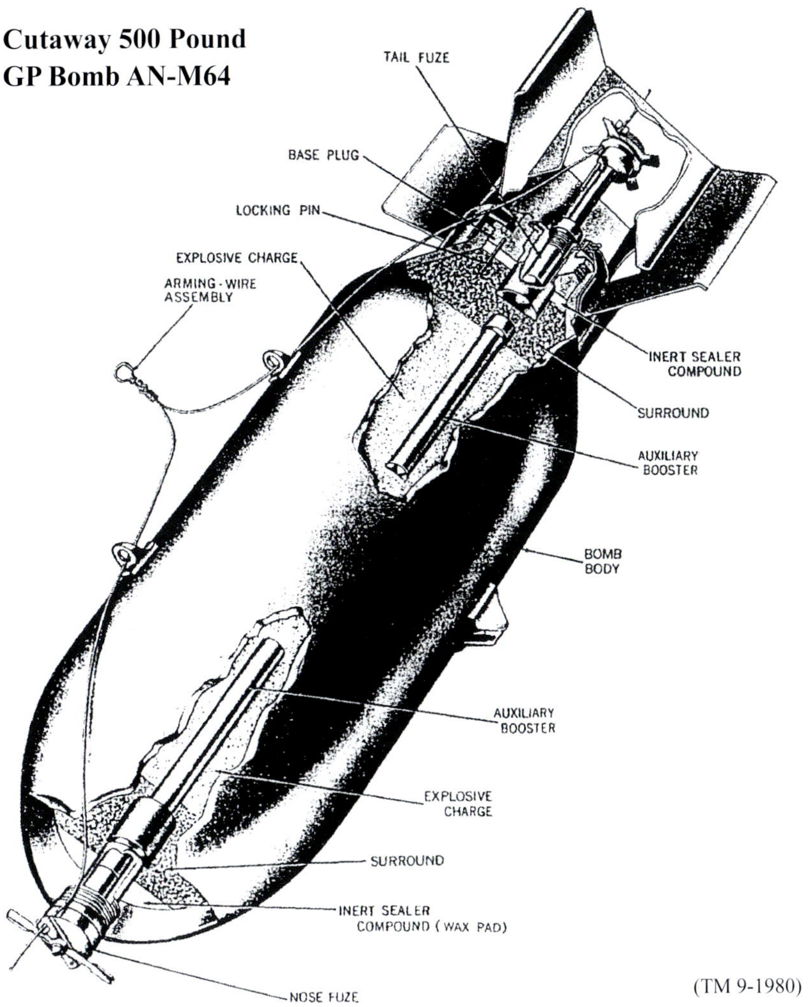

(TM 9-1980)

Armorers load a 500 pound GP bomb onto an A-36 Apache dive bomber in Italy. (AAF)

GP Bomb Sectioned

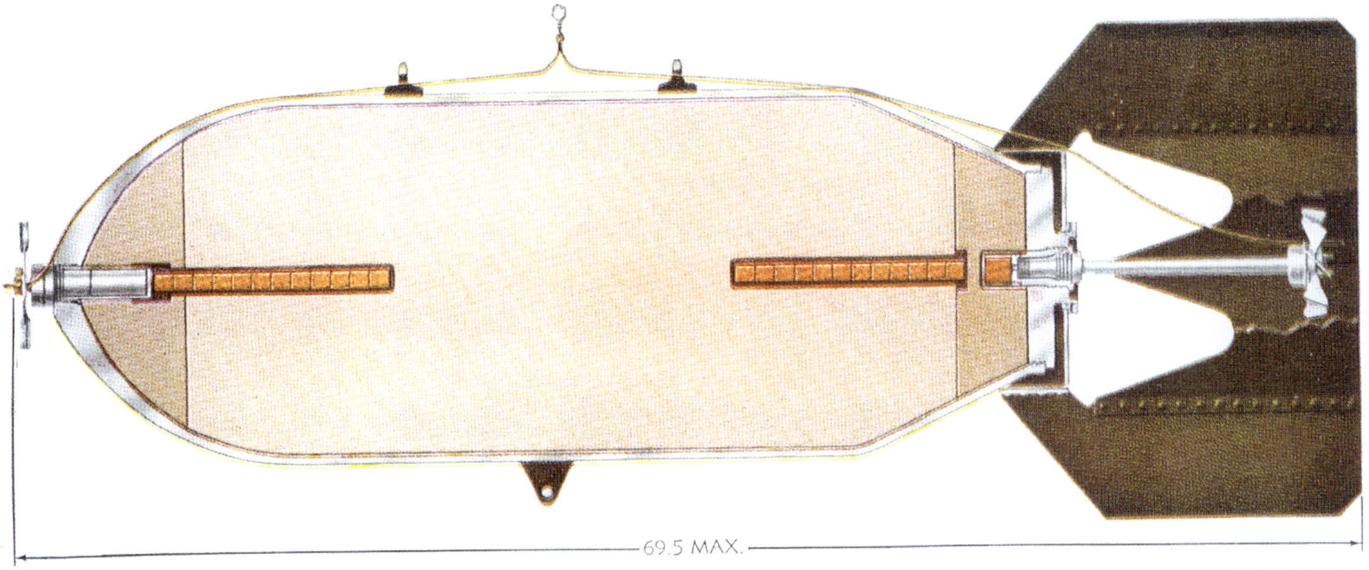

RA PD 15006
(TM 9-1980)

Bomb Types

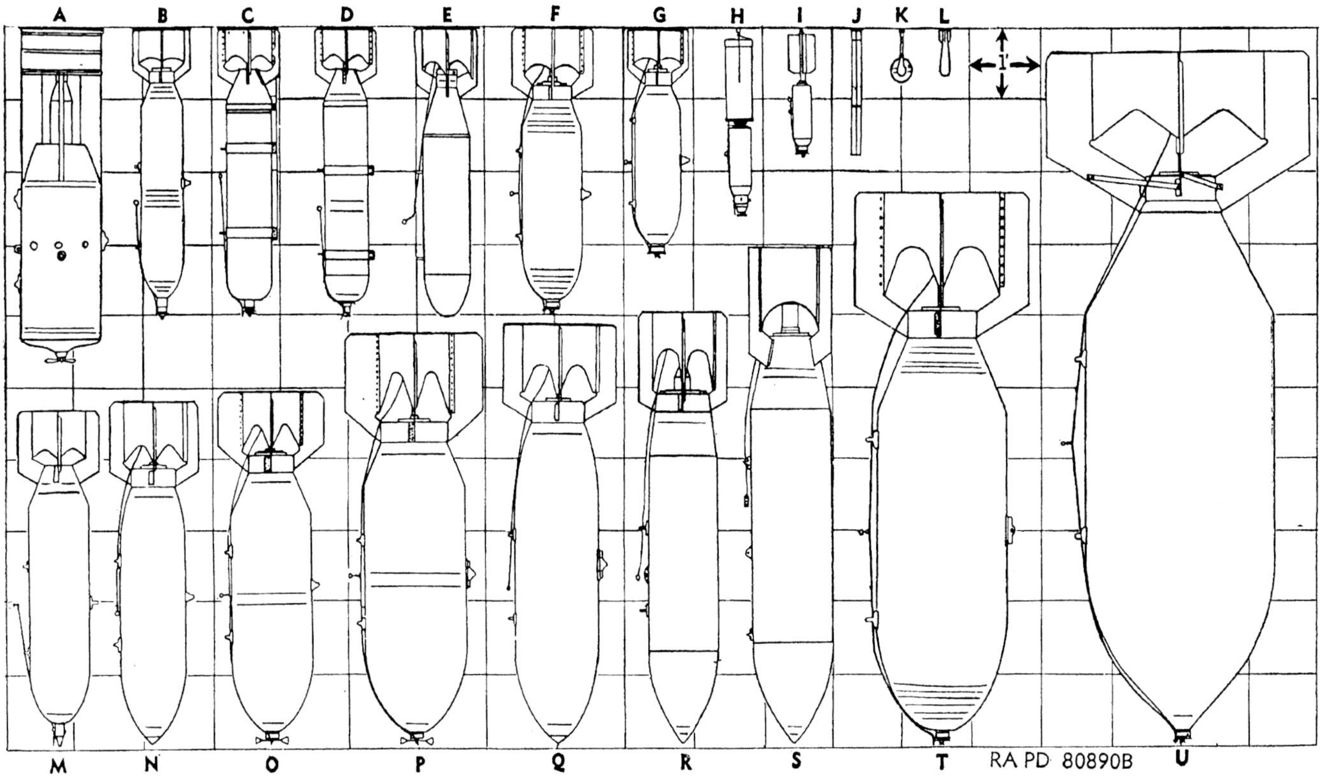

Legend

b. REPRESENTATIVE TYPES AND SIZES. Figures 1 and 2 illustrate various types of bombs and their comparative sizes. The following legend is keyed alphabetically to figures 1 and 2 to aid in identifying the different bombs shown therein:

A—BOMB, depth, TNT, 350-lb, AN–Mk 54 Mod 1.
B—BOMB, gas, HD, 115-lb, M70A1.
C—BOMB, photoflash, 100-lb, AN–M46 (M46).
D—BOMB, smoke, PWP, 100-lb. AN–M47A4.
E—BOMB, practice, 100-lb, M38A2.
F—BOMB, GP, tritonal, 250-lb, AN–M57A1.
G—BOMB, GP, TNT, 100-lb, AN–M30A1.
H—BOMB, fragmentation, TNT, 23-lb, M72A1.
I—BOMB, fragmentation, TNT, 20-lb, AN–M41A1.
J—BOMB, incendiary, 4-lb, AN–M50A2.
K—BOMB, fragmentation, TNT, 4-lb, M83.
L—BOMB, practice, miniature, 3-lb, Mk 23.
M—CLUSTER, fragmentation bomb, M28A2 (100-lb size).
N—BOMB, SAP, picratol, 500-lb, AN–M58A2.
O—BOMB, incendiary, 500-lb, AN–M76.
P—BOMB, gas, 1,000-lb, AN–M79.
Q—BOMB, SAP, picratol, 1,000-lb, AN–M59A1.
R—BOMB, AP, Exp D, 1,000-lb, AN–Mk 33.
S—BOMB, AP, Exp D, 1,600-lb, AN–Mk 1.
T—BOMB, GP, tritonal, 2,000-lb, AN–M66A2.
U—BOMB, LC, TNT, 4,000-lb, M56A2 (AN-M56A2).
V—BOMB, GP, tritonal, 12,000-lb, M109 (T10).
W—BOMB, GP, tritonal, 22,000-lb, M110 (T14).
X—BOMB, GP, tritonal, 44,000-lb, T12.

CLASSIFICATION	WEIGHT	NOMEN-CLATURE	COLOR MARKINGS		HE WEIGHT	FUZES		SHACK-LES	MINIMUM SAFE BA	TARGETS AND REMARKS
			BODY	BANDS		NOSE	TAIL			
GENERAL PURPOSE	100	AN-M30	LUSTERLESS OLIVE DRAB	(1") YELLOW BAND AROUND NOSE AND TAIL	54	AN-M103 or M118 or M119	AN-M100A2 or M112A1	B-7 or B-10	1500	Railroad equipment, trackage, small buildings, ammunition dumps, planes on ground, hangars
	250	AN-M57			123				2000	Railroad equipment, trackage, RR terminals, ammunition dumps, destroyers, subs, transports
	500	AN-M64			262		AN-M101A2 or M113A1		2500	Steel railroad bridges, subways, concrete docks, light cruisers
	1000	AN-M65			530		AN-M102A2 or M114A1		3000	Reinforced concrete bridges, steel RR bridges, piers, approach spans, medium cruisers
	2000	AN-M66			1061			D-6	3000	Massive reinforced concrete and suspension bridges, heavy cruisers, battleships, dams
LIGHT CASE	4000	AN-M56			3245	AN-M103	AN-M102A2		3000	Raze areas equal to a city block or more
SEMI-ARMOR-PIERCING	500	AN-M58A1			145	STEEL PLUG	AN-M101A2	B-7 or B-10		Armor plate, lightly armored vessels, reinforced concrete
	1000	AN-M59			303		AN-M102A2			
ARMOR-PIERCING	1000	AN-Mk33			144	NONE	AN-Mk228			Heavily armored naval vessels
	1600	AN-Mk1			215			B-10		
DEPTH	350	AN-Mk47			252	AN-Mk219 or AN-M103	AN-Mk224 AN-Mk234 (LATERAL)	B-7 or B-10		Submarines and surface craft
	650	AN-Mk29			464					
FRAG. PARACHUTE	23	AN-M40			2.7	AN-M120A1	NONE	N-3	80	Personnel—If detonated at proper angle, almost 100% casualties over 120 ft. radius Tanks—Running gear, 60-90 ft.; light tank, direct hit Planes—Motor, 60 ft.; wings and tanks perforated, 200 ft.; structural damage, 3-4 ft. Telephone wires—100 ft., some cut by side spray
FRAG. FIN	20	AN-M41			2.7	AN-M110A1			800	
FRAG. CLUSTER	500	M26				M111A2				
CHEMICAL MULTI-PURPOSE	100	M47A2	GRAY	*See Below	68	M108	BURSTER M4	B-7 or B-10		Irritating physiological effect on personnel, neutralize areas, contaminate materiel HS produces irritating physiological effect WP produces screening smoke or incendiary effect
	115	M70			64	AN-M110A1	BURSTER M10			
INCENDIARY	4	AN-M50A1		1 PURPLE	1.8	NONE	STRIKER UNIT			Usually in 5 bomb clusters; includes 1 AN-M50XA1 (150 gr. BP burster charge)
PRACTICE	100	M38A2	BLUE		2.6	NONE	MIA1			Training—22 gage, light sheet metal body, filled with about 80 lbs. of dry sand. Actual weight, 98 lbs.
FLARES (PARACHUTE)	44	M24	GRAY	BLUE		NONE	FRICTION IGNITER		2500-3000	Target lighting; dropping rate, 11.6 ft./sec.; burns 3-3.5 min.; yellowish tint, 1,000,000 candle power
	53	AN-M26				M111A2			4000-25,000	Target lighting; dropping rate, 11.6 ft./sec., burns 3-3.5 min.; 800,000 candle power
	16	M8A1				NONE				Emergency landings; can be used for bombing. Burns 3 min.; soft yellow, 400,000 candle power
TORPEDO	2100	Mk13-2			600	EXPLODER MECHANISM	NONE			Effective range, 6000 yds.; speed about 40 mph; has 93-98 hp steam and gas turbine engine

*BANDS: (NOSE, TAIL AND CENTER) 1 GREEN, NON-PERSISTENT; 2 GREEN, PERSISTENT; 1 PURPLE, INCENDIARY; 1 YELLOW, SMOKE; 1 RED, IRRITANT SMOKE (Vomiting Gas)

Light Case Bombs (4,000 pound shown) were designed to carry a maximum charge representing approximately 70% of their total weight. (AAF)

Assembly

Components

The components of the complete round were as follows:

1) Bomb, unfused, without fin assembly, including:
   Bomb body,
   Explosive charge of Tritonal, TNT, COMP B, or Amatol,
   One or more auxiliary boosters,
   Nose fuse-seat liner with closing plug,
   Base plug with fin lock nut,
   Tail fuse adapter-booster with closing plug.
2) Fin assembly or anti-ricochet device (the anti-ricochet device was used, when required, in place of the fin assembly, and then only on the 250 and 500 pound GP bombs).
3) Nose fuse.
4) Tail fuse.
5) Arming wire.

Method of Assembly of a Bomb with a Fin

The complete round was assembled as follows:

1) Remove the shipping bands from the bomb and remove the assembly from its crate. Remove the required number of fuses and arming wires from their packing boxes. Inspect the components and then put them onto a bomb service truck and trailer.
2) Proceed to the assembly point.
3) At the assembly point, cut the shipping wire and remove the fin lock nut and its protector. Remove the protector from the lock nut.
4) Place the fin assembly over the tail of the bomb with one fin in line with the suspension lugs. If bombs were intended for external racks the fin was turned 40° out of alignment with the suspension lugs. Replace the lock nut and tighten it with a wrench.
5) Deliver the bomb to the aircraft and install in accordance with the instructions pertinent to the type of rack in use.
6) When the bomb was securely locked on the rack install the fuses and arming wire. If the space in the bomb bay did not permit fusing, the fuses were assembled to the bomb at the assembly point. Fuses will be assembled to the bomb in accordance with instructions for the particular fuse.
7) If the bomb was not dropped, it was to be defused with the nose and plugs replaced and the bomb returned to storage. The anti-disturbance bombs of the M123, M123A1, and M132 types were not to be defused, and were to be destroyed by bomb disposal personnel.

The method of assembly with anti-ricochet device for the complete round was similar to that of the finned bomb.

Fusing

Light Case Bombs were fused with instantaneous fuses for surface blast effect. General Purpose or Demolition bombs were fused with instantaneous fuses for blast effect, with short delay (0.1 sec and less) for mining or penetration effect, with fuse delay of four to 5 or eight to 15 seconds for low altitude bombing, or with fuses of one hour to six days delay.

Limitations

Light Case Bombs could not be used for penetration, as the case failed on any ordinary impact. Delay fused General Purpose Bombs released from high altitudes failed on impact with armor plate or heavy reinforced concrete, but these were proper targets if the fusing was for instantaneous action, or if the bomb was released from medium or low altitudes.

Types of General Purpose Bombs

Bomb, GP, 100 Pound, AN-M30A1

The AN-M30A1 was a cylindrical bomb which was 40.25 inches long and weighed 112.3 pounds as released with fin assembly. However, when fitted with the M16 anti-ricochet device, the AN-M30A1 was 44.8 inches long and weighed 126.1 pounds. The body (without fin and fuse) was 30 inches long and 8.18 inches in diameter. It weighed 106.7 pounds, of which 66.6 pounds (50.4% of the complete round) was explosive charge—TNT or Amatol. The base plate of the AN-M30A1 was securely locked to the bomb body by two studs which extended from the plate into the solidified explosive charge. The bomb also provided a way of locking the adapter-booster to the base plate; a locking pin was passed through a hole in the adapter-booster and extended into a groove in the base plate. These modifications were initiated to prevent the removal of base plate and adapter-booster to make the anti-withdrawal devices of longer delay fuses more effective.

Other Models

Bomb, GP, Tritonal, 100 Pound AN-M30 differed from the AN-M30A1 in that it was 38.46 inches long and weighed 114.3 pounds as released. The base plate of the AN-M30 could be removed by unscrewing, and no locking device was provided for the adapter-booster. The AN-M30 may be loaded with Tritonal, TNT, or Amatol.

Bomb, Demolition, 100 Pound, M30 was the earlier model of the AN-M30, and differed in that it did not have a lug for single suspension and used a base plate, having internal threads instead of external threads for assembly to the bomb.

Bomb, GP, 250 Pound, AN-M57A1

The AN-M57A1 was a cylindrical bomb that was 47.8 inches long and weighed 267.4 pounds as released with its fin assembly. When the M16 anti-ricochet device was used instead of a fin, the bomb was 51.7 inches long and weighed 279.6 pounds. The bomb body was 37.5 inches long and 10.9 inches in diameter. It weighed 253.7 pounds, of which 131.1 pounds (49.7% of the complete round) was explosive charge—TNT or Amatol.

Other Models

Bomb, GP, 250 Pound, AN-M57 differed from the AN-M57A1 in that the complete round weighed 262 pounds and the weight of explosive charge was 132.2 pounds, or 50.4% of the complete weight. The base plate of the AN-M57 could be removed, and the adapter-booster could not be locked to the base plate.

Bomb, Demolition, 300 Pound M31 was an earlier model corresponding to AN-M57. The M31, although nominally a 300 pound bomb, actually weighed 274 pounds when loaded with Amatol and was three inches longer than the AN-M57AI. The M31 also differed from the M57 series by not having the single suspension lug.

Bomb, GP, 500 Pound, AN-M64A1
The AN-M64AI was a cylindrical bomb that was 59.16 inches long and weighed 560 pounds as released with the fin assembly. If the M17 anti-ricochet device was used instead of a fin assembly the bomb was 62.6 inches in length and weighed 577 pounds. The body was 47.5 inches long and 14.2 inches in diameter. It weighed 535 pounds, of which 278.3 pounds (49.7% of the complete round) was explosive charge; TNT, Amatol, and Comp B. The base plate of this bomb was securely locked to the bomb body, and the adapter-booster could be locked to the base plate. When the AN-M57A1 was used for dive bombing by the Navy it had to be fitted with the Band, trunnion, AN-M1A1.

Other Models
Bomb GP, 500 Pound, AN-M64 differed from the AN-M64A1 in that the weight of the complete round was 524.1 pounds and weight of explosive charge (Amatol, Comp B, or TNT) was 274 pounds, or 52.3% of the total weight. The base plate of the AN-M64 was removable, and the adapter-booster could not be locked to the base plate.

Bomb GP, 500 Pound, AN-M43 was an earlier model corresponding to the AN-M64 series. It weighed 508 pounds, of which 262 pounds was the explosive charge of Amatol. The AN-M43 used the fin assembly M108, whereas the AN-M64 series used the M109 or AN-M109A1 fin assembly.

Bomb, GP, 500 Pound, M43 was the same as the AN-M43, except that it was not fitted with the single suspension lug.

Bomb, Demolition, 500 Pound, M43 was the same as the GP bomb M43, but was fitted with a base cap in place of the base plate.

Bomb, GP, 1,000 Pound, AN-M65A1
The AM-M65A1 was a cylindrical bomb which was 69.5 inches long and weighed 1,080 pounds as released. The body was 54 inches long and 18.8 inches in diameter and weighed 1,042 pounds, of which 572.3 pounds (53% of the complete round) was explosive charge (Tritonal, TNT, COMP B, or Amatol). The base plate of this bomb was securely locked to the bomb body and the adapter-booster could be locked to the base plate. When the AN-M65A1 was used for dive bombing by the Navy it had to be fitted with Band, trunnion, AN-M2A1.

Other Models
Bomb, GP, 1,000 Pound, AN-M65 differed from the AN-M65A1 in that the weight of the complete round was 990 pounds and weight of explosive charge (Amatol) was 530 pounds, or 53% percent of the complete weight. The base plate of the AN-M65 was removable, and the adapter-booster could not be locked to the base plate.

Bomb, GP, 1,000 Pound, M65 differed in not having the single suspension lug.

Bomb, GP, 1,000 Pound, AN-M44 was an earlier model corresponding to the AN-M65 series. It weighed 967 pounds, of which 530 pounds (54.8%) were the explosive charge (Amatol). The AN-M44 used the fin assembly Ml 12, while the AN-M65 series used the M113 or AN-M113A1 fin assembly.

Bomb, GP, 1,000 Pound, M44 was the same as the AN-M44, except for weight of explosive charge (538 pounds), and it was not fitted with the single suspension lug.

Bomb, Demolition, 1,000 Pound, M44 was the same as the GP Bomb M44, but was fitted with a base cap in place of the base plate.

Bomb, GP, 2,000 Pound, AN-M66A2
The AN-M66A2 was a cylindrical bomb that was 92.63 inches long and weighed 2,155.5 pounds as released. The body was 71.8 inches long and 23.3 inches in diameter and weighed 2,098.5 pounds, of which 1,140.3 pounds (52.9% of the complete round) was explosive charge (Tritonal, TNT, Comp B, or Amatol). The base plate of this bomb was securely locked to the body and the adapter-booster could be locked to the base plate. When the AN-M66A2 was used for dive bombing by the Navy it had to be fitted with the Band, Trunnion, AN-M7.

Other Models
Bomb, GP, 2,000 Pound, AN-M66A1 differed from the AN-M66A2 in that it was 92.83 inches long and weighed 2,155 pounds as released. The AN-M66A1 contained 1,156 pounds of explosive (Tritonal), or 53.6% of the total weight. In addition, the nose of the AN-M66A2 was thicker than and not as rounded as that of the AN-M66A, with the AN-M66A2 being more similar in shape to smaller GP bombs.

Bomb, GP, 2,000 Pound, AN-M66 was the same as the AN-M66A1, except that its base plate was removable and the adapter-booster could not be locked in place.

Bomb, GP, 2,000 Pound, AN-M34 was an earlier model corresponding to the AN-M66 series. It weighed 2,049 pounds, of which 1,060 pounds (52.5% of complete round) was explosive charge (Amatol).

Bomb, Demolition, 2,000 Pound, M34 differed from the AN-M34 in that it weighed 1,987 pounds, of which 1,076 pounds (54.2% of complete round) was explosive charge (Amatol). In addition, the M34 did not have the single suspension lug and was fitted with a base cap in place of a base plate.

Bomb, Light Case, 4,000 Pound, M56A2 (AN-M56A2)
The M56A2 was a cylindrical bomb which was 117.25 inches in length and weighed 4,535 pounds as released. The body was 95.6 inches long and 34.25 inches in diameter and weighed 4,397 pounds, of which 3,515 pounds (77.9% of the complete round weight) was explosive charge.

Other Models
Bomb, Light Case, Tritonal, 4,000 Pounds, M56A1 (AN-M56A1) weighed 4,514 pounds, of which 3,619 pounds (78.4% of complete round) was explosive charge. The M56A1 was the only bomb of this series (M56, M56A1, and M56A2) which was modified to receive British-type hoisting and single suspension lugs. This bomb was fitted with a base cap in place of a base plate.

Bomb, Light Case, 1,000 Pound, M56 (AN-M56) differed from the M56A2 in that it weighed 4,201 pounds, of which 3,244 pounds (77.2% of complete round) was explosive charge (Amatol). The M56 was also fitted with a base cap in place of the base plate.

Bomb, GP, 12,000 Pound, M109 (T10)
M109 was a cylindrical bomb which was 21 feet long and weighed 12,622 pounds as released. The body was 10.33 feet in length and 3.17 feet in diameter and weighed 12,448 pounds, of which 5,500 pounds was Tritonal (43.8% of the complete round). Early models of this bomb were loaded with 5,200 pounds of Torpex and a one inch layer of TNT added to the rear end. This bomb was triple fused in the tail, and consequently required three of each of the fusing components. The fuses were 120° apart radially, and fusing was accomplished through three circular holes located in the tail assembly. The M120 tail assembly was attached to the rear of the bomb body with 20 bolts, and resembled a cone with the four fins displaced 5° from its axis. This displacement caused the bomb

to rotate as it fell. A cylindrical metal cowling placed between the body and the tail cone increased the streamlining of the bomb.

Bomb, GP, 22,000 Pound, M110 (T14)

The M110 was a cylindrical bomb 24.42 feet long and weighed 23,037 pounds as released. The bomb body was 12.5 feet inches long, 3.83 feet in diameter, and weighed 22,850 pounds, of which 9,600 pounds was Tritonal (41.6% of the complete round). Early models of the M110 were loaded with 9,200 pounds of Torpex and a one inch layer of TNT added to the rear end. The 22,000 pound and 12,000 pound GP bombs were similar in construction, except that the three fuse seats in the tail of the 22,000 pound bomb were all in a straight line rather than in a circle. The M110 bomb used the M121 tail assembly, and the section of tail assembly to the rear of the fins could be removed when necessary to fit the complete round in aircraft.

Bomb, GP, 44,000 Pound, Tl2

This bomb was under development near the end of the war and was similar to the 22,000 pound, M110. The bomb body was made up of six sections welded together and was 16.67 feet long and 4.5 feet in diameter. The tail assembly was attached to the body with 24 bolts that anchored in the base plate of the body.

(Note: The 12,000, 22,000, and 44,000 pound very heavy bombs are discussed in detail in *U.S. Aerial Armament of WWII***:** *Volume 3: Air-Launched, Air-Dropped, and Secret Weapons*.)

Specialized GP Bombs

"Daisy Cutters"

The 5AF modified 300 and 500 pound GP bombs by wrapping them with heavy 1/4 inch steel wire and installing instantaneous fuses on the ends of six pipe extensions in the nose. When the bomb exploded the wire broke into lengths ranging from half a foot to several feet long that would cut swaths 150 feet in diameter through parked aircraft and any unlucky personnel caught in the open.

Spike Bombs

To prevent bomb ricochets during low-level attacks, the Luftwaffe used a purpose-designed spike bomb, the *Stachebomben*, or *Stabo* for short. A threaded lug was forged into the bomb case nose and the Stabo spike was screwed into this threaded lug with a special handle that fit into a hole in

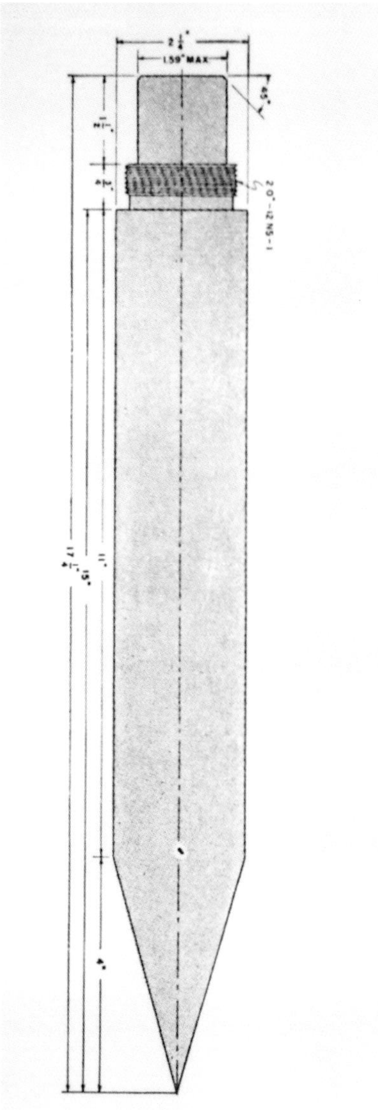

During 10AF attacks on railway lines the bombs would often ricochet, and a method needed to be developed to prevent this. The spike bombs were fabricated from thick two foot iron rods screwed into the nose of a 100 pound bomb armed with an eight to 15 second delayed fuse. (AAF) (Note: 2 photos side-by-side with one caption)

AP Bomb Sectioned

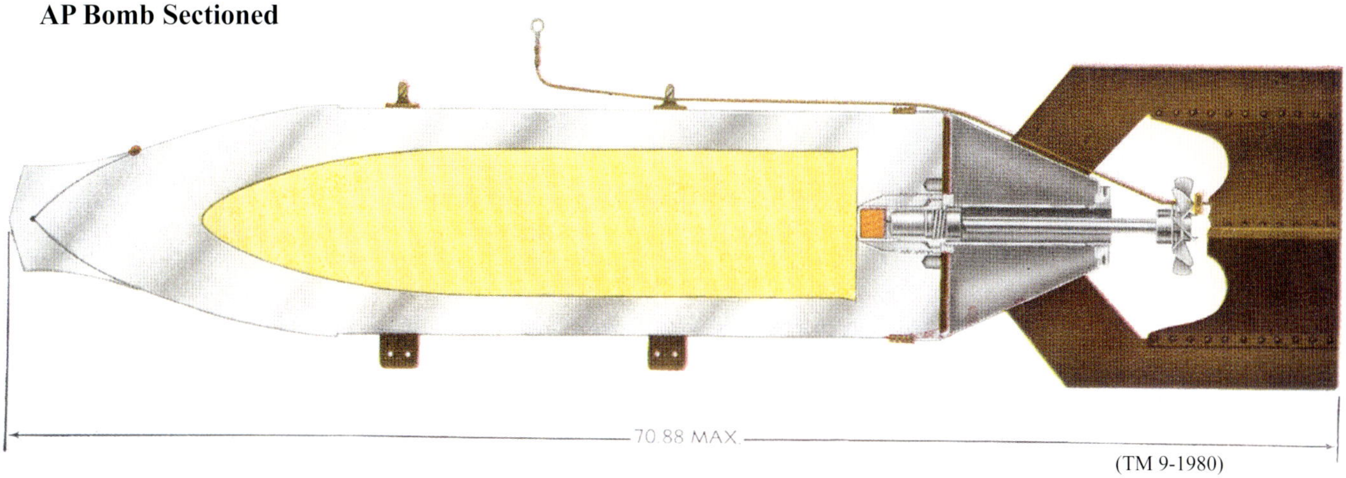

(TM 9-1980)

the spike to insure a tight fit. The German spike bomb was fitted to 50, 70, 250, and 500 kilogram bombs using various fuses.

During 10AF attacks on railway lines the bombs would often ricochet, and a method was needed to be developed to prevent this. Among the various unsuccessful methods tried were "trick" fins, flat concrete filled noses, and metal brakes. The spike bombs were fabricated from thick two foot iron rods screwed into the nose of 100 pound bombs armed with eight to 15 second delayed fuses. The first spikes fractured at the threads upon impact, and the remedy was to extend the shaft several additional inches beyond the threads into the bomb casing.

Attacks were carried out at minimum altitude by individual bombers flying at high speed over long stretches of railway track, dropping a pair of bombs at intervals of up to two miles. Repair crews usually had access to the damaged areas by rail and thus could repair only each successive damaged area one at a time, succeeding in denying the enemy the use of the railway for a maximum length of time.

The Chinese-American Composite Wing (CACW) B-25s flew a few spike bomb missions, but had difficulty in repeating the success of the 10AF in Burma in using spike bombs against railways. The crews flew accurate approach and delivery runs, getting hits with the delayed action spike bombs, only to later find that the bombs had not exploded after the time delay had expired. The cause was found to probably be due to the stocks of undependable "old bombs" supplied by the 14AF.

Armor Piercing (AP) and Semi-Armor Piercing Bombs (SAP)

General

Armor Piercing (AP)

This type of bomb was designed to pierce the heavy deck armor of modern battleships and the case was extremely heavy; as a consequence, the percentage of explosive was only about 15%. The weight and thickness of the metal case was concentrated toward the nose. In order to be effective Armor Piercing Bombs had to score direct hits. The effect of a near miss was small due to the comparatively small amount of explosive. The AP bomb was not to be used against unarmored or lightly armored ships because, being fused with a delay fuse to permit penetration of armor, the bomb would pass entirely through a light target before exploding. Armor Piercing Bombs were streamlined in shape and adapted for a tail fuse only. Suspension lugs were bolted to the body when the round was assembled, and in the case of the 1,600-pound AP bomb locations were provided for either 14 inch or 30 inch spacing. Earlier AP models used suspension bands with the lugs welded to the bands and equipped with locating studs for the 14 inch or 30 inch spacing. AP bombs were loaded with explosive D, which was sufficiently insensitive to withstand heavy impact.

500 Pound SAP Cutaway

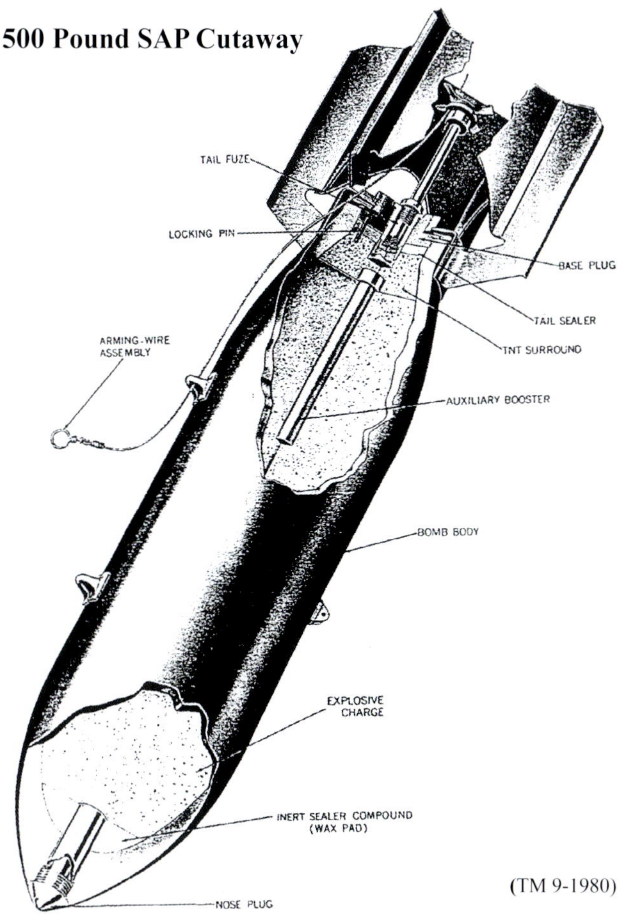

(TM 9-1980)

Semi-Armor Piercing (SAP)

Semi-Armor Piercing Bombs resembled the Armor Piercing Bombs but had a somewhat lighter case, and a tail and nose fuse seat. Except for the 25,000 pound SAP bomb, which was rarely used, the nose fuse seat was ordinarily closed by an Armor Piercing plug. The standard SAP explosive charge was Picratol, representing approximately 30% of the total weight, but SAP bombs containing TNT or Amatol were used.

Assembly
Components
SAP (without fin assembly)
Bomb body:
Explosive charge of Picratol, TNT, or Amatol
One or more auxiliary boosters
Fuse seat liner, with closing plug
Base plug with fin lock nut
Adapter-booster with closing plug
Fin assembly
Tail fuse
Arming wire
Trunnion band (for dive bombing only)

AP: AN-MK series (without fin assembly)
Bomb body:
Base plug with fin lock nut
Adapter and fuse seat liner containing auxiliary booster and fuse hole plug
Explosive charge of Explosive D
Fin assembly crate contents:
Fin assembly
Suspension lugs
Hoisting lug
Guide study
Cap screws
Safety wire
Lock washers
Trunnions
Arming bracket
Tail fuse
Arming wire assembly

Method of Assembly
SAP bombs: Assembly was the same as for the GP bomb.

AP bombs (AN-Mk series).
1) Remove the shipping bands (if present) from the bomb and fin assembly, and remove them from the shipping crate. Remove the required fuse and arming wires from their packing boxes and inspect their components. Load all unpacked and inspected components onto the bomb service truck and trailer and proceed to the assembly point.
2) Remove shipping plugs from the places for fittings as required by the type of suspension. Clean out holes.
3) Attach the required suspension fittings. Tighten cap screw and safety wire the screws holding suspension lug in pairs. Attach the trunnion using a shake proof lock washer under its base and tighten the trunnion securely.
4) Remove the closing plug or snap-on cover from the fuse cavity, being sure the auxiliary booster was in place and that there was no foreign matter present in tail fuse seat.
5) Remove the fin lock nut and place fin assembly over tail with one fin in line with suspension lugs. Replace fin lock nut and tighten. Tighten the set screws.
6) Attach arming bracket loosely to the neck of the fuse.
7) Install the fuse.
8) If bomb was not dropped, reverse the above steps and return the components to their packings and crates.

AP bombs (M-Series)
The assembly for the M-Series was the same as for the AN-Mk series, except for the installation of the suspension bands.

Functioning
AP and SAP bombs were fused for delayed action in order to permit the penetration of the target before the bomb exploded. AP bombs were designed to pierce concrete bombproof construction and heavy deck armor. SAP bombs were designed for use against reinforced concrete construction and lightly armored shipping.

Limitations
If used on unarmored or lightly armored ships AP bombs would usually pass entirely through the target before exploding. Because of the limited explosive content direct hits were required for effect, and because of the high impact velocity required they had to be released at high altitudes.

SAP Bomb Types
Bomb, SAP, 500 Pound, AN-M58A1
The AN-M58A1 was a cylindrical bomb measuring 57.8 inches long and weighing 502 pounds, as released. The bomb body was 47.2 inches in length and 11.8 inches in diameter and weighed 488.5 pounds, of which 144.5 pounds, 29% of the complete round, was explosive charge (Picratol). The base plate of this bomb was securely locked in place and the adapter-booster may be locked to the base plate.

Bomb, AP, 500 Pound, AM-M58A2
The AN-M68A2 was a cylindrical bomb which was 57.8 inches long and weighed 536.5 pounds as released. The bomb body was 47.7 inches in length and 11.8 inches in diameter and weighed 522.5 pounds, of which 143.1 pounds (26.7% of complete round) was Picratol. The base plate of this bomb was securely locked in place and the adapter-booster could be locked to the base plate.

Bomb, SAP, 500 Pound, AN-M58
This bomb was an earlier model which differed principally in having a slightly lighter body.

Bomb, SAP, 1,000 Pound, AN-M59A1
The AN-M59A1was a cylindrical bomb which was 70.375 inches long and weighed 1,033.9 pounds as released. The bomb body was 57.8 inches in length and 15.1 inches in diameter and weighed 1,013.8 pounds, of which 312.6 pounds (30.2% of the complete round) was explosive charge (Picratol). The base plate of this bomb was securely locked in place and the adapter-booster could be locked to the base plate.

Bomb, SAP, 1,000 Pound, AN-M59
The AN-M59 was the only other model of this series. It differs from the AN-M59A1 in that its complete weight was 990 pounds as released, of which 315 pounds (31.8 percent) was explosive charge. The base plate of the AN-M59 is removable and the adapter-booster cannot be locked to the base plate.

Bomb, SAP, Picratol, 2,000 Pound, M103
The M103 was a cylindrical bomb which was 88.45 inches long and weighed 2,039.4 pounds as released. The bomb body was 68.55 inches in length and 18.8 inches in diameter. It weighed 1,983.3 pounds, of which 556.5 pounds (27.3% of complete round) was explosive charge.

Bomb, SAP, 25,000 Pound, T28E4
This bomb was under development at the end of the war. The bomb body was 199.5 inches long and had a diameter of 32 inches. The tail assembly was attached to the bomb body with 16 bolts that were anchored in the base plate of the body. The T28E4, unlike other SAP bombs, had no nose plug, with the nose being a solid piece.

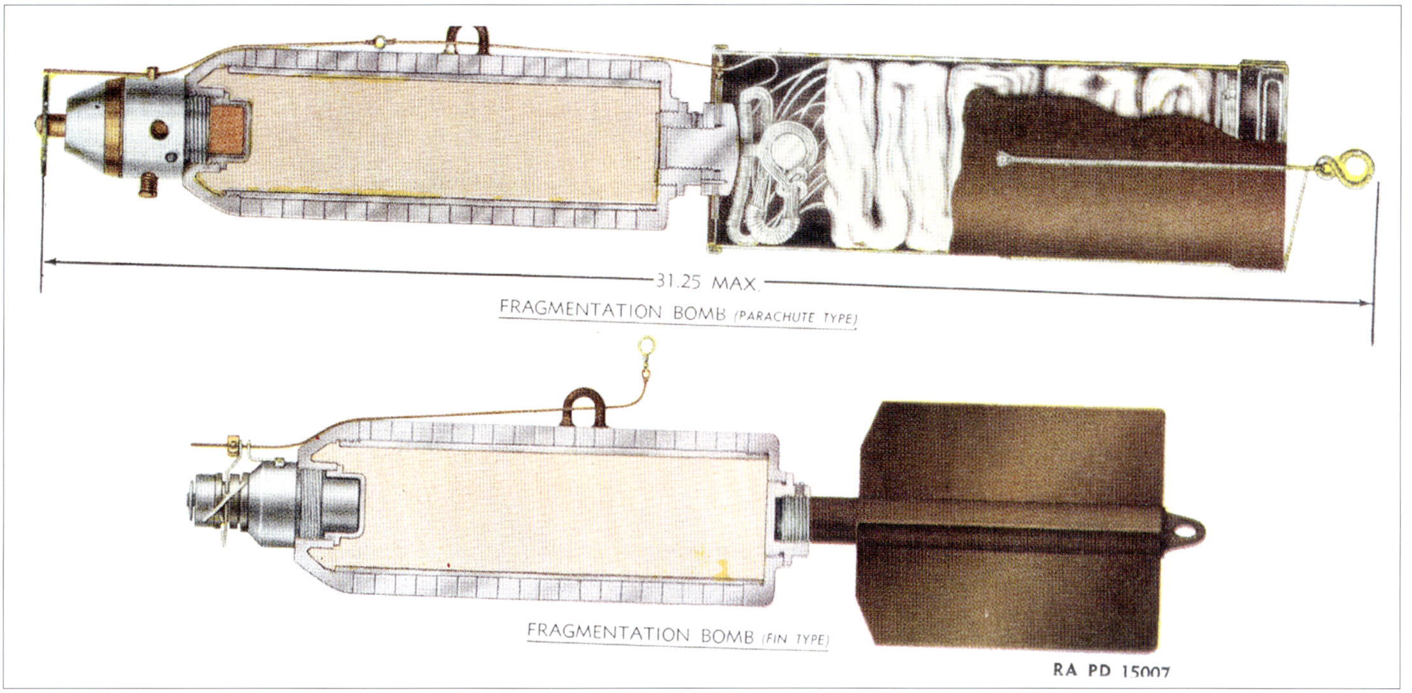

Fragmentation Bombs: Parachute Type (top) and Fin Type (bottom) (TM 9-1980)

AP Bomb Types

Bomb, AP, 1,000 Pound, AN-Mk33

The AN-Mk33 was a streamlined bomb which was 73 inches long and weighed 1,008 pounds as released. The bomb body was 59.75 inches long and 12 inches in diameter and weighed 991 pounds, of which 140 pounds (14% of the complete round) was explosive charge.

Bomb, AP, 1,600 Pound, AN-MK1

The AN-Mk1 was a streamlined bomb which was 83.5 inches long and weighed 1,590 pounds as released. The bomb body was 68.9 inches long and 14 inches in diameter and weighed 1,575 pounds, of which 216 pounds (14% of the complete round) was Explosive D. This bomb was issued unfused, without fin assembly or suspension accessories.

Other AN-Mk1 Models

Bomb, AP, 1,600 Pound, MK1 (Navy)

This bomb differed, as the method of suspension was provided by suspension bands bolted around the bomb body. A stud on the band fit into a recess in the bomb body to prevent shifting. The recesses were located to space the lugs on the bands 14 inches apart center to center. If suspension from the 30 inch racks was required, the bands and studs were removed from the bomb by any available means, such as file or hacksaw. One band was installed with the center of the lug 18.5 inches from the nose of the bomb, and the other band was installed with the center of the lug 30 inches aft of the center of the lug on the forward band. Before final tightening, the lugs were to be lined up with each other and with one tail fin, and then the bands were securely tightened. Extreme maneuvers were to be avoided when carrying a bomb with this modified suspension.

Bomb, AP, 1,600 Pound, Mk1/Mod.1 (Navy)

This bomb was equipped with suspension bands, but these bands were positioned by shallow grooves machined in the bomb body. There were five grooves: the outer pair for locating the suspension bands for 30 inch racks, the next pair for locating the bands for 14 inch racks, and the center groove for locating the hoisting band.

Bomb, AP, 600 Pound, M62

The M62 was a modified artillery shell type of bomb. As released, the bomb was 62.1 inches long and weighed 634 pounds. The bomb body was 47 inches long and 10 inches in diameter. It weighed 606 pounds, of which 33.6 pounds—only 5.5% of the complete round—was Explosive D. The bomb was issued unfused, without fin assembly or suspension bands.

Other M62 Models

Other models of this size and type differed only in details of the adapter-booster assembled to the bomb, since the shells from which these models were converted were fused with different types of artillery fuses.

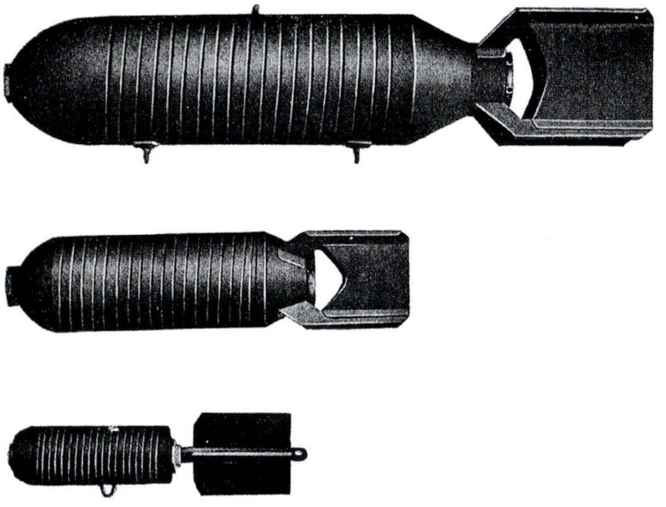

Comparative sizes (L-R): 260 Pound AN-M81, 90 Pound AN-M 82, and 20 Pound AN-M 41. (TM 9-1980)

Bomb, AP, 800 Pound, M61
The M61 was a modified artillery shell type of bomb and was similar to the 600 pound, M61 bomb. As released, the bomb was 58.7 inches long and weighed 853 pounds. The bomb body was 38.6 inches long and 12 inches in diameter and weighed 824 pounds, of which 32.7 pounds (only 3.8% of the complete round) was Explosive D.

Bomb, AP, 1,000 Pound, M52
The M52 was a modified artillery shell type of bomb and was similar to the 600 pound bomb, M61. As released, the bomb was 71 inches long and weighed 1,078 pounds. The bomb body was 50.5 inches long and 12 inches in diameter and weighed 1,049 pounds, of which 58 pounds, or 5.4% of the complete round, was Explosive D.

Bomb, AP, 1,400 Pound, M63
The M63 was a modified artillery shell type of bomb and was similar to the 600 pound bomb, M61. As released, the bomb was 69.1 inches long and weighed 1,412 pounds. The bomb body was 45.74 inches long and 14 inches in diameter and weighed 1,364 pounds, of which 35 pounds—only 2.5% of the complete round—was Explosive D.

Fragmentation and Parachute Bombs
Fragmentation Bombs were designed to produce their effect through the explosive projection of the fragments of the shattered bomb body. These bombs were intended for use against personnel and light materiel. The explosive charge averaged 14%, and the body was of uniform thickness and could be made up of steel coils. One type of Fragmentation Bomb was stabilized by fins, while the other, designed for low altitude bombing, was equipped with a parachute to delay the impact of the bomb until the dropping aircraft had cleared the danger area. Fuses for Fragmentation Bombs were designed to function on or above the surface of the ground. Frags were usually loaded with Comp B or TNT.

Parachute Bombs
The intention of the Parachute Bomb was to slow the forward momentum of the dropped bomb to allow the low-level bomber to escape the blast of the exploding bomb. The parachute was spring-loaded to pop out of the pack.

Parafrags
The Parafrag was developed in the 1920s, but was all but forgotten in the inter-war years. The innovative bomb was a standard 23 pound Fragmentation Bomb that was fitted to a special bomb tail fin unit. The tail fin unit mounted a tube on one side that contained a small parachute whose release ("rip") cord was attached on one end to the bomb bay and opened the chute upon release. The suspension hook inside the bomb bay released the bomb and the arming hook retained the pull out wire, pulling out the container. The pilot disk of the top cord assembly was caught by the airstream and pulled the parachute out of its case. The arming cord was attached to the parachute shrouds, and as the parachute opened and the shroud lines straightened the arming cord pulled the arming wire from the fuse, which was then armed. Meanwhile the bomb, slowed by the parachute, fell with a terminal velocity of about 20 mph. The bomb was fused by a very sensitive proximity or instantaneous fuse that would cause it to explode several feet above the ground, spreading 800 to 1,200 pieces of fragmented bomb casing over a radius of ten to 25 yards, devastating nearby personnel, exploding fuel tanks, and shredding vehicles and aircraft.

Before he left for the SWPA, Gen. George Kenney had discovered 3,000 Parafrags stored in war reserve and had them shipped to Australia. Kenney asked Col. Paul "Pappy" Gunn to design a delivery system for the parafrags and he developed the "Squirrel Cage." The device was a

Curtiss A-12 dropping early fragmentation bombs in 1933. (AAF)

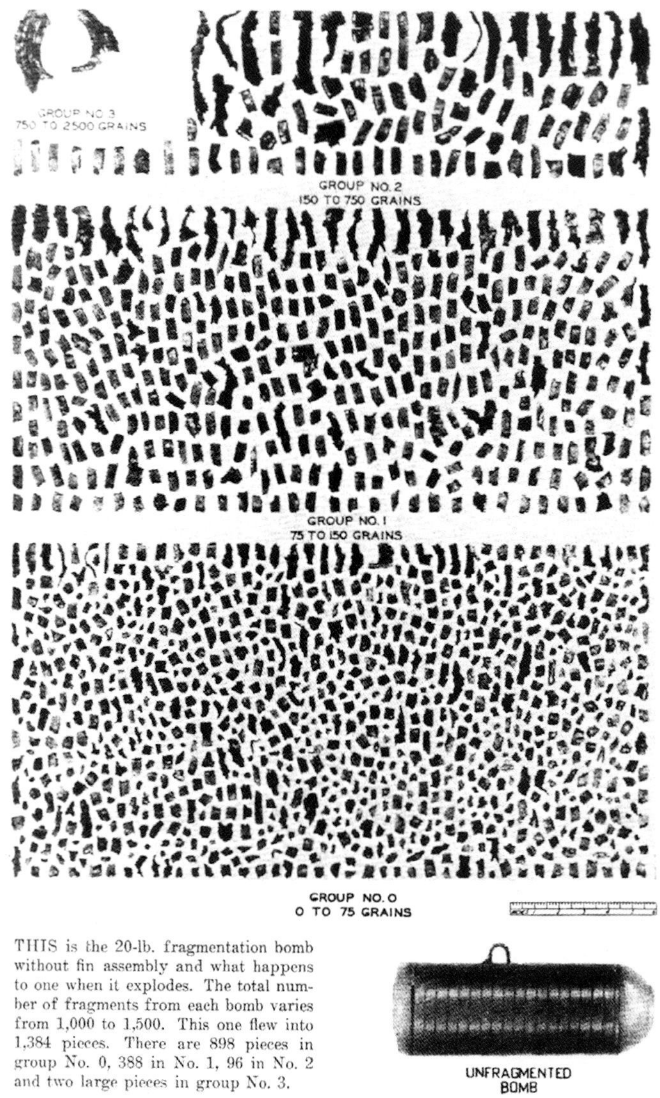

1,384 pieces from an exploded 20 Pound fragmentation bomb grouped into grain sizes. (AAF)

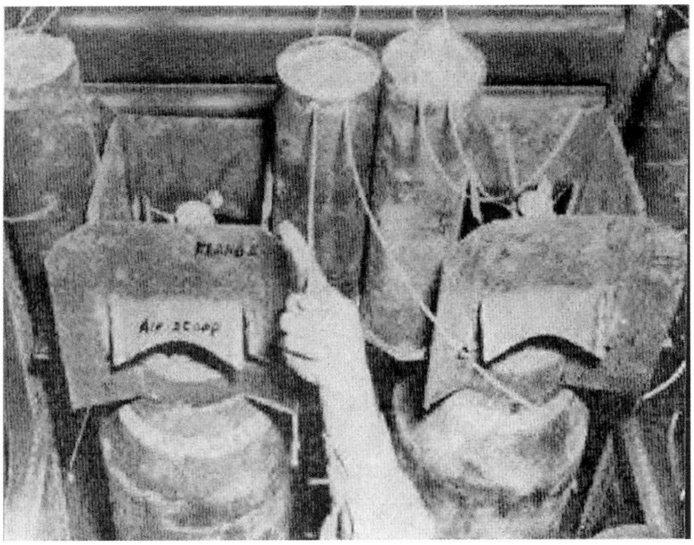

250 pound **parademo bomb**, which was to be suspended by two parachutes and with the tail unit containing an air scoop on the downward-facing fin that was to put the nose in a downward-facing position when it was released so that the parachute could be released upward without interference. (AAF)

honeycomb metal bomb rack that resembled a cage with partitions that stacked four 23 pound parafrags; one on top of another, nose to tail, in 10 stacks per cage. Over the target all the Parafrags were toggled, with the lower bomb in the stack leaving first and with the other three following, from the rear stacks forward, until the cage was empty. The first cages had a complicated arrangement of levers and cables to release the bombs and problems occurred when the parachutes opened before bombs left the cage and hung up and against the bottom of the aircraft. There were no reported aircraft losses because of this, but until the problem was remedied some pilots would salvo the entire cage just to get rid of it. Once the apparatus and technique were perfected the Parafrag became the devastating weapon that became famous in the multitude of combat photos and movies taken from the escaping B-25.

Parademos

It was found that when dropping standard demolition bombs they often ricocheted off the ground away from the target. In August 1943, to prevent the ricochet the parachutes used on the 23 pound Parafrags and a new parachute adapter were fitted on the larger demolition bombs. The 100 pound bomb would require one parachute, while the 250 pound bomb was suspended by two parachutes and the 500 pound bomb by four chutes. The tail unit on the parademo bomb contained an air scoop on the downward-facing fin that put the nose in a downward-facing position when it was released so that the parachute could be released upward without interference. The Parademos could work as demolition bombs or Daisy Cutters with instantaneous or delayed fuses.

General

With the exception of the four pound M83 bomb, the body of a Fragmentation Bomb consisted of a thin steel tubular sleeve closed at each end by a heavy metal cap. A body of heavy steel bar stock, spirally wound, was assembled to the outside of the steel sleeve and provided the principal source of fragments when the bomb was detonated. The nose was threaded to receive an impact fuse, and the tail cap was threaded to provide attachment of the tail assembly or spring-loaded parachute unit assembly. Fragmentation Bombs two pounds and larger were adapted for both nose and tail fuses. The typical targets for Fragmentation Bombs were personnel, unarmored or lightly armored vehicles, and parked aircraft.

Assembly

Components

The components of a complete Fragmentation Bomb (with the exception of the four pound, M83) were:

1) Fin type
   a) Bomb, unfused includes:
      Bomb body, including case, nose, and base.
      Explosive charge, TNT or Comp. B
      Fin assembly.
   b) Vane type nose fuse.
   c) Vane type tail fuse (large bombs only).

No arming wire was necessary for bombs assembled in clusters, since the vane stop of the cluster adapter kept the fuse from arming until the bomb was released from the cluster.

2) Parachute type
   a) Bomb, unfused, includes:
      Bomb body, including case, nose, and base.
      Explosive charge, TNT, or Comp. B.
      Parachute unit assembly, parachute case assembly, and arming wire assembly.
   b) Pin type nose fuse with delayed arming.

3) Fins

The stabilizer assembly of small bombs consisted of an axial member to which four radial fins were attached. One end was threaded for attachment to the bomb and the other end was formed into a lug for vertical suspension of the bomb. Large Fragmentation Bombs had a box type fin.

4) Parachute unit assembly

The parachute unit assembly consisted of a cylindrical parachute case which was attached to the bomb body and contained the parachute and shrouds, arming cord, and parachute top cord assembly; and when bombs were individually suspended a pull-out wire and pull-out wire container. In the latter, the pull-out wire container served to close the case; however, for handling a shipping cover was added and sealed in place. The case was closed, in the cluster bomb, by a loose cap held in place by the cluster adapter.

Method of Assembly

1) Bombs issued in clusters were completely assembled.

2) Large Fragmentation Bombs were assembled in accordance with the directions for GP bombs.

3) Small bombs for individual suspension were assembled and installed as follows:

a) Remove the bomb and fuse from their packing and inspect the components. After inspection the components were loaded on bomb service truck and trailer and taken to the assembly point.

b) The tape holding the arming wire to the case was removed and the arming cord disengaged from the case coupling.

c) Assemble the fuse to the bomb.

e) Remove sealing strip and shipping cover from the parachute cage. Uncoil the pull-out wire from the case, taking care not to loosen its container or to kink or knot the pull out wire.

f) Suspend the bomb in the rack by the "S" hook located on the suspension cable and remove the safety cotter pin from the fuse. Attach the loop on the pull-out wire to the arming pawl.

g) If the bomb was not dropped, the above steps were to be reversed by defusing the bomb, and the components were to be returned to their original condition and packing.

Functioning
Fragmentation Bombs suspended individually function as follows: (The functioning of bombs in clusters is described elsewhere)

Dropped Armed
The suspension hook released the bomb, while the arming hook retained the pull-out wire, pulling out the container. The pilot disk of the top cord assembly was caught by the air stream and pulled the parachute from the case. The arming cord was attached to the parachute shrouds and, as the parachute opened and the shroud lines straightened, the arming cord pulled the arming wire from the fuse and allowed the fuse to arm. Meanwhile the bomb, slowed by the parachute, fell with a terminal velocity of approximately 20 mph. Upon impact the bomb exploded, projecting fragments over an effective radius of 10 to 25 yards.

Dropped Safe
When dropped "Safe," the pull-out was released with the bomb. The container remained in place, keeping the parachute in the case. Since the parachute did not open the arming wire was not withdrawn from the fuse and the fuse did not function on impact.

The fragmentation bomb was slowed by the parachute to fall with a terminal velocity of approximately 20 mph and projected fragments over an effective radius of 10 to 25 yards upon impact (on a Japanese Sally bomber in this case). (AAF)

Limitations
Because of their small size, direct hits or near misses were required for this type bomb to damage armored targets. Aircraft loads were limited by the number of bombs and not by their weight-carrying capacity.

Types of Fragmentation Bombs
Bomb, Fragmentation, Four Pound, M83
This bomb was a small cylindrical bomb used only in clusters. The fuse (M129, M130, or M131) was set into the bomb body and had a cable ex-

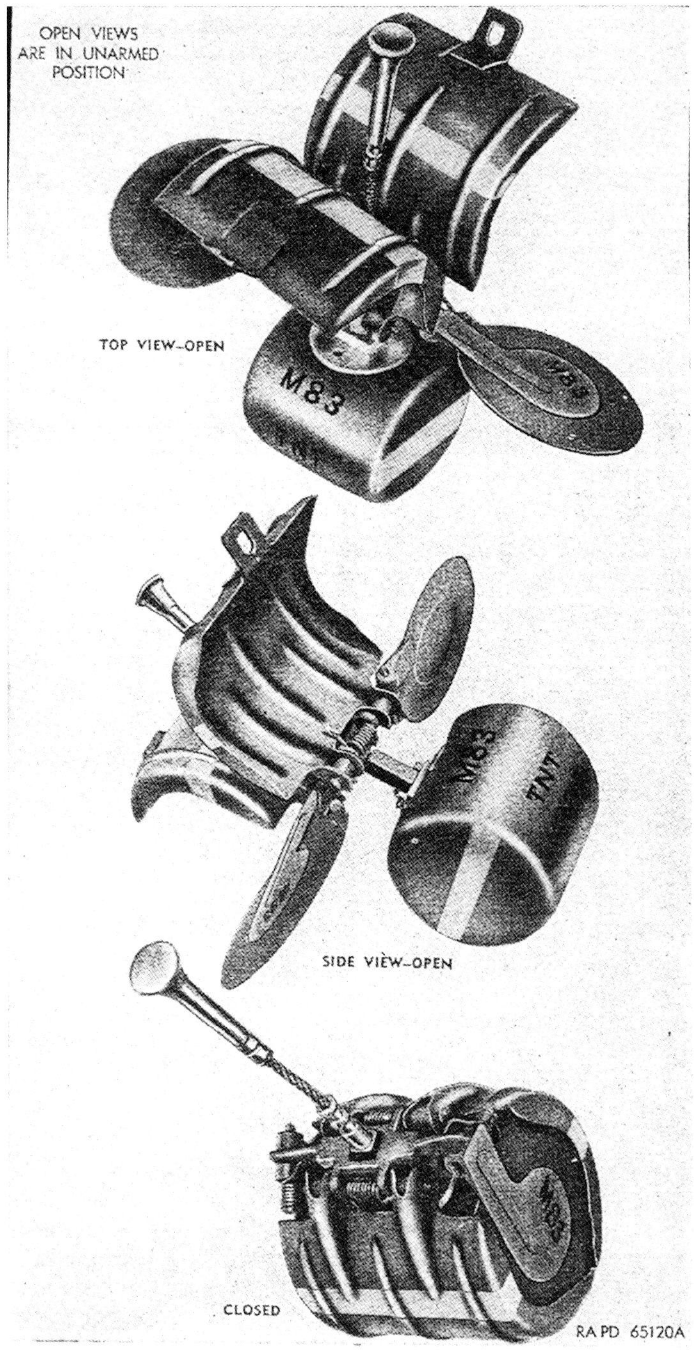

Figure 94. Bomb, fragmentation, 4-lb, M83—steps in operation.

When the **Four Pound M83 bomb** was released from the cluster the wings were opened by spring action and forced by the air stream to the top of the cable extension. In this position the butterfly wings slowed the fall of the bomb and began to rotate, which turned the cable and withdrew the arming stem, thus arming the fuse.

Pound M41 Cutaway

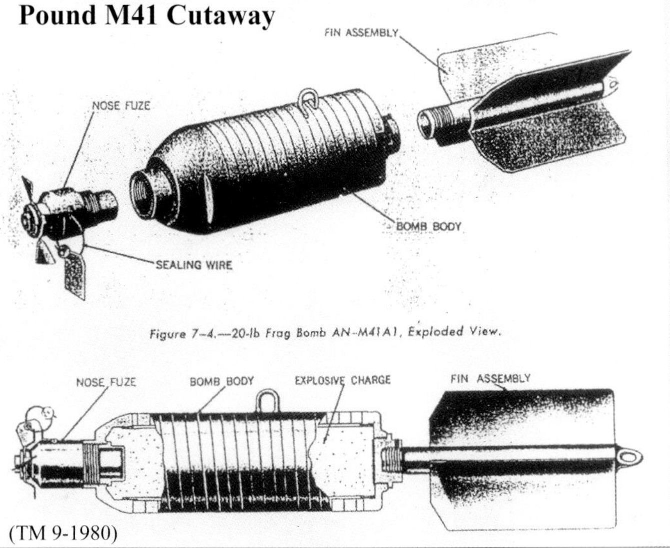

Figure 7-4.—20-lb Frag Bomb AN-M41A1, Exploded View.

(TM 9-1980)

tension on which the bomb case assembly (butterfly wings) was mounted. When the bomb was released from the cluster, the wings were opened by spring action and were forced by the air stream to the top of the cable extension. In this position the butterfly wings slowed the fall of the bomb and began to rotate, which turned the cable and withdrew the arming stem, thus arming the fuse. The bomb was issued in Cluster Fragmentation Bomb M28, M28A1, and M28A2 (the 100 pound size containing 24 bombs), or as a 10 bomb wafer for use in the field. The M29 or M29A1 cluster was a 500 pound size containing nine wafers (ten bombs per wafer) or a total of 90 M83 bombs. The action of the fuse was specified in the marking of the cluster and was airburst, impact, mechanical time, or anti-disturbance.

Bomb, Fragmentation, TNT, 20 Pound, AN-M41A1
The AN-M41A1 was fin-stabilized, with the fused bomb measuring 22.36 inches long, 3.64 inches in diameter, weighing in at 19.8 pounds, and carrying 2.7 pounds of TNT. It was issued in a Fragmentation Bomb cluster, AN-M1A2, and the M26 series Fragmentation Bomb clusters.

Other Models
Bomb, Fragmentation, TNT, 20 Pound, AN-M41 was 1/2 inch shorter than the AN-M41A1 due to a change in design which added a shoulder to the nose of the bomb; this change in design constitutes the "Al" modification."

Bomb, Fragmentation, AN-M41A2 was only issued in cluster form, but could be found in the Fragmentation Bomb cluster M1A1 as well as the M1A2.

Bomb, Fragmentation, TNT, 23 Pound, M40A1, (AN-M40A1with parachute unit)
The M40A1was a parachute type Fragmentation Bomb designed for assembly in clusters, but was also authorized for single suspension use. The fused bomb was 30.15 inches long, 4.37 inches in diameter, and weighed 24.6 pounds. This bomb was used in Fragmentation Bomb clusters M4A1 and M4A2.

Other Models
Bomb, Fragmentation, 23 Pound M40 was 1/4 inch shorter than the M40A1 due to a change in design which added a shoulder to the nose of the bomb; this change in design constitutes the "Al" modification." The M40 is used in forming the M4 cluster, as well as the M4A1 and M4A2.

Bomb, Fragmentation, TNT, 23 Pound, M72AI (with parachute unit)
This bomb was a parachute type Fragmentation Bomb designed for single suspension. It is 30.15 inches long (not including the vertical suspension lug and cable), weighed 24.5 pounds, and contained 2.7 pounds of TNT.

Other Models
Bomb, Fragmentation, TNT, 23 Pound, M72AI did not have the shoulder design type of nose, and consequently was only 29.75 inches long (not including vertical suspension lug and cable). The vertical suspension lug of the M72 was "S" shaped, whereas that of the M72AI was a flat piece of metal with a drilled hole used for suspension purposes.

Conversion of the AN-M41 Type Bomb to the M40 or M72 Type
The conversion of the 20 pound Fragmentation Bombs of the AN-M41 type to the parachute type for single suspension, or for use in the M4 series of clusters, was required at times. A conversion kit was issued for the purpose of making these changes and included three types of nose fuses; three M4 parachute units; one M3 cluster adapter; and associated accessories.

Bomb, Fragmentation, 90 Pound, M82
M82 was designed for use in clusters and only had one suspension lug; consequently, it was not directly adaptable to standard bomb racks for individual suspension. The complete round was 28 inches long and weighed 88.5 pounds. The body, issued unfused and without fin, was 20.5 inches long and 6.06 inches in diameter and contained 12.3 pounds (13.9% of complete weight) of Comp B. Some of these bombs were TNT loaded. This bomb was used in forming the M27 type cluster.

Bomb, Fragmentation, 120 Pound, M86
The M86 consisted of the same bomb body as the 90 pound M82 and the Parachute Unit M5. The complete round was 58.82 inches long and weighed 118.2 pounds.

Bomb, Fragmentation, Comp B, 220 Pound, AN-M88
The AN-M88 was designed for single suspension. The complete round was 43.7 inches long and weighed 217 pounds. The bomb body was 34.1 inches long, 8.1 inches in diameter, and weighed 208.4 pounds, of which 41.4 pounds was included in the COMP B explosive charge and the nose and tail surround. Alternative explosive fillers for this bomb were Ednatol (the first alternative) and then TNT. The assembly of the bomb was the same as described for GP bombs.

Other Models
Bomb, Fragmentation, 260 Pound, AN-M81
The AN-M81 was an earlier modification of the AN-M88, and differed from the AN-M88 in that the complete round weighed 263 pounds, with the weight due to the larger size of spiral wrapping. The AN-M81 bomb body weighed 253.5 pounds, of which 36 pounds was Comp B.

Incendiary (I) Bombs
Of all the bombs dropped during World War II the incendiary bomb inflicted far more damage and casualties than any other type. But during the war the effectiveness of incendiaries versus high explosive bombs was questioned. The lengthy and careful conclusions of the postwar United States Strategic Bombing Survey stated that the M47 incendiary weighing 70 pounds was 12 times as effective, bomb for bomb, than the 500 pound HE bomb against targets classified as readily inflammable, and one and a half times as effective against targets classified as fire-resistant.
There were two types of aerial incendiary bombs: the incendiary bomb usually dropped by bombers on targets far behind enemy lines, and the fire bomb (commonly referred to as the napalm bomb), which were dropped by

fighter bombers at or near the front lines. The bomber incendiary bomb will be discussed in this Volume 2, while the napalm bomb will be discussed in *U.S. Aerial Armament in World War II: Volume 3.*

World War I Incendiary Development

The aerial incendiary weapon was first used in World War I when German zeppelins and airplanes dropped incendiaries on England. These rudimentary bombs were bucket-shaped, and were comprised of a core of thermite wrapped with tarred cotton waste and tarred rope. These bombs were inadequate as incendiaries and had poor ballistic qualities, and the Germans replaced them with a torpedo-shaped bomb filled with gasoline, kerosene, paraffin, and liquid tar. These mixtures were highly inflammable and were only loaded into the bomb shortly before take-off. Later a more inflammable mixture of benzol, tar, and thermite, which burned at temperatures as high as 5,400°C, was developed. Just before the end of the war German scientists had perfected the two pound electron bomb, which was composed of a magnesium-thermite filler in a magnesium alloy casing. These incendiaries were used mainly for anti-personnel attacks, dropped from a bomb rack containing 20 bombs that could be fitted to any two-seater aircraft. Although not used in World War I, it was important as the prototype of World War II incendiaries.

The early British incendiaries were filled with petrol or black powder with a propeller-actuated fuse firing a Very Cartridge. Great Britain's principal incendiary bomb, the Baby Incendiary, weighed 0.4 pounds and was filled with a thermite mixture. These small bombs were carried in containers that held either 144 or 272 bombs. Although these bombs were in production and were effective, only a few were used during World War I. A 40 pound phosphorous incendiary introduced in the last year of the war was more successful and often employed against kite balloons, as the time fuse could be set to ignite at any height above ground and spread a shower of burning phosphorus over a circle of about 750 feet diameter.

America developed several types of incendiary bombs during World War I. The Mark I bomb was intended for use against very inflammable targets. The 40 pound Mark II and 100 pound Mark III were of the "intensive type," which were bombs with a great penetrability (depending on their weight) and an intensive incendiary action. The Mark I, which outwardly resembled the Mark II, was a scatter-type weapon. Both bombs contained a thermite charge that ignited the main incendiary. The Mark II was filled with solid oil, while the Mark I contained a number of waste balls saturated with an inflammable mixture. Two explosive charges ignited these balls and spread them over a radius of 20 feet.

The United States also developed two incendiary darts: one was the Mark I, which consisted of an elongated 12 gauge shotgun shell filled with an incendiary material. This small incendiary ignited on impact and was intended for use to set grain fields and forests on fire. The heavier Mark II dart was composed of a zinc body, a thermite and solid oil filler, and a steel nose, and had the penetrability needed for use against buildings. Neither the incendiary darts nor the other three American aerial incendiaries were used in combat. U.S. air units in France used the French *Chenard*, which was considered to be the most efficient of all Allied incendiary bombs. The early French incendiaries had been filled with phosphorus, but other fillings, such as a mixture of celluloid, paraffin and resin, or cotton, potassium, and resin were developed later.

Inter-war Incendiary Development

Due to the too optimistic appraisal of the capabilities of high explosive (HE) bombs there was little interest in America in developing incendiary bombs in the first 15 years after the war. However, during the 1930s Col. J. Enrique Zanetti, a Chemical Warfare Service Reserve officer teaching at Columbia University, championed the potential of the incendiary bomb. Col. Zanetti was considered the American expert on incendiary weapons, having experience with them in World War I. Aerial gas attacks were seen as the most horrific danger to civilian populations, but Zanetti foresaw incendiary bombs as a greater threat. Zanetti pointed out that small incendiary bombs could do much more damage than the tons of gas that were required to produce lethal concentrations, especially when considering that gas dissipated while fire propagated. Zanetti stated that "Each of these small bombs held within itself the devastating possibilities of Mrs. O'Leary's cow."

By the mid-1930s the Army Air Corps began to recognize the potential of incendiary weapons. In November 1934 the commandant of the Air Corps Tactical School at Maxwell Field, AL, suggested to the Chief of Air Corps to begin developing a filling for an incendiary bomb, and in December the requirements for an incendiary bomb were sent to the Chief of the CWS. By April 1936 the CWS Book of Standards contained a military requirement for an incendiary filling for the 25 pound chemical bomb, and on 30 December 1936 the CWS established a project to find an effective incendiary bomb filling. In 1940 Luftwaffe bombers were burning out large areas of London with hundreds of magnesium electron bombs and 110 kg oil bombs, but there was the continuing belief in America in the superiority of high explosives over incendiary bombs. At the time of Pearl Harbor the U.S. had only one standardized incendiary bomb, the gasoline filled 100 pound M47, and this was due to the efforts of Zanetti and Maj.Gen. William Porter, Chief of the CWS. Porter's previous two assignments before he became CWS Chief had been with the AAC, which made him wholly conscious of the value of aerial incendiaries.

In July 1941 Gen. Porter called Col. Zanetti back to active duty and dispatched him to London to study English research, development, and production of the effective British 4 pound incendiary bomb. Col. Zanetti obtained formulas for incendiary fillings, bomb casing designs, and manufacturing techniques. With this information there was a need for extensive American research, but since 1920 the responsibility for incendiary weapons had been divided between the Ordnance Department and the Chemical Warfare Service. The CWS had responsibility for the procurement of the containers and the storage and issue of the complete incendiary bomb, whereas Ordnance was to develop the incendiary material and fill the bomb. Gen. Porter labored to consolidate the incendiary program under the CWS, as he realized the necessity for its exclusive control by one entity. In the case of the 4 pound magnesium incendiary bomb the argument was particularly strong, and the case and incendiary material were the same. In September 1941 the CWS was granted the complete responsibility for the entire incendiary bomb program.

Early Anglo-American Wartime Incendiary Development

Once the CWS was given control of the incendiary program and the U.S. entered combat there was a continued apathy among AAC officers, particularly at the operational stage. Early CWS incendiaries left much to be desired, as they were hastily developed in the rush to arm for the war. The Luftwaffe's success setting English cities on fire during the Blitz using the incendiary bombs led to English interest in incendiary bomb development and spurred CWS incendiary bomb development.

England established an operational research unit, designated as RE/8 (Research and Experiment Station, Section 8) of the Ministry of Home Security. RE/8 consisted of scientists, statisticians, photo interpreters, and other specialists whose task it was to study the effects of bombing and to make their conclusions accessible to both British and American air commanders. American military and civilian personnel were also attached to RE/8. RE/8 concluded that, in attacks against German industrial cities, incendiaries were more efficient than high explosives. RAF Bomber Command conducted a series of missions on Hamburg in the summer of 1943 to validate this conclusion. Between 24 July and 3 August the RAF, sometimes augmented by American bombers, attacked Hamburg seven times and decisively confirmed the great effectiveness of the incendiary bomb. Nearly 1.5 million bombs were dropped on Hamburg, with 1.3 million being 4 pound incendiaries that caused 45,000 deaths and nearly one third of the residences uninhabitable. The mission of the night of 27/28 July was the most devastating, as it created a fire storm, which is an occurrence caused by numerous fires combining with little or no surface winds. A huge pillar of heated air and gases rises vertically over the inferno and cold air rushes in from all sides of the base of the pillar to replace the hot ascending blast. The velocity of these newly created surface winds is able tear off a person's clothing and uproot large trees. The large numbers of deaths are not only caused from the flames but from asphyxiation, the inhalation of the intense heat, and carbon monoxide poisoning

In spite of the British success using incendiaries the hierarchy of the operational Eighth Air Force remained unconvinced of their effectiveness. Col. Crawford Kellogg, the first chemical officer assigned to the 8AF, was instrumental in persuading the Eighth of the worth of incendiary bombs. Kellogg was enthusiastically supported by a faction of RAF officers who had extensive and successful operational experience with incendiaries. These RAF officers joined USAAF officers to form the Zoroastrian Society, which was an informal Anglo-American group that significantly aided the Eighth Air Force in delineating the composition and characteristics of incendiaries that had the greatest promise.

Meanwhile, both the RAF and the Eighth Air Force conducted extensive incendiary bombing trials. The trials led to the abandonment of the U.S. 6 pound M69 incendiary oil bomb and the interim acceptance of the British 30 and 250 pound incendiaries pending the availability of more suitable American bombs and clusters. The best early U.S. bombs were the 100 pound cluster of 4 pound magnesium bombs and the 69 pound M47 bomb with an oil and crepe rubber filling. However, these bombs could not be supplied in combat quantities because of the lack of the development of manufacturing facilities and the English incendiaries continued to be used.

Development of Jellied Gasoline Incendiary Filler

During World War I, both Germany and the U.S. used an early form of Napalm in infantry combat flamethrowers, but the substance burned out too rapidly to be very effective at igniting targets. Gasoline alone was not an effective burning agent, as it splashed off of the target on impact and then ran off like water. A better thickening agent was required so that the fuel would adhere to the target for a more complete burning effect. During the early months of World War II, the U.S. Chemical Warfare Service (CWS) used latex from the Para rubber tree to jell gasoline that could be ejected further from flamethrowers and adhered to the target better and burned longer. However, the Japanese conquests in the Far East in 1941 cut off the supply of natural rubber.

When the NDRC initiated its investigation of incendiaries in the summer of 1941 it was a rather new bomb concept, with its only extensive use being by the Luftwaffe during the Blitz on England. Pre-Pearl Harbor studies of bombing effectiveness in the war in Europe had shown that the Luftwaffe and RAF use of incendiary bombs was as effective pound for pound as high explosive bombs. American incendiary bombs in inventory at that time were the M50, a four pound magnesium bomb which was a copy of the primary British incendiary bomb; and the M54, a four pound thermite bomb intended as an alternate. In September 1941 the critical shortage of magnesium caused Gen. Arnold to urge NDRC head Dr. Vannevar Bush to develop substitutes. On 7 October the Chemical Warfare Service engaged a group of Harvard scientists led by Dr. Louis Fieser, who had previously done work on incendiary materials, to examine alternate organic incendiary materials. The NDRC also contracted the Standard Oil Development Company to develop a small incendiary bomb filled with a petroleum product.

Dr. Fieser (1899-1977) was a renowned organic chemist who, following his deadly creation of Napalm, went on to do award-winning research that included work on blood-clotting agents, including the first synthesis of vitamin K; the synthesis and screening of quinines as anti-malarial drugs; and steroid research leading to the synthesis of cortisone. He then studied the nature of polycyclic aromatic hydrocarbons, which are one of the most widespread organic pollutants, some of which are known or suspected carcinogens and are linked to other health problems.

In October 1941 the Chemical Warfare Service employed Harvard scientist **Dr. Louis Fieser** to examine alternate organic incendiary materials which led to the development of napalm. Fieser was later instrumental in developing synthetic Vitamin K, anti-malarial drugs, and cortisone. (AFHRC)

Both the Harvard and Standard Oil groups recognized the importance of thickened or jellied gasoline as an incendiary material because of its easy ignition, high heat of combustion, and controlled burning rate. The Fieser Harvard group and Arthur D. Little, Inc., investigated the possibility of using aluminum naphthenate as a thickening agent, and in January 1942 added the aluminum soaps of coconut acids. The earliest thickeners were soaps, aluminum, and magnesium palmitates and stearates. Napalm was named so because it was made from the aluminum salts ***nap***hthenic and ***palm***itic acids (modern Napalm is composed primarily of benezene and is known as Napalm-B). During the next few months the Nuodex Products Company found that the addition of aluminum oleate and the development of a co-precipitation process formed a dry granular soap powder capable of producing a gasoline jelly by simple mixing at ordinary temperatures.

Naphthenic acids are corrosives found in crude oil, while palmitic acids are fatty acids that occur naturally in coconut oil, and individually naphthalene and palmitate are relatively innocuous substances. The M1 thickening powder was chemically a mixture of 25% (by weight) aluminum naphthenate, 25% aluminum oleate, and 50% aluminum laurate or aluminum stearate (soap). It was a highly hygroscopic (liquid-absorbing) coarse tan-colored powder. When gasoline was added a syrupy brownish substance was produced and formulated to burn at a specific rate and adhere to materials. According to the amount of thickener, the resulting viscosity (thickness, or resistance to flow) varied between a syrupy liquid and a thick rubbery gel. The content of long hydrocarbon chains made the material highly hydrophobic (resistant to wetting with water), making it more difficult to extinguish.

The principal application of gasoline jelly at this time was in the M47, which was a 69 pound incendiary bomb being developed by the Chemical Warfare Service. The M47 was a bursting-type bomb activated by an impact fuse and a central burster tube. A burster was an explosive charge used to open an incendiary or smoke bomb and to spread the bomb filling. It consisted of a long plastic or paper and chipboard tube, closed at both ends, and was filled with TNT, black powder and magnesium, Tetryl pellets, or other explosive. It fit into either the burster well or the igniter cavity. In Spring 1942 the Harvard group developed an improved burster for the M47, which consisted of an inner core of TNT surrounded by white phosphorus instead of the conventional black powder burster.

In the meantime, the Standard Oil Development Company tested a variety of mechanisms for incendiary bombs against specially designed targets simulating the attics above buildings. To be effective, an incendiary bomb had to have stability in the air and the correct terminal velocity. If the latter was too great, the bomb would shatter and fail to function; and if it was too low, the bomb would not penetrate the structure. When the incendiary hit the target correctly it had to start a fire quickly on a scale that it could not be easily extinguished. These experiments determined that the radius of effectiveness of the incendiary material in a small bomb was very limited unless a way could be found to project the material over a wider area of the target. A tail-ejection bomb was developed, consisting of a hexagonal steel container 2.87 inches in diameter and 19.5 inches in length. This bomb was filled with gasoline jelly and fitted with a delay fuse that would allow the bomb to assume a horizontal position after penetrating a roof and ignite a powder charge in the incendiary material and eject it through the tail. Another innovation in bomb design was the substitution of cloth streamers for the conventional rigid metal tail. During the spring of 1942 the new gasoline-gel bombs were comprehensively tested in a wind tunnel to set the terminal velocity at the value necessary to penetrate roof structures. The roof structures to be penetrated ranged from the light wood of Japanese homes through medium industrial roofs, and the final figure determined the strength that had to be built into the bomb and the amount of drag on the bomb to be imposed by the tail streamers. (Note: The use of napalm in fighter-bomber operations is discussed in *U.S. Aerial Armament in World War II: Volume 3*)

Testing of Incendiary Bombs

In May 1942 tests of the various gasoline-thickening agents confirmed that an isobutylmethacrylate material produced by DuPont was the most satisfactory, but by 1943 Napalm had been improved and its manufacture standardized, and it replaced the DuPont product for filling both the M47 and the new Standard Oil Development bomb. Both of these bombs were available by the summer of 1942 in sufficient quantities for airborne testing against condemned farm buildings at Jefferson Proving Ground, IN. These tests showed the superiority of the new gasoline-jelly filled M47 over the other small bombs tested and the TNT-white phosphorus burster over the previous burster. This bomb was standardized as the M69 and the Chemical Warfare Service put it into production. The TNT-white phosphorus burster was turned over to the Chemical Warfare Service for final development and production, and was eventually standardized as the M9-M13 burster-igniter, which was used extensively in the bombing of Germany and Japan.

Comparative tests of the M50, M54, and M69 bombs against farm buildings at Jefferson Proving Ground were thought by some to be easier to set afire than German or Japanese buildings. To confront these doubts, Standard Oil constructed full-scale sections of typical German and Japanese urban and industrial structures which could be used as targets for incendiary bombs fired from mortars to simulate bombs dropped from airplanes. In March this project was assigned to the Chemical Warfare Service, but the Standard Oil Development group continued in the important responsibility as architect-engineers. On 29 March 1943, work began on these structures at the Dugway Proving Ground, UT, and by 15 May 12 two-family Japanese houses and a block of six German houses were ready for testing. To be authentic the Hawaiian Islands and the West Coast were scoured for Japanese straw floor mats and other house furnishings, and authentic German and Japanese furniture was manufactured in New York.

Tests were conducted at Dugway from 17 May to 16 July 1943, where bombers in formation dropped clusters of quick-opening incendiaries from various altitudes and detailed records were made for each bomb hit. The results demonstrated that the M69 was the most effective of the three incendiaries. The M36 was a 220 pound cluster of 36 M69s and was the most devastating incendiary cluster dropped in World War II. The M69 was not as effective against German brick and stone structures, but presaged the horrifying infernos it would cause in Japan's crowded cities with a high percentage of wooden construction. In the fall of 1943, following the Dugway tests, plans for the incendiary bombing of Japanese cities were prepared by the AAF Air Force in conjunction with the NDRC.

When Japan became a target, war planners found that the construction of Japanese cities differed from those in Europe, as 95% of German cities were constructed of brick and stone, while 80% of Japanese cities were built from wood and paper products. The construction of many of the Japanese roofs was wood or thatch and easily penetrable by incendiary bombs. Japanese dwellings housed many civilians and were crowded together along narrow streets, making multiple fires started in them difficult to control. It was estimated that 15 primary German urban areas targeted by the RAF Bomber Command for area bombing contained about 12% of Germany's labor force, while studies indicated the 15 major Japanese urban area targets contained nearly 45% of the enemy's labor force. There were thousands of "home" industries crowded in Japanese city centers that were particularly vulnerable to concentrated incendiary attack (30% of the Japanese labor force was employed in factories with less than 30 workers). Key Japanese military industries were concentrated in only a few cities. For example, 40% of Japanese aircraft engines were produced in one city, 30% of aircraft assembly in two cities, 50% of machine tools in four cities, 45% of ordnance in seven cities, and 90% of electronic tubes in three cities. While the key industries in the priority target systems would not be destroyed in a concentrated area incendiary attack, they would be greatly affected by the destruction of the component and subassembly factories that supplied them and the loss of life of the work force and their housing. Another major consequence of incendiary attacks was the collateral disruption to utilities, transportation, and storage. The destruction of these key industries would have to be left to precision bombing.

The success of the incendiary missions depended on two factors. A pattern density of 600 pounds of M69 incendiaries per square acre (roughly 100 of the six pound bombs) was considered necessary, but with no guarantee of success. Area density was the concentration of aircraft bomb loads, their location, and the accuracy with which the incendiaries were delivered. The bombs had to be laid quickly in compact areas so that the fires could merge, and also to prevent the firefighters from gaining control. Surface winds were found to be very important, as they quickly spread and merged the fires, but rain and snow had little effect, as the incendiaries burned so hot that they were able to set wetted combustibles aflame and even fire-resistant buildings were damaged. Firebreaks created in Japanese cities were ineffective as bombs fell on both sides, but the breaks did allow an avenue of escape for Japanese civilians. As mentioned previously, incendiary bomb loadings were mixed with high explosives and Fragmentation Bombs to obstruct firefighters and civil defense personnel.

During the fall of 1943 the AAF formulated new requirements for incendiary bombs. The small incendiary bombs were released in clusters and created a major hazard to formation flight, and in addition were adversely affected in their aim by wind conditions. The AAF directed that all future incendiary bombs were to be produced in aimable clusters, which would fall unopened with the same trajectory as a large demolition bomb until they were within a few thousand feet of the target, at which time the cluster split open, scattering the small bombs. CWS and the Standard Oil group both performed developmental work on aimable clusters, and the final model combined features from both. In late fall 1943, the AAF ordered the rush production of 10,000 aimable clusters for use by the 20th Bomber Command in China. In cooperation with the CWS, the Standard Oil Development group assumed the responsibility for supervising the production of this order and met the deadline for delivery. These clusters were subsequently sent to China and were used in bombing operations there. During 1944 large-scale production of aimable clusters was initiated, and by the end of the war approximately 30,000,000 M69 bombs had been produced.

Once production of the M69 bomb began in the winter of 1943, the Standard Oil Development group began development of a modification containing a small tetryl charge, a heavy nose for production of fragments, and a variable time delay. This promising incendiary and anti-personnel bomb did not go into production until March 1945.

Incendiaries in the ETO

The Eighth Air Force only dropped a total of 97,046 tons of incendiary bombs on German targets compared with 569,751 tons of high explosives and 20,352 tons of fragmentation bombs. The large majority of the incendiaries were M50s in M17 clusters and M47s. The RAF dropped many more incendiaries than did the USAAF, as it was dedicated to a policy of night area raids against German cities. The AAF was initially confident in its pre-war precision bombing strategy of using its accurate Norden bombsight in daylight raids against specific industrial targets and in the protection afforded by its fighter escorts and formation flying. Because of the incendiary bomb's inherent inaccuracy, the AAC felt that it was a bomb that attacked the civilian population and was ineffective against hard industrial targets. Urban areas bombed by the RAF were more susceptible to incendiary bombs than were the individual plants and factories targeted by the 8AF. And while the Eighth Air Force only gradually realized that incendiaries had a part in industrial bombing, the RAF quickly saw the worth of incendiary bombing against larger, easy to hit area urban targets. From early 1943 the AAF no longer followed its prewar Norden Bombsight precision bombing philosophy, and radar (non-visual) bombing was used 60% of the time and accounted for 50% of the bombs dropped by the 8AF and had been used in three successful and deadly high altitude non-precision attacks on Germany (Berlin, Dresden, and *Operation Clarion*). The 8AF's use of incendiaries was effective, but not spectacular, and most of the damage to German cities resulted from RAF operations.

Incendiaries in the Pacific

The most impressive and effective use of the incendiary bomb was in the Pacific. The first significant operational use of the M69 incendiary bomb occurred in March 1944 when the 7AF attacked the town of Ponape on Ponape Island, causing extensive fire damage with about 20 tons of bombs. The first mission dropping M69 bombs on Japan occurred on 6 January 1945, when the 21st Bomber Command dropped 138 tons of bombs on Nagoya. Beginning in March 1945, Gen. Curtis LeMay's concentrated B-29 incendiary attacks against vulnerable Japanese cities played a significant part in Japan's decision to surrender. The use of incendiaries against Japan varied substantially from that against Germany. Airfields for the bombardment of Japanese cities were not immediately available, as was the situation of the 8AF, which had UK bases well within range of German cities. It was not until the Mariana Islands, located some 1,500 miles south of Tokyo, had been captured that AAF bombers were within bombing range of the Japanese capital and the other important cities on the island of Honshu. Japanese cities were extremely vulnerable to fire, and although many German cities were vulnerable to destruction by fire they were less feasible targets for the incendiary bomb than those of Japan. Ninety-five percent of German construction was brick and stone, and roofing, which was a vital consideration in starting fires, was usually constructed of tile or slate. In Japan 80% of the construction was of very inflammable wood and paper, and the buildings in these areas were so packed together and lacking fire barriers that an uncontrolled fire could spread very quickly. Japanese cities had frequently experienced destructive peacetime conflagrations.

The first permanent bases for the XX Bomber Command were in India, and the advanced bases were located near Chengtu, western China, which was only in range of the cities of Kyushu, at the southern end of Japan. Range and logistical problems limited the effectiveness of these operations until B-29 bases could be constructed on the newly captured islands of Saipan, Guam, and Tinian in the Mariana Islands. The first strategic bombing mission against a Japanese Homeland target was flown from Saipan on 24 November 1944, and from then until the early days of the following March, the XXI Bomber Command used conventional strategic bombing tactics against Japanese cities. In Europe the 8AF had developed the concept of precision bombing, and it also appeared to be the answer for conducting the air war against Japan. B-29s flew high altitude daylight missions against individual Japanese industrial targets using high explosives as a large percentage of the bomb load. But precision bombing would not be effective against Japanese targets.

In December 1944 Gen. Arnold was made aware of the vulnerability to fire of Japanese cities and requested that the XXI Bomber Command mount a large scale test of incendiary attacks. XXI BC CO Brig.Gen. Haywood Hansell was a staunch proponent of daylight precision bombing, but nevertheless ordered incendiary test missions. These missions were relatively ineffective, which was unfortunate for the Japanese, as they formed an overly optimistic estimation of their inefficient fire fighting organization.

Brig.Gen. LeMay replaced Hansell on 20 January 1945. Initially LeMay did not change tactics, and although some success was obtained from high altitude precision bombardment of particular Japanese industries, this success fell far below expectations. In order to improve bombing results LeMay made radical alterations in his bombing tactics. The B-29s were no longer to attack individual factories or complexes, but were to drop the most damaging payload possible on Japan's combustible cities, filled with home industries as well as with various military installations. The bombers were to attack from altitudes of 6,000 to 7,000 feet instead of the usual 20,000 and 30,000; a change which was partly caused by the weather encountered over the island of Honshu. At the higher altitudes strong jet stream winds pummeled the B-29s and crews, causing overly large fuel consumption, while the usual heavy cloud formations over Honshu prevented the visual bombardment of targets from higher altitudes. Bombers were to make individual bombing runs against the target instead of attacking in formation, which was the established practice, as it provided an effective defense against attacks by enemy fighters. But formation flying involved rendezvous points for the aircraft, and therefore a greater consumption of precious gasoline needed for the long round trip. LeMay ordered the B-29s to attack at night to achieve surprise and take advantage of the weak Japanese night fighter force and ineffective radar gun-laying facilities. Finally, the bombers were to be stripped of all armament (except tail guns), which meant a savings in weight and the lesser demand for fuel, which meant that a greater bomb load could be carried made up exclusively of incendiary bombs.

The XXI BC first used these tactics on its historic mission No. 40 flown against Tokyo on the night of 9-10 March 1945. The Superfortresses carried the M47A2 and the M69 with the M47s toggled together, six to a 500 pound bomb station by the T19 cluster adapter developed by the Chemical Section of the XXI Bomber Command. Pathfinder units, one squadron of each of the three participating wings, carried the M47s, which served not only as aiming points, but also started appliance fires, which were those fires large enough to be controlled only by special fire fighting apparatus. The M69s used by the rest of the force started a large number of small fires that soon joined to form large ones. The M47 had been used extensively in Europe, but the M69, because of its poor penetrating power, was unsuitable for German targets; this feature made it particularly effective for use against the flimsy construction of Japanese buildings.

The first B-29s left Guam at 1735 on 9 March with the entire attacking force airborne by 2020. Although the aircraft met some bad weather on the way to Tokyo, they identified the initial point on the coast and target without difficulty. The first bombs were dropped on Tokyo just after midnight at 0015. It required only 30 minutes for the fires to become an unstoppable conflagration that burned out 15.8 square miles of Tokyo, which was an area almost four times more than that destroyed by the atomic bomb attack on Hiroshima five months later. There were 83,703 deaths and 41,000 more injured for a loss of only 14 of 279 B-29s. The results achieved by the XXI Bomber Command left no doubt as to the validity of LeMay's revolutionary tactics and the destructiveness of the incendiary bomb.

The exceedingly successful attack on Tokyo was followed in rapid succession during 11-18 March by four major attacks on Nagoya, Osaka, Kobe, and a repeat on Nagoya. These attacks depleted the supply of incendiary bombs in the Marianas, and only two more incendiary attacks were made during the next two months. When sufficient stocks of bombs finally arrived attacks resumed on 15 May, and during the next two months a series of heavy incendiary attacks effectively destroyed all the major cities of Japan except Hiroshima, Nagasaki, and Kyoto. In these attacks about 50% of the total weight of bombs dropped was M69 bombs, with the remaining 50% made up of other types of incendiary bombs, demolition bombs, and fragmentation bombs. This air offensive was a major contributing factor to the surrender of Japan in August. If the enforced bomb shortage delay in the incendiary bombing offensive from 18 March to 15 May had not occurred the war might have ended even sooner; perhaps before the Atomic Bombs were dropped.

Incendiary Bombs

Bomb, Incendiary, Four Pound, AN-M50 A2, AN-M50 XA1, and AN-M50 XA3

In early 1941, Col. J. Enrique Zanetti of the Army Chemical Warfare Service purchased the four pound British Mark II incendiary bomb and made some modifications and redesignated it the M50. The first 100 pound clusters of the M50 bombs arrived in England in 1942, but inspection showed a large number of defective M50s in early shipments, and a testing program had to be initiated to uncover the bad lots. Defective bombs were only part of the problem, as the 100 pound incendiary bomb adapter which clustered the M50s into a container was operationally unusable because of the hazard of released adapter parts hitting other aircraft in the formation, or sometimes the tail of the aircraft that released it, as was revealed on the Eighth Air Force's first use of incendiary bombs on 14 May 1943, when falling cluster parts damaged other planes in the formation. Trials also showed that any degree of accuracy was impossible with bombs released from their clusters at high altitudes. The Eighth Air Force then suspended the use of the M50 until aimable clusters arrived and used the M47 incendiary bomb. In January 1944 the M17 500 pound aimable quick opening cluster for the M50 bomb was first put into operational use and eliminated most of the problems inherent in those clusters, which made the M50 one of the most effective incendiary bombs of the war.

The AN-M50 A2 had a hexagonal magnesium alloy body, an iron nose plug, and a sheet metal tail. The bomb was 21.3 inches in overall length, 1.69 inches across the flats, and weighed 3.7 pounds. The main charge consisted of 1.25 pounds of magnesium alloy, which was the bomb body, and a core of 0.63 pound of Thermite. Upon impact the Thermite was ignited and burned for approximately 1.5 minutes, melting and igniting the magnesium alloy case, which burned for from four to six minutes longer. The M50 had high penetrability and burned intensively, which made it particularly suitable for use against construction in Germany, 95% of which was brick and stone. In this construction, fire divisions (the area which would be burned out by an unchecked fire) could be not only buildings but their individual rooms. The M50 had to have great penetrating power in order to pierce the heavy roofs, and because it was small meant that a bomber, in seeking out the numerous fire divisions, could carry many more than if the bomb were larger.

The AN-M50 XA3 was the same as the AN-M50 A1, except that the nose plug was replaced by a steel shell containing a delay fuse, a detonator, and a Tetryl bursting charge. This bomb burned for about 1.5 minutes, at which time the delay fuse was ignited. The burning fuse provided a delay ranging from a few seconds to several minutes and ignited the detonator, which exploded the charge and projected fragments of the steel shell and particles of burning magnesium. After the M50 was developed it virtually replaced the M47.

Issue

These bombs were issued only in clusters as described later.

Bomb, Incendiary, Oil, Six Pound, AN-M69

The AN-M69, initially designated as the M-56, was hexagonal, 19.5 inches in length, and 2.88 inches across the flats. It contained a main charge of 2.8 pounds of gelled gasoline and an ejection-igniter charge of 0.4 ounce of black powder and magnesium. The bomb, having a terminal velocity of 225 feet per second, was stabilized in flight by muslin streamers which, until release of the bomb from the cluster, were packed loosely in the tail cup. The bomb was fused with the M1 Fuse, which acted upon impact with a delay of three to five seconds delay. An ejection charge was ignited that expelled the incendiary material through the tail of the bomb. Thus, when the bomb came to rest it functioned like a small mortar; when flat on the floor it could eject flaming napalm as far as 100 feet until it struck an object in its path. The fragments of the charge burned for eight to 20 minutes, depending upon their size. The bomb itself was designed to be small so that a large number could be dropped at once and start more fires in more places, making fire fighting more difficult. Its case had to be light

Incendiary AN-M50 4 Pound Bomb

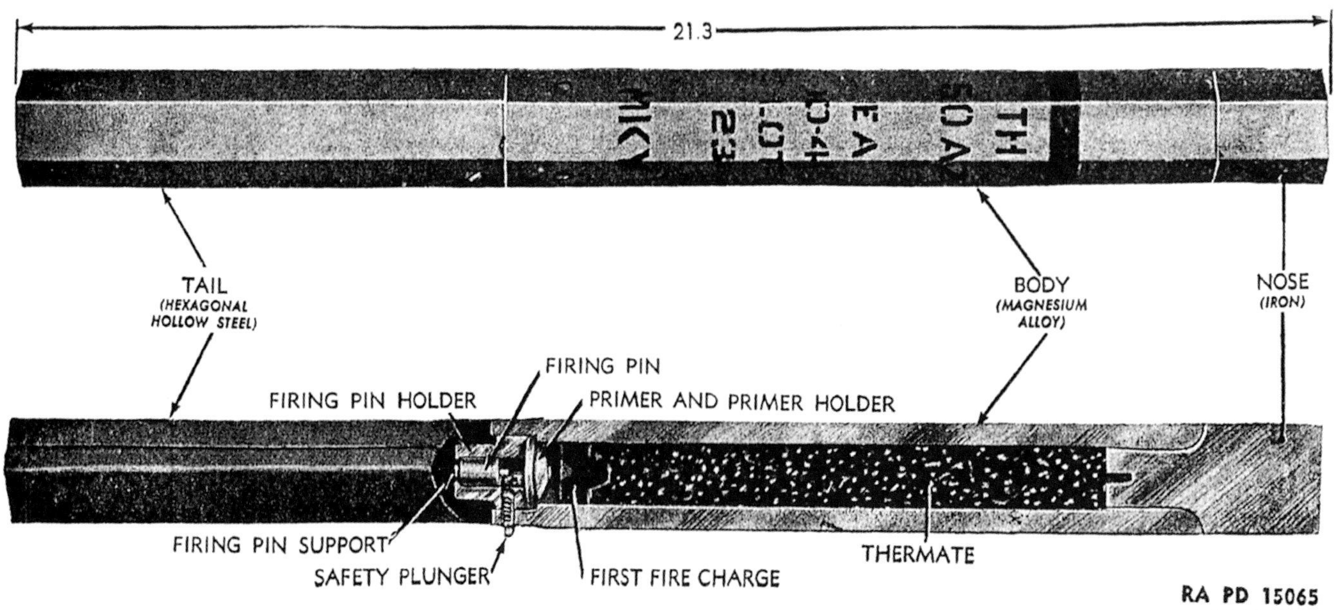

(TM 9-1980)

Incendiary AN-M50 4 Pound Bomb

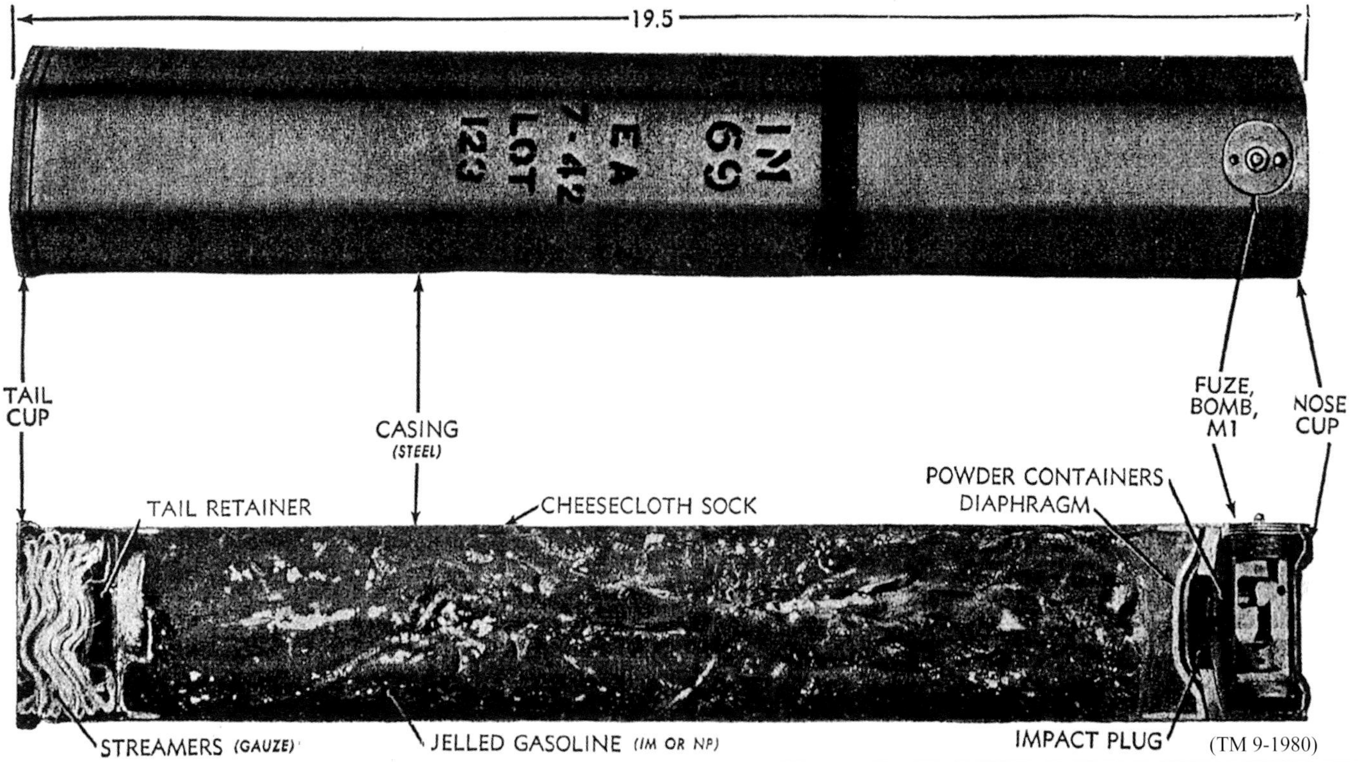

(TM 9-1980)

and thin, but strong enough to penetrate the roof, but not burst prematurely on hitting the roof and be able to propel its incendiary filling throughout the room in which it settled.

The hexagonal case was fabricated of sheet steel and was closed at the nose by a sheet steel nose cup and at the tail by a sheet steel tail cup. The charge of gelled gasoline was contained in a cheesecloth sock. The nose cup contained the fuse, the ejection charge, and a diaphragm. Upon functioning of the explosive train, the gel was ignited and ejected out of the tail of the bomb. The tail cup served as attachment and container for the streamers.

This bomb could also be filled with white phosphorous for use as an anti-personnel bomb to inhibit fire fighting.

Issue

The M69 was issued the Cluster, Incendiary Bomb, AN-M12 (100 pound) but also could be used in an aimable cluster.

Bomb, Incendiary, 100 Pound, AN-M47A2

It was not until 1940 that the AAC developed its first incendiary bomb, the 100 pound, a four feet long and eight inches in diameter M47 incendiary bomb. The Army Chemical Warfare Service filled a stock Chemical Bomb case with a gelatinous mixture created by the British that consisted of rubber, coconut oil, and lye blended with gasoline. Initially, the M47 was filled with straight gasoline or oil, but later a thickener was added. The M47 was the only available American aerial incendiary bomb at the time of Pearl Harbor, and it was in short supply throughout 1942. Late in 1942 Col. Crawford Kellogg located a supply of empty M47 bomb casings in Iceland and shipped them to the UK, and had 10,000 filled and assembled by Air Chemical Sections.

The advantages of the M47 were its aimability, penetrability, and its large 40 pound filling of incendiary material. But the M47 also had problems. Its suspension in the bomb bay allowed only one bomb to occupy the same space that could contain a much heavier bomb. By July 1943 the Air Chemical Sections supplied an in the field measure to resolve this loading difficulty. Bombs paired by the use of a cable loop-sling permitted the suspension of 42 M47s in a B-17 bomb bay, and the number of bombs falling together improved the bombing pattern. After Col. Harold Baum succeeded Col. Kellogg as 8AF Chemical Officer in 1943, he modified the loop-sling into a short cable toggling mechanism that allowed the suspension of 52 bombs in a bomb bay, making this huge cluster of M47s more aimable and creating a better bombing pattern.

In Spring 1943 Eighth Air Force headquarters called for mixed loadings of incendiary and high explosive bombs in a single bomber on operational missions. The VIII Bomber Command decided this request was impractical because uneconomical loads would result, and because of the danger of mixing the two bomb types in the same aircraft. Chemical Officers agreed with the Bomber Command on mixed loadings, but proposed new incendiary loads considering recent M47 developments. During the summer Col. Kellogg convinced Col. Curtis LeMay to authorize M47 incendiary loadings for trial missions against industrial targets in occupied France. Although there was a month long lack of M47 fuses for these trials, these missions conclusively established the effectiveness of incendiary bombing in general and the M47 incendiary bomb in particular. In October 1943, analysis of the results of the first major incendiary raid against a German factory (at Heddernheim) showed that the incendiaries were much more effective, weight for weight, than high explosives. For the following three months the M47 was the preferred incendiary bomb and maintaining a supply became a major problem, as all incendiary expenditures mounted from 408.2 tons in September 1943 to 1,292.6 tons in October, 2,382.9 tons in November, and 4,189.6 tons in December.

The heavy M47 easily penetrated most enemy roofs and just after penetration a burster charge would detonate, exploding the case and

In 1940 the AAC developed its first incendiary bomb, the 100 pound, four feet long and eight inches in diameter **M-47 incendiary bomb**. The Army Chemical Warfare Service filled a stock Chemical Bomb case with a gelatinous mixture created by the British that consisted of rubber, coconut oil, and lye blended with gasoline. (AAF)

Nose Section of a M-47 Bomb

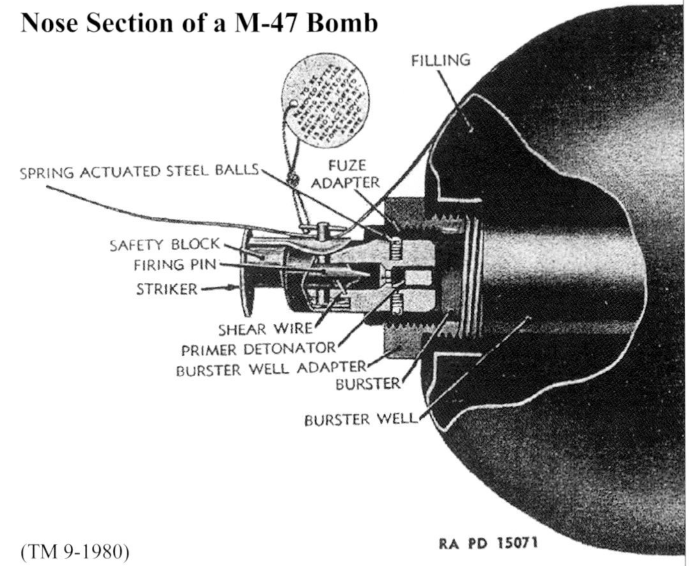

(TM 9-1980)

scattering a cone of flaming globs of gasoline downward and outward, scattering them over a 50 square foot area to burn for about 10 minutes. The resulting small fires were relatively easy to put out if they ignited surrounding structures. This bomb was used mainly by pathfinder forces, as it had a high "appliance fire value" and lit up an area quickly, especially congested highly inflammable areas. The M47 was initially used, as it was in stock, but after the M69 clusters became available it became the incendiary of choice.

The AN-M47A2 was loaded with a 40 pound charge of gelled gasoline IM or NP and the complete round weighed 69 pounds.

Authorized Fuses and Bursters

The AN-M13 burster and the AN-M9 Igniter were authorized for use in this bomb with incendiary filler. As originally designed this bomb was adapted for the M108 nose fuse. If the AN-M126 or AN-M126A1 fuse was available it was preferred to the M108.

Other models

Bomb, Incendiary, 100 Pound, M47A1, differed only in that the interior coating was acid proof paint instead of oil.

Bomb, Incendiary, 500 Pound, AN-M76

In direct contrast with the M50 was the AAF's largest incendiary bomb, the 500 pound M76, popularly known as the "Block Burner." The M76 was developed to meet the request for a large, highly aimable incendiary bomb for use against industrial targets. It contained incendiary gel (PT) which, upon the detonation of an explosive charge, was scattered in large gobs over a 100 foot radius. Although the M76 was first used against Berlin on 6 March 1944 with only moderate success, it was enough to merit priority shipment of these heavy incendiaries from the U.S. However, subsequent operations proved that the effectiveness of these bombs due to the low percentage of incendiary fuel as contrasted with the total weight of the bomb did not justify its further use. Also, there were relatively few targets against which it could be used. By September 1944 no future operational use of the M76 was anticipated, and most of the M76 bombs were returned to Air Force depots.

The AN-M76 consisted of the body for the 500 pound GP bomb modified for field assembly of a burster and igniter, and loaded with a gasoline gel-magnesium mixture. As released the bomb weighed 475 pounds, including 180 pounds of incendiary mixture.

Components of the 500 Pound, AN-M76

The complete round consisted of:

1) Bomb, incendiary, 500 Pound, AN-M76, unfused, without fuse seat liner, adapter-booster holder, igniter, burster, or fin assembly, in shipping bands, with nose and tail plugs and fin lock nut protector.
2) Nose and tail fuse.
3) Fuse seat liner which was packed separately in bulk.
4) Adapter-booster holder, with adapter-booster, M115 or M115A1, packed separately, 12 per box.
5) Igniter, AN-M5, packed separately, 5 per box.
6) Burster, AN-M14, packed separately, 40 per box.
7) Fin assembly for 500 pound GP bombs, AN-M64 and AN-M64A1, incendiary AN-M76 and chemical AN-M78, packed separately, one per crate.
8) Wire, arming, assembly packed 5 per can, 20 cans per box.

Authorized Fuses

The following fuses were used with this bomb: AN-M103 nose set for instantaneous action, and AN-M101A2 fuse with primer detonator, M14, non-delay. The M103 fuse, partially armed if necessary, could be substituted for the AN-M103, and the AN-M101A1 fuse could be substituted for the AN-M101A2. When an air burst was desired, the mechanical time, Ml27 fuse, with adapter-booster M117 could be used. TheM124 tail or M133 tail fuse could be used when required.

This bomb had ballistics that were similar to a GP bomb and was sometimes used with mixed loadings. It was utilized against soundly constructed buildings containing heavy machinery, and because the magnesium burned very brightly it was also dropped by pathfinders in built-up areas of poor inflammability as a marker. The bomb was not used very extensively.

Phosphorous Bombs

The "Kenney Cocktail" was an in-the-field invention of Gen. George Kennedy's 5AF, whose make up varied with the materials on hand. The first Cocktails were constructed of sheet metal with a full length burster well and were usually filled with Tetryl and phosphorous, while the common later version was a standard M47 incendiary bomb loaded with white phosphorous. Air bursts used standard 1,000 pound GP bombs with a special nose fuse that detonated above the ground. This fuse had a standard mechanical time flare fuse for the upper half and a GP nose fuse for the lower half. Since the fuse could be set for a range of five to 93 seconds the bombs could be dropped from various altitudes.

Detonation on hard surfaces under normal conditions resulted in a brilliant burst with a radius of 150 feet for the central portion, with streamers of hot phosphorous shooting in every direction for as much as 100 feet or more. Pieces of burning phosphorous could destroy vehicles, aircraft, and wooden buildings. These bombs were often dropped by the leading bombers to suppress AA fire on those aircraft following. The white smoke often lingered near the ground, blocking the vision of the enemy gunners, and was particularly feared by ground personnel, as it burned through flesh and could not be extinguished.

Bomb, Smoke, Phosphorous, WP, 100 Pound, M47A2
The M47A2 was loaded with a 100 pound charge of phosphorus and the complete round weighed 127 pounds.

Authorized Fuses and Burster
The M14 Burster was authorized for high altitude bombing, while the M18 Burster was authorized for low altitude bombing. The M7 Burster could be substituted for either. As originally designed, this bomb was adapted for the M108 nose fuse. If the AN-M126 or AN-M126A1 fuse was available it was preferred to the M108

Other Incendiary models
Bomb, Smoke, Phosphorus, WP, 100 Pound, M47A1, differed in that it carried a charge of 100 pounds of phosphorus and weighed 127 pounds.

"Homemade" Incendiary Bombs
In order to maintain the bombing campaign, when bomb supplies ran low armorers used their ingenuity and constructed effective homemade bombs using 55 gallon fuel drums filled with any inflammable material ranging from contaminated gasoline to old drained oil. Bomb fins were fabricated from wood or pieces of sheet metal. The igniter was a hand grenade wired so that when the barrel hit the ground its collapse would arm the grenade to explode.

Class C Fire Bombs (Napalm) for Bombers
A refined petroleum jelly known as Napalm became available during the second half of 1944. Handled in bulk, it was intended for filling as required. Tested in various containers, the preferred type was the paper composition fighter fuel tank of 108 U.S. gallon capacity. Known as Class C-Fire Bombs, Napalm tanks were used on a few special missions where blanket fire cover was required, notably against German strong-points on the French coast in April 1945. Usually six Napalm tanks were carried in a B-24 and four in a B-17; small incendiary igniter units were fixed to each tank.

"Kenney cocktails" were various bombs filled with phosphorous devised in-the-field by 5AF units. The common later version was a standard M47 incendiary bomb loaded with white phosphorous. (AAF)

The Incendiary Mission
Twenty to 30 minutes before the main bombing force left two homing aircraft from each Wing, carrying no bombs but the standard defensive armament, took off with additional fuel and radio equipment. They were to orbit the target at 25,000 feet, and expert radio operators were to direct the oncoming bombers. Three marker bombers from each group, modeled after the RAF Pathfinder bombers, also flew ahead. They were manned by the outstanding crews of the group and would set fires in a large "X" across the target area to mark four points in the 10 square mile target area. A number of lead bombers were loaded with Fragmentation and HE bombs with the intention of driving the populace and fire fighters to take shelter and prevent fire fighting. The Fragmentation Bombs were the T4E4, 500 pound cluster of 20 pound Fragmentation Bombs, and 260 pound Fragmentation Bombs, and the HE bombs were the 500 pound and 4,000 pound bombs instantaneously fused or with proximity fuses. The main force flew to the target aided by LORAN, and at about 65 miles from the Japanese coast the radar operators took over. The Bomb Wings climbed to their assigned bombing altitudes (specific 1,000 foot bands for each wing) at about an average altitude of 7,000 feet. When they neared the pathfinder fires they dropped their 500 pound firebomb clusters, not on the fires but adjacent to them. Each cluster was made up of 38 M69 incendiaries fused to separate at

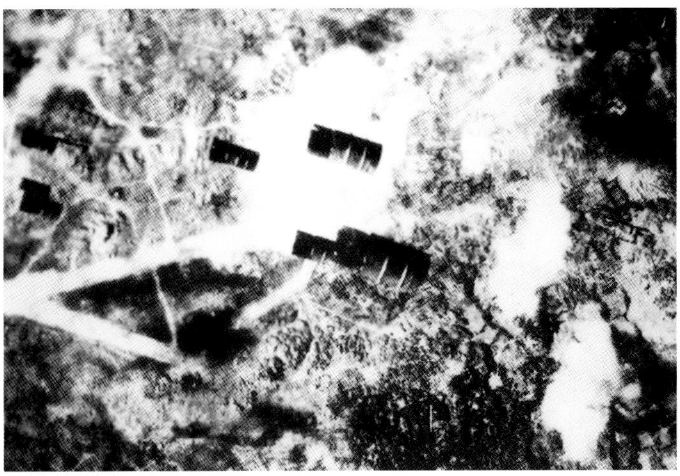

"Homemade" Incendiary Bombs (AAF)

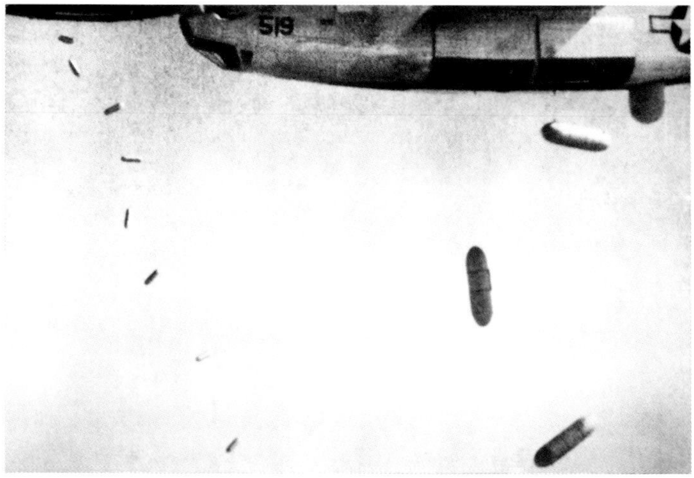

Class C Fire Bombs (Napalm) (AAF)

2,000 to 2,500 feet. The Intervalometers were set to space the release of the bombs and thus the impact point, so that the clusters exploded at 50 foot intervals. The bomb load of each bomber covered a rectangular area of 350 by 2,000 feet (about 16 square acres). The attack plans took into account the wind direction so that smoke would not cover the next areas to be bombed.

Fifteen major Japanese cities had more than 70% of their built up areas destroyed. The 20AF flew 6,960 sorties, dropping 41,592 tons of bombs on Japan's five largest cities. These cities (Kyoto was off limits) suffered 133,000 killed, 117,000 wounded, and 1.4 million homeless, and had 102 square miles burned out. Tokyo had 51% of its city area damaged and 87,000 killed and 60,000 injured, and almost 750,000 homeless. By August there were no more strategic targets remaining, as Japan's largest cities had virtually been burned to the ground, and then its secondary cities had been attacked and an additional 76 square miles of their built up areas was devastated. The fire bombing campaign certainly caused great destruction and suffering among the civilian population and lowered their will to resist, but the Japanese kamikaze/samurai psyche at high levels made surrender impossible. So, despite the debate that continues to rage to this day over the necessity of dropping the atomic bombs, they did give the Japanese government the reason to end the destruction and suffering caused by the incendiary raids.

Cluster Bombs and Adapters

General

A cluster adapter was a mechanical device by which several bombs were suspended in the carrying station for one bomb. There were three types: the Quick Opening (frame), Aimable Adapters, and Hook and Cable.

Function

A cluster adapter was a device by which two or more small bombs could be:

1) Held together for installation in a station for a single large bomb, thus providing for greater loading efficiency.

2) Released from the aircraft as a unit for area bombing rather than point bombing.

3) Released from the cluster to arm and fall separately after the cluster was released from the aircraft, thus providing more efficient coverage of a large target than was possible when small bombs were released individually.

Thousands of incendiary clusters made up of 38 **M-69** incendiaries rain down from B-29s of the XX Bomber Command. (AAF)

Tokyo had 51% of its city area damaged, 87,000 killed, 60,000 injured, and almost 750,000 homeless, while 15 major Japanese cities had more than 70% of their built up areas destroyed. Pictured is Hitachi, which was 78% destroyed. (AAF)

Fragmentation cluster opening from B-25 of the 41st Bomb Group over the Gilbert Islands. (AAF)

Construction

Generally, cluster adapters consisted of two or more longitudinal members for strength and rigidity, two or more cross members to hold the bombs in the correct position, and straps or wires to fasten the bombs in the cluster with a means to release them at the desired time. Three suspension lugs were attached to one longitudinal member to provide for single or double hook suspensions. Each lug was held extended by a cotter pin which could be removed to allow the lug to drop back into the cluster. The release mechanism was operated by withdrawing the arming wire.

Types

Quick Opening (Frame) Adapters

This type of Adapter consisted of a frame to which several bombs were attached by metal straps that formed an assembly that was suspended and released as a unit. The straps were fastened with clamps that were released by withdrawing the arming wire or by the action of a time fuse. The frame was also equipped with a fuse lock which prevented arming of the bomb fuses until after they were released from the cluster. When the armed cluster was released the arming wire was withdrawn and the clamp strap flew open and freed the strap, which then freed the bombs from the adapter. The strap springs aided in forcing the bombs away from the adapter.

Aimable Adapters

This type basically consisted of a streamlined metal body containing the clustered bombs, a fin assembly or other such types of stabilization, and a time fuse that opened the body and released the individual bombs at the desired time.

Hook and Cable

This type of adapter consisted of a set of hook and cable assemblies which suspended several bombs or clusters from the same station and a yoke and hanger assembly by which the arming wires of the individual bomb or clusters could be withdrawn or released as "safe" as desired.

Cluster and Frame Adapters for Incendiary Bombs

Adapter, Cluster, AN-M4

The M4 consisted of an upper and lower longitudinal member each 39.25 inches long, and two end plates each 7.75 by 8.38 inches. Attached to the upper member were three lugs for single and double hook suspension and four mechanical release buckles for the strapping bands. The M4 was used to assemble 14 Bomb, Incendiary oil, AN-M69, into Cluster, Incendiary Bomb, AN-M12.

Cluster, Incendiary Bomb, AN-M12

The M12 was a 100 pound size cluster consisting of 14 AN-M69 six pound incendiary oil bombs in an M4 Adapter, Cluster. It was 39.25 inches long and weighed 105 pounds.

The 100 pound cluster of six pound oil bombs was very successful against light, inflammable construction.

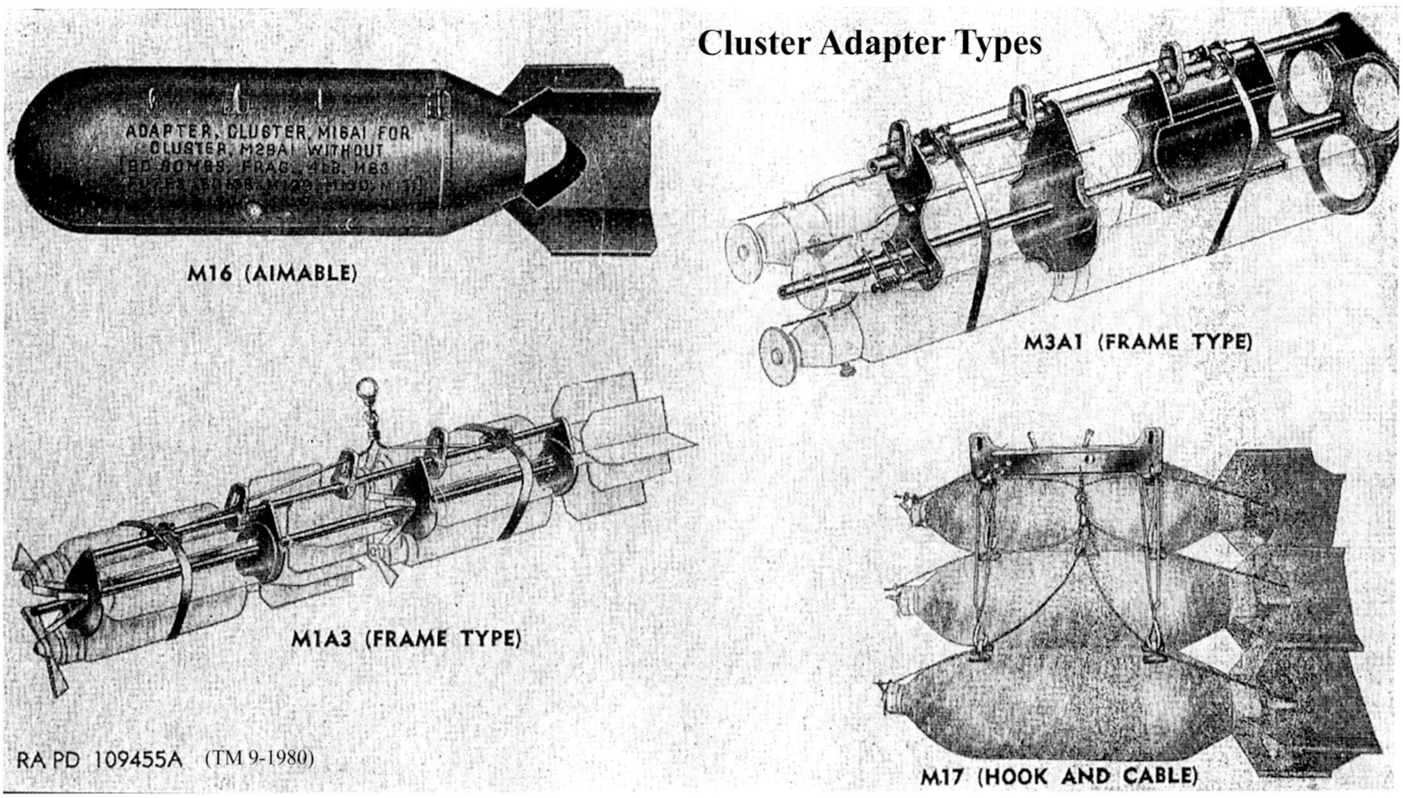

CLUSTER DATA

CLUSTERS

Cluster		Length	Weight	Cluster, Incendiary Bomb	Length	Weight (lb.)
Fragmentation	M1	46.75	125.0	AN-M6 (100-lb. size)	42.78	145
Practice	M2	46.75	124.0	M7 (500-lb. size)	42.78	540
Fragmentation	M1A1	46.6	125.0	AN-M12 (100-lb. size)	39.25	98
Practice	M2A1	46.6	124.0	AN-M13 (500-lb. size)	58.88	417
Practice	M4	31.0	87.2	M17 (500-lb. size)		462
Practice	M5	31.0	76.0	M17A1 (500-lb. size)		462
Fragmentation	M26	52.6	465.0			
Fragmentation	M27	56.0	585.0			
Fragmentation	M28	47.35	155.2			
Fragmentation	M29	59.37	415.1			

CLUSTERS

CLUSTER		BOMBS					ADAPTER	
Code	Model	Size	No.	Wt.	Model	Fuze	Model	Cartridge or Fuze
FRAGMENTATION BOMB CLUSTERS								
S1ZVB	M1	100-lb	6	20-lb.	M41	M110	M1	M6
S1ZVG	M1	100-lb.	6	20-lb.	M41	M110A1	M1	M6
S1ZVD	M1A1	100-lb.	6	20-lb.	M41	M110	M1A1	None
S1ZVH	M1A1	100-lb.	6	20-lb.	M41	M110A1	M1A1	None
S1ZVL	AN–M1A1	100-lb.	6	20-lb.	AN–M41	AN–M110A1	AN–M1A2	None
S1VAA	AN–M1A2	100-lb.	6	20-lb.	AN–M41A1	Unfuzed	AN–M1A3	None
S1ZVF	M4	100-lb.	3	23-lb.	M40	M104	M3	None
S1ZVK	M4	100-lb.	3	23-lb.	M40	M120	M3	None
S1ZVN	AN–M4	100-lb.	3	23-lb.	AN–M40	AN–M104	AN–M3	None
S1ZVO	AN–M4	100-lb.	3	23-lb.	AN–M40	AN–M120	AN–M3	None
S1VBA	AN–M4A1	100-lb.	3	23-lb.	AN–M40 AN–M40A1	Unfuzed	AN–M3	None
S1ZVQ	M26	500-lb.	20	20-lb.	AN–M41	AN–M110A1	M13 (T4E2)	M111,–A1,–A2
ø	M27	500-lb.	6	90-lb.	M82	AN–M103	M16 (T8)	M111,–A1,–A2

(TM 9-1980)

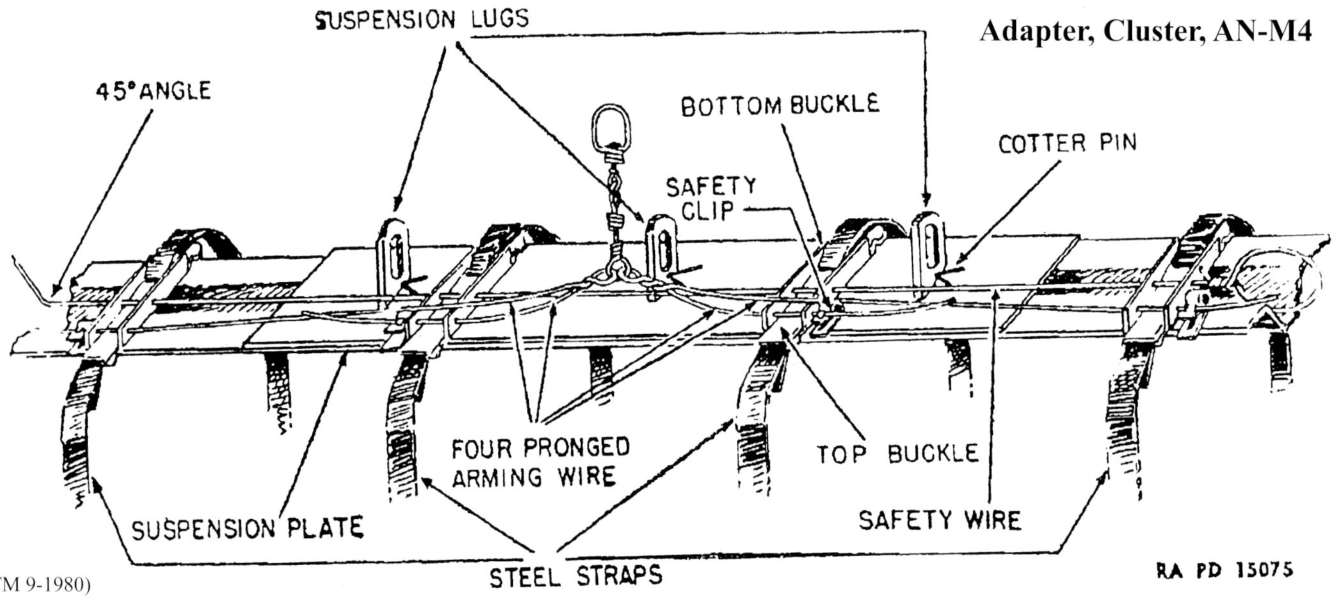

Adapter, Cluster, AN-M4

(TM 9-1980)

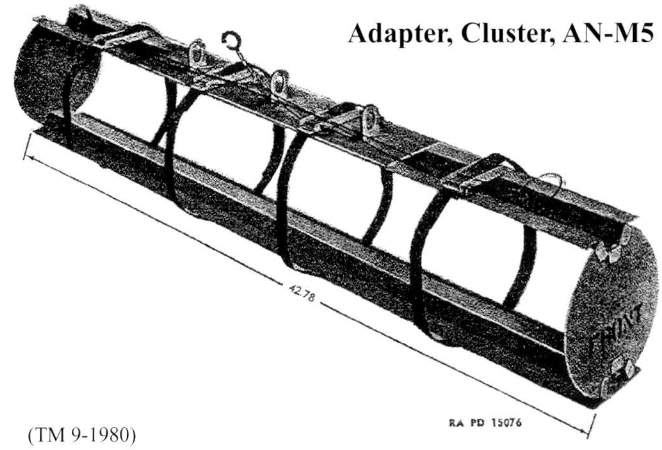

Adapter, Cluster, AN-M5 (TM 9-1980)

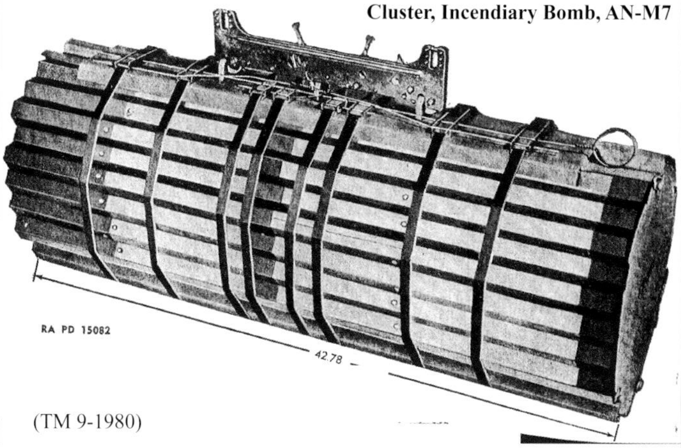

Cluster, Incendiary Bomb, AN-M7 (TM 9-1980)

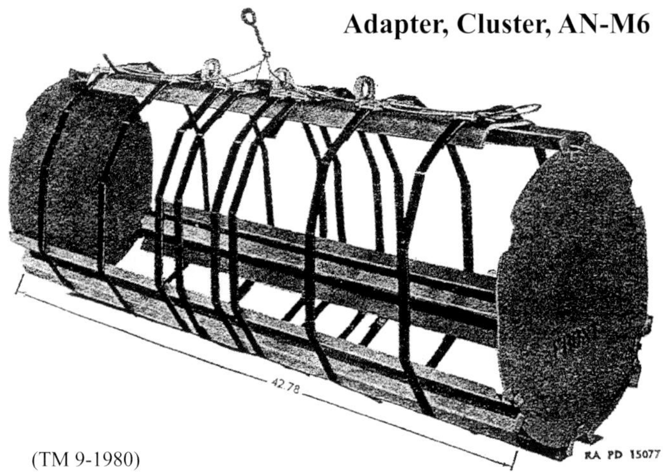

Adapter, Cluster, AN-M6 (TM 9-1980)

Cluster, Incendiary Bomb, AN-M6 (TM 9-1980)

Adapter, Cluster, AN-M5
The M5, formerly designated as the AN-M3, consisted of upper and lower longitudinal members 42.78 inches long and two end plates 6.75 inches in diameter. Three suspension lugs and six mechanical release buckles were assembled to the upper member. Six steel straps were locked in the buckles by a four branch arming wire. When used for two pound incendiary bombs this adapter had six straps and buckles, and when used for four pound bombs only four straps were used. The M5 was used to assemble 34 four pound incendiary bombs into Cluster, Incendiary Bomb, AN-M6.

Adapter, Cluster, AN-M6
The M6 was formerly designated as the Adapter, Cluster, 500 Pound Incendiary Bomb, Ml. This adapter consisted of one reinforced longitudinal member 42.78 inches long, three plain channel members of the same length, and two oval end supports 14.3 inches in vertical and 12.63 inches in horizontal diameter. The reinforced member had three suspension lugs and eight mechanical release buckles assembled to it. The three plain members were attached to the end supports at 5, 6, and seven o'clock in relation to the suspension member being attached at 12 o'clock. A four branch arming wire locked steel straps in the release buckles. The M6 was used to assemble 128 four pound incendiary bombs in Cluster, Incendiary Bomb, 500 Pound, M7.

Cluster, Incendiary Bomb, AN-M7
The M7 was a 500 pound size cluster consisting of 102 AN-M50 -A2 four pound incendiaries. It was 42.78 inches in length and weighed approximately 540 pounds. After the M69 was chosen for the bombing campaign on Japan the M50 was used mainly in the ETO in 500 pound clusters of 102 M50s.

Cluster, Incendiary Bomb, AN-M6
The AN-M6 was a 100 pound size cluster consisting of 28 four pound, AN-M50-A2 incendiary bombs in the Adapter Cluster M5. It was 42.78 inches in length and weighed 145 pounds. After the cluster was dropped an arming wire released the bombs from the cluster and they separated in descent. These Thermite/magnesium bombs would penetrate a roof and lay on the floor, where its filler would ignite and burn intensely, igniting the magnesium casing; the resulting fire would burn at 2400°F for five to seven minutes and was very difficult to extinguish. Bombs were used against heavily industrialized areas that contained machinery or machine tools. Some of these bombs also contained Tetryl explosive heads to discourage fire fighting.

Cluster, Incendiary Bomb, AN-M13
The AN-M13 was a 500 pound size cluster consisting of 60 AN-M69 six pound incendiary oil bombs in an M7 Adapter, Cluster. It was 58.88 inches long and weighed 417 pounds. The bombs were bundled in clusters in the bomb bay, and the clusters separated and the bombs fell free when released.

Cluster, Aimable, Incendiary Bomb (TM 9-1980)

The bomb's casing was without stabilizing tailfins and a three foot cloth streamer, much like a kite tail, was released after separation and stabilized the bomb, controlling the rate of descent. Once the bomb had penetrated the roof it had either come to a stop, laying on its side, or had embedded its nose in the floor. A delay fuse was activated, and after three to 5 seconds it detonated an ejection ignition TNT charge. The TNT explosion would cause the magnesium to ignite the gasoline gel contained in a cloth sock. The explosion of the ignited gel would blow the burning gel out the tail of the casing as far as 100 feet. The gel would burn for four to five minutes, and when in contact with combustible material would burn fiercely and tenaciously.

Cluster, Aimable, Incendiary Bomb, M14, M15, and 17A1
This type cluster was assembled in a closed adapter which resembled a bomb in shape. It contained 110 four pound incendiary bombs and was adapted for fuse, bomb, and mechanical time. The fuse was installed after the cluster was securely installed in the aircraft.

Composition of the various models:

Cluster	Size	Adapter	Bombs Held in Unit
M14	500lb	M10A1	110 AN-M50 T-A2
M17	500lb	M10	88 AN-M50 -A2 & 22 AN-M50 X-A3
M17AI	500lb	M10A1	88 AN-M50 -A2 & 22 AN-M50 X-A3

Quick Opening Frame Adapters for Explosive Bombs
Adapter Cluster, M1
The Ml was constructed of two longitudinal members of tubular steel and four sheet metal supports joining them. The lower member served as the backbone of the cluster. In addition to the four supports, two vane stops were welded to this member. These vane stops prevented the rotation of the fuse arming vanes while the bombs were still in the cluster. Suspension lugs were attached to the upper member, which was closed at the front end by a steel plug. Four holes were drilled through this member, and the wires binding the bombs to the adapter passed through these holes. A pressure relief hole was drilled near this nose plug. A cartridge firing a steel plug and a firing mechanism—containing a spring-loaded firing pin restrained by the arming wire—were installed to the rear end. When the armed cluster was released the arming wire was withdrawn, releasing the firing pin. The firing pin was driven by its spring into the primer of the cartridge, which fired the slug through the tube, cutting the wires that bound the bombs to the adapter. The M1 was used to assemble six fin type fragmentation or practice bombs in Cluster, Fragmentation Bomb, M1 or Cluster, Practice, Bomb, M2.

Adapter, Cluster, AN-M1A2
The AN-M1A2 resembled the Ml, except that instead of the cartridge type release it had a mechanical release. The bombs were bound to the adapter by metal straps that were held in place by a toggle type clamp that was held closed by the arming wire. When the arming wire was withdrawn the toggles opened and the bombs were released. Single and double suspension lugs were installed on the upper member. The AN-M1A2 was used to assemble six fin type fragmentation or practice bombs in the Cluster, Fragmentation Bomb, AN-M1A1 and Cluster, Practice Bomb, M2A1 respectively.

Quick Opening Frame Cluster, AN-M1

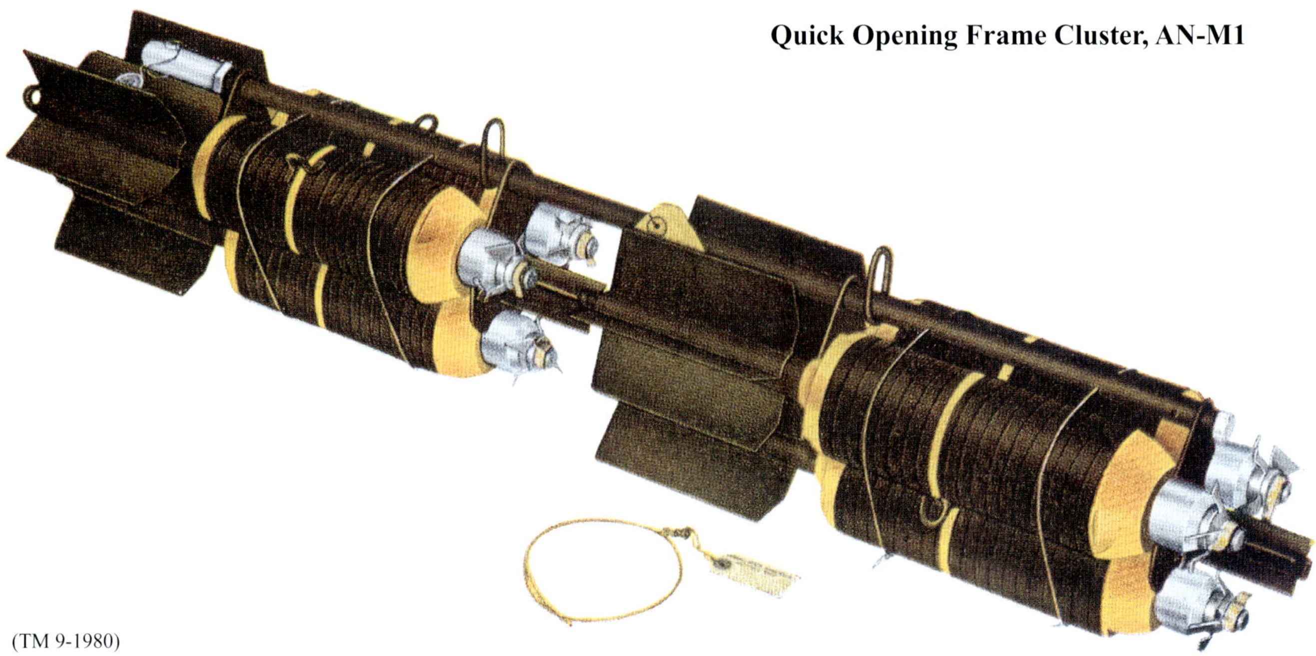

(TM 9-1980)

Adapter, Cluster, AN-M3

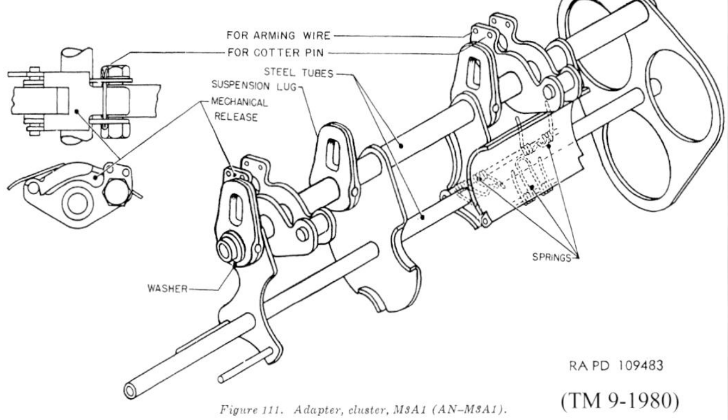

Figure 111. Adapter, cluster, M3A1 (AN-M3A1). (TM 9-1980)

Adapter, Cluster, AN-M1A3
This modification permitted the shipping of the clustered bombs unfused, with the fusing done in the field.

Adapter, Cluster, AN-M3
The AN-M3 consisted of two longitudinal members and three supports. The upper member carried two mechanical release mechanisms and three lugs for single and double suspension. The lower member carried five springs that aided in separating the bombs when they were released from the cluster. The AN-M3 was used to assemble three parachute type fragmentation or practice bombs in Cluster, Fragmentation Bomb, AN-M4 and Cluster, Practice Bomb, respectively.

Adapter Cluster, M12
This adapter consisted of two hook and cable assemblies, with each assembly consisting of a harness hook with a 4.5 inch loop of steel cable attached. The adapter was used to suspend two 100 pound bombs or clusters from a single station. Before the first bomb was installed, the loop of wire was placed over each suspension lug before the shackle was attached. The hook of each cable was then snapped to a suspension lug of the second bomb or cluster. The arming wire swivel looped from both bombs, or clusters were attached to the arming hook of the shackle.

Adapter, Cluster, M13
This adapter resembles the M14, except that it was arranged to suspend 20 twenty pound bombs in two banks of 10 bombs each. It was used to assemble 20 Bomb, Fragmentation, 20 Pound, AN-M41 in Cluster, Fragmentation Bomb, M26. Fuse, flare, mechanical time, M111A2 was used to provide delayed opening of the cluster.

Adapter, Cluster, M14
The M14 cluster adapter was designed for either immediate or delayed opening. The adapter consisted of two longitudinal steel tubes to which four sheet steel plates were welded to form nose and tail supports for two banks of three bombs each. The lower member served as backbone for the cluster and carried a fuse vane stop for each bank of bombs. The upper member carried a pair of suspension lugs, a hoisting lug, two buckles for holding and releasing the steel straps holding the bombs in the cluster, and the adapters for nose and tail fuses. The suspension and hoisting lugs consisted of U-shaped shackles, with the bolt held in place by a cotter pin. When suspension from single-hook racks was required, the hoisting lug was removed and replaced by one of the suspension lugs. The release mechanism consisted of a toggle type buckle. Delayed opening of the cluster was by a shear wire, and when the cluster was to discharge the individual bombs the shear wire was cut off after the arming wire was installed.

Adapter, Cluster, M15
This adapter was a cylindrical sheet metal case which opened longitudinally to discharge 24 four pound Fragmentation Bombs. The case was hinged at the rear and was held closed by a nose cup that was opened by the action of a time fuse. Double suspension lugs were attached to bulkheads and passed through the cover. When single hook suspension was required, the outer double lugs were pushed down into the case and the single lug was attached with the screws. The cluster was issued with the bombs installed and the nose locking cup wired in place.

Adapter, Cluster, M16
This adapter resembled the M15 except in size. It was used to assemble 90 four pound Fragmentation Bombs in Cluster, Fragmentation Bomb, M29.

Aimable Adapters
Aimable adapters resembled a conventional bomb body and box fin. The case was cylindrical and constructed of steel parts consisting of upper (cover) and lower halves that were hinged on the rear and could be opened longitudinally. Double suspension lugs were attached to the bulkheads and passed through the top cover of the case. A square sheet metal drag plate was screwed over the rear end of the fin assembly to slow the descent of the adapter. A round sheet metal spoiler ring contained one central hole large enough to accommodate the threaded end of a nose fuse and a smaller hole through which the arming wires passed. When the cluster was released armed the arming wire was withdrawn from the time fuse, allowing the fuse to arm. When the time set on the fuse elapsed the fuse functioned and blew the nose cup into the adapter, permitting the cluster to open and disperse the bombs.

Cluster, Fragmentation Bomb, M1
The Ml (100 pound size) used six 20 pound fused AN-M41 Fragmentation Bombs and was installed by using the Adapter, Cluster, M1. It was 46.75 inches long and weighed 125 pounds. This cluster was provided with lugs for double hook suspension only. The release mechanism operated by means of a cartridge and firing mechanism.

Cluster, Practice Bomb, M2
The Ml (100 pound size) used six 20 pound fused AN-M48 practice bombs and was installed by using the Adapter, Cluster, M1. It was 46.75 inches long and weighed 125 pounds. This cluster was provided with lugs for double hook suspension only. The release mechanism operated by means of a cartridge and firing mechanism.

Cluster, Fragmentation Bomb, AN-M1A1
The Ml (100 pound size) used six 20 pound fused AN-M41 Fragmentation Bombs and was installed by using the Adapter, Cluster, M1A2. It was 46.75 inches long and weighed 125 pounds. This cluster was provided with lugs for single and double hook suspension. The release mechanism operated mechanically.

Cluster, Practice Bomb, M2A1
The Ml (100 pound size) used six 20 pound fused AN-M48 practice bombs and was installed by using the Adapter, Cluster, AN-M1A2. It was 46.75 inches long and weighed 125 pounds. This cluster was provided with lugs for single and double hook suspension. The release mechanism operated mechanically.

Cluster, Fragmentation Bomb, AN-M1A2
This cluster was a modification of the AN-M1A1 with the bombs shipped unfused and the fuses shipped hermetically sealed in individual containers in the same box.

Cluster Fragmentation Bomb AN-M4

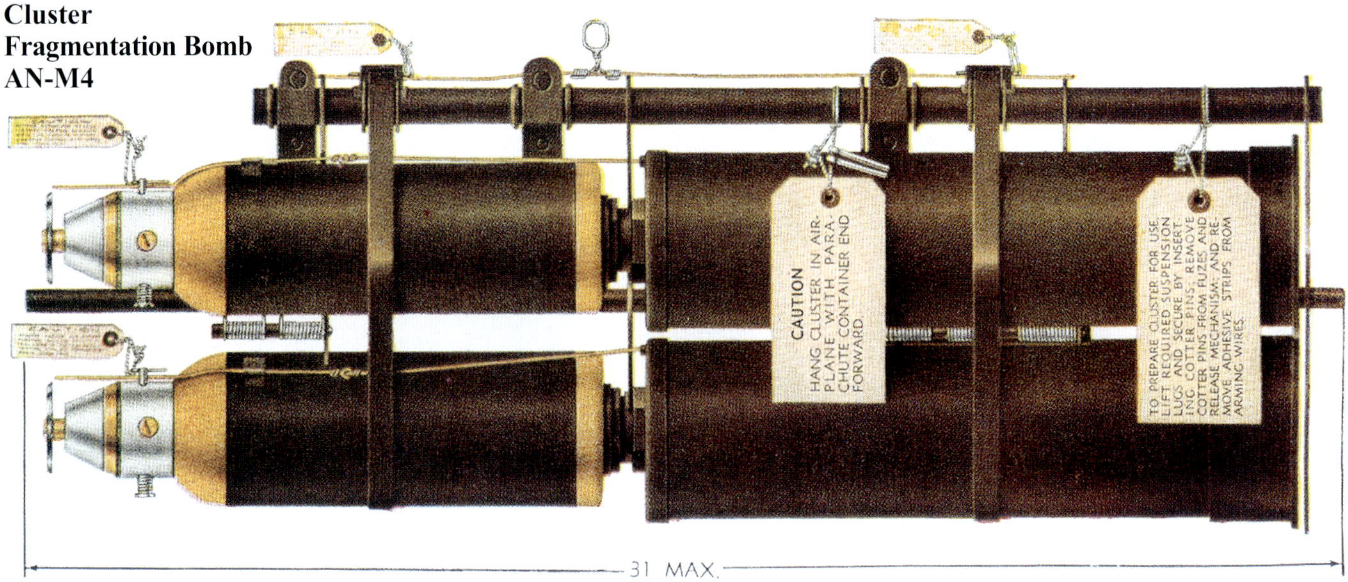

(TM 9-1980) RA PD 15080

Cluster, Fragmentation Bomb, AN-M4 and AN-M4A1
This 100 pound size cluster used three 23 pound AN-M40 or AN-M40A1 fused Fragmentation Bombs. It was installed using the Adapter, Cluster, AN-M3, which was of the mechanical release type. The cluster was 31 inches long and weighed 87.2 pounds, and was provided with lugs for single or double hook suspension. When issued with the bombs unfused this cluster was designated as the AN-M4A1. The bomb body and Parachute B unit were installed with the three bombs bound in the cluster by the two steel straps fastened in place by cotter pins in the outer eyelets in the buckles. The arming wire was then inserted with one branch through the inner eyelets of each buckle and a safety clip placed on each end.

Cluster, Practice Bomb, M5
The 100 pound size M5 used three 23 pound M71 practice bombs and was assembled in the field, and the assembled cluster was 31 inches long and weighed 76 pounds.

Cluster, Fragmentation Bomb, T4E3
The 500 pound size T4B3 used twenty fused 20 pound AN-M41 Fragmentation Bombs and was assembled by using the Adapter, T4E3. The cluster could be set for immediate or delayed opening. When immediate opening was required the shear wires were cut off close to the release mechanisms and the fire branch of the arming wire was cut off close to the swivel loop. When delayed opening was required a mechanical timer was installed in the adapter. When the fuse functioned it blew a steel slug through the horizontal member, shearing the wires and thus allowing the release mechanisms to open and discharge the individual bombs.

Cluster, Fragmentation Bomb, T8
The T8 was a 500 pound size cluster of six 90 pound T8 Fragmentation Bombs assembled with the Adapter, Cluster T3. This cluster could be adjusted to discharge the individual bombs immediately or, by the action of one or two mechanical time fuses, to discharge the bombs 5 to 92 seconds after release of the cluster. The assembled cluster was 56 inches long and weighed approximately 585 pounds.

Cluster, Fragmentation Bomb, T8

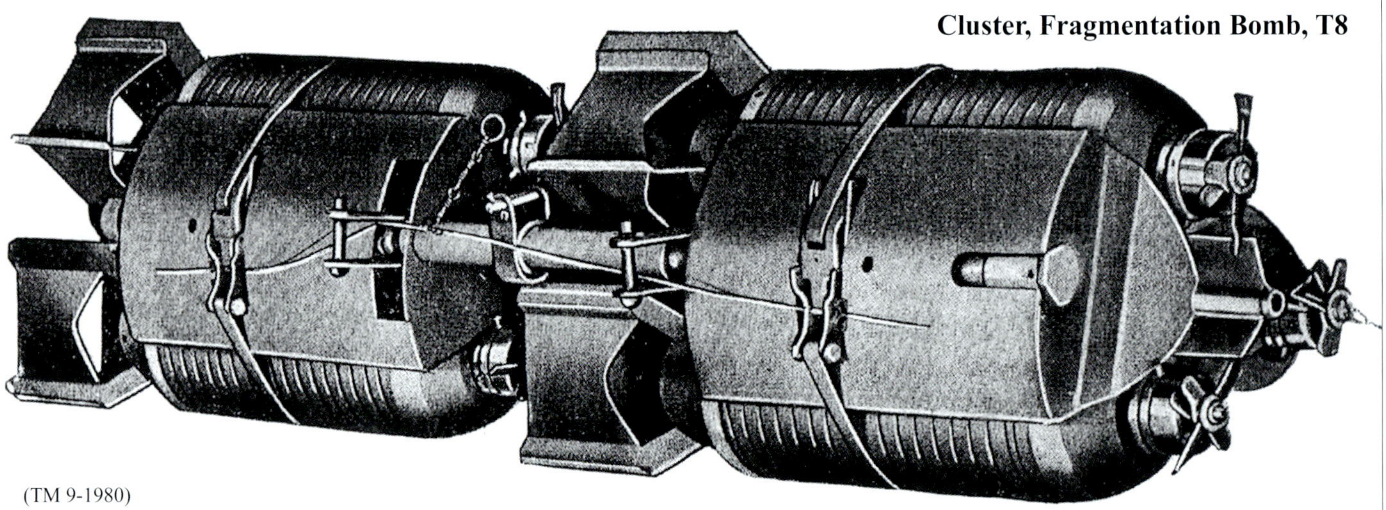

(TM 9-1980)

Fragmentation Bombs Insert Wafers

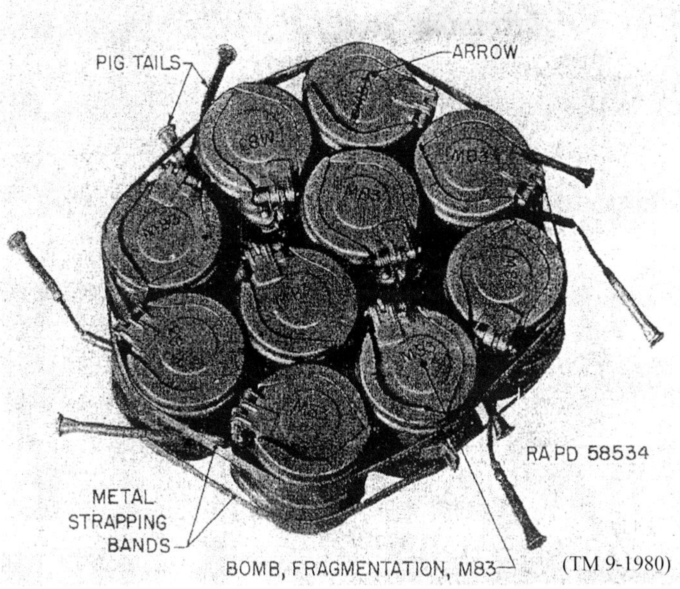

(TM 9-1980)

Cluster, Fragmentation Bomb, M29

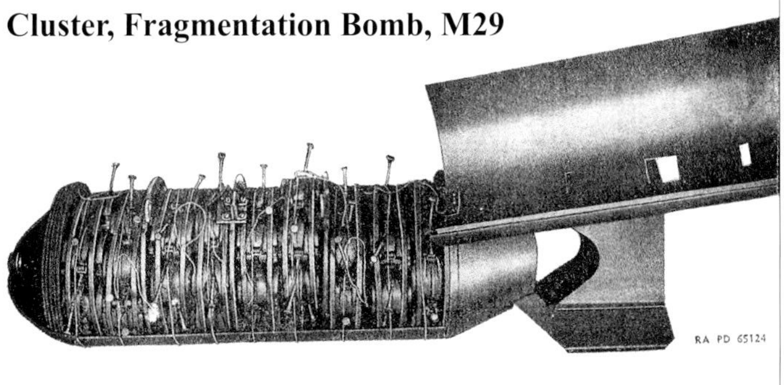

Figure 136. CLUSTER, fragmentation bomb, M29, open. (TM 9-1980)

Cluster, Fragmentation Bomb, M28
This cluster consisted of an Adapter, Cluster, M15, containing 24 four pound M83 Fragmentation Bombs arranged in eight banks of three bombs each. It was adapted for fuse, flare, and mechanical time, with the fuse used indicated in the marking on the cluster. The cluster was issued assembled except for the nose fuse.

Cluster, Fragmentation Bomb, M29
The 500 pound bomb cluster M29 consisted of 90 cylindrical-shaped, four pound M83 Fragmentation Bombs assembled in the M16 cluster adapter, each equipped with a case assembly (butterfly wings) and with a M129, T48, or T49 fuse. The M29 had a hinged top cover with nine partitions inside the body to insert wafers of M83 four pound fragmentation bombs. Each round wafer contained a circle of ten bombs (eight outside and two inside).

The fuse was set into the bomb body and had a cable extension on which the bomb case assembly (butterfly wings) was mounted. When the bomb was released from the cluster the butterfly wings were opened by spring action and were forced by the airstream to the top of the cable extension. In this position the butterfly wings retarded the fall of the bomb and started to rotate. The rotation turned the cable and withdrew the arming stem and armed the bomb. Because of the great dispersion when released from high altitudes the M29 Cluster was to be dropped from 2,000 to 5,000 feet with a fuse setting of five to eight seconds.

Hook and Cable Adapters

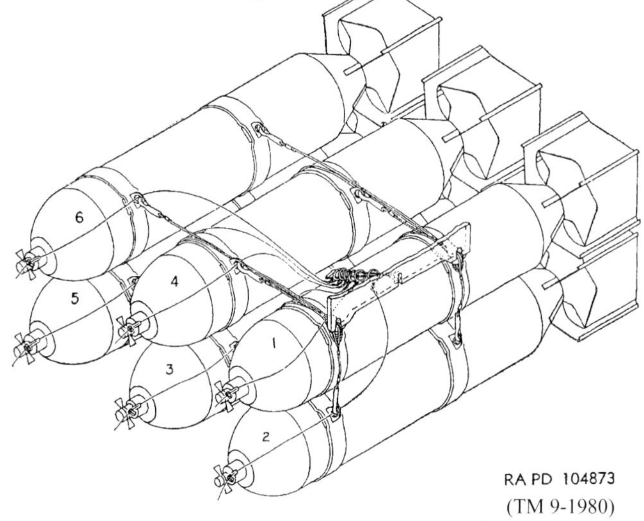

(TM 9-1980)

Hook and Cable Adapters
Hook and cable adapters differed from the quick opening (frame) adapters and aimable adapters by functioning as a method of hanging more than one bomb or one cluster of bombs from one shackle. A hook and cable assembly consisted of a loop of wire stranded cable to which a harness-type snap hook was attached. The bombs dropped in these clusters (100 or 200 pound) were assembled and fused like those for a single suspension. However, the swivel loops of the arming wires were not placed in the shackle, but were placed over the stirrup-shaped wire hanger that connected to the shackle. Once the hook and cable clusters were released all items (bombs or clusters of bombs) in this adapter fell freely as the cables remained attached to the shackle. When the cable cluster was dropped armed the stirrup (hanger) was not released by the shackle, but the hanger held the arming wires that were withdrawn from the fuses, thus arming the fuses.

Adapter, Cluster, M12
This adapter consisted of two hook and cable assemblies comprising of a harness hook with a 4.5 inch loop of steel cable attached. The M12 was used to suspend two 100 pound bombs or clusters from a single station.

Adapter, Cluster, M13
The M13 suspended 10 twenty pound M41 fragmentation bombs in two banks of ten bombs each. It was made up of two longitudinal steel tubes to which four sheet steel plates were welded to form nose and tail supports for two banks of ten bombs each. The lower member served as the backbone for the cluster and carried a fuse vane for each bank of bombs. The upper member carried a pair of suspension lugs, a hoisting lug, two buckles for holding and releasing steel straps holding the bombs in the cluster, and adapters for nose and tail fuses,

Adapter, Cluster, M14
The M14 closely resembled the M14 and was designed for either immediate or delayed opening of two banks of three bombs each.

Adapter, Cluster, M17
This assembly consisted of four hook and cable assemblies and an arming wire assembly consisting of a hanger assembly and three arming wires. The M17 was used to suspend three 100 pound bombs or clusters from a single station.

Adapter, Cluster, M18

The M18 consisted of two hook and cable assemblies, with each assembly consisting of a hook with a loop of wire stranded cable. This adapter was used to suspend two 250 pound bombs or clusters from a single station.

Adapter, Cluster, M24A1

This adapter consisted of two sets of five separate hook and cable assemblies and one hanger assembly with six arming wires (all color coded). This adapter was used to suspend six 100 pound nose fused bombs or clusters from a single station.

Statistical Summary

Number and Tons of Conventional Bombs Dropped by Theater and Aircraft

AAF Number of Bombs Dropped By Theater 1943-45*

Bomb Type vs Germany	vs Japan	Total	
High Explosive	**7,952,020**	**6,284,271**	**1,667,749**
4,000lb	1,220	----	1,220
2,000lb	64,962	48,575	16,387
1,000lb	753,167	564,969	188,198
500lb	3,695,468	3,089,916	605,552
250lb	1,328,458	1,055,289	272,169
100lb	2,102,186	1,520,209	581,977
Fragmentation (Ind.)	**327,322**	**206,179**	**121,143**
260lb	328,877	198,758	120,119
90lb	1,861	1,696	165
30lb	5,829	5,435	394
Fragmentation (Cluster)	**1,157,591**	**768,929**	**388,662**
540lb	4,666	3,976	690
480/400lb	18,030	2,884	15,146
360lb	3,442	3,279	163
120lb	1,025,128	756,304	268,824
60lb (parachute)	104,401	1,979	102,422
Incendiary (Ind.)	**1,762,889**	**868,972**	**893,917**
500lb	64,208	33,905	30,303
250lb (British)	11,612	11,612	----
100lb	1,669,044	806,394	862,560
100lb (White phosphorus)	16,162	15,259	903
Incendiary Cluster	**649,911**	**270,723**	**379,198**
512lb	5,873	1,283	4,590
440lb	360,440	267,023	93,417
360lb	4,469	----	4,469
338lb	9,516	----	9,516
228lb	255,073	----	255,073
136lb	7,788	874	6,914
84lb	4,675	----	4,675
Class C Fire	**36,928**	**12,200**	**24,718**
165/150lb	16,312	1,426	14,886
110/100lb	8,088	6,793	1,295
75/70lb	10,022	3,971	6,041
50lb	1,720	10	1,710
Armor-Piercing	**1,126**	**1,126**	**----**
1,600lb	1,122	1,122	----
Semi-Armor-Piercing	**53,521**	**47,135**	**6,386**
1,000lb	22,528	16,200	6,308
500lb	30,993	30,915	78

* 1,000 bombs or more only

AAF Tons of Bombs Dropped by Theater 1/41 to 8/45

Theater	1941 (Dec)	1942	1943	1944	1945 (Jan-Aug)	Total
ETO	----	1,713	55,655	591,959	322,435	971,762
MTO	----	4,410	98,462	346,993	132,836	582,701
Total	----	6,123	154,117	938,952	455,271	1,554,463
POA	----	35	1,309	17,546	13,843	32,733
FEAF	36	2,633	29,705	92,134	107,988	232,496
CBI	----	697	10,841	27,987	22,636	62,161
Alaska	----	715	2,828	295	493	4,331
20AF	----	----	----	9,064	161,996	171,060
Total	36	4,080	44,683	147,026	306,956	582,781
Total	36	10,203	198,800	1,085,978	762,227	2,057,244

AAF Tons of Bombs Dropped in the ETO by Aircraft Type

Aircraft	1942	1943	1944	1945	Total
Heavy Bomber					
High Explosive	1,713	40,479	389,099	192,850	624,141
Incendiary	----	6,973	57,066	26,539	90,578
Total	1,713	47,452	446,165	192,850	714,719
Medium & Light Bomber					
High Explosive	----	8,153	93,272	62,385	159,858
Incendiary	----	26	351	3,952	4,329
Fighter-Bombers					
High Explosive	----	24	52,171	40,661	92,856
Incendiary	----	----	577	3,672	4,249
Total by Year	1,713	55,655	591,959	322,435	971,762
High Explosive Totals					872,606
Incendiary Totals					99,156

USN Bomb Tonnage Expenditure by Bomb Type, Aircraft Type, and Year

	Carrier-Based				Land-Based		
Bomb Type	**1942**	**1943**	**1944**	**1945**	**1942**	**1943**	**1945**
100# GP	40	115	2,036	3,598	31	475	815
250# GP	0	0	1,281	927	0	83	2,982
500# GP	192	639	7,914	12,878	101	1,347	7,482
1,000# GP	279	426	3,944	1,336	182	2,555	7,652
2,000# GP	0	223	1,119	558	0	2,192	815
500# SAP	0	0	624	160	0	0	93
1,000# SAP	0	113	1,401	209	0	0	294
AP	0	10	264	29	0	0	7
260# Frag	0	2	335	957	0	48	1,257
Totals	511	2,039	18,918	20,652	314	6,700	21,397

Note: No Figures available for Land-Based A/C 1944

Heavy bombs received scant use by the Navy in 1945, except in the heavy anti-shipping strikes of January and July. In the latter month armored warships were the principal targets and 21% of total tonnage consisted of 1,000 or 2,000 pound bombs.

BOMB DATA

Bomb			Body			Charge			Complete Round	
Type	Weight	Model	Length (in.)	Diameter	Weight (lb.)	Type	Weight (lb.)	Percentage	Length (in.)	Weight (lb.)
G.P.	100	AN-M30, -A1	30.0	8.18	101.0	AM 50-50	54.2	51.0	38.46	108.0
G.P.	250	AN-M57, -A1	36.9	10.93	240.0	AM 50-50	122.5	49.0	47.8	252.0
Demo	300	M31	40.16	10.9	262.0	AM 50-50	137.0	50.0	51.0	274.0
G.P.	500	AN-M43	46.9	14.18	489.0	AM 50-50	262.0	52.0	59.16	508.0
		AN-M64, -A1	47.1	14.18	492.0	AM 50-50	262.0	51.0	59.16	512.0
G.P.	1,000	AN-M44	53.1	18.8	965.0	AM 50-50	530.0	53.0	69.5	994.0
		AN-M65, -A1	53.3	18.8	970.0	AM 50-50	530.0	53.0	69.5	999.0
G.P.	2,000	AN-M34	71.0	23.29	2,004.0	AM 50-50	1,061.0	53.0	92.83	2,049.0
		AN-M66, -A1	71.0	23.29	2,008.0	AM 50-50	1,061.0	53.0	92.8	2,053.0
L.C.	4,000	AN-M56	94.9	34.25	4,087.0	AM 50-50	3,245.0	77.3	117.25	4,201.0
A.P.	1,000	M52, -A1	50.5	12.0	1,049.0	D	58.0	5.4	71.0	1,078.0
S.A.P.	500	AN-M58A1, -A2	47.2	11.8	4,885.0	AM 50-50	144.5	29.0	57.8	502.0
S.A.P.	1,000	AN-M59, -A1	57.3	15.1	970.0	AM 50-50	303.0	30.5	70.4	990.0
A.P.	800	M61	38.6	12.0	824.0	D	32.68	3.8	58.72	853.0
A.P.	600	M62 and Mods	47.0	10.0	606.0	D	33.61	5.5	62.1	634.0
A.P.	1,400	M63	45.74	14.0	1,363.5	D	35.0	2.4	69.1	1,412.0
Depth	650	AN-Mk. 29	42.25	17.7		TNT	464.0	71.0	70.0	657.0
Depth	325	AN-Mk. 17	31.14	15.0		TNT	243.0	75.0	52.5	345.0
A.P.	1,000	AN-Mk. 33	59.75	12.0	991.0	D	140.0	14.0	73.0	1,008.0
A.P.	1,600	AN-Mk. 1	68.9	14.0	1,575.0	D	216.0	14.0	83.5	1,590.0
Depth	350	AN-Mk. 47		15.375		TX	252.0	71.1	53.1	355.0
Depth	325	AN-Mk. 41	68.9	15.375	1,575.0	TNT	227.0	68.9	53.1	330.0
Practice Target	100	M75	47.0	8.0	29.0	Hematite	72.0		47.0	101.3
Incendiary	4	AN-M50A2	13.356	1.69		TH	.63		21.3	3.6
						Mg	1.25			
Incendiary	4	AN-M50XA2	13.356	1.69		TH	.58		21.3	
						Mg	1.25			
						Tetryl	X			
Incendiary oil	6	AN-M69	19.5	2.88		Black powder	0.016		19.5	6.1
						Mg	0.011			
						Gel	2.6			
Incendiary	10	M74								
H	100	M47A2	46.88	8.125	26.0	Burster	2.4		48.92	98.0
						H	68.5			
Incendiary	100	M47A2	46.88	8.125	26.0	GA	39.0		48.92	68.1
WP	100	M47A2	46.88	8.125	26.0	WP	100.0		48.92	129.5
WP	100	M47A1	46.88	8.125	26.0	WP	103.6		48.92	133.1
H	100	M47A1	46.88	8.125	26.0	H	73.0		48.92	102.5
Chemical	100	M47	46.88	8.125	17.0	GA	39.0		48.92	59.0
H	115	M70	40.4	8.1	119.5	H	60.6		49.4	126.0
Incendiary	500	AN-M76	45.3	14.2	431.0	PTI	180.0		59.2	475.0
Chemical	500	AN-M78	47.5	14.2	464.0	CG	205.0		60.7	488.0
					359.0	AC	100.0			383.0
Chemical	1,000	AN-M79	53.6	18.8	904.0	CG	417.0		70.9	939.0
					687.0	AC	200.0			722.0
Fragmentation	20	AN-M41	11.31	3.64	17.9	TNT	2.7		21.8	19.8
Fragmentation	23	AN-M40	11.31	4.35	17.9	TNT	2.7		29.5	24.7
Fragmentation	23	M72	11.37	4.35	17.9	TNT	2.7		31.26	24.6
Fragmentation	90	M82	20.5	6.0	80.6	TNT	11.4	13.0	28.0	85.7
Fragmentation	260	AN-M21	34.1	8.1	252.0	TNT	34.8	13.0	43.7	261.5
PF		M46	45.25	8.0	51.0	PF	25.0		48.64	51.9
FL		M26	46.0	8.0	51.5	Flare			50.0	52.5
Practice	3	Mk. 5-1	8.25	2.5	3.0	Signal, AN-Mk.4	0.13		8.25	3.5
Practice	20	M48	11.31	3.64	15.2	Black powder	0.13		21.8	19.7
Practice	23	M71	11.37	3.64	15.2	0	0	0	26.77	21.0
Practice	23	M73	11.37	3.64	15.2	0	0	0	28.53	21.1
Practice	100	M38A2	47.5	8.125	15.7	Black powder	3.0		47.5	100.0
						Sand	80.0			
Target	100	M75	47.0	8.0	36.5	Burster, M4			47.0	101.3
						Hematite	72.0			

3

Bomb Handling and Release and Control Mechanisms

Development

Before 1936 the AAC secured guns, ammunition, and bombs from the Ordnance Department, which stationed Ordnance Service Companies at airfields to prepare, maintain, and repair ordnance and deliver it to combat units. The squadrons put munitions aboard their aircraft and cleaned and maintained their own guns. After transfer of AAC stations to Gen. Andrews' control in 1936, ordnance personnel at the fields became part of the 10th Ordnance Service Company, commanded by Lt. Col. Russell Maxwell, Andrews' Ordnance Officer. The 10th OSC consisted of six platoons, one stationed at each Air Force station.

Bombardment squadrons used 100, 300, 1,100, and 2,000 pound bombs, which the Ordnance Department shipped to the airfields. Demolition bombs arrived filled with TNT, but practice bombs (mostly old demolition bombs) arrived unfilled. Generally, the receiving ordnance platoon added a small amount of black powder in these practice bombs as a "spotting charge" and filled the steel cases with sand to the weight of service bombs. The platoon also attached fins, installed suspension lugs, and inserted fuses. Attack and pursuit units used small bombs of 17, 30, or 100 pounds designed for fragmentation, demolition, smokescreens, mustard gas, or other chemicals.

In July 1935 Capt. Charles De Shields, Armament Officer of the 59th Service Squadron at Langley Field, moved bombs and ammunition to Richmond for a mobility test with the 96th Bombardment Squadron. His stock for the exercise consisted of nine 2,000 pound bombs, eighteen 1,100 pound, and twenty-seven 600 pound, plus seven 140 pound boxes of machine gun ammunition. He and his section (four noncommissioned officers and 20 privates) hauled the sand-filled bombs to Richard Byrd Field by truck, set up a bomb dump, and moved the bombs to the flight line as needed by nine aircraft of the 96th Squadron. De Shields' unit moved each bomb into position on the flight line or in the dump by fastening a rope to it and dragging it along the ground. The 96th used slings and hoists to lift bombs into aircraft, having no special tools, equipment, or mechanical devices of any kind. Since they were testing bomb mobility, not practicing bombing, the bombs were removed from the bombers by the squadron before takeoff. De Shields and his men then took them back to the dump to practice 13 more missions from Byrd Field. He relied on sheer manpower to lift bombs into and out of 1.5 and 2.2 ton trucks to move them from place to place. To raise a bomb from the ground to the truck bed, his men leaned two nine foot long channel irons against the end of the truck and slid the bomb up. Some men pulled on a 0.25 inch manila rope from the truck bed while others pushed from the ground. The trucks had no bracing or other means to keep the bombs from rolling and shifting, which often damaged the fins. To unload the truck, the men used the rope to let the bombs slide down the channel iron. The mobility tests determined that a truck with a boom and hoist and trailers were required to carry bombs efficiently in combat conditions. The new bomb hauling equipment was developed at Langley Field.

In 1937, Col. Russell Maxwell established the School of Aviation Ordnance at Langley Field, which was directed by Capt. Edward Mechling. The school gave students training in supply and maintenance of ammunition, assembly and delivery of ordnance materiel to combat units, and inspection and repair of armament. The early two month classes enrolled about a dozen ordnance officers from various bases who would return to their bases to teach after graduating.

In December 1938 Capt. Mechling, now with the Ordnance Department, conducted bomb handling exercises at Langley Field using newly developed equipment and techniques. A squadron of nine B-17s and two squadrons of B-18s commanded by Col. Carl Connell, based at Mitchel Field, flew two missions with demolition bombs to targets on Plum Tree Island. Brig.Gen. Arnold Krogstad, 2nd Wing CO, decided to use the entire bomb allotment, and the Ordnance Department shipped more than 300,000 pounds of bombs of various sizes (100 to 2,000 pounds) to Langley Field. Capt. Mechling's unit removed the bombs from the railroad cars, took them to storage areas, prepared them for use, and delivered them to the aircraft. Throughout the exercise the unit used 34 trailers pulled two at a time by Prime Movers (trucks and a few light tractors). A railway track-laying tractor with a crane was used for lifting bombs on and off trailers and moving them at storage sites. However, the men continued to do much of the lifting by hand, which was made easier by the low beds on the new trailers.

Bomb and Fuse Handling and Storage

Care and Precautions in Handling: Bombs

Bombs were packed to withstand all conditions that would be ordinarily encountered, but general precautions were necessary to insure that bombs would be serviceable when required for use:

1) Ground crews were to be trained with drill bombs and inert components before attempting to handle service ammunition.
2) Bombs and bomb components were to be stored as shipped, and those items shipped separately were to be stored separately.
3) Bomb packing boxes were not to be opened until the items were required for use or inspection. Complete rounds were not to be assembled in advance of requirements.
4) Partly used boxes were to be resealed, marked, and kept on top or in front of the pile, and the partly used boxes were to be used before opening

other boxes. Damaged containers were to be repaired or replaced, with care given to transferring the markings to the new parts of the container. Packing boxes were not to be opened, repaired, or replaced within 100 feet of a magazine or other store of explosives.
5) Those rounds prepared for use but not used were to be disassembled and returned to storage in their packing containers and resealed with adhesive tape.
6) Assembled rounds were to be carried with sealing wires and safety pins in place at all times up to the time of installation in the aircraft. The arming wire was to remain in place until the bomb was released, or until the safety pins and sealing wire were replaced and secured.

Care and Precautions in Handling: Fuses
1) Fuses were packed in sealed moisture proof containers which were not to be opened until they were required for use. Fuses unpacked and not used were to be repacked and resealed with adhesive tape.
2) Fuses were to be protected against shock, moisture, and high temperature. Boxes were to be lifted or wheeled and not dropped, slid, rolled, or walked on the corners or struck, as in lining up a stack. They were to be shaded from the direct rays of the sun and protected from other sources of high temperature.

Bomb and Fuse Storage and Maintenance
Explosives and ammunition were to be stored in an area reserved for that purpose and were to be located away from operating areas, inhabited areas, public roads, and by distances prescribed in TM 9-1900. This TM also stipulated that each type of ammunition was to be stored separately and in quantities small enough to prevent sympathetic detonation of surrounding stores if a stack or magazine were to explode. Smoking, carrying matches or other flame-producing devices, use of lights other than an approved type, accumulation of inflammable trash or dead vegetation, and hunting were forbidden in storage areas. Ammunition and explosives of any one size and type were to be stored in as many separate storage units as storage facilities permitted, and in no circumstance was the entire supply of any one size and type to be concentrated in one place.

Bomb Storage
The preferred method of storage determined the separation of bombs by type, with only one type being stored in a magazine or igloo at one time. However, in conditions that did not permit individual storage of bombs by type Amatol, Explosive D, Picratol, and TNT-loaded bombs could be stored together. Such storage was permitted provided the quantity/distance regulations outlined in TM 9-1900 were observed and all requirements for each type were met. General Purpose, Armor Piercing, Semi-Armor Piercing, Depth, or Light Case Bombs could not be stored with another type of ammunition or explosives. Bombs shipped with fuses in the same container would ordinarily be stored as shipped. However, for long term depot storage fuses were to be removed from bomb containers and stored separately. Bomb storage areas were to be located at greater than missile distances from artillery ammunition storage. Bombs were to be stored on steel dunnage (storage) stacks that were electrically connected and grounded, and the use of inflammable (i.e. wood) dunnage for bombs was to be avoided. Photoflash bombs were not to be stored with any other type of ammunition, except when the total amount of explosive was less than 1,000 pounds of photoflash bombs and small arms ammunition stored together.

Fuse Storage
Fuses were to be stored in dry, well-ventilated places and were to be protected against sun, excess moisture, and heat. Fuses could be stored with primers, primer-detonators, detonators, boosters, bursters, and small arms ammunition. Under conditions of limited storage, if the total amount of

Large crane lifting 500 pound bombs by shipping bands from a railway car. (AAF)

Crane adaptation on bull dozer body lifting 1,000 pound bombs by lugs into piles in 1,000 pound bomb storage area. (AAF)

Bomb storage areas weren't usually located this close to airfields (390BG/Framington). In this storage area 250 pound bombs are stored in front and 500 pounds in rear. (AAF)

explosive in one location was less than 1,000 pounds fuses could be stored with fixed ammunition. Chemically actuated fuses containing ampoules, which could initiate, directly or indirectly, explosives and explosive-loaded components, had to be stored separately, as did all chemically actuated fuses assembled with ampoules containing acids as the reaction media. Chemically actuated fuses not containing acid-filled ampoules and not containing explosives and explosive-filled components in the normal train could be stored with non-chemical fuses only in accordance with regulations prescribed in the Ordnance Safety Manual.

Inert Component Storage

Fin assemblies, empty bomb bodies, arming wires, and similar inert components could be stored in any area that provided protection against the weather.

Bomb Delivery and Loading

Background

Once the war started new bomb handling equipment had to be developed to reduce bomb loading time intervals as much as possible. Partially loaded bombers sitting on the ground were vulnerable to attack by enemy bombers and fighters, and any hit by an enemy bomb would cause the damage to be multiplied by the explosion of "friendly" bombs waiting to be loaded. Quick bomb loading was essential on days when multiple missions were flown and when reconnaissance missions discovered targets, such as enemy shipping or armor, that required a mission be sent out as soon as possible before the targets escaped or were camouflaged.

The early tear drop-shaped bomb was not easily handled, but ballistic research had shown that the tear drop shape was not essential for streamlining and that cylindrical bombs were just as accurate, much easier to manufacture, and were easier to handle. The new bomb handling equipment was developed for delivering all sizes of cylindrically shaped bombs to the bombers.

Bomb Loading Equipment

The bomb service truck was a standard one ton truck chassis with no cab, mounting a winch and crane that extended over the rear of the truck bed. The M5 bomb trailer was a three-wheeled, 2.5 ton capacity vehicle used for transporting bombs from storage. Up to six M5s could be towed in a train, and each weighed 7,200 pounds fully loaded. The bomb trailer had a lunette (vaulted roof) attachment for towing behind the bomb service truck. It was equipped with channel irons to provide rigid seats for each bomb on the trailer and with a chest to carry fuses, while fin posts for the bomb fins were mounted externally on these chests. Steel bomb cradles also were carried on the trailer to keep the bomb from resting on the ground after it was removed from the trailer and before it was loaded into the bomb bay. The bomb lift truck for moving the finned and fused bomb under the airplane was a modified form of the common garage mechanic's hydraulic jack, with three rubber-tired wheels and a hydraulically operated platform for raising bomb and cradle.

Despite the equipment's relative simplicity, much training was necessary to insure smooth co-ordination under all operating conditions. An aviation ordnance man spent his first month in infantry basic training and then trained in the various special ordnance fields, such as Ammunition, Welding, Vehicle Mechanics, etc. The Ammunition Section had the responsibility for delivering all bombs and ammunition to the aircraft. Bombs were difficult to handle because of their weight and their potential to explode during handling. Teamwork and constant practice was stressed for all Ammunition Section men.

The basic operating unit in an Ammunition Section in an Aviation Ordnance Company was the Bomb Service Crew, which consisted of five men: a Crew Chief and four munitions personnel. Five men were considered the optimal number no matter if the bomber was light, medium, or heavy, since bombs could only be loaded one at a time into the aircraft. Finned and fused bombs could only be delivered to the bomber as fast as the crews could load them. However, once new fuse types were available it was no longer necessary to fuse all bombs as a safety precaution before they were delivered to the aircraft.

Bomb Delivery: From Dump to Aircraft

The bombs were loaded onto the bomb trailers by tractor cranes maneuvered by skilled and coordinated operators. The "bomb dump" was to be located away from the airfield but within easy driving and transporting distance on all-weather roads. Due to safety requirements, the bombs were to be stored in many small piles, rather than a few large ones. Sand bag revetments were then placed on three sides of the piles and the whole area was to be camouflaged if it was to be a semi-permanent location.

The bombs were transported to the dunnage area, where they were separated according to sizes of bomb and were positioned perpendicular to the roads in order to facilitate the loading and unloading of trailers. The bottom bombs were placed on blocks and the others blocked on top of them; their ends without fuses or fins, which were shipped separately to prevent damage during handling. The bombs were then inspected for correct lug spacing, correct fuse threading, and general condition.

To transport a bomb from the dump to the aircraft a steel channel ramp was placed in the rear of the M5 trailer and the bomb was man-handled up this ramp to its correct position by crews using two-man steel bars. Chains were used to secure the bombs to the trailer. As many as six M5s could be towed in a train. After arriving at the bomber, the Bomb Service Crew loosened the chains and placed the channel ramp and a cradle in position to slide the first bomb off the rear of the trailer. Two men immediately placed fins and fused the bomb while two others slid the next bomb off the

M-5 Bomb Trailer carrying four 1,000 pound bombs in photo was a three-wheeled, 2.5 ton capacity vehicle used for transporting bombs from storage. (AAF)

The **Bomb Service Truck** was a standard one ton truck chassis with no cab, mounting a winch and crane that extended over the rear of the truck bed. (AAF)

The **2,000 pound bomb** required special handling, as it was removed from the bomb trailer and placed on a cradle by the bomb service truck and moved under the bomb bay for hoisting. (AAF)

trailer. As soon as the first bomb was finned and fused it was inspected by the Crew Chief and then was lifted by the hydraulic lift truck and pushed under the plane for loading into the bomb bay.

The 2,000 pound bomb required special handling. Instead of sliding it down the ramp, the bomb service truck was detached from the trailer and backed to the trailer's side, and the bomb was lifted by a winch from the channel and suspended in the air. The bomb service truck driver moved slowly forward about 20 feet while two crew members walked along with the bomb to keep it from swinging or turning. A cradle was placed on the ground under the bomb and the bomb gently lowered onto it. Nose and tail fuse, arming wire, and fin were then placed on the bomb while it was in this position. Before rolling the lift truck under the bomb and cradle, the Crew Chief inspected the entire assembly to see that the arming wire had been cut to the right length, the fuses set correctly, and the fin set at the correct angle to correspond to the type of aircraft.

A M-5 trailer could hold a maximum 6,000 pound load for one bomber. With B-17s the trailer could be backed right under the bomb bay, but for B-24s, with their bomb bays close to the ground, it was necessary to offload the bombs onto special steel cradles. These were then picked up on a hand jack trolley that was similar to the hand jack used in automotive shops and maneuvered under the low bomb bay. Bomb fins had been fitted at the hard stands before the bombs were winched into the bays. Once the bomb was moved in place under the bomb bay it was ready for hoisting into the bomber by the bomber crew (to be discussed later).

Bomb Transport and Assembly

Assembly of complete rounds was to be done in an area located at a safe distance from explosives and operations areas as specified by appropriate AAF commanders. At the distribution point, all of the necessary bomb components were loaded on the bomb service truck and bomb trailer and transported to the assembly point. At the assembly point components were removed from their packing and inspected. Nose and tail fuse hole plugs were removed and the cavities and threads inspected. The shipping wire of the fin lock nut was cut and the nut removed from the bomb tail. The fin assembly was then attached with the fins in proper alignment and the fin lock nut tightened securely with proper fin lock nut wrench and fastened in place with set screws (earlier models were not provided with set screws and could not be locked in place). Bombs were installed in the aircraft, and then their fuses were assembled to the bomb as prescribed. When the space in the bomb bay was limited fuses were assembled in the bomb before the bomb was moved into the aircraft.

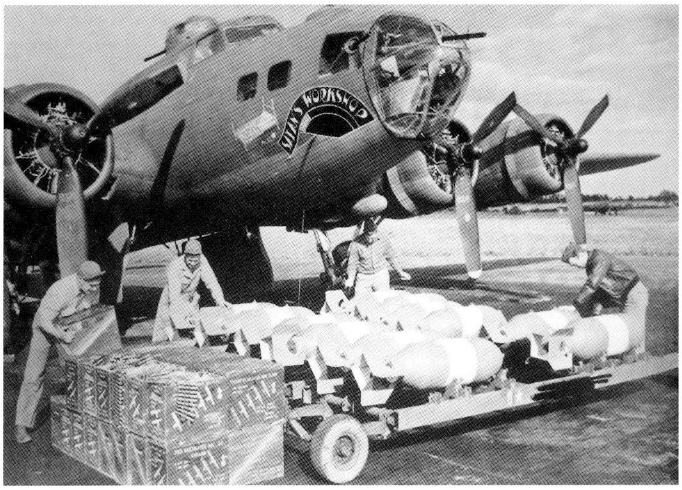

Above: Bombs could be loaded directly into the B-17. (AAF)

To load the low slung B-24, bombs had to be unloaded from the M-5 bomb trailer and then placed on a hand truck to be hoisted into the Liberator bomb bay. (AAF)

Hand Truck (Author/Palm Springs AM)

In attaching the tail fin, the fuse hole plug was removed and the fin assembly was then attached with the fins in proper alignment and the fin lock nut tightened securely. (AAF)

Destruction of Unserviceable Material

"Unserviceable material" was to be destroyed by authorized and experienced personnel in accordance with the provisions of TM9-1900. Bombs weighing more than 100 pounds could not be destroyed without authority from the Chief of Ordnance. Duds were destroyed by personnel specially trained in bomb disposal activities.

Safe Altitudes and Distances

Altitudes and distances safe from fragmentation and blast were specified y the AAF Chief of Staff and FM 1-110.

B-17 Bomb Bay (Author/CAFAZ)

B-29 Bomb Bay (Author/Pima ASM)

Interior construction of B-25 (L) and B-17(R) bomb doors. (Both Author/CAFAZ)

Bomb Bay

A bomb bay was enclosed by the bomb bay doors and contained the bomb hoisting equipment and one or two pair of racks, depending on the size of the aircraft. Each rack held a number of stations (usually five), again depending on the size of the bomb bay. Each station consisted of a bomb release unit and a bomb shackle. The stations were numbered consecutively beginning from the bottom position of Rack 1, reading from bottom to top in succession through the numerical sequence of racks and ending with the top position of Rack 2 (or Rack 4 in large bomb bays with a pair of racks). These shackles were removable from the rack and were supported at each end by spring latches that were permanently fastened to the bomb rack beams. The stations were connected together by a linkage system by which the bomb release unit were set or fired in selective or salvo position. The linkage system passed from the bottom station of each bomb rack up to one arm of a bellcrank located on the forward side of the aft bomb rack beam. A short linkage connected to bellcranks on the right and left bomb rack.

Bomb Bay Doors

The opening of the bomb bay doors increased drag and reduced the bomber's airspeed anywhere from eight to 12 mph, which increased the bomber's vulnerability to enemy interceptors and anti-aircraft fire. Most doors (B-17, B-25, and B-26) were of the standard clam shell configuration—opening and closing on hinges—but Consolidated Aircraft fitted their B-24 and B-32 bombers with flexible corrugated doors that rolled up the side of the aircraft on rollers along a curved track. However, these rollers were subject to freezing at high altitudes, and in early Liberators the bombs sometimes dropped through the doors. Bomb bay doors could be opened either electrically, hydraulically, or pneumatically.

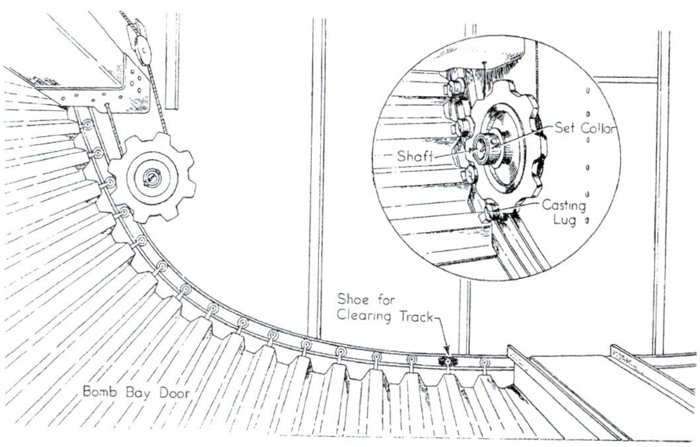

Most bomber doors (B-17 electric motor-driven closer shown on left) were of the standard clam shell configuration, opening and closing on hinges, but Consolidated Aircraft fitted their B-24 bombers with flexible corrugated doors that rolled up the side of the aircraft on rollers along a curved track. (Author/CAFAZ and B-24 E&M Manual)

Electric Doors

Bomb bay doors were operated by electric motors mounted in the bomb bay. The motors drove retracting screws, two on each end of the bomb bay. Power for this mechanism was supplied through central gearboxes to which

the retracting screws attached. Two solenoids, one for retraction and one for extension of the bomb bay door, controlled each motor. Torque was applied to the operating shaft that extended between the two forward retracting screws by an electric motor-driven unit mounted on the bomb bay truss. A shaft from the forward gear unit extended aft along the bomb truss to supply torque for the two retracting units. A link at the front of a bomb bay door operated a mechanical interlock on the bomb release control mechanism in the LOCK position until the bomb doors were open. A latch connected the retracting screws to the bomb bay doors to permit emergency opening of the doors.

Hydraulic Doors

A toggle switch on the bombardier's panel electrically controlled the hydraulic operation of the doors when the bombardier's master circuit switch was ON. When the switch was turned to OPEN it actuated the master selector valve solenoids and the valve directed fluid into the doors OPEN position. The fluid flowed through bomb door restrictors that metered the fluid into four hydraulic motors. These motors opened the doors and were stopped by a microswitch when each bomb door was fully open. Limit switches on each door prevented bomb release until each door was completely opened. Normally, the bomb bay doors operated automatically by hydraulic power as the controls were moved to the operating position. In the event of hydraulic pressure failure the bomb bay doors could be cranked open manually. The bomb bay doors could also be opened by the action of the salvo switches on the bombardier's panel and on the rear bulkhead of the flight deck. If the electric circuit failed the doors could be opened or closed by manual operation of the main selector valves.

Pneumatic Doors

Pneumatic doors literally snapped open and closed, and were used on the B-29 to maintain its aerodynamics. The air pressure for the system was provided by two compressors and was stored in the accumulators. The doors were actuated by the bombsight and snapped open immediately prior to bomb release. This made the bomber more stable on its bombing run, as there was no vibration as was the case in the slowly opening electric or hydraulic doors. In addition to the bombsight salvo switch, the bombardier had a bomb door selector switch that enabled him to open forward and aft doors together or only the aft door. The bombardier's panel had two indicator lights showing which doors were open, and another light that warned when the doors were not latched. The airplane commander had two switches mounted on the aisle control stand that opened and closed both sets of doors simultaneously. There were two emergency pull handles for opening the bomb bay doors; one was located at the airplane commander's station and the other just aft of bulkhead 218. In later B-29 models there were two emergency pull handles for closing the bomb bays. There were electrical safety shut off valves and safety switches to keep the doors opened or closed. The snapping pneumatic doors could be hazardous to maintenance crews, and if the bomb bays were to be left open on the ground the valves were to be closed and the switches turned off. But the ground crews did not trust the safety valves and switches and often placed a 2x4 plank to be certain to hold the bomb bays open. If the bay doors were to be tested on the ground it was suggested that a guard be posted to be sure no one entered them.

Bomb Hoisting and Bomb Loading

Preloading Inspection

The preloading inspection always was to be completed just before the bombs were loaded on the bomb racks and with no droppable bomb bay fuel tanks in place. The Crew Chief was to check the condition of the batteries before the battery power was turned ON, and if the voltage was low an outside source of power was to be used, as the release units would not operate properly on low voltage. The bombing system was inspected for binds and the retainer levers

The pneumatic doors of the B-29 literally snapped open and closed, and were used to maintain the Superfortress' excellent aerodynamics. The doors were actuated by the bombsight and snapped open immediately prior to bomb release. (Author/Pima ASM)

on the bomb shackle support hooks were inspected for proper condition of the engaging spring and the shackle support hooks inspected for security of bomb attachment. All bomb release units were checked for secure attachment to each bomb station to be used and that the racks were clean.

Inspections were done at the various bomb control handle settings. The arm safe levers of the bomb release units were checked in the SELECTIVE setting. They were carefully cocked by moving them first to the rear safe position and then the release lever was cocked by moving it to the forward position. The bomb control handle was then moved to the DOOR OPEN position (the racks were locked in this position) and then all bomb stations were inspected for locking by attempting to turn the tripping screw on each bomb release unit with a screwdriver. A release check screw with an arrow indicating the direction to turn to release the unit was provided on the face of each bomb release unit. The station was not to release during the check. The bomb control handle was then moved to the SALVO position and a test was made to check that the release levers at all stations were released. A number of checks were made with the bomb control handle again in the SELECTIVE position. To determine if the arm safe and the release levers tripped simultaneously, the bomb stations were manually released by turning the tripping screw on each bomb release unit with a screwdriver. All indicator lights were checked again in the SELECTIVE mode. If the indicators did not light the bomb release units and auxiliary switch boxes were checked for proper installation. Finally, it was necessary to determine if each station released and the corresponding indicator lights were extinguished each time the bomb release switch was tripped.

Hoisting Equipment

Type C-3 bomb hoist assemblies were installed on the exterior of the fuselage adjacent to the bomb bay when hoisting bombs. Bomb hoisting diagrams, charts, loading instructions, and adjustment and inspection instructions were included in a folder that was stowed in a holder in the bomb bay. The hoist assemblies were usually stowed in the floor of the forward part of the bomber. 1,000 and 2,000 pound bombs were not to be lifted with the Type C-3 bomb hoist unless the braking device was installed.

Loading Bombs

Typical Loading Procedure:

1) The preloading inspection was to be completed.

2) The bomb control handle was moved to SELECTIVE and a bomb release unit installed only at those stations on which bombs were to be mounted, as indicated on the chart for the desired bomb load. The arm safe lever was cocked followed by the release lever of the bomb release unit. The bomb control handle was then moved to the DOORS OPEN (racks locked) position.

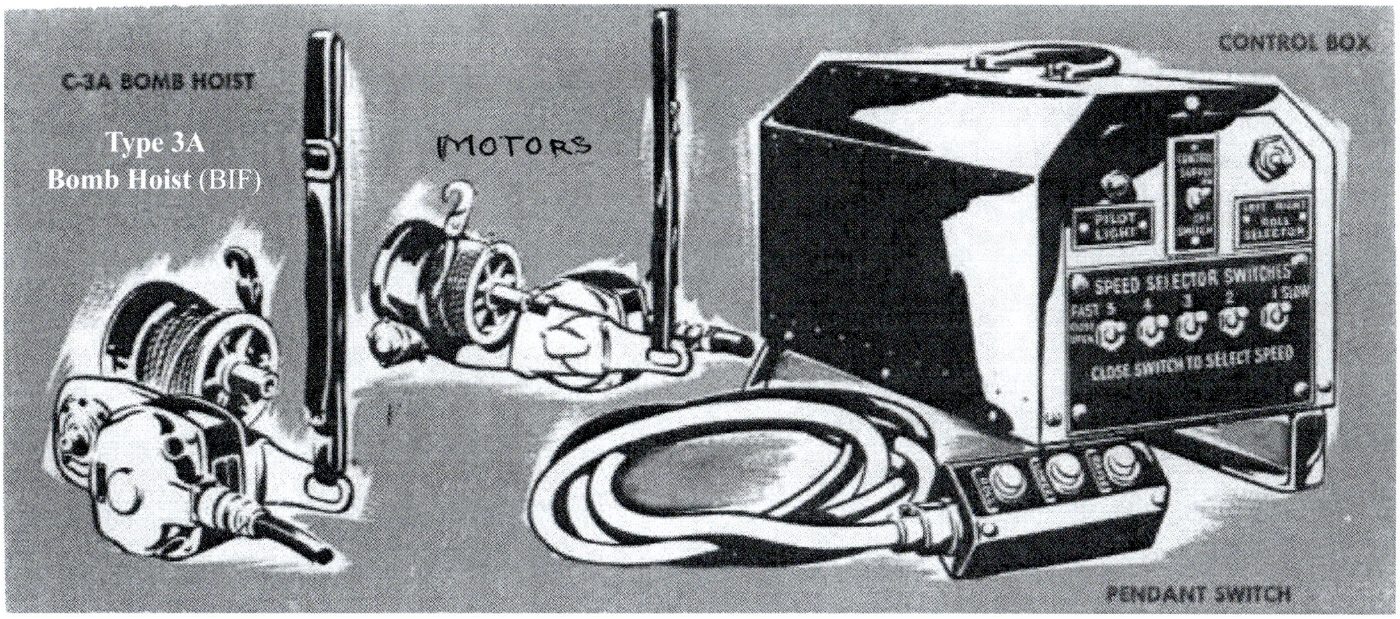

Type 3A Bomb Hoist (BIF)

Type 3A Bomb Hoist (B-17 E&R Manual)

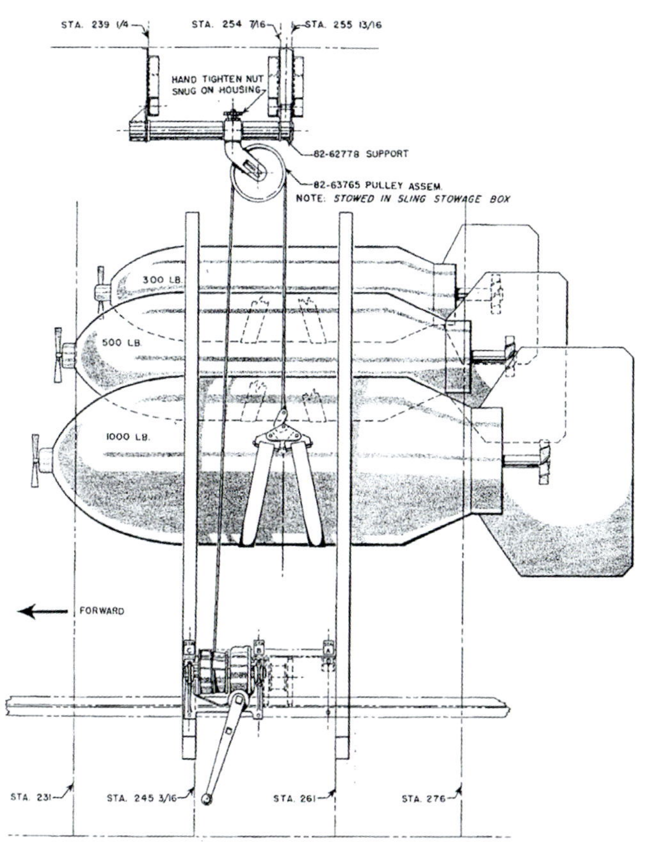

Hoist Mechanism (B-17)
(Author/CAFAZ)

Hoist Motor (B-17)
(Author/CAFAZ)

3) The bomb hoists were installed in the key slots on the sides of the fuselage in hoisting stations B and C, as shown on the hoisting diagram. The cable slot doors on the sides of the fuselage were removed and hoisting cables were inserted through slots.
4) The swivel pulley assemblies (two required) were installed in the pulley support assemblies in the crawlway over the bomb bay. The swivel pulley assemblies were stored in the bomb sling stowage locker in the bomb bay.
5) The bomb hoist cables were threaded around the lower pulleys. The cable was then routed in front of the racks and up through the forward fairlead in the crawl tunnel floor, and then threaded through the swivel pulley. For hoisting on the left hand side, the left hand cable was routed down through the aft fairlead on the crawl tunnel floor to the bomb hoist sling on the ground. The right hand cable was then strung through the snatch block assembly and the blocks attached to supports on the fuselage bulkheads that were stenciled to indicate the location of snatch blocks when hoisting respective size bombs. The cable was then carried down through the manhole in the crawl tunnel floor to the bomb hoist sling on the ground.
6) The Type B-10 shackle was engaged with the first bomb to be hoisted. The bomb was hoisted and engaged the shackle release latch and arming hook arm with the respective bomb release unit levers as the shackle was installed on shackle hooks. The shackle end, marked FRONT, was to be forward.
7) The above procedure was repeated, loading racks on each side from top to bottom until the desired bomb load was completed. Only one bomb sling was used; therefore, the bomb had to be balanced in the sling before hoisting. The tension was not to be released from the hoisting cables until all installation operations were completed and checked.
8) After all the bombs were mounted, either of the battery-disconnect switches and the bomb indicator light switch on the bomb control panel was to be turned ON. The illuminated bomb station indicator lights were to correspond with the bomb stations on which bombs were installed and that no bomb release units were to be installed on empty bomb stations.
9) The hoisting equipment was to be removed and stowed, including idler pulley guides if used.

Hoisting M-69 incendiary clusters into a B-29 bomb bay. (AAF)

Bomb Racks

Fixed Bomb Racks

The fixed ladder-type bomb racks, located on either side of the bomb bay, were fastened to the aircraft's frames and lower longeron. The aircraft was not to be flown unless the bomb racks were installed, as they were integral fuselage structural members. The vertical supports or rails of the racks were made up of two 24ST aluminum channels. The bomb rails were separated by eight die cast spacers that constituted the bomb stations, fastened to the inside face of the bomb rails. The various bomb stations and the type of bombs to be used were printed on each spacer. The lowest bomb station was not attached to the bomb rails, but was fastened to the fuselage lower longeron by a plate assembly. Two bomb bay tank release units, one on each side of the bomb bay aft of the bomb racks, were interconnected to the main bomb rack operating system at bomb stations by bellcranks and link rods.

The bomb rack released and armed bombs electrically or manually. Arming was done only electrically, and the bombs could be dropped in a safe (unarmed) state. The bomb rack release assembly consisted of a solenoid, a release lever that seated in a release pawl, and two bomb suspension hooks that incorporated a connecting link that was actuated by the movement of the release pawl. In electrical release, the release solenoid was energized and retracted the release lever, which freed the release pawl, letting it swing downward. As the release pawl rotated the connecting link slid forward, causing the bomb suspension hooks to open. In manual release, the emergency bomb release cable system actuated the manual release trigger. Movement of the trigger retracted the release lever, causing the suspension hooks to open. When the pull on the release cable was relaxed a spring returned the trigger to its original position. To latch the bomb rack (i.e. close the hooks), it was

Although 100 pound bombs could be hoisted, they were loaded much faster by hand, with the lower bomb stations loaded first and progressing up the rack. (AAF)

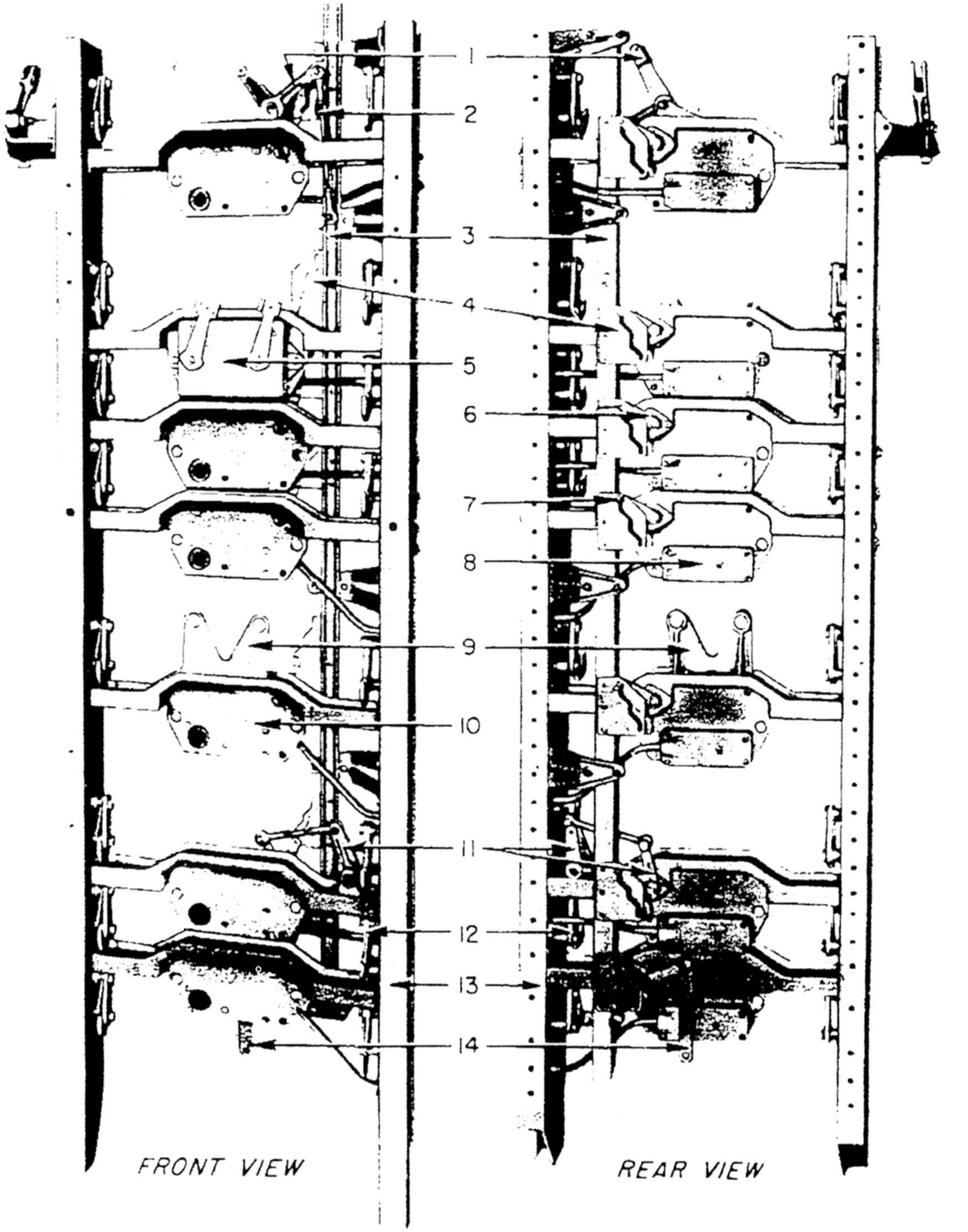

1	BELLCRANK	8	AUXILIARY SWITCH BOX
2	LINK ROD	9	SUPPORT 2000 LB. RACK CONTROLS
3	CAM PLATE SHAFT	10	BOMB STATION OR SPACER
4	CAM PLATE	11	BOMB BAY TANK RELEASE LINKAGE
5	BOMB RELEASE UNIT	12	BOMB SHACKLE HOOK
6	BOMB RELEASE ACTUATING UNIT	13	BOMB RAILS
7	CAM PLATE ROLLER	14	LONGERON STATION CONTROL LINKAGE

Bomb Rack: Front and Rear Views (B-17 E&R Manual)

Bomb Rack (B-25) (Author/CAFAZ)

Bomb Rack Station (B-25) (Author/CAFAZ)

necessary to press upward on the release pawl latching pin, which projected from the outboard side of the bomb rack. A small hole located just aft of the latching pin permitted the insertion of a lock and latching pin. When the pin was installed the downward movement of the release pawl was restricted and could not be released accidentally.

Underwing Racks for Bombers

B-17Fs were provided with underwing racks from Boeing-built -30s and both Vega and Douglas-built -20s. Two removable wing bomb racks attached to the under surface of each outer wing panel were installed to carry additional bombs or depth charges up to 1,000 pounds. The four total underwing bomb racks could carry six to eight 100 to 325-pound bombs. Six 325 pound Mark 17 depth charges could be loaded on the wing racks

100 pound bombs being manhandled onto the wing racks of a B-25. (AAF)

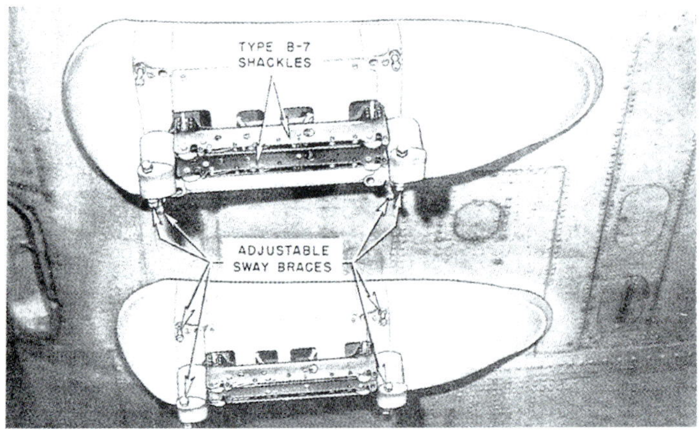

B-25 wing racks showing adjustable sway braces and B-7 bomb shackle. (B-25 Flight Manual)

at stations 3, 4, and 5 on the right wing and on stations 1, 2, and 8 on the left wing by using two Type 3-C bomb hoists. When the Mark 17 was installed on the wing racks, their large size necessitated the use of special sway brace pads. There were a variety of underwing rack adaptations for the mounting of a chemical tank and to carry aerial mines.

The wing bomb racks were fabricated of a cast assembly that was bolted to brackets in the wing. The casting included hooks for supporting the B-7 bomb shackles and two A-2 release units with the necessary electrical and mechanical connections. The casting assembly was bolted inside a pressed aluminum housing that was curved to fit the wing contour and lined with rubber stripping to allow for a snug fit to the lower surface of the wing. Adjustable sway braces aided the carrying of larger ordnance. Each housing had a door hinged on the bottom to give access to the A-2 release units. Each removable wing bomb rack was held to the under surface of the wings by eight bolts, four on each side, the four front bolts making electrical connections which were used to operate the micro switches. When the racks were removed the switch was closed, completing the electrical connection and working in the same manner as the skip station feature of the fuselage bomb racks.

The mechanical controls on the wing bomb racks locked and unlocked the A-2 release units and salvoed the bombs. The connecting cables of the wing rack mechanical controls started at the bomb bay door safety lock and moved through the leading edge of the wing to the outer wing panel junction, where an adjustable push-pull rod that operated cables fastened to the bomb salvo linkage that operated the A-2 release units. The bombardier's control handle was moved from DOORS OPEN to SELECTIVE or SALVO.

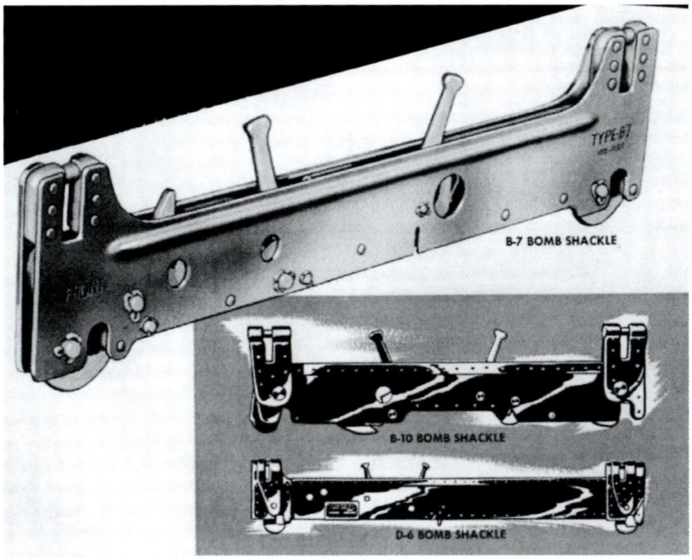

Bomb Shackle Types: B-7 (top), B-10 (middle), and D-4 (bottom). (BIF)

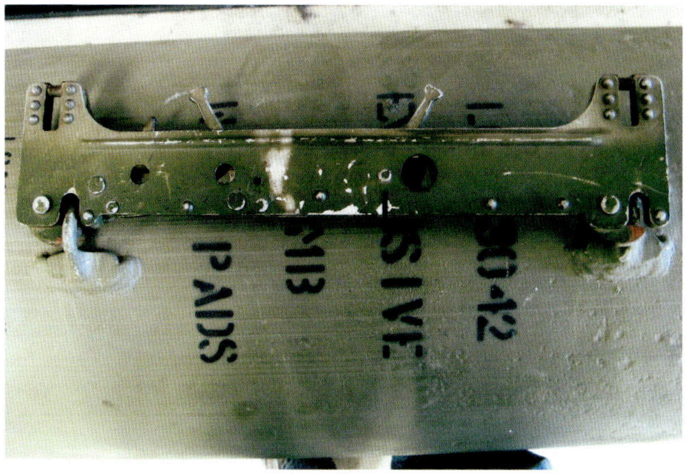

Two rotating bomb support hooks at each lower end of the shackle (B-7) hooked into the "deadeye" bomb support lugs welded to the bomb casing. (Author/CAFAZ)

Parts of B-7 Shackle (AAF)

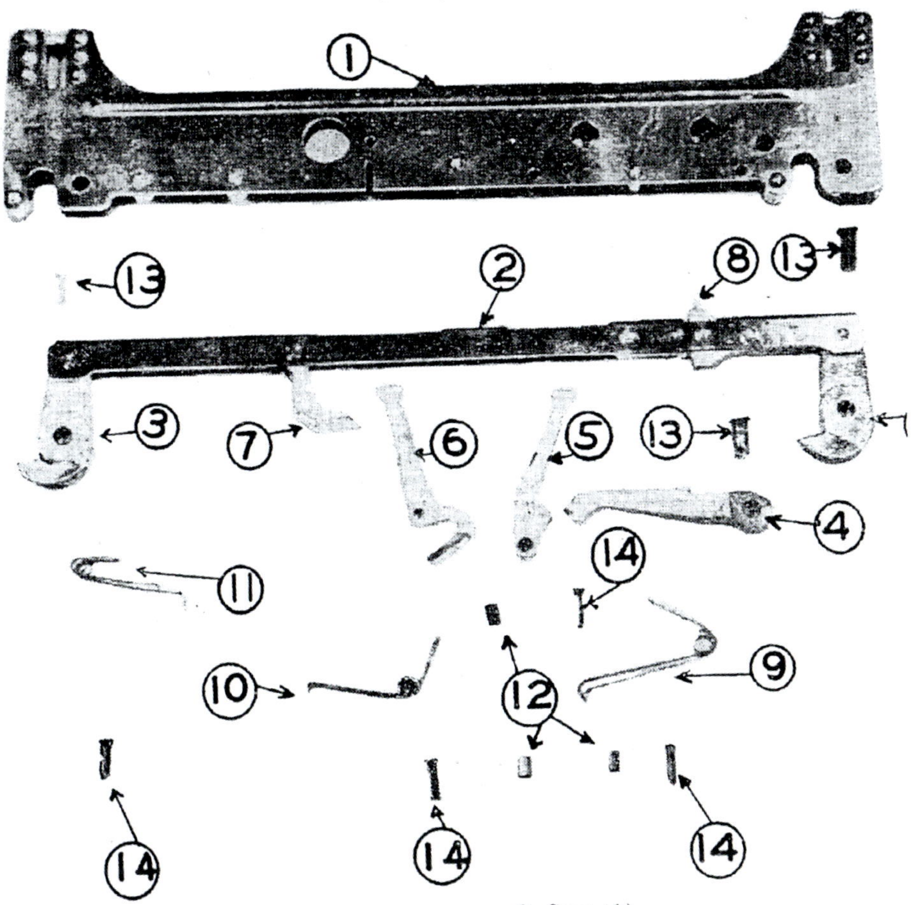

1. Shackle frame (1).
2. Bomb-carrying hook link (1).
3. Bomb-carrying hook (2).
4. Latch (1).
5. Trigger (1).
6. Arming hook (1).
7. Arming wire retainer and spring (1).
8. Sear (1).
9. Latch spring (1).
10. Trigger spring (1).
11. Arming hook spring (1).
12. Bushing (3).
13. Carrying hook and latch pin (3).
14. Assembling pins (4).

(Underwing and centerline fighter pylons will be described in Volume 3.)

Bomb Shackles

Bomb shackles carried, armed, and released bombs. They were attached to the bomb and hung on the shackle suspension hooks of the bomb rack. If this attachment was done correctly, the arming lever and release lever were then correctly positioned in the bomb release mechanism. Two rotating bomb support hooks at each lower end of the shackle hooked into the "deadeye" bomb support lugs welded to the bomb casing. An interval slide bar connected to the two bomb support hooks was actuated by a lever on the top side of the shackle that fit into the release lever of the bomb release unit. A second lever that fit into the arming lever of the bomb release unit retained or released the bomb fusing arming wire. When the arming lever was rotated by the release unit, a hook interconnected to the shackle lever engaged with the ring on the arming wire and retained the arming wire when the bomb fell.

Types of Bomb Shackles

B-5 and B-7 Shackle

B-5 and -7 bomb shackles carried bombs ranging in weight from 100 to 1,100 pounds. They were designed for internal bomb racks but could be used externally with specially constructed adapters. The word FRONT was marked on the frame as a guide to correct installation of the shackle in the bomb station. In the reverse position the shackle would not fit on most bomb racks. Special care had to be taken in the B-17F and B-29, as their bomb racks were symmetrical and it was possible to install shackles backwards in them.

The shackle release lever had two positions, COCKED and RELEASED. When it was COCKED the carrying hooks could not open. When it was RELEASED the locking mechanism of the shackle disengaged, allowing the bomb to pull the carrying hooks open. The shackle arming lever also had two positions, SAFE and ARMED. When the arming lever was SAFE, the release of a bomb pulled the arming wire out of the shackle. When the arming lever was ARMED, the arming wire was locked so that it could not leave the shackle; upon bomb release the arming wire was pulled from the fuse.

D-6 and D-7 Shackles

D-6 and D-7 bomb shackles carried 2,000 and 4,000 pound bombs and were similar in operation; however, they were not entirely interchangeable. Whenever a D-6 or D-7 was to be used, the aircraft technical orders (T.O.) were to be checked to be sure that the correct shackle was chosen for the bomb and bomb station being loaded. If a D-6 shackle was used to carry a 4,000 pound bomb when the aircraft T.O. called for a D-7 it would place too much stress on the D-6 shackle. The D-7 could not be hung satisfactorily on racks designed for the D-6.

The D-6 bomb shackle was approximately 33 inches long and of spot welded steel plate construction, and had a rotating release hook at each end. The shackle was designed to operate with the AN-A2A release unit. It had two levers, one for release and the other for arming, which corresponded to the levers on the release unit. The arming and releasing levers of the D-6 bomb shackle were remotely controlled through the AN-A2A release unit by the bombardier's quadrant handle, the electric release and arming controls, and the pilot's emergency release handle. Opening of the shackle hooks for attachment to a bomb was done by holding the release lever in the release position and pulling on the hooks. To close the hooks, the shackle was forced down on the bomb lugs until the release lever was engaged to lock the shackle hooks in the closed position. To attach the bomb arming lanyard to the shackle, the arming lanyard hook was held open and the arming lanyard loop inserted in the notch.

The procedure for loading a bomb and shackle on the racks was as follows. When the release lever was moved aft, as in salvo, the release hooks were rotated by the weight of the bomb. The bomb was released unarmed as the arming lanyard was pulled from the notch in the shackle. If the arming lever was actuated in conjunction with the release lever as in electrical release, the arming lanyard hook would be locked in position, pulling the arming lanyard from the released bomb.

D-6 Shackle (Author/CAFAZ)

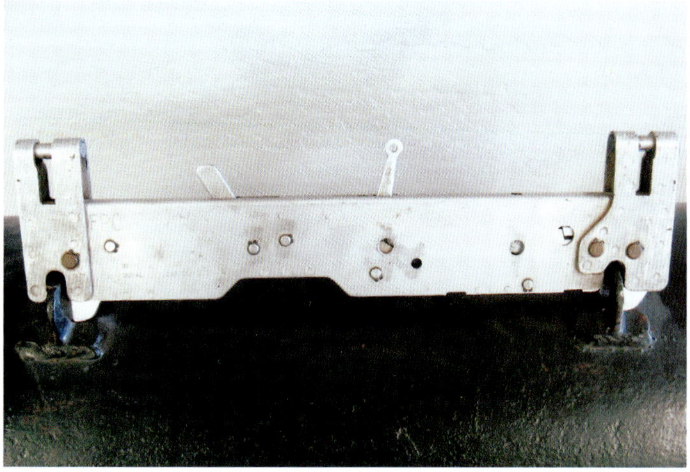

B-10 Shackle (Author/CAFAZ)

B-9 Shackle

B-9 bomb shackles operated much like the B-7 and were used to carry bombs with one lug, which could weigh up to and including 1,000 pounds.

B-10 Shackle

B-10 bomb shackles were similar in operation to the B-7 and were used interchangeably, except that the B-10 had to be used to carry 1,600 pound bombs. The shackles were suspended from locking hooks of each bomb rack station and were removable when not in use. The B-10 shackle consisted of two steel side plates spaced and spot welded together, with a rotating release hook on each end, and arm and release levers designed to fit into corresponding arm and release levers of the bomb release units. Carrying lugs for suspending the shackle from the bomb rack were spot welded and pinned to each end of the shackle. The lugs were designed to fit into locking hooks on the bomb rack.

The B-10 operated as follows. After the bomb racks were checked for correct operation the bomb release lever was set in the SELECT position, and all bomb release units to be used were manually cocked, after which the bomb release lever was set in the SAFE position. The shackle was attached to the bomb lugs before the bomb was hoisted to the rack, attaching the end marked FRONT to the nose of the bomb. The shackle was attached to the shackle hooks in the bomb lugs by pressing a lever. The engagement of the release lever was checked through an inspection hole in the shackle. As a precaution, the release lever was to be toward the front of the shackle. The spring-loaded catch was pulled downward and the arming lanyard loop was inserted into the notch. If the bomb to be hung with both nose and tail fusing the tail fuse was to be armed by the shackle, and the nose fuse was to be armed by the electric fusing units at the front of each bomb station. If there was only one fuse on the bomb it was to be armed by the shackle. To load a bomb rack station, the bomb was hoisted to a position slightly higher than its normal loaded position to facilitate attachment of the shackle to its bomb rack hooks. When bombs were lifted into position by hand they were not to be raised by the shackle, as the release lever could accidentally be moved and the bomb disengaged. The shackle-carrying lugs were snapped onto the bomb rack hooks with a check to be sure that the bomb rack hook latches snapped back into place over the shackle-carrying lugs. If this foregoing procedure was followed the shackle release and arming levers would readily fit into the forks of the corresponding release unit levers.

Bomb Rack Release Mechanisms

The bomb release mechanism was an electrically operated mechanical device designed to cause the bomb shackle to release and arm a bomb.

Type A-2 Bomb Release

One bomb rack release unit was required for each bomb carried, and all units in excess of those required for any particular mission were to be removed. The units, which were readily detachable from the spacer plate, were contained in a small rectangular housing with a back plate, two guide pins, and two latching devices. On the face of the unit were two levers, one of which was for operating the arming lever of the bomb shackle. Inside the unit were springs, levers, and electrical solenoid and switches, and a connection to the servo salvo channel linkage. On the face was an arrow that designated in which direction the unit was to be placed. The trip screw and the release and arming levers were marked by raised letters on the case and an arrow indicated the front of the unit. The left and right hand units were not interchangeable. A salvo coupling, two dowel pins, and an electrical receptacle protruded through a detachable cover on the back of the unit. The A-2 bomb release unit functioned in conjunction with a Type B-7 or B-10 bomb shackle. Two mounting attachments were located on the ears of the bomb release case. Each of these fasteners consisted of a controlled push button and mounting ring permanently secured in the bomb rack mounting plate. By pressing on the heads of the push buttons two projecting prongs were retracted and the bomb release unit could be removed. The arming and release levers could be tripped by inserting a screwdriver or similar tool into the trip screw on the front of the case and turning in the direction indicated on the case. The mechanism would then be in the same condition as if it had been tripped electrically. The bomb release unit was cocked by pivoting each lever away from the center of the box. The arming lever had to be cocked before it was possible to cock the release lever.

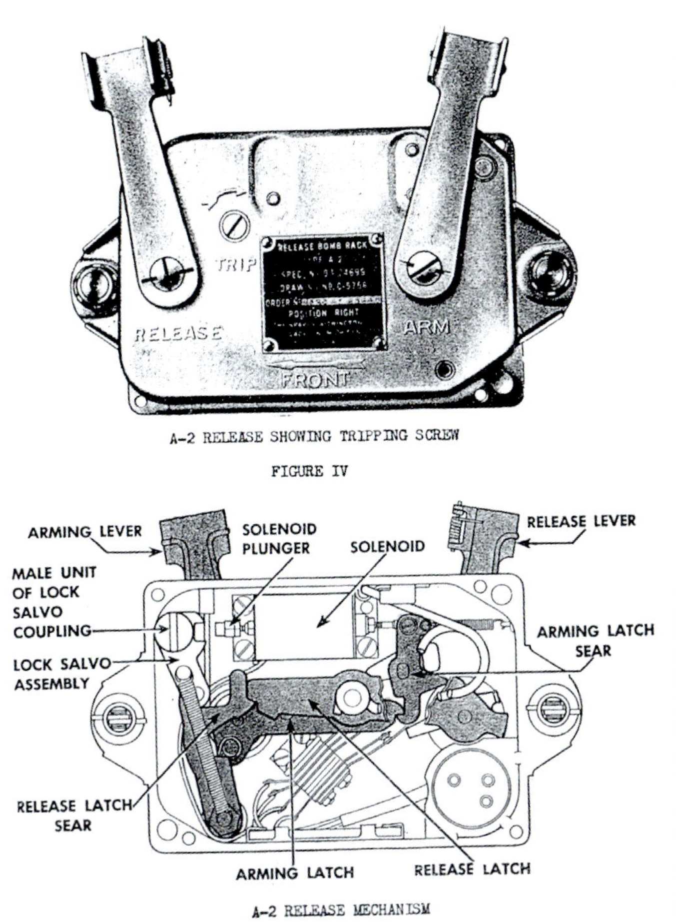

A-2 Bomb Release Mechanism (TM9-1980)

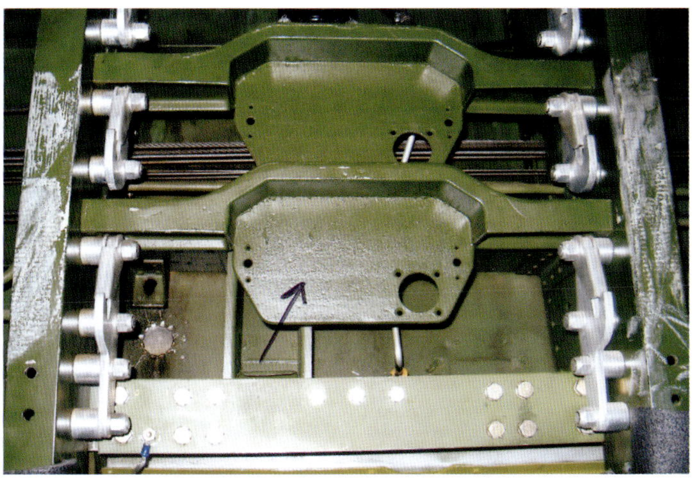

Bomb rack release units were attached to the **spacer plate** (arrow) by two guide pins and two latching devices contained on a small rectangular housing with a back plate. (Author/CAFAZ)

The ends of these two arms were flanged to provide recesses for the operating levers of the bomb shackles. The salvo coupling, which was a locking device operated remotely by the bomb release handle, had three possible positions when the release was cocked: ARM-SELECTIVE, SAFE-SALVO, and LOCKED. When the coupling was in the ARM-SELECTIVE (vertical) position, both levers could be tripped simultaneously by a solenoid within the unit and the bomb was dropped in the armed condition. If the coupling was turned to the SAFE-SALVO position only the release lever was tripped; a bomb dropped in this manner would be safe. With the coupling in the LOCKED position all movement of the solenoid was stopped by a cam, thus preventing the selective release of the bombs. In this position, an arm on the coupling locked the mechanism and prevented mechanical salvo of the bombs. A small switch within the unit operated the corresponding indicator light showing that the bomb release unit was cocked.

A-4 Bomb Release

The A-4 served the same purpose as the A-2 bomb release with modifications for simpler use. In order to release bombs in SELECT or in TRAIN the bombardier's master switch had to be ON, bomb bay doors OPEN, and the rack selection made. The electrical impulse from the bomb release switch or the bombsight automatic release mechanism energized the rotary solenoid inside the A-4. The solenoid rotated to the SELECT position; this tripped the release lever and the arming lever. The indicator light switch had to be OFF while bombs were being released since if it was ON a partial salvo resulted. To salvo bombs the salvo switch was placed at SALVO. The solenoid rotated to the SALVO position and only the release lever was tripped.

To operate the A-4 manually, the trip screw (marked TRIP) on the front of the A-4 was turned in the direction indicated. This affected the rotary solenoid like an electrical impulse, tripping both the release lever and arming lever. If an A-4 had been cocked by mistake the trip screw permitted tripping. When the release was tripped manually the trip screw was always to be returned to the vertical position or it would be impossible to cock the release. When the A-4 release was jammed, preventing normal operation, the bombs were released safely by prying the fork of the bomb shackle release lever over the hinged ear.

AX-6 Auxiliary Bomb Release Switch Boxes

An AX-6 Type bomb release auxiliary switch box was mounted on the outboard side of each bomb station, and an auxiliary switch box was attached to the bottom bomb station. Each switch box had a switch button

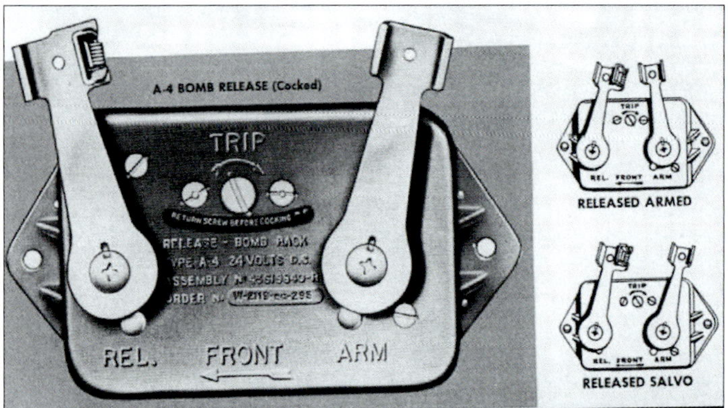

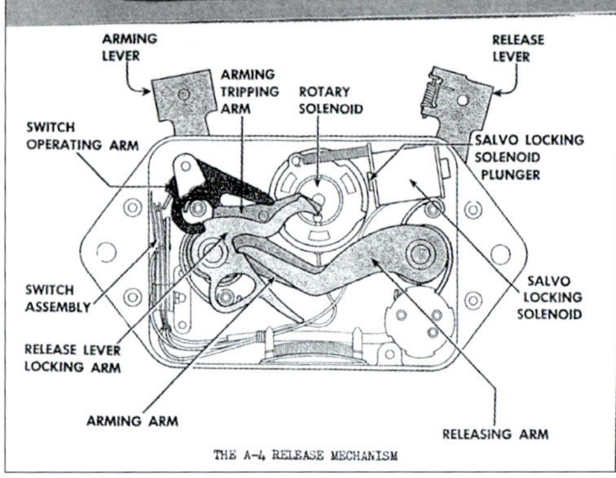

A-4 Bomb Release Mechanism (TM9-1980)

A-4 Bomb Release Mechanism (Author/CAFAZ)

that protruded through the inboard face of the bomb station. The bomb release unit actuated the button switch and broke the circuit between the two adjacent bomb stations, making contact for this station. If the bomb release unit at this station was not cocked, the switch within the bomb release unit again automatically completed the circuit to the two adjacent bomb stations.

Cam Plates

A cam plate shaft (salvo channel) at the outboard side of both bomb racks slid freely within a series of rollers. A cam plate was attached to the shaft at each bomb station to control the bomb release units. The cam was interconnected by an arm with the bomb release unit at each bomb station, and the salvo coupling of the bomb release unit engaged in the slot in the pivot shaft of this arm. A spacer attached to the upper end of the arm rode in the slot of the cam plate, which actuated the arm for the LOCK, SELECTIVE, and SALVO positions. The slot was cut into each cam plate so that when the whole salvo channel assembly was in the lower position (the roller in the top portion of the cam plate slot) all the bomb release units would be locked. The center or intermediate position of the salvo channel placed the release units in position for selective release. When the channel was lifted to the upper position all installed bomb release units would salvo. The slots in the cam plates on the salvo channel were so designed as to allow the bombs falling from the lower stations to clear the racks before the next higher ones were released. This prevented the bombs from bumping when the racks were salvoed. The salvo channel had to be properly adjusted, as improper setting would result in the loss of travel and could prevent salvo of the racks. It might also affect the operation of the bomb door control valve. The salvo channel on the left bomb rack was interconnected with the channel on the right rack by adjustable push-pull rods and bellcranks.

Arming of Bombs

The term ARM was used to describe the removal of safety devices or the setting of a fuse train so that the bomb would explode on impact, or at a definite time interval after release or after impact. Arming of bombs was accomplished either by the bomb release units and its bomb shackle or by the bomb arming controls, or both, depending upon the unit into which arming wires had been inserted. The bomb release units could be mounted on all bomb stations, while the bomb arming units were mounted on the front rail of the fuselage bomb racks. When the arming wires from both the nose and tail fuses had been inserted in the bomb shackle arming slot both the nose and tail fuses of all bombs were automatically armed during a normal release. During a SALVO release, all bombs were automatically dropped SAFE. The bomb arming controls, actuated simultaneously by a switch on the bomb control panel, armed the nose fuses of all bombs, provided the arming wire from the nose fuse of the bombs had been inserted into the arming controls. Normally, during SALVO, bombs would drop in the SAFE condition; however, ARMED salvo would be achieved when the bomb fusing switch was moved to the ON position (bombs were nose fused only).

Bomb Arming Controls Type A-1 and A-2

The bomb arming controls provided an electrically-actuated selective fuse arming system for AAF bombs. These units, installed at the forward position of each bomb station on the racks, were cylindrical in shape

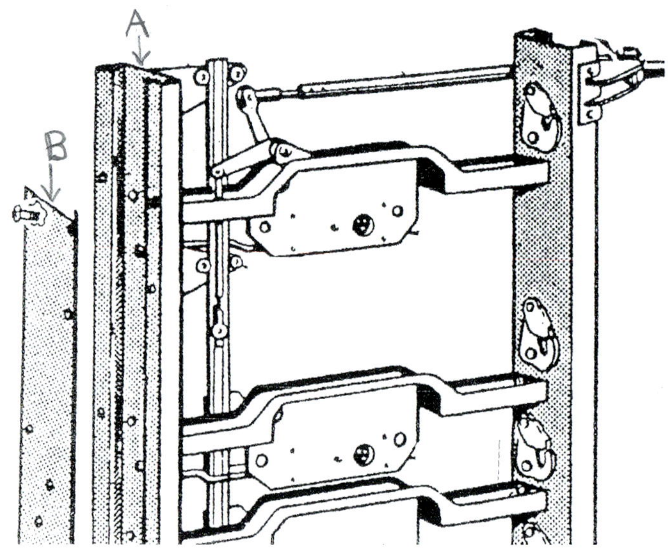

A **cam plate shaft** (A and B), also called a salvo channel, was located at the outboard side of both bomb racks and slid freely within a series of rollers. A cam plate was attached to the shaft at each bomb station to control the bomb release units. (B-17 E&R Manual)

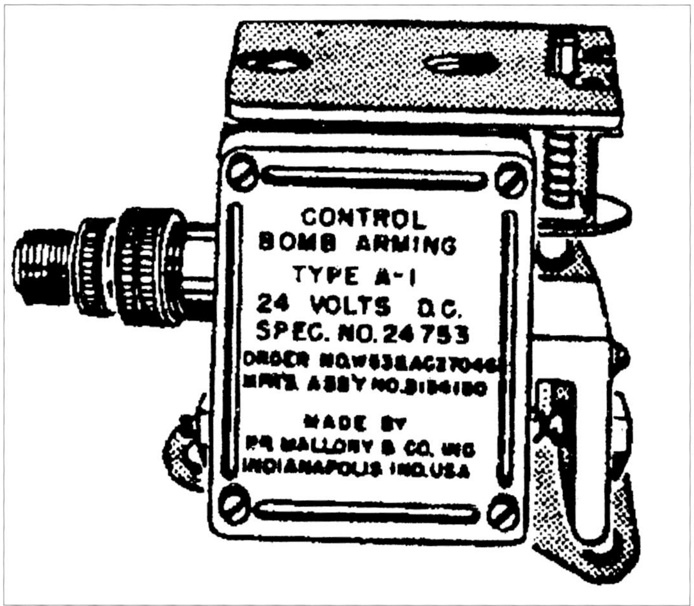

A-1 Arming Control (BIF)

A-2 Arming Control (BIF)

with a moisture proof and dust proof case. A spring-actuated ball catch was locked in the armed position when the solenoid within the case was energized; thus, the arming wire swivel loop was retained. The units were connected to the electrical system by a standard type connector and were grounded through the mounting framework. All arming controls were wired in parallel and were energized by the bomb fusing switch on the bomb control panel. When the units were energized a light adjacent to the bomb fusing switch was turned on. An arming control was permanently mounted to the front rail of each fuselage bomb rack opposite each basic bomb station. An arming unit was provided for the 2,000 pound bomb on the forward face of the 2,000 pound bomb rack. The arming units could be removed and mounted on the fuselage frame located on the first frame forward of the bomb rail for the arming of British bombs.

To operate the bomb arming switch the bombardier placed the bomb nose fusing switch in the OFF position and inserted the bomb arming lanyard swivel loop in the ball catch of the A-2 unit. When it was necessary to release bombs unarmed, as in salvo, the arming wire swivel loop was pulled free of the ball catch by the released bomb. When bomb nose fuses were to be armed the switch on the bombardier's switch panel was placed in the ARM position, closing the circuit to the A-2 unit solenoid. A plunger in the solenoid moved into a recess in the ball catch, locking the arming lanyard loop in place. The arming lanyard was then pulled from the bomb as it was released,

Bombardier's Control Panel

The function of the various lights and switches on the bombardier's control panel was to provide an indication of bombs selected and released and the circuit protection of electrical components. The components of a typical Bombardier's control panel were:

1) The control panel light which illuminated the face of the panel.
2) The rheostat that controlled the panel light intensity.
3) The bomb bay door indicator lights that flashed ON when the bomb bay doors were fully opened. These lights were located on the bombardier's switch panel and on the pilots' instrument panel. They were controlled by two switches located in the lower rear section of the bomb bays. The circuit design prevented the dropping of bombs from the bomb bay section in which either of these switches were located, in the event the doors were not fully opened. The right hand bomb bay door indicator light turned ON when the right rear bomb bay door was opened for photographic purposes.
4) The bomb size indicators identified the size of the bombs carried in each rack. The blocks were six sided and indicated sizes from 100 to 1,600 pounds.
5) The bomb release power circuit breaker-type switch that activated the bomb panel circuit. The guard located over the top of the switch was a safety device to prevent accidental operation of the switch.
6) The bomb sight power circuit breaker-type switch that activated the electrical circuit to the bomb sight.
7) The four rack switches that allowed the bombardier to select the bomb racks from which bombs were to be released.
8) The nose fusing switch that allowed the bombardier to fuse the bomb's nose.
9) The nose fused indicator light that indicated to the bombardier that the nose fusing switch was in the ARM position. The light remained ON as long as the switch was in the ARM position.

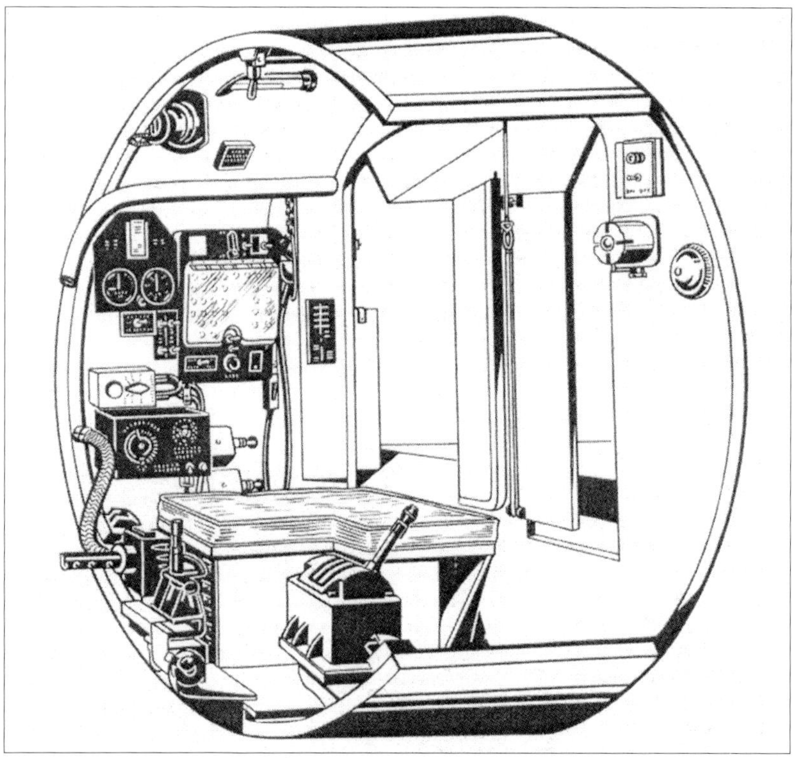

B-26 Bombardier Control Panel (B-26 Flight Manual)

B-17 Control Panel & Intervalometer (lower) (Author/CAFAZ)

B-25 Control Panel & Intervalometer (upper right) (MAAM)

10) The bomb release switch that allowed the bombardier to release the desired number of bombs either manually or automatically. If bombs were to be dropped singly or at varying intervals the switch was placed in the MANUAL position. In this position, if the Intervalometer switch was in the SELECT position a single bomb was released each time the bombardier depressed the bomb release switch (firing key). If the Intervalometer switch was in the TRAIN position a string of bombs was dropped in accordance with the Intervalometer setting. When the bomb release switch was placed in the AUTO position the Intervalometer was activated through the bomb sight circuit, and any predetermined number of bombs could be released automatically.
11) The bomb release indicator that flashed ON for a moment as each bomb left the bomb racks.
12) The bomb station indicator lights that turned ON only if the bomb release units were cocked and if the indicator lights switch was in the BRIGHT or the DIM position. When the 100 to 1,600 pound bomb racks were used only the 100 to 1,600 pound bomb station indicator lights turned ON. When the 2,000 pound bomb racks were used only lights indicating the 2,000 pound bombs turned ON.
13) The bomb station indicator lights that turned OFF when the bombs were released.

Intervalometer (Author/CAFAZ)

Intervalometer

Description

The Intervalometer provided a method of releasing in train a predetermined number of bombs with a predetermined space interval between successive impacts. The space interval in feet between bomb impacts depended on the ground speed of the aircraft and the time lapse between bomb releases. The number of bombs to be released depended on the target.

The front panel of the typical Intervalometer was provided with an interval control knob and associated indicator dial, a counter knob and pointer, a train selector switch, and an indicator lamp. An electrical receptacle was located in the bottom of the Intervalometer casing for a plug-in connection for either 24 or 28.5 Volt DC current supply. The interval control knob dial was graduated in ground speed knots per hour. The inner dial was set in accordance with any desired interval in feet between bombs, as indicated by the outer dial. The counter knob and pointer provided for the selection for the release of any desired number of bombs to 50 inclusive; for the release of more than 50 bombs, the counter had to be set manually to the zero position. The train selector switch enabled the bombardier to choose between a train release of a selected number of bombs—after each momentary closure of the firing switch the selective release of one bomb for each closure of the firing switch. All sizes of bombs ranging from 100 pounds to 2,000 pounds could be released in train.

SELECTIVE Release

With the switch set in the SELECTIVE position, the operation of the Intervalometer was independent of the setting of either the interval control knob or the counter knob. The release solenoid circuit was closed at each closure of the bomb release switch (also called the "firing key"). The counter knob pointer moved counterclockwise one point toward zero each time a bomb was released, which indicated to the bombardier how many bombs remained to be released. With the switch in SELECTIVE position, and the rim of the indicator lamp turned to the ON position, the indicator lamp remained lit regardless of the position of the counter. The indicator remained lit if the indicator lamp switch was in the ON position while the switch was in the SELECTIVE position, regardless of the position of the pointer.

TRAIN Release

With the switch set for TRAIN release, the counter knob had to be set at least one minute before pressing the firing switch. Momentary closure of the firing switch then started a train release, which continued until the release solenoid of the interval control had been closed for the number of times set. The interval dial read directly in feet of spacing between consecutive bomb hits at 100 to 500 miles per hour ground speed. The release solenoid circuit was closed at intervals corresponding to frequencies of one to twenty cycles per second, depending upon the interval selected. With the switch set for train release and the rim of indicator lamp turned to the ON position, the indicator lamp remained lit only while hte counter was set at any number above zero.

In train bombing, the first bomb impact was to be placed so that the center of the train of bombs would hit the center of the target. The train bombing equation converted to mils the number of feet by which the first bomb was to hit short of the target. Either by reducing the Distance Short (DS) or trail the bombardier could place the first impact the desired number of feet short. To determine how much to reduce the Distance Short the bombardier had to double the ground speed GS and divide it by 100, and then divide the result into the number of mils needed to place the first bomb impact the proper distance short of the target. Reducing the trail caused an appreciable cross-trail error unless the bombsight was equipped with a trail spotting device. The Trail Spotting Device reduced the trail setting in the rate end without introducing an error in Crosstrail. It was used in train bombing to get the center bomb (the mean point of impact) of the train on the target. It could also reduce trail to compensate for the Range Component of Crosstrail (RCCT). (See Train Bombing)

Operation

Before reaching Initial Point (IP) when train bombing, the train select switch was set to TRAIN and the counter knob pointer set at number of bombs desired in train. The Ground Speed expected over the target was determined and set opposite the desired bomb spacing. After releasing a train of bombs the counter knob pointer was at 0 and the Intervalometer was OFF. For selective release the train select switch was set at SELECT. To turn the Intervalometer OFF the counter knob pointer was set at 0 and the train select switch at TRAIN.

Calibration of the Intervalometer

The Intervalometer was to be calibrated accurately before takeoff. To set the Intervalometer the train select switch was moved to TRAIN and the counter knob pointer set at 50. On the ground speed dial 500 mph was set opposite 750 feet on the interval dial. At least one minute was allowed for the Intervalometer to reach its operating temperature. The time required for the counter knob pointer to reach 0 was determined after the bomb release switch was pushed, which should take from 45 to 55 seconds. If it took more than 55 seconds, the calibration screw on the back of Intervalometer was to be turned clockwise. If it required less than 45 seconds for th counter knob pointer to reach 0 the screw was to be turned counterclockwise. At least one minute prior to release, the train select switch was to be set at TRAIN and the counter knob pointer at the required number of bombs. The Intervalometer was to be turned OFF when not in use.

Bombardier's Quadrant

The bombardier's quadrant was comprised of a mounting support and two levers located on the floor of the bombardier's compartment and had two functions. The outboard lever opened and closed the bomb bay doors while the inboard lever, through a mechanical linkage, controlled the locking and unlocking of the AN-A2A release units in the bomb bay and mechanically controlled the simultaneous release of all bombs.

The bomb bay doors were never to be operated when the bomber was on the ground without first warning nearby personnel to stay clear. The bomb bay door lever could be set in three possible positions: CLOSED, NEUTRAL, and OPEN. The CLOSED and OPEN positions were stenciled on the top of the mounting quadrant. When the lever was moved to either the OPEN or the CLOSED position, the bomb bay control rod actuated the bomb bay door selector valve to open or close the bomb bay doors. The lever automatically returned to NEUTRAL from either position. If, for any reason, it did not return to NEUTRAL it was to be returned manually.

The bomb release lever had three positions (SAFE, SELECT, and SALVO) and was normally kept in SAFE position. When the bombs were

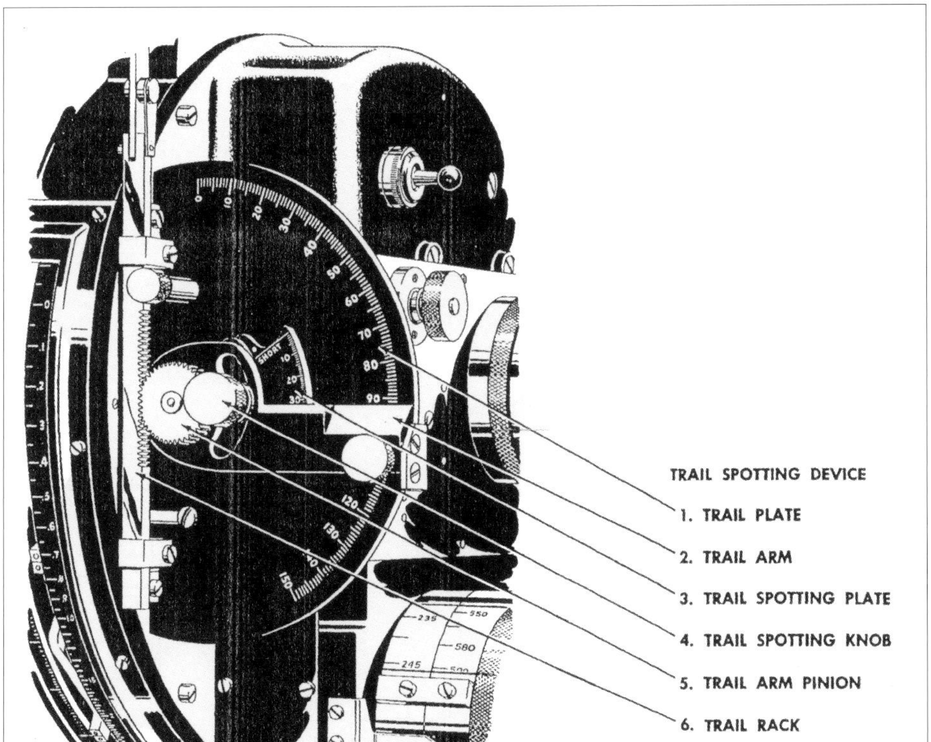

(TM9-1980)

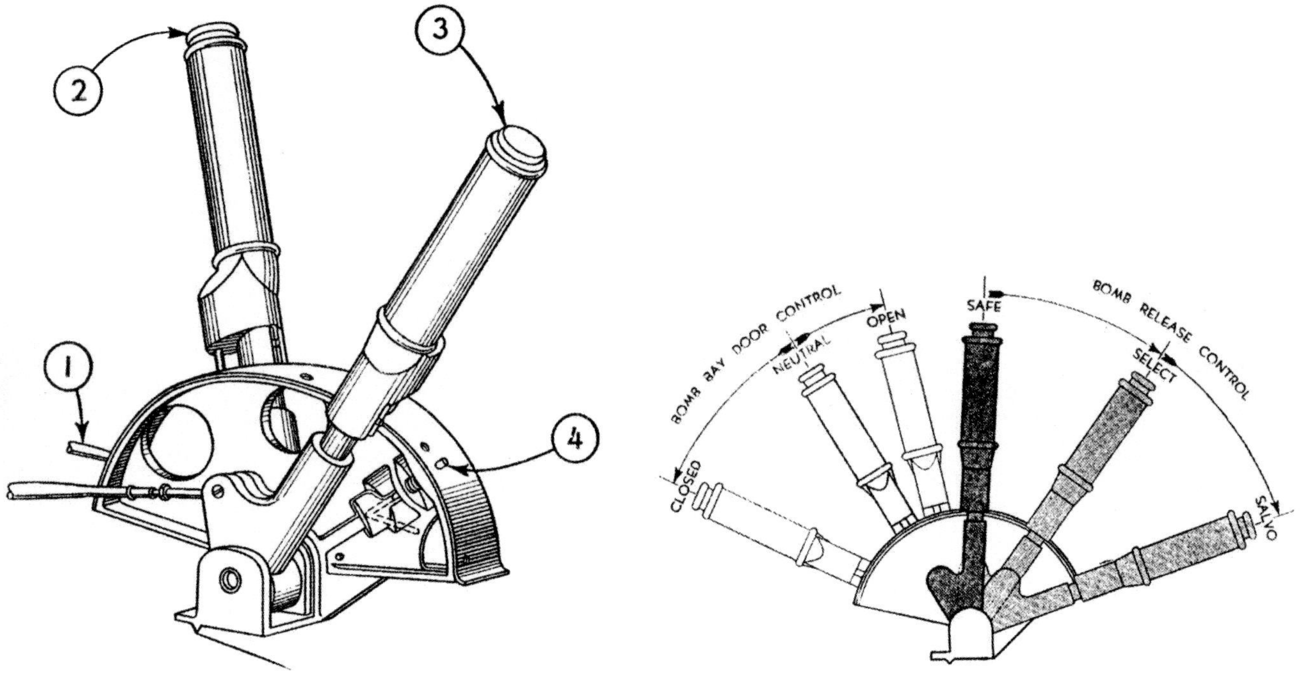

Figure 8—Bombardier's Quadrant

1. Bomb Bay Door Control Rod
2. Bomb Bay Door Selector Valve Operating Lever
3. Bomb Release Lever
4. Salvo Safety Stop Pin

(B-24 E&R Manual)

to be released the lever had to be moved forward to the SELECT position. When in the SELECT position a series of rods, linked together by bellcranks, actuated the sliding cam plate, which unlocked the AN-A2A release units.

The SALVO position was only used in an emergency situation when the bombs had to be jettisoned. When the lever was in the SALVO position the bombs were released unarmed. A safety stop pin was provided to prevent the accidental salvo of the bombs. This pin had to be depressed manually before the lever could be pushed forward to the SALVO position.

Procedure for Releasing Bombs

The battery power switch on the Ignition switch panel, the AC power switch on the pilot's pedestal, and the bomb release power switch had to be turned ON before the following procedures could be executed:

1) Select the bomb racks to be used by placing corresponding rack selector switches in the ON position.
2) Turn the bomb panel indicator light switch ON (BRIGHT or DIM).
3) Place nose fusing switch from SAFE to ARM.
4) Place the train selector switch on the Intervalometer to SELECTOR or TRAIN as required.
a) If a number of bombs were to be released at definite intervals, the Intervalometer switch was to be placed in TRAIN; the number of bombs to be released was selected by counter dial, and set the interval with the calculated ground speed on the interval control dial.
b) If the bombs were to be released singly the Intervalometer train selector switch was set to SELECT. No other setting of the Intervalometer was necessary, as the bomb station indicator lights on the bombardier's control panel would report the bombs dropped.
5) The bomb release switch was set to MANUAL if the bombs were released by the firing key. This switch was set to AUTOMATIC if the bombs were released by the bombsight. Bombsight power was controlled by the bombsight power switch on the bombardier's switch panel.
6) The bomb bay doors were opened by using the bomb bay door control handle on the quadrant. When the bomb bay doors were fully opened the bomb bay door indicator lights lit.
7) The bomb release handle was placed in SELECT. The bombardier had to be sure that the salvo safety stop pin on the quadrant was in position to prevent the bomb release handle from overtravel into the SALVO position.
8) The bomb firing key safety lock was moved away from the firing key.
9) To release the bombs the firing key was moved either up or down. It was not necessary to hold the firing key, as a single operation served either to start the Intervalometer or to release a single bomb, depending on the previous setting of the Intervalometer.

As bombs were released, the bomb station indicator lights on the bombardier's control panel turned OFF in the following sequence: Left Front, Right Rear, Right Front, and Left Rear. The bomb release indicator light flashed ON momentarily with the release of each bomb.

After the bombing operation was completed the bomb release handle on the quadrant was moved from the SELECT to SAFE position. Also, the bomb bay doors were closed by using the bomb bay door control handle. The bombardier's control panel was cleared by moving the nose fusing switch to the SAFE position and setting all other switches to the OFF position. The guarded bomb release power switch was not to be turned OFF, as this switch was a circuit breaker for circuit protection and was to be left ON at all times.

Virtually all Eighth Air Force bombing was formation bombing, which by its nature caused large bomb patterns. Thus, in order to make for smaller bomb patterns and thereby increase the concentration of bombs on the target, it became the practice to *bomb on the leader* (that is, on the Pathfinder plane) and to bomb by salvo. The intervalometer was seldom used.

4

Bombsights

Development

World War I

In the early days of World War I bombs were mostly dropped by hand, but the pilots had two advantages which somewhat compensated for the lack of a mechanical sighting device. Aircraft could fly in daytime and at sufficiently low altitudes to give a good view of the target, because the only resistance was from disorganized gunfire from the ground. Pilots learned to make allowance for the effect of the speed of their aircraft on the trajectory of the bombs and from experience, the first elementary sighting system was simply three nails pounded into the side of the aircraft, to be lined up on a target. Another simple sighting method producing a more accurate drop was to dive the aircraft at a target, which gave the pilot a better view and increased the stability of the aircraft, and was the first step toward dive-bombing.

As fighter aircraft developed and defenses improved a more sophisticated sighting method became necessary. Hitting a target with a bomb from a fast-moving airplane was a difficult task. Even if traveling at 100 mph and only a few thousand feet above the ground, a bomb dropped just half a second too late could miss its target by hundreds of feet, and that error would be amplified by flying higher to avoid ground fire. In addition, the bombardier would have trouble seeing a small target tens of thousands of feet below, but simply using a telescope with crosshairs as a bombsight would not be enough. Any turbulence would bounce the airplane and throw off the aiming, and the bombsight needed internal stabilizers to counter the movement of the aircraft. A bombardier had to use a complex formula that incorporated the trajectories of different size bombs with the effects of altitude, airspeed, true ground speed, cross winds, and other variables, such as hitting a moving target. Because making all these computations in combat would be almost impossible, a bombsight was required that could automatically perform all these calculations for the bombardier. In addition, the bombardier needed a simple method of transmitting minor course corrections to the pilot on the final approach to the target.

Initially German bombsights were superior because the Zeppelin dirigible was to be used as a bomber. Before the war, the Zeiss Optical Company produced a telescopic device intended for operation in the Zeppelin, which was at altitudes higher than most aircraft could then fly. By 1916 the German Air Service had adapted this sight for use in aircraft that flew faster than airships. By using a stopwatch to record the time it took for a landmark on the ground to pass across a certain part of the sight the sight could set at the correct aim point by relating this to the altitude, based on predetermined tables. A Gorz telescopic sight was developed for night use, and near the end of the war the Gorz-Borjkow sight was introduced, which by a built in clock mechanism could automatically determine the correct moment at which to release a bomb.

In spring 1915, when Trenchard took over command of the RFC, there were no effective bombsights, with only two crude sights available: the nail sight and the lever sight, both of which had been developed by the RNAS. The nail sight was a hand-held board with an attached spirit level and two nails positioned to indicate the dropping angle, and the bombs were released when the two pins came into line. This sight was only practical for dropping bombs from a fixed height and at a fixed speed. The lever sight incorporated modifications which allowed for the dropping of bombs from varying heights and varying speeds. The two pins, one the foresight and the other the backsight, pivoted on a lever, allowing the line of sight to be set at a dropping angle determined by referring to tables for height and groundspeed.

It was not until mid-summer 1915 that the first standard British bombsight, the CFS, became operational. This sight, which was similar to the German Gorz sight, was developed by 2Lt. R.B. Bourdillon of the RFC who, after serving as an intelligence officer, was assigned to the newly created experimental flight at the Central Flying School, Upavon, in December 1914. While there he collaborated with Lt. Strange on a simple "wires and nails" sight that resembled the sight developed several years earlier by American Lt. Riley Scott. The timing scale enabled the pilot, with the aid of a stopwatch, to measure his groundspeed by two sightings taken on one object. To give the correct angle for bomb dropping, the moveable foresight was then set on a timing scale to correspond with the time interval recorded in seconds on the stopwatch between the two sightings. Using the CFS sight, it was still necessary to bomb directly up or down wind. The CFS (for Central Flying School) sight would be in service for three years and was first used by the RFC in the Battle of Loos. A similar system was adopted by the French in 1915 with the Dorand and Lafay sights.

During the last year and a half of the war bombing theory evolved and bombsights became considerably more complicated. Sights, with spirit levels and then gyrostats for leveling, were installed in large bombers. These sights could take into account the height of an aircraft above the target, its airspeed, the wind velocity, and the amount of drift when flying cross wind. In single-seat aircraft simpler sights were developed with which the pilot could view the ground through the cockpit floor. These sights were notably inaccurate, as usually they were calibrated for use only at three heights: about 6,000 feet, 10,000 feet, and 15,000 feet. The pilot had to estimate the wind direction and velocity from a previous knowledge of the weather forecast or by watching the smoke bursts of shells fired from the ground. The French developed the Michelin sight, which was considered the most accurate bombsight of the war. However, it could not compensate for

Lt.Cdr. Harry Wimperis of the Royal Naval Service introduced his **Wimperis Course Setting Bombsight (CSBS)** in 1916, but the improved version did not reach combat in WWI; it did, however, see notable use by various nations in the interwar years. (AFHRC)

wind, forcing the pilot to fly directly into or against the wind and making the bomber an easy target for anti-aircraft.

The British began experimenting with more sophisticated bombsights in 1916, with the most promising developed by graduate engineer Lt.Cdr. Harry Wimperis of the Royal Naval Service's Imperial College of Science. The rudimentary sight was a board fitted with a bubble level and two adjustable rifle sights, and the "bombardier" used predetermined bombing tables and levers to adjust for altitude and speed. After adjusting the sight for altitude, airspeed, and somewhat for the wind the bombardier essentially aimed it like a rifle. The bombsight was used at low altitudes and could achieve an accuracy of "hundreds of feet." Because the Wimperis did not have a stabilizer the normal random pitch and roll of the aircraft in flight affected its accuracy during the bombing run. Wimperis improved his Course Setting Bombsight (CSBS), which enabled the bomber to attack its target from any direction without considering airspeed or wind direction. The Wimperis sight was scheduled to equip the bombers of the new British Independent Air Force to bomb Germany in retaliation for the bombing of London by German Gotha bombers and Zeppelins. However, the war ended before the IAF was a viable force. After the war the Wimperis CSBS was used by foreign air forces, including the USAAC, which had purchased

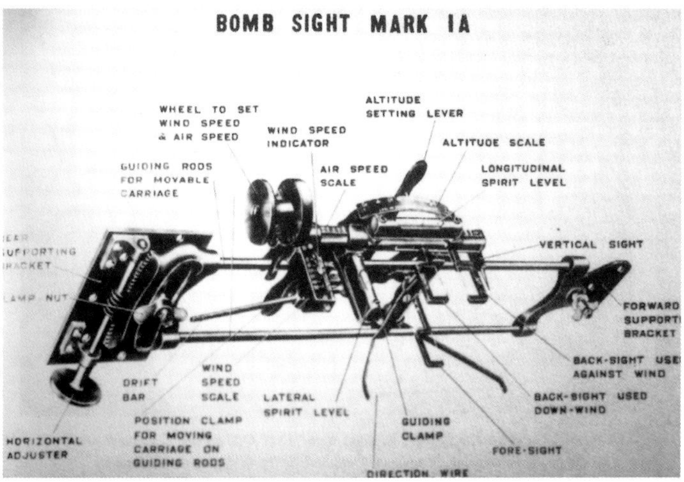

After WWI the U.S. Army Air Service Engineering Division developed the **Mark IA Bombsight** from the British wartime Wimperis. (AFHRC)

or built under license over 11,000. The Japanese developed a CSBS sight based on the Wimperis which they used until early World War II.

The Army Air Service Engineering Division at McCook Field, OH, undertook the development of a new bombsight after WWI. The sight was developed from the British wartime Wimperis and designated as the Mark IA, and was mounted on the DH-4 for use by the observer. The Army engineers incorporated a series of modifications that improved its use at high altitudes, but these improvements were limited, and the sight proved to be so inadequate that Gen. Billy Mitchell borrowed U.S. Navy Mark IIIA bombsights to sink the *Ostfriesland* in 1921. The sight was the Navy's first stabilized bombsight; an upgraded Wimperis version mounted on a newly built Norden base.

As will be discussed, Carl Norden initially worked to improve the Wimperis Sight, but after the long development of his renowned bombsight Norden would abandon the principles of the CSBS bombsight for the much greater accuracy that sight stabilization would afford.

British Bombsight Development

The British continued to develop several variations of the CSBS to permit bombing at low and high altitudes that were suitable for the speeds of the post-war biplane bombers, which did not increase much beyond 100 mph until the mid-1930s. When the RAF rearmed in the mid to late 1930s the change to speedy, high flying monoplane bombers led to the increased development of the CSBS, culminating in the introduction of the Mk VII ("A") in 1932 and the Mk IX ("C") in 1939. The "A" was graduated in mph and intended for light bombers with restricted range, while the "C" was graduated in knots and intended for longer range operations using dead reckoning (DR) plotting. Both models were superseded, but the Mk IXC remained in use in training aircraft in the UK and Commonwealth until the end of WWII. The CSBS demonstrated outstanding accuracy in pre-war bombing training and maneuvers where targets were attacked individually under an exacting regimen and did not at all duplicate operational situations in the future war, especially since it was believed that Bomber Command would be operational mainly during daytime. During testing an important problem with the CSBS sight was not identified; to achieve this accuracy the bomber had to be flown at a constant speed, straight and level to the target, which was not possible under combat conditions and could have been improved by using stabilization.

As reports about the development of the stabilized Norden Bombsight filtered into England in the mid-1930s it was considered that the CSBS should be simplified, and the Automatic Bombsight (ABS) was developed at Farnborough. The ABS had a difficult development, with many changes in sight requirements and problems in procuring suitable test aircraft, as modern high performance contemporary bombers were not readily available for testing. Despite much discussion the ABS lacked stabilization, which would double the accuracy. A decision was finally made to add stabilization to the ABS, but only when it was in full production, causing production to almost be brought to a halt.

Concurrently to ABS development was a redesign of the CSBS as the MkX which, while using the same principles, displayed little resemblance to its MkIX precursor. With the developmental problems of the ABS the then successful CSBS MkX was specified for the new British four engine bombers as well as those ordered from America (e.g. the Liberator and the Baltimore). To provide the quantities required for the new aircraft, companies in Canada and Great Britain discontinued Mk IX production and were re-equipped to manufacture the new MkX. During testing there was little emphasis given to night operations, and 5,000 were manufactured before the MkX was recognized as nocturnally unsuitable and was immediately cancelled.

Once the MkX was cancelled, remaining supplies of the MkVII and MkIX bombsights were selectively installed in the new bombers whose performance was appropriate, and a new similar Sperry tachometric bombsight was quickly developed; these Sperry sights were purchased to replace the MkX for the RAF Liberators and other bombers. The few ABS sights available went to the new Manchester bombers and later to Hampdens.

It was not long before RAF bomber crews, led by CO Arthur "Bomber" Harris, expressed their intense dislike of both the MkIX and the ABS and demanded their replacement ASAP. The influential Tizard Committee and a Committee founder, Dr. Patrick Blackett, decided to design a new sight to meet the requirements of Bomber Command. The Mk XIV bombsight was developed at Farnborough and was regarded as the "wonder sight of the day," and would be the standard Bomber Command bombsight until the end of the war and after. Shortly after its operational introduction its manufacture was subcontracted to the Sperry Gyroscope Company in America who, after re-engineering it to meet American standards, arranged for A.C. Spark Plug—a Division of General Motors—to manufacture it in quantity. Some aspects of the American T1 were a mechanical improvement on the British manufactured sight, but it was fully compatible with it in every way. The sight's chief source of error was the requirement to set the wind speed and direction on the computer, which in combat conditions were often inaccurate. The American T1A version was produced for use with the faster Mosquito and to allow for the greater operating height, while the British manufactured T2 and T4 versions were developments based upon the T1 bombsight and would be used on post-war aircraft. The MkXV and MkXVII versions were intended for Coastal Command but never entered production. The T1 will be discussed in more detail later.

Farnborough continued its ABS development, and in August 1943 the outstanding SABS Mk IIA tachometric precision bombsight was ready for manufacture. The SABS provided a more complex mechanical computer which was able to calculate the wind and to automatically release bombs, which were qualities it had in common with the Norden. So it was not unexpected that the RAF rejected the Norden when it was belatedly offered in 1944. Less than 1,000 SABS bombsights were manufactured, and after the war in Europe there weren't enough sights to equip two Lincoln squadrons intended for precision bombing against Japan.

The Theory of Bombing and the Bombing Problem

Before any examination of bombsights a brief discussion of the theory of Bombing and the bombing problem needs to be undertaken.

Forces Affecting the Bomb

From the moment a bomb is released a number of forces begin to act upon it; gravity, airspeed, air resistance, and wind, all of which determin the path the bomb will follow and the point of impact.

Gravity

Gravity pulls the bomb toward the earth at a continually increasing speed. It exerts the same force on all bodies, whatever their size, shape, or weight.

True Airspeed

At the same time that gravity is pulling the bomb downward, velocity is driving it forward, as the aircraft is traveling at a definite speed with respect to the air. Since the bomb is a part of the aircraft up to the moment of release, it leaves the aircraft with the same forward velocity. In bombing, this forward velocity of the airplane and the bomb relative to the air is called true airspeed (TAS). Gravity and true airspeed act on the bomb at the same time. During the time between release and impact the bomb follows a path between the direction of these two forces. This time is called the actual time of fall (ATF).

Air Resistance

The third force is called air resistance, which affects the bomb in its flight and is one which acts against the first two. While true airspeed is driving the bomb forward, the air through which the bomb moves is resisting this motion (i.e. air pushes back against the bomb, causing it to lag behind the aircraft). The distance on the ground resulting from this resistance to the forward motion of the bomb is called horizontal lag. In the same way air resistance acts against the force of gravity, horizontal lag tends to keep the bomb in flight longer. During the extra time required for the bomb to fall the aircraft continues to fly forward. The distance on the ground over which the airplane travels during this extra time is called vertical lag.

Wind

Wind could affect the bomb from four directions: headwind, tailwind, and right and left crosswinds.

Bombing Problem

The bombing problem has two parts: the course problem and the range problem. Course means that the bomb has to travel in the right direction; toward the target. Range means that it has to be released the correct distance back from the target so that it will not fall short of the target or over it. The course problem is fairly simple. A bomb always falls in the direction in which the aircraft is headed at the moment of release, and therefore the course problem is solved by directing the bomber on the correct heading.

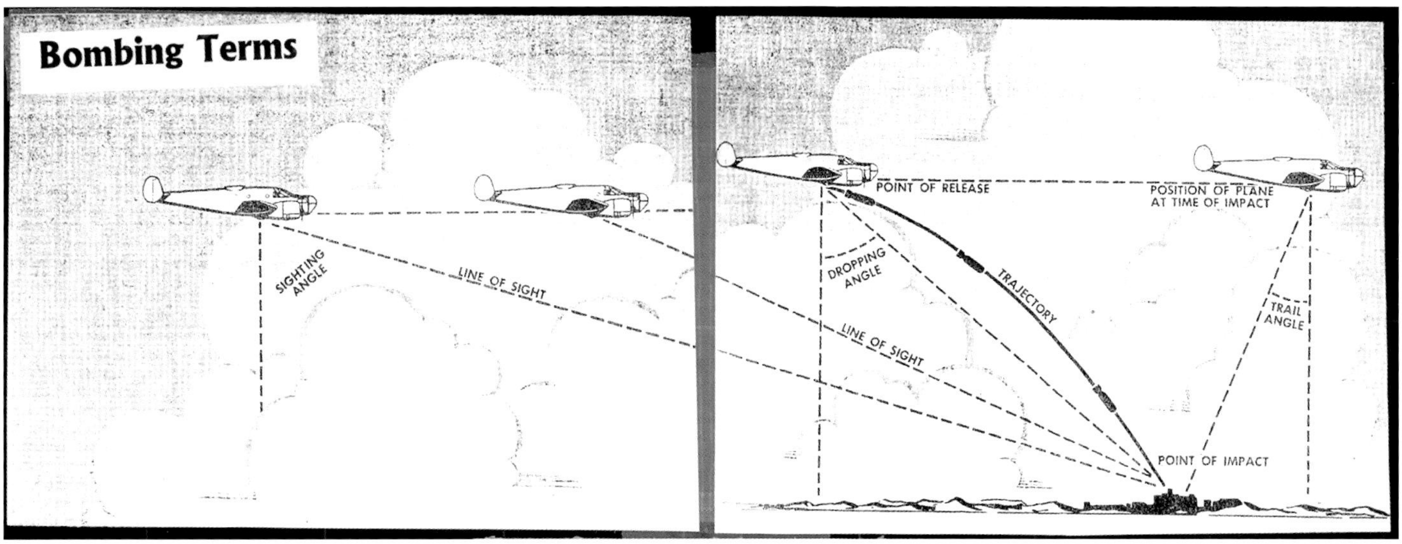

(BIF)

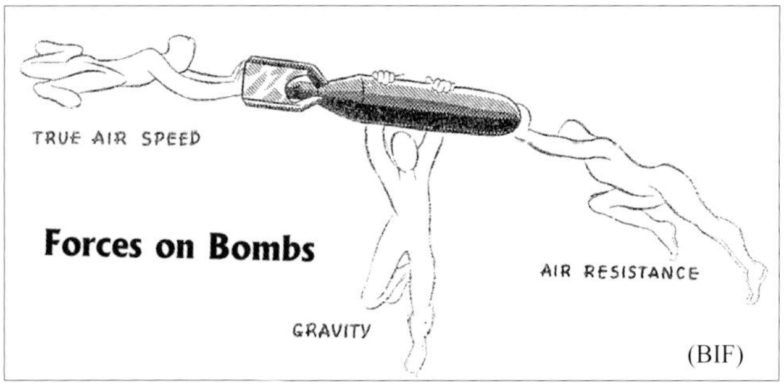

(BIF)

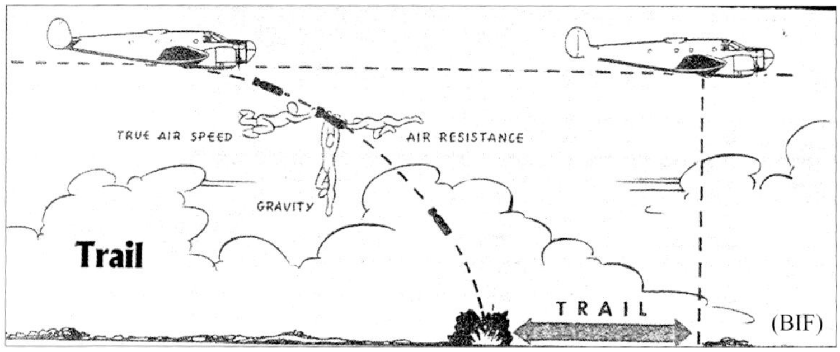

(BIF)

Course Problem

If a bomber airplane is flying directly into a headwind or with a tailwind, its True Heading (TH) and True Course (TC) are the same. To obtain a hit on a target under these circumstances it is necessary only to track over the target. When there is a crosswind, however, the bomber has to crab into the wind at an angle equal to the angle of drift in order to track over the target. This presents another problem, since the bomb always trails along the TH, or longitudinal axis of the bomber; it is affected by the same wind. Therefore, in a crosswind the bomb does not fly the same track as the bomber as it flies downwind a distance called Crosstrail (CT). The size of this Crosstrail distance depends upon the drift angle and the trail of the bomb. The bomber has to fly a course parallel to the collision course and Crosstrail distance upwind of the target. Since your radar set has no way of taking care of Crosstrail, and since the Crosstrail error is minor in relation to the inherent errors in the radar equipment, the solution of the bombing problem is concerned with range.

The Range Problem

Because a bomb leaves a bomber with the same forward speed as the aircraft, it falls forward as well as downward. To place a bomb on a target, therefore, the bombardier has to consider the forward distance it is going to travel as well as the direction it is going to fall in determining its actual release point. That distance depends on several aspects. If a bomb could be streamlined perfectly, so that it would offer no air resistance and would retain its initial velocity, the airplane dropping the bomb would be directly over the target at the time the bomb struck it. However, since there is no such thing as perfect streamlining, the bomb lags or trails behind the bomber. At the moment of impact the bomber is some distance beyond the target. This distance, measured along the ground, is called Trail (T). The Trail value varies for different bombs and is given as a mil value in the bombing tables. A mil is a tangent value which subtends a distance on the ground equal to .001 of the altitude.

Trail is the result of several forces which are acting on the bomb. While True Airspeed is driving the bomb forward, air resistance is tending to hold it back; while gravity is pulling it down, air resistance tends to hold it up. If true airspeed increases, the resistance of the air increases; thus, the horizontal lag is greater. Therefore, as True Airspeed increases Trail increases. Likewise, if the downward velocity increases, the resistance of the air to that force increases and the vertical lag is greater. Since the downward velocity depends on the bombing altitude from which the bomb is dropped, as bombing altitude increases Trail increases. The amount of resistance which the air offers to the bomb depends on the size and shape of the bomb. Ordnance engineers classified bombs into different types according to the Ballistic Coefficient of the particular bomb; the relative amount of resistance the air offered to it. A bomb with a high Ballistic Coefficient falls faster and with less Trail than a bomb with a low ballistic coefficient. Therefore, as Ballistic Coefficient increases Trail decreases.

The distance along the ground that the bomb actually travels in its flight is called Actual Range (AR). The Actual Range plus the Trail, then, is the distance that the airplane flew during this same time. That total distance is called Whole Range (WR). Whole Range is determined by multiplying the Actual Time of fall (ATF)—the number of seconds from release point to impact—by the ground speed in feet per second. When the Whole Range is determined the Actual Range is found by subtracting the Trail.

Slant Range (SR) is the distance from the bomber's position in the air to the target measured by the radar set. To determine the Slant Range that equals the Actual Range of the bomb, the problem is one of solving a simple right angle triangle learned in high school geometry. The sum of the squares of the two sides is equal to the square of the hypotenuse: $(\text{Slant Range})^2 = (\text{Actual Range})^2 + (\text{Altitude})^2$

The actual time of fall (ATF) of the bomb depends primarily on the exact height of the bomber above the target, or the vertical distance which the bomb has to fall, but it is also affected by true airspeed and bomb ballistics. The Actual Time of Fall for each bombing altitude, True Airspeed, and type of bomb is determined by trial and error and was tabulated in bombing tables.

Trail and Actual Time of Fall were the two factors that the bombardier had to set into the bombsight. The Actual Time of Fall was set into the M-Series Bombsight as a disc speed, but when using some sights the Actual Time of Fall was set directly. Trail was set into the bombsight as a mil value. The tables gave the correct Actual Time of Fall or the correct disc speed for each bombing altitude, true airspeed, and type of bomb. Similarly, the tables gave the correct Trail for each bombing altitude, True Airspeed, and type of bomb. Therefore, before the sight could function accurately the bombing altitude, True Airspeed, and type of bomb had to be set. Once the correct Trail and Actual Time of Fall were correctly set into the bombsight it had

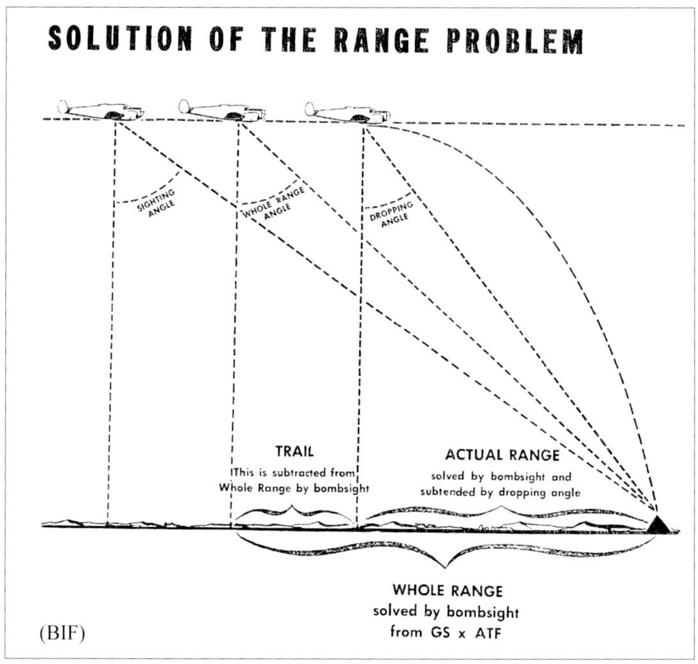

(BIF)

Estoppey D-Series Gallery

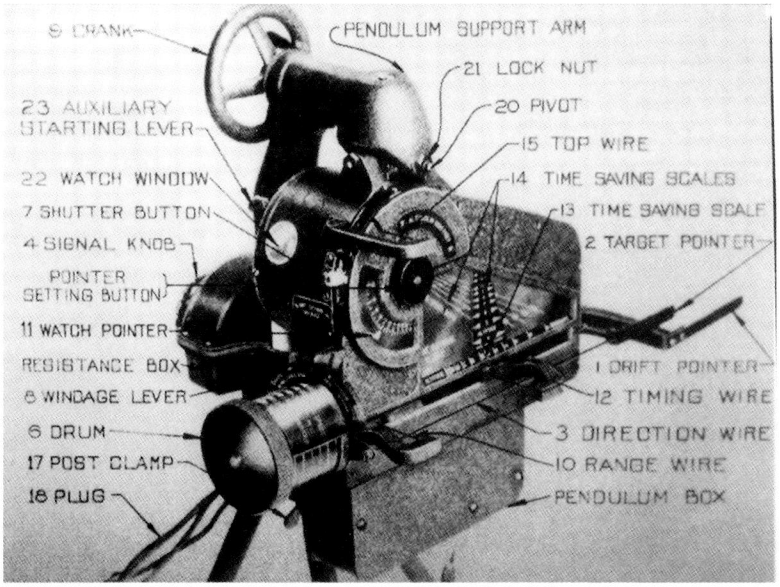

Estoppey D-1 (AFHRC)

Estoppey D-2 (AFHRC)

Estoppey D-4 (AFHRC)

Estoppey D-7 (AFHRC)

Estoppey D-8 (AFHRC)

to be synchronized for course and range. If these few steps were done correctly the bombsight automatically solved the bombing problem.

Conventional Bombing and Bombsights
Estoppey D-1 through D-8

The D-1 bombsight was devised by Swiss émigré George Estoppey, who was a civilian employee at the McCook Field Engineering Division in July 1921. The pendulum-stabilized D-1 used a stop watch to synchronize the speed of the aircraft with the true ground speed. In 1926 the AAC standardized the D-4 bombsight, which integrated an internal timing mechanism. A brand new D-4 was able to attain good results in ideal conditions at altitudes up to 8,000 feet, after which the sight became very inaccurate. In 1939, due to the acute shortage of bombsights, the AAC ordered the new, upgraded Estoppey D-8 into quantity production by the National Cash Register Company (NCR), and later by International Business Machines (IBM). The D-8 was very simple to operate, consisting of wire-type sighting elements that were hand operated to establish synchronization relative to target movement. Time of bombfall was set into a timing mechanism to compute the ground speed, thus solving the bombing problem with provisions made to dial in drift, angle, and trail. The sight was stabilized through a pendulum and dashpot mounting system. The D-8 was discontinued by October 1943 when the Norden M-9 became the standard sighting device.

Sperry Bombsights

Early Sperry Bombsights

The Sperry Gyroscope Co. of Brooklyn, NY, which had been founded by Elmer Sperry in 1909, had begun designing and manufacturing bombsights as a progression of its development of gyroscopes for military and commercial aircraft, as well as ocean vessels. Sperry would become the CEO of the Elmer A. Sperry Company and would hold more than 70 patents, and was generally considered at the time as being only second to Thomas

Sperry Mk1A (AFHRC)

Elmer Sperry founded the Sperry Gyroscope Co. of Brooklyn, NY, in 1909, and began designing and manufacturing bombsights which were a progression of its development of gyroscopes for military and commercial aircraft and ocean vessels. He held over 70 patents and was generally considered at the time as being only second to Thomas Edison as an inventor. (AFHRC)

Edison as an inventor. In 1914 Sperry, with Carl Norden as a key employee, had developed and built a vertically stabilized bombsight that used a vertical gyro assembly energized by DC power. The company went on to develop improved models of this first synchronized sight in 1915, 1918, 1924, 1927, 1929, 1930, and 1933.

In 1922 Sperry tried to improve the Wimperis Mark IA bombsight by attaching it to a Sperry gyroscope, but it failed to meet the Air Service's needs and Sperry looked for an entirely new sight. During 1921-23 Alexander de Seversky worked with the Sperry Company to develop the first fully automatic synchronous bombsight. While serving with a Russian bombing squadron in World War I de Seversky had developed a crude bombsight, stabilized by means of pendulums. He had considered using gyroscopes, but they had not developed enough, and later considered inertial navigation, which also had not advanced to a usable state. Then, while working for the War Department as an aeronautical engineer and test pilot, he collaborated with Sperry and combined a Sperry gyroscope to an analog computer to build a bombsight which used manual inputs of airspeed, altitude, and bomb ballistic characteristics. One master gyro controlled other instruments through remote transmitters, which were equipped with differentials that could be adjusted to remove errors. De Seversky had considered automatic inputs of airspeed and altitude, but with the slow, low altitude aircraft of the time the manual inputs were almost as almost as efficient. The bombsight provided an indication of groundspeed (the first such device to do so) as well as drift on dials. By using horizontal and vertical gyroscopes, a direct course could be automatically set up with the target, which could itself be moving, since the bombsight incorporated a "fourth vector" capability. The sight was tested successfully off the Virginia Cape and contract for more than $2 million was signed by the U.S. Army Air Corps. De Seversky was paid $50,000 for the patent and formed his first company, Seversky Aero Corp.

The Inglis C-1 was another bombsight developed by the Army Air Service and built by Sperry in 1928. The C-1 synchronized the airspeed, altitude, true ground speed, and the bomb's ballistics. It also had a gyroscopic stabilizer and an automatic bomb release. The addition of pendulums or gyroscopes helped stabilize bombsights, but none of these bombsights achieved the accuracy then expected. Sperry continued the development of the C-1 into the C-4 by 1934, when the famed Norden MkXV came online.

But like the future Norden Bombsight, the Sperry gyros encountered major problems along the process of development, and since there was no inter-war demand for the Sperry bombsights funds for development were lacking. It was not until 1936 when the AAC began having problems pro-

Inglis C-1 (AFHRC/AAF)

Sperry C-4 (AFHRC/AAF)

During 1921-23 **Alexander de Seversky** worked with the Sperry Company to develop the first fully automatic synchronous bombsight that could be used on a moving target. (AFHRC)

curing the Norden Bombsight that interest in the Sperry O-1 increased. In January 1936, the Navy suspended all deliveries of the Norden sight to the AAC until its own requirements were fulfilled, which naturally concerned the AAC. Maj.Gen. Frank Andrews, the Commander of the GHQ Air Force, expressed this concern in a memo to the Chief of the Air Corps and to the Navy, in which he openly encouraged Sperry to develop the O-1 Bombsight to meet Air Force specifications.

Bombsights of the 1930s

In the 1930s, relatively simple bombsights assured reasonable accuracy in hitting targets from altitudes below 5,000 feet, which made them vulnerable to enemy anti-aircraft guns. But at altitudes above the effective range of AA guns bombers flew too fast for standard computation of bombing data.

The bombardier's problem was not merely an airborne version of the artillery gunner's problem of hitting a moving target, but also involved aiming at the moving target from a moving platform. The bombing equipment of the time could not calculate in real time the correct moment for releasing a bomb. The calculations had to take into account that a bomber flew rapidly in three dimensions and rotated about three axes, and was often buffeted by turbulence. The flight of the dropped bomb was a function of the acceleration of gravity and the speed of the dropping aircraft, and was then influenced by altitude, wind direction, and the ballistics of the specific bomb.

Originally, bombing missions were concluded by bombardier-pilot teams using Pilot Director Indicator (PDI) signals. While tracking the target, the bombardier would press buttons that moved a needle on the bomber's control panel, instructing the pilot to turn left or right as needed. The pilot had to maintain straight and level flight at the precise altitude and airspeed the bombardier had predetermined for the mission. If the pilot allowed those factors to vary, it would disrupt the bombardier's attempt to track the target; similarly, if the bombardier operated the azimuth tracking of the bombsight unevenly, the uncertain PDI signals would cause the pilot to fly the plane inaccurately. It took expert pilots and expert bombardiers working in harmony to aim a bomb accurately, and in the heat of combat that ideal combination was the exception rather than the rule.

Sperry S-1

The Sperry S-1 Bombsight was the first bombsight with all-electronic servo systems, and compared to the Norden's electromechanical controls was faster and easier to gain a proficiency which could equal that of the fabled Norden. The Sperry S-1 was used in conjunction with the first all-electronic autopilot, the A-5, which was so effective that it became the basis for future post-war autopilots used for years in commercial and military aircraft.

Development of the S-1 Bombsight

In 1937 Orland Esval, Sperry's leading electrical engineer, developed a new type of gyroscope which used a heavier gyro. The gyroscopic effect is due to the moment of inertia of the wheel, and the greatest effect is achieved by a huge gyro spinning fast. Esval's new gyro had double the mass of the existing gyro in the Sperry O-1 bombsight and about the same weight as the vertical gyro in the Norden Mark XV. However, Esval's gyro was designed to spin at 30,000 rpm, which was approximately four times faster than the Norden Mark XV gyros. This increased gyroscopic effect overcame friction in the gimbal bearings that was a source of precession (a slowed gyration of the rotation axis).

Sperry development engineer Carl Frische, who years later would become Sperry's president, developed the first self-erecting system for the new vertical gyro. When engaged, this self-erecting system would automatically find the exact vertical, eliminating the necessity for a pilot and bombardier to use valuable time during a bombing run aligning liquid levels. The self-erecting system could be turned off during banking maneuvers, so as not to precess the gyro to a false vertical, and when switched back on again after the aircraft returned to level flight it would again automatically seek the true vertical.

Esval's high speed gyro and Frische's self-erecting system, and an optical gyro-balancing machine that speeded manufacture, significantly improved the vertical tracking accuracy of Sperry's O-1 bombsight. Next, Esval and Frische turned a second gyro wheel assembly on its side to create an azimuth gyro.

Sperry O-1 Bombsight (AFHRC/AAF)

Sperry O-1 Bombsight (internal) (AFHRC/AAF)

Sperry S-1(left) and S-M2 Bombsight (AFHRC/AAF)

Esval and Frische used the azimuth gyro as a sensor, only using an electromagnetic pickoff mounted on a non-spinning ring that was centered on the spinning rotor and controlled by the azimuth servo motor. This eliminated the physical linkage that caused friction in the Norden Bombsight. When aircraft movements caused the slightest angular deviation of the gyros from the bomber's axes the E-pickoff generated electric signals that, when amplified, controlled a servomechanism that compensated for the bomber's movement and thus stabilized the bombsight optics in azimuth.

The new gyros were self lubricating and induction powered, which eliminated the DC brushes that caused carbon dust, but they required their own AC power source. However, in the late 1930s U.S. aircraft instrumentation was powered only on DC power or on vacuum suction created through venturi tubes mounted outside the aircraft, but the Sperry bombsight was so promising that the AAC implemented induction electrical systems for aircraft. A 400 Hertz electrical system was adopted that spun the new gyros at a slightly reduced speed of 24,000 rpm, which still was more than three times faster than the Norden gyros. With the addition of these new gyros the new Sperry bombsight was designated the S-1.

The new precision S-1 bombsights required new precision autopilots to maintain the bomber's course, altitude, attitude, and trim to a greater degree than was currently possible with a Sperry A-3 commercial autopilot in use. The A-3 used slow pneumatic hydraulic servo systems which could only distinguish the simple angular displacement of the aircraft from its chosen course. The A-3 did not determine velocity or acceleration, and overcompensated in rough air and oscillated. To complement the new S-1 bombsight Frische conceived the first all-electronic autopilot, designated as the A-5. The new autopilot was based on three very reliable dual element vacuum tube amplifiers, each corresponding to a different axis (roll, pitch, and yaw) in the aircraft's control system. Each tube amplified the weak signal measured from the autopilot's set of sensors on the high speed induction gyros. These amplified signals controlled independent electro hydraulic servo-mechanisms, providing quick response in stabilizing the aircraft. The system was damped, which allowed for the aircraft's inertia, and was much more responsive than the electromechanical technology with wind and command signals from the bombsight.

Sperry T-1 (Mark XIV) Bombsight and Computer

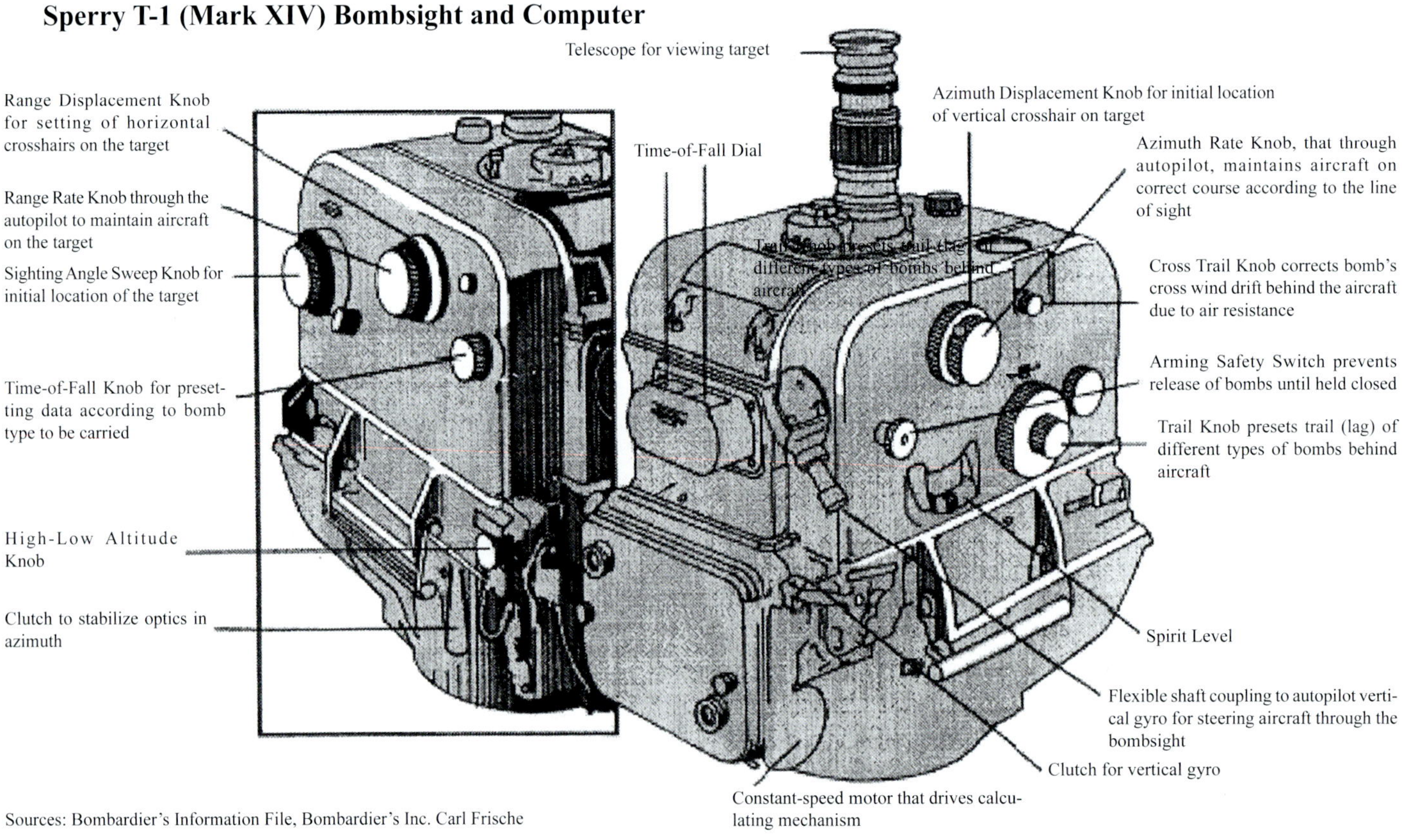

Sources: Bombardier's Information File, Bombardier's Inc. Carl Frische

S-1 Bombsight controls were connected electrically to the A-5 autopilot, and the combination resulted in exceptional accuracy for the time. When the bombing run was started the pilot relinquished the control of the bomber to the bombardier, who then flew the bomber by tracking the target through the bombsight. When the bombsight determined that the release point had been reached it alerted the bombardier, who dropped the bomb.

The inadequate production of Norden M-Series bombsights caused the AAF to equip all B-24Es onward and the B-32 program with the Sperry S-1 bombsight and the A-5 autopilot. Problems with the first Sperry S-1 sight and A-5 auto pilot caused the removal of the S-1/A-5 from the B-32 program. Norden Mark XV production continued to inadequately meet the AAF requirements, and the Navy could make no promises regarding future production, so the AAF had to look to the Sperry S-1 as a substitute

On 17 June 1941, the government approved an 186,000 square foot facility in Great Neck, NY, for manufacturing the A-5 autopilot and S-1 bombsight. The AAC also decided that in the future "all production models of bombardment airplanes to be equipped with the A-5 Automatic Pilot and have provisions permitting the installation of either the M-Series Bombsight (Norden) or the S-1 Bombsight."

Meanwhile, Norden developed an autopilot called the Stabilized Bombing Approach Equipment (SBAE) for the Navy which was known as the Automatic Flight Control Equipment (AFCE) by the AAF. Since the SBAE/AFCE was also based on the same technology as commercial autopilots it consequently was no better than the Sperry A-3 commercial autopilot. In 1940 and 1941, the Norden XV bombsight was installed in AAC B-17s while the Sperry S-1 was installed in B-24Es used by the 15th Air Force in the MTO and in Lend Lease B-24s sent to the RAF (the Navy declined to release Norden sights to foreign governments). A Sperry S-1 bombsight first saw combat on 30 April 1941 installed in a British Lockheed Hudson MK V of Coastal Command 220 Squadron, which hit an 800 ton German supply ship from 8,000 feet off the Denmark coast.

Norden had always begrudged Sperry its growing reputation; perhaps due to Carl Norden's early work with the Sperry Company. Norden left Sperry to launch his own engineering firm, but then had to return to work for Sperry as a paid consultant to keep his new firm afloat. During a Navy, AAC, and Norden conference convened at Norden's New York City offices on 29 July 1937, Maj.Gen. Frank Andrews stated that he would persuade Sperry to develop a bombsight for AAC aircraft because Norden could not meet the AAC's demand for the sight because it was supplying the Navy. After the meeting, Norden President Theodore Barth "spoke somewhat disparagingly of the Sperry Company" and "stated he was very much grieved that the Air Corps was purchasing...an inferior sight" from Sperry, and offered to establish another Norden Bombsight factory exclusively for the Air Corps; a proposal that clearly irritated the Navy.

Andrews and the Air Corps further proposed that Norden collaborate with Sperry to make the Sperry A-5 the standard autopilot even on Norden-equipped aircraft. Of course Norden summarily rejected this plan, even though Sperry signed an agreement that it would not "take any steps in the way of the filing of suits, etc., regarding the possible infringement of patents on the part of the Norden Company that may be incorporated in the Norden Sight." In January 1942, in order to circumvent Norden and the Navy, the Air Corps acquired a manufacturing license from Sperry and contracted Honeywell Regulator Company of Minneapolis to manufacture autopilots designated as the C-1. With the Sperry licensing Honeywell would be free to incorporate certain features of the A-5 into the C-1, which was based on the Norden SBAE gyros but integrated the electronic rate circuits and servos from the Sperry A-5, producing a superior autopilot.

Meanwhile Barth, the affable and colorful Norden President/salesman, used his extensive links to both the Navy and the Army to promote his company's bombsight and autopilot. As is discussed next in the Norden section, even though by Pearl Harbor the classification of the Norden Bombsight had been downgraded from "*Top Secret*" to "*Confidential*," Barth continued to promote his bombsight as the *Top Secret*, "hit a pickle barrel" bombsight; a charisma that surrounds the Norden Bombsight to this day.

The Sperry bombsight was also classified as *Top Secret*, but it was strict company policy not to publicize the fact that the Sperry Gyroscope Company even made bombsights. Fred Vose, the company's head military marketing representative, had established a strong business relationship with the AAC through Maj.Gen. Frank Andrews, but in April 1942 Vose was killed in an airplane crash near Salt Lake City, and in early 1943 Andrews was lost over Iceland; consequently, Sperry lost two powerful S-1/A-5 advocates.

Also, at the time there were reservations about Sperry's position as a multinational commercial company which, before the war, had licensees not only in the UK, but also in Germany and Japan. Barth took advantage of these suspicions by publicly highlighting the fact that as a dedicated source of bombsights, the Norden Company could not only "devote its entire attention to the interests of the Government," but also could "maintain a high degree of secrecy not possible with an international organization engaged in world trade."

Sperry/Norden Comparison Tests April-July 1943

The Second Air Force was assigned to conduct comparison service tests between the Norden and Sperry bombsights during April-July 1943. In August 1943, the Chief of the Air Staff charged a Board of Officers from various Commands and high level departmental heads to consider the unacceptable Norden/Sperry bomb sight situation. The Board of Officers was ordered to meet to consider both precision bombsights and their allied automatic pilot equipment, and to make recommendations as to standardization. The Board drew on a number of expert sources to make a comparative analysis, including the comparative service tests done by the Second Air Force, the Office of the Chief of the Air Staff, Materiel Maintenance, the Air Force Proving Ground, the Air Materiel Command, Production Engineering at Wright Field, the Training Command, and representatives from combat theaters.

On 15 September 1943 the Board of Officers met to review the data that had been gathered on the two systems. Both sights were synchronous with their optics fixed to the target, which they tracked as the bomber neared the target. Both were stabilized by directional and vertical gyroscopes, and both computed ground speed and crosswind drift. The main advantage of the Sperry sight was that it had controls conveniently located on each side of the instrument that were easy to operate. The Norden bombardier had to awkwardly reach around and under the sight itself to simultaneously manipulate the controls on the right side of the base with both hands while sighting through the eye piece. Both the Sperry and Norden utilized the A-5 autopilot to control the aircraft during the bombing run. The Sperry sight was larger at 75 pounds and was unwieldy to install and remove, and took up too much space in the cramped bombardier's compartment as compared to the more easily handled 35 pound early Norden sights and later 45 pound standard M-9 sight. The Board's conclusions were that the data generally favored the Norden sight/autopilot over Sperry.

Long bombing runs under manual control and on autopilot gave the edge to the Norden sight, as experience using the Sperry A-5 autopilot was very limited due to installation and operating problems. No comparison was available on short bombing runs due to the lack of necessary design features in the Sperry units. The Board considered that even with the proposed improvements the Sperry unit would not be as accurate as the Norden.

In the areas of visibility, target search capabilities, and orientation of the line of sight the S-1 was definitely inferior to the Norden. Light transmission through the S-1 sight was definitely less than the Norden due to the inherent design of the optics, which in turn would require redesign of the sight itself to change. This feature was especially important under conditions of poor visibility, especially in the European and Pacific areas, where smoke and haze often restricted clear views of the target. The Sperry optical system admitted approximately 20% less light than the Norden, and this excessive loss of light would be a severe handicap to bombing accuracy in the European and Pacific Theaters. Accuracy in night bombing with the Sperry was also severely handicapped due to this deficiency.

The operational design features of the Norden were far superior, but the Sperry equipment was capable of being improved to a suitable standard in most of the features. However, the improved versions would not be available in adequate quantities in the combat theaters for at least six months.

In the areas of serviceability and reliability the Norden sight and the C-1 autopilot had fewer malfunctions and required less maintenance per operating hour than the Sperry equipment.

The training of Sperry bombardiers and Sperry maintenance personnel for all echelons was inadequate in both quantity and quality, largely due to the lack of sufficient and suitable Sperry equipment for training. It was estimated that it would take about five years before reaching self-sufficiency and overall experience would reach the level of the Norden equipment.

The Norden sight and the C-l autopilot were superior concerning voltage requirements in both sensitivity to small variations in voltage and maintenance requirements of the aircraft electrical system. The voltage and current requirements were extremely critical, and any small variation resulted in malfunction.

The tests concluded that the S-1 sight and A-5 autopilot were operationally unsatisfactory and were not to be installed operationally**.** The Board recommended nine modifications that were essential in order to render the Sperry bombsight and autopilot suitable for operational use. The recommendations included adding a tangent scale for sighting angle and dropping angle; degree scales for sighting angle and dropping angle; trigger lock trail angle and fall of time lock; automatic cross trail setting; improved visibility through optical system; protection of the optical system from oil, foreign particles, and moisture; installation of a locking mechanism on the front window of the sight to keep dirt and moisture out of the sight and permit an easy removal of the window when fogging occurred; and providing suitable turn control for the pilot.

Sperry engineers and the AAF Materiel Command estimated that these recommended changes would take from four to six months to be developed before they were ready to be installed in the bombsights then in production. An additional four to six months would be required for training bombardier and maintenance personnel. Altogether it was estimated that it would require approximately one year before the Sperry would be the equal of the Norden. But even if the Sperry system did match the Norden system in the future there would be the problem of providing both systems with an adequate flow of materiel and personnel for production, not to mention the wasteful duplication in doing so.

However, by May 1943 the Navy, after years of complaining about the Norden Bombsight shortage, now revealed that there was a bombsight surplus, which was due to the fact that the Navy was not engaged in strategic bombing and jealously withheld the sight from the AAF because it had contracted and developed it. A month later the Navy decided to dispose of its newest bombsight factories. The surplus of the Norden, which had cost millions, sounded the death knell for the Sperry S-1/A-5. On 4 August 1943 Gen. Barney Giles, GHQ Chief of Air Staff, had recommended that the Norden be standardized, and a week later Maj.Gen. Davenport Johnson, 2AF CO, sent a letter to AAF CG Gen. H.H. Arnold, declaring that the Sperry equipment was not as accurate as the Norden. Giles then recommended that all contracts for Sperry S-1 bombsights and A-5 autopilots be immediately canceled.

Upon being notified that their contract was recommended to be canceled, Sperry sent representatives to Washington to meet with each Board of Officers member to discuss their decision, as numerous modifications had been made since the S-1 had been reviewed by the Board. The AAF Chief of the Air Staff was also contacted and informed that the new equipment integrating all of the most recent modifications had not been given a fair test. The Sperry arguments must have been persuasive, as on 23 October 1943 HQ AAF directed that the cancellation of Sperry contracts be held in abeyance pending complete reports from operational theaters using the latest types of Sperry equipment. The AAF Materiel Command contracted the International Business Machine Company to build 150 of the S-1 bombsights incorporating all of the recommended changes. Ten were to be available ASAP for transfer to the 8th Air Force in England, and the sights were delivered by air, together with officer personnel who were completely familiar with their operation. On 21 November 1943 a report was sent to the Board stating that all of the latest modifications were a distinct improvement over the original equipment, but the problems "were basic in the bombsight and automatic pilot." This report confirmed the previous recommendations to standardize the Norden system. The next day AAF Brig.Gen. Edwin Perrin, the Deputy Chief of The Air Staff, instructed the Materiel Command to immediately cancel all contracts for Sperry S-1 bombsights and A-5 autopilots with Sperry and Sperry's licensed contractors (International Business Machines and National Cash Register) as directed by the Board of Officers. A meeting attended by the AAF, Navy, and the War Production Board was held in late October 1943 to review bombsight facilities and production schedules versus Army and Navy requirements. The intention of this meeting was to summarize the requirements of both the AAF and USN in comparison with existing facilities in view of the Sperry equipment cancellation, which would necessitate an increase in facilities for the additional manufacture of M-Series bombing equipment and C-l autopilots, and also to investigate the possibility of utilizing the facilities vacated by the Sperry program for other high priority war work. The Air Service Command took the necessary action to insure that Norden equipment was available for installation in B-24 airplanes at the time these bombers were coming off the production lines.

Although it was the general consensus and policy to adopt the Norden M-Series bombsight and C-l autopilot as standard equipment in all heavy bombardment aircraft, this decision presented problems of obtaining sufficient numbers of Norden sights without using the Sperry sights. Norden sight production had to be increased from BuOrd facilities and also by increasing AAF allocations. Sperry production was to stop when a sufficient number of S-1 sights and A-5 autopilots were accrued for B-24 bombers that could not be equipped with the Norden sight, with this change over to one type of bombing equipment to take place as early as practical. The Materiel Command and Sperry engineers had worked long hours to improve the Sperry bombsight and the A-5 autopilot so ample numbers of this improved S-1 type could be obtained so that maximum bombing operations would be continued before the standardization of Norden equipment.

In late October 1943 the AAF ordered all B-24 bombers to be engineered for the installation of the Norden M-Series sights and C-1 autopilots, but until that time the Sperry S-1 sight and A-5 autopilot would continue to be installed. Sperry contracts for sights and autopilots, in addition to the equipment required for this installation, were canceled. It was also proposed that Sperry equipment was not to be replaced on bombers that had been delivered. Norden equipment production was to be available to ensure installation in the E and H model B-24 bombers as soon as they were suitable for the changeover. In addition to the installation of this equipment, Sperry established a program to supply sufficient spare parts for their units in use, and complete units were to continue to be manufactured for training and combat aircraft.

There was a plan for any surplus Sperry sights and autopilots to be used in Lend Lease bombardment aircraft instead of Norden equipment. The Sperry Company would be out of production by May 1944, and over the years many millions had been spent on Sperry equipment. The AAF had procured 6,719 Sperry bombsights and A-5 autopilots, of which 5,140 had been installed, leaving 1,579 surplus units for use as spares, replacements, and for ground training. It was estimated that it would take approximately 250-350 man hours per aircraft to remove the Sperry sight and autopilot and replace them with the Norden. If the kits were made in the U.S. and forwarded to the operating units the man hours required would be less, however, the AAF Air Service Command considered that it would still take too long and be too difficult for the operating squadrons to complete this work. When done in American-based facilities the AAF could only convert 30 to 50 B-24s in training units per month. The kits themselves required the procurement of a large number quantity of brackets, bombsight mounts, and the fabrication of a new electrical harness, along with many other miscellaneous items, meaning it would require three to five months for the first kits to become available. On bombing missions over Europe the 8th Air Force was using the majority of the Sperry-equipped bombers and were using "bomb leader tactics" whenever possible (a Norden-equipped bomber was delegated as the lead aircraft so it was not necessary for all the bombers in the formation to be equipped with the Norden system).

The AAF directed that all Sperry-equipped training aircraft in the Continental U.S. (approximately 500 B-24Hs and 200 AT-11s) be converted to the Norden system ASAP. The Assistant Chief of the Air Staff, Training, was concerned by the cancellation of Sperry equipment, especially since 100 of the 200 AT-11 bombardier training aircraft scheduled for the Sperry S-1/A-5 autopilot had already been equipped and would be useless to the bombardier schools until modified for the Norden sight.

No conversion was ordered for combat B-24Hs in the 8th and 15th Air Forces, but Sperry-equipped bombers were to be replaced as soon as possible and brought back to the U.S. for use in four-engine and gunnery schools and for training bombardiers. The conversion of these airplanes to Norden equipment was accomplished at the Air Materiel Command depots. By March 1944, M-Series sight production was sufficient to sustain installation of Norden Bombsights in production aircraft and approximately 200 kits were available per month for conversion, and were divided between training and overseas Sperry-equipped B-24 airplanes.

The Deputy Chief of The Air Staff considered transferring surplus Sperry sights to the Russians for installation on Lend-Lease B-25s. To re-engineer and install Sperry bombsight equipment in the Russian B-25 would require too many man hours, and if accomplished the everyday wear and tear requiring sight replacement and the need for spare parts would not leave enough Sperry sights for use in AAF aircraft deployed in the combat theaters at the time. Since there was a surplus of D-8 Estoppey and the T-1 (British Mark 14) sights available they were installed in the Soviet Mitchells.

All major Sperry bombsight contracts, except for some repair and rework contracts, were completed by May 1944, and by the end of that month all bomber production included Norden installation. Only 5,000 S-1s were deployed before it was discontinued, with most being used in the B-24 Liberator. So until VJ-Day the Air Force's standard heavy bombing equipment was the Norden Bombsight and Honeywell C-1 autopilot, both of which integrated technology developed at Sperry.

Sperry T-1 (Mark XIV) Bombsight

Although the T-1 Bombsight was British in origin it is included as a footnote here since it was manufactured in large numbers by Sperry, an American company, and was briefly considered as a substitute for the short-in-supply Norden Bombsight.

In late December 1939 Air Chief Marshal Sir Edgar Ludlow-Hewitt, Commander of the RAF Bomber Command, asked for a new bombsight for British bombers to replace the inadequate existing ABS Mk IX bombsight. Eminent physicist and scientific advisor to the Air Ministry Dr. Patrick Blackett took on the task and developed the Blackett Bombsight prototype known as the Mk XII, which consisted of only a sighting head with a second crew member entering data into the sight. The sight was the first to provide acceptable accuracy in combination with wide scale tactical freedom. The two-man operation was soon replaced with a computer cabinet that allowed the sight to be operated by the bomb aimer only and the new sight was designated as the Mk XIV.

The new, smaller Mk XIV needed to be mass produced to equip the Bomber Command's heavy and medium bombers, and Mk XIV manufacture used relatively unskilled labor compared to the Norden sight and required less sophisticated assembly, which had caused significant delays in Norden production. The urgent demand for the Mk XIV led to the British decision to subcontract production to an American company.

Fred Vose, Sperry's head military marketing representative, was very interested in manufacturing the sight under licence as the T-1, and in his sales pitch also implied that the USAAF might be interested in the sight. Later the AAF experimentally equipped a Lockheed Hudson with the MkXIV but rejected it, because wind speed and direction had to be manually set and also because it lacked connection to the aircraft through the automatic pilot; both features which were attributes of the Norden and Sperry S-1 sights. Sperry was selected because of its years of experience in bombsight manufacture, which included the S-1 tachometric bombsight currently in production. Once the initial developmental work had been completed Sperry, which was already over-extended with wartime contracts, subcontracted the work to A.C. Spark Plug Company, Flint, MI, a division of General Motors. Work on preparing the bombsight for mass production began in May 1942, with the first T1 being ready for testing in November. A.C. Spark Plug engaged 15 subcontractors to manufacture components for the 12 main bombsight assemblies, which were then assembled by A.C. Spark Plug, with the final assembly of the T-1 at Sperry, Flint.

Three versions were proposed for manufacture: one for British Blenheim and Wellingtons; a second for the B-24D Liberator; and the last for B-25C and B-25D Mitchells. But by August 1944 only one model of the bombsight was being manufactured, and modification centers in the U.S. and UK were to adapt the bombsight to match the flying characteristics of aircraft designated to use it. Although the T-1 was never installed in American combat aircraft, an amazing total of 23,450 T1 bomb sights were produced by Sperry from November 1942 until June/July 1945, with an optimum 54 completed sights per day

Sperry T-1 (Mark XIV) Bombsight and Computer (AFHRC/AAF)

delivered by two shifts working eight hours per day, six days a week. Further development of the MK VIV sight in the UK was based on the American T1 series of bombsights rather than the original British version. Towards the end of the war bomber aircraft were flying higher, so the bombsight design had to be modified to allow for this change. In December 1944 the T1A and B versions were produced for installation in the fast-flying Mosquito.

Norden Bombsight
Carl Norden, Early Years

Dutch immigrant **Carl Norden**, after a confrontational working arrangement with Elmer Sperry, left Sperry in 1915 to launch a consulting engineering business and became a leading authority on gyroscopes and bombsights. (AFHRC/AAF)

Carl Norden was born on 23 April 1880 in Semerang, Java (Indonesia), and returned to Holland five years later when his father died. The family moved to Dresden, Germany, in 1893, and in 1904 he graduated as a mechanical engineer and immigrated to America. After working for several engineering companies Norden was hired by the Sperry Company in 1911 to refine gyro-stabilizing equipment for the Navy. Norden and Elmer Sperry had continual problems with each other, and in 1915 Norden left to launch a consulting engineering business in Brooklyn. Norden's firm needed extra funds to remain in business, and he worked another two years for Sperry as a paid consultant on work contracted with the Navy and became a leading authority on gyroscopes and bombsights.

Navy Marks III through XI

After the First World War the Navy BuOrd decided it required a precision high altitude bombsight capable of bombing moving ships. At the time the Navy and the Army Signal Corps had not developed a bombsight of their own and were using the course setting-type British Wimperis Sight, which the Navy found to be unsatisfactory. In January 1920 Norden was solicited to submit a preliminary design on a new gyroscopically-stabilized bombsight. Due to the many unresolved problems of bombing and bombsight design Norden did not believe that a completely new bombsight was required at this time and suggested that a redesign of the U.S. Wimperis Mark III. Norden integrated a telescope and added a mechanism that could set the speed and course into the high altitude type of the Mark III, which the Navy accepted after testing with Norden's stipulation that the Wimperis was a finished design and further extensive redesign would not be possible. The redesigned Mark IIIA, the Navy's first stabilized bomb sight, was mounted on a newly built Norden base and sent to the Naval Proving Ground at Dahlgren, VA, for testing in July 1920. The sight performed acceptably, even though the gyro functioned erratically, and it was felt that the Mark III merited additional testing despite Norden's assertion that it was a "finished" design.

As Norden expected, while reworking the design problems developed in determining the direction and degree of the drift relative to the moving target, but designing a sight for use against moving vessels was very complex and at that point there were no solutions, and significant costly testing and engineering would be required before a practical sight could be developed.

When the Army Signal Corps learned of the Navy's experimentation with stabilized sights it formed the Army Bomb Board in 1919 with a group of three Army officers from the Air Service Command and two Navy officers from the BuOrd. The Bomb Board was to develop a policy for future bombsight development, including bombs and fuses, after conducting an in depth examination of the bombing problem.

Previously, at the end of World War I, the American Expeditionary Force published a booklet "High Altitude Bombsights" (20 August 1918) which stated:

> "...in order to drop a bomb so that it will strike at least in the vicinity desired, the use of a bomb sight is imperative. However, this sight must be simple enough...to use it even under hostile fire."

So it was not surprising that the Bomb Board came to the conclusion that the bombsight was the most important item for achieving satisfactory bombing results. After extensive testing the Bomb Board decided in late 1920 that the French Michelin sight was the best sight available because it was partially stabilized. However, the Michelin could not compensate for wind, which forced the pilot to fly low directly into or against the wind, which made the bomber an easy target for anti-aircraft gunners. Therefore, developing a high altitude bombsight capable of correcting for crosswinds became an important project for the Army Air Service. The Board also determined that at the time of determining the correct settings and other adjustments to sight, as well as when the bomb was being dropped, the sight had to be absolutely level and at true vertical to the surface of the earth. The Board suggested that gyroscopic stabilization be used in obtaining a solution for a high altitude precision bombsight.

The Bureau of Ordnance had not yet decided which tack they would take in developing an accurate bombsight, and in 1921 the Navy hired Norden at $35 per day plus expenses to investigate the feasibility of designing an accurate timing sight. In using timing sights, it was necessary to have a timing mechanism or clock to determine the speed in which the aircraft was closing on the target. From January until June 1922 many lengthy discussions were conducted and the submission of numerous drawings, sketches, and engineering designs submitted to Norden and the BuOrd. In June 1922 the Navy awarded a contract (#56166) to Norden for three experimental models of a timing sight at a fixed price of $10,700, including three Pilot Director Indicators (PDI) Mark I. The cost of the equipment required by the Bureau of Ordnance was particularly

French Michelin Bombsight (AFHRC/AAF)

expensive, and to reduce the cost it was decided to simplify the engineering (i.e. manufacture) and improve on the original design.

This new bombsight was designated as the Navy Bombsight Mark XI. The Navy and U.S. Army Air Service had previously signed an agreement to use the same series of bombsight marks, and the Mark I, III, XI, and XV were assigned to the Navy and the IV to X to the Army. The surplus World War I pilot directors were inadequate and unreliable and Norden submitted various new designs, and in 1922 the Navy ordered these new units, designated as the Pilot Director, Mark I. With this new Mark XI bombsight and Mark I PDIs began the lengthy and difficult transition of the bombing problem into an instrument that would be capable of precision bombing.

This new Navy contract necessitated the enlargement of Norden's Larchmont, NY, shop to fabricate the three contracted experimental sights and PDIs. Since these new instruments had to be handmade by trial and error they required a much longer time to complete and be thoroughly tested. The Pilot Directors were not ready to be sent to the Navy until 1923, and the three Mark XI bombsights until March 1924. The new sights were accepted and sent to the Naval Proving Ground, Dahlgren, VA, for thorough bench testing before any air testing was to be begun. Once the bench testing was completed and many modifications made the results of the air tests were very disappointing. The sight was considered to be too complicated and required too much time to keep calibrated. Norden and the BuOrd believed that the sight was viable and that the project should continue, and the BuOrd awarded another contract (#63111) for the modification of two of the Mark XI sights. The modification of these sights was completed in 1925 and they were again tested at Dahlgren.

Norden took different approaches on each of the sights. One sight was equipped with a pendulum design while the other was gyroscopically-controlled. Again, the results of the testing of both sights was disappointing, but valuable data was gathered to formulate the ballistic coefficient of various bombs, the creation of bombing tables, and the mathematical computation concerning sighting angles, which would be invaluable in future bombsight programs.

Despite the problems modification, redesign, and testing continued because the BuOrd would not abandon the dollars already spent along with the engineering and testing time that had already been invested in the project (although much of the redesign and rework on the sights was assumed at no cost by Norden). Norden believed his engineering and design of the bombsight was correct and that the fault was due to the Pilot Directors and course changes during approach to the target.

In April 1926 BuOrd awarded a contract for $21,650 to Norden and Theodore Barth (who had become Norden's administrative partner in 1924)

Norden Mark XI Bombsight (AFHRC/AAF)

to develop two new Mark XI bombsights, three Pilot Directors, and two additional bombsight clocks. By March 1927 two experimental sights were completed and again, despite all of the redesigning, engineering, and testing the results were still not acceptable to the BuOrd, and also to Norden, who continued to be convinced that the sight itself was engineered correctly but the fault lay in the PDI. He continued modification, testing, and the development of the PDI automatic pilot, but again, because of the many mechanical, electrical, and maintenance problems being encountered it appeared that the Mark XI would not be ready for production.

Meanwhile, the Fleet Squadrons continued to use modified Mark IIIA sights and were anxious for a modern bombsight. In 1926 the Navy ordered 40 D-4 Army-type Estoppey bombsights from Geartner Scientific Corporation as an interim measure, as it would not be until late 1927 or early 1928 that the Mark XI would be ready for production. Parallax appeared to be a major problem. Parallax was "the apparent change in the direction of an object, caused by a change in observational position that provided a new line of sight." Norden consulted a number of experts, and it was determined that the parallax problem was not optical but mechanical, which led Norden to develop a new adjustable fork which corrected most of the problem.

Finally, by late 1927 the Mark XI was ready to be tested against other sights and the results, for once, were positive, and BuOrd placed an order for 25 sights; with further modifications the sight was considered to be the best available and the order was increased to 80 sights. The contract totaled $348,700, with the unit cost set at $4,050 and 26 spare parts boxes at $950 each. With this large order Norden and Barth founded a new company in early 1928 called Carl L. Norden, Inc., with Carl Norden as the Consulting Engineer and Theodore Barth as the President. Before contract authorization and production could begin a determination as to the propriety rights on patents and patent liability was needed. It was finally agreed that any patent rights on bombsights produced by Carl L. Norden, Inc. were to revert to the U.S. Government with assignors to the Untied States of America as represented by the Secretary of the Navy and, in turn, the Bureau of Ordnance.

This new contract would require the massive expansion of Norden production facilities, including the addition of new floor space and machine tools; the hiring of experienced machinists, mechanics, and draftsmen; and the hiring and training of assembly line workers. In addition to this expansion, it would be necessary to find subcontractors to supply the many parts of the subassemblies, castings, optics, hardware (such as machine bolts and screws), electric wiring, precision ball bearings, etc. The sophisticated and complicated Mark XI, with tolerances of plus or minus one or two ten-thousandths of an inch, was the first instrument of this tolerance to be mass produced, and it would be many months before any sights would be ready.

Soon, it became evident that no one bombsight design could meet all requirements, and in April 1929 BuOrd issued a Memorandum for Bombsights concerning the Navy's requirements for bombsights. The Memorandum determined that three main sights were needed:

1) High altitude sight of great accuracy
2) High altitude, high precision sight
3) A general utility sight

The Memorandum noted that at the time the Navy was dependent on Norden for its bombsights, and the BuOrd decided to look to other companies and tried to interest General Electric and the Ford Instrument Company, which were already experienced in developing and manufacturing fire control instruments. Ford declined to participate, but a contract was awarded to GE to study bombsight development. General Electric worked on a $10,000, 200 pound high altitude precision sight which was to have a theoretical average error of about 50 feet at 11,000 feet. However, this sight was to be delayed for testing, as a comprehensive study of the problems of gyro-stabilization and a compilation of bomb ballistic data was needed. It was to be ready for testing by the mid-1930s at the earliest, and this delayed date led the company to terminate the project.

Another possible source of bombsights mentioned in the Memorandum was the rival Army Air Corps, which was having problems with their own bombsights. At the time the Army Air Corps was using the Estoppey (D-4) and the Sperry-Inglis (C-1) bombsights, which were not as accurate as the Mark XI, and in early 1929 the AAC had asked the Navy Department for a Mark XI bombsight system for test purposes. Norden quoted the Navy a price of $4,500 for a complete Mark XI, plus $200 for spare parts and a tool box for this additional AAC unit. The transaction contained numerous conditions and guidelines concerning the AAC's acquisition of the sight, which would be the first in a protracted and occasionally rancorous relationship between the two services concerning the Norden sight.

At this time there was no general utility sight available, and the Navy was using the MKIII Wimperis, which was unsatisfactory, as it did not have any stabilization, thus making it erratic. The D-4 Estoppey was better but mechanically substandard, and both sights required special maneuvering on the bombing approach. The Norden Company was requested to look into designing a general utility sight and to submit estimated developmental and manufacturing costs for two experimental sights. In April 1929, Norden informed BuOrd that the cost would be a pricey $20,500 for the two units, and that it would take an additional six months to complete the first instrument because every part had to be hand made, which added to its high cost. Work on the utility sight progressed slowly, as emphasis was on the Mark XI.

By December 1929 one bombing squadron was completely equipped with one Mark XI sight per aircraft, and by the end of 1930 all 80 sights on the contract would be deployed. Tests demonstrated that a novice bombardier using a Mark XI had an average error of 190 feet compared to 286 feet using the Wimperis, Estoppey, or Sperry sights. Also, when using the Mark XI every bomb salvo would straddle the target, while when using the other sights the average was one in every four straddles.

During Individual Battle Practice conducted on 11 November 1929, the San Diego-based U.S. Fleet, Aircraft Squadron, Battle Fleet, Torpedo and Bombing Plane Squadron Two experienced multiple problems with the sight when over 30% of the aircraft were forced to return to their base with sight problems. The exercise subjected the sights to extreme operating conditions with very little time allowed for maintenance. The causes of the problems were analyzed, and it was determined that the Mark XI required scrupulous mechanical and electrical adjustments that were so complicated that under continuous and demanding operational conditions numerous malfunctions occurred. There were not enough trained personnel available to maintain, much less overhaul the delicate sights (which would require three days). To improve the situation, more personnel were to be given sufficient training either by the Navy or Norden, and enough spare sights were to be supplied to the squadrons to compensate for those under maintenance or overhaul.

The Mark XI had met the requirements for a high altitude, highly accurate sight with a theoretical accuracy of 1% of altitude. However, it could not be used accurately under 2,500 feet, it was extremely complicated, required significant maintenance, and was very expensive. The Navy Five Year Plan called for 150 Mark XI sights, of which 80 had already been contracted, and the remaining 70 were to be contracted as soon as the design had been proven under simulated combat conditions.

In early 1930 the first group of 80 sights, which had been issued two or three at a time to the *USS Saratoga*, was returned to Norden for overhaul. Inspection of the returned sights revealed that the instructions requiring extreme care be taken in their shipment had been completely disregarded and the sights were extremely dirty. The Chief of BuOrd sent a strongly worded letter to the Fleet demanding that all instructions in the care of these instruments be followed without delay. To assist in the care of their sights Norden offered instruction in the techniques involved in the disassembly, overhaul, reassembly, and testing. However, the care and maintenance of the sights was an ongoing serious problem that had to be sorted out if the sights were to operate properly.

On May 27, 1930, Norden and Barth filed an application for a patent on the Mark XI bombsight system, but because it was placed on a Secret status the patent was not issued until October 7, 1947.

Navy Mark XV

Even before the Mark XI was introduced into Fleet aircraft Norden and the BuOrd were not entirely satisfied with the sight. The ideal level bombing bombsight required not only the greatest possible accuracy, but also speed and simplicity of operation, low maintenance, and adaptability to quantity, low cost mass production. The most important factor was the speed of operation, of which there was to be a minimum of elapsed time over the target beginning with the bombing approach and ending with the dropping of the bomb. During this time the bomber was flying straight and level, making it vulnerable and an easy target for enemy interceptors and anti-aircraft fire. So with these parameters Norden began the development of the Mark XV in early 1929. The new sight would not be a timing sight but a synchronizing type, which Sperry, Estoppey, and General Electric were also developing.

In a synchronizing sight the altitude and air speed were set, and the line of sight automatically established a motion which the bombardier could control. The sight provided ground speed, drift angles, and true air speed, and would also hold a true compass course for hours and compensate for earth rotation, all in knots per hour. These calculations were to take only about 10 seconds, but in practice the actual time was closer to 20-30 seconds. The new constant speed governor made these calculations possible, as it was very accurate and responsive, and adaptable to a wide range of revolutions per minute. The new rate end contained the synchronous drive transmission in the new sight. The sight was able to transfer the bombing problem to the sight by determining the correct dropping angle.

On 9 February 1931 Norden sent the first Mark XV Bombsight, Experimental Model #1 and #2, to the Dahlgren Naval Proving Ground for wide-ranging and rigorous flight testing. During the initial tests the servo motors were affected by temperature changes in the range of 40° to 50F°, making the sight unusable and suspending testing until this problem was resolved. A more powerful servo motor was substituted with excellent results. Problems also arose in determining the best spotting methods for bombing fixed targets, and two spotting rules were devised by the use of tables developed by the Naval Proving Ground. During the tests on Exp. #1 and #2 Dahlgren submitted 33 pages of deficiencies, along with suggestions on the remedies that should be taken.

Despite these deficiencies, the Mark XV Experimental Model #2 was scheduled to be used in comparison to the Mark XI from an altitude of 5,000 feet in October 1931 in bombing tests on the anchored target ship *USS Pittsburgh*. Using the Mark XI 14 bombs were dropped, scoring three hits for 21% success, while using the Mark XV a total of eight bombs were dropped with four scoring four hits for 50%.

In November 1931 more tests were conducted to determine vulnerabilities and to establish the feasible life of this sight. The most serious defect were the bearings, as they ran dry after several hundred hours of running time. There were other miscellaneous defects that were immediately corrected, and generally these experimental models withstood the rigorous

The Mark XV, Experimental Model #2 was used in comparison to the Mark XI in October 1931 in bombing tests on the anchored target ship *USS Pittsburgh*. (USN)

testing and surpassed expectations. The shortcomings detected in these experimental models allowed Norden to make corrections and improvements. Once Norden corrected these deficiencies the BuOrd recommended the manufacture of the Mark XV bombsight, provided that enough time be allowed for the Proving Ground to conduct air testing and calibration with service bombs.

On 11 February 1932 the AAC acquired 15 Mark XI sights, which were to be delivered immediately, and 25 Mark XVs, which were to be delivered as soon as production began. The Mark XI was obtained to establish a bombsight school to train Ordnancemen to maintain both types of sights. First the Navy granted a limited number of AAC Ordnancemen entrance to their Ordnancemen's School at Hampton Roads, VA, for special bombsight training, after which the AAC graduates would establish their own school.

At the start of 1933 the AAC had realized that its current Estoppey (D-4) and the Sperry-Inglis (C-Series) bombsights, and even the Navy/Norden Mark XI sights were obsolete or inadequate, and coveted the Navy's superior Mark XV sight; after all, bombardment was the AAC's bailiwick. By October 1933 the entire Air Corps still had only three Mark XV sights and demanded that the Navy supply enough XV sights to be able to allocate their major tactical organizations (March, Rockwell, and Langley Air Bases) three sights per month for six months. Despite the Navy's cooperation in supplying the Mark XV sets the series of service tests conducted by the AAC were not completed until the end of April 1934, which badly affected the schedule of their bombsight program. Also, due to the modification of the sights it would be until August 1934 when any further testing could begin.

The large number of fundamental changes in the Mark XV caused Norden and Barth to patent a large number of the modified sights to protect the company in a period where there were an increasing number of bombsight inventors. On 15 July 1931, during the development of the Mark XV, Theodore Barth filed a patent for a Speed Controlling and Speed Measuring Centrifugal Mechanism which was issued on 23 November 1933. This important device provided for the manufacture of a control mechanism having a high degree of precision for maintaining constant speed in rotary motion. It also provided for the manufacture of an improved governor mechanism for rotary systems that ensured constant speed without using large or complicated parts.

The Norden Company had become the leader in producing a small, accurate, and simple-to-operate high altitude precision bombsight that had finally solved the bombing problem. Accordingly, a patent was taken out on the Norden Synchronizing Bomb Sight in the name of Theodore H. Barth and filed on 28 September 1932, but again was not issued until 30 March 1948 because of its secrecy. From 1932 to 1935 the Mark XV underwent many modifications, with some major and others minor; none of which merited a patent. However, with all these changes, on 5 April 1935 Barth filed another patent for a Synchronizing Bomb Sight that was issued in 1950. The U.S. government retained the patent rights and patent liability.

The Mark XV synchronized bombsight had solved the bombing problem. The bombsight's parts were synchronized to move in conformity with the apparent movement of the target while keeping the sight trained on the target. The optical parts of the sight were stabilized so that they would not be affected by the roll or pitch of the bomber, which would also afford an accurate method for correcting trail and cross-trail of the bomb. The Mark XV was designed so skillfully that throughout its service life from 1935 to its final combat use in 1967-68, its basic configuration amazingly remained virtually unchanged. Although many modifications and attachments were developed over the years, these had no effect on the use and basic design and could be incorporated without redesigning the entire sight.

AAF Mark XV

On 6 March 1933 the AAC, Engineering Division at Wright Field was awarded a contract for 35 Mark XV sights, which was later reduced to 23 due to a lack of funds. The first model was to be furnished to the Army Air Corps for testing in April 1933, and if any modifications were required they were to be incorporated in the new production model being produced.

In early April 1933, BuOrd and representatives from the AAC Materiel Division at Wright Field attended acceptance tests at the Dahlgren Naval Proving Ground, where the Mark XV was being shop and air tested. On 5 April 1933, 12 bombs were dropped from an altitude of 5,000 feet in "disturbed air conditions" with excellent results. The next day the Navy provided a sight to the AAC, Wright Field for testing.

The AAC test results were also very good, and on 10 April 1933 the AAC requested 78 (later reduced to 77) additional sights besides the 35 (reduced to 23) Mark XV sights; eventually giving them 100 sights. BuOrd, the AAC, and Norden agreed on a policy of strict secrecy to prevent disclosure of any design features of the sight and issued explicit instructions regarding the shipment, storage, and use of the sight. They also required a special course of instructions in the care, maintenance, and operation of the sight to be taught by specially selected officers.

By April 1934, eight sights had been sent to the Air Corps, with 12 more delivered in April and three in May for 23 total. The AAC was very impatient over the slow delivery of the new sights, but secrecy and the intricate and precise workmanship required in building them slowed production, as it would until late 1944. The contracts for the bombsight program were awarded to the Norden Company without advertising for bids, which was in violation of existing government regulations concerning the purchase of ordnance materiel, but Norden was the only manufacturer capable of producing these precision bombsights. The unit cost of the sight was comparable to and in some cases lower than other types of sights in production. Under the terms of the contract the Navy was to acquire complete patent rights.

A cost study conducted in November 1934 showed that labor, overhead expenses, and additional expenses resulted in a cost per sight of $3,683, which, after adding 10% for profit placed the per unit cost at $4,051. The net profit for Norden for the Mark XI and Mark XV for six and one half years, from 1928 to 30 June 1934, averaged about 10%, with neither Carl Norden nor Theodore Barth receiving a salary! Because of the delivery of 81 sights to the Air Corps and 72 to the Navy for a total of 153 sights the unit price dropped from $4,725 to $4,555.

In January 1935, after several hundred Mark XV sights were in use by the Navy and AAC, the usual failures (called "casualties") were being reported but on a very large scale. The most serious problem involved the slicking brush, which caused the gyro commutator to malfunction, critically affecting the gyro and making the sight useless. Norden engineers found that problem stemmed from a rough cloth used to clean the commutators.

Although the Mark XV was extremely accurate, the addition of an automatic pilot would greatly enhance this accuracy, as it replaced the human with an automatic pilot during a bombing approach. In the early years of bombsight development Norden and BuOrd were not satisfied with the existing Pilot Director of the Mark XI, and many types of directors were developed, redesigned, and modified, but none were thought to be more than adequate. The use of an automatic pilot was not new, as Sperry Gyroscope and other companies were developing them, as was the Navy. In December 1933 BuOrd awarded Norden a contract for an experimental model for automatic flight control equipment to be used with the Mark XV sight. The Stabilized Bombing Approach Equipment (SBAE) was designed by the Navy and contracted to Norden for manufacture. It was sent to Dahlgren Naval Proving Ground on 14 February 1935 to be installed in a XT3D-2 aircraft and was ready by 28 March 1935 for flight and bombing tests. The weight of this automatic flight control system was 126 pounds, to which was added the 52 pounds of the Mark XI and XV sights. The required base for this equipment was 30x30 inches. Only "Acceptable" bombing accuracy was achieved from 1,300 and 1,600 foot altitudes at 70 knots airspeed using the low altitude bombing device, but no attempt was made to bomb from higher altitudes. The tests showed this directional flight gyro to be superior to the Sperry gyro, as it produced sufficient stability about the lateral and longitudinal axis for bombing approaches and its power was at least twice of what was required. However, this set did have its limitations, as it was not quite as easy to operate as the Sperry set; its proportionate banking element had not been successfully established; its durability and dependability had not been determined; and the adjustment of the rudder control to give automatic flight sufficient steadiness for bombing approach was not satisfactory. As these results were not as good as anticipated it would be several years before an operational unit was developed. On 7 April 1936 Norden had prepared new engineering drawings, data, and charts for use in the installation of the SBAE, and this data was forwarded, showing the exact dimensions for the major sub-assemblies; two possible installations; and the approximate dimensions of the mounting surfaces required for the SBAE units, but again the unit did not meet expectations.

In the mid-1930s the BuOrd was looking for an adequate low-level bomb sight to meet the requirements set in April 1929. The U.S. air services continued to use the World War I modification of the British Mark III. In April 1936 a Low Altitude Bombing Comparative Test of the Mark III and the Mark XV was conducted by the U.S. Fleet, VP Squadron One based at Pearl Harbor, HI. Tests determined that the Mark III was very simple compared to the Mark XV and was more readily adapted for use by inexperienced operators. Although the Mark XV was not designed for low altitudes, it was easily adapted to low altitude bombing by using established techniques. Since most bombs were approximately similar in their ballistic coefficients this allowed the use of tables and curves already established, and could be readily utilized for all altitudes. During these tests 10 bombs were dropped at altitudes of 1,000, 1,500, and 2,000 feet. In all cases the Mark XV outperformed the Mark III, with the average radial errors for the Mark III at different altitudes being 97.9 feet and for the Mark XV were 62.2 feet.

With the resurgence of militarism in Europe BuOrd requested that Norden formulate a wartime emergency production capability. In January 1936, Norden informed BuOrd that monthly production by the end of the year could be about 75 sights and increase to about 400 sights per month in 12 months thereafter. This would require Norden to expand its facilities, hire and train new personnel, acquire new production machines, and gather sub-contractors.

Even though the AAC was finally receiving the Mark XV in quantities there continued to be a serious shortage of the sight, and the AAC continued to use the Sperry C-4 and the IBM Estoppey D-4. A new D-4 in perfect condition, providing all circumstances were perfect, could achieve very good results at an altitude of 8,000 feet, but above 8,000 feet its errors became extreme. The C-4 sight was considered to be very unsatisfactory under any conditions. Because the AAC was dependent on the Navy for the Mark XV the Materiel Division at Wright Field sent a letter to the Chief of the Air Corps outlining the problems with the other sights and the urgent need for the Mark XV.

By January 1936 the AAC had purchased 206 Mark XVs from the Navy, but by the end of 1936 only 100 had been delivered, and BuOrd was unable to give the Air Corps any definite delivery date for the remainder. BuOrd was unable to supply enough bombsights for both services without expanding the Norden manufacturing plant. It was becoming a critical issue for the AAC, as the new Martin B-10 Bombardment aircraft were being delivered at a rate of three per week and the Navy had been promised delivery of 10 sights per month.

So it was obvious that a single source of supply for the sight was becoming highly unsatisfactory, as the Navy was unable to furnish the sight for itself and the AAC. It was the view of the HQ, GHQ Air Force that future bombardment aircraft should be designed around the bombsight rather than have the bombsight installed as a removable accessory. The structure of the sight lent itself to a built-in installation, with shock proof mountings as well as constant temperature and moisture control regardless of altitude. The bombardier was to sit in a natural, comfortable position with no movement of his body other than his hands, so that he would be capable of precision equal to that of the sight; otherwise, physical and mental exhaustion would induce errors which no sight could eliminate. Previously, the nose of the aircraft had to be modified to install the sight after the aircraft was built and contractors were required to make this modification. All future bombardment aircraft were to provide for the permanent installation of sights as part of the aircraft's structure, with the nose designed for maximum comfort for the bombardier and unlimited approach vision while he was seated at the sight.

To further compound matters, the production of bombsights was seriously affected by the continuing shortage of the vital precision ball bearings. This shortage was to last for many months before the bearings would become available in sufficient quantities to supply all of the bombsight manufacturers. In spite of all the shortages, the Navy was able to furnish approximately 70% to 80% of the anticipated bombsight production, but the full needs of the AAF could not be met. In 1942 Theodore Barth and Carl Norden founded the Barden Company (hence the name "Bar-den") to make precision ball bearings for the Norden bombsight. The bearings they manufactured were of exceptional quality, featuring tolerances beyond the scope of the technology then available.

Wartime Production and the Mark XV M-9

The introduction of the Norden Mark XV in 1933 marked a milestone in the development of a precision bombsight which automatically solved the bombing problem. During the next decade the speed of bombardment aircraft increased from 100 mph to 200 to 300 mph, while the bombing altitude increased from 5,000 to over 25,000 feet. As the bombing altitude increased bombing problems were magnified and caused a decrease in bombing accuracy. But, as was expected of an instrument this intricate and delicate, many deficiencies became apparent in the Mark XV. Carl Norden, his engineering staff, and the BuOrd continually worked to solve these problems, resulting in various Mark XV MOD numbers. There were several models in use, among them the M-2, M-4, M-6, M-7, and M-9, with the even-numbered models using 12-volt direct current; the later odd-numbered models used 24 volts. The reason for the voltage difference was that the newer type bombers had 24-volt circuits.

There were two types of M-4 sights. The early sights were modifications of the Navy MOD 3 and the M-2 sight, while the later M-4s were manufactured as the M-4 and not modifications of the earlier sights. The M-5 was identical to the later batches of M-4s except for using 24-volts, while the M-6 was also identical to the M-4s except for operating on 24-volts and having modifications to the bombsight gyro. The M-7 was identical to the M-4 except for operating on 24-volts. The Navy MOD3 was equivalent to the AAF M-2; the Navy MOD4 to the AAF M-5; and the Navy MOD 5 to the AAF M-7. These models were very similar in principle and operation, so that if the bombardier learned to use any one of them he could use all of them.

The Norden Company improved its bombsight from the Mark XV to the M-7, and then to the M-9, which was introduced in late 1943. With the M-9 the closing speed of attack could be established at any time during the approach and a fixed speed and altitude needed only to be maintained for 15 to 20 seconds by the use of the Norden produced gyro-stabilized automatic pilot, which was called the Automatic Flight Control Equipment (AFCE) by the Army, while the Navy named it the Stabilized Bombing Approach Equipment (SBAE). The AFCE was an internal computer consisting of an intricate system of numerable gears and cams and mirrors, as well as lenses and prisms that controlled the aircraft on the bombing approach and eliminated manual control.

In June 1940, BuOrd asked the AAC for its requirements for bombsights in view of FDR's request to Congress for 50,000 aircraft. The AAC estimated that, due to deteriorating conditions in Europe, their requirements in 1941 would be 316 sights, followed by 3,645 in 1942, 5,000 in 1943, and 5,115 in 1944. Norden replied that production could be increased to 120 sights a month on three months notice. To fulfill the AAC's 1942 requirement the BuOrd would expand the Norden facilities by adding a new plant in Indianapolis, IN, to produce 400 sights per month as soon as possible.

By the summer of 1941 the bombsight supply situation was becoming critical, because the AAC estimated that its requirements would now be at least twice the quantity considered sufficient in the summer of 1940. To meet these new requirements, the Bureau of Ordnance concluded that a minimum of $5-6 million in additional tools and equipment would be required by the bombsight manufacturers. By December 1941, American aircraft production programs were quickly reaching the point where they surpassed all bombsight production and the allocation of bombsights could not be maintained. By the next December the bombsight shortage had reached a very critical juncture, as the AAF was unable to meet the demands of conducting bombing operations in both the European and Pacific Theaters. Previous correspondence with Navy C-in-C Adm. Ernest King, in November 1942, concerning the bombsight situation had come to naught, as King, protecting his turf, maintained there were other potential bombsight manufacturers other than Norden to supply the AAF. The AAF did have facilities (the Victor Company and the Cardanic-Burroughs Company), but their factories had not yet produced one complete sight and were experiencing significant difficulties and delays before they could mass produce satisfactory bombsights. (Note: the Cardanic Corporation was named after the cardan ring around the gyroscope.) Approximately ten months planning was involved in the production of sights, and therefore it was necessary to plan months in advance to keep production lines moving to meet the increased schedules. As previously discussed, the Sperry Gyroscope Company was producing alternative precision S-1 bombsights at the rate of 200 per month, but this sight had yet to be proven satisfactory. The AAF strongly implored the Navy to make additional Mark XV bombsight allocations available, as the mission of the AAF was strategic bombing.

The AAF was especially concerned with higher aircraft speeds and a wider range of altitudes used in contemporary bombing operations, and so the Mark XV, MOD 5 underwent extensive modifications to meet these new bombing requirements. When America entered the war the Mark XV, MOD 7 (called the M-7 sight) was ready for production and was considered to be the ultimate precision bombsight available to any combatant. But in 1941 BuOrd requested that Norden begin a new high priority project to explore the possibility of bombing from 60,000 feet, even though there were no bombers, in fact or on the drawing board, that could reach that altitude. To meet this goal Norden thought that the Mark XV, MOD 7 could be modified with an attachment designated as the MOD 9 series, called the M-9 sight.

The M-9 was a synchronizing type bombsight designed so that, when correctly operated by the bombardier, it would solve the bombing problem by determining the dropping angle at which the bombs should be released and the course on which the bomber should be flown to obtain a direct hit on the target. This was achieved by a mechanical system that set up a "line of sight" between the bomber and the target, and measured the angle which this line of sight made with vertical. Gyroscopic stabilization was used to allow instantaneous and continuous measurement of the angles which ex-

The **Norden M-7 Bombsight** (head shown) was identical to the M-4 except for operating on 24-volts. (Author/CAFAZ)

Norden modified the Mark XV, MOD 7—designated as the **MOD 9** series and called the **M-9** sight—for use at higher altitudes. The M-9 would be the ultimate wartime Army/Navy Norden bombsight. (Author/CAFAZ)

isted between the line of sight and the true vertical. To accomplish this the line of sight had to be maintained on the target. The sights, having only the trail modification, were designated as type M-9A, and the sights having both trail and disc speed modification for high altitudes were designated as type M-9B. The Mark XV, M-9 series was to become the standard Army-Navy production model during World War II and for many years thereafter.

In January 1943, once the M-9 was accepted after testing at the Dahlgren Naval Proving Ground, the BuOrd asked Norden for a quotation for the production of 3,000 Mark XV, M-9 sights with one Pilot Directional Indicator (PDI) but without the stabilizer (part of the Auto Pilot). The cost per unit was quoted at $3,500 plus a fixed fee at 6% ($210), and the total cost of this contract was to be $11.1 million dollars. An additional order of 900 Mark XV M-9 sights with one PDI but without the stabilizer was to be manufactured by the Burroughs Adding Machine Company as the sub-contractor at a cost of $7,102 per unit, with the contract totaling $6.5 million dollars. These proposed per unit costs would prove to be too low, especially that from Norden.

However, the Navy made no additional bombsight allocations and on 30 December 1942 the AAF approached the Joint Aircraft Committee (JAC) to request additional critically needed bombsights, stating that the present allocation did not take into account the needs and responsibilities of the two services. To justify the allocation of more bombsights to it the AAF, which rightly considered itself America's strategic bombing arm, argued that the Navy should concern itself with its over water pursuits, which did not require high altitude precision bombsights. The JAC brokered an increase of bombsight allocation from the BuOrd which would also allow the AAF to plan their bombsight installation and determine in which of their bombing aircraft the sight would be installed. But again, this proposed increase in sight allocation would not begin to satisfy AAF requirements, and the months passed before the increases in deliveries of the Norden sight actually occurred.

Throughout 1942, the BuOrd had continued its efforts to increase the output from the Norden plant and to bring the new Naval Ordnance Plant at Indianapolis into production. The construction and equipping of the Remington Rand factory was facilitated so that it could start production of bombsights as soon as possible. Also, it was expected that the other new non-Norden factories coming on line would fill this huge sight production disparity (which they would accomplish).

With the growing number of factories manufacturing the Norden sight and associated equipment, it became compulsory to identify and serially number the bombsights made by the various facilities to eliminate confusion as to where the sight was made and which was responsible for the instrument. In October 1942, the Office of Naval Inspector of Ordnance issued a directive to identify each bombsight and the location where it was manufactured. Beginning with the Mark XV, MOD 5, each sight was ordered to have a letter and number. The following facilities were assigned letters as follows: N= Carl L. Norden; L= Lukas-Harold; R= Remington Rand; B= Burroughs Adding Machine; V= Victor Adding Machine; and C= Cardanic Burroughs. The serial number assigned to the manufacturer would start with the number 1, such as N-1 for Norden. The name plate showed the name of the company making the bombsight, and was not to refer to Carl L. Norden, unless the instrument was actually manufactured at the Norden New York city facilities. The design of the Army and Navy bombsight name plate did not allow for sufficient space for the letter "N."

Because of the huge investment involved in the production of bombsights and auxiliary equipment, the AAF and Navy Budget Offices requested information to compare the costs of a sight manufactured by the new companies and Norden. The cost of M-9 Series sights purchased by the AAF from the Navy (Norden) and the Victor Adding Machine were compared. The first contract for 1,000 sight heads from Victor cost $7,625 per unit; the first 4,013 Norden sights cost $8,800 per unit, and a subsequent contract for 4,065 were produced for a reduced cost of cost $6,051 per unit ($7,560 total average).

By February 1943 the number of Norden Bombsights manufactured was not sufficient to supply the AAF's requirements. It was estimated that the AAF orders would not be completed before February 1944, and by that time the monthly production rate would drop off to one third, which would mean a reduction of bombsights to the AAF. BuOrd notified the AAF that in order to obtain sufficient bombsights their future orders should be sent to C.L. Norden, Inc., by March 1943 so that production would continue uninterrupted. The bombsight allocations were based on the estimated monthly production from the War Production Board Report of 30 November 1942, which stated that after satisfying the Navy requirements the AAF would be allocated the remainder of the sights. The schedule of allocation as of 30 June 1943 showed an undelivered total of 12,382 bombsights for the Navy and 10,432 for the AAF for a total of 22,814 scheduled but undelivered sights. It would not be until late 1943 that sufficient quantities of bombsights would be available to the AAF. It was expected that bombsight production for 1943 from all sources would be 14,438, with 7,536 allotted to the AAF and the rest for the Navy. During the war there was the continual but unanswered question as to why the Navy required so many high altitude precision bombsights when their bombers did not engage in strategic bombing to anywhere near the global extent as did the AAF.

The bombsight supply situation became so serious that the AAF considered substituting the inferior Estoppey D-8 bombsight for the Norden M-9 on aircraft that could later be easily re-equipped with the Norden sights when they became available. M-9 bombsights were to be made available only at staging areas, so that all aircraft taking off for overseas combat would be fully equipped. A substantial time would pass before Modification Centers could be completely supplied with the M-9, and an even longer period before the bombsights could be furnished to the various bomber production lines for installation. The BuOrd agreed that its "lower group" aircraft, which actually had no use for a precision high altitude bombsight, would not be equipped with M-9 sights until sufficient sights later became available. At the factory level, in order to speed up to maximum production each bombsight contractor made direct patriotic appeals to its workers to encourage them to do their best to achieve peak production.

Victor and Cardanic-Burroughs were late getting into production due to problems in obtaining specialized machine tools, training their labor force, and understanding and implementing the manufacturing techniques of using extremely small tolerances, as well as due to the complicated character of the bombsight itself. Provisions were made for all manufacturers and subcontractors to exchange information on their problems and to sell to each other surplus parts and materials.

In mid-July 1943, the manufacture and delivery of maintenance spare parts for the M-Series of bombsights became an immediate problem that appeared to have a solution in the near future. Before the war spare parts supply did not present a difficulty, as the bombsights were returned to Norden for repair or modification. Once the war began it became impossible to return the sights to the manufacturer or repair depots because the distances and logistical problems from the extended battlefront were too far. Hypothetically, it would be thought that all bombsight parts manufactured by the different contractors would be interchangeable, but this was not the situation because of the extremely close tolerances of many parts. Cannibalization—the using of parts from other bombsights—was suggested, but many essential parts of the bombsight, after they had been in operation for some time, became "run in" and could only be used in that sight. The Navy always had priority over the AAF concerning the allocation of spare parts, and the answer to the spare parts problem was for the new bombsight manufacturers to come on line and supply new replacement sights. To further compound matters, the production of bombsights was seriously affected by the continuing shortage of the vital small precision ball bearings, which was to last for many months before the bearings would become available in sufficient quantities to supply all of the bombsight manufacturers.

By late 1943, as the bombing of Germany and Japan escalated, the AAF bombsight situation became even more critical, and the Navy was unable to anticipate more than 30 days in advance what the increased bombsight allocations would be to the AAF. Then, at this point, to make matters worse the stabilizer came into as short of supply as the bombsight. However, there was the promise of significant production from the Victor Adding Machine and Cardanic-Burroughs by late May or June 1944.

Despite the emergency measures taken by both the AAF and BuOrd, a large shortage of sights extended into November 1943. Victor, Lukas-Harold, and Cardanic-Burroughs were only beginning to manufacture sights, while Remington Rand was undergoing significant difficulties in getting their production lines up and running. Every effort was being made by the Navy and the prime sight contractor, C.L. Norden Company, to bring its plant to capacity production as soon as possible. But by 8 May 1943, Victor had produced only 14 sights and Cardanic-Burroughs 10, which meant that, at that rate, it would not be until the first quarter of 1944 that these contractors would reach their peak scheduled production of 700-750 units per month.

As a result of the meetings held in October 1943 between the AAF Air Materiel Command, the BuOrd, and the War Production Board, the Navy increased the peak production of the Norden factory and Lukas-Harold from 600 to 650 sights per month each, which would give the AAF an additional 100 sights. In December 1943 the AAF received 911 bombsights from Navy facilities, and by January 1944 this figure increased to over 1,000 sights per month and continued to increase to over 1,500 sights per month. In January 1944 total bombsight production was 1,700 sights, of which the Navy took about 600 and 1,100 were sent to the AAF. In case additional bombsights were required, any expansion would have to be assumed by AAF contracted manufacturers, as the Navy manufacturers were running at full capacity to supply the AAF with as many sights as possible.

By fall 1943 the monthly production by Navy controlled facilities would be 1,800 bombsights, 1,600 SBAEs, and 2,500 directional stabilizers, plus other related equipment. Production from AAF activities, which began in February 1943, reached a maximum monthly production by September 1943 with 1,400 bombsights, 1,700 SBAEs, and 2,400 stabilizers. In December 1943 the flow of sights increased to a point where the AAF Materiel Command felt that no additional new manufacturing plants would be required, nor would the expansion of any current factory be necessary. If bombsight shortages occurred, the allocation of spares could make up these shortages until production again became adequate. With more sights available the AAF could begin installing the sights in all very heavy, heavy, medium, and light bombers equipped with so-called bombardier glazed noses.

In January 1944 the AAF requirements for sights and stabilizers for the rest of the year were 20,960 units. To fulfill this quantity, the Navy estimated that production from October 1943 to January 1945 for both bombsights and stabilizers from all Navy and AAF sources (Norden Company, Remington-Rand, Burroughs, Lukas-Harold, and the Victor Company) was 32,024 sight heads, with the Air Force receiving 20,960 units, and that all the sights ordered on contract by the AAF would be delivered by November 1944. The stabilizer production for this same period was estimated at 31,024 units. However, using finished stocks on hand at the manufacturers' plants, this shortfall of 1,000 stabilizers could be met. At the same time provisions were also made to supply 33,072 spare parts kits while spare parts supply was operating normally.

During the fall of 1944 maximum bombsight production was finally realized and, after all the in-fighting and shortages, there was an excess of bombsights available for Army and Navy requirements, so in October 1944 the production of 2,365 bombsights was cancelled. However, in the beginning of December 1944 the AAF found that they required more sights than they had planned on, as war in Europe was not going to end as early as predicted and would continue into well into 1945. The earlier cancellation of October's 2,365 sights was reinstated, and on 4 December 1944 BuOrd was informed that the AAF would require approximately an additional 4,200 sights from Navy sources. The BuOrd placed an order for 2,620 sights with Norden at a rate of 350 per month, and the remainder of the order at the same monthly rate was to be fulfilled by Lukas-Harold. Production continued until May 1945, when at the end of the war in Europe production was reduced about 50%, and at V-J Day in August 1945 all bombsight production ceased.

In late December 1944, a Manhattan Federal Grand Jury charged that Carl L. Norden, Inc. tried to protect its monopoly on manufacture of the sight by blocking production by other companies of the critically needed sight. The Grand Jury indicted company President Theodore Barth and Vice-President Ward Marvelle, along with Cdr. John Corrigan, USNR, Robert Wells, and Corrigan, Osbourne & Wells, their large industrial engineering firm. Bombsight inventor Carl Norden was no longer associated with the company. The indictments were mainly based on Truman Committee findings that charged the Norden Company had blocked Remington Rand production of the sight. The Navy Department ordered Norden to turn over bombsight plans to Remington Rand, Inc., which was to build 8,500 "football units." Norden was charged with withholding engineering advice; furnishing incomplete and inaccurate specifications; and rejecting completed Remington Rand Norden units. In July 1943 the CIO's United Electrical Workers complained to the Navy of a production slowdown at Norden's New York plant, but Cdr. Corrigan, the Navy's production-management supervisor for both plants, investigated and absolved Norden. The indictment charged that Corrigan then persuaded Norden officials to hire his firm, with which he had supposedly severed all ties when he was commissioned, for a fee of $104,000. As a result of Corrigan's recommendations the Navy took over the Remington plant and turned it over to Norden to manage. It was also charged that Corrigan allegedly forced other manufacturers to employ his firm, threatening to submit critical reports to the Navy on those who refused. His firm allegedly collected $109,000 as Corrigan's share in fees thus received. The Norden Company categorically denied all charges in the indictment. The Justice Department tried the case, which was dismissed for lack of evidence.

An estimated 52,000 Norden Bombsights were manufactured during the war at an estimated cost of a half billion dollars. The major contractors were Carl L. Norden, Inc., NYC (21,437 sets); Lukas-Harold Corp., Indianapolis (12,743 or 14,000?); Minneapolis Honeywell Regulator Co. (8,257); Victor Adding Machine Co., Chicago (7,000 est.); Burroughs Adding Machine Co., Detroit, including Cardanic-Burroughs, Elmira, NY (6,041); and Remington Rand, Inc., Elmira, NY (3,450). Honeywell and Victor were direct contractors to the AAF; and the other companies were direct contractors to the Navy, and the additional AAF bombsights (all but about 6,500) were procured from the Navy contracts.

Production of Bombsights

Bombsight	**AAF**	**Navy**
MarkXV Mod1/M-1, 2, 3	100	179
MarkXVMod2/M-4	81	72
MarkXVMod.3/M-5	82	102
MarkXVMod.4/M-6	469	80
Mark15Mod5/M-7	8,805	7,920
M-9	27,500	----
M-9A	1,500	----
M-9B	43,000	----
Norden Total	**81,537**	**8,353**
Sperry S-1	5,563	----
T-1/MarkXIV*	23,000	----
Estoppey D-4B	2,080	----
Estoppey D-8	10,080	----
Other Total	**40,723**	**----**
Total	**122,260**	**8,353**

***For English use**

Production of Bombsight Accessories

AFCE/SBAE:	90,000
Bombsight Disc Speed Tachometers:	55,000
Pilot Direction Indicators (PDI):	52,000
Glide Bombing Attachments (GBA):	35,000
Low Altitude Attachments:	16,000
Formation Sticks:	15,500
Tangent Scale Kits:	10,500
Reflex Sight Kits:	9,000
Rotor Speed Tachometers:	3,500
Rate End Computers:	1,000

Comparative Costs of Bombsight AFCE/SBAE Combinations

Model	Year	Bombsight	AFCE/SBAE	Total
Estoppey D-4	1926	$286	None	$286
Norden XI	1929	$4,500	None	$4,500
Norden XV-1	1934	$4,275	None	$4,275
Norden XV-1	1934	$4,725	$2,375	$7,100
Norden XV-2	1934	$5,145	$2,375	$7,520
Norden XV-3	1937	$4,993	$2,375	$7,368
Norden XV-4	1939	$5,845	$3,560	$9,405
Sperry O-1	1939	$9,480	None	$9,480
Norden M-6	1940	$6,442	$3,992	$10,434
Sperry S-1	1942	$8,130	$9,426	$17, 529
Norden M-9	1944	$8,800	$3,559	$12,359

Conclusion

The entire American strategic bombing doctrine was based on the precision of the Norden Bombsight, and although planners realized that it alone could not win the war, it could hasten its end. Gen. Ira Eaker, the first commander of the 8AF, summed up the initial Allied bombing philosophy in 1942 when he stated, "We should never allow the history of this war to convict us of throwing the strategic bombing at the man in the street" (i.e. unlike the indiscriminate bombing of Warsaw, Rotterdam, and then London by the "murderous" Luftwaffe). RAF Bomber Command tried precision daylight bombing and took terrible losses while obtaining unsatisfactory results. Arthur "Bomber" Harris switched his RAF Bomber Command to nighttime "precision" bombing and was lucky to hit the target city, much less a target within the city, and became guilty of bombing the man on the street. The 8AF continued to espouse daylight precision "pickle barrel" bombing, but a study in early 1944 concluded that only 7% of all USAAF bombs fell within 1,000 feet of their aiming point. The Norden Bombsight in combat conditions was unable to hit the pickle barrel or the pickle factory, but more often hit the cucumber patch outside town! The original mid-1930s "pickle barrel tests" were conducted in good weather by very experienced bombardiers flying in the Douglas B-18A at 150 mph at 12,000 feet without facing flak or enemy fighters. The Norden-equipped B-17, B-24, and later the B-29 flew higher and faster, often in bad weather, facing disconcerting enemy AA and fighters. With the failure of precision bombing the USAAF concluded that area bombing, which was nothing more than the continuation of inaccurate precision bombing, was justified because of "the contributions in numerous ways of the civilian population to the fighting strength of the enemy and to speed securing of unconditional surrender." (USSBS)

The last combat use of the Norden Bombsight was by Navy VO-67 during the Vietnam War, when the unit dropped electronic acoustic sensors from high altitudes along the Ho Chi Minh Trail to track enemy troop movements.

Norden Security

Whenever the Norden Bombsight is discussed the subject of it being "*Top Secret*" is brought up. Although the Mark XI bombsight was initially clas-

Despite propaganda hoopla, such as this training manual cartoon, the Norden Bombsight could not hit the pickle barrel or even the pickle factory, but quite often hit the cucumber patch outside town! 8AF studies showed that only 7% of all USAAF bombs fell within 1,000 feet of their aiming point. (BIF)

sified as "*Secret*," this classification was found to be too restrictive to be effective in the handling of the sight per se and the exchange of data on it and the BuOrd changed the sight's security classification to "*Confidential*." *Confidential* was defined as "although not endangering national security could be prejudicial to the interest of the nation." Interestingly, the decision to downgrade the sight to *Confidential* rather than *Secret* was made only to permit sending correspondence within the continental United States by Registered Mail rather than by messenger, as would have been required under the *Secret* classification. When an item was sent by registered mail it was handled under armed guard and kept in a special vault, and was to be signed for at each transfer.

The design, development, testing, and production of the Mark XV by the Navy were conducted under conditions intended "to insure an unusual degree of secrecy." The AAC was obliged to abide by the same security classification as the Navy and "strict compliance with these instructions were mandatory on all concerned." Keeping the source of the bombsight manufacture secret was relatively easy, as Norden was the only manufacturer. No visitors were allowed in the plant, including Navy and AAF commissioned officers, except by the authority of the Chief, Bureau of Ordnance. The Chief of the Air Corps issued regulations to include the inspection, calibration, acceptance of sights, and the distribution of spare parts, tools, storage, and receipt of each bombsight and packing case keys. The Depot Supply Officer was to personally inventory all articles on the shipping ticket prior to their issuance to a commissioned officer in charge. A bombsight log book was sent with each sight, and the keys to the packing case and the log book were sent to the receiving activity by Registered Mail. All spare parts were to be stored and treated on *Confidential* status. When a bombsight was installed in an aircraft it was to be covered while on the ground, so that it was not visible through the bombing window from the ground. When the bombsight was not scheduled for a mission it was to be removed from the directional stabilizer and placed in storage, and if proper storage was not available the sight was covered, and a guard was to be placed. Photographs were absolutely not permitted of the bombsight. Each station using the sight was issued a pamphlet that contained information on the precautions required in preventing unauthorized personnel from gaining access to the sight, and a bombsight log book was provided for each sight. There are prewar photos that show a bombardier carrying the bombsight in a canvas bag accompanied by two armed guards. It was supposed that bombardiers were to take an oath to protect the sight, which was perpetuated by a scene in the 1943 RKO movie "*Bombardier*," but

Prewar photo showing a bombardier carrying the bombsight in a canvas bag from a storage vault accompanied by a armed guard. (AAF)

there is no evidence to validate this. However, it was compulsory for any person, either military or civilian, who dealt with the bombsight to read and sign the Espionage Act of 1917.

Classification

In May 1941, in order to facilitate the installation of the Stabilized Bombing Approach Equipment (i.e. automatic pilot), BuOrd reclassified the SBAE and associated equipment from *Confidential* to *Restricted*. BuOrd informed the AAC of this change of classification of the SBAF (which was the AFCE, Automatic Flight Control Equipment, in the AAF), which was then later reclassified to *Restricted* by the AAF.

In July 1942 HQS, AAF issued a new policy governing the M-Series bombsight unit and complete bombsight assembly, consisting of bombsight stabilizer, glide angle attachment, descriptive matter, unsatisfactory reports, correspondence, and drawings, which were to be *Confidential*. The Automatic Flight Control Equipment (AFCE) pertaining to performance, malfunction, design, unsatisfactory reports, drawings, basic instructional manuals, and technical instructions were to be treated as *Confidential*. The Flight Gyro, rudder, elevator, aileron servo motors, banking motor, sector panel, requisitions, shipping tickets, purchase orders, contracts, etc., were to be classified *Restricted*, along with the pilot director indicators, tachometers, and bomb trainers when not equipped with the bombsight. Radiograms or telegrams referring to the bombsight equipment were to be properly coded.

In December 1942 the AAF issued broad new directives reclassifying equipment concerning the M-Series bombsights: the AFCE and SBAE equipment (Type B and C) and attachments and the Low Altitude Bombing (LAB) System from *Restricted* to *Confidential*. Otherwise, the elements of security remained basically the same as described in the July 1942 Directive.

In January 1943 BuOrd issued another directive for the proper handling of the Mark XV bombsight and associated equipment when it became evident that this equipment was not being handled in accordance with the prior guidelines. The classification was changed to *Restricted* from *Confidential* to expedite shipment and distribution of information referring to this equipment, which continued to be *Confidential*. New precautions were added for shipment, stowage, security, and packing. Sights and stabilizers, when shipped singly or together, had their gyros caged, the sights strapped to the base and safety wired, and then were secured in a metal or wood packing

Staged propaganda photo with the covered Norden sight ready for removal back into its canvas carrying bag. (AAF)

Bombardiers were supposed to take an oath to protect the sight which was perpetuated by a scene in this 1943 RKO movie "*Bombardier*," but there is no evidence to validate this. (Author/RKO)

box by shock proof type mounting. The packed box was then enclosed in a wooden non-tip crate. In addition to stenciled caution "Extremely Delicate Instrument," the stenciled caution "Handle with Utmost Care" was added. The bombsight was to be placed in a L-shaped vault, if available. Storage rooms were to be maintained at a temperature range of 65° to 95°F and be equipped with a dust filter and a dehumidifier. If a vault was not available then a suitable locked room, barred to other than authorized personnel, was to be used. All other provisions remained the same and were to be followed as outlined in previous directives.

The Doolittle Tokyo Raid

For the Doolittle Tokyo raid of April 1942 the top secret Norden bombsight was removed from the B-25s, as the Air Force was concerned that it could be captured. Doolittle decided that the mission that was to be conducted below 4,000 feet on a short bomb run using abrupt evasive maneuvers, during which the bombardier would be unable to sight targets moving swiftly under the aircraft. The Norden would not be effective at this altitude using these tactics, so Capt. Ross Greening, a group pilot and armament officer at Eglin, developed the "Mark Twain" sight, which was a simple sighting bar and plate apparatus. The name "Mark Twain" was conferred by Greening, and it referred to the simple "lead line" depth finder used on Mississippi river boats. Greening was able to connect his bombsight to the linkages of the Norden, allowing the bombardier to set wind drift and to relay turn directions to the pilot through the PDI without relying on voice communications. Before the bombing run the dropping angle was computed and set on the sighting bar, giving the bombardier an open field of vision over the sight. He could then direct the pilot on to the target, and when the target became aligned with the sighting bar the bombs were released.

German Intelligence and the Norden

By mid-1937, despite the secrecy of the new bombsight the *Abwehr*, the German Intelligence Service, gleaned its existence from pieces of intelligence, but German operatives in New York reported that no one in the ring had access to the Norden factory there. In September, intelligence documents arrived in Hamburg which included unidentified drawings from a source who worked at the Norden plant at 80 Lafayette Street and was willing to meet with a special envoy in New York.

At the same time, Nikolaus Ritter returned to his native Germany after ten years as an unsuccessful textile manufacturer in America and rejoined the Army; he was made Chief of Air Intelligence in the *Abwehr*. Ritter was assigned to observe the American air force and aviation industry, so in October he sailed on the *Bremen* for New York and began to establish a new identity as a German businessman. Immediately, he went to meet with the man who had forwarded the unidentified drawings, codenamed "*Paul*," who was Hermann Lang, a 35 year old machinist and draftsman. Lang had come to America in 1927 and was about to become a naturalized citizen; he was employed as an assembly inspector at the Norden factory.

Lang told Ritter that the bombsight manufacture was carried out by different groups at different locations, even different companies, and each had no awareness of what the others were doing. However, one of Lang's responsibilities was to obtain and hand out drawings to the different groups and place them overnight in a safe if they were needed again the next day. When he had overnight document access he would then take some home and copy the drawings on tracing paper. Lang would be unable to get all the drawings, but the *Abwehr* felt clever German engineers would be able to engineer a complete bombsight. Ritter was overjoyed at his quick success, but faced the problem of getting what turned out to be an overly large drawing back to Germany. Ritter had contact with a steward on the *Bremen* who was an *Abwehr* agent and the drawings were smuggled back to Germany. Ritter persuaded Lang with a 10,000 mark inducement to return to Germany to help in the rebuilding of the Norden. The Germans built a model from the drawings, but because of the missing parts it did not work.

By mid-1944 enough B-17s had been shot down over Germany that it was probable that the Germans had captured at least one intact sight and, consequently, the equipment was downgraded with all security removed. After the war complete Norden sights were captured by the advancing Americans but could not be used, as the Luftwaffe bomber force had been decimated.

The **"Mark Twain" Bombsight** was developed for the Doolittle Tokyo raid of April 1942, as the top secret Norden bombsight was removed from the B-25s due to concern that it could be captured. (Author/Hornet Museum)

Storage and Shipping

At the end of a bombing mission, or when the aircraft was moved to a hangar, the bombsight was to be removed and locked in the bombsight storage vault by the base Armament Officer, who had the keys. The keys were forwarded under separate cover by Registered Mail for bombsight shipping boxes to AAF and Navy consignees designated to receive the bombsight.

Originally, the Norden Bombsights were stored in wooden buildings that contained five or six individual concrete vaults and an area for sight testing and repair. After the Norden was downgraded from *Secret* to *Confidential* in 1943 second generation vaults were introduced. These rectangular 11x14 or L-shaped vaults with one door stood alone and were used only to store the bombsights. The 10 foot walls were about eight inches thick, and the slightly sloping roof was steel reinforced concrete and had heavy steel or vault type doors installed and locked, with at least one armed guard. The vault was surrounded by a square-shaped fence 50 feet on each side and eight feet high, with a double strand of barbed wire on top. When operating in the field, or where no adequate storage was available, the bombsight was left in the aircraft and a guard or guards were posted.

Identifying lettering as to type, manufacturer's name, bombsight assembly, and PDI was concealed from view on the shipping box. Code words were to be used when shipping a bombsight. In place of the word "Bombsight" the code word *Siding* was to be used if the sight was shipped on Sunday; *Latent* on Monday; *Telescope* on Tuesday; *Mickey* on Wednesday; *Dusty* on Thursday; *External* on Friday; and *Talon* on Saturday. If it was shipped by Railway Express the code word was *Relax*, by Army truck it was *Truax*, and by air transport it was *Pinay*. When conveyed by Army truck the driver and a guard were to be armed during shipment. Later the Norden was shipped in a corrugated box with the actual contents stenciled on the side.

The Norden Bombsight was stored in a L-shaped vault with ten foot walls, about eight inches thick, one door, and no windows. The vault was maintained at a temperature range of 65° to 95°F and equipped with a dust filter and a dehumidifier. (AAF)

Corrugated Norden Shipping Box (AAF)

Exterior view of the Norden Bombsight installed in a B-17. (Author/CAFAZ)

Destruction to Prevent Capture

When the bombsight was installed in the aircraft the bombardier was to be armed with a pistol at all times. Prior to a forced landing over enemy territory the bombsight was to be destroyed by firing two rounds with a .45 caliber service pistol: one into the rate end mechanism and the other round through the telescope. If time permitted the bombsight was to be removed and jettisoned overboard. An explosive "destruct" mechanism was mentioned in several directives but was never developed or used.

The Norden Bombsight Described

General

The Norden Bombsight weighed 45 pounds and was comprised of over 2,000 parts, many of which were manufactured to minute tolerances. The Norden sight was a two-part system: the sight proper and the base unit, which contained the electronics and incorporated the Automatic Flight Control Equipment (AFCE)/Stabilized Bombing Approach Equipment (SBAE)). The AFCE/SBAE was connected to the C-1 autopilot and allowed the bombardier to control the lateral movement of the bomber by his adjustments of the sight. The detachable upper half of the Norden contained the gyroscope for vertical stabilization of the instrument. The stabilizer consisted of the directional gyro, which was to detect deviations from the bomber's set course, and the flight gyro, which recorded any inclination for the bomber to either roll or to nose up or down. The sight was located on top of the stabilizer and was equipped with a 2.5 power telescope that was driven by a variable speed electric motor with a gyro to keep the sight stable.

During preflight, the bombardier had to enter basic data into the computer from pre-calculated tables. These tables provided data for the bomb trail (the distance the bombs would hit the ground behind the aircraft) and the time it would take the bombs to fall based on the scheduled speed and altitude of the approach. Approximately five minutes from the target the bomber's course was checked for drift from cross wind data that was then entered into the computer. When the target came into view the bombardier trained the telescope on it and adjusted the telescope drive so that the bombsight maintained its course to the target. When the bombsight clutches were operated they immediately actuated the stabilizer-controlled autopilot. The flight and directional gyros both had electrical brushes fitted to them. If the bomber went off course, the gyro maintained its orientation and in response moved inside its case. The brushes would make contact with the solenoids, which engaged electric servo motors that then operated the aircraft's control surfaces and corrected the deviation. There was a link between the rudder and aileron servo motors that caused a bank in turns, but a designated switch could be operated that gave all directional control to the rudder and eliminated bank. The bombardier could control the stabilizer to take evasive action in case of heavy anti-aircraft fire, but these controls were

Interior view of the Norden Bombsight installed in a B-25. (Author/CAFAZ)

During the war a myth arose that the Norden's crosshairs were made from spider silk, as this photo and accompanying article on Dr. John Albright in the July 1942 issue of *Flying* magazine purports to be true. (AAF/*Flying*)

limited by mechanical stops in the autopilot that eliminated steep banking. During the bomb run the bomber was kept extremely straight and level by the stabilizer. The telescope tracked the target until it reached the precise dropping angle when the bombs were automatically released.

Synchronous Sight

Synchronous defines as "one thing will maintain the same relationship to another under constantly changing conditions." In a synchronous bombsight that meant that the rate of angular drive of the optics kept pace with the rate of angular change of the sighting angle. For example, when the sighting angle was 50° the transverse crosshair rested synchronized upon the target; then, when the sighting angle moved to 40°, the transverse crosshair would likewise be at 40° from the vertical and in that state also rested upon the target.

When sighting through the telescope optics there were two points: one above and one below the transverse crosshair. The first was the position of the eye which sighted to the transverse crosshair; the second was the point of projection to the ground of this line of sight. As the bomber approached the target, with the sight synchronized, the point of projection would move along the surface of the earth at a speed equal to the velocity of closure. The reality was that the transverse crosshair (and therefore this point of projection) remained on the target and didn't move relative to it. This was because the forward velocity of closure of the bomber was equaled exactly by the rearward velocity of the point of projection relative to the target. Thus, the rate of angular closure of the transverse hair was exactly equal to the rate of change of the sighting angle.

No sight synchronized itself, as it had to be properly adjusted and operated for synchronization. Manual synchronization caused the optics to drive at the correct speed for synchronization and set up the correct actual range angle for the given altitude, velocity of closure, and trail characteristic of the bomb. With this correct actual range angle set up, the bomb should be caused to be released at the correct actual range distance away from the target. The Norden Bombsight, when synchronized, caused a rate quadrant to be positioned at the correct actual range angle measured off from its 0° position.

During the war a myth arose that the Norden's crosshairs (reticles) were made from spider silk, and the myth was later further enhanced by reports that it was Black Widow silk. The July 1942 issue of *Flying* magazine has a small article and photo of Dr. John Albright of the Case School of Applied Science about his research on using spider silk for bombsight crosshairs. The article stated that Albright established a spider "ranch" at Fredericktown, OH, where 200 spiders (the Golden Garden Miranda type) were "in production for Uncle Sam's war program." The article went on to state that extracting silk was "much like milking a cow," and as it emerged from the spider's pouch it was wound on reels which sold for $9 per 100 feet. The spiders were harnessed to a "contraption" that prevented them from snipping the silk with their rear legs. Spider silk, while extremely strong, was too coarse and irregular for use in sighting. Another story circulated that the reticle of the Norden was so fine that it required exceptionally fine human hair plucked from the head of a blonde named Mary Babnick, who was known as "Arcadia Mary" because she taught dancing to soldiers at the USO's Arcadia Ballroom at the Pueblo, Colorado, Army Air Base. All these crosshair myths persist, even though Carl Norden's 1932 patent stated that the reticles were etched in the telescope's glass. The crosshairs were initially engraved by a $15,000 pantograph that etched only ten telescopes simultaneously but with a rejection rate of 50%. Minneapolis Honeywell Regulator developed a basic $600 pantograph with a much higher productivity and a lower rejection rate.

Sight: Operation and Nomenclature

Basically, the purpose of the bombsight was to enable the bombardier to drop bombs with the greatest degree of accuracy. In so doing the bombsight set up or established a line of sight which, at the instant of bomb release, would determine the actual range distance on the ground, or the horizontal distance that the bomb would travel on its path through the air. The bombsight also determined the proper course of the bomber in order to maintain the necessary line of sight according to the prevailing conditions.

The bombsight was a stabilized instrument. The cross hairs of the telescope were mechanically stabilized: in the vertical by the vertical gyro

Norden Bombsight Gallery

Norden Bombsight installed in B-17 (left) and B-25 (above). (Author/CAFAZ and Pima)

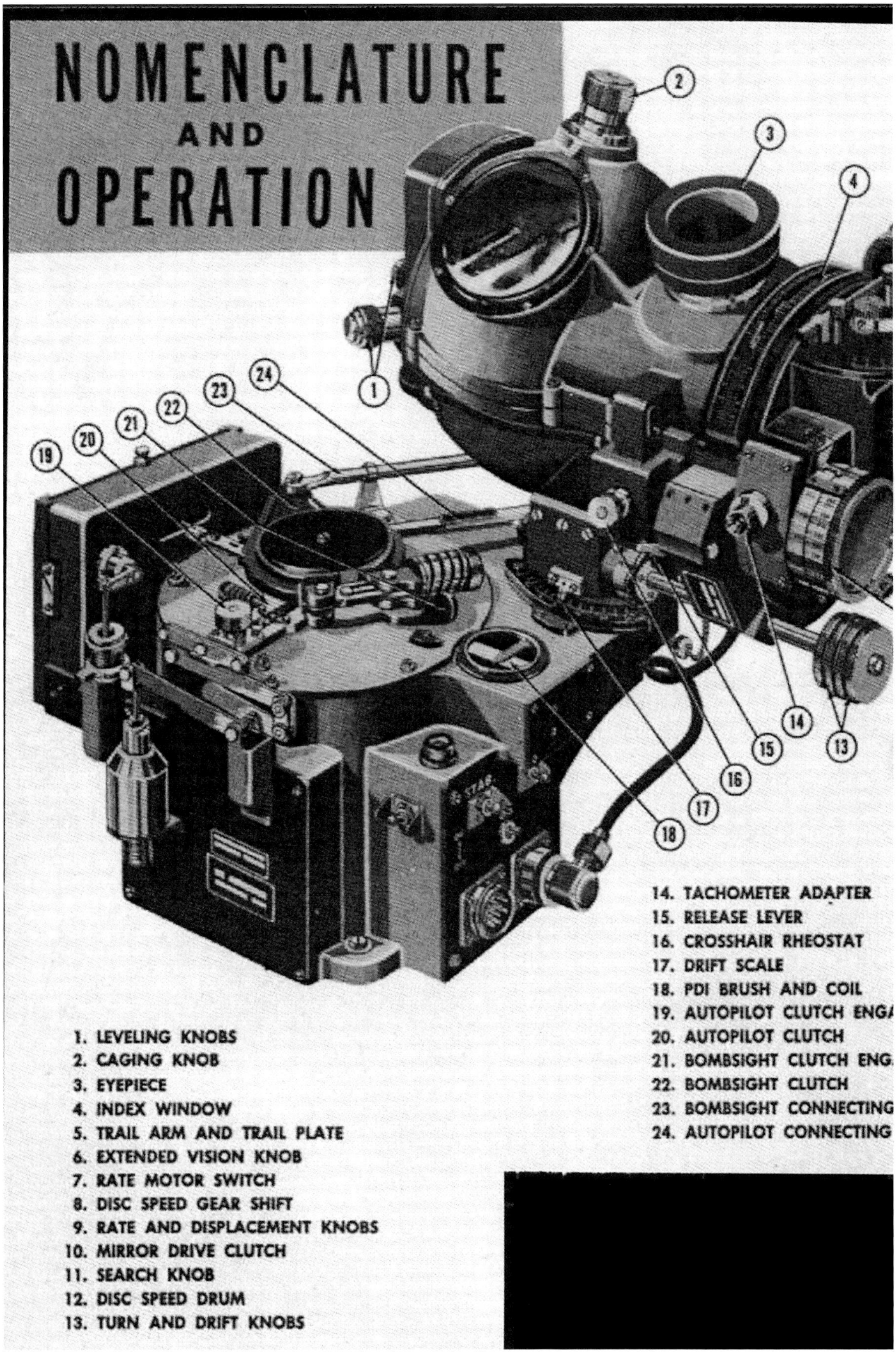

(Norden Bombsight Maintenance Manual)

and about the vertical or in the horizontal plane by the directional gyro. The Norden sight was a synchronizing mechanism, in that the bombardier could, by properly adjusting the course, rate, and displacement knobs, cause the intersection of the cross hairs to remain on the point of aim or target by causing the mirror in the M-6 model and the telescope in the M-3 model to turn about its lateral axis at the correct speed (i.e. a speed proportional to ground speed). When the sight was properly calibrated and was correctly synchronized it would accurately solve the bombing problem. The power for operating the bombsight was provided by the bomber's power source.

Exterior

In describing the exterior of the sight, the right and left, front and rear were determined from the bombardier's position. The rate end of the sight is to the bombardier's right and the vertical gyro to his left. The rear of the sight is toward the bombardier and the front away from him. The Navy description reversed these positions.

On the left end of the sight were the precession, or leveling knobs, which gave the bombardier control over the vertical gyro so that he could level it at any time. The center knob caused the gyro to process about its transverse axis and in the fore and aft plane. The knob to the rear of center caused the gyro to process about the fore and aft axis and in the transverse plane. It was to be remembered that the gyro had to be running to secure the above precessions (the motion of the axis of the gyro when there was an external force acting on its axis), otherwise the gyro and cardan would move in the opposite directions. The case which housed the gyro and cardan was divided into two parts, the upper and lower housings. The upper housing was attached to the lower part of the case with eight screws. The two screws in the upper part of the left end had to be removed in order to remove the upper housing.

Located in the center and rear of the lower housing was the Crosstrail knob, which was turned to the left to set in trail. When this knob was turned an eccentric disc and stud were moved to the rear of the center of the sight stem. The purpose of this eccentric disc will be discussed later. This knob was only found on the M-1, M-2, and M-3 sights. On the upper half of the housing, center top left, was the caging knob, which was a push-pull knob, and locked the gyro in a near vertical position when not actually making a bombing run. Near this knob but to the rear of the housing was a window that allowed the bombardier to see the optics. In the M-3 the telescope moved, while in the M-6/9 it consisted of a stationary eye piece. Just below this window, but on the lower half of the sight housing, was the telescope light knob, which lit up the cross hairs by means of two slots: one in the case, and a matching slot in the telescope tube.

Anti-glare filter lenses made by Polaroid were supplied in a hinged rectangular case to help the bombardier to see the target by cutting down on glare and haze that were obscuring the target. The kit had five interchangeable filters that fit into a special rubber eye piece that fit into the sleeve of the regular sight eye piece when it was removed. There were two uncolored filters: one cut out up to 60% of the light, while the other was adjustable to cut out from 60% to all the light. These Polaroid lens were used to reduce the glare from water, snow, or searchlights, and had to be twisted in the sleeve to the desired amount of light. The light yellow or dark yellow filter was used to reduce glare from sandy soil or white sand, or heading into the sun. The dark yellow of red filter was used to reduce haze, fog, overcast, or shadows.

The extreme right end of the sight was made up of a switch and four knobs, the altitude, rate, displacement, and search knobs. At the top and jutting out from the rate end was a semicircular calibrated plate and a movable arm, which was the trail setting mechanism and by the arm trail was set. Just beneath this mechanism was a toggle switch which turned the telescope motor on and off. On the left side of the rate end, as the bombardier faced it, was the altitude knob, which was calibrated in disc speed and altitude in feet. This knob controlled the speed of the telescope motor and disc. Just below the center of the diameter of the rate end were the rate and displacement knobs. The outer knob was the displacement knob, which allowed the bombardier to displace the optics independently of the rate of drive. The inner knob was the rate knob and controlled the angular speed of the optics. These knobs will be described in detail later. At the very bottom of the rate end was the search knob, which entered the rate end at an angle and which quickly displaced the optics. Located within the displacement knob was a locking clutch (locked when pushed in and unlocked when pulled out) which simply engaged the displacement knob. The search knob was never to be used when the clutch was engaged. The rate and displacement knobs were located together so that they could both be used at one time by double gripping.

The course knob assembly was attached on the rear and lower part of the sight case. This assembly consisted of the turn knob, the drift knob, the turn worm, the drift worm, and the intermediate gears that drove the drift worm. The turn knob was fastened to the inner turn rod and carried the turn worm directly. The turn worm acted directly upon the rack of the stabilized sector.

The drift knob was fastened to the outer shaft, which was connected to the drift worm through two gears. The drift worm acted directly upon the drift gear, which was collared around the sight stem sleeve. The drift worm was mounted in a swivel housing and was adjustable, so that proper clearance between the drift gear and drift worm could be maintained. The course knobs were used to set up the course of the bomber in relation to the line of sight. When the turn knob was rotated the turn worm tracked around the rack of the stabilized sector, which was stabilized by the bombsight clutch.

The drift worm dragged the drift gear as the sight tracked about the rack of the stabilized sector. When the drift gear turned the stabilized brush was displaced and a reading was registered on the PDI, which then informed the pilot which way to turn the bomber to bring it back to straight flight. If the drift knob was turned the drift worm rotated the drift gear, which would displace the stabilized brush, giving a reading on the PDI.

Polaroid Anti-glare Filter Lens Kits were supplied in a hinged rectangular case containing five interchangeable filters that fit into a special rubber eye piece. (Author/CAFAZ)

When both knobs were rotated at once this was called "double gripping." To set up the course properly the knobs could be double gripped. The bombardier had to remember that the autopilot clutch was a slip connection between the directional gyro and the stabilized PDI brush, and unless the autopilot clutch was disengaged the PDI brush would be displaced when the course knobs were rotated. With the bombsight clutch engaged and the autopilot clutch disengaged, the PDI brush would be displaced and the sight rotated in azimuth as the course knobs were double gripped. The over-correction factor was the amount the aircraft was turned more than the line of sight while double gripping.

The stabilized sector was the gear connection between the sight and the sight clutch connecting rod. As part of the bombsight, the stabilized sector was stabilized in azimuth by the stabilizer gyro through the sight clutch connecting rod. The entire bombsight case was also stabilized in azimuth.

The altitude knob was important in the solution of the bombing problem because the springs controlled the speed of the telescope motor. The altitude knob assembly was composed of a removable outer knob calibrated in revolutions of disc speed, and in feet of attitude on some units. There were two altitude springs and two cases. The outer spring supplied the tension only when high disc speeds were necessary, as in low altitude bombing; the inner spring supplied the tension for low disc speed used in high altitude bombing, but its tension was always being employed, even for high disc speeds, in which case the outer spring began to add its tension to that of the inner spring. These springs converted their torque through the altitude shaft to the breaker arm. This torque kept the contact points closed until the tension of the altitude springs was overcome by the telescope motor governor. The inner altitude spring case fit over a friction collar. The inner altitude spring case was held in place on the friction collar by three adjustable set screws that had to be loosened to rotate the case or the collar. The outer case fit over the inner case and was held in place with three adjustable set screws; in order to maintain the spring tension on the springs a fiber friction ring frictionally engaged the flange of the friction collar. The tension of the friction ring was regulated by two leaf springs called friction adjusting springs, one on the top and one on the bottom of the friction ring. The tension of the leaf springs had to be sufficient to hold the altitude knob at any desired position. Keyed to the altitude shaft was the high altitude clutch holder, against which the low altitude clutch holder contacts as the outer case is rotated clockwise. A continued rotation of the outer case in a clockwise direction increased the tension of the outer altitude spring. The necessary screws and bearings completed the assembly.

Interior

To get into the interior of the sight it was necessary to remove five screws holding the rate end. The rate end motor half housed the telescope motor assembly, displacement and rate knob assembly search knob, and disc assembly.

The telescope motor assembly consisted of a parallel-wound constant speed motor, field coils, carbon brushes, governor, breaker arm and necessary bearings, pin screws, and wiring. The telescope motor drove and controlled the speed of the disc. The speed of the motor was controlled by having a set of breaker points wired in series with the armature. The breaker points were kept closed by the tension of the altitude springs until the governor overcame that tension.

As the motor sped up the arms of the governor tended to become parallel, pulling the connecting links and collar toward the center of pivot of the governor while at the same time moving the breaker arm with them. The breaker arm was attached to the altitude shaft and, as it was pulled toward the governor, pivoted the altitude shaft, overcoming the tension of the altitude springs and breaking the contact between the points. When the circuit to the telescope motor was broken the motor slowed down; the pull of the governor became less than the tension of the altitude springs and the breaker points were closed, and the circuit was again completed. This action was so rapid that the speed of the telescope motor remained constant.

This assembly consisted of the rate knob (inner knob), displacement knob, displacement clutch engaging knob and shaft, displacement shaft, bevel pinion, and intermediate gears. The rate knob enabled the bombardier to set up the correct rate of drive so that he could synchronize by positioning the roller on the disc. The displacement knob enabled the bombardier to move the optics independently of the rate of drive.

The disc assembly consisted of the disc, tachometer shaft, tachometer shaft springs, bearing blocks, bearings and screws, inspection plate, and tachometer connection. The disc drove the roller, which translated the drive to the rate and telescope drive mechanisms. The tachometer shaft spring supplied the tension that held the disc against the roller; the tachometer shaft and connection transmitted the speed of the disc to the tachometer when the tachometer was applied.

The search knob, shaft, and bevel pinion were parts of the search knob assembly. It was used to displace the optics quickly and independently of the displacement knob. The search knob was not to be used without disengaging the displacement clutch because of the danger of shearing the displacement clutch pin.

The trail assembly consisted of the trail plate, trail arm, trail setting gear, nut gear, thrust washer, and spindle screw. When the trail arm was rotated toward maximum trail the trail setting gear rotated the nut gear, which moved up on the threaded upper spindle bearing and against the thrust washer, which then carried the spindle screw in translation against the tension of the spindle spring. The roller was then moved up from the disc center a distance proportional to trail without affecting the rate mechanism. The spindle spring forced the spindle screw in translation downward as the trail arm was rotated toward minimum.

The rate assembly consisted of the rate knob intermediate gears, rate bevel pinion, rate bevel gear retaining pin, thrust spring, spindle screw, roller and roller carriage, spindle gear, rate drive gear, rate rack pinion, rate rack cam follower or stud, rate quadrant camway, rate index, automatic release points, ground speed drum, and ground speed scale.

This synchronous assembly set up the rate of drive necessary to synchronize on the target.

The bombsight gyro assembly consisted of a case which was in two parts (held together with screws), gyro caging pin, leveling bubble tubes, fore and aft and transverse gyro balance weights, two carbon brushes, armature, field, two rotor ball bearings, and rotor.

The bombsight gyro rotor was an inverted cup-shaped wheel driven clockwise at about 7,800 rpm by direct current. The gyro spun on an axis

Interior of Norden Head (Author/CAFAZ)

Norden Bombsight Gyro (Author/CAFAZ)

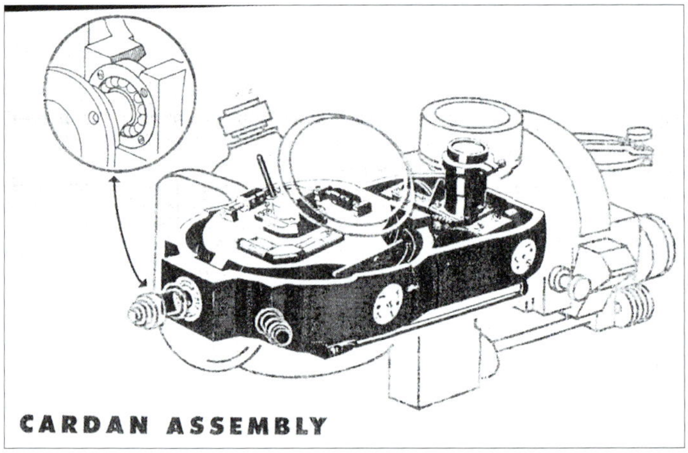

(Norden Bombsight Maintenance Manual)

which, for the correct solution of the bombing problem, had to be vertical. Around the top and lower edge of the rotor were 10 balance screws that were never removed except when balancing the gyro. Inside the wheel and bolted to it was the armature of the motor that powered it. The entire wheel or rotor was enclosed in a gyro casing. The upper part of the case carried the gyro caging pin, the upper rotor bearing, the fore and aft and transverse leveling bubble tubes, and the fore and aft and transverse gyro balance weights. The lower half of the gyro casing carried, on its inside, the field coils, which fit between the gyro rotor and motor armature, and lower rotor bearing. Extending through the lower casing and at right angles to the commutator were the brush tubes that held the carbon brushes. Attached to the bottom of the casing were fixed lead weights used in balancing the bombsight gyro.

The sight cardan was a pear-shaped metal ring that pivoted at both ends in the sight head. One of the pivots, known as a gudgeon bearing, was located at the left end of the sight head, and the other was at the right end in the plate between the rate end and cardan assembly. It provided support for the fore and aft bearings of the gyro in its left half and support to the fore and aft bearings of the telescope cradle in its right half. The cardan was supported by gudgeons (pivots) working in ball bearings in the case (right and left cardan). The right cardan was drilled to allow the telescope cable to pass through its axis and was a fixed bearing.

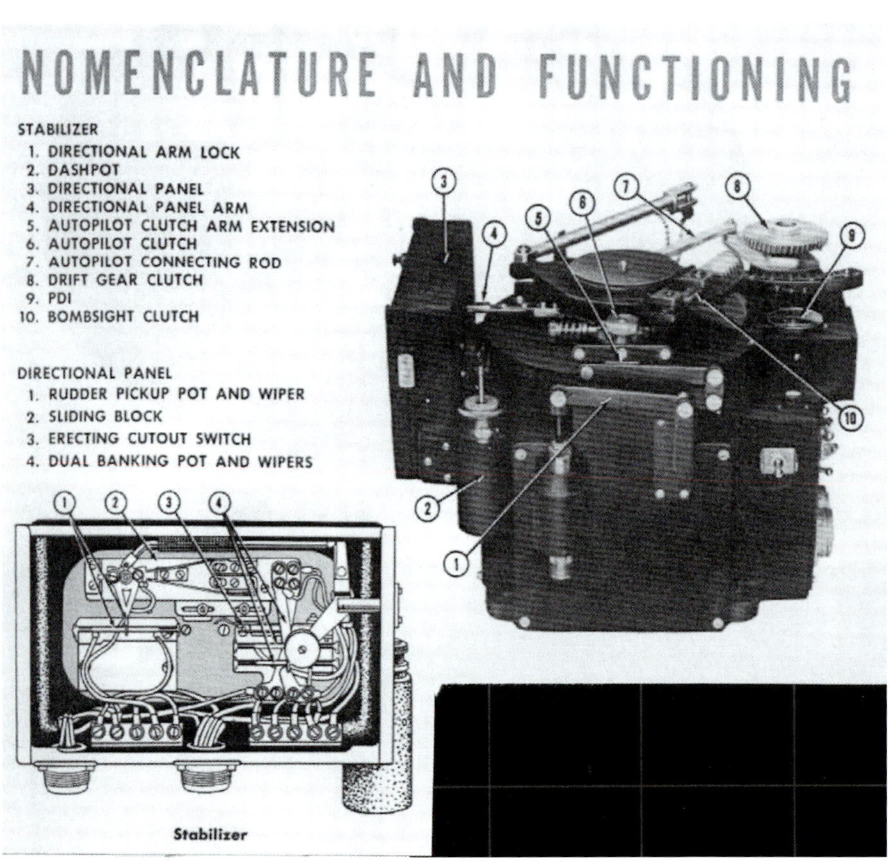

(Norden Bombsight Maintenance Manual)

Stabilizer: Operation and Nomenclature

The stabilizer was used as a base for the bombsight and provided the housing and mountings for the mechanical devices used to maintain an azimuth reference line, or more specifically, to stabilize the bombsight case (i.e. entire case, including the fore and aft hair) in azimuth and with AFCE/SBAEs in operation to stabilize the entire bomber against deviations from course.

In describing the stabilizer, the terms front and rear, right and left were used as the stabilizer was seen by the bombardier. On the rear of the stabilizer housing was an inspection plate or cover that was fastened to the housing with four screws. The removal of this cover permitted inspection of the horizontal gyro and cardan (a universal joint that transmited rotary motion).

To the right of the rear cover was the PDI switch. On the top of the stabilizer were the following: clutch cover plate, bombsight clutch, bombsight clutch connecting rod, bombsight clutch connecting rod clamp bracket, autopilot clutch, directional arm, PDI coil and brush view glass, drift gear and clutch assembly, and drift scale.

The PDI coil mounting plate, the switch panel containing, as designated, the stabilizer, servo and bombsight switches, the stabilizer and the bombsight male cannon plugs, were on the right side of the stabilizer housing. Located on the front of the stabilizer housing was the torque or servo motor, which was

AFCE/SBAE Stabilizer Gallery

accessible by removing the inspection cover, which was attached with four screws. On the left side of the housing were the projections for mounting the directional panel.

The Norden Solves the Bombing Problem

In any discussion of the bombardier and bombing and the Norden Bombsight the term "Solving the Bombing Problem" appears repeatedly and needs to be discussed and defined in its fundamental parts.

Solving the Range Problem

The Norden Bombsight had two main units: the sighthead and the stabilizer. The sighthead was attached to the stabilizer by a pivoting connection and two locking pins. Solving for range was the sighthead's principal function and was carried out by three main parts:

1) The rate end, which computed the exact release point for the bomb.
2) The optical system, through which the target was observed.
3) The vertical gyro, which stabilized the optics so that the roll and pitch of the aircraft would not move the line of sight from the target.

The rate end combined the values of automatic track finding (ATF), groundspeed, and trail to compute the dropping angle. From the bombing tables, the values of ATF and trail were entered into the sight, leaving groundspeed as the only unknown factor. Groundspeed was then solved by using the rate knob located on the rate end. By turning on the rate motor switch, a motor was started that turned a disc in the rate end. The speed at which the disc turned represented the ATF. The desired speed was set by positioning the disc speed drum, and to find the correct disc speed setting the ATF was divided into the bombsight constant, which was 5,300.

The disc drove a roller that could be moved from the center of the disc to its upper edge. When the roller was in the center of the rotating disc it did not turn; when it was just off center it turned very slowly. The farther the roller was moved from the center of the disc the more rapidly the roller turned. The position of the roller on the disc was controlled with the rate knob and the trail arm.

In trail was set by moving the trail arm to the desired position on the trail plate. This moved the roller out from the center of the disc a distance proportional to trail. Then, looking through the optics, the bombardier turned the rate knob until the lateral crosshair appeared to stay on the target. By doing this the roller moved an additional distance on the disc, with this additional distance being proportional to the actual range. The distance from the center of the disc to the roller was then proportional to whole range and the roller's speed of rotation was proportional to groundspeed.

At the same time that the rate knob positioned the roller on the disc it positioned the dropping angle index on the tangent scale, thus setting up the correct dropping angle. The roller drive was transmitted to a mirror that reflected the image of the target into the telescope. The mirror was hinged so that the roller changed the angle of reflection as the bomber approached the target. The sighting angle at any moment was shown by the sighting angle index on the degree scale in the index window.

When the sighting angle index was exactly opposite the dropping angle index, the sight automatically released the bomb if the release lever was up. There were three types of release levers: one that was held up manually; another that locked in the ON position when it was raised and had to be released after the bomb was released; and the third was locked in the ON position and was released automatically after the bomb was released.

Before synchronization was started, however, the bombardier had to place the line of sight manually on the target. At higher altitudes the search knob was used to give rapid displacement of the mirror for sighting angles from 70° to 0°. When the target was picked up the mirror drive clutch was engaged to connect the drive of the roller to the mirror. At lower altitudes, when more than 70° forward vision was required, the extended vision knob was used, permitting vision up to 90°. When using the extended vision knob the mirror drive clutch was not engaged until a sighting angle of 70° was reached.

The displacement knob was used if the crosshair was to be moved while the mirror drive clutch was engaged, thus changing the position of the crosshair without changing the speed at which the roller drove.

The vertical gyro stabilized the optics in roll and pitch. The gyro and optics rode on pivots which had the same effect as a universal joint, making it possible for the gyro and optics to stand upright and hold their own horizontal plane regardless of pitching and rolling of the bomber.

The fore and aft bubble and the lateral bubble (spirit levels) were located on top of the gyro. The gyro was leveled with the fore and aft leveling knob and the lateral leveling knob, which were located on the left end of the sight case. The caging knob was on the sighthead directly over the gyro. This knob was used to lock the gyro to the sight case when the gyro was not being used on a bombing run.

A stem that projected from the lower part of the sighthead fit into a hole on the front right corner of the stabilizer. This connection permitted the sighthead to be turned in relation to the stabilizer. The shaft, which passed through the center of the stem into the sighthead, was locked to the stabilizer by the dovetail locking pin.

Another connection between the sighthead and stabilizer was the clevis pin, which is a fastener with a head at one end and a hole at the other used to join a clevis to a rod. A clevis is a yoke with a hole formed or attached at one end of a rod. When an eye or hole of a second rod was aligned with the hole in the yoke, a clevis pin could be inserted to join the two. A cotter pin could then be inserted in the hole of the clevis pin to hold it in, but was readily removable. This joint is used for rods in tension where some flexibility is required. This clevis pin attached the bombsight clutch arm to the sighthead. When the bombsight clutch was engaged the directional gyro stabilized the entire sighthead in yaw through this linkage.

To turn the directional gyro on, the switch on the stabilizer case marked "Stab" was flipped and left on for three minutes before turning on any other switch. Other switches on the stabilizer case were the bombsight switch marked BS, which sent current to the sighthead through a cable and turned on the vertical gyro and the bubble light. The switch, marked PDI, activated the PDI circuit to the Pilot Director Indicator. The torque unit switch, marked Servo, activated the torque unit.

The directional gyro did not have enough power to maintain stability without some assistance provided by the torque unit, which held the spin axis of the gyro horizontal in relation to the stabilizer case.

Solving the Course Problem

The concentrically mounted course knobs, located on the lower right side of the sighthead, were used to make drift and course corrections. The turn knob—the outer of the two—changed the line of sight and the bomber equal amounts. The inner knob was the drift knob, which changed the heading of the bomber without changing the line of sight, thus establishing the drift angle. Although it was correct to use the turn knob alone, the drift knob was never single-gripped and was always used in conjunction with the turn knob (double grip), in order to establish the drift angle and displace the line of sight toward the target in one operation. The drift angle was read from the drift scale located on the stabilizer. The PDI sent electrical signals to the pilot with the corrections to make in the heading of the bomber when the course knobs were used.

Solving for Crosstrail

When drift and trail were combined the result was called Crosstrail. The Crosstrail mechanism located in the sighthead automatically combined these two factors and gave Crosstrail by tilting the telescope laterally so that the angle between the line of sight and vertical subtended Crosstrail distance on the ground.

X-1 Norden Reflex Sight

The Reflex Sight was an auxiliary sighting device for the Norden M-Series bombsight, providing a greater field of vision and enabling the bombardier to make his initial alignment of the bombsight crosshairs on the target in a minimum amount of time. The Reflex Sight was only to be used to establish the initial course and range synchronization.

There was a minimum loss of light transmission through the optics of the Reflex Sight, making it particularly adaptable for bombing at night and at extremely high altitudes, where visibility was limited. The optics of the Reflex Sight were mechanically geared to the bombsight mirror drive quadrant, and when correctly engaged with the optics the sighting angles indicated by both the Reflex Sight and the bombsight were identical. To align the sighting angle indices the bombardier pulled the Reflex Sight clutch to the right; rotated the sighting angle index of Reflex Sight to the same angle as the sighting angle index of the bombsight; and engaged the clutch. The additional drag of the Reflex Sight optics on the bombsight's mirror drive mechanism was not enough to cause roller slippage, so the Reflex Sight clutch could remain engaged after properly aligning sighting angle indices. Before using the Reflex Sight the indices had to coincide.

The Reflex Sight was rigidly attached to the bombsight housing and the optics were not gyroscopically stabilized, so when the sighting angle indices were aligned the bombsight needed to be level after the bomber

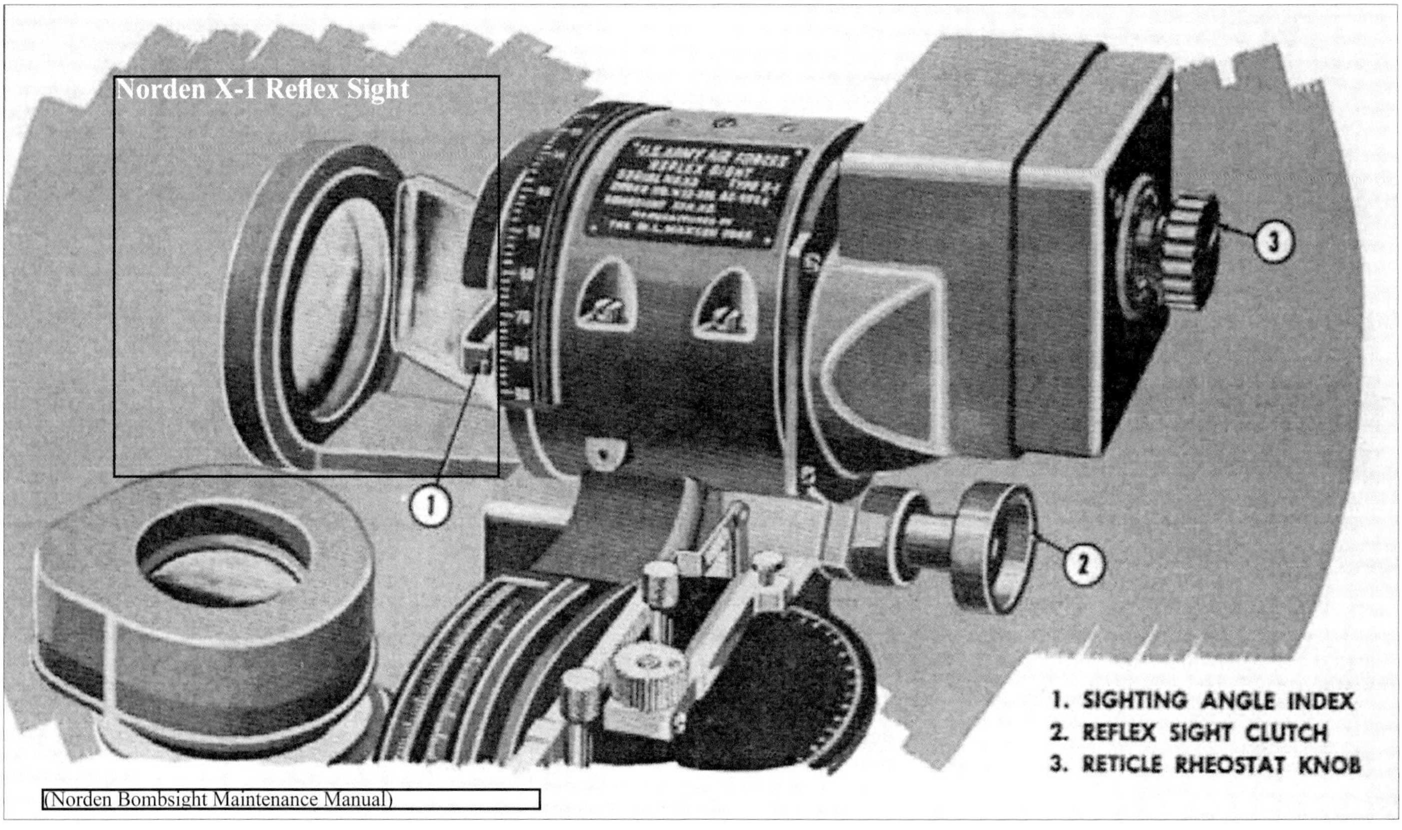

(Norden Bombsight Maintenance Manual)

Norden Glide Bombing Attachment (GBA)

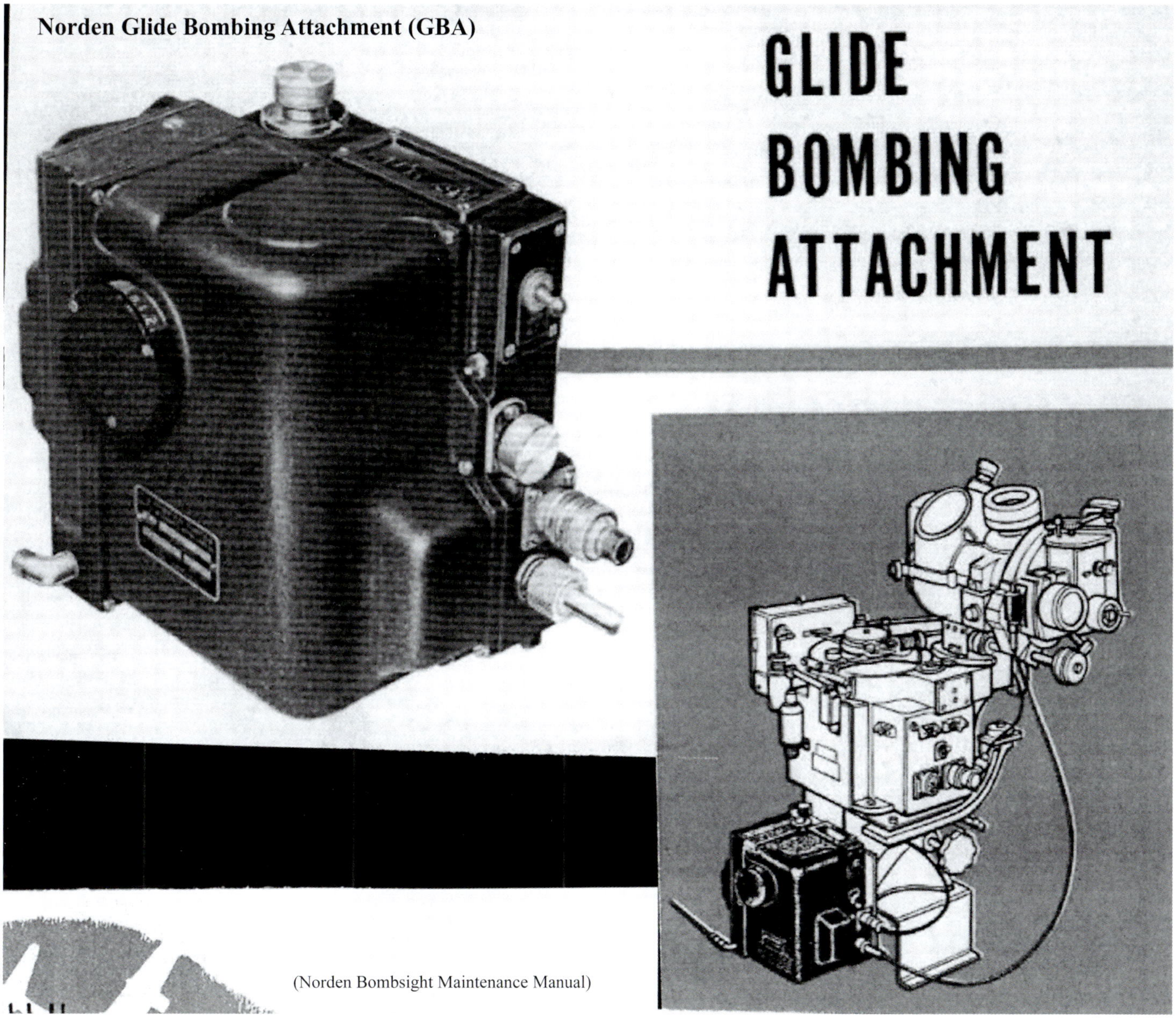

(Norden Bombsight Maintenance Manual)

(Author/CAFAZ)

had been trimmed for normal flight. The vertical gyro was caged and the leveling bubbles used as a reference for adjusting the stabilizer mount, giving the Reflex Sight the same vertical reference as the bombsight. The crosshairs of both bombsights then coincided on an object which was more than 2,000 feet away. The Reflex Sight did not have a Crosstrail mechanism, and if the bombsight was set at any drift angle other than 0° the Reflex Sight crosshairs would be in a lateral error in an amount equal to Crosstrail (the distance between the bomber's true course and the collision course).

The Reflex Sight could be used for dropping angles up to 70° when engaged with the bombsight and an additional 20° by disengaging the Reflex Sight optics and setting them at the desired angle manually. The center of the Reflex Sight optics was several inches above the center of the bombsight optics, and in some bombers part of the aircraft structure interrupted the line of sight, limiting the sighting angle. A two filament lamp illuminated the reticle of the Reflex Sight, and the amount of light could be controlled by rotating the rheostat in either direction from OFF. If one filament burned out the other could be used by rotating the rheostat in the opposite direction.

Norden Glide Bombing Attachment (GBA)

The glide bombing attachment was an auxiliary instrument for use with the Norden M-Series bombsight, enabling its use in climbs and glides as well as in horizontal flight. The attachment significantly simplified bombing problems even in horizontal flight. All settings could be made well in advance of the bombing run with a small loss in accuracy.

The automatic track finding (AFT) of a bomb dropped during a climb or glide varied with the bombing altitude and the vertical velocity at the time of release. The GBA measured altitude and vertical velocity by a barometric element connected to the pitot static system. It computed the disc speed required for that bombing altitude and vertical velocity and drove the bombsight disc at the proper speed.

The vertical velocity was shown on the drum type scale viewed through the window on the side of the main cover. The scale was graduated in feet per minute, with each division on the scale being 200 fpm. On the right side the scale read from 0 to 3,000 fpm for climb and on its left side from 0 to 9,000 fpm for glides.

The altitude scale indicated pressure altitude, plus any correction that was set in, and was read through the window in the top of the computer case. The main scale indicated intervals of 1,000 feet, while the vernier read from 0 to 1,000 feet in intervals of 50 feet. (Note: A vernier scale was a small auxiliary graduated scale located parallel to a main graduated scale and calibrated to indicate fractional parts of the subdivisions of the larger scale.)

The altitude knob was used to set bombing altitude into the GBA. The instrument indicated pressure altitude until the bombardier made a correction for pressure and temperature variations by pulling out on altitude knob, turning it, and then working it back in.

The GBA computed the disc speed on the basis of the time it would take a bomb to fall in a vacuum (VTF). Therefore, a correction needed to be made by turning the disc speed correction knob at the left of the altitude scale so that the disc speed in the bombsight was based on ATF. The amount of correction in rpm was indicated on the scale attached to the knob.

Power to the GBA was supplied through a cable connection on its right side below the altitude knob. The flexible drive shaft between bombsight and GBA connected it with the attachment at the lower right side of the computer case. The other end of the shaft connected with the bombsight disc through a special tachometer shaft bracket that replaced the standard tachometer shaft brace.

A total of just over 18,100 GBAs were manufactured for an average unit cost of $2,836 each and a total contract of approximately $51.4 million, not including design, engineering, and test costs.

Lawrence Sperry was the third son of Elmer Sperry and developed a gyroscopic stabilizer for aircraft that would enable an aircraft to maintain its course and attitude under all circumstances. The brilliant Sperry's life was cut short at 31 when he was killed in an airplane crash. (AFHRC)

Autopilots

Sperry Autopilot

Lawrence Sperry was born in Chicago on 22 December 1892, the third son of famed inventor Elmer Sperry. After spending his youth interested in flying he enrolled in the aviation school run by Glenn Curtiss at Hammondsport, NY, and became the youngest licensed pilot in the United States. Sperry soon developed an interest in a gyroscopic stabilizer for aircraft that would enable an aircraft to maintain its course and attitude under all circumstances.

The Wright brothers, with their familiarity with bicycles, had briefly investigated the gyroscopic phenomenon, and Sperry had also been interested by the inclination of a motorcycle or bicycle to remain upright when it was moving. While the principles of the gyroscopic effect were understood at that time there had been no attempt to utilize the gyroscope's capabilities in stabilizing an aircraft. Sperry was granted funding by the U.S. Navy to investigate gyro-stabilization.

Without pilot input on the controls an aircraft could stray through the three flight axes of an aircraft (yaw, pitch, and roll), but Sperry believed that a spinning gyroscope could maintain an aircraft's original course. Sperry proposed that if the three flight axes could be linked to the stability of a gyroscope an automatic control system could be developed. Yaw is lateral deviation from the course heading, pitch is the up and down divergence from level flight, and roll is the lengthwise rotation around the axis of flight. Sperry linked the control surfaces with three gyroscopes, which permitted flight corrections to be introduced based on the angle of deviation between the flight direction and the original gyroscopic settings.

The Sperry guidance apparatus would perform mechanically what the pilot performed instinctively. Sperry's control gyroscopes were designed to maintain a zero setting for all control surfaces unless corrective action was required. The transmission of corrective commands to the controls required a mechanical linkage to the control surfaces. The gyroscopes required electrical power to maintain rotational rotor speed as the actuating medium. The source of power for the gyroscope motors was obtained by mounting a wind-driven generator in the slipstream on the upper wing.

The Sperry autopilot weighed 40 pounds and was compacted into a small box measuring 18 inches by 18 inches by 12 inches. Sperry's stabilizer required four gyroscopes rotating at 7,000 rpm and was mechanically linked to the aircraft control mechanism. When one of the gyroscopes moved in opposition to the movement of the aircraft, linkage to valves would actuate pistons operated by compressed air and connected by levers to the control surfaces. Also, an anemometer that could sense inadequate airspeed and incipient stall was also linked to the device and would cause a corrective action.

A problem arose, as different manufacturers had different methods of operating control surfaces. Pilots had to learn a completely different cockpit layout for each different type, making it unfeasible for Sperry to design a stabilizer for the unique control actuation methods employed in different aircraft. The problem was solved for Sperry by the universal implementation of the simple Deperdussin control system, which is in use today. The Societé de Production Armand Deperdussin (SPAD) had developed the method of using a central control stick to manipulate the elevators and ailerons, with pedals or a rudder bar controlling the vertical rudder. The Deperdussin control system was to prove to be ideal for the Sperry gyroscopic system.

The U.S. Navy moved gyroscopic stabilizer trials to San Diego, CA, to avoid the poor weather at Hammondsport and had assigned Lt. Patrick Bellinger to assist and supervise him while using a Curtiss C-2 as a testbed. In flight tests with Sperry, Bellinger had a penchant to take over the controls if the gyroscopic operation seemed slow or reluctant. After a while Bellinger controlled his tendency to seize the controls, but one time he waited too long and crashed the C-2 into the waters of the Spanish Bight. Sperry managed to save the gyro stabilizer and both men escaped unharmed. Sperry finally solved most of the problems in further tests. He offset the rudder position to overcome engine torque and corrected the aileron settings to compensate for the location of the center of gravity for each aircraft. Once Sperry was confident that his system was perfected he climbed out onto the wing during a test with Bellinger in the cockpit and the system corrected the banking momentarily caused by the transfer of Sperry's weight to the wing.

The Aero Club of France and the French War Department sponsored an international aircraft safety competition, the Concours de la Securité en Aéroplane, scheduled for 18 June 1914. Curtiss, seeing a good public relations ploy, sent one of his C-2s and Sperry to provide his stabilizer and flying expertise. There were 57 specially equipped planes entered in the competition, featuring such improvements in aircraft technology as magnetos, self-starters, carburetors, and other innovations. Sperry, the sole participant equipped with a gyroscopic stabilizer apparatus designed to improve stability and control, was listed last on the program.

On his first run, the Curtiss C-2 flew down a river directly in front of the judge's stand. Sperry engaged his stabilizer, extricated himself from the shoulder yoke that controlled the C-2's ailerons, and passed by the judges with both his arms held high, the aircraft continuing on a straight and steady course. During the second pass his mechanic, Emil Cachin, climbed out on the starboard wing and moved about seven feet away from the fuselage with Sperry's hands off the controls. As Cachin moved out on the wing the aircraft banked momentarily due to the shift of weight, but the gyrostabilizer immediately acquired control and corrected the attitudinal change, and the Curtiss continued to fly properly down the river. On the C-2's last pass Cachin was on one wing and Sperry on the other waving to the spectators, with the pilot's seat empty. Sperry was awarded first prize (50,000 francs/($10,000)) and became famous overnight. The handsome, personable 23 year old had become a well-known inventor.

With the outbreak of World War I weeks later Sperry's life changed, and he began to think about producing a dual-purpose aircraft; a flying boat could carry a retractable landing gear so that it could also operate from a land base, which was developed by the end of March 1915. Sperry voyaged to Britain in 1916 and secured numerous orders for his automatic pilot. In 1916 he was also commissioned a Lt(jg) in the U.S. Navy and was assigned as a flight instructor. After the United States entered World War I on 6 April 1917, Sperry and his father continued research on an aerial torpedo that was actually a guided bomb, and the two then joined automotive inventor Charles Kettering, who produced a prototype of a pilotless aircraft equipped to fly a preset course to a designated target. (The Sperry and Kettering *Bug* are described in detail in Volume 3.)

When World War I ended aviation endeavors turned to civilian activities, and Lawrence Sperry designed and built an inexpensive sport plane, the Sperry *Messenger*. On 23 December 1923 he took off in his *Messenger* from England for France over a fogged-in Channel, but crashed and was killed at the age of 31. Although the Sperry Aircraft Company did not endure the loss of Lawrence Sperry, between 1915 and 1923 he had pending or granted 23 patents. Among his inventions were instruments that permitted aircraft to be piloted when visibility was zero, and variations of his bank-and-turn indicator and artificial horizon equip modern aircraft. He also invented a variety of other instrumentation, including an airspeed indicator, a drift indicator, and a considerably improved liquid-filled magnetic compass. Today all major passenger ships use a Sperry-type stabilizer actuating a wing-like device to dampen rolling. A type of Sperry autopilot linked to a Sperry gyrocompass is commonly used today on every ship of any size.

AFCE/SBAE Autopilot

General

The C-1/B-1 autopilot was known as the Automatic Flight Control Equipment (AFCE) by the AAF, while the Navy version was known as the Stabilized Bombing Approach Equipment (SBAE). The AFCE was manufactured by Minneapolis Honeywell Regulator for the AAF, and the SBAE was manufactured by the Navy. The only difference between the C-1 and B-1 was that the C-1 autopilot operated on 24-volt direct current and bombers with 12-volt circuits were equipped with the B-1 autopilot. Approximately 55,000 sets were manufactured at an average cost of just under $3,100 per set.

The C-1 Autopilot was an electronic-mechanical device that automatically controlled the bomber in straight and level flight, or maneuvered it in response to the fingertip control of the pilot or bombardier. The precision of even the most skilful human pilot was limited by his reaction time. Reaction time in turn varied with fatigue, inability to detect deviations the instant they occurred, errors in judgment, and muscle coordination. The autopilot, on the other hand, detected flight deviations the instant they occurred, and just as instantaneously operated the controls to correct them. When properly adjusted, the autopilot neither over-controlled nor under-controlled the bomber, but kept it flying straight and level with all three control surfaces operating in proper coordination.

When used with the Norden M-Series bombsight it controlled the course of the bomber, and the course corrections caused the autopilot to make the correct turns. When the bombardier finished training to join a combat crew he usually was the only man in the crew who understood the operation of the autopilot. The bombardier was responsible for setting up the autopilot, and to get maximum performance from it he had to know how it worked and how to set it up for proper operation and teach the pilot and co-pilot how to use it. Although its main purpose was for use on bombing runs to give a stabilized bombing platform, it was also used to relieve pilot fatigue and as a navigational aid.

How the Autopilot Operated

Before Takeoff

Before takeoff the autopilot turn control was to be centered, and all switches on the control panel were to be OFF. When the temperature was below 32°F the autopilot needed to run up for 30 minutes before engaging. It could be warmed up on the ground prior to takeoff for immediate use after takeoff by turning on the master switch during engine run up. Before engaging, each centering knob was to adjust the autopilot control reference point to the straight and level flight position of the corresponding control surface. The autopilot had to be OFF during takeoff, but after takeoff the master switch was turned ON.

After Takeoff

After 10 minutes the Pilot Direction Indicator (PDI) switch was turned ON and the aircraft was trimmed for level flight at cruising speed. The PDI was a remote indicating device operated by the PDI pot, and when the autopilot was used the PDI indicated to the airplane commander when the system and aircraft were correctly trimmed. When engaging the autopilot the aileron telltale lights were put out with the aileron centering knob and then the aileron engaging switch was tripped. Once the ailerons were engaged on the autopilot, with the PDI centered, the autopilot could make aileron corrections automatically. The bombardier then disengaged the autopilot clutch, recentered the PDI, and locked it in place. The PDI remained locked and centered until the pilot had completed the rudder engaging procedure. The rudder telltale lights were put out with the rudder centering knob and the rudder engaging switch was tripped. When the rudder was engaged the autopilot clutch was re-engaged and the PDI lock released. The same procedure was then repeated for the elevator rudder. The final autopilot trim corrections were made, and if necessary the centering knobs were used to level the wings and center the PDI.

Operation of the Autopilot

After the C-1 was operating the pilot was to scrupulously analyze the action of the aircraft to be certain that all adjustments had been made correctly for smooth and precise flight control. When the two telltale lights in any axis were out it indicated that the autopilot was ready for engaging in that axis. In the Student's Bombing Manual the autopilot operation was compared to that of the human body.

Operation of the Autopilot

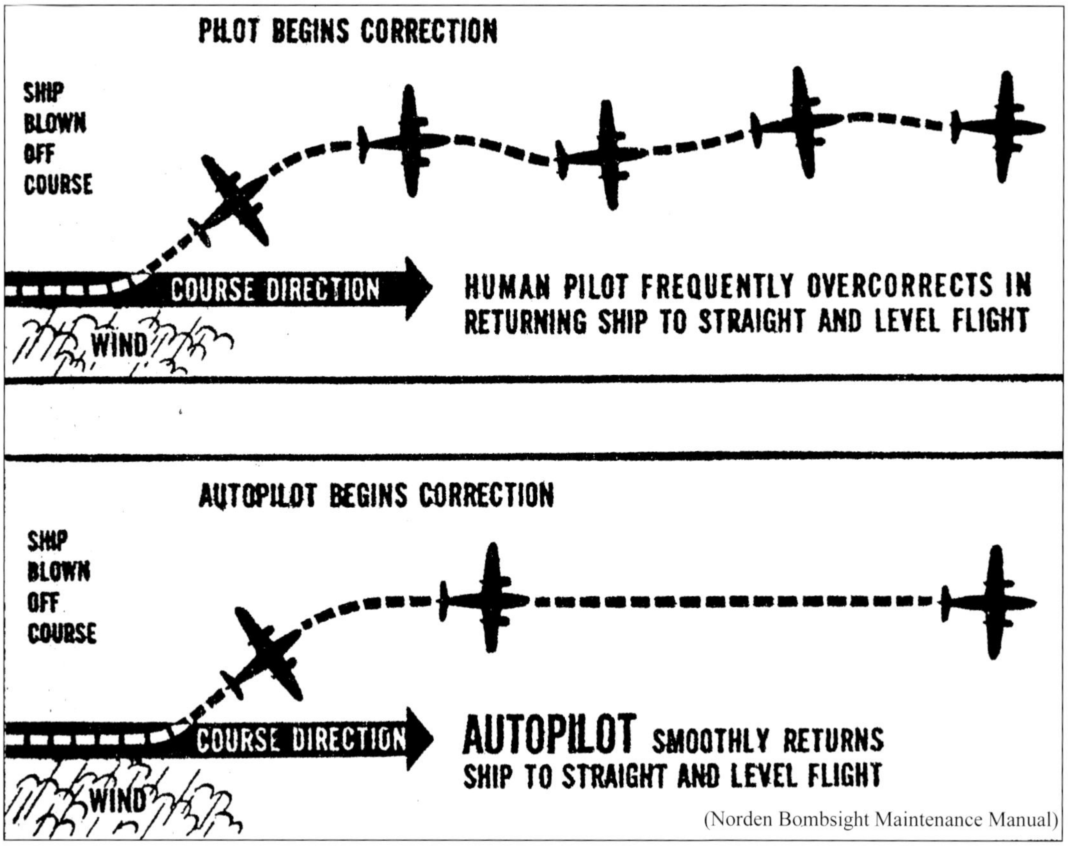

(Norden Bombsight Maintenance Manual)

The Autopilot's "Eyes"
A human pilot watched the horizon or his instruments to see if the bomber was flying straight and level. The "eyes" of the autopilot were two gyros: one was the directional gyro located in the bombsight stabilizer, which detected any deviation of an aircraft from straight flight (i.e. its spin axis was in the horizontal and provided stabilization about the bomber's yaw). The other, which had its spin axis in the vertical, was the flight gyro, and was usually located near the center of gravity of the aircraft. The cases which held these gyros were attached to the aircraft, and when it angled the cases moved with the bomber, but the gyros tended to maintain their fixed position in space. Two wipers were placed in a fixed position to the flight gyro: one around the roll axis and one around the pitch axis. Another wiper was placed in a fixed position to the directional gyro, around the yaw axis. These wipers were similar to the PDI brush of the bombsight. Each of these three wipers were positioned on a potentiometer mounted to the gyro case. These potentiometers were just coiled wires. If the wiper moved from the center, or "dead" spot on the potentiometer, it unbalanced an electric bridge circuit. So when the airplane angled from normal, the gyro and wiper maintained their position in space, but the potentiometer, which fastened to the airplane, moved under the wiper. In this way the autopilot "saw" when the airplane was not flying straight and level.

The Autopilot's "Nerves"
A human pilot's brain must receive and send signals through his nervous system so the proper muscles of his body will react to apply a force on the airplane's controls to correct the attitude of the airplane's flight. The autopilot's "nerves" were a system of electric bridge circuits and wires that carried signals between the various units.

The Autopilot's "Brain"
Just as the pilot's eyes sent a signal to his brain, the gyros of the autopilot, through wipers and potentiometers, sent an electric signal to the amplifier, which was an "electric brain."

The Autopilot's "Muscles"
Signals from the amplifier caused servo units in the autopilot system to operate. These servo units corresponded to the human pilot's muscles. They were attached by cables to the bomber's control surfaces. Thus, when the airplane deviated from straight and level flight the gyros signaled the amplifier, which in turn sent the proper signals to the servo units. This caused the servo units to move the controls mechanically in the proper direction and return the airplane to straight and level flight.

Parts of the C-1 Autopilot
Autopilot Control Panel (ACP)
The Autopilot Control Panel (ACP), located in the pilot's compartment, contained the switches, lights, and knobs for engaging parts of the autopilot and adjusting its operation to compensate for changes in flight conditions. The ACP afforded the pilot with fingertip control through which he could easily engage or disengage the system, adjust the sharpness or speed of its response to flight deviations, or trim the system for various weight and flight conditions. It consisted of various separate units interconnected electrically to operate as a system:

Tell-tale lights showed when the electrical trim of the autopilot agreed with the manual trim of the airplane.

Autopilot Gyro

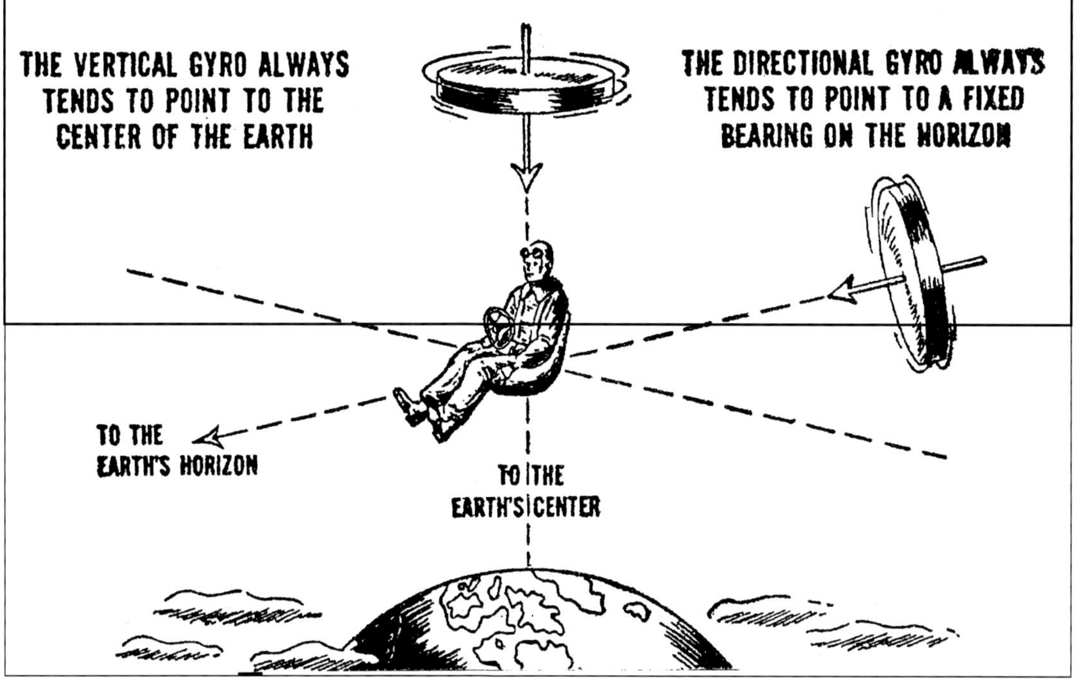

Tell-tale light shutter knob regulated the brightness of the tell-tale lights. *Centering knobs* changed the electrical trim of the autopilot to agree with the manual trim of the airplane.

Sensitivity knobs regulated the distance the airplane was allowed to deviate from straight and level flight before the servo units applied control to correct the deviation. The sensitivity control was comparable to the human pilot's reaction time. When the sensitivity was set high the autopilot responded quickly to effect a correction for even the slightest deviation. If the sensitivity was set low, the flight deviations had to be relatively great before the autopilot made any corrections. There were three sensitivity increase knobs, one each for the aileron, the rudder, and elevator, that were turned clockwise to increase and counterclockwise to decrease sensitivity.

Ratio knobs regulated the amount the servo units moved the control surfaces for any given deviation of the aircraft. The ratio control was the amount of control surface movement exercised by the autopilot when correcting a given deviation. The ratio control directed the speed of the aircraft's response to corrective autopilot actions. The correct ratio adjustment depended on airspeed. If the ratio was too high then the autopilot over-controlled and the flight corrections were too great. If the ratio was too low then the autopilot under-controlled and the flight corrections were too small. The ratio panel resembled the sensitivity panel with three increase knobs, one each for the aileron, rudder, and elevator.

Turn compensation knobs regulated the amount of control necessary when the directional panel was used in making a coordinated turn. The turn compensation was adjusted by having the bombardier disengage the autopilot clutch and move the engaging knob to the extreme right or extreme left. The aircraft then was to bank 18° as indicated by the artificial horizon. The recovery from this turn needed to be coordinated. If the PDI returned to center before the wings were level the rudder ratio needed to be decreased or the aileron ratio increased, depending on the speed of recovery. If the wings were level before the PDI was centered the rudder ratio was to be increased or the aileron ratio decreased, depending on the speed of recovery.

Turn control enabled the pilot to make coordinated turns with the autopilot with as much as 40° of bank.

Aileron and rudder trimmer screws regulated the amount of aileron and rudder control necessary to make a coordinated turn with the turn control.

Remote control transfer knob shifted the turn control operation to a remote turn control station in either the bombardier's or navigator's compartment.

Servo Units

The three servo units, one for each axis of the airplane, were identical, and provided the mechanical force via a cable drum driven by an electric motor necessary to move the aircraft's control surfaces. There was one servo unit for each control surface (rudder, aileron, and elevator), and it was located as close as possible to the control surface that it moved. Servo units were connected to control surfaces by cables clamped to the regular control cables of the bomber. Servo units were built so that they were easily overpowered if, in an emergency, the pilot had to take over control of the airplane.

Amplifier

The amplifier controlled the operation of the servo units, causing them to move the control surfaces of the aircraft in one direction or the other in response to corrective signals from the gyros. The amplifier received the electrical signals sent by the other units—bridge circuits (wipers and potentiometers)—and amplified these signals, which directed the proper servo units to apply a definite amount of control in the desired direction.

Directional Stabilizer

The directional stabilizer was located in the bomber's nose and contained the horizontal gyro, which served as the directional reference for the Autopilot. The directional panel was connected to the side of the stabilizer and supplied the electrical signals to steer the bomber. The directional stabilizer was connected to the stabilizer gyro through the Autopilot clutch. When the clutch was engaged the stabilizer steered the aircraft; when it was disengaged, the bombardier could steer the bomber manually.

(Norden Bombsight Maintenance Manual)

Figure 250 – Auto Pilot C1 Control Panel

Dashpot

The dashpot ("pot") was a device consisting of a piston that moved within a cylinder containing oil and was used to dampen and control motion. It was linked to the mechanism in the directional panel that produced the signal for rudder control. It increased the signal for initial rudder correction as the speed of the aircraft's yaw increased. The degree of increase in that signal could be controlled by adjusting the knurled nut on top of the dashpot. Likewise, if the aircraft's nose dropped the vertical flight gyro detected the vertical deviation and operated the elevator pick up pot that sent an electrical signal to the elevator section of the amplifier. This signal was amplified and relayed by electrical impulses to the elevator servo unit, which raised the elevators the correct amount to bring the aircraft back to level flight. If a wing dropped considerably the vertical gyro operated the aileron pick up pot, the skid pot, and the up-elevator pot. The signals from the operation of these units were transmitted to their respective aileron, rudder, and elevator sections of the amplifier. The electrical impulses to the aileron, rudder, and elevator servo units caused each of these units to operate its respective control surfaces just enough to bank and turn the aircraft back to level flight.

Rotary Inverter

The rotary inverter was a generator operating on the direct current from the aircraft's power supply (batteries), which converted it to the alternating current necessary for use in the amplifier and bridge circuits of the autopilot.

Junction Box

The junction box provided terminals to connect the wiring from the various units of the autopilot and as a central wiring station; it saved wire and made it easier to check the various circuits. The C-1 autopilot operated on 24-volt direct current. However, bombers with 12-volt circuits were equipped with the B-1 autopilot, which was identical except for operating on different voltages.

Directional Panel

The directional panel contained two electrical devices: the banking pot and rudder pick up pot that signaled to the aileron and rudder section of the amplifier whenever the directional panel was activated by a change in course. The signals were amplified and converted by magnetic switches or relays into electrical impulses that caused the aileron and rudder servo units to operate the ailerons and rudder of the aircraft in the correct direction and amount to turn the aircraft back to its original heading.

(Norden Bombsight Maintenance Manual)

Steering by AutoPilot

Pilot Steering

For the pilot or bombardier to steer the bomber by the autopilot the autopilot clutch needed to be disengaged, disconnecting the directional gyro from the directional panel. The pilot or bombardier was then in control of the directional panel and, through it, the servo units were also controlled. When the autopilot clutch was moved it caused the bomber to turn. The bomber resumed straight and level flight when the autopilot clutch was again engaged to the directional gyro, or when the clutch was returned to center manually.

If the pilot wished to make a turn, he set the turn control knob to the degree of bank and in the direction of intended turn. His control command sent signals through the aileron and rudder sections of the amplifier to the aileron and rudder servo units that operated the ailerons and rudder correctly to achieve a completely coordinated turn without slipping or skidding. As the aircraft banked the vertical flight gyro operated the aileron, skid, and up-elevator pots. The signals from the aileron and skid pots canceled the signals to the aileron and rudder servo units and streamlined these controls during the turn. The up-elevator pot sent signals that caused the elevators to raise just enough to maintain altitude. When the intended turn was finished the airplane commander turned the turn control back to 0 and the aircraft leveled off on its new course. The directional arm lock on the stabilizer was energized by a switch in the turn control and prevented the stabilizer from interfering with the turn by carrying out its normal direction correcting function.

Bombardier Steering

The autopilot clutch was located on the directional gyro at the bombardier's station and was used to disengage the directional stabilizer. When the clutch was engaged the pilot, navigator, and bombardiers steered the aircraft, but when it was disengaged only the bombardier could steer the airplane using his turn control. The bombsight clutch on the directional stabilizer engaged the bombsight and autopilot, allowing the bombardier to steer the airplane by turning the bombsight. When the bombsight clutch was engaged the autopilot clutch was to be disengaged. The bombardier used his turn control knob to turn the airplane when he had control.

The Effect of High Altitude on the Autopilot

At high altitudes of 30,000 feet and above there were several factors that affected the autopilot. High altitude affected the normal flight characteristics, and the pilot had to compensate for these changes. The aircraft flew tail low, especially when fully combat loaded. The controls became increasingly soft and the aircraft sluggish. Pilot control errors showed up more slowly and took longer to correct, and could take the aircraft far out of the formation before they were corrected. Low temperatures affected the autopilot, and it had to be properly warmed up and set up as soon after takeoff as practical. While in the climb the autopilot was to be adjusted with the necessary controls on the way up. At high altitudes the insulation of electrical wires lost efficiency and could affect the autopilot, and the generators needed to be checked periodically. The pilot had to know the characteristics of his aircraft under various conditions, be thoroughly familiar with the operation of the autopilot, and anticipate any correction the same as if he were flying the aircraft manually.

Formation Stick

The formation stick provided a means by which the pilot could maneuver the bomber with the autopilot with easier, faster, and more efficient control, especially when flying in formation. The system consisted of two sticks and pedestal assemblies, two release switches. and one function selector switch located adjacent to the two pilots' seats. The formation stick assembly consisted of a fighter aircraft type stick grip, a control transfer switch button, and a trigger microphone switch. Two potentiometers picked up signals from the movement of the stick and transferred them to the autopilot amplifier. The control transfer button on top of the grip was used to transfer control of the aircraft from one stick to another. Only one stick had control at a time, and the pilot could override the co-pilot's transfer button and maintain control by constantly holding down his own control button. The release switches allowed immediate disengaging of stick and autopilot.

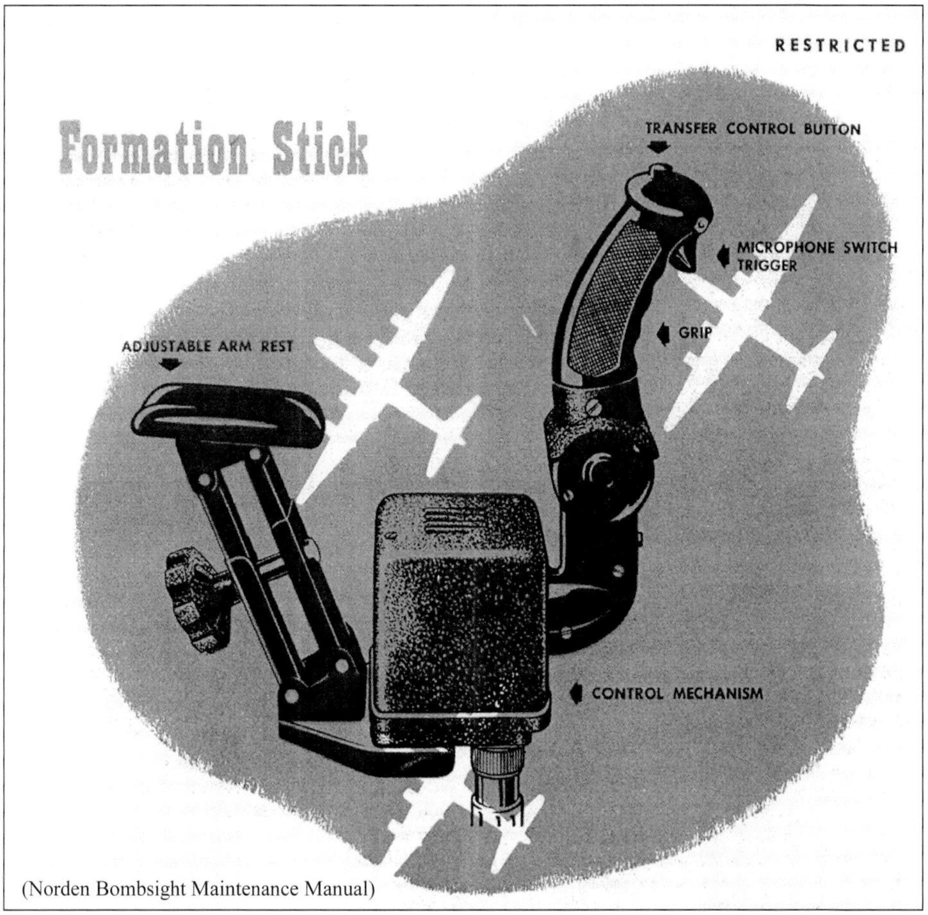

(Norden Bombsight Maintenance Manual)

Handheld Bombing Computers

The Bombardier's Information File stated, "If you have to make many calculations and you have to make them in a hurry, computers, if you know how to use them, can solve your problems accurately, and they can do it quickly and easily."

E-6B Computer

The E-6B computer was designed to calculate nearly all of the bombardier's computations in navigation and bombing. The slide rule on the back of the E-6B computer had a stationary outer scale and an identical movable inner scale on a rotating disc. During making calculations, the outer scale usually represented units of measure (i.e. miles, gallons) while the inner scale represented units of time (i.e. hours and minutes). Since these scales

E-6B Computer

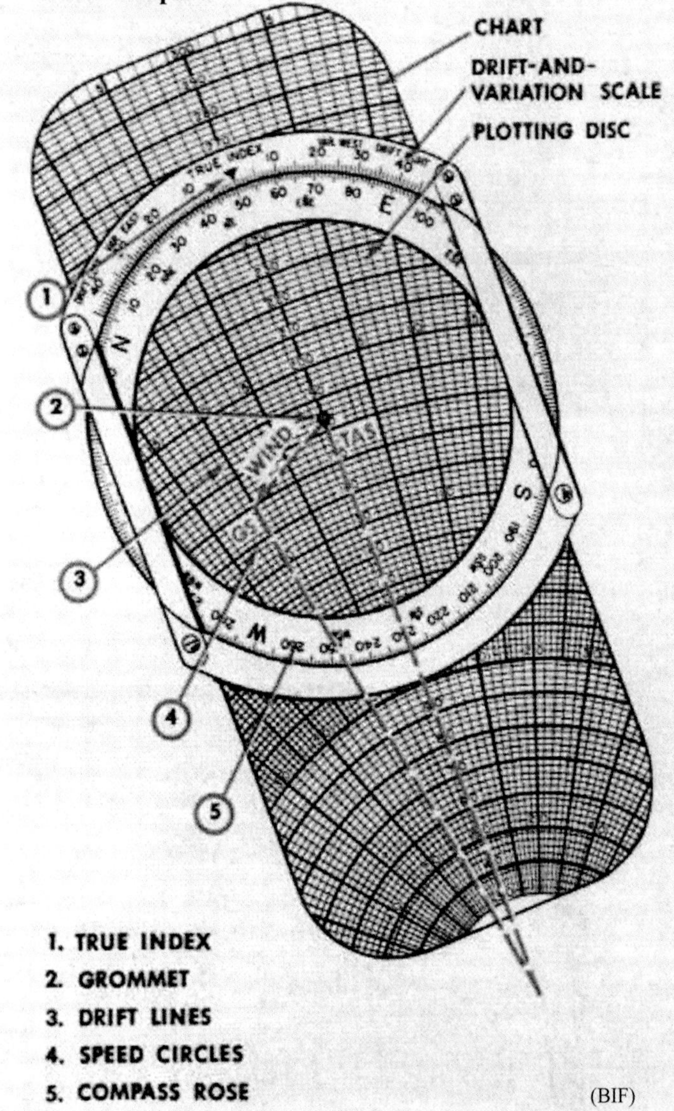

(BIF)

were standard logarithmic scales, the E-6B could also be used to solve any problem in multiplication or division like a standard slide rule.

Description

To find bombing altitude (BA) using the E-6B, the circular slide rule and the window marked "For Altitude Computations" were used. This window consisted of two scales. Air Temperature in the window was set opposite Pressure Altitude under the window. On the outer scale of the slide rule the True Altitude (Cor. Alt.) and opposite it the Pressure Altitude (Cal. Alt.) on the inner scale were found.

Operation

There were two possible methods of operation, depending on whether or not the atmospheric conditions at the target were known (known was the most accurate method).

Automatic Bombing Computer (ABC)

The Automatic Bombing (ABC) computer, which was used with the M-Series Norden Bombsight, allowed the bombardier to solve for wind and automatically indicated the drift angle and dropping angle for any heading of the bomber.

Purpose

The Automatic Bombing Computer was used with the Norden M-Series bombsight. If the proper data was entered the ABC would solve the vector triangle just as the E-6B did, but more rapidly. For this reason it was used to great advantage in short combat approaches. With the ABC the approximate dropping angle and drift for any heading could be determined. This data could be pre-set into the bombsight, and it was possible to make a short bombing run with accurate results.

Description

Since the ABC was used to solve the vector triangle, certain known values had to be entered in order to find the unknowns. Set the magnetic heading on the compass rose, under the lubber line. The compass rose was locked to the clutch drum of the stabilizer by the compass rose lock. The wind direction was entered on the compass rose by positioning the wind arrow on the wind gear, which was mounted on top of the compass rose, and locked by means of the wind gear lock. An idler gear connected the wind gear to the wind disc. The wind gear and the wind disc were the same size and had the same number of teeth; therefore, a turn of one would give an equal turn of the other and in the same direction. On the wind disc was mounted the wind speed scale and the wind speed indicator. The wind speed indicator was set at the wind speed on the wind speed scale and locked with the wind speed lock, which operated freely in the slot of the groundspeed bar. On the right side of this bar was the groundspeed scale. Attached to the left side of the bar was the tangent scale. This scale was selected for the true airspeed, bombing altitude, and the type of bomb used. At the lower end of the slot was the airspeed lock, which locked the true airspeed indicator on the true airspeed scale. On the lower end of the groundspeed bar was the drift pointer, which operated freely over the drift scale.

When the true airspeed and wind were set on the computer and the wind gear locked to the directional gyro, the wind gear and wind disc were held in a fixed position in space. Therefore, the computer automatically determined the drift, groundspeed, and dropping angle for any heading that the bomber flew. The drift and dropping angle were then pre-set into the bombsight for the bombing run.

C-2 and AN Computers

Description

The C-2 and the AN computers solved for bombing altitude and were exactly alike, except that they were printed in different colors. The black figures were the same on both computers, but the C-2 had red figures and the AN had light fluorescent figures. Both computers consisted of two concentric discs and two arms. On the small inside disc were two spiral logarithmic altitude scales. On the outer side of the spiral was the (true altitude) scale with light (or red) figures, on which was found Bombing Altitude (BA). On the inner side of the spiral was the Indicated Altitude Scale with black figures for setting Pressure Altitude above target (PA above T). The large outside disc had a Pressure altitude scale, in black figures, for setting Target Pressure Altitude (TPA). It also had a Temperature scale, in light (or red) figures, for setting the Mean Temperature. The clamped arm was used for Pressure Altitude (PA) settings, while the free arm was used for Mean Temperature and the Bombing Altitude (BA) setting.

Operation

The clamped arm was set at the Target Pressure Altitude (TPA) and locked. The small disc was then rotated until the Pressure Altitude was above target (PA above T in black figures) was under the clamped arm. The free arm was set at the Mean Temperature and the Bombing Altitude (BA) was found the in light (or red) figures under the free arm.

(BIF)

C-2 and AN Computers

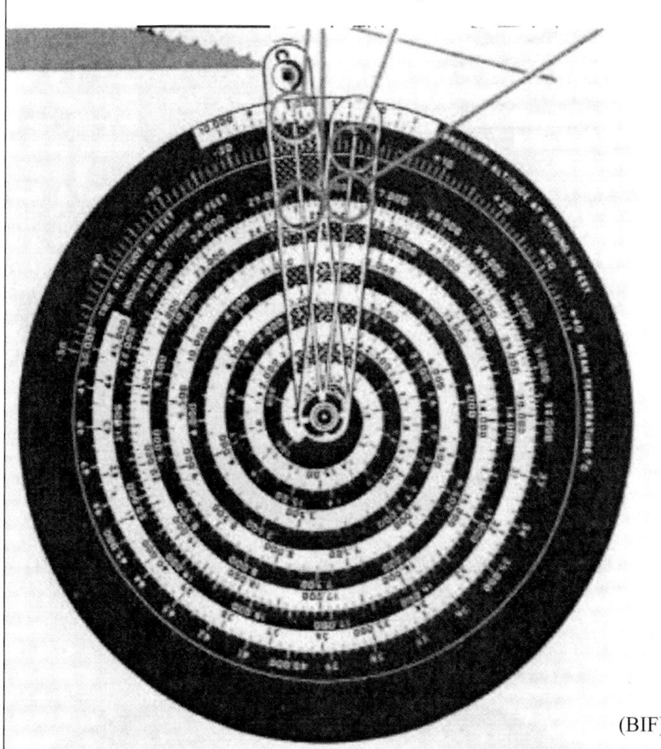
(BIF)

G-1 Computer

The G-1 computer solved for True Airspeed (TAS) when flying at high altitudes and airspeeds when the compressibility of air became an important factor and had to be taken into consideration. The G-l computer made the necessary correction for compressibility.

Radar Bombing and Bombsights

Airborne Surface Vessel Detection (ASV) Radar

Because of the dire U-Boat threat at the beginning of the war, Airborne Surface Vessel (ASV) Detection Radar was given priority for development. Once ASV radar was developed many of its basic principles were applied to bombing radar.

Long Wave Radar ASV MkI

The British development of ground-based radar in the late 1930s is well known through the movies and documentaries on the Battle of Britain that show the massive "Chain Home" radar antennas that gave the RAF "few" the forewarning that saved England from Göring's Luftwaffe. But the development of airborne radar would prove to be much more difficult. A radar transmitter required an antenna to send out its signal and a receiver needed an antenna to pick up that signal. The basic antenna was the dipole, which was reciprocal, being able to produce radar waves at a particular frequency and also was effective in receiving them. The dipole antenna functioned best if its length was half of the wavelength of the radar beam, so the objective in developing airborne radar was to develop a shorter wavelength beam. With the longer wavelength apparatus available to focus the beam in any direction a large array of dipole antennas were required, which limited the number and length of the dipoles. The airborne radar needed to be able to automatically sweep, and simple manually guided radar with an A-scope was the first step toward ASV (airborne surface vessel) and AI radars (airborne intercept), which were essentially similar. The next step was to develop 360° radar, which was difficult, as a dependable rotary coupling system needed to be designed so that the electrical connections between the antenna system and the radar electronics would rotate freely. Also, radar's accuracy depended on the focusing (e.g. "spotlighting") of the beam, as a narrow beam would pinpoint the direction of a distant target more accurately than a broad beam.

In 1936 Edward "Taffy" Bowen formed a team at the Telecommunications Research Establishment (TRE) at Swanage to investigate airborne (AI) radar. Installing radar in an aircraft was difficult due to the size and weight of the set and its antenna, its power supply, and its operation in an environment of cold and vibration. Bowen and his group solved most of the problems over the next year and developed early experimental sets using very long 6.8 meter waves, which made the transmission of narrow beams unfeasible. Most of the transmission return was from the ground and limited AI radar to the height of the aircraft from the ground. In early 1937, during flight testing Bowen flew over the ocean and discovered that ships could be detected at short ranges and ASV radar was conceived. By the summer of 1937 the Telecommunications Research Establishment (TRE) had developed shorter wavelength ASV radar which was based on the Western Electric 316A valve that developed 100 watts of power at a 1.25 meter wavelength. This radar was installed in an Avro Anson and first flown on 17 August 1937 in weather so poor standard reconnaissance

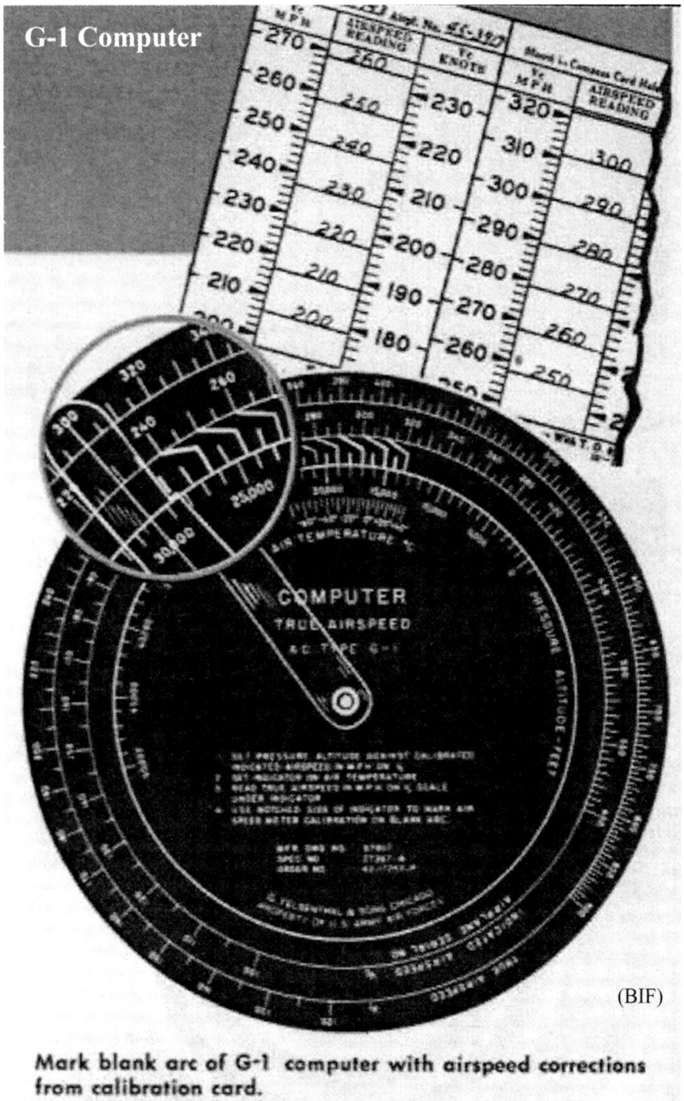

(BIF)

was impossible. The Anson was able to track the aircraft carrier *HMS Courageous* and aircraft taking off from her decks, the battleship *HMS Rodney*, and the cruiser *HMS Southampton*. However, this radar was not ready operationally due to antenna difficulties, along with administrative and priority problems. As the prospect of a European war approached in 1939 ASV and AI were given increased priority, and the wavelength was increased to 1.5 meters and two antenna designs were developed. One antenna design utilized a dipole transmitting antenna with a reflector that sent a broad forward directed beam. Two receiving antennas that had overlapping polar diagrams were installed on the aircraft's wings. The target's direction was ascertained by comparing the signals from the two receivers that were displayed on a cathode ray tube (CRT), which was a vacuum tube containing an electron gun (a source of electrons) and a fluorescent screen, with internal or external means to accelerate and deflect the electron beam, and used to create images in the form of light emitted from the fluorescent screen. The AI CRT had a center vertical baseline, one to the right and the other to the left of the vertical line. If the target was to the left then the left receiver gave the stronger signal. The vertical time base displayed the distance to the target with a 1,000 ton vessel detected at 10 miles and an elevated coast line at up to 40 miles.

In late 1939 a test was conducted using a Hudson of the Coastal Command 220 Squadron and RN submarine L 27. The submarine was detected broadside at three miles when the Hudson was flying at 1,000 feet and later at six miles when flying at 6,000 feet. The encouraging results led the Coastal Command to equip 12 Hudson bombers of its 220, 224, and 233 Squadrons with the first ASV radar, designated as the ASV MkI in January 1940. The radar had its fixed antenna located in the aircraft nose and was only able to search forward. At 3,000 feet the MkI could detect a U-Boat at 5.5 miles, but at 4.5 miles the target was lost in reflections from the water's surface

Edward "Taffy" Bowen, a leading authority on radar, formed an English team at the Telecommunications Research Establishment (TRE) to investigate airborne (AI) radar, and would become instrumental in aiding American radar development. (Author)

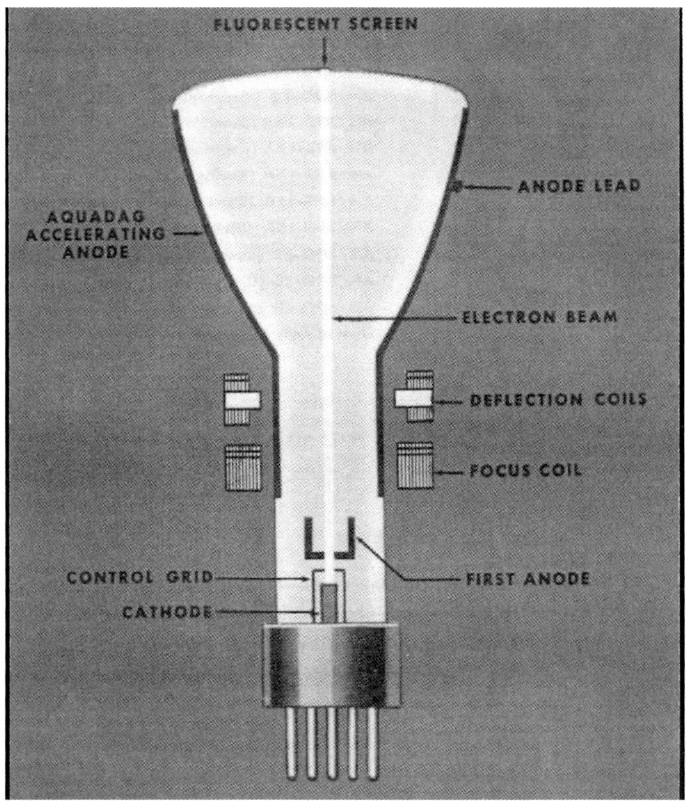

In using AI radar, the target's direction was ascertained by comparing the signals from the two receivers that were displayed on a **Cathode Ray Tube (CRT)**, which was a vacuum tube containing an electron gun (a source of electrons) and a fluorescent screen. (ROBIF)

called "sea clutter." Flying at 200 feet was found to be more effective, as the U-Boat could be detected at 3.5 miles and the sea clutter would not obscure the target until reaching a vicinity of a half mile, but flying at 200 feet proved to be difficult to maintain for long periods. The forward looking MkIs were greatly improved when a second antenna system was developed called the Long Range ASV (LRASV), which was a sideways looking system. The transmitter was an 18 foot long array of 10 dipoles installed in five pairs (later four) on top of the fuselage, while the two 12 foot receiving antennas were installed on the sides of the fuselage. Because of their length these antennae were nicknamed "stickleback" by the British. The nose or side antennas had to be used individually, but the side antennas could be quickly switched from side-to-side. Routinely the side antennas swept 10 miles on each side, so a patrolling aircraft flying at 125 mph could theoretically scan 20 miles on each side, covering 2,500 square miles in an hour. This antenna array gave a much better resolution and range (2.5 times better) and was able to detect a submarine at 10 to 15 miles.

MKI reliability was poor due to inferior manufacturing quality control of its components. It required skilled tuning by a highly trained operator and was difficult to maintain, and in practice was considered to be inadequate for U-Boat detection, but was very good for navigation in bad weather and for rendezvousing with convoys for escort duty. By the end of 1940 some 200 sets were manufactured and placed in Coastal Command Hudsons and Sunderland flying boats, but another radar system using a shorter wave length was needed.

Long Wave Radar ASV MkII

The MkI was replaced by the more reliable and a better performing shorter wavelength ASV MkII developed by the spring of 1940 by Pye Radio Ltd. and E.K. Cole Ltd. The MkII was very similar to the AI Mk4 and also operated at 176MH. Whereas early ASV sets required separate receivers and transmitters that used multiple sets of separate antennae, the MkII had an Aerial Coupler that used a motor driven switch to allow the transmitter and receiver to send and receive radar beams through a single set of antennas. The MkII had a more powerful transmitter than the MkI that could focus a narrow beam either through the nose or the two port and starboard scanning antennas. However, a variation used a large antenna array placed on top of the fuselage which was used to sweep shipping lanes, or as a receiver beacon at ranges up to 90 miles. Radar returns were received through a new and more powerful receiver and indicator units. When the side scanners detected a suspected target the aircraft would turn at 90° towards the target. The nose radar was switched on and the pilot closed on the target. During test flights at 1,000 feet the MkII could detect a surfaced submarine at 10 miles through its side antennas or at seven miles through its nose antennas. The first MkII success was on 30 November 1940 when a Whitley MkIV bomber damaged U-71 in the Bay of Biscay, and half a year later more sets and more experience had increased attacks on U-Boats by 20% and night patrols were initiated.

The MkII receiver used the early Range Azimuth screen (A-scope), which was an oblong screen with a vertical base line running down the middle. All ground returns came up as blips from the bottom, either to the right or left of the base line depending if the signal were to the port or starboard, and the distance from the bottom of the trace was equivalent to the range. Three distance ranges were selectable on the indicator and the suitable scales were imprinted on the cursor. There were two blips on the screen: the lower and larger was the simulated sea echo at the height of the aircraft, while the upper blip was the simulated target. The radar operator had to line up the target blip on the base line and determine the distance to the target. The A-scope returns made it difficult for the operator to determine the U-Boat's location in relation to the aircraft and distorted images below. So it was almost useless for range and bearing navigation in U-Boat detection or for navigation on anything but a coastline. When a blip was seen the radar operator gave the pilot course corrections so that he could approach the target head on, and the radar return would move from either side of the base line and the operator would give directions, such as "right, right, left, left." The echo would grow larger on the screen as the target was approached and would move down the screen, and the range was measured by a graticule attached to the front of the screen. Using the operator's directions the pilot was constantly maneuvering, which meant that the aircraft would be banking over the target and dropping all the depth charges in salvo instead of in string, which was a much less accurate method.

Long Wave Radar ASV Mark II

(AAF)

The interference called "noise" at the bottom of the screen was sea clutter, and the target echo could merge into it and be lost. The MkII was far less susceptible to sea clutter and, while it did occur at a half mile, it was at a time the U-Boat would be visible. However, at night, unless there was bright moonlight, a surfaced U-Boat once detected by radar would become lost in the radar's sea clutter return at one half mile. The initial response was to drop a string of flares to light up the U-Boat, which hopefully should be directly under one of the flares, and the bomber would turn to make its attack run. However, by the time the bomber returned to attack the U-Boat had plenty of time to dive. The next fix was to drop a buoy into the sea containing time delayed flares near the U-Boat. As the bomber circled and approached for its attack run the flares would be shot into the air, hopefully silhouetting the U-Boat. RAF HQ administrative officer Humphrey Leigh suggested that a better solution would be to mount a powerful forward pointing searchlight on the aircraft that could be switched on to the U-Boat as it disappeared into the radar sea clutter. Contractors Savage & Parsons developed the "Leigh Light," but had problems installing the searchlight due to its size and providing a sufficient power source. In the meantime, the Air Ministry also considered the Turbinlite searchlight, which had been initially developed to intercept enemy bombers at night, but in testing had failed. Savage & Parsons continued to work on Leigh's searchlight, called the Leigh Light (L/L), and developed a powerful new 24 inch searchlight that could swivel about 20° downwards or sideways that was initially powered by a generator but later by a battery pack. On 4 May 1941, Leigh personally piloted a radar/Leigh Light equipped Wellington to illuminate the Royal Navy submarine H-31 that had been lost in the radar's sea clutter at a half mile. On 21 December 1941 a MkII radar equipped Swordfish made the first successful night attack on a U-Boat using the Leigh Light. By June 1942 ASV/L/L equipped patrol aircraft were swarming the U-Boats attempting to cross the Bay of Biscay to reach the Atlantic. They were so successful that by August Doenitz decided that it would be more advantageous for his U-Boats to fight it out on the surface.

Short Wave Microwave ASV Radar

Cavity Magnetron

In the 1930s high microwave frequencies were found to produce more focused beams with greater resolution. But at the end of the decade there was no source that was powerful enough to generate short waves, and the British Admiralty established a committee to study radar operating at 10 centimeter microwaves. A team at Oxford's Clarendon Laboratory was assigned to develop a microwave receiver, and another team at the University of Birmingham was to develop the microwave transmitter. To test their designs microwaves had to be generated for the circuits to detect. At the time there were two methods to generate microwaves: the magnetron and the new American invention, the klystron. Englishmen Drs. John Randall and Henry Boot combined the features of both and made the initial breakthrough in centimetric radar when they built their 3,000 Mc (10cm) magnetron oscillator called the Cavity Magnetron. They completed their first microwave transmission on 21 February 1940, which had a maximum power output three times that of any other device. The Cavity Magnetron was sent to Cambridge's Cavendish Laboratory, headed by Dr. Philip Dee, which built a 9.1 centimeter radar system which was referred to as 10 centimeter for expediency. On 12 August 1940 the Cavendish radar system was used to track an aircraft, and the next day it tracked a technician carrying a metal sheet on a bicycle without any of the previous radar crippling ground clutter.

Magnetron Tube in a radar set. (AAF)

British Centimetric ASV Radar

The British developed ASV MkIII centimetric, radar but the record of its evolution was a checkered one. The original team that developed British airborne radar was disbanded as its head, Taffy Bowen, was in America and personal conflicts arose, causing a new group to be assembled to develop centimetric radar for night fighters. Centimetric radar had the benefit of having a small parabolic reflector to focus an accurate beam that produced better range and resolution and eliminated strong ground returns that were inevitable with the broad beams of the long wave MkI and MkII sets. When Drs. Randall and Boot developed their Magnetron the first sealed unit suitable for airborne use was produced by the GEC (General Electric Company) Research Laboratories, Wembley, London, in June 1940. While centimetric radar development concentrated on AI use, in fall 1940 the Royal Navy conducted ground based experiments under Captains B.R. Willett and C.E. Horton. They were able to track the submarine *HMS Usk* over seven miles on 11 November 1940. After testing and refining the equipment and antennas the first operational

Far Left: Englishmen **Drs. John Randall** (shown) and **Henry Boot** combined the features of the magnetron and the new American invention, the klystron, to make the initial breakthrough in centimetric radar when they built their 3,000 Mc (10cm) magnetron oscillator called the Cavity Magnetron. (Author)

Near Left: **Dr. Philip Dee**, the head of the Cavendish Laboratory at Cambridge, England, used the new Cavity Magnetron to develop a 9.1 centimeter radar system that was referred to as 10 centimeter for expediency. (Author)

British centimetric radar was the Type 271 S-band shipboard set that was put into production within months and underwent sea trials in March 1941. The rudimentary set had manual direction and separate large box-like transmit and receive antennas, and led to a series of other naval and ground radars. By March 1941 the Type 271 was put into operation only because it was the straightforward option for both utility and the placement of its large antennas in the large areas available. On 16 November 1941 the Type-271 equipped Royal Navy corvette *HMS Orchis* sank U-433 near Gibraltar, and by mid-1942 the Royal Navy had equipped 236 ships with the Type 271 radar.

However, the priority was for S-band AI radar for night fighters and ASV radar for anti-submarine aircraft. In April 1941 tests on the AIVII were conducted against the RN submarines *HMS Sea Lion* and in August against the *HMS Sokol* that demonstrated that the radar was effective, but the development of centimetric ASV was lagging, and the first prototype ASV radar was not test flown until December 1941. The production version was being finalized by the summer of 1942 by Ferranti Ltd., a major supplier of electronic fuses and valves located at Moston. However, on 30 September 1942 the company was ordered to halt work; a directive that astounded Coastal Command. The reason was that Bomber Command was simultaneously developing H2S ground mapping radar, which was very similar to ASV radar, under Philip Dee and Bernard Lovell at TRE. The first test of H2S was conducted on 1 November 1941 and was very successful, as it picked up the outline of a town 35 miles away, and the first production model was ready by mid-March 1942. H2S radar attracted the attention of Churchill and centimetric ASV was halted in favor of the H2S, which was to equip four-engine bombers flying at 20,000 feet. Coastal Command leaders were piqued that H2S was selected over ASV radar and were unwilling to continue to work with the Bomber Command concept for ASV purposes. Finally, Coastal Command was forced into an attitude adjustment and reluctantly began to redesign the Bomber Command high altitude H2S concept for ASV functions at 2,000 feet or less. It would not be until 1 March 1943 when a Wellington of 172 Squadron flew its first patrol over the Bay of Biscay. The small 28 inch scanner was mounted in the nose, giving a 60° scan that was received on a Plan Position Indicator Screen that represented the area below as a map on a TV-like screen (to be described later).

America Develops British Centimetric ASV Radar

The RAF ordered 4,000 ASV MkII sets, but production problems due to the demand for other types of radar, particularly bomber H2S targeting radars, slowed its delivery, and the MkII was not available in numbers until early fall 1940, when 45 sets were delivered to Coastal Command. Thus, in mid-1940 Britain found that its scientific, engineering, and manufacturing resources were being stretched thin, and it was apparent that the development of centimetric radar would require the time, money, and engineering capabilities of the United States to develop. Churchill wisely decided to share Britain's secret technological developments, including the cavity magnetron, with American scientists. In August 1940 the prominent British scientist Sir Henry Tizard, with eminent physicist Dr. John Crockett as his deputy, "Taffy" Bowen as the British radar representative, and four other scientists made up the so-called "Tizard Mission" that was sent by Churchill to meet with American Dr. Vannevar Bush. Bush had recently created the National Defense Research Committee (NRDC), which was "to coordinate technology development between civilian scientists and military officials, and to conduct preliminary technical research studies using such funds as they were available." The initial British technical information was examined by Alfred Loomis, who was a very successful investment banker and an avid lay scientist and researcher, and in this position Loomis was put in control of the NDRC's "Microwave Committee." In September Loomis hosted a gathering for members of the Tizard Mission who unveiled the cavity magnetron, and at once the perceptive Loomis realized its potential in saving U.S. scientists "two years of development." Bush and Loomis understood that for the prompt development of cavity magnetron technology it would have to be kept out of military control and a civilian research laboratory would have to be established using NDRC funding. Both Bush and Loomis had strong bonds to the Massachusetts Institute of Technology (MIT) and set up the Microwave Laboratory there. Soon the Microwave Laboratory was referred to as the Radiation Laboratory, or "Rad Lab." At the time American long wave radar was generally on a par with its British counterpart due to the work of the Navy's NRL and Army Signal Corps Laboratories.

In October 1940 Loomis and Bush began to enlist scientists and researchers for the Radiation Lab, and Edward Bowen of the Tizard Mission proved to be an important recruiter, enthusiastically promoting the new British technology. The knowledgeable and genial Bowen has been credited with establishing the amiable Anglo-American scientific collaboration during the war. Among the top scientists signing on with the Radiation Laboratory were physicist Dr. Isidor Rabi and a number of his top students and Dr. Ernest Lawrence of the University of California, Berkeley, who also was accompanied by a number of top students and researchers, including the brilliant Luis Alvarez. By mid-November 1940 the Radiation Lab was ongoing, and a month later 30 physicists were conducting research under the management of Lee DuBridge, another Lawrence protégée, and under the supervision of the NDRC and Loomis.

The Radiation Laboratory had a 6 January 1941 deadline to demonstrate its centimetric radar, and on 4 January the large prototype, consisting of a very large transmitter and receiver, was set up on a MIT roof. Radar beams were bounced off surrounding buildings in an unimpressive demonstration of the impractical unit. A 1 February deadline was set for an airborne demonstration that meant that the size of the set had to be significantly reduced. To achieve this goal the same antenna had to be used for transmission and reception of radar beams. Although the scientists developed a rudimentary duplexer that allowed a single antenna to transmit and receive beams, at the deadline there was no functional airborne radar ready for testing. The MIT researchers increased their efforts, and on 10 March a B-18 was fitted with a prototype centimetric set that was used for initial calibration tests, and on 27 March the first tests using the B-18 set successfully picked up surface shipping. The prototype set was sent to the Research Construction Company division of the Radiation Laboratory for construction of sets to be supplied to the Air Corps and Navy for refinement for operational use, as neither service had operational ASV radar of its own.

Dr. Vannevar Bush was the influential head of the newly formed National Defense Research Committee (NRDC), which coordinated technology development between civilian scientists and military officials and conducted preliminary technical research studies. (Author)

On 10 March the adapted British AI centimetric radar had successfully detected a flying aircraft.

Meanwhile, since the centimetric radar was in the slow developmental stage, U.S. Secretary of War Henry Stimson desperately wanted examples of the secret and reportedly successful long wave British MkII ASV radar and ordered the Chief Signal Corps Officer to purchase sets, with the Army and Navy to split the cost on a 60-40 basis at $6,000 per set. In late February 1941 the MkII radar was shipped under guard from Canada and reached the Army Signal Corps Aircraft Radio Laboratory (ARL) at Wright Field. However, these sets were not provided with the necessary antenna, as each had to be fabricated for the specific aircraft that was to carry the MkII. Also there were no spare parts supplied for maintenance, and these omissions delayed the American ASV radar program. By mid-April the Aircraft Radio Laboratory was ready to demonstrate its progress using a laboratory test version of the set that was installed in a B-18 at Wright Field. The B-18, with ARL technicians on board, flew to Lake Erie, successfully detecting ore freighters, and the tests seemed to be successful enough for the Signal Corps to procure 30 service test models from Western Electric. The AAC trumped the Signal Corps order with a production order for 500 sets on the Air Corps Test Board's supposition that further tests would be as successful. However, there was concern among the scientific community about the Test Board's conclusions about the tests, which had been conducted by skilled technicians, and particularly about the standardization of the British design to American production specifications. The British had great faith in their design and were using it operationally, and the American had nothing else and ordered a further 6,000 sets from Research Enterprises Ltd., a Canadian Company, and another contract was licensed to Philco Radio Company. The production standardization and quantity manufacture did prove to be arduous as predicted, as the Metric measurements, external antenna layout for U.S. aircraft, wiring, British built components that had to be modified for American use, and defective oscilloscopes all caused delays in the program. Research Enterprises had promised initial delivery by December 1941, but by February 1942 the 1st Bomber Command had outfitted only four B-18s with the "Americanized" MkIIs, which were designated as the SCR-521. With the U-Boats devastating merchant shipping off American coasts and the Navy unable to cope with the problem, the War Department was eager to have the Army Air Force and Signal Corps utilize the SCR-521 sets on a large scale operational basis as soon as possible. An investigation reported that the AAF did not have sufficient long range B-24s and B-17s available and would have to manage with the B-18 medium bomber for the new anti-submarine campaign. Compounding the problem was the continued lack of necessary radar antennas and personnel to install them. The manufacture of antennas was delayed by the shortage of steel tubing and insulators, while the ARL had only one crew capable of installing the antennas, which required a day per aircraft. The investigation concluded that by mid-April the AAF would have 150 sets available, but only 33 were installed.

Although the long wave SCR-521 could dependably locate a surfaced U-Boat at six miles with a trained operator, the operational results were disappointing, as many operational contacts were false, usually being floating debris or high waves, but nonetheless the set saw extensive American ASW service through default as nothing else was available. Later the Germans captured a MkII set from a downed RAF Wellington in Tunisia during the North African campaign, and soon the Germans developed the long range *Metox* (FuMB-1) radar detector. *Metox*, named after its French manufacturer, was quickly installed on U-Boats, and by September 1942 almost all U-Boats sailing from French ports into the Atlantic were equipped with it. The wooden, cross-shaped antenna, which had to be taken inside before diving, was the distinguishing feature of the unit and was called the "Biscay Cross" by U-Boat crews. The *Metox* receiver was able to detect radar wavelengths between 1.25 and 2.5 meters that were within the range of the 1.5 meter MkII radar beams of an approaching Allied patrol aircraft. It could detect these airborne radar signals at distances up to 30 miles, which was well within the six to 10 mile range of the SCR-521 and thus rendered this radar ineffective, as the U-Boat would identify an approaching attacker and dive long before it arrived.

By mid-1941, both the British at TRE and the Americans at MIT were developing 10 centimeter AI-10 radar, which was designated as the **SCR-520** Air Interception radar set and built by Western Electric. (AAF)

With the disappointing operational performance and then negating of long wave MkII ASV radar by *Metox*, the necessity for operational centimetric ASV radar became a priority. The strategic priority for centimeter radar sets before 1941 was for detection of aircraft by aircraft (AI radar), but after the Battle of Britain Hitler's U-Boats, not aircraft, became the priority, as hundreds of merchant vessels were being sunk almost without Allied air intervention. By mid-1941, both the British at TRE and the Americans at MIT were developing 10 centimeter AI radar, called AI-10. Studies of the two receivers and transmitter units found that the British AI receiver was better while the American AI transmitter was better, and it was decided to use the best in a new system which increased the range three fold. The new AI-10 sets were tested by ARL, and though very bulky at 600 pounds were found to be very successful, and were designated as the SCR-520. The Signal Corps ordered several hundred sets to be built by Western Electric, and the first pre-production set was available in December 1941 for air-to-air testing. However, in early 1942 the priority had shifted from the aircraft threat of 1941 to the very real U-Boats operating off the U.S. coast. By now Gen. Arnold had SCR-520 sets available for air interception, but he needed an ASV radar unit better than the 6,000 long wave SCR-521s he also had on order from Canada and Philco. Fortunately, both the ARL and Radiation Laboratory had made great strides in 10 centimeter radar research and were able to convert the air-to-air SCR-520 AI sets into anti-submarine ASV-10s that were designated as the SCR-517A ("A" denoting a conversion set). The SCR-517A units employed a compact dish antenna that could be mounted entirely inside the nose of a bomber and could be focused into a narrow beam that radiated from a rotating scanner able to cover the surface in a full 360° circle under the aircraft. The set presented much more distinct reflections and experienced less interference from sea clutter. Ten SCR-520 sets were quickly modified and installed in B-18s at Wright Field for further testing as the SCR-517A. On 27 March 1942 a SCR-517A equipped B-18 flew over Block Island Sound to test its set against the submarine *USS Mackerel*. During this successful demonstration radar echoes were being received as far away as 19 miles. By the beginning of April four SCR-517A B-18s were stationed at Westover, MA, and six at Langley Field, VA, for further field testing by the First Sea Search Attack Group (1SSAG). The new radar was to be tested operationally

SCR-517A Radar Gallery

Dome (exterior) on a Douglas B-18B (Author/Pima ASM)

Radar Receiver (above) with PPI Screen and Synchronizer (below) (Author/Pima ASM)

Dome (interior) with Radar Antenna and Junction box (Author/Pima ASM)

Radar and Antenna Tilt Controls (Author/Pima ASM)

Radar Transmitter Unit (Author/Pima ASM)

along with MAD equipment against U-Boats. In the first three months of operational field testing the Group's history reports that 11 contacts were made, resulting in six attacks where depth charges were dropped with three reported as "possibly successful." On 1 April 1942 a B-18 of the Attack Group detected a surfaced U-Boat 11 miles away by radar, tracked it, and made a "definitely successful" attack. This claim and the first three have been denied, as postwar *Kriegsmarine* records do not show a U-Boat sunk in those areas on those dates. Because of the increased U-Boat activity in the south Caribbean the Attack Group operated from Trinidad between 24 September and 16 October 1942 in an attempt to more extensively test the new radar operationally. The Group conducted patrols at a search rate of 50 square miles around the aircraft and 12 contacts were reported, but only four resulted in a depth charge attack. The final report concluded that no U-Boats were sunk, but the Germans were unable to detect the centimetric radar as they had been able to with the long wave SCR-521 sets.

Converting the SCR-520 sets to the SCR-517A configuration caused problems that arose from changing short range air interception (AI) radar to long range air to surface radar (ASV). It would not be until into the fall that these conversion problems would be solved so that scratch built SCR-517s (designated with no "A") could be scheduled for manufacture. The major conversion difficulties were in changing the speed of rotation of the spinner and the angle of rotation of the reflector, and work progressed very slowly while the U-Boats continued to ravage Allied merchant shipping. Western Electric was contracted to supply 10 sets in February 1942 and 20 for each of the next two months, but that schedule was not met, and was reset to 60 SCR-517 sets for the Navy in June and 40 in July; 28 SCR-520 sets for the AAF in June and 35 in August; and 60 SCR-520 sets for the British in July, 100 in August, and 40 in September. Obviously the Americans were beholding to the English for their development and sharing of the cavity magnetron. As the demands for ASV (SCR-517) and AI (SCR-520) radar shifted these allotments were changed several times during the summer of 1942, and production numbers and delivery dates suffered. To make the situation more difficult, the Navy decided that it needed 100 of the SCR-517 sets to install on its small subchaser vessels. To escape this subchaser allocation responsibly the Signal Corps said that the Air Force was to decide the allotment. Surprisingly, the AAF agreed to let the Navy have 100 SCR-520s to be converted to SCR-517As, provided that the AAF first receive its scheduled delivery of 100 SCR-517s and an additional 25-30 SCR-520 sets for AI service tests. Despite the reshuffling and agreements neither the Army, Navy, nor British were receiving very many SCR-517As nor -520s, because the spinner manufactured by General Electric was in short supply and Philco had to be awarded a contract to manufacture additional spinners. At the end of June the AAF only had 11 aircraft equipped with the SCR-517A, but these did not have spinners, and so far the Signal Corps 1942 target of 1,142 sets to be manufactured had reached only 203! In the meantime, improvements on the SCR-517A were being made, with the B (heavier due to the addition of beacon and IFF features) and the C (lightweight) versions being introduced, causing further delays. The lack of certain raw materials, such as mica, and components such as switches, condensers, and potentiometers slowed production. Since Arnold and the AAF had ordered thousands (but fortunately only hundreds were manufactured) of the inferior long wave SCR-521 sets they were stuck with them, and by the end of summer 1942 over 90 B-18s were equipped with either the SCR-521 or the SCR-517A, and many with a Leigh searchlight. The Navy was able to equip ASV in one PBY each of VP-71, VP-72, and VP-73, and two PBMs of VP-74. By October Patrol Wing 7 had a large number of aircraft equipped with AVS radar and began demonstrations off Quonset Point, RI, for the NDRC, when a Catalina detected submarine S-48 during tests.

Western Electric had to labor to convert the 102 available AI-10 (SCR-520) into the ASV-10 (SCR-517A), and it would not be until late summer that the conversions were completed and SCR-517As could be built from scratch as SCR-517 (no A). In September, Arnold felt he could safely justify replacing the inferior SCR-521s with the SCR-517A version; fortunately, he was soon vindicated when the SCR-521 sets were compromised by German *Metox* detection. The SCR-520s would continue in production as AI equipment with the possibility of conversion to -517As. By the end of September 1942 the Army and Navy had each received 100 SCR-517A sets, but 48 of the new SCR-517C sets had gone to the Army. Sixty-two of the Army's SCR-517A sets were installed in B-18Bs, while the remainder went as spares and for parts, or to maintenance and operational training schools. The failure of the delivery schedules caused problems, as aircraft remained out of ASW operations while parked in depots awaiting ASV sets for installation. The AAF was under the gun of Secretary of War Stimson and his advisor, Dr. Henry Bowles, who were impatient for the AAF bombers to get on with the war against the U-Boats. Ten SCR-517A equipped B-18s of the 1SSAG under Col. William Dolan had been operating out of Langley Field, VA, and Jacksonville, FL, and Gen. Arnold reported to Stimson that he was "enthusiastic over the possibilities of this equipment." The success of Dolan's ASV B-18s led to the establishment of the Sea Search Attack Development Unit (SADU), which was to be the operational testing unit for new types of ASW weapons (the SADU and 1SSAG will be discussed in depth later).

So by the fall of 1942 Secretary Stimson's avocation of ASV radar for patrol aircraft was finally coming to fruition and had proved to be the most effective means of combating the U-Boat menace. But the days of the stopgap ASV equipped B-18A were numbered. In September 1942, the first two B-24s with their longer range, especially with auxiliary fuel tanks, were equipped with the SCR-517, and in December the 1SSAG had its first squadron of SCR-517 B-24s to complement its aging B-18s.

The SCR-517A radar apparatus included a rotating three foot diameter concave dish-type antenna mounted behind a bulbous egg-shaped dome that replaced the shark nosed Plexiglas windows covering the bombardier's compartment in the B-18A. The spinner was the rapidly rotating and highly accurate antenna mechanism that allowed a narrow radar microwave beam to scan a wide area. The antenna was connected to the antenna junction box (AB-874) by two braided connections. The junction box was connected by three braided connections to the radar control unit (MD-7/ARC-5), which was located just adjacent to the dome enclosure on the port side just below the window. The two knob control box was situated on top of a 28 volt DC unit. The left knob controlled ON> STB> NORM> CNR> MAP> TEST, while the right knob controlled antenna tilt to +10° UP and -15° DOWN. The BC-1040 radar transmitter resembled two black stove pipes and was located in the nose compartment on the starboard fuselage wall. The Signal Corps BC-1101-A Receiver (indicator) was placed on top of the Western Electric BC-1043-B Synchronizer in the radio operator's position in the cabin.

Training determined that the chief operational deficiency of the early SCR-520 and SCR-517A sets was that they used the early Range Azimuth screen (A-scope) of the MkII sets, rather than the Plan Position Indicator (PPI) screen. The PPI scope was divided into compass headings, with a "lubber line" extending from the center of the circle (the true heading of the aircraft) toward the target with a rotating time base that gave a blip out from the center. The PPI screen presented the terrain below much like that on a TV screen, and so was much easier to use. The PPI could be adjusted in range to enlarge the image of the area below on the scope and to bring out the light and shadows on the scope that could represent a U-Boat. As the bomber closed on the target the blurred images on the scope slowly moved nearer the center of the scope, which constantly represented the position of the bomber. Unlike the A-scope, the PPI scope could plot the position of the target it was homing and track it until the bomber was directly over the target. Using the PPI, the radar operator could direct the pilot on an attack track so that he could drop the depth charges at intervals that would have a greater chance of doing damage. In night patrols the radar operator would not know the nature of the target—native fishing boat, merchantman, or U-Boat—until the Leigh searchlight was switched on at a mile or less. The pilot had to make a quick target ID to decide if he should drop the depth charges immediately, or if he was too late or uncertain of the ID he had to switch off the searchlight and turn at once to circle quickly to make an attack, but there was the good chance of the U-Boat escaping in a crash dive.

Early tests determined that under ideal conditions ASV radar could detect individual U-Boat-sized targets at 25 miles and a group of ships at even greater distances. The range of ASV radar was then acknowledged to be 25 miles in every direction and capable of sweeping an area of 50 square miles around the aircraft. The 1SSAG used these range assumptions as the basis to train combat crews in the tactical use of the new equipment for the ASW patrol concept in the Caribbean. However, operational conditions were not always ideal, and results mostly depended on the skill of the operator.

In operational training missions flown by the 2nd Anti-submarine Squadron, the first ASW unit in the UK, the new ASV radar proved to be difficult to use, and an initial report found a 55% failure rate due to poor maintenance. 2nd Squadron CO Lt.Col. Jack Roberts did not believe the high maintenance failure rate and defended his maintenance personnel by ordering another study. But this new study found the sets operated satisfactorily only 63% of the time, with 42% due electrical equipment failures (mainly defective vacuum tubes, 65%), 33% due to "undetermined" causes, and only 5% due to maintenance deficiencies. However, it appears that the majority of the 33% "undetermined" category actually fell into the maintenance deficiency category.

In August 1942 the U-Boat war had reached a perilous phase, and the Air Force began an ASAP program to convert 122 B-18A to the B model with the ASV radar conversion configuration. The B-18As were ferried to San Antonio for the conversion, which removed the glass in the upper bombardier's position and replaced it with a bulbous ASV radome and the installation of a rudimentary Metallic Anomaly Detector (MAD) boom located aft of the tail. Radar equipped B-18Bs did not appear until October 1942, when the four old B-18s of the 35BS that were nearly worn out from flying exhaustive patrols off the east coast were replaced by four radar-equipped B-18Bs that were immediately sent to the Caribbean. Here the squadron was to suffer many teething problems with the newly installed radar. By October 1942 three ASV B-18Bs were being delivered per week to the Caribbean. By December 1942, there were 45 B-18Bs and nine old B-18s in the Antilles, and only three B-18s and two B-18As in the CZ. Some 43 B-18Bs served with the 6AF and Antilles Air Command, and probably even more with the assorted ASRONs of the Anti-submarine Command.

ASV radar was obviously the foremost and continual obsession of the ASW combatants, as it was the essential factor for the success of the campaign. Training of operators and technicians was a major problem, as was the shipment of parts, particularly because the equipment was constantly being improved and changed. By early 1943 well tuned radar equipment controlled by experienced and skilled operators could identify landmarks at 100 miles and even buoys at 35 to 40 miles. A surfaced U-Boat could be distinguished at more than 50 miles, and the conning tower of a U-Boat running with its decks awash at 15 to 30 miles. But ASV radar continued to have its limitations, as the equipment was not reliable and required constant and expert maintenance.

Magnetic Anomaly Detector (MAD), Retro-bombs, and the Sonobuoy

While Airborne Surface Vessel Detection (ASV) radar promised to detect surfaced U-Boats, a technique needed to be devised to find submerged U-Boats, and the solution seemed to point toward a Magnetic Airborne Detector (MAD, later the Magnetic Airborne Detector). When a ship's steel hull is constructed it undergoes heating by welding and impact through riveting. Ferrous metal is comprised of clusters of iron molecules called "domains," each of which is a minute magnet with its own north-south magnetic field. Normally these domains are arranged randomly, but with heating and hammering they tend to align themselves so that their south poles point north and their north poles point south, so that the accumulative effect is that the ship's hull acquires a permanent magnetic field that is quite substantial in comparison to the earth's magnetic field. Also, the steel in a ship's hull causes the earth's lines of force, called "flux," to move out of their normal positions and be concentrated at the ship, which is called the "induced field." The ship's total magnetic field, or "magnetic signature," at any point on the earth's oceans is the sum of its permanent and induced magnetic fields. The earth's natural magnetic field does not always run in straight north-south lines, but weave in places to the east and west and dips at different angles to the horizontal. These directional changes and dips in the area of a large mass of ferrous matter are measurable by a sensitive magnetometer. An airborne magnetometer was to detect a metal submarine in the earth's magnetic field. The depth at which a submarine can be detected is a function both of the size of the submarine and how close to the water's surface the magnetometer is flown. Since magnetic fields, unlike radio waves, were unaffected by passage through earth or water, prewar investigation on a Magnetic Airborne Detector was based on magnetometers used by mining companies to detect distortions in the earth's magnetic field that

The **Douglas B-18A** (shown flying over Miami in January 1941) and B-18B (the primary anti-submarine version) were America's most numerous bomber at the time of Pearl Harbor. The Bolo would play a primary ASW role in the Army Air Corps in the Caribbean and off the American East Coast, freeing other more modern bombers for bombing duties. (AAF)

The Consolidated **PBY Catalina** and **Blimps** were the U.S. Navy's U-Boat hunters. (USN)

Magnetic Airborne Detector (MAD) extending from the end of the tail of a B-18 because the metals used in constructing the aircraft would interfere with the device. (AAF)

would indicate large underground mineral deposits. However, contemporary devices could not locate small objects such as submarines.

Late in 1940 Dr. Victor Vacquier of the Gulf and Research Development Company introduced the "saturable-core" magnetometer for mineral prospecting that was two to three times more sensitive as previous types. Early in 1941 the National Defense Research Committee (NDRC) recognized the potential of Vacquier's device and began its development for anti-submarine warfare. The detection of a submarine presented the NDRC with a very challenging dilemma, as Vacquier's device had to measure the distortion of a comparatively minute ferrous object like a submarine in comparison with the earth's powerful magnetic field. The strength of the earth's magnetic field varies with the distance from the poles (e.g. latitude) but averages about 50,000 gammas, while the magnetic field of the World War II U-Boat was only 10 gammas at 400 feet. This strength decreased with the cube of the distance so that at twice the distance (800 feet) the sub's magnetic field was only 1.25 gammas. In addition, there were other problems to contend with involving the aircraft and equipment. If the magnetic detector in the search aircraft were not kept in alignment with the earth's magnetic field to within only 0.1° its sensitivity would drop off noticeably. Because the metals used in constructing the aircraft would interfere with the device, it had to be positioned in the furthest end of the tail or wing tip and ferrous components had to be replaced with non-ferrous ones. Even so, the range of the NDRC device was so short that the search aircraft had to fly at 100 feet and directly over a submarine submerged at 300 feet to locate it. This drawback meant that the device could not be used at night or in poor visibility for fear of colliding with the ocean's surface.

The next investigation of a MAD device was started in early 1942 by Westinghouse and the Airborne Instruments Laboratory. Trials began in the spring using Navy patrol aircraft and airships, and when German U-Boats appeared off the U.S. East Coast the MAD apparatus was used operationally for the first time, but only for a short time, as the Germans shifted their U-Boats to southern waters. Trials showed the range of the MAD to be very short, and the operator received signals of a contact only when he was directly over the submarine. If depth charges were released at that time the forward speed of the search aircraft would cause the depth charges to fall forward of the submarine's location.

Thus, it was obvious that a special bomb that would fall vertically even though the aircraft was moving forward needed to be developed.

Retro-rockets/Retro-bombs

In early 1941 Prof. Philip Blackett chaired a committee which was to study means for the Fleet Air Arm to cope with the German U-Boat menace that was endangering her merchant shipping lifeline. The committee proposed a rocket-propelled spear with a cast iron fluted head that could tear a large hole in the pressure hull of a surfaced U-Boat, preventing it from diving. The idea received little enthusiasm because of its relative unscientific simplicity. The anti-shipping testing of the three inch rocket with the 25 pound solid steel warhead led to the subsequent fortuitous accidental discovery of its good underwater trajectory with shallow-diving aircraft. Admiral Sir Max Horton, who was directing the Battle of the Atlantic, pressed for the development of this rocket weapon to operational status. In a short several months a sight was developed, the aircraft fitted with launching apparatus, and the air crews trained.

By mid-1942 Dr. Carl Anderson, the California Institute of Technology head of Aircraft Projects, developed a 65 pound "retrobomb" which was filled with 37 pounds of Torpex, impact fused, and with a solid fuel rocket installed in its tail. Rocket propulsion had two characteristics that made it an ideal solution. Firing backwards it would cancel out the forward motion of the aircraft, and having no recoil relatively large missiles could be carried without damaging the aircraft structure.

The U.S. began its anti-submarine rocket development in conjunction with MAD, developed by Division C of the NDRC, which gave a signal when the carrying aircraft flew over a mass of metal, such as a submarine. Since MAD signaled when the aircraft was directly over the target it was too late to drop a depth charge or bomb. In February 1942 California Institute of Technology (CIT) scientists suggested firing a rocket from the aircraft towards the rear at the same speed as the aircraft's forward speed. Therefore,

Rearward-firing 65 pound "**Retrobomb**" mounted under the wing of a PBY. The Retrobombs, which were actually rockets, were filled with 37 pounds of Torpex, impact fused, and had a solid fuel rocket installed in their tails. (AAF)

Retrobomb being fired rearwards from a B-18. Rocket propulsion had two ideal characteristics. Firing backwards, it would cancel out the forward motion of the aircraft and, having no recoil, relatively large missiles could be carried without damaging the aircraft structure. (AAF)

this retro-rocket should be propelled straight downwards. Speedy development of a suitable rocket was possible due to the previous work done on the "Hedgehog" and "Mousetrap" anti-submarine shipboard-launched rocket program. Testing posed a problem for CIT, as difficulties arose in obtaining a suitable aircraft from the Navy because of the state of alert on the U.S. West Coast caused by the Pearl Harbor attack a few months earlier. Finally an obsolete B-18 in dubious mechanical condition was transferred for testing. Lt.Cdr. James Hean was assigned to the project and did yeoman duty, not only by piloting for the tests, but also in working with CIT scientists in making the rocket adaptable to the carrying aircraft.

The Squadron (Hedron 14) Experimental Unit was unofficially organized in San Diego and equipped with a TBF aircraft, a pilot, Lt.Cdr. Thomas Pollack, and a mechanic, William Camp; but soon four more staff and a PBY Catalina were added. Hedron 14 received its name from **He**adquarters Squa**dron** 14, which was its parent organization and supported Fleet Air Wing 14, located at the Naval Air Station, San Diego. Pollack had just returned from a combat tour in the Pacific and had participated in a test flight of the MAD Retro-rocket in a PBY before coming to the unit. During April and May 1943 Hedron 14 was assigned to test MAD equipment, sonobuoys, and retro-rockets and floating retro smoke lights in their PBY and TBF aircraft.

The Magnetic Anomaly Detector was an instrument that could sense changes in the earth's magnetic field caused by the presence of a large metallic object, such as a submerged submarine. The sonobuoy could be dropped in the water by an aircraft and would report submarine propeller noises and underwater explosions by radio. The retro-rockets were rocket-powered missiles that could be fired in the direction opposite to the aircraft's travel, canceling out the aircraft's speed to strike the water at the point where the MAD signal was the strongest: directly over the submarine. The floating retro smoke lights were dropped during several runs and would mark the underwater course of the U-Boat.

On 26 June 1942 six retro-rockets were test-fired from a grounded PBY Catalina patrol bomber at North Island, near San Diego. These ground tests were mostly trial and error, and damage to the wings indicated a need for blast deflectors. By 3 July 1942 the first rockets fired from an American aircraft were ready for testing, and a PBY was assigned for the test at the San Diego Naval Air Station. The first firing run was successfully made with the target being hit.

The retrobomb went into service in mid-1943. When a MAD operator made a contact he fired the retro-bombs, and the rockets propelled the bombs backwards off their launching rails, bringing them to a mid-air stop. After their solid rocket fuel was expended the bombs would drop vertically into the water over the submarine. A B-18 could carry 16 under wing retro-bombs, eight under each wing on special launching rails, while a PBY could carry 24, 12 on each wing. They were launched in salvoes of eight, four from each wing, with a second salvo of eight, again four from each wing, being launched automatically a half second later (followed by another eight in another half second on the PBY installation). The retrobomb launchers were divided into groups of three, with each group being set at a slightly different angle so that the bombs from each salvo hit the water in a line about 100 feet long and at right angles to the aircraft's line of flight. The half second intervals between salvoes gave 90 foot spacing between these lines. Before the attack was initiated the crew tracked the submerged submarine with smoke markers so that they could attack it lengthwise, hopefully resulting in at least two of the bombs exploding over the target. Of the 122 B-18Bs, 79 had MkIV magnetic anomaly detection equipment installed in a tail boom.

The further development of the program was accelerated, and in the spring of 1943 two squadrons were trained and outfitted with the retro-rocket. One squadron was sent to Tulagi, which lies near Guadalcanal, but by that time there were few Japanese submarines in the area. So the 50,000 retro-rockets that had been manufactured by CIT saw little employment after the spring of 1944, being supplanted by the conventional forward firing rocket.

Sonobuoy

The British Admiralty established a special committee for anti-submarine measures headed by the brilliant Dr. Patrick Blackett, who won the Noble Prize in physics in 1948. In May 1941 the committee proposed an expendable sonar buoy that could be dropped from ships to listen for trailing submarines. Tests showed the idea to be practicable, but due to limited funding the British abandoned the idea. Fortunately, RCA had supplied the sonar buoy prototypes and continued the tests with the Navy, which found when using MAD equipment the operator had problems distinguishing if the object detected was indeed a submerged submarine or another metallic object, such as a wreck. To remedy the problem Colombia University's Undersea Laboratory at New London, CT, developed a passive hydrophone buoy with a radio transmitter based on the RCA design designated as the AN/CRT-1 sonobuoy. The 14 pound cylindrical, 3.75 foot long, and four inch in diameter device consisted of a small floating transmitter under which a hydrophone was suspended on a cable. The parachute at the top of the buoy slowed its fall, and on impact with the water the hydrophone's 24 foot long connecting cable was released and the buoy's batteries were turned on. The cable had to be long enough so that the sounds of the waves splashing the canister would not interfere with any faint U-Boat propeller sounds. Underwater sounds were transmitted to the floating transmitter and then to an operator in the aircraft patrolling overhead, who listened to the sonobuoy's HF transmissions on a special receiver. The operator had the challenging job of trying to decipher U-Boat sounds from those produced by the sea and its inhabitants.

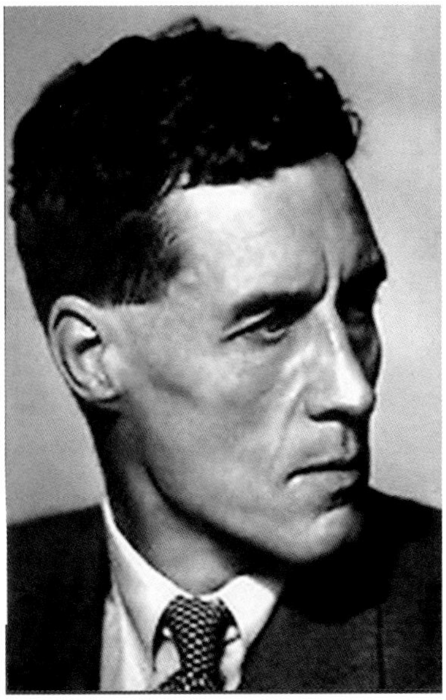

The brilliant **Dr. Patrick Blackett**, who won the Noble Prize in physics in 1948, was the head of the British Admiralty special committee for anti-submarine measures that developed the sonobuoy. (Author)

The range of the hydrophone depended significantly on conditions, but the U-Boat's propeller had to be turning to produce cavitation, which is the sound of bubbles produced by a turning of propellers and varied with depth (i.e. more depth meant lesser cavitation). Detection could be as high as 3.5 miles if the U-Boat were moving at seven knots submerged at 60 feet in calm water or as little as 300 feet if the U-Boat were moving at three knots at a depth of 250 feet in a rough sea. The early sonobuoys were non-directional, and the operator was unable to determine the direction of the noise's origin. To obtain an approximate location of possible U-Boat noises it was necessary to lay a pattern of five sonobuoys. The life of the batteries was about four hours, and to prevent the enemy from recovering a buoy a stopper was slowly dissolved by seawater, and the buoy would sink once the batteries ran out.

Although sonobuoys had been developed in 1941 the concept was not embraced; meanwhile, MAD-equipped Navy blimps were expending time and weapons after detecting sunken ships and old wrecks. The blimps needed a sensor to validate and corroborate their MAD contacts and the passive sonobuoy concept was resurrected. In February 1942 the Navy's Coordinator for Research and Development requested the National Defense Research Committee to develop an expendable radio sonobuoy that could be used by lighter-than-air (LTA) aircraft. In March

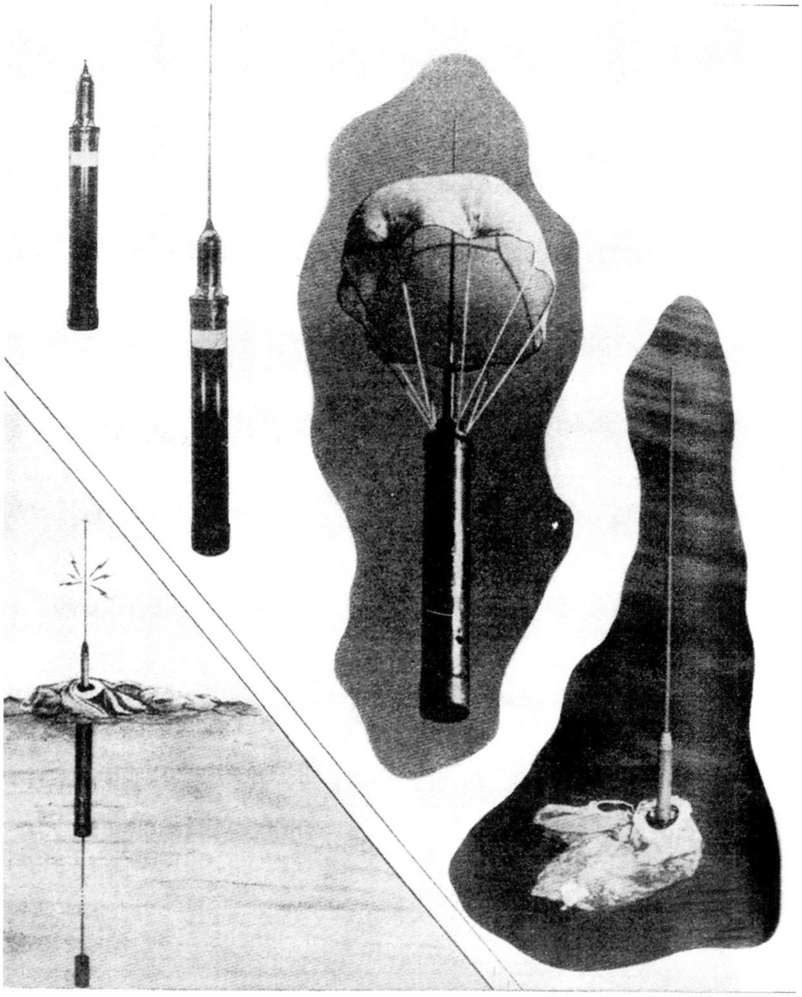

Above: **Expendable Radio Sonobuoy:** The drawing at top left shows the buoy with its antenna withdrawn, while the drawing second left shows the antenna extended. The third drawing shows the sonobuoy floating to the water suspended by a parachute. The bottom right shows the sonobuoy floating in the water with its antenna aloft. The lower left drawing shows the bottom compartment, containing the hydrophone, separated and submerged by a cable to a depth of 24 feet. (USN)

Near Left: **Sonobuoys** and depth charges (to rear) loaded into the bomb bay of a TBF off the escort carrier *Bogue*. (USN)

1942 the practicality of sonobuoys was demonstrated off New London, CT, as a blimp detected the propeller sounds of the submarine S-20 at maximum distances of three miles. Radio reception of the signals, however, was limited to five miles. In October 1942 the Bureau of Ships began sonobuoy procurement by purchasing 1,000 sonobuoys and 100 ASW receivers.

In June 1942 *Project Sail* was initiated at Quonset Point for MAD system research and testing by the Naval Ordnance Laboratory and the NDRC. In July, the first so-called "fast drops" of sonobuoys were made by parachuting a sonobuoy from a B-18 cruising at 120 mph, and after success of the tests 200 units were ordered; the AN/CRT-1 went into production in the fall of 1942. The first operational use of a sonobuoy was in August 1942, and the first U-Boat (U-568) sunk in conjunction with a sonobuoy occurred on 30 October 1942 by a Canadian145 Squadron RCAF Hudson.

In 1942 U.S. Navy Blimp Squadron ZP-12, Lakehurst, NJ, equipped Blimp K-3 with a MAD set that was operated by civilian scientists on actual ASW missions in an effort to perfect the system. During 1942 ZP-12 flew 865 flights, but only K-3 was equipped with MAD radar, and it often malfunctioned or detected the many ship wrecks lying off the U.S. Atlantic coast. On 14 January 1943 the first positive MAD U-Boat contact by an airship was made by K-3, which marked the contact spot with a flare. The U-Boat was depth charged by a destroyer without observable results. Four days later K-3 made another MAD contact on a surfacing U-Boat off the New Jersey coast. K-3 dropped a bomb that malfunctioned, as did the marker flares. On the following attack one of its two bombs dropped was a dud and the U-Boat escaped. On 22 January K-12 dispatched three airships and another MAD contact was made by K-3, which dropped three bombs, bringing up large air bubbles. K-4 then made its bombing attack, which brought up debris and oil and was followed by USN destroyers that made three depth charge attacks. Despite the evidence no official credit for the destruction of a U-Boat was given. USN MAD-equipped blimps were not credited with any U-Boat victories during the war, but airships of ZP-42 played an important role in the detection and sinking of U-883 on 5 May 1945. K-16 was patrolling in the fog off the eastern U.S. coast and made a MAD contact and marked the area with dye markers and flares, enabling destroyers *Ericsson* and *Atherton* to make depth charge attacks. After contact was lost K-16, joined by K-58, used sonobuoys to make new contact. K-16 made a rocket attack, and some debris surfaced as the destroyers made a series of heavy surface attacks that brought up a large amount of conclusive debris. Official credit for U-883's destruction was given to the *Atherton* and Coast Guard frigate *Moberly*.

During the war the MAD/Retrobomb/Sonobuoy combination had limited operational usefulness, as the U-Boats changed their tactics and remained on the surface using an increased AA armament capability to fight it out, making it too dangerous for the attacking aircraft to fly directly over the bristling U-Boat to drop their retro-bombs.

VP-63: Combat Use of the MAD/Retro-bombs

Patrol Squadron 63 (VP-63) was commissioned on 19 September 1942 at Alameda, CA, Naval Air Station, and happened to be near Goldstone Lake, where scientists from the California

Blimp ASV Gallery

The **K-type Blimp** was the major USN blimp used in ASW operations during the war with the **M-type Blimp** introduced later in the war. (USN)

K-29 being released for operations. Its ASV radar dome can be seen suspended from the cabin just behind the nose wheel. (USN)

ASV Scopes located in the blimp cabin. (USN)

Five Sonobuoys next to two dropping tubes on left (USN)

Institute of Technology were testing the retro-bombs, and the C-in-C of the U.S. Fleet ordered the new equipment installed in VP-63's PBY-5As for testing. The Squadron's CO, Lt.Cdr. Edwin Wagner, helped set up a training program and supervised the installation of the MAD equipment and retro-rockets in three of the amphibian -5A Catalinas equipped with landing gear. However, these PBY-5As were found to be too heavy with the added MAD/rocket equipment and the landing gear. Between January and March 1943 VP-63 received 15 new and lighter, all amphibian -5s equipped for MAD operations. Later it was found these lighter -5s suffered damage from large ocean swells and five more -5As were equipped with MAD sets and tail cones. The installation of the new MAD retro-rocket equipment required some revamping of the aircraft. A long probe extended from the tail of each PBY and specialized rails were fabricated and installed under the wings to mount 12-15 retro-bombs on each wing. The retro bombs weighed 65 pounds each, including warheads filled with 37 pounds of Torpex. The bombs could be fired automatically or manually by the pilot or MAD operator, all at once or in salvoes of eight. The bombs were impact fused so that a U-Boat would not become aware of an attack if they missed. On each pass retro smoke lights were dropped through the tunnel hatch to mark the position of a submerged U-Boat. After several passes the course of the U-Boat could be determined.

After the equipment was tested all 12 VP-63 PBYs were equipped with MAD gear. Since MAD was the acronym Magnetic Anomaly Detection and the PBY Catalina was called the "Cat," VP-63 became known as the "MAD CAT" squadron. On 13 March 1943, after rigorous training off the San Francisco coast VP-63 flew across country to Elizabeth City, NC, where three more MAD-equipped Catalinas joined the squadron. Detachments of the unit operated from Elizabeth City; Quonset Point Naval Air Station, RI; Jacksonville and Key West, Florida; and Bermuda. While operating off the east coast the deficiencies of the MAD equipment became apparent. Although it was very accurate, it had an extremely short range of only 400 feet, and the two U-Boats that were reported, one off Key West and the other off Bermuda, escaped the MAD-equipped PBYs, probably due to the MAD's short range. During an April 1943 test off Key West, four PBYs flew abreast about 1,300 feet apart at 100 feet off the water, turning in formation at the end of each sweep to start the next. The MAD gear seemed to work,

VP-63 "**MAD CAT**" (MAD-equipped CATalina) with tail-mounted MAD antenna. (USN)

VP-63 PB5Y with 12 retrobombs mounted under each wing. (USN)

as five charted shipwrecks were found, but the spacing between aircraft left an area of 500 feet uncovered between each aircraft.

Soon Doenitz' *Kriegsmarine* U-Boats shifted their emphasis from the U.S. east coast and sightings decreased, and VP-63 was deployed to Iceland on 7 June, where they detected no U-Boats on their patrols. In July they were transferred to the 19th Group of the Royal Air Force Coastal Command to support a maximum offensive in the Bay of Biscay against U-Boats traveling into the Atlantic to and from their bases on the northern French coast. The 15 PBYs of VP-63 arrived on 25 July at Pembroke Dock, South Wales, UK, to begin five months of operations. Three days after their arrival the unit's first U-Boat sighting was made when Lt.(jg.) Sam Parker sighted two U-Boats on the surface. He closed on the enemy, and when he encountered heavy anti-aircraft fire Parker, following tactical protocol, did not attack, but called for more aircraft. While waiting for help to arrive the PBY's gunners scored a few hits on the conning tower and crew of one U-Boat. The U-Boats dove when two RAF Sunderland flying boats arrived. Parker quickly dropped two depth charges and then unsuccessfully tried to track them with the MAD unit.

VP-63 made no more U-Boats on its tour, and in late December 1943 the *MAD CATS* were ordered to Port Lyautey to fly routine anti-submarine patrols and convoy escort duty near the Strait of Gibraltar. There were fewer U-Boats, and they were wary of being sighted. The boats ran submerged into the Mediterranean, slipping through the Strait of Gibraltar just before dawn and benefiting from the east-west current; their screws turning so slowly that destroyer hydrophones could not detect their sound. New VP-63 CO Lt.Cdr. Curtis Hutchings thought the narrow Strait could be sealed off by his Catalinas, even with their short range MAD equipment. Hutchings developed a plan in which two PBYs would create a magnetic wall across the Strait by flying a race track course, with straightaways four miles long and three-fourths of a mile apart over the deepest part of the strait, from Point Gamarinal on the Spanish coast to Point Malaba in Spanish Morocco. The flying boats would patrol at 50 to 100 foot altitudes, constantly maintaining position directly opposite each other. Using this method a patrol plane would be passing any given point on the circuit at one to two minute intervals, which a U-Boat could not pass through without being detected. The patrols changed shifts at noon in order to avoid the morning fog at Port Lyautey. The afternoon shift would fly until dusk, landing to stay the night at Gibraltar. The morning patrol would takeoff before dawn to set up the barrier and fly until noon. The barrier patrols began on 8 February 1944, along with their regular patrols and escort duties. Remaining on the oval course during barrier patrol was demanding, and often, when approaching the Moroccan coast, the PBYs were fired on by anxious AA gunners, with one suffering minor damage.

On 24 February two *MAD CATs* flown by Lts.(jg). Howard Baker and T.R. Wolley became the first aircraft using MAD equipment to locate and sink a fully submerged enemy submarine. The enemy was contacted around 1500, and Baker and Wolley flew a cloverleaf circuit and marked the U-Boat's course with retro float lights. Two British destroyers, *HMS Anthony* and *HMS Wishart*, came on the scene and scattered the lights. The destroyers radioed the PBYs that they had found a school of fish and left. The *MAD CATs* had lost contact with the U-Boat, but at 1557 they found it again and fired their retro-rockets two minutes later. Some of the rockets hit their target and, alerted by the explosions, the two Royal Navy warships returned and fired depth charges. The U-Boat immediately surfaced and the crew abandoned ship. The destroyers picked up about fifty crewmen and the captain, who confirmed that the first explosions had severely damaged his U-Boat (U-761), and that he was preparing to surface when the destroyers arrived.

This action demonstrated that there was a need for cooperation between surface craft and aircraft. A tactical procedure was established in which the senior patrol aircraft commander would be in tactical command of all ships and aircraft when a MAD contact was made. All warships would remain away until the *MAD CATs* had attacked, after which they were allowed to move in slowly and attack. The attacking vessels were to warn the PBYs when they were about to throw depth charges and hedgehogs into the air, so as not to shoot down one of these low-flying planes with an underwater weapon!

On 15 March periscope sightings and radar contacts were reported by patrols on the Atlantic Ocean side of the Strait, and the barrier patrol was alerted that U-Boats were attempting to slip through. A third PBY was sent out to fly an individual barrier patrol east of the normal patrol. At 0845 Lt. R.C. Spears and Lt.(jg). V.A. Lingle made contact with a U-Boat, tracked it and verified its course, then directed *HMS Vannock* to the attack. The *Vannock* hurled 24 hedgehog depth bombs and moments later oil, bubbles, and debris rose to the surface, confirming the destruction of the U-Boat (later identified as U-392). For this action the two Navy pilots and Lt.(jg). M.J. Vopatek, the pilot of the third PBY, were awarded the Distinguished Flying Cross while the crew received the Air Medal.

Since the barrier/MAD technique worked best in daylight it was necessary to force the U-Boats to cross the barrier at that time. VP-63 CO Cdr. Hutchings asked to have a British searchlight squadron illuminate the strait at night so that any U-Boat entering the Mediterranean in darkness would have to travel submerged. The U-Boats would have to charge their batteries further west for a submerged run and they would not be able to reach the barrier before sunrise.

On 15 May Lt.(jg.) Vopatek and copilot Lt. A.L. Worrell were flying the afternoon barrier patrol when propeller noises were picked up by the sonobuoy. At 1530 the *MAD CATs* closed and fired 30 retro-bombs. Debris was observed on the ocean surface, but the sonobuoy showed that the U-Boat continued under way. The PBYs continued to track the wounded U-Boat, dropping retro float lights. The PBY guided the *HMS Kilmarnock* to the area, where it fired its hedgehogs ahead of the line of float lights. The crew of the PBYs observed the shock waves from two underwater explosions, which were followed by the release of two large air bubbles bursting on the surface. No further contact was made with the U-Boat (which was later identified as U-731, and was the last U-Boat to attempt to enter the Mediterranean, as losses had been exorbitant).

In June MAD-equipped blimps of ZP-14 joined VP-63 to patrol at night, making the barrier patrol a round-the-clock operation. Toulon and Marseilles continued to be bases for the remaining U-Boats in the Mediterranean, but enemy activity stopped after the Allied invasion of Southern France.

A detachment of VP-63 was sent to the UK during the final months of the war. On 30 April 1945 Lt. F.G. Lake sighted a submerged U-Boat using a snorkel in the Bay of Biscay, west of Brest. Lake put the PBY into a dive from 2,000 feet, following the snorkel's wake, and when the MAD magnetometer needle pegged he fired all of his retro-bombs. The crew spotted debris on the surface, plus an oil slick a mile and a half long that confirmed the victory (over U-1107). Lake was awarded the Distinguished Flying Cross for this action.

The **Oboe** apparatus in the aircraft consisted of a receiver-transmitter automatically triggered by the pulses from the ground stations that controlled each Oboe aircraft. (AFHRC)

Oboe Radar Operation

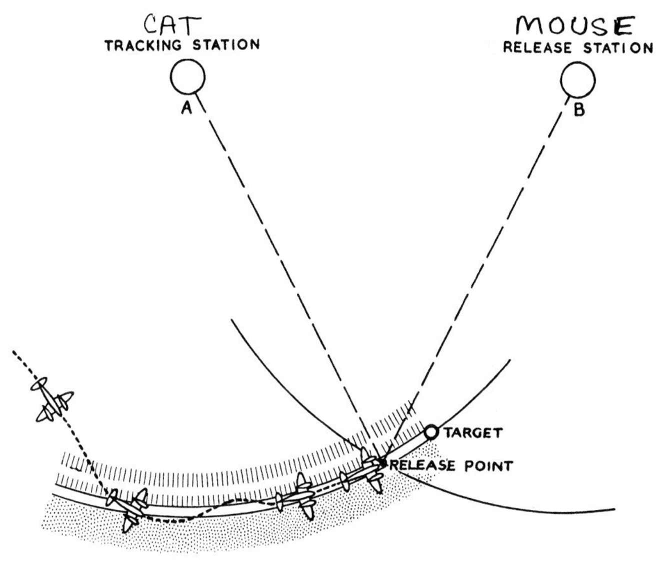

Bombing/Target Identifying Radar

Once ASV anti-submarine radar was developed the use of radar was explored for use in bombing in poor visibility. Experience showed that a target was often covered by clouds and smoke, and the line of sight view through the Norden Bombsight would be obscured. On 4 November 1939 Maj.Gen. Arnold ordered the Materiel Division to explore methods of bombing through overcast. Among the suggestions were to use optical filters in the Norden telescope or to employ a pilot aircraft to fly below the overcast to control the bomber flying above or in the overcast. Another suggestion was the use of radio waves, which offered two possible solutions. The first was to use radio ranging using ground control stations using beacons (beams) and no bombsights, while the second solution was to use self-contained systems from which radio transmissions were sent from the bomber.

Oboe Navigational Bombing Radar

Oboe was the creation of Alec Reeves, of Standard Telephones and Cables Ltd, who, along with Frank Jones of TRE (Telecommunications Research Establishment) at Great Malvern developed the PCM (Pulse Code Modulation) basic principle of Oboe. Oboe was the reverse of Gee, in that two Type 9000 ground stations established an aircraft's position by measuring distance by re-radiation of signals directed at an aircraft.

The Oboe apparatus in the aircraft consisted of a receiver-transmitter automatically triggered by the pulses from the ground stations that controlled each Oboe aircraft. Two ground stations (code named *Cat* and *Mouse*) were used that emitted trains of pulses on the same carrier frequency but with different recurrent frequencies. The bomber carried a responder that replied to the interrogations of both ground stations so that each recognized the range to the bomber. For use in bombing one of the ground stations (*Cat*) was known as the tracking station and the other (*Mouse*) as the releasing station. The range of a European target, measured from two widely spaced ground stations in the UK, was derived from pre-war ordnance survey maps and aerial photographs.

The bomber flew on a course of constant radius from the tracking station that would bring the bomber over the target. The train of pulses sent from the *Cat* tracking station was changed to audible Morse dot and dash signals to convey information to the aircraft on its track to the target; a steady note when the aircraft was on the correct course, as dots when it was to the left, and as dashes if it veered right.

The *Mouse* ground station signaled the bomber as it passed a number of course markers along the radius to the target until it reached the release point, which was the intersection of the *Cat* and *Mouse* ranges. At this point the bomb release signal (five dots and a dash) was automatically given to release the bombs. It took approximately 10 minutes to control an Oboe bomber on a target run. The precise release point was influenced by many factors: time of bombfall, trail distance, weather, and the velocity and heading of the bomber just before release. These were taken into account by the *Mouse* computer, fittingly called *The Micestro*, the release point being continuously and automatically corrected to ensure that the predicted impact point of the bomb was within the target zone. Oboe was considered somewhat more effective than Gee. Its range was limited to 280 miles at 28,000 feet, although by using repeater aircraft it could be extended.

The RAF use of Oboe in the winter of 1942-43 was restricted to fast Mosquito bombers operating at night. The British wanted to avoid the premature capture of the Oboe equipment installed in slow, vulnerable bombers, which could cause the frequencies used to be compromised and jammed. In March 1943 the 8th Air Force agreed not to use Oboe in its daylight missions until it was in mass production and the next generation Oboe MkII was ready for production in case the Germans were able to counteract the original by jamming. Meanwhile, several AAF heavy bombers received Oboe Mk I installations, and in February 1943 six men from the VIII BC were sent to the TRE for instruction in Oboe technique. In March two 305BG B-17s (42-5745 and 41-24359) were sent to Wyton, the RAF pathfinder base near Huntingdon, for Oboe installations by RAF mechanics and the AAF mechanics who had previously trained at TRE. These Oboe B-17s were transferred to Alconbury and were used to train more personnel. Two more Oboe B-17s arrived during the summer and the total reached 12 by the late autumn, augmented by six B-24s fitted with Oboe. At Alconbury a trial installation to link Oboe signal with the B-17's AFCE system was attempted.

Oboe was released for operational use by the 8AF's 482nd Bomb Group B-17Fs. The Oboe ground stations were known as Type 9000, and those for the MkI (ARI 5148) used the Eastern chain transmitters at Swingate, Trimingham, Hawkeshill Down, and Winterton. It was first used during a daylight mission on 15 October 1943, and the first mission led by Oboe B-17 pathfinders was flown five days later during an attack on Duren, with one of the two Oboe pathfinders aborting early and the other was unable to pick up signals in the target area. Five more missions were led by Oboe B-17s during November but none met expectations. On the fifth mission there was a deterioration of signal strength probably due to atmospheric conditions prevalent at the high altitude and further Oboe-led operations were suspended.

However, operational tests were conducted at night with two B-17s equipped with the new Oboe MkII, which used nine cm wavelength compared to the 1.5 meters of the MkI. The MkII was virtually free from jamming but had slightly less range. A version of Oboe MkII, using a higher frequency, was given operational trials under the code names *Album Leaf* and *Aspen*, which covered its use with components of U.S. Navy sea search radar (ASG-3). By the end of January 1944 it was clear that other existing radar bombing systems would more adequately meet 8AF requirements. After considering Oboe's range limitations and jamming possibilities, a decision was made to hand over all Oboe equipment to the 9AF, other than sets used for operational experimentation. The 9AF B-26 Marauder medium bombers needed an overcast bombing system, and Oboe was ideally suited to their short range requirements and medium altitude attacks; Oboe-guided bombing would achieve outstanding accuracy. By 7 February 1944 most Oboe MkII equipment and trained maintenance personnel were transferred to the 9AF together with five Oboe B-24s. These aircraft, in which Oboe MkII sets had been installed, were later returned to the 8AF after the sets had been removed.

SHORAN Navigational Bombing Radar

In 1938 RCA engineer Stuart Seeley, while attempting to remove "ghost" signals from an experimental television system, discovered that he could measure distances by time differences in radio reception. In summer 1940 Seeley proposed building SHORAN (**SHO**rt **RA**nge **N**avigation) for the AAC, and a contract was awarded nine months later; the system made its first military flight tests in August 1942 aided by Dr. William Alexander of Wright Field's Armament Laboratory.

In 1943 Seeley flew to England to demonstrate the early system to the AAF and RAF and compare it to the British Oboe system. They observed that the Oboe could guide only a single aircraft, unlike SHORAN, which could guide multiple aircraft. Unfortunately, on the return flight from the UK all records and experienced engineers and technicians involved in the design and development of the system were killed in a plane crash in Newfoundland. Seeley was forced to recreate the SHORAN system from the hand written notes and sketches left by the original design crew and his memory.

The SHORAN system was reconstituted, and in September 1944 a SHORAN-equipped B-17 and two ground sets were assigned to MATAF, where weather had been seriously hampering both strategic and tactical operations in Italy for months. Four more complete sets were obtained and installed into B-25s of the 310th Bomb Group, and by December crews had been trained and the ground sets relocated for operations.

A SHORAN-equipped aircraft was able to determine its position in space by measuring distances from two ground stations whose positions were known. This was done by sending out a pulse to each of the two ground stations, which received and retransmitted the pulse back to the aircraft. By measuring the time required for the pulse to make a round trip to ground station and back the distances to the aircraft could be determined. The control dials were read directly in distances. For navigational purposes the bombardier carried a map with the SHORAN distances overprinted.

The operator saw three small clear pips on his airborne radar scope. A transmitter in his aircraft sent a constant stream of impulses back to each of two SHORAN stations on the ground. These signals were reflected back to record as drift and rate indicators on the airborne operator's scope and could be compared with the stationary marker pip. Since the frequencies used depended mainly on line of sight conditions, the actual area from the ground stations over which navigation or bombing could be completed depended both on the altitude of the

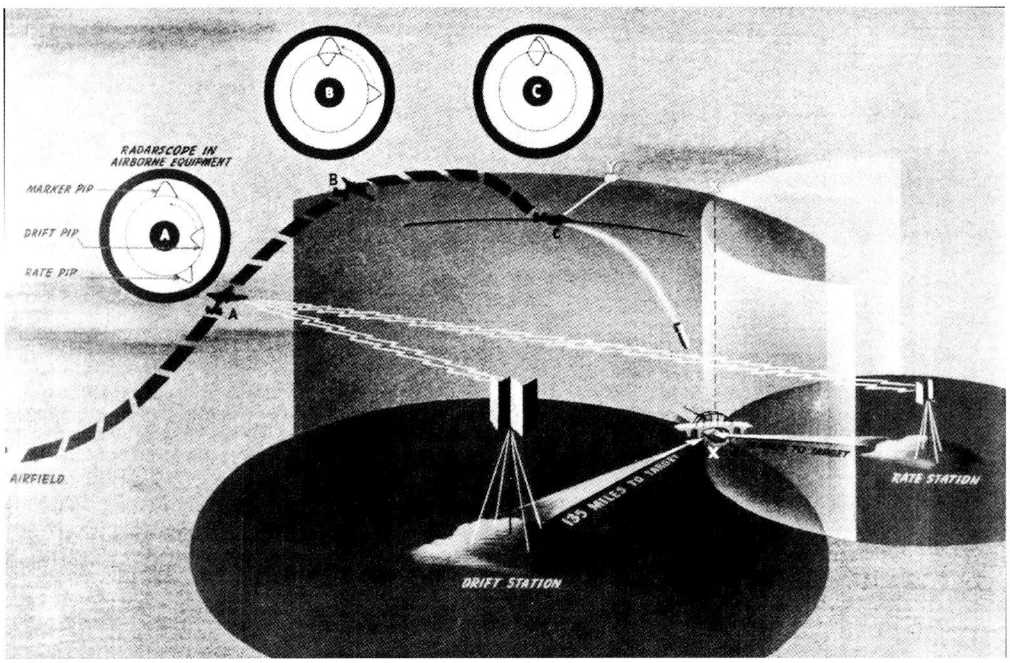

SHORAN Mission: The bomber locates the target by broadcasting signals to the Drift and Rate ground stations. The radarscope in the bomber is shown on the top circles. (AAF)

aircraft and the elevation of the ground stations. For example, an aircraft operating at an altitude of 12,000 feet had a range of 173 miles around a ground station located at an elevation of 200 feet. Distance had no effect on the accuracy of SHORAN (good to about 25 feet) or the clarity of its signals.

Associated with the SHORAN equipment was a very accurate airborne bombing computer into which was preset and inserted the bomb release point data. The computer incorporated a circuit that released the bombs when the aircraft was over the pre-computed release point.

The combat evaluation reported the following advantages of the system:

1) The engagement of pinpoint targets was independent of target visibility.
2) Flak losses should decrease, as the enemy was forced to rely completely on radar-controlled AA fire.
3) Close cooperation with ground troops could be maintained under overcast conditions.
4) Accurate night bombing was possible.
5) Navigation was simplified.
6) Target misidentification was minimized.
7) Up to 20 aircraft could contact a pair of stations at once.

The limitations of SHORAN included:

1) Because the system was line-of-sight limited, an aircraft operating at 12,000 feet had a range of 173 miles around a ground station located at 200 feet, while one flying at 35,000 feet had a range of 285 miles. Altitudes over 20,000 feet were not easily attained by fully-loaded bombers.
2) A maximum range of 300 statute miles and a clear radio path
3) The station angle had to be between 30° and 150°, and the exact geographical position of each of the two ground stations and the target had to be known.
4) Complex calculations made prior to the flight could not be changed during the bomb run.
5) There were only four possible approaches to any one target, which were all predefined by the system.
6) Only stationary targets could be attacked

SHORAN equipment was light, at 650 pounds for each ground set and 290 pounds for the complete airborne set, readily transportable, and could be set up in a few hours. Its signals were strong and resistant to enemy electronic jamming. The airborne computer, preset with data as to altitude, speed, type of bombs, drift, etc., directed the pilot to the proper release point. It had crystal-based accuracy in its sweep and timing circuits with an excellent computer geared into the electronics equipment. The PDI (Pilot Direction Indicator) indicated not only the space error, but also the true correction rate of the space error by utilizing two meters. The lower meter, which was displacement, indicated distance from the desired track, while the upper meter, which was rate, indicated the velocity with which the aircraft was approaching the correct track. Although no new techniques were integrated in SHORAN, it was a very effective system that gave the most accurate bombing results during World War II.

In March 1944 the MATAF sent an operational pilot to the United States to observe tests on the SHORAN, and by July it had been decided to proceed with the technique. In mid-September a B-17 equipped with a SHORAN airborne set and the equipment for two ground stations were received and assigned to the 310th Bomb Group of the B-25 equipped 57th Bomb Wing. After the training of the pilots and bombardiers the first mission was led by Maj. Bud Berge on 10 December 1944, when four boxes of six B-25s, each led by a SHORAN aircraft, successfully attacked a railway bridge at Fidenza, Italy.

After the B-26 equipped 42nd Bomb Wing transferred from Corsica to Dijon, France, it also was equipped with SHORAN (code named *BAT*) and the secret Gee-H radar navigation apparatus to cope with the chronic cloudy weather. MIT's Dr. Charles West was sent to supervise the Wing's SHORAN project aided by Dr. William Alexander and Maj. Ray Dickinson, who trained Wing personnel, while Capt. Robert Romero directed the installation of the equipment. Lt. Frank Paradise and Lt. Robert Whitlock, both skilled radar technicians but who had no previous SHORAN experience, were transferred to the 42nd from the 64th Fighter Wing to operate the equipment. Eight officers and Maj. Bud Berge were detached from duty with the 57th to be the nucleus for the new SHORAN training program. The SHORAN and Gee-H training of pilots, bombardiers, and navigators from the 320th and 17th Bomb Groups would be conducted under Lt.Col. Harvey Keene, Wing Training Officer, at the recently established Wing Training Center at the Istres Airdrome on the Rhone Delta, near Marseilles.

The SHORAN ground station equipment were set up: one high in the Vosage Mountains, and the other at the monastery of Montelima, in Southern France. They also gave coverage, by turning the antennas, over the three practice bombing ranges out of Istres. Airborne SHORAN components were installed in two aircraft, and on 23 January 1945 the first bombardier-navigator teams came to Istres to start *BAT* training and familiarization.

During a period of poor weather that prevented normal operations the first SHORAN practice mission was carried out on 7 February 1945, but the target was missed by an unexpected mile and a half. However, a quick inflight analysis discovered that the bombardier had made a computing mistake that was rectified, and on the next bomb run the practice bomb hit the target. Meanwhile, the Wing's bombardier-navigators were sent to the 8AF in England for Gee operational training and returned for further SHORAN training at Istres on 3 February under Capt. Walter Ashley, who was on Detached Service from the 1st TAF. By late February ten trained *BAT* "lead teams" returned to their units after 35 hours of SHORAN practice bombing achieving an average circular error of only 200 feet. When compared to H2X the SHORAN system proved to be not only more accurate, but more mobile and durable, and didn't require recalibration as often.

The decision to use SHORAN or Norden for a mission depended on the particular target and the weather prediction for the day. Targets were analyzed with reference to their from-the-air physical characteristics and rated good visual (Norden) or good SHORAN. When a *BAT* mission was assigned to the Wing, it issued a Field Order to the Group furnishing the target, bomb loads, times and size of formation, and the Group, then made the final choice as to target approach and returned that information to Wing. Aiming points were then decided and the data was sent to the SHORAN Computing Section. Initially computing was completed at Wing headquarters, but when enough trained personnel were available Computing Sections were set up at each Group. The briefing of SHORAN pilots and bombardiers was relatively easy compared to visual bombing briefings. In addition to the discussion of the data sheet figures and SHORAN navigational charts, only the route to the Initial Point and evasive action, if any, was considered. Once the formation was airborne and assembled, the Gee-H operator and the SHORAN bombardier in the lead aircraft of the formation navigated to the IP, after which the SHORAN operator assumed control while the Gee-H operator continued to take fixes to check against gross error or equipment malfunction. The main problem was drift indicator adjustment, and the pilot kept in contact with the bombardier during the approach to the drift arc and through the bomb run. After the bombs were dropped the Gee-H navigator generally guided the bombers back to base with the bombardier using auxiliary SHORAN navigation.

Each lead aircraft for each flight—nine aircraft in the 320BG and six in the 17BG—were to be equipped with a SHORAN system for a total of 44 SHORAN B-26s in the Wing with 22 spares. However, an initial shortage of equipment caused one SHORAN-equipped bomber to lead as many as 36 B-26s with the formation divided in half. One half would fly 1,000 feet above and ahead of the others. The SHORAN pathfinder bomber would lead the first flight, and when it released, the second flight would wait until the bombs had dropped to their level, then they would release. The speed of the second flight's aircraft, plus the delay in the forward speed of the first flight's bombs once they had left the bays, was to result in a perfectly timed concentration of bombs on the target.

In the "Pick-up the Leader" procedure there were not enough SHORAN sets available to service all formations. Two formations would follow a lead SHORAN aircraft, and at the Orbit Point the second formation broke away and circled while the first went in and bombed. The leader released only three bombs at the release point, which would signal the release point to the formation. The Deputy Leader took over the formation on the break-away, allowing the SHORAN-equipped lead aircraft to return to the Orbit Point, pick up the second formation, and take them over the target.

By early March 1945 equipment installation, personnel training, and target planning were completed, and the first operational SHORAN mission by medium bombers in the ETO was scheduled for the 320BG. The first mission, on the Hauenstein supply depot in Germany, was led by Col. Ashley Woolridge and Lead Pilot 1Lt. Elmer Schrantz. Three boxes of six 320th B-26s were each led by a SHORAN-equipped aircraft, and each dropped 6x500 pound bombs on the rail yards at 1335. The SHORAN bombardier made a few miscalculations and used incorrect rate and true altitude settings. There was a weak signal from one of the ground stations during part of the bomb run which was subsequently corrected by flying at a higher altitude. On 11 March 18 B-26s led by Maj. Lawrence Haywood and Lead Pilot Jackson Brainerd each dropped 4x1,000 pound bombs at 1324 through 10/10ths cloud on the Bad Munster railroad bridge. The cloud cover both days was 10/10, which tested SHORAN's blind bombing capabilities but prevented immediate photographic evaluation, but recon photos taken on 13 March showed the two missions to be successful.

On 15 and 16 March SHORAN, directed by a 15th Corps ground controller, was to be used against targets in the long, narrow Zweibrucken defense zone of the Siegfried Line. The intention of the bombing was to leave the German defenders in a state of shock before a U.S. infantry advance, but to leave no bomb craters that could impede the tanks. These targets were a problem for visual bombing even under conditions of CAVU (Ceiling And Visibility Unlimited), but when using SHORAN the target was only map coordinates. On 15 March the 320th flew two *BAT* missions and placed 70% and 99% of its bombs in the target areas, respectively. These missions of the 15th were so successful that all the missions of the 16th were SHORAN, and the Group flew four more assessed *BAT* missions to the Siegfried Line area and achieved accuracy grades of 56%, 77%, 64%, and 74%. Although the bombs were on target they did not achieve their objective, as the U.S. infantry was not in position to advance and most German troops were not in the bombed area.

Near the end of the war the key to the German defenses at Bordeaux was the small fortified island of D'Oleron that blocked the sea passage to the city, and a combined air-ground assault was scheduled to take the island. An analysis of reconnaissance photos showed that visual bombing of its defenses would be difficult because of target identification. Also the Metrological Unit forecast poor long-range weather which limited visual bombing, so SHORAN bombing was selected to be used. D'Oleron was at a too great distance from coverage by the ground SHORAN stations then located in Eastern France, so the two ground stations from the training range at Istres were transferred, specially sited, and calibrated for the operation. A very accurate captured German survey of the area that included accurate current maps was used for siting and calibrating the SHORAN equipment. The attack began in the morning of 30 April with a diversionary amphibious landing of French infantry on the west coast of the island followed by a main landing to the south. The 320th's B-26s then bombed German positions and troop concentrations in eight morning and afternoon close support SHORAN bombing missions with good to excellent results. On the second day the SHORAN targets were gun positions on the northern tip of the island, with two Marauder missions dropping effective patterns of demolition bombs supporting advancing French Commandos, and at 1845 the German commander surrendered.

Strike photo of the excellent SHORAN bombing results of the small fortified island of D'Oleron. (AAF)

In January 1951, during the Korean War SHORAN units were installed in B-29s and B-26s, but their use was not maximized, as the ground stations were often improperly located or too far from the targets; the ground and aircraft equipment was not correctly maintained; many technicians were improperly trained in its use; and operators were too unfamiliar with Korean geography. Corrections were made, and by June 1951 the ground stations were relocated to areas which would give range, such as islands and mountaintops; and SHORAN operators and technicians were given better training to familiarize them with the system. By November 1952 these changes had developed SHORAN into a reliable accurate blind-bombing system that was well-used by B-29s and B-26s for the remainder of the war. After the war SHORAN was used extensively for mapping the U.S. in the Geodetic Survey.

Gee Navigational Bombing Radar

Gee, or AMES Type 7000, was a crude aerial navigation and bombing through the overcast British radio navigation system used by the Royal Air Force beginning in March 1942. The Gee system utilized an airborne transmitter which interrogated two ground beacons and, while it was able to find the city where the target was located, finding a target at night with the Gee's accuracy was difficult. The basic problem with Gee was that it was essentially a navigational and not a blind bombing aid.

There were three Gee transmitter stations—one master and two slaves—with about 100 miles between master and slaves that sent out precisely timed pulses. The master sent a pulse followed two milliseconds later by a double pulse. The first slave station sent a single pulse one millisecond after the master's single pulse, and the second slave sent a single pulse one millisecond after the master's double pulse. The whole cycle repeated on a four millisecond cycle. The signals from the three stations were received by equipment on an aircraft that would display the two slave's signals as blips on an oscilloscope type display (radar scope). Since the display timing was controlled by the pulses from the master station, the display equipment gave the difference in reception time of the pulses and thus the relative distance from the master and each slave. This data gave Gee coordinates and, by referring to data charts, the navigator could fix the aircraft's position by finding the intersection of the two transmissions representing the two slave stations.

Gee Radar Set

(AAF)

Gee accuracy decreased with increased range, but a competent navigator could usually place the aircraft with an accuracy of five miles of true position at 250 miles. Maximum Gee range was about 350 miles, but depended on atmospheric conditions and was easily jammed by the Germans. Unlike the German beam systems, where the bombers flew to their targets along the beam, the Gee pulses were radiated in all directions, so even if detected they would not reveal the bomber's likely destination. As the system was passive, unlike H2S, there were no return signals that could give away the bomber's positions to night fighters.

In the 8th Air Force it was first used in B-24Ds of the 93rd Bomb Group assigned to *Moling* (see next) operations in the winter of 1942-43, and thereafter it was adopted as a general navigation aid for all VIII BC bombers. Commencing April 1943, 12 aircraft in each Group were to receive Gee in the initial program, with the 92nd, 305th, and 306th having been equipped by early June. By the end of the year 515 B-17s and B-24s had Gee, about half the total on hand. All 8th Air Force bombers were not equipped until the following spring. The Gee MkII set used by the 8AF was identified as ARI 5083, comprising receiver R1335 and the indicator as Type 62. VIII BC navigators mostly used the Eastern Gee Chain, which had stations at Daventry (7111), Stenigot (7122), Gibbet Hill (7123), and Clee Hill (7124).

The Gee technology was developed by the Americans into the LORAN system and was used for general navigation, especially by the U.S. Navy and Royal Navy during World War II. After the war LORAN came into common civilian use world wide for coastal navigation until Global Positioning Satellite (GPS) technology made it obsolete.

Moling Operations Using Gee

In fall 1942, meteorologists informed VIII BC planners that the approaching European winter would restrict their normal bombing operations. In response strategy was directed to using British navigational radar in harassing raids by small units operating over enemy territory in thick cloud. The primary objective of these raids, called "*Moling*," was more disruptive than destructive. The presence of aircraft in poor weather was intended to keep the enemy's interceptor and AA defenses and civilian air raid system on alert and disrupt industrial production, while the negligible bomb load, mostly poorly aimed, would have little effect. The early *Moling* missions were mainly directed to developing the technique and tactical doctrine for blind bombing, but also, in the future, could be used by specially equipped pathfinding aircraft to guide bomber formations over cloud cover to unobstructed targets.

Moling operations were to utilize a single B-24 operating under strict restrictions. A pilot was to abandon the mission if icing or other severe weather was encountered and if armament, ordnance, or the radio failed. When flying over enemy territory the bomber had to fly inside or near the top of the cloud cover and continually employ prescribed systematic evasive action. Cloud cover of 8/10 to 10/10 was ideal *Moling* weather, but if there was insufficient cloud the mission was to be aborted. The primary method of navigation was to be dead reckoning using Gee for confirmation.

On 24 October 1942 a single B-24 squadron of the newly arrived 44th Bomb Group was to be trained and equipped, but the Group was under strength, having only three squadrons instead of the normal four. So in early December the 329BS of the 93BG, under Maj. George Brown, was chosen and transferred to the satellite airfield at Bungay, where Gee sets were installed in eight B-24Ds. The Ruhr was selected as the prime target area, but it was not until 2 January 1943 that the weather over the target was 10/10. Four B-24Ds took off, but over the North Sea the cloud thinned and all the bombers returned to base. On 11 and 13 January *Moling* missions were similarly aborted, as were three in February. In March, the 329BS was returned to the 93BG for conventional daylight bombing missions, but participated in a final *Moling* mission on 26 March, which was again turned back by thinning cloud cover, and the *Moling* was permanently abandoned.

Gee-H Navigational Bombing Radar

Along with the range restriction Oboe had another major drawback, as it could only effectively be used by one bomber at a time. Consequently, the British revised Oboe into a new system named "Gee-H" that was basically Gee plus Oboe in reverse, but requiring the use of a bombsight.

In August 1943 Dr. W. Norris Tuttle of the Operational Research Section (ORS) recommended that the Bomber Command use the British Oboe equipment for short range radar bombing and the British H2S and American H2X for long range bombing. For security reasons the Oboe equipment was not released for daylight bombing, and as an alternative Dr. Tuttle recommended British Gee-H equipment for short range bombing (less than 300 miles). Dr. Tuttle and Maj. Warren Bales (ORS) and the Radar Subsection administered the Gee-H program, training crews in Gee use and maintenance, preparing lattice charts, and computing data for the combat crews. It coordinated activities with RAF beacon operators and analyzed the operations. Despite these preparations the 8AF did not fly its first Gee-H mission until 28 January 1944.

As stated, Gee-H was Gee plus Oboe in reverse, but required the use of a bombsight. A bomber carried a transmitter and a receiver, bouncing signals off two ground stations to determine range, which appeared on a scope in the aircraft; thus, its presentation was visual instead of aural. While on average it was never as accurate as visual bombing, Gee-H was far superior to H2X against small targets, as the point of attack could, theoretically, be pin-pointed by the ground station to within a few feet. Accuracy was similar to Oboe, but with greater range due to a longer radio beam, giving it an effective range of 170 miles at 20,000 feet and 200 miles at 25,000 feet. Gee-H was first used in January 1944, and the Eighth Air Force would achieve an average circular error of 1,864 feet on Gee-H missions.

Multiple aircraft could use the two stations in parallel because random noise was inserted into the timing of each aircraft's pulse output. The receiving equipment on the aircraft could match its own unique pulse pattern with that transmitted back by the transponder. Each receive-reply cycle took the transponder 100 microseconds, allowing it to manage a maximum of 10,000 interrogations per second and making "collisions" improbable. The practical limit was about 80 aircraft at one time.

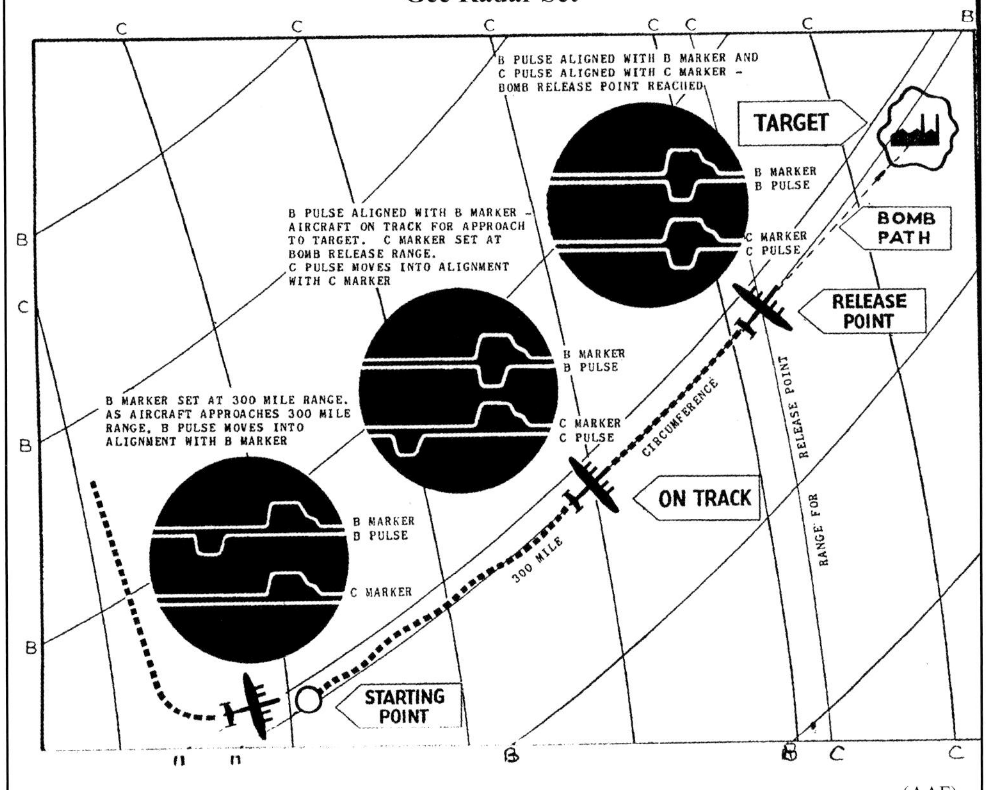

Gee Radar Set

(AAF)

In the synchronous procedure, the navigator determined the track and furnished the bombardier with information, enabling him to set up the bombsight, which dropped the bombs automatically when the indices of the sight met. Analysis of the warning point system led to the development of this refined Gee-H method of operation. As had been successfully accomplished with the H2X system, a method of connecting the Norden Bombsight with the Gee-H technique was developed. Basically, it consisted of synchronizing the bombsight at a number of Gee-H checkpoints. At the briefing, both the navigator and bombardier received data for a series of checkpoints that had been computed to a high degree of precision by the Gee-H section. During the mission the navigator identified each checkpoint to the bombardier. At the first checkpoint he called "Check 1," and the bombardier immediately adjusted his bombsight to the pre-determined sighting angle listed for that checkpoint in the Gee-H data sheet. This procedure was repeated as each checkpoint was reached and, if necessary, corrections were made until the bombsight automatically released the bomb load. This method was considered superior to the warning point system in that it gave

There were two techniques for Gee-H bombing, the warning point procedure and the synchronous procedure. In the warning point procedure, the Gee-H navigator determined both the track and the release point.

In the warning point procedure, the Gee-H system was controlled by the Gee-H navigator of the bomber who turned his equipment on after leaving the English coast. He provided rate information to the bombardier, who also used visual sightings when possible to improve accuracy. The Gee-H bomber's transmitter unit pulsed a signal which triggered the two Gee-H responder ground stations, which pulsed answering signals on another frequency that were received by the receiver in the bomber and were represented as two blips, one from each station, on the scope of the Gee box. One ground station pulsed a range, or "Cat" signal, while the other pulsed the releasing "Mouse" signal. The navigator watched the Cat blip to verify the bomber was following the desired course, which was an arc of a circle that cut through the target location. Any deviations from this course were immediately corrected by directions relayed to the pilot. About 15 to 20 minutes from the target the navigator determined the calibration figures for the position of the Mouse blip. A chart near the Gee scope listed a series of predetermined figure/time check-points computed for each operation by Gee-H specialists. The navigator compared the calibrations on his scope with this data, which gave him his movement towards a final check-point, called the "warning point." The instant the Mouse blip reached the warning point he called "Check" over the interphone to the bombardier. The bombardier carried a stopwatch set for a timed run based on a figure previously supplied by the navigator and derived from the warning period tables based on true altitude, ground speed, and type of bomb. At the end of the timed run the bombardier used the toggle switch to release the bombs, and other aircraft in the formation then released their bombs on the leader's release of bombs and sky markers. The 1st Air Division Gee-H units continued to use the original warning-point method of operation for some time, but during October and November 1944 gradually converted to the new synchronous technique.

a lesser margin for error at the critical point, which was the warning point. This synchronous method was first used by the 2nd Air Division when Gee-H operations recommenced in September 1944, and from December 1944 all Gee-H operations were conducted in this way.

In September 1943 a B-17 (42-29994) and three mechanics were sent from Alconbury to RAF Newmarket for the initial Gee-H installation. This aircraft was flown extensively after its return to Alconbury, but as Oboe was at that time the chosen beam radar for B-17 pathfinders, Gee-H was eventually earmarked for B-24s. After eight test installations were completed in early November it was decided that the Gee-H should be employed operationally by a 2nd Bomb Division unit leaving the 482nd Bomb Group to concentrate its efforts on perfecting Oboe, H2S, and H2X.

The eight Gee-H B-24s were transferred with one officer and two mechanics to the 329BS at Hardwick, the unit which had pioneered 8AF Gee bad weather operations a year earlier. The first operational use of Gee-H was on 28 January 1944 when four 329BS pathfinders led its parent group, the 93rd, and the 446th Group to bomb a V-1 site near Bonnieres, France. When visual sighting was not possible Gee-H was, because of its reasonable accuracy, the logical method for this target system. V-weapon sites were nearly the only target for the 31 Gee-H missions flown up to the time of the D-Day invasion in June.

In May 1944 Gee-H equipment was fitted in selected B-17Gs of the 41st Combat Wing at Grafton Underwood, Kimbolton, and Molesworth, and while these aircraft were used primarily to lead their own group formations, they also provided leads for units in the 1st Air Division. Gee-H was also allocated to the 3rd Division's 486BG, and when this unit converted to B-17s in July 1944 these Gee-H B-24s were passed to the 34BG.

In the latter part of July 1944 the Gee-H program was threatened by two factors. The improved summer weather made visual bombing possible much more often for the targets in the range of Gee-H beacons. The other factor, though less important, was that advancing Allied armies began to overrun some of the V-weapon sites along the French coast, which were the principal Gee-H targets up to that time. Gee-H Pathfinder crews became discouraged by the lack of activity, and many of the trained personnel were sent elsewhere. The resourceful Dr. Tuttle and Maj. Bales, struggling to keep the program alive, explored the possibility of using Gee-H on tactical support missions.

After D-Day Gee-H attacks were expanded to many other types of targets, notably airfields, bridges, rail junctions, and arms dumps. After June, however, there was a decline in this type of beacon bombing, as Allied advances put most targets beyond the range of the ground stations in England, and by mid-August all were out of reach. Gee-H was not resumed until late September when the British, who operated the ground stations, established new ground station sites on the Continent. In June 1944 alone, approximately 3,000 AAF and RAF bombers were led by Gee-H aircraft. In the last quarter of 1944 15% of 8AF missions used the Gee-H system.

Micro-H Navigational Bombing Radar

The Micro-H technique, a combination of Gee-H and H2X, was developed by the British Branch of the Radiation Laboratory (BBRL). Dr. W. Norris Tuttle and a representatives of BBRL decided to employ this form of blind bombing along with Gee-H and H2X. At that time, it was decided that BBRL personnel would supervise the installation of the equipment, help train crews, do essential calculation, and advise and control operational problems. In the spring of 1944 Microwave-H, later called Micro-H, was under rigorous operational development at Alconbury by the 482BG.

In employing Micro-H, the navigators followed Gee-H beams emanating from Gee-H ground beacons whose signals appeared on a H2X radar scope in the aircraft as two bright white dots. Gee-H range information was added to the ground returns of the radar equipment until approximately 35 miles from the target, at which point the navigator switched to H2X. The dots had to remain approximately equidistant from the center of the scope for the bomber to be following the correct course; like Gee-H, this was an arc running through the target. The radar operator called out predetermined check-points, allowing the bombardier to synchronize his bombsight. At the commencement of the bomb run the radar navigator set up his first check-point on the scope in the form of a range circle. As the aircraft moved towards the target the two white dots moved simultaneously towards the circumference of the range circle. When they touched it the navigator called to the bombardier "Check 1." The bombardier immediately synchronized his bombsight to include the sighting angle from the predetermined data in his brief. Likewise, each check-point was synchronized into the bombsight until the aircraft reached the release point, a similar procedure to that of synchronous Gee-H.

While the synchronous procedure using the bombsight to determine when to drop the bombs was used with Micro-H, there were two techniques used to establish track. In the first of these, the difference in the distances of the aircraft from the two beacons was kept constant. The bomber approached the target along a hyperbolic curve. In the second technique its distance from one of the beacons was fixed. The system differed from that employed in H2X bombing; in H2X bombing the bombers were guided to their targets by the use of airborne radar alone, whereas in Micro-H bombing the bombers were positioned exactly with reference to the ground stations (beacons).

Micro-H originally had three intrinsic restrictions: range, target handling capacity, and course. The range restrictions were unchangeable, but the limitations of the other two could be reduced by converting the ground stations to pulse range and release signals as was done for the Gee-H system. The two white dots on the H2X scope thus represented "Cat" and "Mouse," which could be used similarly. Instead of being restricted to a single approach course and a single target of the original Micro-H concept four target approaches were possible. Four targets could be attacked by setting up the beacons to pulse, creating several Cat ranges for tracking and several Mouse signals for different release points.

Micro-H was used exclusively by the First Air Division throughout the war. Because Gee-H operated on the same frequency as Gee, which had already been successfully jammed, both the 1st and 2nd Divisions trained to use Micro-H, which could not be jammed. The 1AD Gee beacon personnel were on detachment from the 482BG, and all the computations were made by the British Micro-H section at High Wycombe. Originally two beacon stations were built, one near Namur, Belgium, and the other at Verdun, France, but the opening of another beacon at Nijmegen, Holland, in January 1945 improved ground beacon bombing accuracy to approximately 1,500 feet. Micro-H entered combat in the Eighth Air Force on 5 August 1944, and the improved Cat and Mouse Micro-H bombing began on 18 December 1944. During the last quarter of 1944 3% of 8AF missions used the Micro-H technique.

H2S Target Identifying Radar

Gee and Oboe were limited to a range of 300 to 400 miles by a line of sight to their transmitters, but a bomber carrying its own, self-contained night targeting system would not be limited in range to a UK-based transmitter. Taffy Bowen, during his early AI experiments before the war, noticed that the radar returns from open areas, cities, water, and other areas had noticeably different appearances on the radar scope, and suggested the development of targeting radar. However, in the turmoil of the Nazi invasion in 1939 the subject was ignored. In late 1940, after the Battle of Britain subsided, RAF Bomber Command increased its night attacks against German cities in retaliation. Bomber Command reported outstanding results to the English media, but an analysis based on air reconnaissance showed that half the bombs exploded miles from the target, and only 10% of the bombs actually hit the intended target.

The targeting radar concept re-emerged in 1941 when Philip Dee's group at TRE had installed a 10 cm (3 GHz) Air Intercept (AI) set in a Blenheim in March. The experimental set was known as AIS, referring to its S-band operation. During the tests of the AIS, Philip Dee's team rediscovered that radar reflections could reveal different types of terrain. In October 1941 Dee attended a meeting of the RAF Bomber Command where the night targeting problem was discussed. On 1 November 1941, Dee used an AIS radar set mounted on a Blenheim bomber to scan the ground and was able to distinguish the outline of a town 35 miles away. In response, the TRE established a team under Bernard Lovell to develop S-band airborne targeting radar based on AIS. The new targeting radar was designed to be installed in a blister mounted on the lower fuselage of a bomber. The antenna would rotate to scan the terrain and send the reflections to a PPI display, producing a crude map of the terrain below.

H2S target identifying radar was the TRE's top priority, and assigned its development to Bernard Lovell's team headed by the gifted Alan Blumlein and other top EMI engineers. British targeting radar was initially designated as BN (Blind Navigation), but quickly became H2S; an acronym whose origin is debatable. Some sources claim it meant "Height to Slope" or "Home Sweet Home," but it is possible the acronym was intentionally ambiguous as a security measure.

TRE established a team under **Bernard Lovell** to develop S-band airborne targeting radar based on AIS, which led to H2S target identifying radar. (Author)

The H2S set transmitted high frequency electrical impulses downward through a revolving antenna, these impulses being reflected back and converted into light images on a cathode ray tube. The reflections, varying in intensity depending on the nature of the terrain below, were discernible on a screen, popularly known as the "scope." The contrast between land and water was particularly clear; built up areas could also be discerned and, with skill, identified. At 25,000 feet the cover of H2S was a radius of about 50 miles.

The first test of the H2S occurred on 23 April 1942 with the radar set installed in a Halifax bomber. The tests revealed that in order to display a uniform map of the terrain the radar had to have low sensitivity, or "gain," for targets directly underneath the bomber, with the gain increasing with the angle of the radar away from vertical. This method was called "cosecant-squared" scanning, after the mathematical function that defined the change in gain.

Churchill's scientific advisor, Dr. Frederick Lindemann (Lord Cherwell), wanted the TRE to design the H2S using the klystron rather than the magnetron so as not to have the top secret revolutionary magnetron fall into German hands, as the Germans could quickly develop countermeasures against it. The klystron wasn't as powerful as the magnetron, but could be much more easily destroyed in an emergency, as the magnetron's copper anode block that housed the resonant cavities from which the operation of the device could be determined could survive large demolition charges. Tests of an H2S set using klystrons instead of the cavity magnetron showed a decrease in the power output by a very large factor of 20 to 30. Lovell asserted that if the Germans did capture a magnetron they would need two years to develop centimetric radar.

On 7 June 1942 the Halifax conducting the H2S tests crashed, killing everyone on board and destroying the prototype H2S, but the greatest loss to the program was the death of the irreplaceable Alan Blumlein. On 3 July 1942, despite all the H2S developmental problems and the loss of personnel, the urgent need for H2S prompted Churchill to bewilder the TRE radar designers by demanding the delivery of 200 H2S sets by 15 October 1942. The H2S design team was given priority on manpower and resources and was allowed to abandon the klystron-based H2S program. Nonetheless, TRE failed to meet the 15 October deadline, and it was not until 1 January 1943 that H2S sets were installed on 12 Stirling and 12 Halifax bombers for trials and fine tuning before operations. The transmitter/receiver equipment was officially known as TR3159 (H2S Mk I/ASV VIB) or TR3191 (H2S Mk II).

Finally, on the night of 30 January 1943 H2S Pathfinder bombers took off to drop target markers on Hamburg for over 100 Lancasters following in the bomber stream. General use of H2S did not occur until summer 1943. On the night of 24 July 1943 the RAF began *Operation Gomorrah*, a large scale multi-day attack on Hamburg. H2S-equipped Pathfinders marked the city for RAF bombers which bombed the city with high explosive and incendiary bombs, and then returned on the 25th and the 27th, with the USAAF carrying out two daylight attacks in between the three RAF raids. A fire storm was started and large parts of the city were utterly destroyed, and about 45,000 people, mostly civilians, were killed.

On 15 March 1943, with the success of the RAF H2S Pathfinders' Hamburg raid, 8AF CO Brig.Gen. Eaker sent Air Chief Marshal Portal, RAF Chief of Air Staff, a pressing official request for the installation of H2S systems in 18 VIII BC B-17s and B-24s to cope with the European overcast. The first B-17 to be equipped with H2S arrived at Defford in June. TRE faced the problem of making equipment originally designed for operating at a ceiling of 15,000 feet to operate at 30,000 feet. Without any type of pressurization problems were greatly increased at 30,000 feet, and the electronic equipment had constant problems during testing. The major problem was the effect of the increased altitude on the polar diagram of the scanner. Bernard Lovell and his TRE team worked to perfect the H2S, and Flt./Lt. Len Killip made the first flight from Defford on 4 August 1943 in a B-17F (25793).

Meanwhile, there was no American component in the VIII BC at Alconbury to install the H2S, and the TRE was only obligated to complete H2S installation by the end of 1943. Meanwhile, the single H2S-equipped B-17F dropped two tons of bombs on Frankfurt on 17 August. The first major raid of the 8AF guided by H2S took place on 27 September when 244 Fortresses attacked the port of Emden. There was thick cloud, and the major bombing attack was carried out on marker flares released by the H2S aircraft. A second attack led by the H2S-equipped Fortresses was made on Emden on two October by 337 B-17s. Subsequent reconnaissance showed that very severe damage had been inflicted on the most vital areas of the target. The TRE completed the equipping of 18 8AF bombers with H2S, but

H2S transmitter "bath tub" located under the mid-fuselage of a Bomber Command Pathfinder Halifax. (Author/RAF)

H2S set mounted in the fuselage of a Halifax. (Author/RAF)

RAF Lancasters mounted their **H2S Mark III bath tub transmitters** under the rear fuselage behind the large bomb bays. (Author/RAF)

The initial **bath tub** mounting on a 92nd Bomb Group B-17F was to be located in the ball turret position, but due to concern over decreasing defensive protection it was located under the bombardier's position. (AAF)

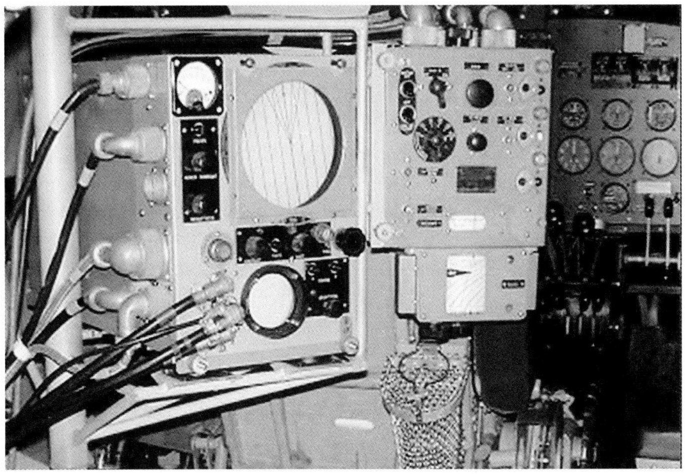

The USAAF **H2S radar scope and tuning set installation** was situated on the left side of the navigator's position and necessitated that the left hand nose gun be repositioned further forward. (AAF)

in the meantime, the Americans had quickly developed their three cm H2X system, and on three November 1943 completed their first H2X mission. All told, the 482BG received nine B-17Fs, one B-24D, and eight B-24Hs with H2S installations.

TRE perfected its 10 cm H2S, and its use by Bomber Command Pathfinders was crucial in the success of the series of large raids on Berlin and other cities from November 1943 until March 1944. Special Pathfinder aircraft equipped with H2S dropped illuminating flares in the area of the target and then bombing proceeded visually. Berlin was out of range of radio navigation aids, such as Gee and Oboe, and was often hidden by cloud cover in the winter. It was anticipated that H2S could be used to distinguish the many lakes and rivers in the city, but the early H2S sets were unable to do so. The RAF continued to use S-band H2S, and when they learned that German fighters could home in on its emissions, they were cautious not to turn the unit on until they were near the target and then turned it off immediately after they dropped their bombs. It would not be until the first days of December 1943 that the H2S Mark III, which operated on the better three cm wavelength (like the American H2X) and could identify open and built up spaces, made somewhat accurate bombing possible.

In March 1943 four AAF radio mechanics and two officers were sent to TRE to learn about H2S. That same month a 92nd Bomb Group B-17F (42-5793) was sent to RAF Defford for installation of H2S. Initial proposals were to install the scanner in the ball turret well, but this would delete valuable defensive armament. Instead, the scanner was placed below the B-17's nose where, shielded by a bathtub-shaped plastic cover, it easily cleared the ground during takeoffs and landings and also gave the radar set anti-interference advantages. The radar scope and tuning set were situated on the left side of the navigator's position and necessitated that the left hand nose gun be repositioned further forward. Although the primary installation made at Burtonwood was completed in April, many difficulties arose in trials at Defford and were not satisfactorily overcome for several weeks. The aircraft was returned to Alconbury in August, and later that month a second B-17F with H2S was received and put into the intense training program. However, the radar sets were found somewhat temperamental, and polar diagram troubles were a recurring problem at this time. A further two H2S B-17s arrived in the first weeks of September, and all four aircraft of the 813th Bomb Squadron took part as combat wing leaders on the first combat mission, 27 September 1943. On 11 October 1943 a H2S B-17 (42-5793) crashed, but the Group was augmented by four additional H2S-equipped B-17s. H2S pathfinders were used on several missions during the following winter, with four successfully leading the combat wings of the 2nd Air Division to the Brunswick area on 11 January 1944. But there were continuing difficulties with the equipment, and two aircraft were MIA (42-5909 on 8 February 1944 and 42-3357 on 8 February 1944). An H2S B-17F (42-30731) led the first 8th Air Force bombing raids on Berlin on 4 March 1944. However, the pathfinder, piloted by 1Lt. William Owens, had its radar fail on the bomb run. Two days later the same aircraft was more successful, taking over the lead when the lead aircraft aborted in the major attack on the German capital. The surviving H2S B-17s (42-3398, -5819, -5970, -30731, and -30729) were withdrawn from operations in late March 1944 and their H2S equipment was removed, and these aircraft were assigned to conventional combat missions as deputy leads when the H2X B-17s began operations on 3 November.

The **retractable H2S radome** in a B-24 was shaped like a trash can with a scanner plastic cover and was housed in the ball turret well. (AAF)

H2S Installation in the B-24

The installation of the prototype H2S in a B-24 was made in cooperation with the British radar research unit at Defford during April 1943. Much more difficulty was experienced during the installation of H2S in a B-24 than in the B-17, and the problems were still not fully resolved when the aircraft was delivered at Alconbury in October. The close proximity of the B-24 fuselage to the ground meant that the scanner had to be retractable, and after some experiments it was placed in the rear fuselage. Considerable difficulty was experienced in design and engineering, and in obtaining a satisfactory performance with the equipment. The prototype H2S was installed in B-24D 42-40987 and tested at Alconbury late in 1943. The retractable H2S radome was shaped like a trash can with a scanner plastic cover and was housed in the ball turret well. During November 1943 to January 1944, eight B-24H-1s were scheduled for operational installation with the 482BG at Burtonwood. These scanners were also housed in retractable radomes in the ball turret well, with the radar scope and operator located on the flight deck. They operated from 11 January 1944, continuing in service until the 482BG was withdrawn from regular operations in late March when their H2S equipment was removed. The original operational H2S B-24s of 814BS were: 41-29120, 41-29163, 41-29177, 42-7644, 42-7645, 42-7646, 42-7669, and 42-7672. Three of these aircraft were lost in 1944 (42-7672 in a collision on 23 January; 42-7669 in a collision on 29 January; and 42-7645 missing on 3 February).

H2X (AN/APS-15 and -15A) Target Identifying Radar

Development and Background

Once America was at war the MIT Radiation Laboratory (Rad Lab) was slowly developing targeting radars in parallel with the British. Only Luis Alvarez was doing any significant work, but this was on a long-term, advanced concept designated as *Eagle*, which is discussed later. In June 1942 the Rad Lab initiated a more conventional project designated NAB (**N**avigation **A**nd **B**ombing) that was patterned on the British H2S, but the small Rad Lab NAB group was given a low priority and made little progress.

George Valley, a Rad Lab scientist working on gun-laying radar, had endured a German bombing attack on London in late 1942 and had observed how inaccurate the bombing had been. When he returned to America he left the gun-laying project and took over the NAB group, determined to develop effective targeting radar.

As the 8th Air Force continued its build up in England during 1942 and 1943, it became obvious to leaders of the VIII Bomber Command that the success of a strategic bombing offensive would be dependent on the ability of the VIII BC to operate above the chronic bad weather and bomb through overcast. By December 1942 the VIII BC had an average of 72 heavy bombers available for operations. The weather during that month did not permit one mission to be dispatched, and it was not until mid-January 1943 that a mission was dispatched. 8AF Meteorologists estimated that visual bombing against targets in Germany would exist on average between 20 and 30% of the year.

In March 1943 Gen. Ira Eaker requested eight H2S units from the RAF for installation in 8th Air Force B-17s. In March 1943 four AAF radio mechanics and two officers were sent to the British Telecommunication Research Establishment at Great Malvern to become acquainted with H2S Radar. At the same time, B-17F (42-5793) was sent to RAF Deford for installation of a H2S set. The scanner and radar dome were placed under the nose and were shielded by a bathtub shaped plastic cover. The radar scope and navigation unit was placed on the left side of the navigator's station, which required some equipment movement. The H2S radar units were found to be unreliable during early test flights, so in early 1943 pressure on the Rad Lab to build reliable targeting radar increased.

Valley improved the NAB S-band targeting radar to the point where it functioned as well as H2S, but still the system needed improvement. The Rad Lab's efforts to develop a three cm (10 GHz) ASV set were in the advanced testing stage, however, and Valley felt that a X-band (10 GHz) could be used for targeting radar. At the time the Rad Lab was concentrating on the advanced *Eagle* radar, which was to have much greater accuracy, but that project was moving slowly, and Valley continued to work on X-band targeting radar as a backup to *Eagle*.

Valley referred to his X-band system as "H2X" in imitation of the British H2S. As he worked, Valley worried that the H2X wouldn't be accurate enough until he analyzed bombing tactics. AAF heavy bombers flew in huge formations, with the aircraft staggered horizontally and vertically to provide overlapping fields of defensive fire, and the bomb pattern from such an extended formation was not going to be precise, so theoretically H2X provided as much accuracy as was necessary.

The *Eagle* project continued to be mired in technical difficulties while the progress on H2X moved quickly forward. Using principals of the S-band ASV being developed by Norman Ramsey, Valley redesigned the antenna system so that, instead of performing a 360° search, it scanned down and in front of the aircraft. The NAB team developed precision ranging capabilities while Valley built an analog bombsight computing system. Using the bombsight was easy, as it included a rotating drum that was calibrated with altitude settings that the bombardier could rotate to determine how far to lead the target at a specific altitude. The drum's position was sent to the PPI display used by the H2X system, bringing up a circle on the display. When the circle was on target the bombardier released the bombs.

In April 1943, a high-level conference was held in England between the Rad Lab, the TRE, and senior military officials. At the meeting Lee DuBridge made the audacious proposal that the Rad Lab take over the development of targeting radar, as DuBridge felt that American-developed H2X, not H2S radar, was the targeting radar of the future for both the RAF and the USAAF. Of course, the suggestion shocked the British. The USAAF had previously stood behind the precision of its fabled Norden Bombsight and been firmly against area bombing, which essentially the BTO H2X was thought to provide. The NAB had been openly contemptuous of the TRE's H2S, which was at a developmental dead end, and while not out of expertise was out of funds and resources after two years of continual and exhausting work. The Rad Lab was given more funds and manpower for its radar programs, and by this time the American effort was beginning to surpass British radar research.

By June 1943 the American H2X program was moving rapidly forward, as the USAAF desperately needed targeting radars. *Eagle* was clearly not going to be ready in the near future, while the RAF Bomber Command did not have enough H2S sets to equip their Pathfinders, much less to supply the USAAF. More importantly, combat experience had demonstrated that H2S was only a slight improvement over pure blind bombing.

The H2X in production was officially designated as the AN/APQ-15. Western Electric was selected to manufacture the AAF version of H2X, while Philco was selected to build the USN version. By September 1943 the Eighth Air Force had a dozen B-17 Pathfinders equipped with H2X sets, which were also referred to as BTO (Bombing Through Overcast), or as *Mickey* radar. The naming of H2X radar as "Mickey" has been credited to 1Lt. Fred Rabo, who was working on the MIT Radiation Lab hand-built H2X sets at Grenier Field, NH. Rabo referred to the retractable radome as looking to be "Mickey Mouse." The remark became the H2X's nickname, which was subsequently shortened to "Mickey," and the radar operators as "Mickey Operators" or "Mickeymen."

In order to gain time the Radiation Laboratory at MIT hand made 20 sets, which were enough to equip 12 B-17s and provide necessary spares. The first H2X set was installed on a B-17F and the remaining eleven of the batch were installed on the newer B-17G equipped with a chin turret. These hand-built installations took place in Rome, NY, and the unit was placed under the nose similar to the H2S in placement. The H2X was semi-retractable and cylindrical in shape. H2X consisted of a receiver and an antenna located in the bomber's fuselage in a retractable housing known as a Radome, which replaced the ball turret in the B-17. The radio compartment of the bomber contained a cathode ray tube along with the necessary

The original hand-built H2X units were placed in semi-retractable and cylindrical in shape radomes, and were placed under the nose similar to the H2S in placement. (AAF)

1Lt. Fred Rabo was a H2X radar technician who is credited with coining the H2X nickname "**Mickey**." (AAF)

electrical equipment needed for its operation.

These dozen bombers (11 B-17Gs and the prototype B-17F), manned by crews partially trained in H2X use, arrived in England in October 1943 to join the 482nd Bomb Group under now Major Fred Rabo. Rad Lab Scientists set up a laboratory at Alconbury, England, to coordinate their work with the Eighth Air Force. During October the H2X crews trained in simulated bombing missions over England but they required more training. Because of bad weather the H2X crews were to complete their training in missions over Germany; each H2X crew was to lead a combat wing of 60 bombers. At the time the 482BG had four H2S-equipped B-17s from TRE.

In January 1944 the first contingent of trainees arrived from the divisions for instruction as *Mickey* operators. The plan was to first form a PFF squadron in each division, later in each combat wing, and eventually in each group. The initial units selected were the 422nd Bomb Squadron of the 305th Bomb Group, the 564th Bomb Squadron of 389th Bomb Group, and the 413th Bomb Squadron of 96th Bomb Group. However, there was some transferring of personnel to other squadrons of the parent groups, as the PFF squadrons were to receive several crews drawn from other units. Each group in each division was to send two crews to Alconbury for training and assignment to the squadron supporting their division. On completion of the training the squadrons returned to their home bases with 12 new H2X aircraft each and began providing PFF leads for their respective divisions. Whenever possible, the crews selected to lead specific groups were those who were on detachment to the PFF unit from that group. During this operational training in 1944 four of the 12 H2X B-17s were MIA (42-3486 on 11 January; 42-3500 on 4 February; 42-30280 on 22 February; and 42-3491 on 6 March). In late March the remaining seven of the original 12 B-17s (42-3483, -3484, -3485, -3487, -3492, -3511, and -37745) were taken off operations, with their H2X equipment removed and their scanners sent to equip RAF Mosquitoes.

Production B-17G equipped with H2X sets began to arrive in the UK in February 1944. The H2S sets in these bombers had their scanners placed in a semi-retractable radome located in the ball turret position and the instruments in the radio room. By the middle of March the 422BS/305BG had 12 H2S pathfinders, while the 413BS/96BG had 11. Bomb squadron strength doubled on 1 May when the 324BS at Bassingbourn, the 66BS at Shipdham, and the 333BS at Bury St Edmunds were established as H2X pathfinder units and were assigned to the 1st and 94th, 14th and 20th, and 4th Combat Wings respectively. On 1 June five B-17s were sent to the 1st Air Division to form a new unit and 10 B-24s to 2AD to expand existing PFF units. By August each combat wing possessed PFF squadrons, and by December all groups had their own PFF aircraft. In some cases pathfinder bombers were concentrated in one squadron of a group, while in others each squadron in a group had one or two PFF aircraft. By the end of 1944 every group had its own H2X B-17s, and H2S became an important bombsight in poor visibility when the Norden was unable to function. At the end of the war there was an average 12 PFF bombers in each group for a total of 260 H2X B-17Gs.

Production B-17Gs equipped with H2X sets began to arrive in the UK in February 1944 with their scanners placed in a semi-retractable radome located in the ball turret position and the instruments in the radio room. (AAF)

The 482BG received the first H2X-equipped B-24s in February 1944 with the placement of the equipment similar to that of the H2S B-24s, except that the scanner had a more prominent shape in a fully retractable dome. (AAF)

Interior view of a H2X scanner apparatus. (AAF)

H2X Installation in the B-24

The 482BG received the first H2X-equipped B-24s in February 1944. The placement of the equipment was similar to that of the H2S B-24s, except that the scanner had a more prominently shaped dome. The H2X radome in the ball turret well was fully retractable, but in the lowered position reduced a Liberator's speed by an estimated 10 to 15 mph. The newly formed pathfinder squadron of the 389BG was assigned the majority of the H2X B-24s during March 1944. Subsequently, all 2nd Air Division groups received their own H2X aircraft, and by March 1945 there were approximately 100 in the Division. The 2nd Air Division required some changes to H2X aircraft as received from the U.S., and from the summer of 1944 these were subject to a modification program. The operator's position was changed from rearward-facing to forward-facing on the left side of the flight deck directly behind the pilot. A table and other navigation facilities were provided at this position, and a K-24 camera remote scope installation was mounted against the bulkhead behind the operator. H2S B-24s were retired as soon as sufficient H2X-equipped models were available. Original H2X B-24H-DTs assigned to 564BS on 18 March 1944 were: 41-28653, 28673, 28690, 28696, 28700, 28713, 28714, 28715, 28763, 28767, 28676, and 28789.

H2X Training

Langley Field, Hampton Roads, VA, became the first training center for H2X *Mickey* operators who, on completion of training, were assigned to units of both the 8th and 15th Army Air Forces to fly as lead bombardiers for Groups, Wings, and Divisions. The *Mickey* operators were "loners," in that they were not assigned to any particular lead crew, but flew where or when they were needed. *Mickeymen* quickly became a very scarce commodity in combat areas due to the staggering losses of lead crews, and additional navigators were trained in England at Alconbury. This base was also used to provide advanced training as improved equipment was introduced.

AN/APQ-15A Components

The AN/APS-15A was a modification of the AN/APS-15 and was operated similarly, but there were differences, of course, that are listed on the accompanying chart. The location of the equipment varied with different types and models of aircraft, but once the Radar Operator recognized each component part he was able to easily orient himself in any aircraft.

AN/APS-15A, like the AN/APS-15 set, was designed for high-altitude navigation and bombing through overcast and had the advantage of providing accurate beacon ranging. It was a combined transmitter-receiver for high frequency radio pulses that operated on a 26-28 volts DC electrical supply. Its maximum range for reception of ground returns was 100 miles and was able to receive signals from a radar beacon as far as 250 miles away.

The four major units of AN/APS-15A were the Receiver-Indicator, the Control Unit, the Range Unit, and the Computer.

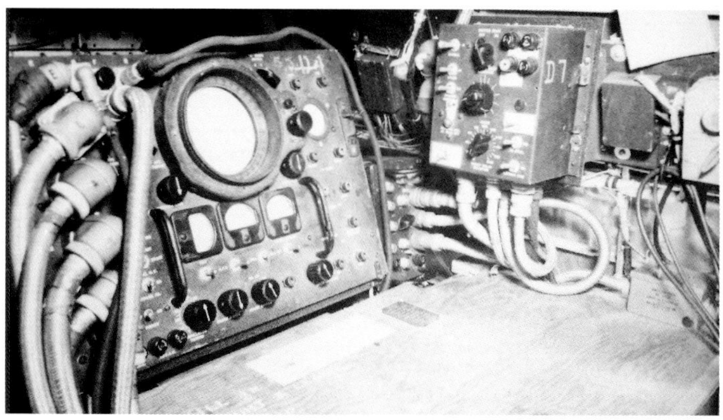

B-17 H2X installation (AAF)

Operational Differences

	APQ-15	APQ-15A
PRESENTATION	PPI scope on rec-ind and remote PRI scope for target presentation. A scope on rec-ind for tuning and monitor use.	PPI scope on rec-ind and remote PRI scope for target presentation. A scope on rec-ind for tuning and monitor use.
MONITOR SCOPE	A scope on rec-ind with 4-position switch to choose signal: 1. Video output for tuning and determining altitude. 2. Transmitter triggering pulse. 3. AFC tuning indication. 4. 10:1 divider (range unit) calibration.	A scope on rec-ind with 4-position switch to choose signal: 1. Video output for tuning and determining altitude. 2. Transmitter triggering pulse. 3. AFC tuning indication. 4. Five-mile and 1-mile range marks for count check.
SCOPE CONTROLS	1. A-scope brilliance, focus, and centering controls above and below A scope on rec-ind. (All screwdriver controls.) 2. PPI scope centering control to left of scope. Focus and brilliance controls below and to the right on rec-ind. (All screwdriver controls.) 3. Remote or PRI scope centered by same controls on rec-ind. Focus control on top of PRI case.	1. A-scope brilliance, focus, and centering controls above and below A scope on rec-ind. (All screwdriver controls.) 2. PPI scope centering control to left of scope. Focus and brilliance controls below and to the right on rec-ind. (All screwdriver controls.) 3. Remote or PRI scope centered by same controls on rec-ind. Focus and brilliance controls on top of PRI case.
INDICATION OF RANGE ON SCOPE	None.	None.

(ROBIF)

Receiver-Indicator

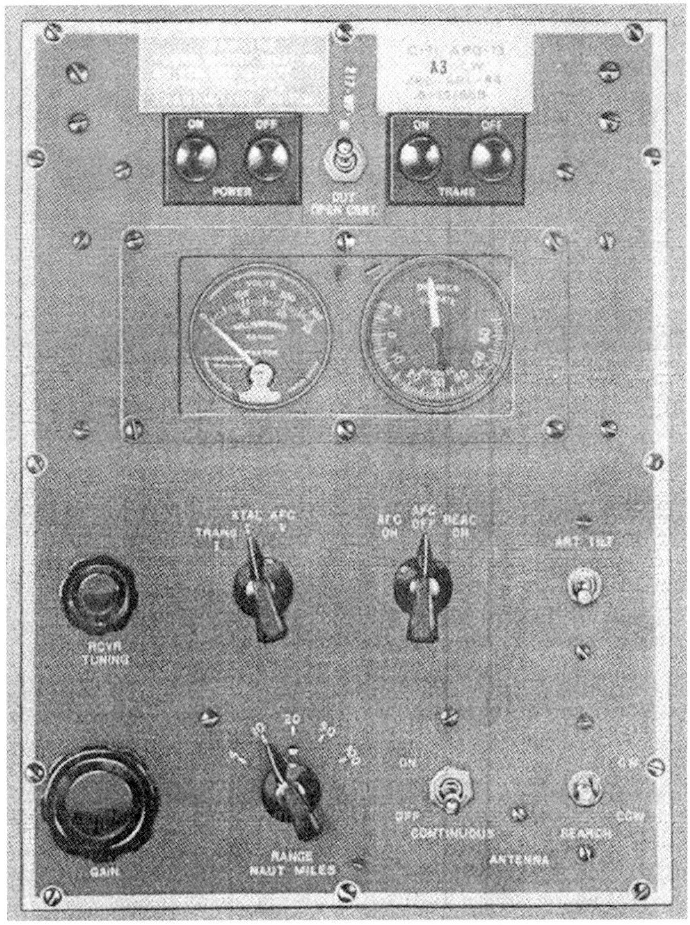

(ROBIF)

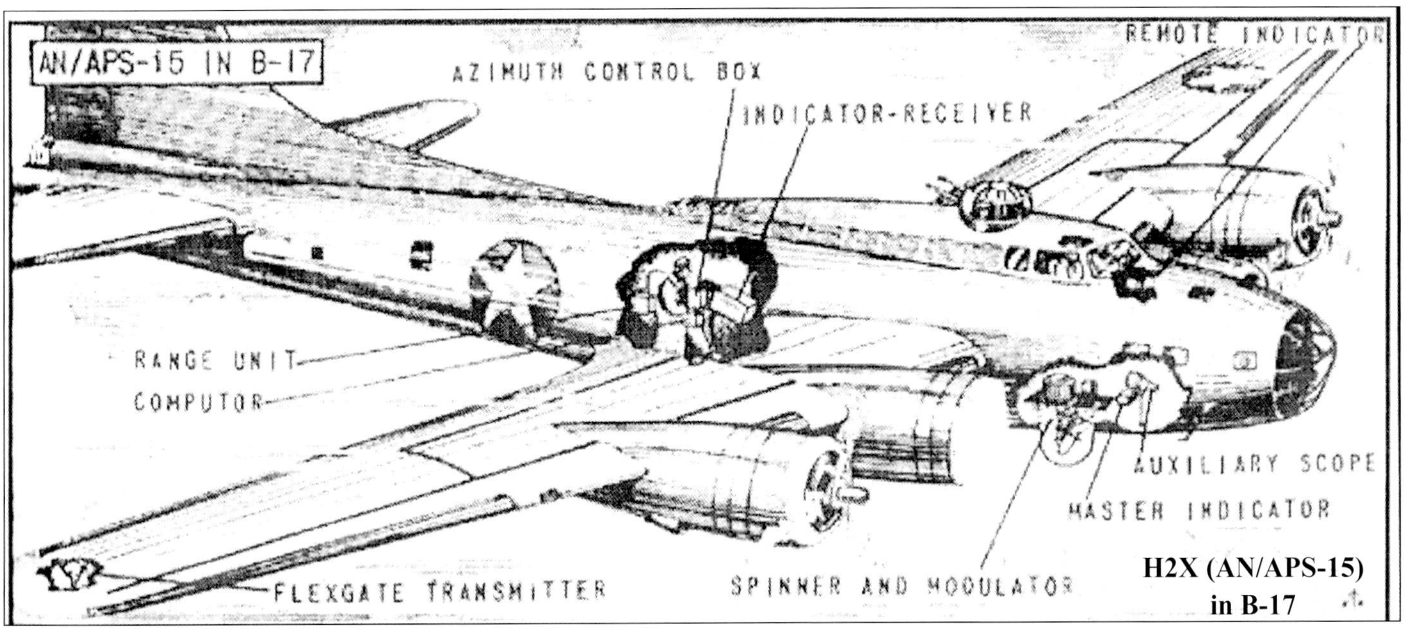

H2X (AN/APS-15) in B-17

Receiver-Indicator
One section of the Receiver-Indicator contained indicators, indicator circuits, and power supplies. The other section consisted of IF, video, and AFC circuits. The main controls were:

RECEIVER GAIN: Control knob which adjusted signal intensity by increasing or decreasing the sensitivity of the received signal in the IF circuit. It varied the brilliance of the returns on both local and remote scopes. In the counter-clockwise position it provided minimum brilliance; in the clockwise position, maximum brilliance.

SEARCH-BEACON: Toggle switch for changing equipment from search to beacon operation.

TRANS HV: Momentary-contact toggle switch for energizing a starting relay, which sent high voltage to the modulator.

TRANS FIL: Toggle switch for turning on the filaments of the tubes, starting the modulator blower motors, and provided high voltage for the receiver.
POWER: Toggle switch which controlled the 115-volt, 400-cycle AC power supply and the 28-volt DC power supply.

TILT UP-TILT DOWN: Toggle switch for starting and changing the direction of the tilt motor, which varied the tilt of the antenna.

MAN-AFC: Toggle switch for cutting the AFC circuit into or out of operation with the IF circuit of the receiver. When the switch was at MAN, the receiver operated without automatic-frequency control and the R/O adjusted the frequency with the OSCILLATOR TUNING control.

LINE VOLT-XTAL CUR: A momentary-contact toggle switch which caused the dial above it to indicate either the crystal current or the line voltage. The dial indicated crystal current at all times except when the R/O checked for 115-volt line voltage by holding the switch briefly at LINE VOLT.

RCT CUR-MOD CUR: Toggle switch for reading transmitter current. When the switch was at RCT CUR, the meter above it indicated average current flowing from the rectifier to the transmitter. When the switch was at MOD CUR, the meter indicated average discharge current of the capacitor into the output tube.

RANGE SWITCH: Control knob with three settings: 5-to-50 mile variable range and 50 and 100 mile fixed ranges.

VARIABLE RANGE CONTROL: Selector switch, not labeled but at the right of the RANGE SWITCH, used for varying the range of the equipment when RANGE SWITCH is at 5-30. It varied the range from approximately 5 to 30 miles.

LUBBER-LINE INTENSITY: Screwdriver control for varying the brilliance of the lubber line in the scope.

VIDEO GAIN: Control knob for adjusting signal intensity on PPI and A scopes by increasing the mount of video amplification. In the counter-clockwise position it provided minimum intensity; in the clockwise position, maximum intensity.

A SCOPE FOCUS: Screwdriver control for focusing the electronic beam on A scope to make images more distinct.

A SCOPE BRILL: Screwdriver control for increasing the brilliance of the sweep trace on the Y scope.

LOCAL PPI FOCUS: Screwdriver control for narrowing the electronic beam which produced the race on the local scope. It brought the beam into focus and made the images more distinct.

LOCAL PPI BRILL: Screwdriver control for increasing the brilliance of range marks on the local scope. In the counter-clockwise position it produced minimum brilliance; in the clockwise position, maximum brilliance.

RANGE MARK INTENSITY: Screwdriver control for regulating the brilliance of range marks on both the local and remote scopes. In the counterclockwise position it provided minimum brilliance; in the clockwise position, maximum brilliance.

A SCOPE SWITCH: Control knob with four settings. Position 1 checked the operating condition of receiver. Position 2 checked the operating condition of transmitter. Position 3 checked the AFC circuits. Position 4 checked the 5:1 divider of the range unit. Position 4 also checked coincidence of bomb release marker with one mile mark when the altitude dial was calibrated. The bomb release marker was continuously applied to one plate of the A scope.

RANGE MARKS: Control knob for selecting 1, 5, or 10 mile range marks on any range of the equipment. In the BR position it set up the bomb release circle.

OSCILLATOR TUNING: Selector switch for adjusting the frequency of the heterodyne oscillator to a difference of 30 mc from the frequency of the transmitted pulse. This control only functioned when MAN-AFC switch was set at MAN, but could be used in either search or beacon operation.

DIAL LIGHTS: Control knob for illuminating the azimuth ring on the edge of the PPI scope.

Control Unit
This unit contained most of the controls for operating the antenna. It controlled the spinner, made adjustments for any degree of sector scanning required up to 360°, provided tilt and azimuth stabilization, provided a lubber line, and selected any amount of sweep delay chosen from 0 to 200 miles. There were four fuse holders mounted at the upper right hand corner of the panel. The two at the left were for AC, the one at bottom right was for DC, and the one at top right was a DC spare. The main controls of the Control Unit were:

MANUAL L-R: Momentary-contact toggle switch controlled the rotation of the antenna manually to the left or right.

Control Unit

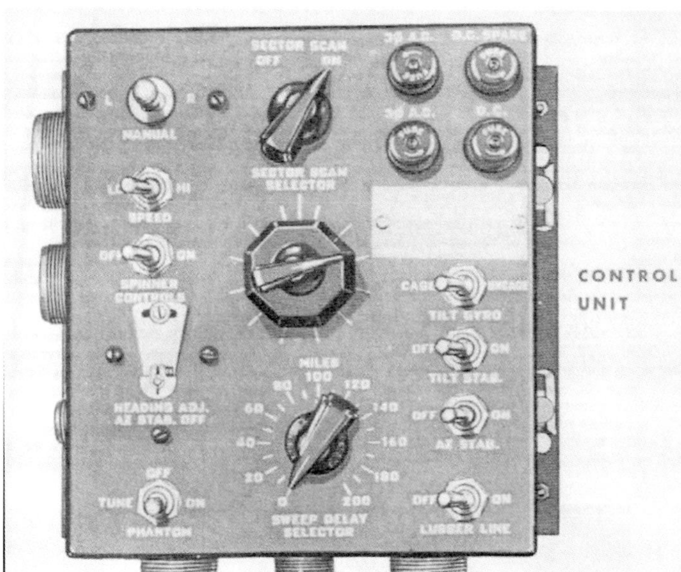

(ROBIF)

SPEED LO-HI: Toggle switch for controlling speed of antenna's rotation. At LO it provided 12 rpm; at HI, 24 rpm.

SPINNER: Toggle switch started and stopped the rotation of the antenna.

PHANTOM: Momentary-contact toggle switch for controlling phantom target.

SECTOR SCAN: Selector switch for turning sector-scan action on or off.

SECTOR SCAN SELECTOR: Dual, concentric control knobs, one mounted above the other. Settings determined the position and width of the sector to be scanned.

SWEEP DELAY SELECTOR: Selector switch with 21 positions which varied range of equipment from 0 to 200 miles by delaying sweep in 10 mile steps.

Range Unit

The primary function of the range unit was to provide crystal-calibrated circuits for all functions of the AN/APS-15A equipment. In addition, it provided delay and gate circuits, which made possible long range navigation.

The front panel had seven screwdriver controls, three receptacles, two fuses, and two pin jacks for testing.

The screwdriver controls, DC fuse, and pin jacks were protected by a cupped door hinged at the left side of the panel. The door was secured by two captive screws which were released to open it.

With the exception of the fuse holders, the only adjustments the R/O may have to do during actual operation were the 5:1 divider, the RANGE ZERO, and the RANGE SLOPE screwdriver controls. These were corrective controls adjusted when the bomb-release circle was calibrated.

AN/APS-15A Computer Box

The dial-type APS-15A computer was designed primarily for the H+B method of direct bombing. In this method, the slant range at which the bomber must be from the target at release point was divided into two components: an H factor (absolute-altitude component) and a B factor (ground speed component). These components were combined electrically to produce a bomb-release circle at the proper slant range.

Greater accuracy was achieved because the ground speed calibrations were more widely spaced on the ground speed dial. Also, it was possible to determine the trail factor of the bombing problem more accurately through the use of various B factor discs for various types of bombs. Twelve discs were supplied with the equipment for three basic bomb types.

A Sweep Timing Knob controlled both open center and altitude delay. When the knob was turned to the left the scope returned, and the bomb-release circle moved out from the center of the scope. This was an advantage in direct bombing, since the bomb-release circle became less defined as it approached the center of the scope. When the knob was turned to the right an altitude delay was introduce in the sweep circuit, making it possible to remove the altitude hole for any altitude up to six nautical miles. The main controls were:

SWEEP TIMING: Control knob for varying the beginning of the sweep. By turning it to the left from 0 (center) as much as six miles of open center could be introduced on the scope. By turning it to the right from 0 as much as six miles of altitude delay could be introduced.

ALTITUDE: Crank knob for varying the position of the BR marker on the scopes. It was geared to the counter above it, which measured altitude or slant range (in feet) up to 90,000 feet. When the GROUND SPEED IN KNOTS control was at its 0 position the altitude indication was the slant range.

GROUND SPEED IN KNOTS: Control knob, geared to the dial above it, for automatically adjusting the BR marker on the scope to agree with the proper bomb release point for a given groundspeed and type of bomb.

DIAL LIGHT: Control knob on side of computer for varying the amount of illumination on altitude and groundspeed dial. In completely counterclockwise position this knob turned the dial lights off.

Twelve interchangeable discs were available for use on the computer covering various types of bombs at various true airspeeds.

APQ-15 Computer Box

The computer box on the APQ-15 radar set solved the range problem through the operation of two knobs: a range knob and an altitude knob.

Range Unit

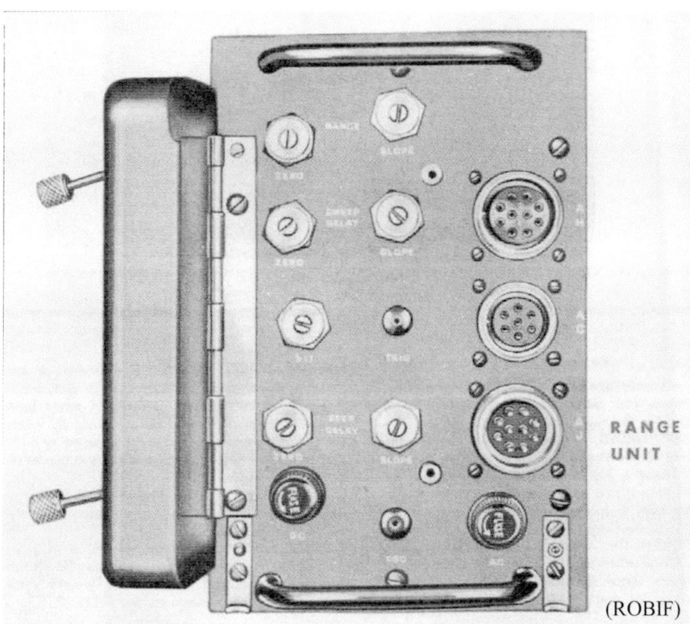

(ROBIF)

Computer Unit

(ROBIF)

The range knob controlled a potentiometer in a bomb-release circuit which introduced electrically a signal or bright spot into the sweep line on the scope. This range signal appeared a specified number of microseconds after the transmitted pulse left the antenna. The delay in microseconds between the transmitted pulse and the range signal equaled an exact distance that the radar wave traveled. The delay time could be changed by varying the potentiometer. A range drum which was controlled by the range knob was calibrated in nautical miles of slant range. By turning this drum (varying the potentiometer) the bright spot (range signal) could be moved along the sweep line between 0.5 and 15 nautical miles of relative distance. Since the sweep line moved around the face of the scope, the range signal appeared as a circle and was called the bomb-release circle.

The altitude knob controlled a potentiometer in an altitude-delay circuit. This was another timing device that delayed the beginning of the sweep a specified number of microseconds after the transmitted pulse. Its purpose was to delay the beginning of the sweep until the transmitted pulse had time to be reflected from the ground directly below the airplane. By using altitude delay the altitude hole (the gap on the scope between its center and the first ground return) could be eliminated.

When the altitude knob was turned, a cursor moved up or down on the face of the computer drum against an altitude scale in nautical miles which denoted how much delay had been introduced.

Altitude delay did not affect the slant range as read from the range drum. The bomb-release circuit was completely separated from the altitude circuit; the pip appeared a specified number of microseconds after the transmitted pulse regardless of altitude delay.

To bomb accurately, a slant range had to be determined that subtended the actual range of the bomb at the point of release. This slant range varied with altitude and ground speed.

It would be impractical to compute a slant range for every combination of altitude and ground speed, but a graph on the computer drum helped the radar operator determine the proper slant range. This graph was lined at the proper slant ranges for a given bomb at all practicable altitudes and a constant ground speed. These slant ranges were plotted as a ground speed line on the chart. Ground speed lines were established for ground speeds from 170 to 350 mph. In order to plot slant range in degrees on the computer chart, the slant range for a given number of degrees (70°) was determined geometrically for certain altitudes. It then was plotted for each altitude, and these points were joined by a degree line. A degree line also was plotted for 68°, 65°, 60°, and so on.

The degrees of slant range selected for the computer drum were not chosen haphazardly, as they depended on the apparent movement of the target. For example, it took the target about the same time to appear to move from 70° to 68° as it did for it to appear to move from 53° to 46°.

Pathfinders, Lead Crew, and SOP as Part of Radar Bombing

AAF Pathfinders

Maj. William Cowart, a VIII BC HQ officer, had been assigned as an advisor to the 329BS by Gen. Eaker during its *Moling* operations. Cowart saw the potential of blind bombing aids such as Gee, and the advantages of establishing a Pathfinder Force similar to that in RAF Bomber Command. Eaker sent Cowart to Washington to get approval to form a special unit to develop and conduct pathfinder operations.

In April 1943 the AAF plan for bad weather pathfinder force development authorized a separate unit under direct VIII BC control at Alconbury, UK, because of its proximity to RAF pathfinder headquarters at Wyton. This unit was to consist of three squadrons: one operating the American version of H2S, one using British H2S and Oboe in B-17s, and the third mounting the same equipment in B-24s. The 325BS of 92BG was selected to train crews with combat experience drawn from other units to be ready for operations by one September, when its aircraft were to lead combat wing formations. The Squadron had four Oboe and two H2S-equipped B-17Fs available for training.

Col. William Cowart (2nd Left) was an 8AF radar bombing pioneer and instrumental in developing the H2X radar apparatus and BTO techniques. **Col. Clement Bird** (5th left) was the CO of the 482BG at Alconbury, UK. (AAF)

On 20 August 1943 the pathfinder unit was officially activated at Alconbury as the 482BG under Col. Baskin Lawrence, a former commander of 92BG Bomb Group, with pathfinder expert Lt.Col. William Cowart named as the Air Executive. Its three Squadrons consisted of the 812BS under Capt. Fred Rabo, who was in the U.S., to return with the first B-17s fitted with the American-built version of H2S. The 813BS, under Capt. William Anderson, was now the redesignated 325BS, which had been directing pathfinder training at Alconbury. The 814BS under Capt. Clement Bird was to operate the B-24s, using personnel including crew who had been part of the unsuccessful *Moling* project. The 482nd was scheduled to move from Alconbury to Podington in July, but as improvements were being made to the runways at Podington the move was postponed until mid-September.

The 482nd Bomb Group participated in its first pathfinder operation on 27 September 1943 using H2S over Emden and continued to provide pathfinder lead aircraft for the 8AF throughout the winter of 1943-44. The AAF decided to eventually end the Group's operational role, and as more equipment and trained personnel became available the AAF planned to institute pathfinder units in each conventional bomb group. On 26 March 1944 the 482nd was taken off regular operations and operated as the ETO radar school and conducted experiments with new equipment.

On 6 March 1944 482BG Pathfinders led the first maximum effort H2X mission on Berlin. Major Fred Rabo's Pathfinder B-17 led the 4th Combat Wing of the 3rd Air Division with former Medal of Honor Medal winner 1Lt. John "Red" Morgan as his co-pilot and Gen. Russell Wilson, the CO of the 3rd Division, as an observer. On the pathfinding run Rabo's B-17 was hit three times by AA fire over Berlin. An engine caught fire and the bomber began to burn and suddenly exploded. Rabo, Morgan, and two waist gunners were able to escape from the bomber, but the other crewmen, including Gen. Wilson, perished. Rabo and the others were taken prisoner.

Lead Crews

From the onset of AAF bombing operations, it soon became apparent that the success of a mission basically depended upon the abilities of the men flying in the lead bombers in group and squadron formations. In July 1943 the VIII BC ordered that each squadron would select four of its most experienced crews to lead bombing missions. After additional training these crews would alternate the lead position on every fourth combat mission. Two bombers in each squadron were outfitted with all the latest navigational

The H2X B-17 Pathfinder of Pilot **Maj. Fred Rabo** (R) and Co-pilot and Medal of Honor winner **1Lt. John Morgan** (L) was shot down on the first maximum effort Pathfinder mission to Berlin. (AAF)

and sighting equipment aids, and whenever possible they were exclusively reserved to serve as leading bombers.

The pilot, navigators, and bombardier, after undergoing especially rigorous training, were the key lead bomber crewmen. On many combat missions a Command Pilot, who usually flew in the co-pilot's seat of a group lead bomber, acted as Combat Wing or Task Force commander. The 482BG furnished pathfinder bombers that led divisions and combat wings while the "host" units supplied bombardiers, Dead Reckoning (DR) navigators, and Air Commanders.

The early Pathfinder (PFF) missions were always accompanied by a deputy with a regular lead crew. When separate PFF units were formed in each division in March 1944 only an Air Commander was usually provided by the host group. Eventually H2X, Gee-H, or Micro-H equipped aircraft were available in every group for the use of lead crews. As soon as sufficient PFF aircraft were available in each group the deputy lead was also so equipped. In many groups lead squadrons were formed; that is, all lead crews were concentrated in one existing squadron by shifting personnel among units in a group. When groups acquired their own PFF aircraft it became standard practice for group leads to carry three navigators: DR, pilotage, and radar. Each squadron maintained four lead crews and always had two in training. If the policy was for all lead crews to be concentrated in one squadron, the total was 16 operational and eight in training. Lead crews were required to fly 30 missions instead of the normal 35 to complete their tour. To denote their status as lead crew they were approved to wear a special blue and gold combat patch.

A lead pilot was selected for his unique capabilities, as the compactness and smooth flight of a formation was mainly dependent upon his skill and judgment. Changes in speed, altitude, and course needed to be made smoothly and gradually. If a lead pilot flew inconsistently the following bombers would have difficulty in maintaining a compact formation. Pilots of lead squadrons were trained not to keep their eyes fixed continually on the group lead, as this tended to make them fly erratically. The preferred way to fly was to continually shift his gaze from the horizon to the group lead. Turns were to be made slowly, for if they were made too fast the formation would become scattered in attempting to follow. Sudden increases in speed had similar effects, but applications of power through a succession of small increments could prevent this. When the lead pilot flew S-turns, trying to lose time to make a control point, the indicated airspeed had to be reduced to 150 mph and the formation was to be warned by radio. The IP turn was to be a definite bank of eight or 10° so that following units had no doubt that it was the IP turn. At all times the lead pilot had to fly a smooth, steady course with no abrupt changes of speed or altitude that could cause problems for the rest of the formation.

Navigation on a lead bomber was provided by three sources: the regular navigator, the pilotage navigator, and the radar navigator. The regular navigator of a lead crew used DR (Dead Reckoning) as he maintained a constant Air Plot which, apart from being the simplest and most accurate means of determining winds being encountered, provided both the pilotage and radar navigators with key information for commencing or recommencing their methods of navigation. While the DR navigator calculated the course by reference to time, ground speed, and drift, with confirmation from his Gee set while in range, the pilotage navigator of the combat wing or group lead plane pin-pointed landmarks he could visually identify. His work, of course, was made more difficult when there were only a few breaks in an undercast on which to make a contribution to confirming correct course.

Cloud cover over northwest Europe was a regular occurrence that made navigation difficult, so during the summer of 1943 frequently lead crews added an additional navigator who practiced "pilotage." A pilotage navigator was usually a senior group or squadron navigator who flew with a map in the nose turret of a B-24 or from a position behind the bombardier in a B-17. Sometimes pilotage was performed by the bombardier in lead B-17s.

By using his H2X equipment to make regular fixes from radar scans the *Mickey* operator (Radar Navigator) provided a third source of navigation. The introduction of H2X radar during the winter of 1943, while primarily intended for bombing through overcast, provided another valuable navigational aid, as it could indicate the bomber's position through the dense undercast. A regular dialogue was conducted by all three navigators to ensure confirmation of course and time at control points. If cloud was present on the bomb run from the IP the radar navigator worked in cooperation with the bombardier. Correct navigation along the planned route was the most critical factor in the execution of a bombing mission. Not only did it place the bombardier at the correct location to drop bombs on the target, but it also ensured that the formation would be at the correct rendezvous points with the fighter escort and avoided the heavy flak concentrations to and from the target.

Standard Operating Procedure (SOP)

The SOP established during the early H2S, Oboe, and H2X-led missions was applicable to all pathfinder techniques. The PFF bomber, loaded with two target smoke marker bombs, would proceed to the airfield of the group scheduled to lead the mission for the division, arriving before briefing. While this aircraft was refueled and bombed up its crew participated in the host group briefing. The Combat Wing Commander for the mission and the lead navigator flew in the lead PFF aircraft. A DR navigator furnished by the host group flew in the deputy PFF aircraft if one was assigned. All other personnel on the PFF bombers were furnished by the PFF squadron involved, although often the rear gunner of the lead aircraft was replaced by an officer of the host group to monitor the formation. If weather prevented the PFF bomber arriving at the host group airfield in time for briefing this was conducted at the home base, and the PFF bomber took off and joined the assigned group at its assembly area. Except in emergencies, all PFF aircraft returned directly to Alconbury when 482BG conducted this service, and the host group had to collect their aircrew from there.

During the mission the lead PFF bomber was responsible for navigating the briefed course, signaling when to open bomb doors, and the dropping of marker flares. The host group provided a deputy for visual bombing who flew the other wing position of the lead element. If bombing was to be by visual means the PFF lead signaled by Aldis lamp to the visual deputy to take the lead at or before the IP, and this aircraft pulled forward slightly ahead of the PFF bombers. At the IP the PFF lead fired double yellow pyrotechnic flares and double red at "Bombs Away" when the smoke markers were also released.

In the first PFF missions there were only sufficient aircraft to mark for the leading combat wings of a division, with succeeding wings having to bomb on smoke trails left by the groups ahead, which were often dissipated by winds. More smoke bombs were dropped by succeeding group leaders as replenishment of the marked spot, but this was far from accurate and led to bomb loads being widely scattered. As soon as more aircraft were available a H2X pathfinder was placed to lead each combat wing, but it was obvious that to achieve a more accurate concentration of bombs a PFF lead was desirable in each group.

PFF Procedure was basically unchanged once a pathfinder bomber could be provided for each group box. The PFF lead also assumed responsibility for visual sighting and carried the group bombardier for the mission.

H2X Bombing Techniques

Solving the Bombing Problem

In radar bombing, the aircraft's H2X radar set (AN/APS-15) helped solve the bombing problem by:

Indicating a track over the target.
Determining the absolute altitude of the airplane.
Computing a slant range equal to the actual range of the bomb.
Indicating the point of release when this slant range is reached.

Crew Duties in Radar Bombing

Prior to the Bombing Run

Prior to the bombing run the bombardier had to calibrate the AN/APQ-15 completely with the aid of the checklist. He made certain that all bombing equipment was ready for use and aided the pilot in setting up the autopilot, if it was to be used. The R/O had to calibrate his radar set completely, being sure that it was ready to use; then to search the target area and pick up the targets to be bombed. The pilot, in addition to setting up the autopilot, had to check to see that the APN-1 (low altitude absolute altimeter) was ready for use and set up his pressure altimeter.

Teamwork between the bombardier and the pilot was essential to a good bombing run. Interphone procedure was particularly important between the R/O and bombardier, and all other crew members were to stay off the interphone during the bombing run, except in an extreme emergency, in order to avoid confusion.

The Pilot's Duties

The pilot followed the radar operator's directions, calling "Level" after he completed each course correction, to let the R/O know that the bomber was level. As soon as the bombardier called that the PDI was ON the pilot followed the PDI (when not using autopilot) and called "Level" after each PDI correction was washed out. During the bombing run the pilot maintained constant altitude and airspeed.

Bombardier's Duties

As soon as the target was identified in the scope, the bombardier bisected it with the tracking line and switched from SEARCH to TRACK. If he already had the target dead ahead by his corrections to the pilot most of the drift was taken out by this time. When the target was within a few degrees of center, horizontally, he engaged the bombsight clutch and disengaged autopilot clutch, if he was using it. He notified pilot that the PDI was ON and killed rate with the rate knobs. He double gripped the rate knobs to keep the target on the tracking line, and in order not to lose the target he rode it on top of the tracking line. He stopped synchronizing on the target at 1.5 miles. With the position knob only he held the target with its bottom edge barely protruding below the tracking line. He set up a collision course with the bombsight's course knobs. If the target was not dead ahead when the run started he brought it to the center with the outer (turn) knob. Any movement of the target from center normally was a result of drift. After each course correction was made he waited for the pilot to call "Level" before he put in another correction (on PDI runs only). This prevented false indications of the target on the scope.

At the three mile mark he unlocked the bomb racks. As soon as the bombs were released he called "Bombs away," switched from TRACK to SEARCH, locked bomb racks, engaged autopilot clutch (if autopilot was being used), disengaged bombsight clutch, and instructed the pilot that it was OK to turn.

Radar Operator's Duties

The R/O was to pick up the target as soon as possible by tuning for maximum target return, so that the bombardier's scope gave him a clear picture. It was vital to the success of a bombing run that the R/O adjusted the tilt and receiver gain so as to keep a clear target return on the bombardier's scope. He gave the pilot the necessary directions to enable him to fly towards the target, always giving azimuth indication or correction first (for example, "Right, 15°") so that the pilot could put the bomber on the heading to the target immediately, and then the R/O called out the range. He continued to guide the pilot, giving azimuth, then range, until the bombardier called "PDI ON." From this point on the azimuth indications were discontinued and only range was given. He called off range every mile until he reached the five mile point, where he then called out range every half mile until the bombs were released.

High Altitude Radar Bombing (HAB)

After Takeoff

In HAB (or HI-OUT) bombing the computer switch was at HI-OUT. The radar operator (R/O) calibrated and tuned his radar set to its maximum efficiency. The bombardier set the SPREAD DIAL at 0, the rate knob at the approximate ground speed (which the radar operator relayed to him), and the altitude dial

Radar Operator's view through **H2X scope**.

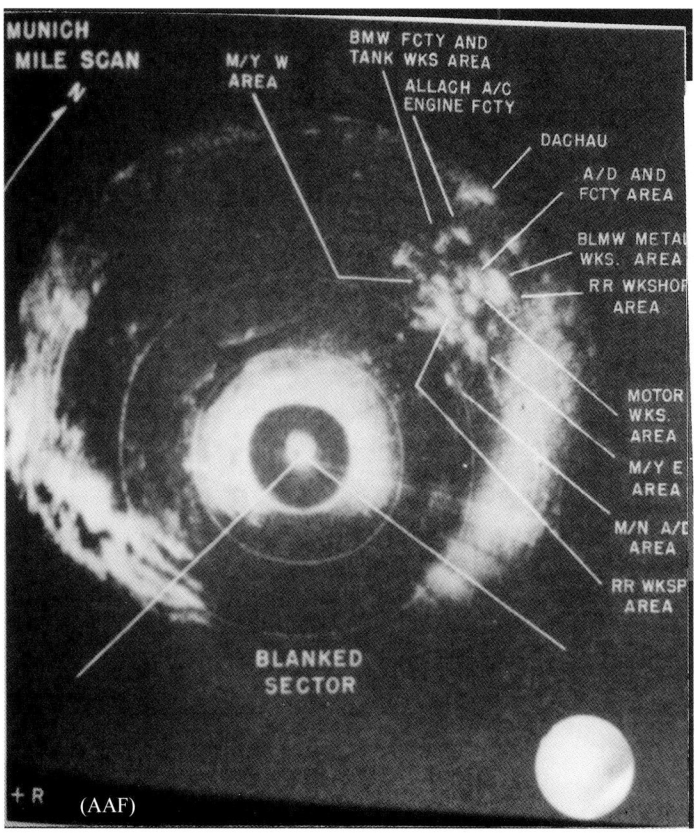

(AAF)

at the normal or minimum setting of 65 feet. He calibrated the AN/APQ-15, determined the absolute altitude of the bombing run, either with the SCR-718 altimeter or his E-6B computer, and helped the pilot set up the autopilot.

On the Bombing Run
R/O: Must pick up the target at 20-25 miles and direct the pilot's flight towards it. Must give correction (for instance, "Left, 30°) and call off range every mile.
Bombardier: Called "Down tilt."

R/O: Must set the spinner at -5° and turn sector scan ON.

Bombardier: Must determine altitude with the AN/APQ-15 by placing SEARCH-TRACK switch to SEARCH and rotating the position control until the tracking line was about one-quarter of the distance up the scope. This placed the release line on the B scope at a distance equal to altitude.

Switched to TRACK and lets the clock run so that the tracking line moved toward the release line (this could be accelerated by using the position knob.

The altitude ring moved up from the bottom of the scope, and when it reached a point halfway between the bottom of the scope and the tracking line the bombardier switched CALIBRATE to RATE ZERO (or used the AUX RATE ZERO control) in order to stop the clock. By careful use of the altitude control, the release line could be moved up to coincide with the altitude ring. When this was done, the bombardier placed the SEARCH-TRACK switch to SEARCH, placed CALIBRATE switch to OPERATE (or released the AUX RATE ZERO button), and rotated the position control until the range line was again at its maximum setting. The SPREAD DIAL was checked to make sure it was on 0. The bombardier informed the R/O to resume normal tilt, and as soon as the target appeared at the top of the B- scope he set the tracking line on the target.

R/O: Stopped making course corrections from this point on and called range every mile.

Pilot: Called "Level' after each PDI correction (if he was not using the autopilot).

Bombardier: Starts "killing" course as soon as the target appeared at the top of the scope and made initial course corrections on SEARCH and refined course on TRACK. As soon as he sets up his approximate course on SEARCH he had to set up his rate and B factor as follows:

1) On SEARCH he bisected the target with the tracking line.
2) Switched to TRACK.
3) Held the target on the tracking line by double gripping the rate knobs; avoiding large double grip corrections.

R/O: Must call off range exactly at seven miles.

Bombardier: Stopped synchronizing at this point and reads his ground speed from the RELATIVE VELOCITY dial. Entered the HAB tables with altitude and ground speed to find the B factor setting for the SPREAD DIAL and entered the proper setting on the SPREAD DIAL.

R/O: Must keep calling the range to the bombardier until he calls "Bombs away."

Bombardier: Turned the rate knob (inner knob) to a velocity of 125, continued to refine the course, and kept the target on the tracking line with the position knob (outer knob) only. He held the target on the tracking line so that the bottom edge barely protruded beneath it as the range decreased and the bomber approached the release point. After the bombs were dropped the bombardier locked the bomb racks, switched from TRACK to SEARCH, engaged autopilot clutch, disengaged the bombsight clutch, and informed the pilot: "Your ship."

Radar Bombing Techniques

Direct Radar Bombing

Radar equipment helped the radar operator to solve the bombing problem in two principal ways. The first of these, called direct bombing, used a pre-computed slant range for the release of the bombs. Since the primary problem was to find a slant range equal to the actual range, the R/O needed to know the altitude and ground speed during the bombing run. With this data and the specific type of bomb both the actual range and slant range could be determined.

For the bombing run altitude was simple to determine, but ground speed was more difficult to determine accurately. The common method of determining ground speed was to find a wind in the vicinity of the target and use an E-6B computer to obtain the ground speed. Then, with whatever type of computer box utilized a bomb-release circle was positioned on the scope at the proper slant range. After the bomb-release circle was set, the R/O tracked the bomber over the target and released the bombs when the target return and the bomb-release circle coincided.

Direct bombing was inaccurate because distortion took place as the target approached the center of the scope. The target was sometimes lost in the "bloom" of the ground returns before the bomb-release circle was reached, requiring the R/O to guess at the release point. Even when the return was not lost there was the widespread tendency to release too soon or too late. If the ground speed used was not accurate a considerable error could be introduced. At 20,000 feet this error can be as much as 400 feet for every 10 mph of ground speed.

Coordinated Radar Bombing

Coordinated bombing coordinated the bombsight with the radar return to overcome some of the shortcomings of the direct method of bombing. It made it possible to synchronize the bombsight for rate, thus canceling out a change in the wind or heading, or any inaccuracy in the computed wind velocity.

The line of sight of the bombsight was identical to the slant range determined by the radar. The R/O had to work closely with the bombardier to coordinate the bombsight with the scope return so that the sighting angle change on the bombsight took place at the same rate as the slant range change shown on the PPI scope. When this was achieved, the bombsight determined a rate of closure and established a dropping angle for the particular bomb that was being used. When the sighting angle (slant range) equaled the dropping angle the bombsight automatically dropped the bombs.

Coordinated bombing has the advantage of partly eliminating faulty judgment. The bombsight was synchronized for ground speed with the synchronization made early in the bombing run so that distortion of the target return or loss of it didn't affect the release point. The correct trail could be set into the bombsight. In case a break in the cloud cover occurred the bombardier was all set to take over.

In order for the R/O and the bombardier to carry out the synchronization of the bombsight the R/O had to furnish the bombardier with specific data. From the bombing altitude, type of bomb, and expected ground speed the bombardier could set the correct disc speed, trail, and approximate dropping angle in the bombsight. The bombardier set the sighting index at 70° while the R/O set the computer drum at 70° of slant range. When the target crossed the 70° slant range marker on the radar indicator the R/O signaled the bombardier to start the rate mechanism of the bombsight. Degrees of slant range then were checked against the successive sighting angles as the target was closed. The rate end of the bombsight was adjusted until the target closed on the scope at the same rate as the sighting angle changed on the bombsight. The bombardier then lifted the trigger, set the racks, and the sight automatically released the bombs.

Synchronous H2X Bombing

With the arrival of production H2X there was a greater effort towards improving the concentration and accuracy of bombing by this technique. While in general H2X could not locate the average pin-point target, it could locate sufficient area targets through cloud to increase 8th Air Force's bombing capability to a marked degree. Additionally, it was found to be of great value in locating targets on visual bombing days by aiding the locating of check points and correcting navigation over cloud on the way to the target. Photographs of the images on H2X scopes taken over enemy territory were used to train radar operators in identifying precise locations. From study of such photographs operational analysts concluded that there were industrial targets situated beside cities or shore lines that might be pin-pointed with some accuracy through reference to the irregular shape of the landmark image. These light images were known as "blips," as a few very large targets produced this blip of their own, which was discernible on the H2X scope. By approaching the identifiable landmark from the appropriate direction a target could be bombed by the aid of its known distance and direction from the landmark. This led to intensive investigation and ultimately the institution of a technique using H2X in conjunction with the Norden Bombsight and automatic pilot system.

Where a landmark could be positively identified from the radar scope blip a calculation of altitude and distance from a nearby target gave a sighting angle, enabling a bombardier to incorporate this setting in the Norden to synchronize the instrument. As the bomber proceeded along the track towards the target the H2X operator provided additional sighting angles to the bombardier to allow him to recheck the synchronization of the sight. The bombs released automatically at the point computed by the sight, as if it were a visual drop. A further benefit of this link between radar operator and bombardier was that in cloud breaks the bombardier could easily take over for visual sighting, as only minor corrections would be necessary. To aid this development tables were prepared for use in converting distance and altitude into sighting angles for the bombsight. By adding sighting angle data to the H2X computer drum the radar operator had the means of furnishing the bombardier with data on ground speed, drift, and distance for every mile until the aircraft was within four or five miles of the target.

This coordinated method of bombing was first tried in April 1944, and was soon shown to improve overcast bombing with H2X. Its most notable application, in the early period of development, was the bombing of coastal defenses in Normandy on D-Day, 6 June. As a lateral bomb pattern was required, multiple elements of 18 to 36 bombers flew line abreast with an H2X pathfinder in the center of the line. The radar operators had been intensively trained to recognize the coastline patterns on their scope and, despite a complete overcast, bombing was accomplished without any of the 1000-plus bombers dropping short of a line 300 yards beyond the beaches.

On 24 June the first major attempt to bomb an important strategic pinpoint target by synchronous H2X was carried out against an oil refinery at Bremen, where there were clear coast and river images on the radar scopes. The target survived, but several bomb patterns were very close, showing that this technique had great potential. Further study of synchronous bombing established that while a reasonable degree of success could be achieved against city areas or isolated industrial complexes, its use against small targets gave only a slight chance of bombs being placed on the desired MPI. Several other factors affected the accuracy of H2X attacks, most notably that one out of every four sightings proved ineffective because the H2X equipment failed, although this position improved during the final months of the war. It was also found that a much longer bomb run was required than for visual attacks (approximately 40 miles) to give a higher chance of success. Moreover, there was a striking correlation between the degree of cloud cover on the bomb run and bombing errors. Even a small break in the overcast enabled the bombardier to synchronize his bombsight and achieve considerable accuracy.

AN/APQ-13 Radar

In the ETO the AAF had used both the British H2S and American H2X/APQ-15 beginning in the fall of 1943. In August the AAF decided to develop another new X-Band bombing radar set from "off the shelf" components to be developed and built by Bell Laboratories and its Western Electric subsidiary and MIT's Radiation Laboratory.

In the Pacific Theater, combat-ready B-29s were to be equipped with this improved ground scanning H2X radar, designated as the AN/APQ-13. The radar was used for high altitude area bombing, search, and navigation. The radome was carried on the aircraft belly between the bomb bays and was partially retractable. The radar operated at a frequency of 9375 ± 45 megahertz and used a sperheterodyne receiver. Computation for bombing could be performed by an impact predicator. A range unit permitted a high degree of accuracy in locating beacons. Major Japanese cities were generally on coastlines or rivers, which made them excellent radar targets. Emulating RAF Bomber Command tactics, the B-29s flew in streams, rather than formations, over Japanese targets, dropping their incendiaries with devastating effect.

The new radar operator was stationed in the only space available in the B-29; the former bunk area in the aft of the rear pressurized compartment, a position that separated him from the navigator in the forward compartment. The first B-29 radar installations had one radar operator facing forward on the left side of the bomber, but later models provided for two operators facing outboard on the left side of the bomber. Initially, the radar operator and scope were mounted inside the aircraft, but the physical unit was mounted in the unpressurized rear compartment; however, difficulties with air pressure, cold temperatures and electrical problems occurred at high altitudes. The main unit was then mounted at the radar operator's station in the rear pressurized

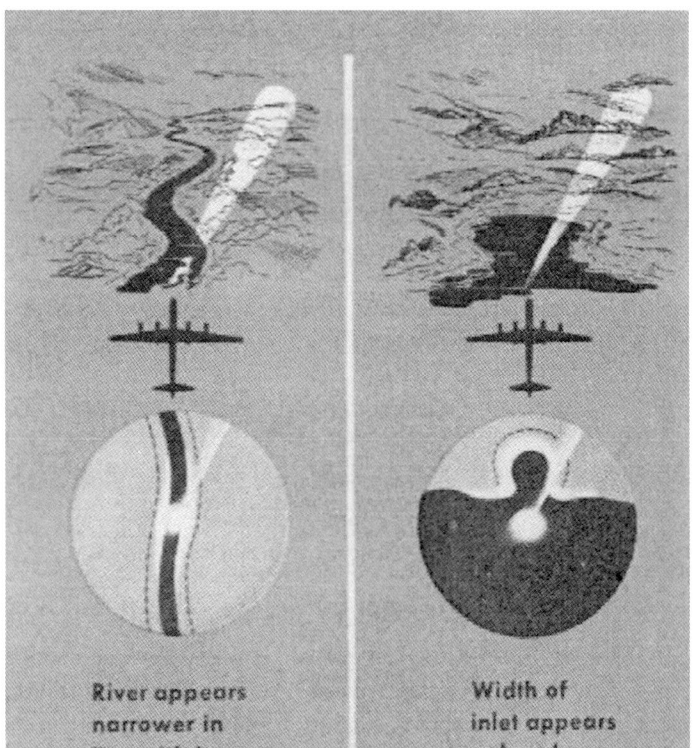

Radar operators view through **AN/APQ-13 Radar scope**: river view (left) and inlet view (right). (AAF)

compartment except for the inverter, which was located beneath the floor near the radar operator, and the radio frequency unit, which was located in the barrel-shaped enclosure just behind the radar antenna dome.

APQ-13 radar was the most advanced bombing radar available when the B-29 became operational and provided accurate fixes on the bomber's position when used with radar beacons. In November 1944 60% of the XXBC's sorties encountered radar malfunctions due to the inverters and lack of spares and inadequate maintenance by poorly trained personnel. However, in the early stages of the bombing offensive radar did make it possible for the bombers to reach their briefed land fall points by computing the winds at bombing altitude, in navigating the bombers over the initial point (IP), and getting it accurately aligned on the axes of attack.

APQ-13 radar was less accurate than conventional optical bombing, with less than 1% of its bombs hitting within 1,000 feet of the aiming point. In early operations it was limited by the following:

1) The radar operators were hastily and insufficiently trained in the United States, which left them unable to evaluate the information depicted on their radarscopes in combat conditions. The radar operators also lacked sufficient navigation skills, and the aircraft navigator had to complete the computations required for bombing and navigation from his remote radarscope in the forward compartment.
2) During the early combat missions from the Marianas the bombers' routes avoided the Japanese-held islands south of Japan to prevent early warning, and thus the radar operator and bombardier were unable to use these landmarks for navigational checkpoints. The B-29s were then left to fly over open water for seven hours with no checkpoints between takeoff and landing.
3) The high bombing altitudes caused 25% of the airborne radar to malfunction, and the return signals at these altitudes were too weak to be of much use.
4) The strong jet stream winds at the high bombing altitudes limited the axes of attack to a downwind bombing run that precluded the maximum use of the radar, as the target approaches with the more distinct radar markers were rarely used.
5) Without the MX-344 bombing computer, effective bombing by radar of priority industrial targets using HE bombs could not be expected because of accuracy limitations.

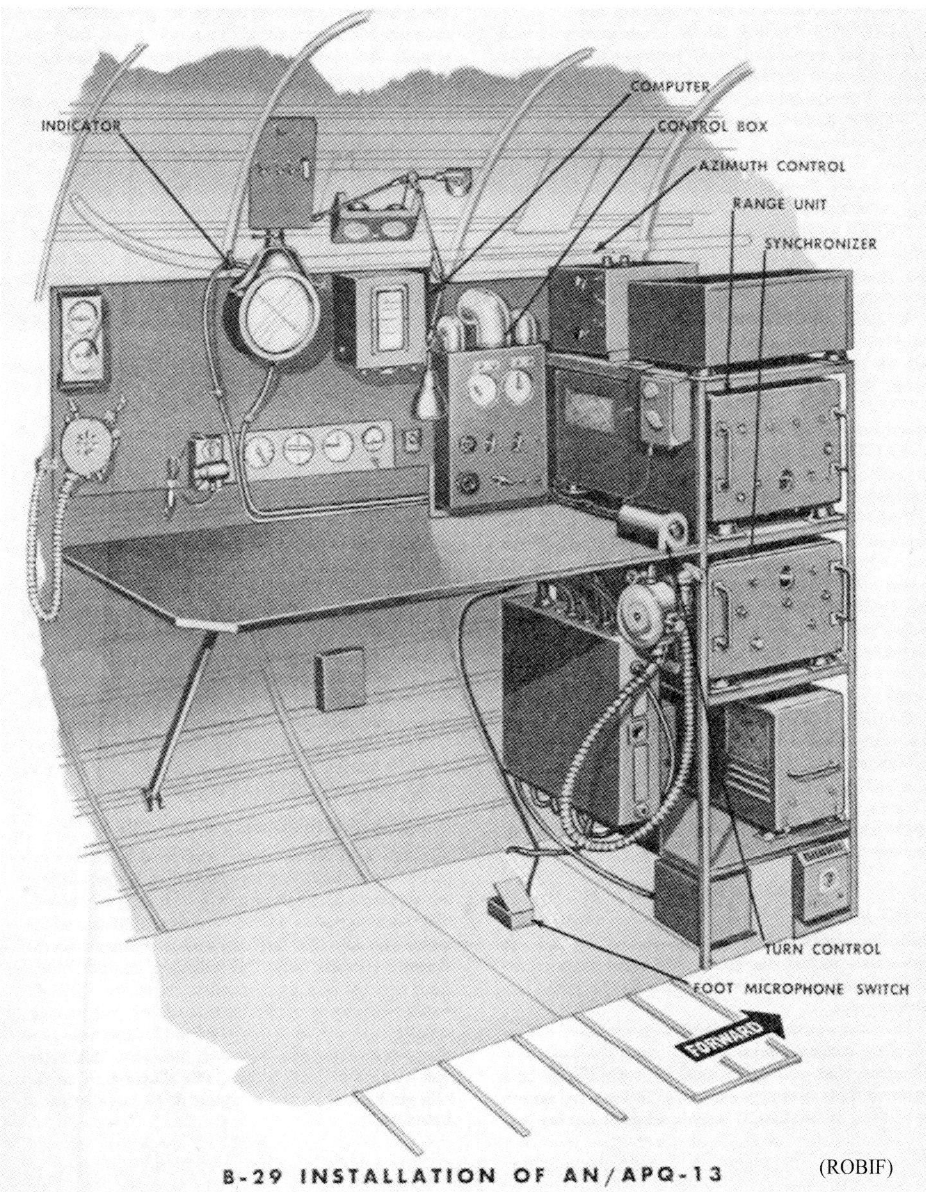

(ROBIF)

During Phase One of operations radar did assist initially in enabling aircraft to reach briefed landfall points, in computing the winds at bombing altitude, in navigating the aircraft over the initial point (IP), and getting it properly aligned on the axis of attack.

With intensive theater radar training of both radar operators and navigators, the initiation of low-level incendiary attacks presented an operation well within the capabilities of crews and equipment. This permitted bombing using clearly defined land-water contrast points as checkpoints. As radar attacks progressed to the smaller industrial concentrations lack of enemy defenses made it feasible to give radar requirements prime consideration in mission planning.

Steady improvement in operating techniques, target, materiel, and mission planning resulted in the achievement of an acceptable degree of radar bombing accuracy, with reference to incendiary destruction of urban areas. Indications were that 18% of bombs were falling within 2,000 feet, 50% within 4,000 feet, and 75% within 6,000 feet of aiming points.

Dr. William Shockley, who was awarded the Nobel Prize for his invention of the transistor in 1956, developed a ground-based radar trainer. The complicated device was used at Smokey Hill AFB in early 1944 to train personnel for radar bombing in simulated bombing runs on Japanese targets. The radar operators were extensively trained in navigation and target identification utilizing clearly defined land-water contrast points. This improved intensive Stateside operational radar training, along with the initiation of low-level incendiary missions, led to conditions that were within the competence of the operators and capabilities of the equipment. Once Japanese defenses diminished over the more important targets the smaller, virtually undefended cities were attacked, and radar was given primary consideration in mission planning. As time passed there was a continuous improvement in radar techniques when used in incendiary attacks. Improved target information and mission planning resulted in satisfactory radar bombing accuracy. This satisfactory accuracy was not of the "pickle barrel" standard by any means. Post attack analysis documented that 18% of the bombs fell within 2,000 feet of the aiming point, 50% within 4,000 feet, and 75% within 6,000 feet, all of which were sufficient when using incendiaries to burn out large urban areas. In late 1945 the APQ-13 became the first military radar converted to a domestic peacetime application as a storm warning radar. About thirty systems were converted and installed on military bases and replaced by the AN/CPS-9 system in 1949.

Typical Installation of AN/APQ-13

In the B-29, for example, the R/O's seat and table were just behind the waist turrets and on the left side of the bomber. The range unit, synchronizer, and rectifiers were mounted on a rack at the right side of the table. The azimuth box and selsyn phasing unit were above the range unit. The indicator, computer, and main control box were mounted above the table directly in front of the R/O. Also in front of the R/O and not installed as part of the AN/APQ-13 equipment were a repeater compass, airspeed indicator, altimeter, and a bomb-release switch.

AN/APQ-13 Described

The AN/APQ-13 radar system was designed for high altitude navigation and bombing through overcast with the additional worth of providing highly accurate beacon ranging. The system functioned efficiently both day and night in temperatures ranging from -40°F to +122°F, in relative humidity as high as 90%, and at altitudes up to 35,000 feet. The total installed weight, including interconnecting cables and mountings for the various units, was approximately 630 pounds. Basically, the AN/APQ-13 was a combined transmitter-receiver for high frequency radio pulses designed to operate from an electrical supply of 26-28 volts DC. Its maximum range for reception of ground returns was 100 miles, but it could receive signals from a radar beacon as far as 300 miles away.

Function

Briefly, the system functioned in this manner: a train of extremely short but intense pulses of radio frequency energy was transmitted in a beam from a rotating antenna. An object in the path of the beam reflected some of the energy, and the transmitting antenna intercepted a portion of this reflected energy. The received pulses, or echoes, were detected and amplified on the Plan Position Indicator (PPI scope), where the Radar Operator (R/O) could determine both the distance to and bearing of the object.

The **AN/APQ-13** radar system in the B-29 was designed for high altitude navigation and bombing through overcast with the additional worth of providing highly accurate beacon ranging. (Author/Pima)

AN/APQ-13 Control Box

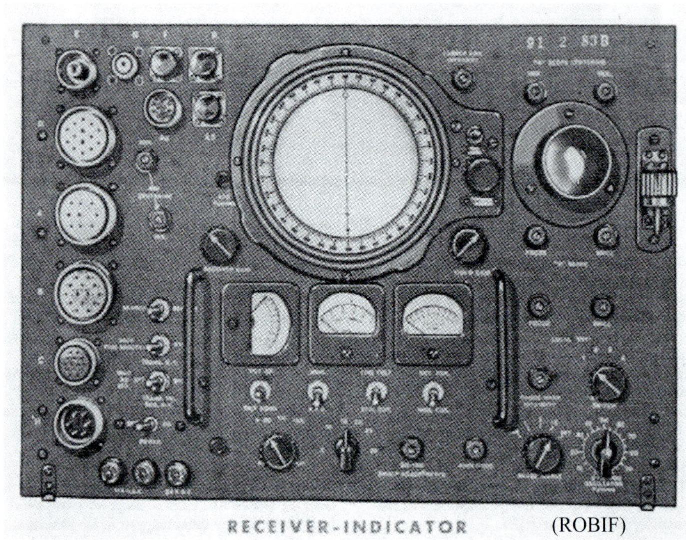

(ROBIF)

Components of the AN/APQ-13

The APQ-13 consisted of:

Antenna Equipment	AS-53/APQ-13
Modulator	MD-12/APQ-13
Radio Frequency Unit	BC-1276-A
Synchronizer	SN-7/ APQ-13
Indicator	ID-41/ APQ-13
Control Box	C-71/ APQ-13
Inverter	PE-218-D
Rectifier	RA-90-A
Voltage Regulator	TF-12-A
Phasing Unit	CN-6/ APQ-13
Torque Amplifier	AM-19/ APQ-13
Azimuth Control Box	C-72/ APQ-13
Computer	CP-7/ APQ-13
Range Unit	CP-6/ APQ-13
Turn Control	GE 1027

Principal parts of the AN/APQ-13

The principal parts of the AN/APQ-13 equipment were the main control box, indicator, computer box, azimuth control box, synchronizer, range unit, and antenna unit.

Main Control Box

The main control box contained the switches that governed the operation of the system. Two meters indicated the various operating currents and voltages and the elevation tilt of the antenna. The main controls were:

POWER: Pushbutton switch. The ON button started the inverter which supplied power to all units, except the modulator and transmitter, which required high voltage. The OFF button stopped the inverter.

TRANS: Pushbutton switch which controlled the supply of high voltage current to the modulator and transmitter units. It was dangerous to apply high voltage immediately to the high frequency transmitting tube and the R/O had to remember to wait at least five minutes after pushing the POWER button before pushing the TRANS button ON.

RCVR TUNING: Control knob with which the receiver (RCVR) was tuned to the intermediate frequency to obtain the best possible picture on the scope.

RCVR GAIN: Control knob with which the sensitivity of the receiver and the brilliance of the picture on the scope was changed. By keeping the receiver-gain control down as far as possible, the R/O could differentiate between small and large targets because a large target gave a brighter and larger return than a small one. When searching for rivers or bodies of water, however, the receiver-gain control had to be turned up, making the terrain give an especially bright return on the screen in contrast to the weak return from the water.

RANGE NAUT MILES: Five position switch with which a maximum range of 4, 10, 20, 50, or 100 miles could be selected. When the switch was at 4 the scope covered four miles of range only if the OPEN CENT switch was IN.

OPEN CENT: Toggle switch which allowed the four mile sweep to begin either at the center of the scope or at a distance from the center equal to a one mile interval. The latter position was used to expand or separate returns from nearby targets when on search.

AFC BEACON: Three position switch which selected the type of operation desired, enabling the R/O to use the set with or without AFC (Automatic Frequency Control). With the switch at BEACON the set was used as a homing device or navigational aid in conjunction with a radar beacon. When the switch was at AFC OFF there was no automatic frequency control and the set had to be tuned manually. When the switch was at AFC ON the set automatically kept itself in tune and the manual tuning control had no effect. The AFC voltage had to be kept properly adjusted in order to have the AFC circuit work satisfactorily.

TRANS-XTAL-AFC: Three-position selector switch used in conjunction with the volt meter on the control box. By placing the switch at XTAL I the current in the rectifying crystal of the receiver was measured. When the switch was at TRANS I the current in the transmitting tube of the radio-frequency unit was read. When the switch was at AFC V, with the AFC-BEACON switch set at AFC ON, the voltage at the output of the AFC unit could be read. With AFC OFF the repeller voltage supplied to the radar beat frequency oscillator could be read. In the first two positions of the switch give a current indication, while in the last switch position voltage was measured.

ANT TILT: Three position toggle switch which controlled the tilt of the antenna from 10° above to 45° below horizontal. The degree of tilt on a tilt meter was read on the control box. The ANT TILT switch was held either up or down to tilt the antenna, and when the switch was released it snapped back to a neutral position.

CONTINUOUS: Toggle switch used to keep the spinner rotating continuously clockwise at above 20 rpm. Before turning this switch ON the R/O

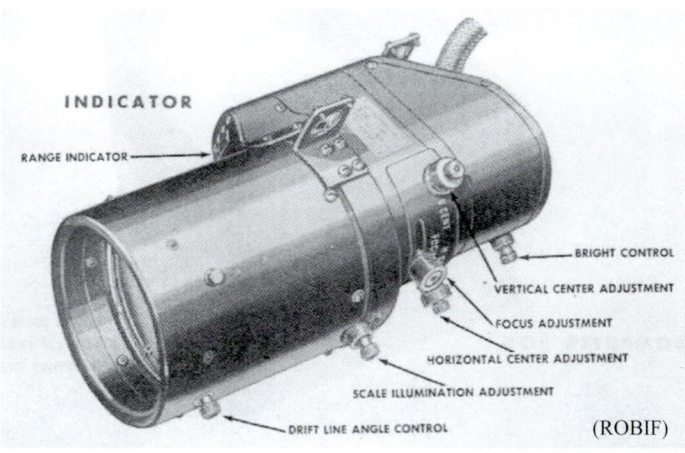

(ROBIF)

AN/APQ-13 Indicator installation with red bomb release switch above. (Author/Pima)

Radar Operator (R/O) during a B-29 bombing run. The indicating equipment consisted of two identical PPI scopes, one for R/O and the other for the navigator. (AAF)

had to be sure the indicators were correctly phased. The spinner was to be rotated two or three times with the SEARCH CW-CCW switch to avoid damage to the selsyn system.

SEARCH-CW-CCW: Three position toggle switch similar to the ANT TILT switch, which rotated the azimuth motor either clockwise or counter-clockwise. It could be used only when the CONTINUOUS switch was OFF. When the switch was released it snapped back to a neutral position.

Indicator
The indicating equipment consisted of two identical PPI scopes, one for R/O and the other for the navigator. In these scopes the radial sweeps were synchronized with the transmitter pulse (to determine target range), and the circular sweeps were synchronized with the azimuth of the rotating antenna (to determine target bearing). The azimuth or bearing of the target could be read directly from a scale on the scope marked clockwise from 0° to 360°. Bearings obtained when azimuth stabilization was not being used were all relative to the position of the interceptor.

The Plan Position Indicator (PPI scope) was a cathode ray tube in which a map-like view of the area scanned was produced on a fluorescent screen by a rotating sweep line. On its face was a movable plastic scale with five etched concentric circles which could be used for estimating distances on all ranges. Cursor lines were etched on this scale for use in navigation. Degrees of azimuth were lettered on a fixed ring on the outside edge of the scope. The main scope was located in the radar compartment and the auxiliary scope in the navigator's compartment. The main controls were:

BRIGHT: Varied the brilliance of the sweep line on the scope.

SCALE CONTROL: Turned the bearing cursor to enable the reading of an accurate bearing from the azimuth scale.

SCALE ILLUM: Adjusted the illumination of the plastic scale on the face of the scope.

H CENT: Shifted the sweep trace horizontally to the right or left, enabling the setting of the sweep starting point equidistant from the right and left sides of the scope.

V CENT: Shifted the sweep trace vertically, enabling the setting of the sweep starting point equidistant from the top and bottom of the scope. When the sweep was correctly centered with the H CENT and V CENT controls, its starting point was directly underneath the intersection of the etched drift lines on the plastic scale.

FOCUS: Varied the sharpness of the returns on the scope as the knurled knob was turned.

Computer Box
The computer box was designed to determine range and altitude accurately for the solution of the bombing problem. Two potentiometers regulated the voltage supplied to the range and altitude delay circuits in the range unit. The range control positioned a range signal at a slant range which varied between 0.5 and 15 nautical miles. The altitude control delayed the beginning of the sweep on the scope for a time interval determined by the altitude set into the computer. The main controls were:

NORMAL-CAL ZERO: Toggle switch, which at NORMAL provided an altitude delay of from 15,000 to 35,000 feet in the altitude circuit. The crosshair was set according to altitude by rotating the altitude knob. When the switch was at CAL ZERO the altitude delay circuit was by-passed.

ILLUM: Knob that adjusted the amount of illumination desired for the computer box.

BOMB-RELEASE MARKER: Toggle switch, marked ON-OFF, that placed or removed the bomb release circle on the scope.

ALTITUDE CONTROL: Knob which controlled the amount of altitude delay set into the altitude delay circuit when the NORMAL-CAL ZERO switch was at NORMAL. This control removed the altitude hole from the scope entirely or varied its size as desired. The control didn't work when the NORMAL-CAL ZERO switch was at CAL ZERO.

SLANT RANGE CONTROL: Knob that controlled the range delay circuit in the range unit. This knob set the proper ground speed, sighting angle, or slant range on the computer chart. The knob rotated the computer drum and its attached bomb release chart to indicate from 0.5 to 15 nautical miles of slant range. When this control was rotated it also caused the bomb release circle to move a relative distance on the scope. Additionally, it could be used in combination with the altitude control to determine the absolute altitude or bombing altitude of the airplane.

SLANT RANGE VERNIER: Used for fine adjustment of the range control.

Azimuth Control Box
The azimuth control box directed the antenna sector-scan, sweep delay, and azimuth stabilization. The main controls were:

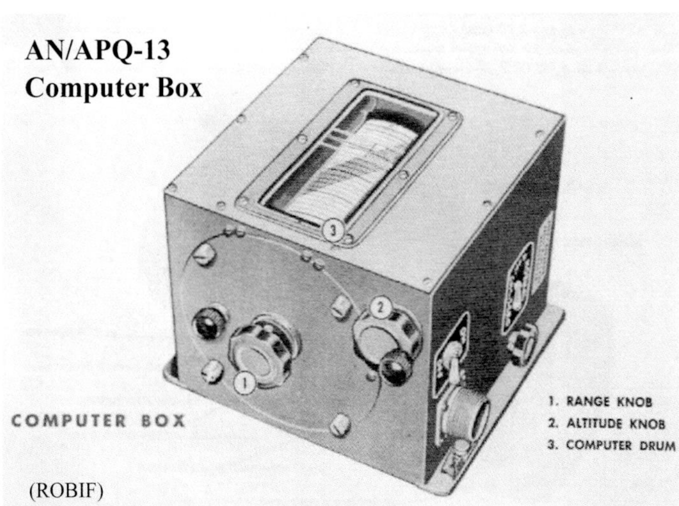

AN/APQ-13 Computer Box

(ROBIF)

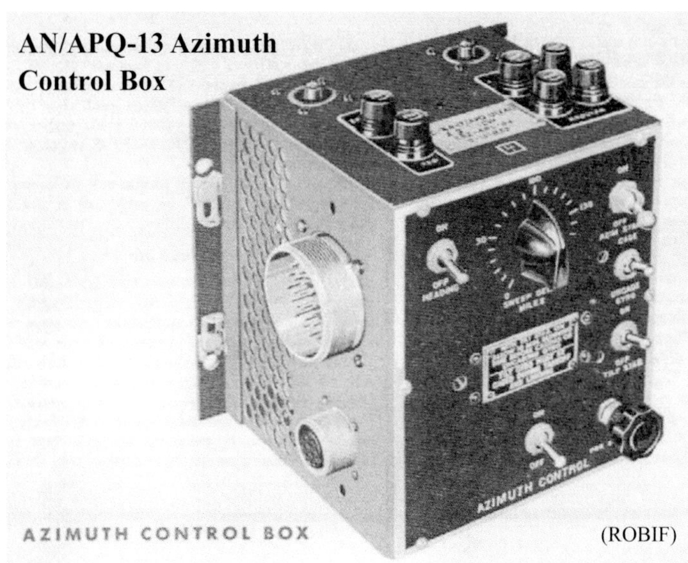

AN/APQ-13 Azimuth Control Box

(ROBIF)

HEADING: Toggle switch which tied in a pulse from the microswitch and cam of the antenna with the scope. When the switch was ON, a lubber line appeared on the scope to show the aircraft's heading; and when it was OFF, no lubber line appeared.

SWEEP DELAY MILES: Knob with 21 positions that delayed the start of the sweep on the scope from 0 to 200 nautical miles in 10 mile steps. It allowed the use of ranges not available on the RANGE NAUT MILES switch and was designed primarily to extend the area for beacon operation. For example, if the beacon was set at a range of 220 miles the SWEEP DELAY MILES switch was set at 150 and the RANGE NAUT MILES switch at 100, and the scope could receive signals from any beacon between 150 and 250 miles away.

AZIM STAB: Toggle switch marked ON-OFF. When this switch was ON the flux gate compass was coupled to the radar system, thus maintaining true north at the top of the scope. This control made the scope an oriented map, with the bomber's true heading indicated by the heading line. When the switch was OFF the top of the scope always represented the bomber's heading.

GYRO: Toggle switch marked CAGE-UNCAGE in early systems.

TILT STAB: Toggle switch marked ON-OFF in early systems.

SECTOR SCAN: Toggle switch marked ON-OFF. When this switch was ON scans could be made of any 60° sector within the forward 180° of the bomber's direction of flight, or within 90° on each side of the bomber's true heading. This switch worked only when the ANTENNA CONTINUOUS switch on the control box was OFF.

POS ADV: Knob selected any 60° sector to be scanned through 90° on each side of the bomber's true heading.

Synchronizer
The synchronizer unit had two functions. One part contained the AFC circuit, several stages of intermediate frequency amplification, the detectors, and the video amplifiers necessary for the receiver portion of the set. The other part of the synchronizer controlled the sweep voltages and range markers applied to the scope. The sweep circuits produced sawtooth voltages to control the speed of the sweep for different ranges. A range marker generator produced the range pips applied to the sweep. By synchronizing the sweep with the received signals this unit made it possible to determine range and azimuth. The main controls are:

AN/APQ-13 Synchronizer Unit

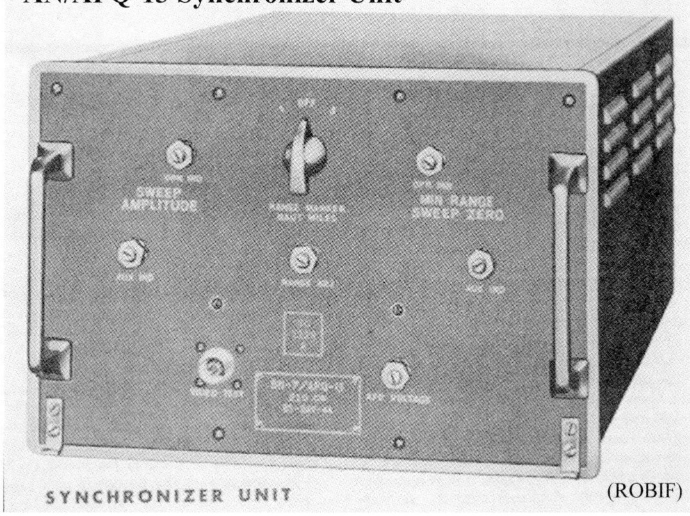

(ROBIF)

SWEEP AMPLITUDE: Screwdriver control that changed the amplitude (physical length on the scope) of the sweep without changing the range (time) it covered. As the sweep line lengthened, the number of range marker pips remained constant but their spacing increased. The scale of the map thus was altered in proportion to the amplitude of the sweep. The end of the sweep was to be just within the limits of the scope.

RANGE ADJ: Screwdriver control that changed the range represented by the sweep line. The sweep line was lengthened and another pip added at the proper interval, but the physical spacing of the pips remained the same. The extent or range of the map thus was altered, but the scale remained constant as the amplitude of the sweep varied. The correct adjustments were made by placing the correct pip, for a given range, at the end of the sweep line.
RANGE MARKER NAUT MILES: Three position switch which placed the one mile and five mile range markers (concentric circles of light) on the scope. Thus, on all ranges there was a range marker for every mile, or one for every five miles, of slant range.

MIN RANGE SWEEP ZERO: Screwdriver control which was used to change the size of the open center on the scope. To set it correctly OPEN CENTER switch on the control box was turned to IN, the RANGE switch set to 4, and the open center circle was to coincide with the first etched circle from the center of the scope.

AFC VOLTAGE: Screwdriver control changed the AFC voltage to give maximum target returns. If the AFC switch on the control box was ON this voltage was maintained and the set remained constantly in tune.

Range Unit
The range unit was the heart of the AN/APQ-13 radar set. It contained six major circuits: crystal-oscillator count divider, range-delay, altitude-delay, sweep-delay, calibrating, and 250-volt rectifier circuits. The unit controlled the timing of the sweep and the bomb release pulse circuits. The sweep delay was used to vary the distance at which the selected range became effective. The delay in the bomb release circuit controlled the indication of the current bomb release time for a target depending upon the prevailing speed and altitude of the bomber. The altitude delay circuit delayed the beginning of the sweep. The main controls of the range unit were:

ALTITUDE SLOPE: Screwdriver control that adjusted the amount of delay between the transmitted pulse and the beginning of the sweep on the cope. This adjustment was used to calibrate altitude.

SWEEP SLOPE: Screwdriver control used to calibrate the sweep delay circuits on the 10 mile delay or any multiple thereof up to 200 miles. This control was to be adjusted by a technician.

AN/APQ-13 Range Unit

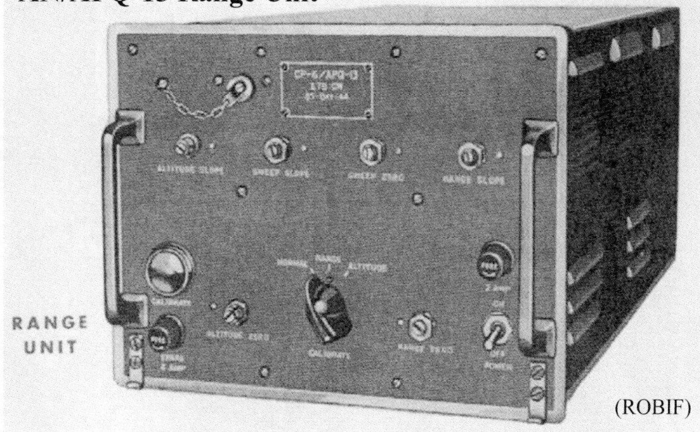

(ROBIF)

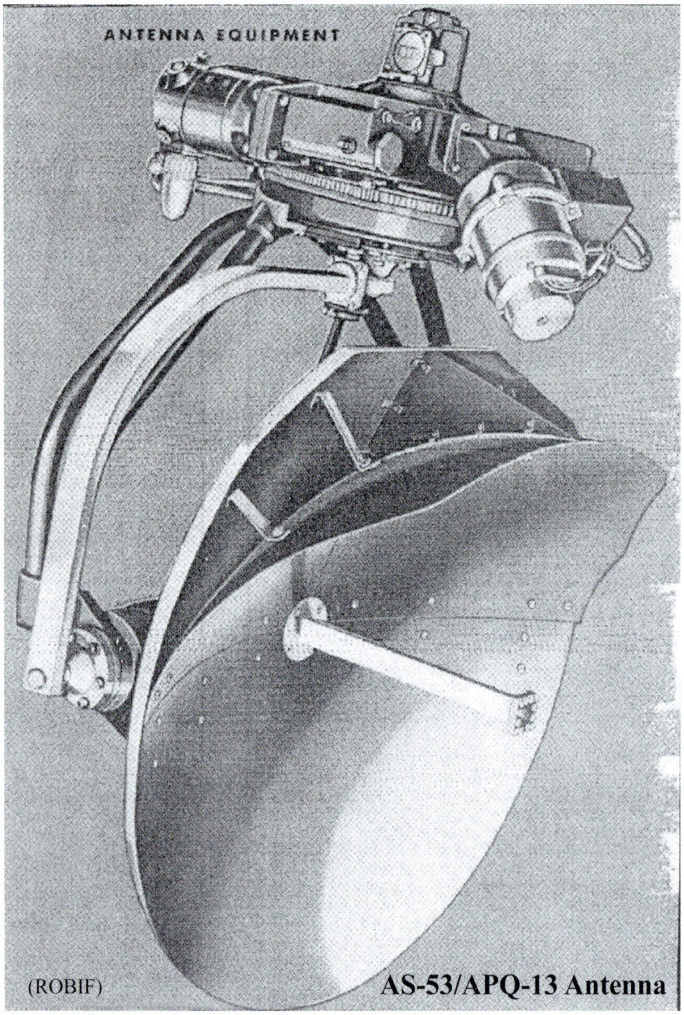

The radar antenna for the APQ-13 radar was mounted in a hemispherical radome (arrow) that was installed on the bottom of the fuselage between the bomb bays. (AAF)

Close up of the B-29 radome that enclosed the 30 inch AS-53/APQ-13 antenna. (Author/Pima)

SWEEP ZERO: Screwdriver control that directed the start of the sweep to allow zero range to correspond to the zero mile echo (the delay inherent in the modulator). This control was to be adjusted by a technician.

RANGE SLOPE: Screwdriver control used to calibrate the range delay circuit, enabling the setting of the range on the chart to represent exact slant range distances.

CALIBRATE (lamp): Neon lamp which dimmed or blinked when two pulses under calibration coincided.

ALTITUDE ZERO: Screwdriver control used to set altitude delay at exactly three nautical miles on the calibrated scale of the computer.

CALIBRATE: Three-position switch, marked NORMAL-RANGE-ALTITUDE. The NORMAL position was used during all operations except when calibrating the range unit. The RANGE position was used when calibrating the range delay circuits against the slant range scale of the computer chart. The ALTITUDE position was used when calibrating the altitude delay circuits in the range unit against the computer's altitude scale.

RANGE ZERO: Screwdriver control used to set one mile of slant range at exactly one mile on the calibrated scale of the computer.

NORMAL-TEST COUNT: Toggle switch that permitted the normal operation of the set when it was set at NORMAL. The TEST COUNT position was for maintenance only.

Antenna Equipment and Radome

The 30 inch AS-53/APQ-13 radar antenna was mounted in a hemispherical radome that was installed on the bottom of the fuselage between the bomb bays. Wartime photos were usually censored and the radome was painted out. The antenna (called a "spinner") was dish pan-shaped and was mounted on edge, was rotated about its vertical axis, and could be tilted through a small angle about a horizontal axis while rotating. The radome could be extended or retracted by the radar operator by a retracting motor located under the wing.

The function of the antenna was to transmit the radio frequency energy into space and receive the reflections of this energy. An RF waveguide transmission line connected the antenna to the radio frequency unit. The unit consisted of a feed horn antenna with a reflector mounted on a spinner unit. The unit was so arranged to rotate it continuously in a horizontal plane at approximately 20 rpm for search operation, or to oscillate it over a selected arc for sector scanning. It could be tilted in a vertical plane through 55° (from 10° above to 45° below the horizontal). An elevation position indicator on the main control box related the antenna's position. The antenna drove a selsyn transmitter through a 1:10 gear ratio, and the selsyn repeaters in the indicators were reciprocally geared 10:1 to their deflecting coils, so the coils were interlocked to reproduce the position of the antenna in azimuth. Because of these gear ratios, the deflecting coils could interlock in any one of 10 angular positions with respect to the antenna. To overcome this problem and to insure that the antenna and indicator coils always maintained the same angular relationship, cam-driven phasing switches were installed on both the antenna equipment and the indicators.

The antenna equipment usually was mounted in an inverted position, with its fore-and-aft line parallel to the fore-and-aft line of the aircraft. The antenna conveyed the direction of the bomber's flight when the heading switch closed when the antenna was in a position that coincided with the longitudinal axis of the bomber. This action applied extra bias to the indicator sweep and, consequently, the sweep that coincided with the bomber's heading momentarily brightened.

Auxiliary antenna equipment was comprised of an azimuth control box, torque amplifier, and the selsyn phasing unit. The primary purpose of these units was to place and keep true north at the top of the scope regardless of the bomber's heading (called azimuth stabilization). A second purpose was to provide sector scanning, in which the antenna beam was oscillated across one target rather than sweeping the entire 360° azimuth.

AN/APQ-5B

Low altitude bombing created a unique problem for radar and required the use of a different type of equipment in the APQ-5B. The apparent movement of the target at low altitudes was approximately equal to the ground speed of the aircraft, and at low altitudes the ground range and slant range were approximately equal. These two factors made it possible to tie the radar return into a tracking unit on the APQ-5B and thus control the speed at which the return was moved toward the radar operator on the scope. A bomb-release line (similar to the bomb circle on the APQ-13 and APS-15A) could be introduced into this equipment and positioned correctly by means of a rate knob and an altitude knob.

The Search Track Switch on the tracking unit made it possible to locate the target out to 18 miles. The drift knobs of the bombsight were then used to determine the track over the target. When the track was approximately established the Search Track Switch was moved to TRACK, which selected a one mile sweep on the scope. The rate knob determined the rate at which a tracking line was driven on the scope. Ground speed was established by adjusting the rate knob until the tracking line moved at the same rate as the change in slant range to the target. A slant-release range factor was then entered into the computer circuit automatically and combined with the absolute altitude, which had been set into the altitude dial.

The combination of these factors created a bomb-release line which determined the point of release. As the tracking line was moved toward the bomber it combined with the bomb-release line at the point of release. The voltages of these two electronic beams triggered a bomb-release circuit and a bomb was dropped.

The LAB APQ-5B equipment also could be used for medium or high altitude bombing. A switch on the synchronizer unit controlled the bomb computer in three positions:

1) LOW-IN: The computer was operative and the slant-release distance was computed automatically.
2) LOW-OUT: The computer was inoperative. Slant-release distance was determined by setting an altitude-dial reading calculated from a conversion chart.
3) HI-OUT: The computer was inoperative. Slant-release distance was determined by the altitude-dial setting and a B factor entered in the spread dial (on control box).
(Note: The LOW-OUT and HI-OUT positions were used for fixed-angle bombing only.)

AN/APQ-5B was auxiliary radar equipment installed in the bombardier's compartment that depended on the associated radar equipment. The bombardier operated the set in cooperation with the R/O, and in combination with the usual equipment for visual bombing and the radar equipment, to make blind spot-bombing possible. Although it was designed for low altitude operation, the AN/APQ-5B could be used with realistic accuracy up to 40,000 feet. It functioned efficiently day or night at temperatures ranging from -40° to +122° F, and in relative humidity as high as 95%.

AN/APQ-5B was normally used with airborne search radars such as SCR-717A, SCR-717B, AN/APS-15A, AN/APQ-13, and the ASC, ASD, ASD-1, and ASH types. If the unit was properly installed it did not interfere with the normal functioning of associated equipment. It also could be used as a search indicator with a range of 18 statute miles, and was used when the bombardier was trying to locate a target at the beginning of a bombing run. The AN/APQ-5B could release a train of bombs, centered on the target, with a normal spread of 830 feet between the first and last bombs in the train. A train of three bombs should have given a direct hit. Operational tests made at an average airspeed of 160 mph indicated a radial error of less than 150 feet at altitude of 500 feet; 175 feet at altitude of 1,000 feet; 185 feet at altitude of 1,500 feet; and 240 feet at altitude of 2,000 feet. Most of this error was in range rather than deflection.

AN/APQ-5B indicator equipment contained eight major assemblies: synchronizer, control box, tracking unit, indicator, rectifier, junction box, capacitor unit, and compensator. Additional equipment required to obtain most effective results with the AN/APQ-5B, other than the usual search-radar installations, included a bombsight stabilizer and Adapter Kit MX-30/APQ-5A.

Synchronizer

This unit was considered the heart of the AN/APQ-5B set. Operating from the radar trigger and video pulses, and from data supplied by the control circuits, the synchronizer generated the necessary sweep for the scope. It also produced the desired track and release pulses at the proper instants. When the bomber approached the release point in flight the synchronizer fired the release relay electrically. The main controls were:

ALT COMPUTER: Selector switch with three settings: LOW IN, LOW OUT, and HIGH OUT.

At LOW IN the range of the set was from 65 to 2,000 feet. The computer was operative. The slant-release distance was computed automatically. The velocity and altitude dials (on tracking unit) indicated correctly.

At LOW OUT the range was from 2,000 to 5,000 feet. The computer was inoperative. The slant release distance was computed by setting the altitude dial manually. The spread dial (on control box) indicated directly in feet.

At HIGH OUT the computer was inoperative. The slant release distance was determined by altitude dial setting and B factor inserted on spread dial.

VIDEO: Screwdriver control that adjusted the video signals on the B scope as they came from the associated radar set.

AN/APQ-5B Synchronizer

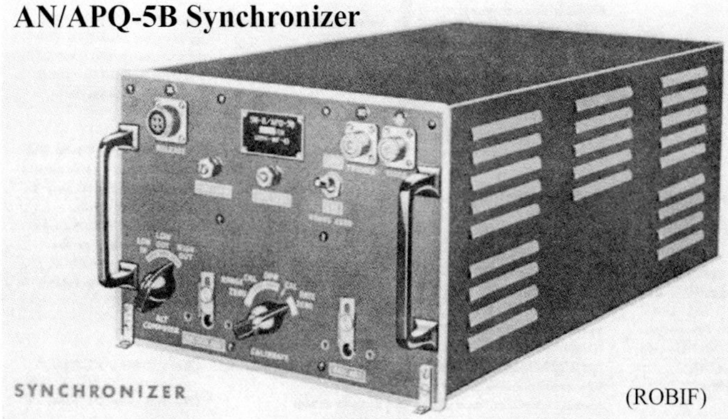

(ROBIF)

RATE ZERO: Screwdriver control that was used to set the tracking pip at zero velocity when the operator of the set was using the rate zero control.

RATE ADJ: Screwdriver control used to calibrate the relative velocity dial.

RANGE ZERO: Toggle switch used to insert trigger into video circuit.

CALIBRATE: Selector switch with five settings:

1) At RANGE ZERO the trigger pulse from the associated radar equipment was inserted into the bomb release circuit for use in calibrating the release line by the R/O on the spread dial.
2-3) At the two settings marked CAL the ground mechanic calibrated the set for range and rate.
4) The OPR position was used on the bombing run.
5) At RATE ZERO the R/O calibrated the set for altitude with the ALT COMPUTER at HIGH OUT. The position of the CALIBRATE switch kept the tracking pip from moving down the time base when the SEARCH-TRACK switch was at TRACK.

Control Box
The control box was located at the bombardier's right, facing the front of the bomber. The main controls were:

POWER: Toggle switch that directly controlled the DC current and indirectly controlled AC current to the set.

SLANT RANGE INCREMENT FEET: Commonly called the spread dial, it was a control knob geared to dial that was read directly in feet. The spread dial had two functions:

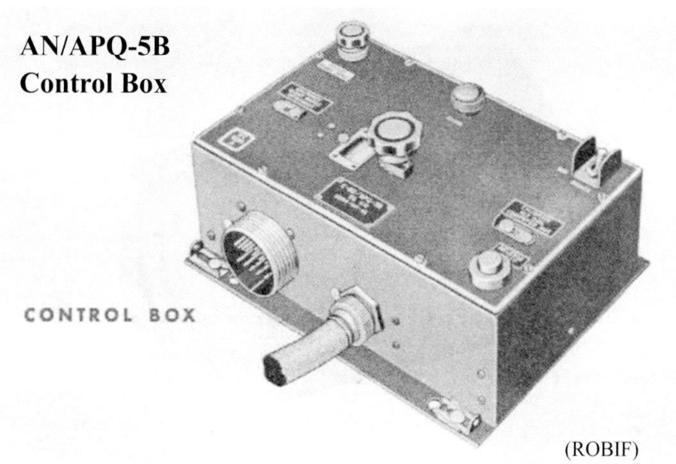

AN/APQ-5B Control Box

(ROBIF)

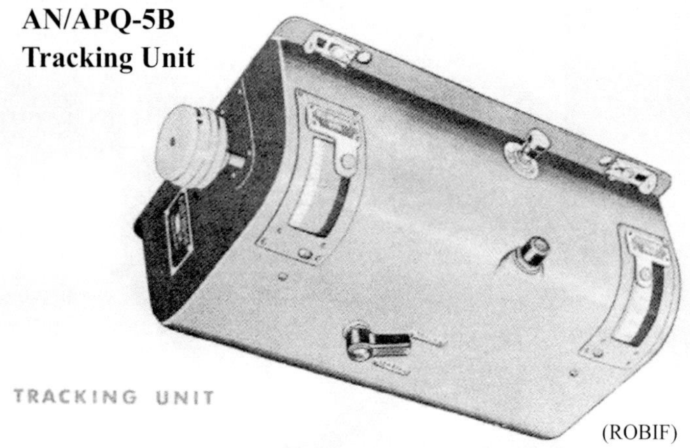

AN/APQ-5B Tracking Unit

(ROBIF)

1) For LAB it was used to add and subtract from the slant range release distance. Increasing the setting provided correction for bombs falling long. Decreasing the setting provided correction for bombs falling short.
2) For HAB, it was used to insert the B factor of total slant range release distance. In this case the dial reading was multiplied by 10 to show the B factor in total feet.

RELEASE RESET: Pushbutton used to re-set the bomb release circuit during calibration, resetting the release relay, which was closed when the set was fired.

ILLUM: Control knob that regulated the amount of light on the ground speed, altitude, and spread dials.
ADJUST RANGE ZERO: Positioned the release pip on the leading edge of the trigger when the equipment was being calibrated for range zero.

CALIBRATE SLANT RANGE, INCREMENT: Screwdriver control used to calibrate the proper range on the slant range increment dial for HAB.

CALIBRATE ALT DIAL COMPUTER OUT: Screwdriver control used to calibrate the altitude dial for computer out bombing.

Tracking Unit
This unit contained the position, altitude, and ground speed circuits. The main controls were:

ALTITUDE: Control knob and dial used in three ways, depending on operating conditions:
1) In LAB, the operator set the absolute altitude into the dial, establishing the basic altitude factor used in automatically computing slant release distance.
2) In computer out bombing, the operator set a slant release range into the altitude dial.
3) In HAB, the operator used the altitude knob and dial to determine absolute altitude. The absolute altitude, when combined with indicated ground speed, determined a B-factor setting for the spread dial in computing slant release range.

REL VELOCITY MPH: Dial which indicated rate of closure.

RATE KNOB: Determined the speed of tracking line.

POSITION KNOB: Determined the position of tracking line.

SEARCH-TRACK: Selector switch with two positions: SEARCH, which provided a range of 18 statute miles on the scope (Bomb release circuit was not cocked); and TRACK, which selected a one mile sweep on the

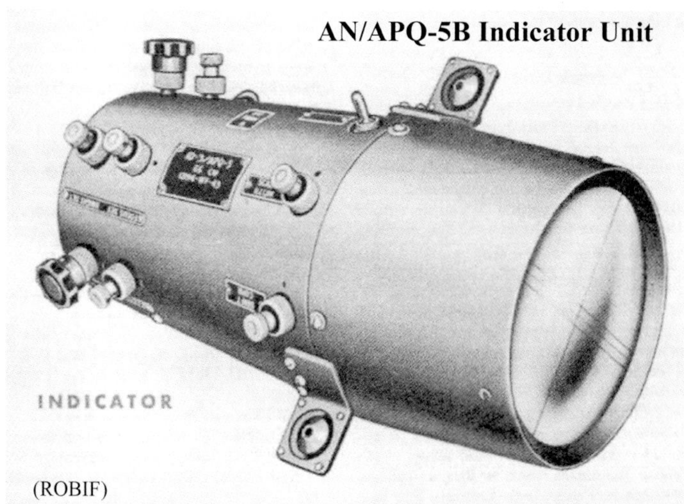

AN/APQ-5B Indicator Unit

(ROBIF)

scope. Cocked the bomb release circuit and made the velocity control effective.

PILOT LIGHT: Indicated when the power was on and when the release circuit fired.

AUX RATE ZERO: Pushbutton used to stop the tracking line.

Indicator
The indicator, or B scope, contained a cathode ray tube and associated equipment, and provided radar pictures on a fluorescent screen for the bombardier. A rubber hood shielded the screen from stray light. The high voltages that the B scope required were supplied by the associated radar system. The B scope obtained its sweep currents from the sweep circuits of the synchronizer, and they could be brightened by range, echo, and release impulses from the video section of the synchronizer. The indicator provided a vertical sweep corresponding to approximately 19 statute miles for search operation, or an expanded sweep of approximately one mile for track operation. In track operation, the horizontal range line appeared as a trace in the center of the B scope. For satisfactory tracking, the intersection of the center vertical crosshair with the horizontal range mark was to coincide with the target trace. When the bomber was approximately a half mile from the bomb release point the horizontal release trace appeared at the bottom of the scope, and appeared to move upward toward the range mark. When the release trace coincided with the range mark the bomb was released automatically. In search operation the returns were similar to those picked up on most search radar systems that used a B scope. During search, depending on the setting of the position control, the range marks appeared between 0 and nine miles on the scope, while the release trace appeared near the bottom. The main controls of the indicator were:

FOCUS: Control knob that focused trace on the scope in both search and track operation.

FOCUS SET: Thumbscrew that provided additional focus for trace in search and track operation.

H CENT: Thumbscrew that centered the trace horizontally.

DRIFT CORR: Thumbscrew with which the R/O determined the ratio between movement of bombsight and the shifting of trace on scope. The ratio was to be 1:1.

SCALE ILLUM: Thumbscrew that controlled the amount of illumination for the vertical lines on the scope.

BRIGHT: Control knob that governed brilliancy of the returns in the track operation.

BRIGHT SET: Thumbscrew that controlled the brilliancy of returns in search operation.

V CENT: Control knob which centered the trace vertically.

AZIM ON-OFF: Toggle switch which controlled flow of azimuth voltage from radar antenna.

AN/APQ-7 *Eagle* Radar System

Although the development of MIT's Radiation Laboratory's APQ-7 radar system had begun before their development of H2X, the innovative and complex APQ-7 did not attain operational status until long after H2X was in production. At first the design team called it "*EHIB*" (Every House In Berlin), but at Lee DuBridge's insistence in early 1942 it was renamed "*Eagle*."

In November 1941 Rad Lab's Luis Alvarez discussed radar targeting with British radar guru Taffy Bowen and went back to MIT to work on the project. Alvarez had originally envisioned the array as a waveguide, a hollow pipe with a square cross section through which microwave energy could flow and with slots cut into it at intervals to act as transmitting antennas. In practice an array of dipole antennas was used instead, but initial tests showed that such an array didn't produce a precise forward beam. It also generated "side lobes" (beams that went off at unwanted angles), wasting transmitter energy. Alvarez redesigned the system by introducing a new array configuration that featured twice the number of dipoles with half the spacing. The dipoles alternated in polarity, and this "reversed dipole" scheme cancelled out the side lobes. The redesign was a 20 foot long linear array of 250 transmitting dipole antennas built into the leading edge of the wing of an aircraft. By properly arranging and controlling the antennas, their emissions would interfere with each other and focus the radar beam into a tall and narrow strip, which would be ideal for targeting. Interference effects could also be used to electronically steer the beam over an angle of 60° in front of the aircraft. The antenna was designed to be linked up to the Norden Bombsight, though it was designed to be easily connected to other bombsights as well. The development of an operational *Eagle* unit promised to be a drawn out and complicated process, and the project was given low priority. A prototype *Eagle* was not successfully flight-tested until 16 June 1943, at which time it was installed on a B-24 and was found to be superior to the H2X. Both the AN/APQ-13/H2X and AN/APQ-7 *Eagle* used the ground-scanning three cm "X" band. Initially the *Eagle* antenna was to be mounted to the wing, but finally it was housed under the fuselage in an aluminum vane that measured 40 inches wide, 36 inches long, and eight inches high. Soon the antenna was lengthened to 18 feet and ran parallel to the aircraft's wing, causing it to resemble a second shorter wing when viewed in the air. This new type of antenna was fixed, but scanned electrically side-to-side and narrowed the beam to 60° (30° to either side of the aircraft's heading), generating excellent (10 times better) resolution (return beam definition) but limiting its use as a navigational instrument. It produced 10 times more resolution than APQ-13/H2X radar, which used rotating antennas that scanned 360° but generated poor definition. The large size of the vane antenna produced drag that reduced the performance of the bomber. It was more difficult to operate and maintain and was exceptionally fragile, as the runway materials stirred up by the props and flying through rain damaged its leading edge, and it had to be replaced after approximately half a dozen missions. Nonetheless, the AAF ordered 650 sets in November 1943.

The operational prototype of the *Eagle* was not flight-tested until 16 May 1944. The improved set had a very narrow beam width, giving it much improved accuracy relative to H2X. The set's range of 160 miles, resolution (its narrow beam allowed it to pick out a single large building in a city), and accuracy were imposing. Though the *Eagle* had been specifically developed

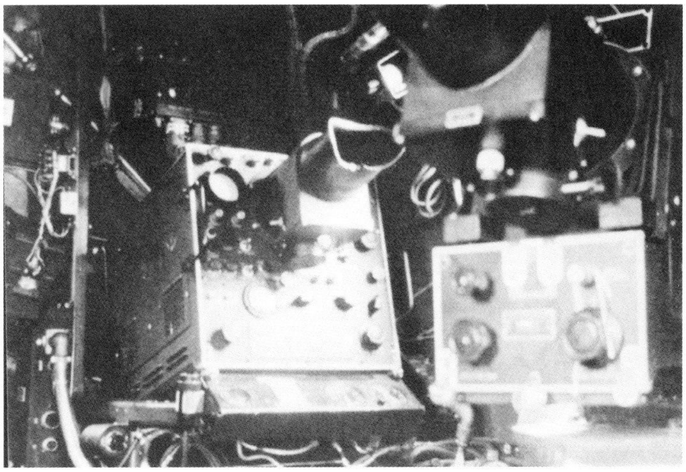

AN/APQ-7 *Eagle* **Radar** unit and scope installation in a B-24. (AAF)

The **AN/APQ-7** *Eagle* **Radar Antenna** was 18 feet and ran parallel to the aircraft's wing, causing it to resemble a second shorter wing when viewed in the air. Shown are antenna installations on a B-24 (top), B-29 (middle), and B-17 (bottom). (All AAF)

AN/APQ-7 ***Eagle*** **Radar System**

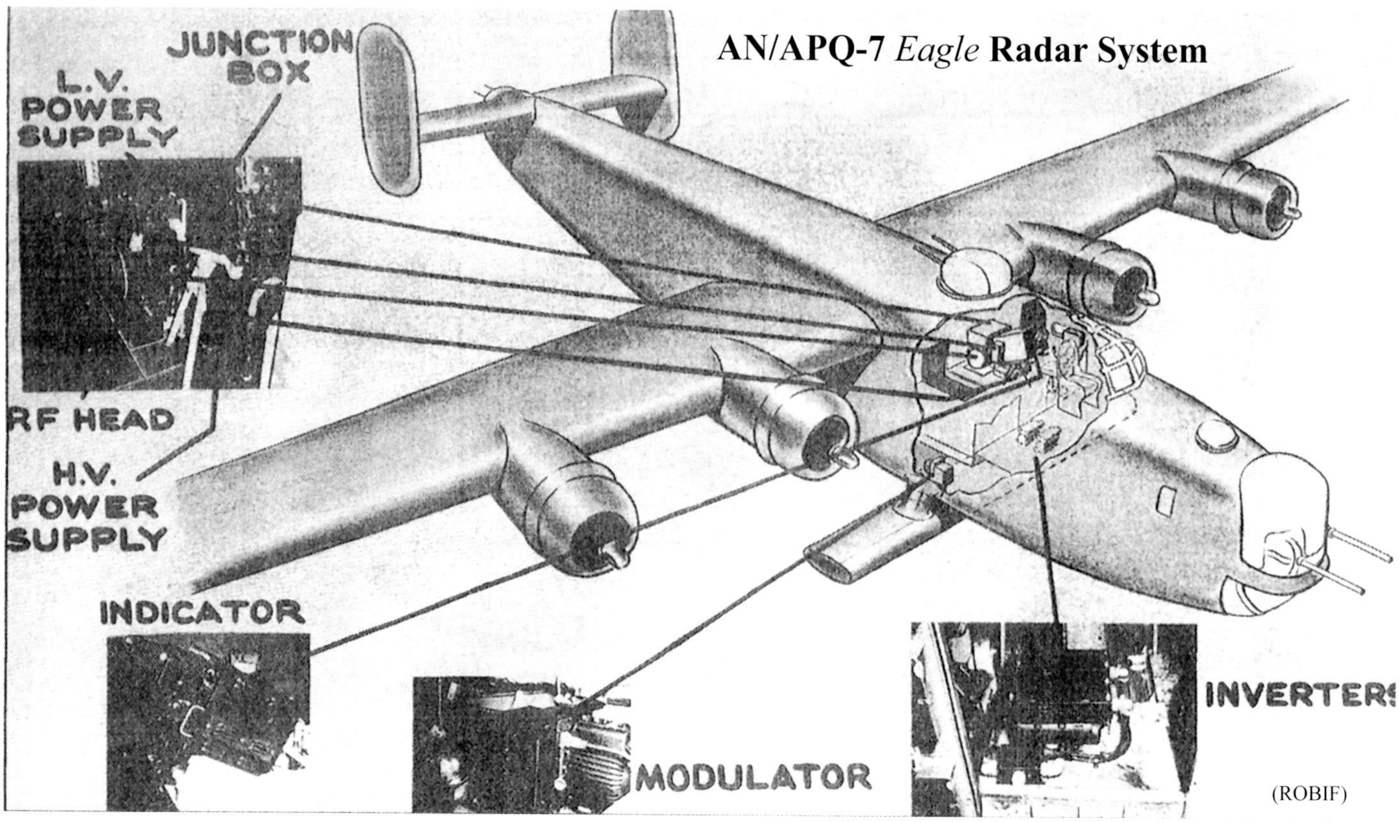

(ROBIF)

for the B-29, the first sets were sent to England in October 1944 for testing by the 482BG at Alconbury, which equipped a B-17G with the set. There were numerous technical problems with the sets, and the first experimental combat operations were not flown until 2 April 1945, when the Group had 11 *Eagle*-equipped B-17Gs on hand. Only two of these *Eagle* B-17s (44-6252 and 44-6990) were used in the 13 experimental combat operations. At VE-Day in May the Eagle aircraft were transferred to the 96BG for the Occupational Air Force, where continued problems in testing caused the cessation of testing.

The B-29-equipped *Eagles* did not enter the APQ-7 program until December 1943, and in January 1944 the AAF stipulated that a mockup was to be ready by mid-June. Problems with the B-29 development by Boeing further delayed *Eagle*-Superfortress use until mid-August. Meanwhile, the AAF increased its *Eagle* order to 1,650. By early November 1944 the AAF was becoming impatient and set a 1 December deadline for the completion of all engineering and a 15 December date for the start of testing, but as was usual with the B-29 program neither deadline was met. The new radar was finally tested in B-29s at Boca Raton, FL, in February 1945, by which time orders had reached 2,650 sets for both the 20AF and the 8AF (the ETO orders would be canceled in April).

In November 1944 Gen. Arnold authorized the B-29s of the 313BW to be equipped with the APQ-7 and increased this order to two wings (315BW and 316BW) in late January 1945. These Wings were to fly stripped bombers for night and bad weather operations. The large APQ-7 antenna reduced the bomber's speed by eight mph and range by 412 miles compared to reductions of 3-4 mph and 312 miles respectively for the APQ-13. Although the established APQ-13 was scheduled for significant improvements, the APQ-7 offered some significant upgrades over the APQ-13, the most important being that it had a much better level of target resolution on its radarscope that gave more accurate direct radar bombing. The APQ-13 radarscope showed a 360°picture, and was thus the better navigational device when approaching the target. Even though the APQ-7 only showed a 60° picture (30° on each side of the bomber's heading), it could be effectively used in bombing. The average bombing run for the APQ-7 was 70 miles and the APQ-13 average was 33 miles. When the APQ-7 became operational it flew unopposed nighttime missions, so its increased bombing approach was of little consequence. But since its targets were smaller the APQ-7's better target resolution produced a more precise bomb drop.

Operations planners had long envisioned night operations for the B-29, and in September 1944 tests showed that removing turrets and blisters and most armor diminished drag, reduced weight by 7,500 pounds, and increased airspeed by seven to 13 mph (depending on altitude). The *Eagle* radar unit was usually reliable, with about 10% failures, and with tweaking the set's range increased over 40% from 67 miles to 96 miles by the last mission. Flame dampers were considered to reduce its visibility at night by enemy interceptors, but by March this idea was discarded, as the dampers increased weight and reduced engine power, and the Japanese night fighter force was found to be small and ineffective. The first production *Eagle* B-29 was stripped of 3,500 pounds of equipment, and the drag of the deleted four turrets almost compensated for the loss of speed and range caused by its huge belly antenna. The stripped B-29 first flew from Seattle on 15 January 1945, and by the end of the month the 315BW was ready to receive their *Eagle*-equipped B-29s, but Bell-Marietta was delayed in its delivery of the bombers. In the meantime, the 315BW radar operators had to take their training in *Eagle*-equipped B-24s. It would not be until March 1945 that the Bomb Wing would acquire its first combat ready B-29B bomber from the Bell factory for training. The wing's *Eagle* B-29s finally reached Guam, in the Marianas, on 1 June under its excellent veteran leader from the ETO, Frank Armstrong, who made two changes: the bomber's underfuselage was painted gloss black to lessen searchlight detection and the bombing altitude was decreased. Training and tests had demonstrated that if the bombing altitude was halved from 30,000 feet the demand on the engines was reduced and the fuel efficiency increased to allow for a heavier bomb load, and also, at 15,000 feet the APQ-7 was more dependable. The *Eagle* sets did not have the operational teething problems of the AN/APQ-13, as its operators had received extensive training with the set itself and spent no time on formation flying or visual bombing. The 315BW did not enter combat until 26 June 1945, and its initial targets were the oil refinery and tank farms on the Honshu coast. The petroleum industry had proven to be the German war machine's Achilles' heel, and Japanese oil was a virgin target to test the viability of the APQ-7. The land/water disparity of these coastal targets made for excellent target definition on radar, and the results of the bombing could be more easily studied, as there were no previous bomb craters or damage to interfere with the assessment. Ten percent of all bombs fell within 1,000 feet of the AP, 30% within 2,000 feet, and 50% within 3,500 feet.

Operations

Between its first mission on 26 June 1945 and its last on 14 August, the 315th flew 15 night missions against 10 targets with a total of 1,180 combat sorties, of which 1,095 bombed the primary target using radar 95% of the time. A total of 9,084 bombs were dropped, most of which were 500 pound GP bombs. A substantial portion of Japan's oil storage tank capacity, as well as 10 individual synthetic and refining facilities, were destroyed or heavily damaged; comprising a major segment of Japanese oil refining and storage capacity. However, the 315BW's attack on the Japanese oil industry was found to be futile in postwar analysis, since it was not refining oil, as its imported oil source transported by shipping had been cut by submarines and the sea and aerial mining campaign.

As the war was about to end the *Eagle* was ready for wide scale installation, with the R/Os using the APQ-13 becoming very proficient operating their sets. The AN/APQ-23, an upgraded APQ-13 system, was also about ready for operations. Despite being touted as the "radar bomber," only 23% of the XXI Bomber Command's B-29s' bombs were aimed by radar during the war. After the war all *Eagle* sets were removed from operational B-29s.

NOSMO Radar System

Late in the war the Bell Telephone Laboratories X-band AN/APS-7 *Eagle* radar was used in conjunction with a Norden M-9 Bombsight for increased accuracy and deployed by the AAF as the NOSMO system (**NO**rden **S**ight **MO**dification). The Eagle's rangefinder system was electronically attached to the Norden Bombsight's viewfinder, in essence creating a system where

NOSMO system (**NO**rden **S**ight **MO**dification) was AN/APS-7 *Eagle* radar used in conjunction with a Norden M-9 Bombsight for increased accuracy. (AAF)

the radar system would automatically input standard bombsight range and drift data. Radar data was fed directly and continually into the Norden Bombsight, rather than having the H2X operator transfer the information to the bombardier verbally. Allowing continuous synchronous range tracking and visual-radar coordination, it would allow accurate bombing from 30,000 to 35,000 feet. Although Norden Bombsights were still used for daylight and clear weather missions, NOSMO would eventually be scrapped in favor of wholly electronic systems.

NOSMEAGLE

Also, late in the war the NOSMO set was improved, as the Eagle radar determined ground speed, wind speed and direction, and altitude; the bombardier set the disc speed on the Norden Bombsight according to this information while the radar operator killed drift and synchronized the sight with the target. Thus, the radar data was fed directly and continually into the Norden Bombsight rather than having the H2X operator transfer the information to the bombardier verbally, allowing continuous synchronous range tracking and visual-radar coordination. Known as NOSMEAGLE, this first true radar bomb-sight proved twice as accurate as H2X. In test bombings at Eglin, NOSMEAGLE achieved a circular error of 800 feet from an altitude of 20,000 feet with the Norden Bombsight. The war ended before NOSMEAGLE could be tested in combat.

AN/APQ-30

This unit was a late war system that provided 360° scanning and a 3° beam width, and was an improved radar system over the AN/APQ–7, even though both had similar pulse widths.

Advantages of Beacon and Radar Bombing

Despite the limitations of radar and beacon bombing, these technologies allowed the Army Air Forces to bomb when weather otherwise would have prevented it. Crews especially appreciated electronic attacks; protected by clouds, the chances of getting home safely from a blind-bombing mission were nearly six times greater than from a visual-bombing mission. If the Allies had been forced to await weather conditions conducive to visual bombing, the number of bombs dropped on Germany would have declined by 52% in 1944 and 1945. These additional 195,000 tons of bombs, nearly 20% of all bombs dropped by the Army Air Forces on Germany during the war, were an integral part of the bombing campaign to destroy the German war economy.

Beacon aids and radar allowed American bombardiers to aim their bombs at specific targets in the German industrial complex through clouds and smoke, though bombing inaccuracy made such missions area attacks in effect. These techniques meant that Eighth Air Force dropped 3.7 bombs on clear days to achieve one hit within 1,000 feet of the target, 13.4 on days of poor visibility, 23.2 with Gee-H, 24.1 with Micro-H, and a huge 567.4 bombs with H2X in total 10/10 cloud cover. Missions relying on blind-bombing aids remained officially "last resort attacks."

Radar Navigation and Bombing

With the advent of instrument bombing the radar navigator assumed new importance. He was responsible for advising the airplane commander of navigational hazards, such as thunderheads and mountains. The navigator depended on radar for ground speeds and drift readings. Since an estimated 40% of the bombs were dropped through clouds the radar man was vital to the bombardier.

The APQ-13 radar returns from the Japanese coast were picked up from 50-60 miles, and the coastline features were so distinctive that any radar operator could easily recognize the point he should make landfall from the terrain features he had studied in preparing for the mission. The standard radar bombing procedure required the cooperation of the radar operator, navigator, and bombardier. The wind speed and drift were determined as soon as landfall was made. The airplane commander was then to fly straight and level at bombing altitude to permit the navigator enough time for a precision turn onto the axis of attack before passing over the IP.

Scope interpretation was the radar man's most important job, no matter how well he operated his set and how well he knew the bombing procedure; if the radar operator and navigator could not orient themselves with what they saw on the set then the mission would fail. To make the mission successful the radar operator and navigator spent many hours studying the maps, charts, target folders, and PPI Radarscope pictures of the route to the target and the target vicinity. Artist's drawings (based on maps, aerial photos, and topographical studies) of what the radarscope image might look like over the target were studied. Later, simulators arrived that by means of accurate terrain models of the area that the missions were to be flown in were able to duplicate the actual scope presentation of the target. There were several factors, both external and intrinsic, that affected the radarscope picture. Among the external factors were terrain and geographic factors, such as lakes, rivers, and islands, and man made factors, such as railway facilities, roads, and buildings. The inherent and operational characteristics of the radar set also affected the scope picture. Because of these influencing factors set tuning, the use of brilliance, tilt, and gain, and the constant study of the scope function and target area were important.

From a navigational standpoint, the APQ-13 Radar Set was a fixing apparatus. The set was only as good as the operator and the accuracy of the fixes he obtained from it, and then his accurate use of the computers and plotting equipment. Radar was not a substitute for standard navigation but an aid and supplement. Experience showed that the APQ-13 had a range of only 40 miles, radar resolution of landmasses was very limited, and the radar operator had to make use of experience and old fashion "dead reckoning" in radar piloting.

Bombing Accuracy of Visual, Beacon, and Radar Sighting

Norden Visual Bombing

Initial Bomb Sighting Learning Curve, 1943

As soon as the VIII BC arrived in Britain and conducted its first missions in mid-August 1943, all over to German-occupied countries, the American doctrine of daylight precision bombing of industrial and military targets using the vaunted Norden Bombsight was put to the test in order not to harm friendly civilians. British Prime Minister Churchill, Air Chief Marshal Sir Charles Portal, and Air Chief Marshal Sir Arthur Harris did not expect daylight "selective" bombing to succeed in light of their early daylight bombing failures and wanted the Americans to join them in the night area bombing of German cities.

The bombing results of the AAF's first 30 combat missions were judged to range from bad to good. Consistent accuracy, the heart of American strategic bombing, had been achieved from high altitudes on practice missions back in the United States. However, bomber crews bombed targets on established and familiar bombing ranges under conditions very different from combat. The crews had no problems in finding the familiar bombing range, but locating a target one had never seen before was a problem in combat. The training crews did not encounter AA fire or enemy interceptors to and from the practice range as they did in combat. However, analysis of these missions showed that Norden bombing by individual aircraft as practiced in training was ineffective and exposed the bombers to enemy fighters that inflicted heavy losses (8.8%) during these missions. A better method needed to be developed.

Col. Curtis LeMay, CO of the 305th Bomb Group, experimented to find the best formation for defense against fighter attacks, as the existing one-level formation (combat box) did not offer adequate bomber protection. In practice flights LeMay developed the first version of the multi-level box formation, consisting of staggered three-plane elements within each squadron and staggered squadrons within each group to provide a compact, maneuverable box formation. This formation could not be maintained on the bomb run, however, if each plane maneuvered for accurate range sighting, so LeMay decided this problem could be avoided if each plane maintained its position in formation and dropped its bombs on a signal from the leading plane in the aircraft box. Thus, the leader of the combat box aimed for deflection and range for his entire box. The first mission to use LeMay's "bombing-on-leader" technique occurred on 3 January 1943, on the well-defended U-Boat base at St. Nazaire. The results were inconclusive, and further sufficient data needed to be assembled and analyzed. On 17 March Gen. Haywood Hansell was presented a report and enthusiastically ordered the full-scale use of the bomb-on-the-leader technique. The next day an attack was made on Vegesack, Germany, which was the first VIII Bomber Command mission in which all the groups were instructed to drop on the leader. The results were extraordinarily successful.

On 20 March 1943, after the Vegesack mission, the Bombing Accuracy Subsection released a report, "Advantage of Dropping on the Leader over Sighting Individually for Range when Bombing in Formation," which made the following recommendations:

1) All groups should be instructed that the bombardiers in each combat box should release their bombs when the bombardier of the lead ship of the combat box releases his, i.e. "bomb-on-the-leader."
2) The aiming point for the lead ship should be selected to place the formation pattern most effectively over the target area.
3) Every effort commensurate with defensive needs should be made to reduce the length of the bomb pattern.

The first recommendation was adopted immediately, and within two or three weeks sighting on the leader was the only technique used during all 8AF missions. The second recommendation, which was the logical consequence of the first, was also adopted and, of course, modified the whole concept of aiming point selection. The lead bombardier was now aiming not just his own bombs but a pattern, or Mean Point of Impact (MPI). Previously, specific aiming points for attack were selected but now specified MPIs instead, and left the selection of aiming points to the groups. The third recommendation, shorter bombing patterns, important though it was, took longer to comprehend and become accepted throughout the command. Nevertheless, this set of recommendations laid the groundwork for very significant improvements in bombing accuracy.

Visual Bombing Accuracy in 1943 and Early 1944

In 1943 the Eighth Air Force grew from an operational force of four to 26 heavy bomber groups, and by the end of March 1944 30 heavy bomber groups were in the Eighth. During the first six months of 1943 the operations analysts had established, by scientific analysis of actual operations, the fundamentals of visual by the Norden Bombsight by the "bomb on the leader" technique. This technique had been put into use to improve subsequent visual bombing operations, and the accuracy of Eighth Air Force operations improved considerably from one October 1943 to one March 1944.

Only 55 to 60% of the visual attacks made by the B-17s were against targets with preassigned aiming points, but because bad weather decreased visibility over the targets it was often impossible to bomb either the assigned primary or secondary target. Instead, bombers would drop their bombs visually on a "target of opportunity." The poor European weather and the AAF's need to press their bombing campaign on a daily basis despite bad weather caused the AAF to develop Bombing Through Clouds (BTO), or blind bombing techniques.

Norden Bombing Accuracy Under Conditions of Good Visibility

The study found that even under conditions of good visibility the bombing accuracy of the Eighth Air Force fell off in the period under study. For June, July, and August an estimated 40% of all bombs dropped under conditions of good visibility fell within 1,000 feet of preassigned aiming points. For the period 1 September through 31 December 1944 the figure dropped to approximately 30%. It dropped even lower, to 22.6%, in the three-month period 1 October to 31 December 1944.

The study identified two causes for this decrease. First, bombs were dropped from much higher altitudes than before. In the first quarter of 1944 only 37% of the bombing with good visibility was done above 21,000 feet. In the second quarter 50% was done above 21,000 feet. This rose to 75% in the third quarter. Finally, in the fourth quarter of 1944 97% of all bombing was done at altitudes of 21,000 feet or higher. The bombers had been driven up by the heavy defenses at German industrial targets. Furthermore, by the fourth quarter almost all targets were in Germany.

The second cause for the decrease in accuracy had to do with the size of the AAF and, more specifically, the size of the attacking force. The study showed that as an attack progressed bombing accuracy decreased. Though the level of accuracy was reasonably high for the first three groups (nine to twelve combat boxes) in a formation, bombing accuracy for subsequent groups dropped by approximately half.

During the last quarter of 1944 the number of visual bombing missions done in large forces of more than nine combat boxes was more than twice that of previous quarters. The larger attacking forces decreased bombing accuracy during the period, but the larger attacking forces did serve a purpose. Assume that to achieve a given bomb density on a single target 500 aircraft and five attacks were required. To achieve the same density on a single mission only 900 aircraft would be needed. Because good flying weather and visibility were rare, the AAF wisely chose to mount a few large attacks rather than several small attacks despite the resulting decrease in accuracy.

Norden Bombing Accuracy Under Conditions of Poor Visibility.

In the last four months of 1944 the amount of visual bombing done in poor visibility was much greater than in preceding months, which was due to the dominance of poor weather during the period and the extensive use of smoke screens by the enemy over oil targets. Of the total visual bombing done under conditions of poor visibility, slightly over 25% was due to the effective use of smoke screens by the enemy. The analysts found that four to five times the force was required to achieve the required density of bombs on a target protected by smoke screens than would be necessary otherwise. No effective countermeasure was devised.

The remaining 75% of the total visual bombing done under conditions of poor visibility was caused by cloud cover and haze. Whereas 30.2% of the bombs dropped under conditions of good visibility fell within 1,000 feet of the preassigned aiming point, only 9.4% of the bombs dropped visually but with cloud cover and haze fell within 1,000 feet of the aiming point. The recommendation of the study was to use radar aids.

H2X Accuracy

Initial H2X Bombing

At the end of the first quarter of 1943, so-called Pathfinder Bombing (H2X) bombing had only been in use since 3 November, and the first report from the Bombing Accuracy Subsection on its effectiveness was eagerly anticipated. The first, dated 31 January 1944, "Report on Results of Pathfinder Bombing on Certain Targets," prepared by Col. Philip Scott, came to the dismal conclusion that H2X missions had averaged only 5% of their bombs falling within one mile of the aiming point.

Opinions differed. Some factions flatly denied the results, while others insisted that the Radiation Laboratory equipment was of a high-quality, but that the Air Force did not know how to properly utilize it. Scott and the Bombing Accuracy Subsection were anxious that the AAF was pursuing a program of inaccurate bombing whose resources could be better used for improving visual or Gee bombing. These misgivings were suppressed for fear that the further development of the promising H2X technique would be hindered.

The official USAAF history of this period further supports the Bombing Accuracy Subsection's evaluation:

"The bomb patterns made by pathfinder-led forces in November and December were too scattered to effect more than accidental damage to any particular industrial plant or installation of importance. The aiming point became a highly theoretical term. On only two missions did bombs fall in the assigned target area."

During this initial period heavy bombers were sent out whenever it seemed possible to bomb either visually or by radar, but often missions were scrubbed before takeoff and often were recalled after takeoff because of weather. But in the next quarter the weather improved and daylight increased. The Eighth Air Force was able to mount bomber attacks on 11 days in January 1944, 17 days in February, and 22 days in March, but during each month radar bombing was a big factor. The H2X Pathfinders were, in bad weather, invariably used for the longer missions, with Gee-H used for some of the shorter missions within its range. But although the H2X radar bombing improved slightly in January, February, and March 1944, it definitely was not precision bombing. While the accuracy of visual bombing could be expressed in units of 500 feet, the accuracy of H2X bombing at this stage was expressed in terms of miles, so appropriate targets for H2X Pathfinders were seaports and large industrial areas.

It was plain, due to the chronically bad weather and the need to keep daily pressure on the Germans, that H2X bombing would assume a significant place in Eighth Air Force operations. Thus, on 30 March 1944 Col. John Harlan, chief of the ORS, assigned Drs. Baley Price and Forrest Immer of the Bombing Accuracy Subsection to analyze H2X blind bombing accuracy.

Bombing Accuracy 1 January 1943 to 1 March 1944
Average percentage of bombs dropped that fell within x feet of aiming point

	500 ft.	1,000 ft.
1 Jan. 1943-1 Oct. 1943	5.5	16.0
1 Oct. 1943-1 Mar. 1944	14.5	37.0
Improvement	9.0	21.0
(percent)	163.6	131.3

This remarkable improvement can be explained by the target systems of the Eighth Air Force for both periods (1 January to 1 March 1944 inclusive), which were easy to hit by H2X: seaports, airfields, and various production centers, such as ball bearing factories, aircraft factories, and shipyards.

However, in December 1943 a large new target system was assigned to the Eighth Air Force; the V-1 Buzz Bomb launching "ski sites" being constructed in the Pas-de-Calais, on the French coast. On 24 December 1943 the first attack with 670 bombers was mounted, followed by 1,034 sorties in January and 733 in February. Two aspects of these targets increased the bombing accuracy. One was the proximity of V-weapon sites to England, decreasing the threat of GAF attack. Attacking combat boxes could be smaller, and were often of squadron size rather than group size. The lower bombing altitude also improved accuracy. Initially, AA defenses around the sites allowed heavy bombers to attack at altitudes considerably lower than their usual 19,000 to 23,000 feet. However, as the antiaircraft defenses around missile sites strengthened the bombers were gradually driven up to higher altitudes.

The report showed that the growth of the AAF to 31 groups had introduced a problem that was negligible when it consisted of only four groups. The data showed that if from one to three groups attacked a given target, 39% of the bombs could be expected to fall within 1,000 feet of the aiming point. If from four to six groups attacked the same target, 34% of the bombs could be expected to fall within 1,000 feet of the aiming point. If from seven to nine groups attacked, the percentage dropped to 25%; and if from 10 to 19 groups attacked the same target, only 20% of the bombs could be expected to fall within 1,000 feet of the aiming point. Such a finding virtually dictated the policy of splitting an attacking force among many targets.

It was discovered in May 1943 that the bombing accuracy of groups bombing the same target decreased as the number of groups bombing increased if they followed one another closely. This was caused by groups interfering with each other on the bomb run and by smoke and debris obstructing the target. Bombing accuracy improved considerably for the following groups if they separated from one another by at least a few minutes, but this increased the bombers' vulnerability to AA fire.

During this period the Eighth Air was growing rapidly. On 13 December a record-breaking 649 bombers were dispatched to targets in Germany, followed by another record-breaking 763 bombers on 29 January and then by a 1,000 bombers sent out on 20 February 1943 during "Big Week."

In February 1944 18,903,000 pounds of bombs (excluding fragmentation bombs) were dropped visually by the Eighth Air Force, whereas in March 17,460,000 pounds (excluding fragmentation) were dropped. However, excluding bombs dropped on targets of opportunity in February 12,426,000 pounds were dropped, with 41% percent within 1,000 feet of the aiming point and 72% percent within 2,000 feet. Excluding targets of opportunity, in March 16,240,000 pounds were dropped with 31% falling within 1,000 feet and 61% percent fell within 2,000 feet of the aiming point.

From 1 September to 31 December 1944 (a period when it was at its maximum strength of 40 heavy bomb groups) the Eighth Air Force conducted heavy bombardment operations on 73 days, an average of slightly over 18 days per month. In these operations, between 60,000 and 65,000 heavy bomber sorties were flown for an average of approximately 900 sorties per operation. On 26 of the 73 days of operations some or all of the bombing was done visually. On the remaining 47 days (64% of the days) all the bombing was done with some form of radar under varying conditions of cloud cover.

H2X Bombing

The analysts viewed H2X as an aid to visual bombing and as a last resort means of bombing through heavy clouds. However, the air force wanted to keep up its strategic bombing and needed to frequently bomb its strategic targets again, especially oil targets. Consequently, 58% of all Eighth Air Force bombing from 1 September to 31 December 1944 was done with the aid of H2X, and 35% was done through 10/10 cloud cover. Thus, in practice, H2X had become the dominant mode of bombing.

Inherent Inaccuracy of H2X Bombing

Radar-assisted bombing was inherently inaccurate. Operator error contributed from 1,000 to 3,000 feet of inaccuracy, beam width up to 1,500 feet, data transmission 250 feet, and the spot size of the target on the radar screen 200 feet. If all factors involved in the radar sighting method worked perfectly inherent uncertainties in the radar system could cause errors up to 2,750 feet. Because the radar received information from other instruments, additional errors in the determination of air speed, wind speed, altitude, and roll rate could account for another 3,700 feet of error. When dropped by radar alone circular errors of two miles were average. With Norden visual assistance errors below one mile were common.

The Problem of Locating H2X Bombfall

The biggest problem of all H2X blind bombing for the analysts was determining its accuracy. Analysts used four sources to locate the bombfall of H2X bombing: photographs of the H2X scope made during the course of the mission; PRU (Photo Reconnaissance Unit) photographs taken after the mission; the strike photographs of the falling bombs; and mission reports made by crew members and others involved in the mission. Scope photographs and the PRU photographs were determined to be subjective. For example, the PRU photographs were of the target area only and never included bombfalls five or more miles from the aiming point, thus giving a misleading sample of all H2X bombfalls.

The analysis of H2X bombing contained in the above report was based on information obtained from strike photographs and mission reports. In many cases, even when the cloud cover on the bombing run was reported as 10/10 small breaks in the cloud enabled the strike photographs to show either the bombfall or sufficient ground detail to calculate the position of the bombfall. In many cases it was possible to check the calculated position of the bombfall with PRU photographs. These checks indicated that, on the average, the pattern center was within a quarter of a mile of the calculated position.

In the period 1 September 1944 to 31 December 1944, 3,025 squadrons (combat boxes) attempted to bomb with H2X and reported cloud cover at the target of from 4/10 to 10/10, and of these 2,933 dropped their bombs. However, the bombfalls of 1,589 combat boxes were not identified, so this study of H2X bombing was based on the knowledge of approximately half of the bombfalls. The report reasonably assumed that the accuracy of the half not identified was to be the same as the half identified.

Cloud Cover: The Main Factor in H2X Bombing Accuracy

The degree of cloud cover in the target area affected the accuracy of the H2X missions more than any other factor. For example, the percent of the pattern centers of bombfalls which fell more than five miles from the aiming point was 42% for 10/10 cover, 18% for 8/10 to 9/10 cover, 9% for 6/10 to 7/10 cover, and 5% for 4/10 to 5/10 cover.

The Relation of H2X Bombing to the Percent of Bombs Landing within Standard Distances from the Assigned Aiming Point Based on Reported Cloud Cover (1 September 1944-31 December 1944)

Reported cloud cover	**Estimated percent of bombs dropped that fell within:**				
	1,000 ft.	0.5 mile	1 mile	3 miles	5 miles
10/10	0.2	1.2	5.6	39.8	58.5
8/10-9/10	1.0	7.3	22.5	67.4	82.0
6/10-7/10	2.0	12.5	36.5	84.0	90.5
4/10-5/10	4.4	22.8	48.5	89.1	96.0

The table shows that visibility was all-important for H2X bombing accuracy, and also no definite line of demarcation between visual bombing and H2X bombing existed. Instead, there was a progression of bombing accuracy, in relation to a scale of visibility, with pure visual bombing at one extreme and pure H2X at the other.

The following example illustrates the two extremes. For targets of the order of one mile in diameter, visual bombing under good visibility was, on the average, approximately 50 times more effective than H2X with 10/10 cloud cover. For targets two miles in diameter the ratio was approximately 15 to 1, while for targets of the order of six miles in diameter the ratio was approximately 2.5 to 1. As an instrument for precision bombing with 10/10 cloud cover H2X was ineffective, but was, however, a practical method for area bombing of large targets; the morality of area "terror" bombing was becoming less of a priority in the 8AF strategy.

The table shows, for example, that in order to put a given density of bombs on a target approximating in size circles with diameters of one mile or less 20 times the force would be required, on average, if the attack were made by H2X under 10/10 cloud rather than by H2X under 4/10 to 5/10 cloud cover.

Other Reasons for H2X Inaccuracy

The H2X was used to drop bombs in four ways: a H2X bomber could drop bombs; an H2X bomber could drop smoke markers, upon which other bombers released bombs; an H2X bomber could drop bombs with the Visual Assistance (VA) of the bombardier; and bombs could be released on smoke markers dropped with visual help. The most accurate was the VA sighting with bombs on smoke markers, while H2X marker, or VA marker were less accurate than those dropped by H2X and VA. Bombs were also dropped accidentally during equipment failure due to combat damage.

The H2X bombing of targets in small cities was more accurate than H2X bombing of targets in large cities. If the objective was only to drop bombs on built up areas the efficiency of H2X attacks on cities of various sizes would vary little. The RAF could place 50% of its bombs in built up areas regardless of the size of the city. Alternatively, if the objective was to place bombs accurately on a target represented by a circle from 2,000 feet to one mile in diameter, it is obvious that the efficiency of attacks on such targets would be greater when they were located in small cities than when they were located in large cities. The analysts felt that this was caused by "an inherent inability of the equipment to locate the target with precision and certainty." H2X-aimed bombs inherently fell short of the aiming point by 0.53 miles on the average.

Why H2X Bombing Accuracy Did Not Improve

A great handicap to improving H2X bombing was the difficulty in getting speedy and thorough information about past operations.

Strike photographs supplied more and better information on visual attacks and were analyzed and reported periodically to the operating units. No such complete analysis for H2X missions was possible, as half of the H2X bombfalls were never identified. The reports that were made became available only weeks or even months after the mission and made it difficult to improve H2X performance.

The H2X part of the report on bombing ends with the following pessimistic summary:

"The accuracy achieved on our H2X missions has been substantially lower than that achieved with the beacon type radar systems as well as with visual bombing. Indeed, except for extremely large area targets, it has been less effective than our visual bombing by factors ranging from about 45 times for targets of the order of one half mile in diameter to six times for targets of the order of two miles in diameter. Similarly, it has been less effective than the beacon type radar systems thus far employed by this Air Force by factors ranging from about seven times for targets of the order of one half mile in diameter to about four times for targets of the order of two miles in diameter.

"With the employment of the synchronous procedure the discrepancy between the results obtained under conditions of solid cloud and under conditions of partial cloud is extremely large. Any system of planning, therefore, which would result in increasing the proportion under partial cloud would greatly increase the effectiveness of the overall effort.

"From the standpoint of possible improvement, nothing in our experience to date has given a basis for expecting any substantial improvement with our present equipment on our present type of targets."

In its first report of 31 January 1944 on the accuracy of H2X missions, the Bombing Accuracy Subsection had estimated that 5% of all bombs had fallen within one mile of the assigned aiming point. For the four-month period 1 September 1944 to 31 December 1944, 5.6% of all H2X bombs dropped with 10/10 cloud cover fell within one mile of the assigned aiming point. After a year of operations there had been no improvement in accuracy with this equipment.

Gee-H and Micro-H Accuracy

Only two types of radar bombing which depended on beacons were used to any great extent by the Eighth Air Force: Gee-H and Micro-H.

Gee-H Accuracy
During the period 1 October to 31 December 1944, 83 attacks made primarily with Gee-H with a total of 794 squadron formations were dispatched. Somewhere between 25% to 40% of the bombs dropped on Gee-H missions resulted in errors of over one and a half miles, while the remaining 60% to 75% approximated a normal distribution with an average error of approximately 0.7 miles, or 3,700 feet. Figures for visual bombing under conditions of good visibility at the higher altitudes showed that 20% to 25% of the bombing resulted in errors of over 3,000 feet, while the remaining 75% to 80% approximated a normal distribution with an average error of about 1,000 feet. H2X bombing with 10/10 cloud resulted in 35% to 45% of the bombs distributed over five miles, while the remaining 55% to 65% had average errors of approximately 2.5 miles. Micro-H accuracy was about the same as that of Gee-H.

Micro-H Accuracy
Since Micro-H was operational for only about the last six weeks of the time period covered by the report the number of bombfalls that could be analyzed was too small to draw reliable conclusions. However, the indications were that its accuracy was about the same as that of Gee-H.

Summary of Gee-H and Micro-H
The Gee-H and Micro-H portion of the report concludes with the following summary:

"Gee-H and Micro-H bombing, while far behind visual bombing, have nevertheless achieved a significant measure of success. Several different techniques have been used but none shows a clear advantage over the others. This problem of the choice of the best technique will continue to be of importance certainly until the introduction of a radar bombing device with an automatic computing system as an integral part....The fundamental limitation of all beacon bombing is its range, and in view of the large errors in H2X bombing, it would appear desirable to make every effort to extend substantially the range of beacon bombing."

Comparison of Visual, Gee-H, and H2X Accuracy
The following table compares the expected percents of bombs within standard distances in Gee-H Bombing, Visual Bombing under Conditions of Good Visibility, and H2X Bombing under Conditions of Total Cloud:

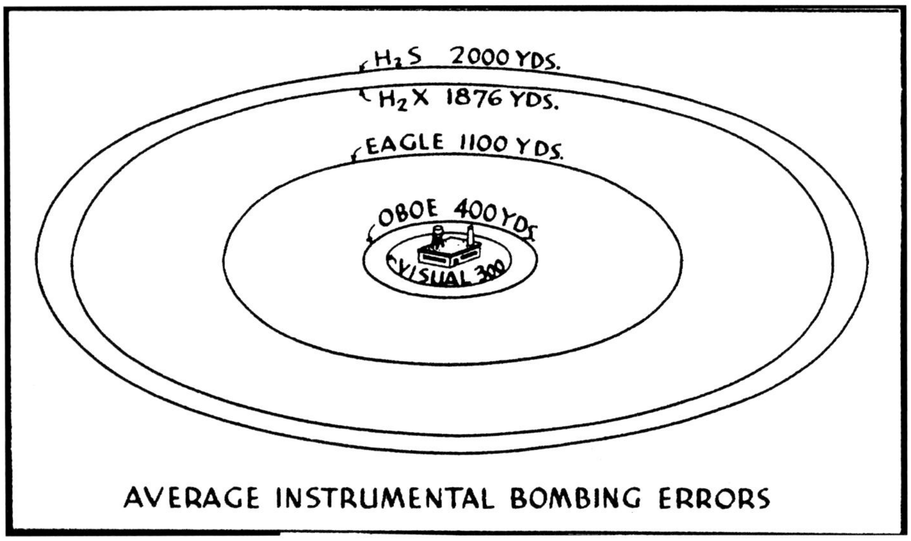

Estimated percent of all bombs dropped that fell within

	1000 ft	0.5 mile	1 mile	3 miles	5 miles
Visual bombing in good visibility	30%	64%	82%	91%	92%
Gee-H	5%	26%	56%	90%	94%
H2X (10/10 cloud)	0.2%	1.2%	6%	40%	59%

Estimated percent of all bombs dropped that fell within

	1000 ft	0.5 mile	1 mile	3 miles	5 miles
Visual Bombing in	30%	64%	82%	91%	92%
Gee-H	5%	26%	56%	90%	94%
H2X (10/10 cloud)	0.2%	1.2%	6%	40%	59%

Table compares the three modes of bombing.

The table shows that for targets of 2,000 feet in diameter Gee-H was approximately 1/6 as effective as visual bombing with good visibility, and it was 25 times as effective as H2X under total cloud. For targets of the order of one mile in diameter Gee-H was approximately 2/5 as effective as visual and 20 times as effective as H2X under conditions of total cloud.

Distribution of Total Effort by Categories of Bombing (1 September 1944-1 December 1944)

Category of bombing	Percent of total effort
H2X (10/10 cloud)	35%
H2X (8/10-9/10 cloud)	15%
H2X (6/10-7/10 cloud)	5%
H2X (4/10-5/10 cloud)	3%
Micro-H	3%
Gee-H	15%
Visual (poor visibility)	10%
Visual (good to fair visibility)	14%

AAF Bombing of German Cities
The policy of the Eighth Air Force was not to bomb German cities as a target system, but nevertheless, the Eighth Air Force was responsible for a large part of the destruction of German cities.

While AAF mission planners and the bomber crews showed great concern about the civilians in occupied countries, their concern for the civilians in Germany was patently less, as bomb groups were less reticent in selecting targets of opportunity when they were unable to drop their bombs on assigned primary or secondary targets in Germany. Often the bomber crews had no idea what they had dropped their bombs on, as the 7 October 1944 entry for the Eighth Air Force in *Combat Chronology* demonstrates:

"Over 1,300 heavy bombers, in four forces, bomb 5 synthetic oil plants, an armament, a tank, and an aero engine works in central and northeast Germany, plus 16 identified and 19 other unidentified targets in the area."

The official justification for bombing German cities was "spillage," which was defined as bombs aimed at military targets that fell in nearby areas. American bomber crews were seldom assigned city areas as aiming points, but the majority of their targets in Germany were in cities or their outskirts. The aiming points given the bomber crews were usually military or economic targets, such as oil plants, rail centers, marshalling yards, factories, etc, within the metropolitan area of a city. Fifty-eight percent of all bombs dropped on German cities by the Eighth Air Force (1 September to 31 December 1944) were the extremely inaccurate H2X bombs, which certainly produced "spillage."

Bombing Accuracy in the Pacific

The capture of Guam, Tinian, and Saipan in the summer of 1944 allowed the XXI Bomber Command to begin its strategic bombing of Japan from the Mariana Islands in November 1944. The Joint Chiefs of Staff ordered its commander, Brig. Gen. Haywood S. Hansell Jr., to "achieve the earliest possible progressive dislocation of the Japanese military, industrial, and economic systems and to undermine the morale of the Japanese people to a point where their capacity and will to wage war was decisively weakened." Targets were the aircraft industry, arsenals, electronic plants, oil refineries, and finished military goods. Hansell's orders also included incendiary bomb attacks on Japanese cities to test their vulnerability.

Hansell was an important figure, supporting daylight precision strategic bombing both at the Air Corps Tactical School and as a member of the Air War Plans Division. He sent 24 B-29s after the Nakajima Musashino aircraft engine plant in Tokyo on 24 November 1944. Although skies were clear for this first mission, bombardiers discovered the 200 mph easterly flowing jet stream would make precision bombing from altitudes above 30,000 nearly impossible, and all bombs missed the Musashino plant. Flying against the jet stream winds slowed aircraft and exposed them to enemy defenses, while flying at an angle to them caused so much drift that the Norden Bombsight could not compensate. Flying with the winds occasionally pushed ground speeds above 450 mph, which was too fast for Norden Bombsight synchronization. When flying against the jet stream B-29 bombardiers would be fortunate to place 10% of their bombs within 1,000 feet of the assigned aiming point.

H2X radar was developed because the AAF anticipated that the Norden Bombsight could not function when used in future 400 mph plus bomber designs. But H2X radar sighting was found to be even more ineffective. A B-29 radar mission on the Nagoya Mitsubishi assembly plant was so ineffective that post strike reconnaissance found hundreds of craters 30 to 40 miles from the aiming point!

A crisis in daylight precision strategic bombing was imminent, as 22 bombing missions against Japanese industries stopped production at only one factory. In multiple raids against the Musashino Aircraft Factory, 835 B-29s dropping 2,300 tons of bombs damaged only 4% of the large facility. The only obvious solutions to bombing inaccuracy were bombing from lower altitudes or area incendiary bombing of Japan's inflammable wooden cities. Hansell was committed to Air Corps Tactical School doctrine and objected to both solutions. To bomb at lower altitudes would bring greater losses of half million dollar B-29s and their 11 man crews, while area bombing would not destroy the Japanese war waging capability. The Air Staff and Arnold urged him to fly incendiary test missions on Tokyo on 29 November 1944, and to Nagoya on 3 January 1945, as tests. These test missions were flown from high altitude and the results were limited; although many fires started, they were widely dispersed and easily controlled.

Gen. Arnold replaced **Haywood Hansell** (right) with **Curtis LeMay** (left), who had helped save daylight precision strategic bombing in Europe. By late January 1945 Hansell's XXI Bomber Command could claim only one successful precision attack, but LeMay would change bombing tactics and devastate Japanese cities. (AAF)

By late January 1945 Hansell's XXI Bomber Command could claim only one successful precision attack when a 19 January raid on the Kawasaki Aircraft Industries plant near Akashi caused serious damage. The next day Gen. Arnold replaced Hansell with Curtis LeMay, who had helped save daylight precision strategic bombing in Europe. LeMay was described by Brig.Gen. Lauris Norstad, 20AF Chief of Staff, as "an operator, while the rest of us are planners." As an operator LeMay would not have Hansell's concern over "incidental" Japanese civilian casualties.

LeMay's initial bombing efforts were no more successful than Hansell's. Weather, high altitude, and high winds made bombing ineffective, including a test incendiary attack on Kobe. On 19 February 1945 Norstad assigned incendiary test raids on aircraft assembly plants as a priority, and LeMay responded with a maximum effort against Tokyo six days later. High altitude drops again limited its effectiveness against the actual target, but the 172 B-29s burned one square mile of the surrounding built-up urban area to the ground.

After four months the 20AF B-29 precision bombing campaign against Japan's industrial complex had not destroyed any of the nine top priority targets due to long and fatiguing 3,000 mile round trip missions encountering the strong jet stream winds and the chronically cloudy Japanese weather, all of which lessened the effectiveness of the fabled Norden Bombsight. Even so, the 20AF's bombing percentage of hits within 1,000 feet of the aiming point was 7% better than that of the 8th and 15th Air Forces in the ETO and MTO. A study of the average accuracy of both the XX and XXI Bomber Commands estimated that visual bombing from 31,000 feet averaged only 5% hits within 1,000 feet of the aiming point, 12% from 24,500 feet, and 30% from 20,000 feet. Radar aiming was even more inaccurate, with less than 1% of the bombs hitting within 1,000 feet of the target (the average was two miles!). More troubling was that 22% of the bombers failed to bomb the target at all. The Navy had done more damage to the Musashino plant in one attack by dive bombers than 2,148 B-29 sorties and 5,398 tons bombs dropped from high altitude.

A new air strategy was needed, and target planners had known for some time that the Japanese cities were much more prone to fire and incendiary bombing than European cities. The planners also knew that incendiary bombing of Japanese cities would cause huge conflagrations that would inflict terrible civilian casualties. When LeMay decided to switch to area incendiary bombing he used the justification that Japanese industry and residential areas were commingled into the flat topography of its large cities, much more so than in Germany, where industry was concentrated into specific areas. It was unavoidable that while bombing the factories the civilian population would also be bombed. So, unable to destroy the machines of war, LeMay resolved to kill the Japanese who operated the machines and to destroy the cities that housed the machines. Terror bombing had replaced precision bombing. There was no precision in dumping clusters out of the bomb bay once the bomber was over the target.

With 6,821 American Marines dying on Iwo Jima LeMay wrote in his memoirs:

"No matter how you slice it, you're going to kill an awful lot of civilians. Thousands and thousands. But if you don't destroy the Japanese industry, we're going to have to invade Japan. And how many Americans will be killed in an invasion of Japan? Five hundred thousand seems to be the lowest estimate. Some say a million.... We're at war with Japan. We were attacked by Japan. Do you want to kill Japanese or would you rather have Americans killed?"

LeMay believed high altitudes would limit effectiveness, as poor ballistics made the M69 incendiary cluster aimless from high altitudes. Low-altitude missions were thought to be too dangerous, but LeMay's intelligence sources told him that Japan had not deployed low altitude antiaircraft artillery because of its experience against high altitude B-29s. Area bombing did not need the precision of daylight, so the darkness of night and surprise made low altitudes safer. Low altitudes, unhindered by the jet stream and heavy cloud formations, compensated for the lost accuracy of night bombing, but the aiming points were to be huge bonfires. The X-l Reflex Sight Attachment with coated optics to increase light transmission made the Norden M-9 bombsight an acceptable aiming mechanism for night missions. Although not designed for this purpose, the APQ-13 radar worked well at low altitudes. It was the greatest gamble of his career. Lower altitudes and stripping the big bombers of their defensive weapons reduced gas consumption and increased bomb loads.

LeMay did not have sufficient bombers available to carry out the fire bombing campaign until March 1945, and was forced until then to continue the strategic bombing campaign using high explosive bombs. On 9 March 282 B-29s dropped 2,000 tons of M69 jelled-gasoline incendiaries from 7,000 feet on Tokyo by intervalometers set at 50 feet. The aiming point was a large burning cross marked by pathfinder aircraft dropping M47 Napalm bombs across a three by four mile rectangle in the center of the city inhabited by more than one million Japanese. Packed in 500-pound clusters, the six pound M69 bomblets scattered over 15.8 square miles of Tokyo. Later crews aimed at unburned areas between fires. Only 14 aircraft were lost, but high winds created a fire storm and at least 78,000 Japanese died. After the war LeMay ruthlessly explained his objectives, "I'll tell you what war is about; you've got to kill people, and when you've killed enough they stop fighting."

XXI Bomber Command's next target was Nagoya on 11 March. Planners increased intervalometer settings to 100 feet to get a larger path of destruction, but the decreased bombing density reduced the intensity of the fires. The next unfortunate targets were Osaka, Kobe, and Nagoya with 50 foot intervalometer settings. Running short on M69 clusters, LeMay's bombers carried M17 magnesium thermite bombs. Although less effective against urban areas, they kept the fire bombing campaign going. LeMay's fire bombing campaign left five of Japan's largest cities blackened shells. Exhaustion, the depletion of incendiary bombs, and the diversion to support the Okinawa invasion halted the fire bombing effort, and strategic bombing with high explosive bombs continued until incendiary bomb stocks arrived on 13 April.

Until VJ-Day, the 20AF Superfortress incendiary bombs burned out city after city, culminating in the dropping of the two Atomic Bombs.

XX Bomber Command Operations
(in tons, including mining operations)

Date	High Explosives	Incendiary	Mining	Total
November 1944	1,415	215	0	1,630
December 1944	678	878	0	1,556
January 1945	1,584	422	233	2,239
February 1945	1,261	604	36	1,901
March 1945	1,019	417	259	1,695
Total	**5,957**	**2,536**	**528**	**9,021**

Source: Twentieth Air Force, Statistical Operations, September 1945

Temporarily without incendiaries, XXI Bomber Command was unable to mount a fire raid against Japan between 19 March and 13 April 1945, and the Bomber Command experimented with variations in bombardment. Encouraged by the XX BC to try nighttime, high altitude precision attacks, LeMay first sent 251 B-29s against the Mitsubishi aircraft facility at Nagoya on 24/25 March 1945. The results were poor, as of the 1,533 tons dropped only 60 tons fell in the main target zone. On 30/31 March LeMay next sent an attack by a single B-29 wing with differing mixes of bombs and flares, but none of the 50 tons of bombs hit the Mitsubishi works. On 1/2 April another bombardment wing of 115 B-29s dropped 1,019 tons on the Nakajima-Musashino complex, but a mere four tons hit the target with virtually no effect.

On the evening of 3/4 April 1945 LeMay tried a new combination by sending one bombardment wing against each of three aircraft engine and assembly plants on a single raid. Tachikawa was hit by 503 tons by 61 B-29s and Mitsubishi-Shizuoka by 181 tons from 48 B-29s, while another 48 bombers dropped 275 tons on Nakajima-Koizumi. Again the results were poor, with Shizuoka untouched, Tachikawa suffering medium damage, and the effect on Koizumi was light. These mediocre results convinced LeMay that the technology for high altitude nighttime precision bombing was unavailable.

At last precision bombing results improved. In the afternoon of 7 April two B-29 wings launched a high-altitude precision attack against the XXI Bomber Command's number two priority target, the Mitsubishi plant at Nagoya. Dropping 614 tons of high explosive bombs, many the new 2,000 pound HE bomb, from approximately 20,500 feet in good weather, 154 B-29s finally devastated the Mitsubishi engine works, destroying or damaging 90% of the building area and essentially putting the facilities out of action for the remainder of the war.

On 14 April 119 B-29s of the 73BW, armed with 2,000 pound bombs, returned to finally eliminate the Musashino plant. That same day 94 Superforts dropped 490 tons of HE bombs on the Nakajima works, and essentially XXI Bomber Command's top priority target was finally eliminated, but it had taken 11 B-29 attacks plus a U.S. Navy carrier strike to accomplish the job.

XXI Bomber Command's support of the Okinawa campaign was continuing when new stocks of incendiaries allowed LeMay to mount more low altitude area attacks on the arsenal district of northwest Tokyo. For more than 3.5 hours on 13/14 April 327 B-29s dropped about 2,130 tons of incendiaries (two-thirds by radar) which, fanned by brisk winds, generated an enormous firestorm that razed an estimated 11.4 square miles of Tokyo.

The next evening, on 14/15April, another force of 303 B-29s, including 109 over Tokyo, dropped 1,930 tons of incendiaries, all by radar from low altitudes. Another 11.1 square miles was razed, over half of it in western Tokyo, with more than a third in Kawasaki and the rest in Yokohama. In these two fire raids combined Tokyo and Yokohama lost more than 217,000 structures, and Kawasaki nearly 32,000, but because of the movement of civilians from the cities to the countryside casualties were much fewer than they had been during the first onslaught of 9/10 March.

Precision bombing continued during the incendiary onslaught, as B-29s attacked strategic industrial targets in daylight. On the morning of 24 April 1945 101 Superforts visually bombed Hitachi's Tachikawa aircraft engine plant at Yamato, north of Tokyo, dropping about 474 tons of standard bombs from only 2,000 feet and causing very heavy damage. Then, on the morning of 5 May, 148 B-29s bombed the Hiro naval aircraft plant at Kure from 20,000 feet and 578 tons of HE flattened the plant. On 11 May 60 B-29s smashed Kawanishi's Konan airframe factory.

After Germany capitulated on 8 May Gen. Arnold asked XXI Bomber Command's LeMay when he could expect Japan to collapse. LeMay confidently declared that destruction of 60 Japanese urban areas would force the country to surrender by 1 October. LeMay proceeded to launch a month long series of area fire bombings to complete what he had begun in March and continued in April. At the same time, precision targets would be hit as appropriate, per the two-track system devised earlier. The new round of incendiary raids began with a maximum-effort 529-plane daylight attack against northern Nagoya during the early morning of 14 May 1945. This was the first incendiary raid in which the bombing was conducted visually. Flying between 12,000 and 20,500 feet, 472 B-29s dropped 2,515 tons of bombs, which burned out approximately 3.2 square miles of the city, but the swirling smoke diminished the bombing accuracy of later formations.

On the night of 16/17 May 522 B-29s struck Nagoya again when 457 bombers flew in at 6,600 to 8,300 feet for one hour, but smoke and thermal currents compelled half of them to bomb from 15,000 feet, expending much more time in the process. The B-29s dropped 3,600 tons of incendiaries to burn out about 3.8 square miles, as 30% of Nagoya's built up area had been leveled and Nagoya was removed from the prime target list. Only Tokyo sustained as many air attacks, but then most of what remained of Tokyo was obliterated in two subsequent fire raids. On the night of May 23/24, 1945, the western section, with its assortment of industrial and residential structures, came under attack again by 520 B-29s and 44 pathfinders. In poor weather, and relying almost entirely on radar, the bombers dropped 3,646 tons of incendiaries in two hours from heights of 7,800 to 15,000 feet. In the second mission of the night Tokyo was struck once again after 0130, and for two and a half hours 250 B-29s flew in, mostly individually, dropping 76,518 incendiary bombs. Strong winds drove the flames into a huge fire storm, destroying 5.3 square miles of Tokyo, but this raid was considered the least effective of the six major attacks on the Japanese capital. Consequently, on the night of May 25/26, 1945, the B-29s bombed Tokyo again, attacking the western section of the city. A combination of light clouds and smoke necessitated radar bombing as the bombers dropped 3,256 tons of incendiaries (three-fourths by radar) from heights of 7,900 to 22,000 feet. This time almost 17 square miles of the capital burned (the largest area destroyed thus far in any raid on Tokyo) and nearly 600,000 inhabitants were made homeless.

XXI Bomber Command continued its unremitting incendiary campaign of area bombing against Japanese urban targets, and Yokohama was next to come under attack. Yokohama was Japan's fifth largest city, possessing the country's largest harbor, but between November 1944 and April 1945 B-29s dropped only 28 tons of bombs on Yokohama. While the highly industrialized harbor area of neighboring Kawasaki was hit hard by 1,110 tons of bombs on 15 April, the XXI Bomber Command did not designate Yokohama a primary target before the end of May.

During the two nighttime attacks on Tokyo at the end of May 1945 the XXI Bomber Command lost 43 B-29s and an additional 169 damaged. For the Yokohama attack LeMay and his staff decided on alternative tactics to cut losses. The B-29s would fly in during daylight in carefully timed formations at high altitude and with P-51 fighter escorts from Iwo Jima. At 0930 on 29 May 517 Superforts escorted by 101 P-51s bombed the center of Yokohama in good weather and dropped 2,570 tons of incendiary bombs, first visually and then by radar when the usual billowing smoke began to cover the targets. Twenty priority targets were destroyed and seven square miles of the city's center was demolished for the loss of only five B-29s.

On Japan's main island of Honshu, two of the three largest and most important urban-industrial centers were now burned out: Kei-Hin (Tokyo-Yokohama-Kawasaki) and the region centering on Nagoya, and only the third urban-industrial zone known as Han-Shin (Osaka-Kobe) was considered to have any value as targets. LeMay dispatched three daylight fire raids against Osaka on 1, 7, and 15 June 1945, and one against Kobe on 5 June. In the first of these Osaka attacks, 458 B-29s flew at 18,000 to 28,500 feet and dropped 2,788 tons of bombs, all but 81 tons being incendiaries, and burning out about 3.5 square miles of the city. On 7 June at 1000 409 B-29s bombed northern and northeastern Osaka at altitudes ranging from 17,900 to 23,150 feet. In heavy undercast the B-29s, using radar, dropped 1,795 tons of incendiaries and 797 tons of high explosive bombs, which were aimed at the vital Osaka army arsenal, the only area attack to include such a large proportion of high explosive tonnage. The attack did significant damage, and the B-29s returned to Osaka a week later. From 0845 to 1045 444 B-29s, at an average altitude of 21,500 feet, dropped 3,157 tons of incendiary bombs (the largest incendiary load of the month). Though the targets were scattered, nearly two square miles were burned out in eastern, southern, and northwestern Osaka. On 5 June, between the first and second attacks on Osaka, B-29s flew a daylight attack against Kobe, across the bay. Flying at lower altitudes of 13,650 to 18,000 feet, 473 bombers dropped 71 tons of high explosives and 3,006 tons of incendiaries that burned out 4.35 square miles, and Kobe was written off as a target.

Between 9 March and 15 June 1945 B-29s had flown 6,960 sorties, dropped 41,592 tons of incendiaries, and burned out 102 square miles of the most densely populated and most important Japanese industrial zones. Japan's 50 or 60 smaller remaining urban areas were now the only worthwhile targets remaining, because they had industrial value and because they were vulnerable in terms of flammability and congestion. Only enough bomb tonnage was to be dropped on every target to destroy it on the first strike, and LeMay had more B-29s available than were needed. Separate B-29 forces were to attack separate targets, adapting to weather conditions on a daily basis. When visibility was satisfactory, the B-29s would fly daylight precision missions against priority strategic objectives, primarily in the aviation industry sector, employing squadron formations of nine to 11 planes that would come in at medium altitude with the formation leader handling the primary sighting task. In times of poor weather night radar bombing would be employed for area incendiary attacks.

LeMay planned to concentrate 70% to 85% of his bombing offensive on radar-guided incendiary fire bombing, which was thought to be adequate to destroy all remaining key industries within the three month period that LeMay thought necessary to cause Japan to surrender, or at a minimum to paralyze the enemy before the first surface invasion took place. LeMay's *Empire Plan* was complicated but flexible. While conventional incendiary attacks required a large amount of prior attention to detail, this plan needed particularly vigilant and continuous photo interpretation; information on force requirements, bomb type, tonnage, and bombing route; carefully selected aiming points; and accurately computed area densities and requirements for radar bombing.

Through July 22% of the overall B-29 effort involved daylight precision attacks. B-29s dropped 7,045 tons of bombs during precision attacks on industrial targets, many on airframe plants and related aviation factories. Eight other precision raids between June and August attacked five arsenals with another 5,270 tons of bombs. The Superforts also visually bombed two light metal processing plants, dropping 1,020 tons, and a heavy electrical equipment factory, with 806 tons. In June 1945, when the weather proved better than expected, 25% of the HE bombardment campaign was directed against 20 important industrial targets. The XXI Bomber Command distributed its forces to achieve maximum results in good weather.

As Japanese air defenses collapsed, LeMay took full advantage by stripping the defensive armament, except for tail guns, on 315th Bombardment Wing B-29s, which carried increased bomb loads and were equipped with the improved APQ-7 Eagle radar-bombing system. The stripped B-29Bs increased their bomb loads from seven to 10 tons per aircraft. In the first of 15 night attacks launched against 10 oil refineries and related installations through mid-August, these specialized bombers, known as B-29Bs, attacked the oil refinery at Yokkaichi on 26 June 1945. The unopposed attack by 30 bombers was made in nearly zero visibility by radar and dropped 223 tons of high explosives (891 500 pound bombs) on the target with satisfactory results. From late June 1945 until the end of the war in August 1,095 of 1,200 aircraft dispatched by the 315BW dropped 9,084 high explosive bombs on primary target oil facilities. Altogether, an estimated 7% of the total bomb tonnage dropped on Japan was directed at 17 oil-industry targets.

The B-29B raids destroyed much of Japan's oil storage tank capacity, but actually had little effect, as nearly all production had stopped because of the lack of crude oil. But in terms of bombs causing damage, the attacks against oil installations in Japan were more effective than they had been in Europe because of the compactness of Japanese plants, their lighter construction, inadequate defensive measures, and the higher average American high explosive tonnage and heavier bombs employed against these Japanese targets.

The Last B-29 Raids

XXI Bomber Command's effective sortie rate and delivery of bomb tonnage increased appreciably during the last few months of the war. Sorties numbered 5,243 in June 1945, 6,168 in July (by which time 979 B-29s were on hand), and 3,145 in the first half of August (when B-29s in inventory reached 1,000). In June, the B-29s dropped 37,542 tons of bombs; in July, 43,091 tons; and in the first two weeks of August, 21,873 tons. When the 8AF was transferred from the ETO it was scheduled to have 600 bombers by November, when the invasion of Kyushu (*Operation Olympic*) was to take place. By then, the Eighth Air Force and XXI Bomber Command would be able to fly 3,500 and 6,500 sorties per month, respectively, and drop a combined total of 70,000 tons of bombs in November, and if the B-29s flew around the clock thereafter, an unbelievable maximum of 715,000 tons of bombs could be dropped per month on Japan.

About 70% of the ongoing strategic air offensive was allocated to incendiary bombing of built-up industrial locations, mostly by radar at night. From mid-June to mid-August 1945 B-29s struck individually from altitudes between 8,000 and 14,000 feet and burned out another 76 square miles of Japan's secondary urban areas. In July alone 42 Japanese cities were burned in radar-directed night area attacks. By mid-August a total of 52 urban regions had been substantially destroyed and six others partially damaged. In 15 areas the destruction of built-up areas exceeded 70% percent: Toyama, 99.5% percent; Numazu, 89.5%; Fukui, 84.8%; Tsu, 81%; Hachioji, 80%; and Hitachi, 78.2%. In another 14 attacked areas the destruction ranged from 50 to 70%. In all cases these cities were eradicated on the first try. Only three of the 58 targeted cities had to be attacked a second time, mainly due to adverse weather over the target.

The continued incendiary bombings everywhere in Japan, with their devastating effect on vulnerable towns and cities, were generally responsible for the subsequent lowering of civilain morale. Increasingly civilians began to doubt the ability to win the war. When America changed its bombing tactics in June 1945 and began to make indiscriminate and brutal attacks on obscure and militarily insignificant villages and towns these attacks only served to strengthen the Japanese people's hate of the United States.

By early July 1945 the Japanese home islands were completely at the mercy of XXI Bomber Command, as medium-sized and small urban areas were not protected by AA defenses and the Japanese Air Forces offered little aerial resistance because of the shortage of aircraft and aviation fuel, and the policy of saving the few remaining aircraft to stave off the expected ground invasion of the homeland. Consequently, B-29s were able to bomb at will. By early August 1945 the AAF had 3,700 B-29s in inventory, and existing bases in the Marianas could accommodate only 1,000, while 600 or 700 more were to be based in Okinawa by November, before *Operation Olympic*.

Summary

The precision bombing campaign of Japan by the B-29s of the 20th Air Force obtained unsatisfactory results that were compounded by long 3,000 mile missions encountering the strong jet stream winds and the chronically cloudy Japanese weather, all of which lessened the effectiveness of the fabled Norden Bombsight. Even so, the 20AF's bombing percentage of hits within 1,000 feet of the aiming point was 7% better than that of the 8th and 15th Air Forces in the ETO and MTO. The purpose of a bomber was, of course, to drop bombs accurately on a target, and that was a primary problem for the B-29 and its Norden Bombsight, which was renowned for its accuracy. A study of the average accuracy of both the XX and XXI Bomber Commands estimated that visual bombing from 31,000 feet averaged only 5% hits within 1,000 feet of the aiming point, 12% from 24,500 feet, and 30% from 20,000 feet. Radar aiming was even less accurate, with less than 1% of the bombs hitting within 1,000 feet of the target (the average was two miles!). More troubling was that 22% of the bombers failed to bomb the target at all.

XXIBC Bombing Totals and Results

During the war the 20AF B-29s dropped 159,862 tons of bombs, 91% of all the bombs dropped on Japan by all services. At the end of the war the 20AF used the following bomb ratio:

HE Bombs:
40% 500lb GP
30% 2,000lb GP
20% 4,000lb LC
5% 1,000lb GP
5% Miscellaneous and special purpose

There were no HE bomb shortages during the war, but the 4,000 pound bombs were not initially ordered in sufficient quantities.

Incendiary Bombs:
40% 100lb gelled gasoline M47
40% 500lb clusters M69 (6lb oil and 10lb oil WP)
20% 500lb clusters M50 /M-52 (4lb magnesium)

There were times when the stocks of incendiary bombs were exhausted, and incendiary missions were curtailed until supply could catch up with demand; often an available bomb was chosen for the mission rather than the best bomb type. Frequently incendiary bombs were unloaded from the arriving ships and transported directly to B-29s waiting on their hardstands for loading.

In March 1945 the ratio between percent incendiary and percent HE was 72/28, in July 74/26, and 80/20 in August. For the entire B-29 bombing campaign (June 1944 to August 1945) the bomb ratio was 61% incendiary (as compared to 14% in Europe), 33% HE and fragmentation, and 6% mines. (20AF, *A Statistical Summary of Its Operations Against Japan*, June 44-August 45)

A brief synopsis of the destruction caused by the 159,862 tons of bombs (1,193 tons per day during the last three months of the war):

65 major cities were severely damaged or almost totally destroyed.
178 square miles of industrial urban areas were destroyed.
602 major factories were destroyed.
83% of oil production was destroyed.
75% of aircraft engine production was destroyed.
330,000 killed and 476,000 wounded (Direct civilian casualties in the concentrated 10 month span of B-29 attacks were more than Japanese military forces suffered in three and half years of war.)
2.3 million homes were destroyed.
8.5 million civilians were homeless and 21 million were displaced.

At the end of the war the 20AF had dropped almost 160,000 tons of bombs in 37 weeks, but had another 160,000 tons stocked and ready to drop in the next 11 weeks if the Atomic Bombs had not ended the war.

5

The Bombardier

Bombardier Training History

In the 1930s each bomb group was responsible for training its own bombardiers, who were enlisted men. After war began in Europe in September 1939, Gen. Arnold prepared a 16 week bombardier program at Lowry Field, outside Denver, CO, to meet anticipated personnel requirements. Gen. Delos Emmons, CO of the GHQAF, wanted the school to be under his control, but in July 1940 Gen. George C. Marshall put Gen. Hap Arnold in charge of the program. Fred Anderson became CO of the Lowry bombardier school, and the first class of 18 candidates made up of pilot training washouts graduated in October, followed by 52 in November, and 50 more in December. Once they graduated these bombardiers were given an additional 10 week service test class to qualify them as instructors. In 1941, seven months before Pearl Harbor, Arnold expanded the program to Barksdale Field, LA, and one month before the school at Ellington Field, TX, was established. The first class of combat bombardiers was not graduated until May 1941. By the end of 1941 only 206 bombardiers had graduated, which was far short of the 1,367 planned. In December 1941 and February 1942 new schools were opened at Albuquerque, NM, and Midland, TX, to meet the new bombardier requirement that was increased to 5,590. However, in March 1942 the requirement was raised to 14,000 bombardiers and then to 22,400 in July 1942. To meet this incredible demand Arnold established the Flying Training Command (FTC) on 23 January 1942, which opened eight new schools in New Mexico, Texas, and Arizona. Because of the demand for combat aircraft many aging B-18s were pressed into service as bombardier training aircraft. Kirtland AFB, Albuquerque, NM, was a major bombardier training center opening in February 1942 with an initial training aircraft complement of 28 B-18s and 50 AT-11s.

The length and content of the bombardier course of instruction underwent numerous changes. The course was lengthened from ten weeks to 12 and then to 18 weeks. Here the Bombing Problem is discussed. (AAF)

The length and content of the bombardier course of instruction underwent numerous changes. The course was lengthened from ten weeks to 12 and then to 18 weeks. The course content of the preflight and advanced curriculum was changed and refined by the training experience and then the combat experience of bombardiers. The bombardiers' 12 week course was comprised of the first three weeks in preliminary ground training; the fourth through ninth weeks inclusive consisting of ground and air training; and the tenth through twelfth weeks inclusive consisting of air training to include tactical bombing and reconnaissance missions.

Bombardier Training Aircraft

Beechcraft AT-11 Kansan

The AT-11, called the "Kansan," was the standard AAF World War II bombing trainer. Like the C-45 transport and the AT-7 navigation trainer, the Kansan was a military version of the Beechcraft Model 18 commercial transport. It was powered by two 450 hp Pratt & Whitney R-985s which gave it a cruising speed of 150 mph, a maximum speed of 215 mph, a range of 750 miles, and a service ceiling of 20,000 feet. The AT-11 measured 34.16 feet long; 9.65 feet high; 47.65 foot wing span; and a maximum weight of 9,300 pounds. A total of 1,582 were ordered by the AAF between 1941 and 1945, 36 of which were modified as AT-11A navigation trainers. About 90% of the more than 45,000 USAAF bombardiers trained in AT-11s, while the reminder trained in the Douglas B-18 and other obsolete bombers. Modifications for the AT-11 bombardier training conversion included a transparent nose, a bomb bay, internal bomb racks, and provisions for two flexible 0.30 caliber machine guns for gunnery training for Bombardiers who would also serve as gunners.

Douglas B-18 Bolo

The Douglas B-18 Bolo was a military adaptation of the DC-2 commercial transport to the long-range bombing role. By the end of 1941 it was obsolete, but was numerically the most important long-range bomber in service with the AAC at the time of Pearl Harbor. The B-18 served an important role in early anti-submarine patrols off the southeast American coast and the Caribbean, but was replaced by Navy blimps and other more contemporary AAF bombers. The B-18 always needed to find a new niche, and one was as a bombing training aircraft. An estimated 30 to 35 B-18s were employed as Bombardier training aircraft.

The **AT-11 "Kansan"** was the standard AAF World War II bombing trainer, and like the C-45 transport and the AT-7 navigation trainer, the Kansan was a military version of the Beechcraft Model 18 commercial transport. About 90% of the more than 45,000 USAAF bombardiers trained in AT-11s. (AAF)

The **Douglas B-18 Bolo** was a military adaptation of the DC-2 commercial transport to the long-range bombing role, but by the end of 1941, although it was the most numerous bomber in ACC inventory, it was obsolete, and was used in an ASW and bombardier training role as pictured. (AAF)

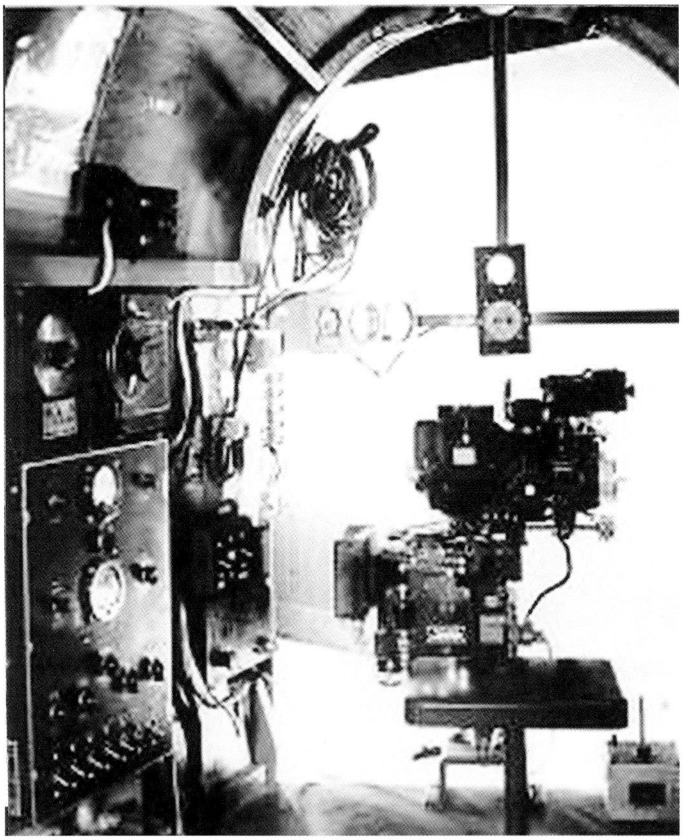

Modifications for the AT-11 bombardier training conversion included a transparent nose and the installation of the bombardier's position. (AAF)

Cadet Aerial Bombing Training

For air bombing training, the classes were divided into teams of three or four students who would train with the Norden bombsight in B-18s or mostly AT-11s crewed by a pilot, co-pilot, and instructor. After 30 September 1943 the AT-11 usually carried a Norden Bombsight and a C-1 automatic pilot, which allowed the bombardier student to guide the aircraft during the bombing run. The Norden Bombsights were so highly classified that they were stored in a guarded vault, and when the students were scheduled to fly a practice mission they had to get clearance to enter the vault area to be issued a bombsight to be carried in a canvas case. When they left the vault the required two students per bombsight were accompanied to the aircraft by an armed guard.

The first AT-11 training missions had three Bombardier students and one instructor flying in the former passenger compartment. The students sat on their parachutes on a backless seat in the noisy aircraft, which had no padding or sound proofing. Each cadet took his turn coming forward into the nose compartment past the bomb bay and the pilots. The training in the ground trainer had accustomed the cadet to the location of the seat position, bomb sight, and bombing equipment. The AT-11 flew at 7,000 feet toward the practice target, which was three concentric circles with a building in the center. The first practice missions were dry runs carrying no bombs, in which the students became familiar with the Norden bombsight and sighting the target. The cadets checked altitude and drift and then called directions to the pilot with a final faux "bombs away." With each dry run the student became more proficient, resulting in the bomber's vulnerable straight and level run over the target becoming shorter and shorter.

The next step was to divide the teams into pairs for practice runs with practice bombs. One cadet would be placed in the nose with the instructor while the other cadet was in the rear with the automatic camera to take photos of his classmate's hits and misses. The 100 pound sand-filled practice bombs had 2.5 pounds of black powder packed in the nose that would explode in a big puff of smoke in the daylight and a flash at night. In flight the student had to enter the bomb bay and pull two safety pins. Practice included dropping single bombs with and against the wind and in cross winds, followed by dropping trains and salvoes of bombs. After each run the student would note the results, which would be entered on the official 12-C form after landing. In 1943 the AAF established a minimum proficiency standard of 22% hits on target for trainees. Typical combat training missions took continuous evasive action within a 10 mile radius of the target with straight and level final target approaches that lasted no longer than 60 seconds.

Probably the most important change made to the Bombardier Program was the institution of dual (bombardier-navigator) training. Dual training had been planned before Pearl Harbor but was necessarily abandoned to meet immediate wartime requirements for bombardiers. By the end of 1942 there was a demand for bombardiers to man both medium and heavy bombers, which were coming online in large numbers. For the medium bomber, the combination of the bombardier-navigator function would reduce the size of the aircrew. For the fatiguing long range heavy bomber missions there would

Practice Bombing Gallery

The AT-11 approaches the target centered in three accuracy marking circles. (AAF)

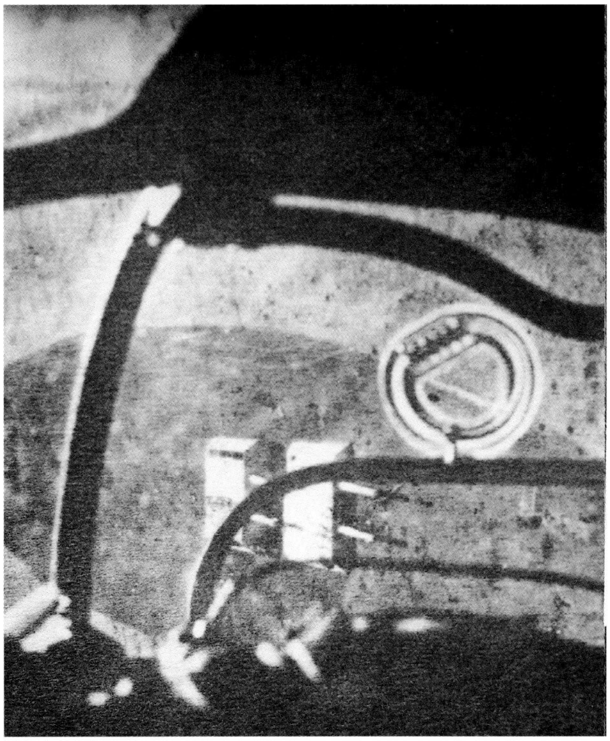

Student bombardier's view of a faux target warship. (AAF)

The student bombardier drops bomb with the center of the target located at the very top of the photo (the shadow of the AT-11 and target rings are seen). (AAF)

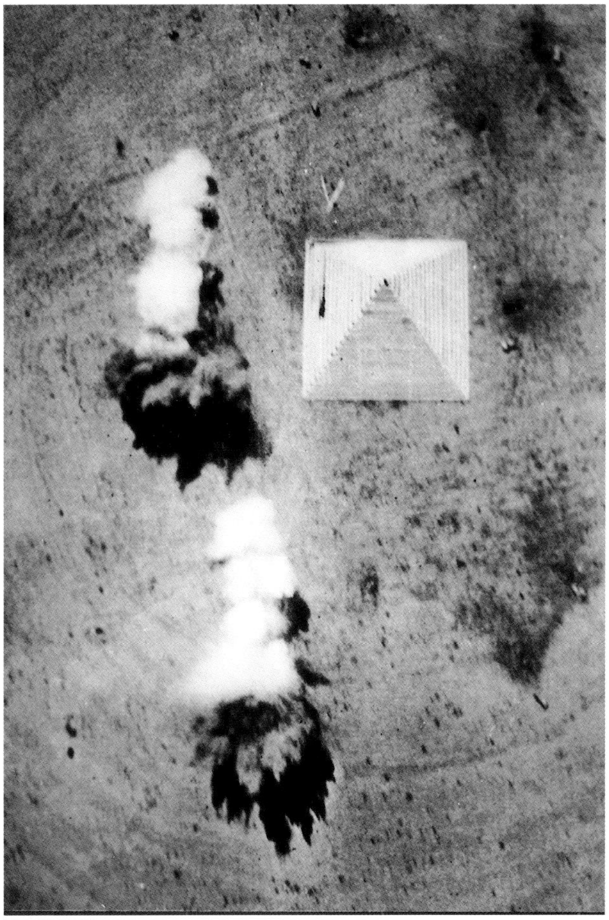

The automatic camera in the rear of the aircraft records the bomb hits near the pyramidal target building. (AAF)

Student bombardier taking his turn on the camera after his practice bombing run. Unknown to him was his "black eye," which was gotten when he pressed his face to the doctored bombsight eyepiece. (AAF)

be a definite advantage in having a replacement for either the navigator or bombardier. Navigators were trained as D-8 bombardiers for medium bombers and as Sperry S-1 or Norden precision bombardiers for heavy and very heavy bombers. Meanwhile, precision bombardiers were trained as dead reckoning navigators for both medium and heavy bombers. Dually trained personnel for the very heavy program were also given radar training.

USAAF Bombardier Training Graduates

Type	1942	1943	1944	1945	Total
Instructor	----	1,140	2,110	2,186	5,436
DR/Navigator					
Instructor	----	84	22	----	106
Preflight	3,678	17,678	19,364	----	40,720
Navigator Preflight	7,349	----	192	----	7,541
Bombardier School	4,082*	5,053	----	----	9,155
Precision for B-29	----	9,053	391	----	9,444
Pre-basic Training	----	----	----	1,477	1,477
Refresher	----	----	----	4,346	4,346
Bombardier/Navigator	----	292	1,257	997	2,546
D-8 Bombardier/					
Navigator	666	225	----	----	891
DR Bombardier/					
Navigator	----	1,475	17,504	5,958	24,937
Total	15,575*	35,000	40,840	14,964	106,579

* Includes 224 in 1941

Bombardier Training Aids

Training Films

In September 1942 BuOrd approved the production of training films on the operation of the Norden Bombsight to train bombardier cadets. The AAF Training Film Production Laboratories at Wright Field produced a number of motion picture training films.

BIF and ROBIF

The Bombardiers' Information File (BIF) and Radar Observers' Bombardment Information File (ROBIF) were general manuals of instructions and information with which all AAF bombardiers (BIF) and Radar Observers (ROBIF) in the Continental United States were required to comply by AAF Regulations. These manuals were designed to conveniently keep the Bombardier current on developments affecting bombing techniques, instruments, and equipment. It was to be checked frequently, and the Bombardier was required to have read and understood the information it contained. The Bombardier was to sign an enclosed receipt (Form 24BA) in his manual and return them to the operations office. Any revisions were to be inserted into the manual and the pertinent sections removed.

A-2 Bombing Trainer

The A-2 bombing trainer was the main method of training the bombardier in the use of the Norden Bombsight. It was used inside a hangar, simulating the principal characteristics of an actual bombing mission. It served two purposes: to help the bombardier learn how to operate the sight, and to help him learn the procedure he would use in the air.

The trainer consisted of two platforms mounted in a framework that rolled on three wheels with seats for the bombardier, driver, and instructor. The upper platform was used for synchronous bombing and the lower to simulate fixed-angle bombing missions. An electric motor drove the trainer, with the newer types including a reversible motor, which made it unnecessary to push the trainer backward after each run. The trainer was driven with a steering wheel connected by cables to the rear wheel of the trainer. The driver controlled the direction of the trainer through signals from the bombardier. These signals were registered on a standard PDI (Pilot Director Indicator). Later A-2s could be equipped with the C-1 autopilot, which made it unnecessary to have a driver.

The trainer target was attached to the "*Bug*," which was a box-like device rolling on three wheels. The electrically-driven *Bug* moved at a constant speed, and could be positioned to move in any direction. The bombardier's "hits" using the sight were marked on the target by a marker solenoid that was mounted on a metal plate connected to the trainer between the two front wheels.

Bombardiers' Information File (BIF)

(BIF)

Radar Observers' Bombardment Information File (ROBIF)

(ROBIF)

Form 24BA Bombing Receipt (BIF)

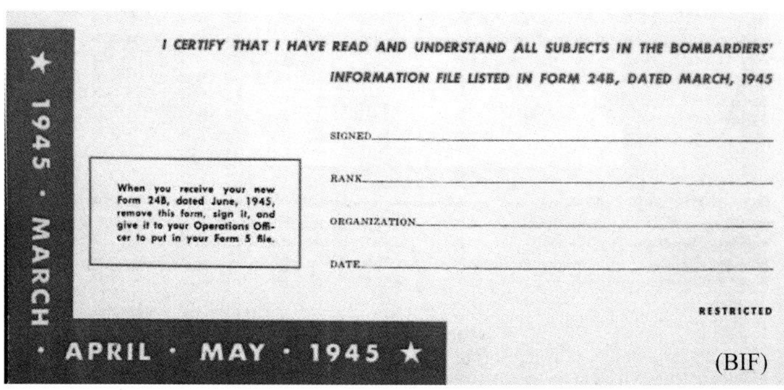

★ 1945 · MARCH · APRIL · MAY · 1945 ★

I CERTIFY THAT I HAVE READ AND UNDERSTAND ALL SUBJECTS IN THE BOMBARDIERS' INFORMATION FILE LISTED IN FORM 24B, DATED MARCH, 1945

When you receive your new Form 24B, dated June, 1945, remove this form, sign it, and give it to your Operations Officer to put in your Form 5 file.

SIGNED________

RANK________

ORGANIZATION________

DATE________

RESTRICTED

(BIF)

The **A-2 Bombing Trainer** was the main method of training the bombardier in the use of the Norden Bombsight. The trainer consisted of two platforms mounted in a framework that rolled on three wheels with seats for the bombardier, driver, and instructor. The "bug" can be seen on the floor at the foot of the A-2. (AAF)

Bombing altitude from the upper platform was considered to be the distance from the center of the optics in the sight to the top of the *Bug*. This distance was 10 feet (120 inches), and since a mil was 1/1,000 of the bombing altitude, a mil on the trainer target was .12 inches (1/1,000 of 120 inches).

For example, if during the simulation of a bombing run from 10,000 feet the plunger impacted 1.2 inches from the center of the target, there would be an error of 10 mils, which would equate to a real ground error of 100 feet during an actual bombing run from 10,000 feet (10x10). If this simulated bombing run was being made from 5,000 feet and the plunger fell at the same 1.2 inch point from the center of the target then the error would simulate a real error of 50 feet on the ground (5x10).

To simulate the time that it would take the bomb to fall from the simulated bombing altitude (ATF) on the trainer a clock was used which energized the marker solenoid ATF seconds after bomb release. The ATF was set in seconds on the clock and the corresponding disc speed into the sight: Disc Speed= 5,300 divided by ATF.

When the sighting angle index met the dropping angle index and the release lever was up, the sight's automatic release system sent an electric signal to start the clock running. When ATF had "run out" the clock sent the signal on to energize the marker solenoid. It plunged downward, marking the trainer target to simulate a bomb impact.

True airspeed was simulated by the speed at which the trainer moved across the hanger floor. This simulated true airspeed generated the same relationship to the actual speed of the trainer as the simulated bombing altitude did to the actual height of the trainer.

Wind direction and speed were simulated by the direction and speed at which the *Bug* moved across the hangar floor. The direction toward which the *Bug* moved simulated the direction from which the wind was blowing. Thus, if the *Bug* was moving toward the east it simulated a wind blowing from the east. The simulated wind speed had the same relation to actual speed of the *Bug* as the simulated bombing altitude did to the actual height of the trainer.

Groundspeed and true airspeed were identical during a run on a stationary *Bug*. The speed at which the distance between the trainer and the *Bug* was covered or closed was called the speed of closure. The moving *Bug* represented a wind or a moving target, but ordinarily the moving *Bug* represented the wind and the speed of closure represented the groundspeed.

When the *Bug* was moving not directly toward or directly away from the trainer then drift was simulated. The direction the *Bug* moved simulated the direction from which the wind was blowing. When seen through the optics, a *Bug* moving from west to east appeared the same as if the bombardier were in a bomber drifting west through the air because of a wind blowing from the east. In both examples, the target moved in the same direction from the west to the east across the field of vision in the optics of the sight.

The metal arm which held the marker solenoid was pivoted so that it could be moved either to the right or left on its drift scale. This was compulsory, because when the bombardier entered drift into the sighthead the optics moved in an arc around the pivot point, the sight stem, and changed their position in relation to the marker solenoid. The marker solenoid arm was moved to a position matching the direction and amount of drift set on the sight. This was done to keep the solenoid either directly under the center of the optics or directly behind it if trail was being used. This was not done to simulate Crosstrail, as when trail and drift were entered into the sight; it automatically set up Crosstrail. The optics were tilted, causing the trainer to be steered upwind. At the moment of impact, the solenoid would be Crosstrail distance downwind and trail distance behind the optics. Thus, Crosstrail was automatically simulated on the trainer and could be ignored.

A-2 Drive and Controls

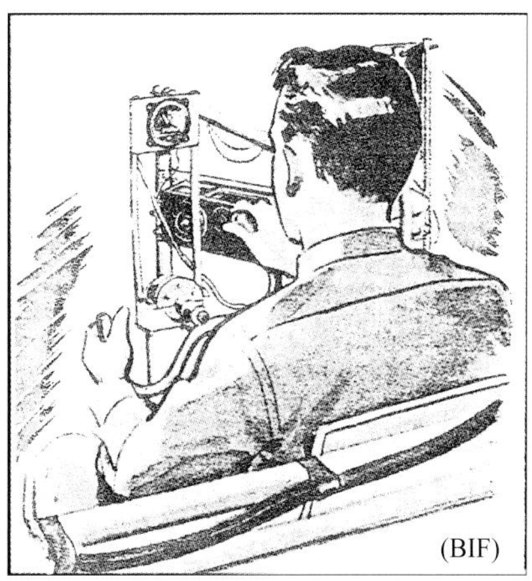

(BIF)

Operating the A-2 Trainer

Before the generator was switched on, supplying current to the sight, the bombardier had to check if the sight used 12- or 24-volts. When the generator was turned on the voltage regulators were set to the correct voltage and the bombsight was preflighted and turned ON.

The marker solenoid was to be directly under the crosshairs when the sight's optical system was in the vertical, since the action of the marker solenoid simulated the bomb impact, which was called the "zeroing of the trainer." Steps in zeroing the trainer were:

1) Roll the trainer up to the *Bug* to eliminate any error that could result from an uneven floor.
2) Set the marker solenoid arm pointer to zero drift on the marker solenoid plate.
3) Set zero drift on the sight and engage the bombsight clutch.
4) Engage the mirror drive clutch and set the sighting angle index at 0°.
5) Uncage and level the gyro.
6) Look through the optics and direct someone to move the marker solenoid plate until the center of the marker solenoid was directly under the crosshairs. Recheck the previous setting, particularly the gyro level, to be sure they were correct.

Although these were not as sophisticated as the new trainers that were being developed and deployed, they were used to train thousands of student bombardiers as late as October 1944.

Link Visual Trainer

In November 1942 BuOrd modified stored Link Visual Trainers, installing AFCE/SBAE autopilots and stabilizers. The project would include all the features for AFCE/SBAE instrument training and also expand the capabilities of the current Link Visual Trainers. Soon a basic model was developed to accommodate an AFCE/SBAE using the Norden Mark XV, the Sperry S-1, and Honeywell control equipment. Link Aviation Devices, Inc. was contracted by BuOrd for 25 modified units, the first of which were completed in early 1943. In September 1944 the existing 25 unit contract with Link Aviation Devices was increased by 55, and the first units were in production and were delivered the early part of 1945. By the end of the war 80 modified Link Visual Trainers had been built.

7A-3 Trainer

The Bureau of Aeronautics proposed a new concept in bombardier training when it designated International Business Machines Corporation to develop synthetic training equipment that was to replace the use of a moving vehicle equipped with a bombsight suspended several feet above the hangar floor. This previous method could not teach target recognition, nor did it simulate actual flying conditions.

IBM developed the 7A-3 Trainer, which was a replica of a B-24 bomber compartment in which every condition of actual bombing procedure was reproduced so accurately that the student was able to correctly perform his bombing function immediately in an actual bomber. Using very accurate photographic maps of actual target areas taken at various bombing altitudes, a movie projector showed a moving image of the ground or target area. The correct impression of altitude was recreated in the exact proportion to the speed of the aircraft and the drift was exactly simulated as when the bomber was influenced by cross winds. The 7A-3 trainer saved in air training time and the cost of fuel, practice bombs, and aircraft maintenance.

A-6 Photographic Trainer

The A-6 (McKaba Trainer) was a later version of the A-2 and A-5 trainers, and did not appear until the spring or summer of 1945 as an intermediate and advanced trainer for bombardiers. It was a simplified and less expensive version of the A-5 and consisted of a mock up of a bombardier's compartment positioned over a screen upon which a traveling terrain was projected. The instruments, controls, and switches were the same as in a bomber and had to be placed in correct positions to enable simulated bomb release. The Instructor, acting as the pilot, had controls to set drift, altitude, temperature, trail, heading, airspeed, and reset, and to further duplicate combat conditions provisions were made for interphone, machine gun noise, motor noise, vibration, and anti-aircraft gun flashes. The point of impact of the simulated bombs was shown by a flash of light projected on a screen.

AFCE/SBAE Training Table Mock up

The AFCE/SBAE training table had all of the necessary bombsight and automatic pilot control equipment installed on a table so that pilots and bombardiers could observe the entire functional unit. It was a simplified version of the actual Norden equipment with all the essential controls provided, but without the instruments, which were to be installed by the training bases. They were manufactured by the AAF at the Sacramento Air Depot (SAD).

Bombsight Repair Training

Classroom Training

In the mid-1930s it was policy to return sights to Norden for repair and modification, but many delays occurred, especially when the sights sent from American foreign bases left squadrons without bombsights. To improve the situation the AAC established an eight week curriculum for the first bombsight repair school at Chanute Field in September 1936. The prospect had to be a high school graduate, a non-commissioned officer with at least six years service, graduate of an armorer course, or have three years in a bombardment organization, or be an air mechanic with at least six years service. Students were selected after a close investigation of their qualifications and a background check was completed, and their applications were forwarded to the Commandant of The Air Corps Technical School for approval. With the increasing numbers of Norden Bombsights field service support was needed, especially in combat theaters. Norden established a school in October 1942, after which there was a constant supply of factory-trained personnel which continued until the end of the war.

The AAC established a **Norden Bombsight Repair School** to supplement the overburdened Norden factory repair facilities and to carry out in-field repairs. (AAF)

Bombsight Training

With the development of AFCE/SBAE in November 1940, the bombsight school at Lowry added a four week, 160 hour training course for this equipment. The qualifications for this course were the same as for the bombsight

Norden Bombsight: Maintenance and Calibration Manual

(NBMCM)

Instruction on radar bombsights. (AAF)

Camera Bombing

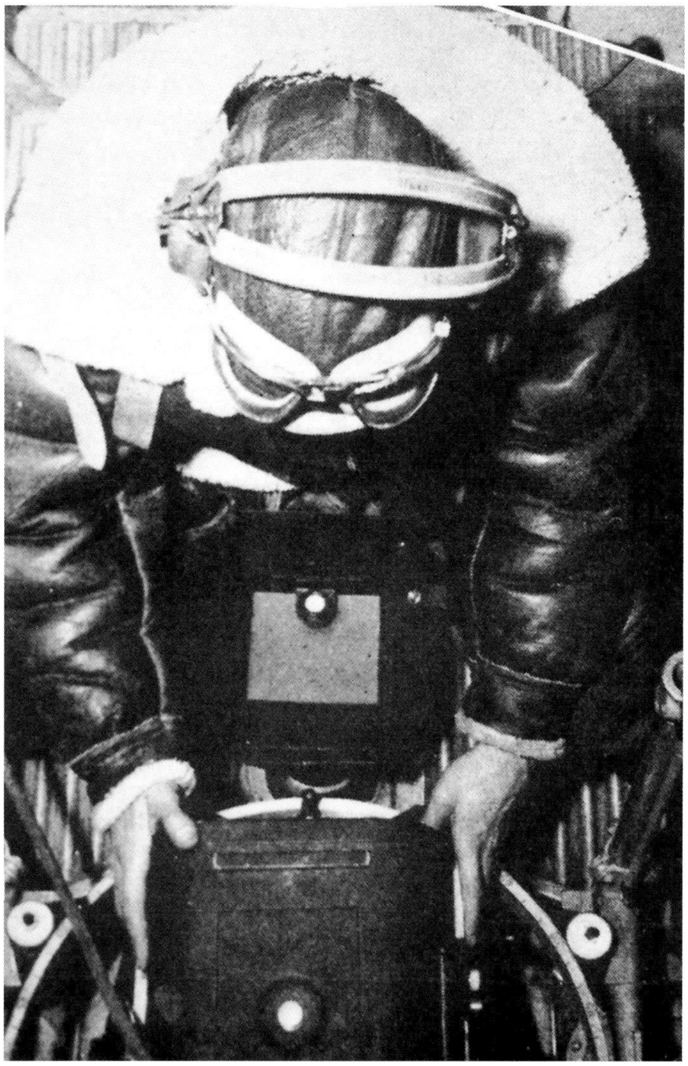

(AAF)

repair course. After Pearl Harbor qualifying requirements were upgraded, and the training at both the bombsight repair and AFCE/SBAE schools was increased in time and in the quantity of course material. The students were given concentrated, six days a week, and comprehensive instruction covering all facets of the equipment being studied. The *Norden Bombsight: Maintenance and Calibration Manual* was the Bible for all Bombardiers and maintenance men. The training program was divided into five blocks:

Block #1 consisted of 72 hours of instruction on manual skills, tools, DC electricity, and Norden Stabilizer;
Block #2 included 216 hours on bombing problems, the Norden sight, the D-8 sight, and the Automatic Bombing Computer;
Block #3 was 36 hours on the Glide Bombing Attachment;
Block #4 was 36 hours on the Bombsight Box, Field Repair, and care and maintenance of the Norden Trainer; and
Block #5 included 216 hours on the calibration and maintenance of the C-1 Automatic pilot.

A two week course was also given on manual skills, tools, DC electricity, supply, technical orders, and the Norden Stabilizer. The course for the C-l Auto Pilot, due to the complexity of the equipment, was increased to 48 academic days.

Camera Bombing
The camera bombing mission was developed to improve the bombardier's target identifying skills. It was considered a better approximation of an

actual bombing run to replace training missions using practice bombs. The bombardier was to take a photo of the IP and the briefed target as his apparent aiming point. Analysis of the photos indicated the accuracy he would have made with a real bomb. For low or medium altitudes, the A-4 35 mm bomb spotting camera was used by the bombardier to take a photo through the bombsight optics at the time he would have released a bomb and, again, when the bomber was directly over the target. For high altitude camera bombing the equipment was a combination of the B-7 camera intervalometer using either the K-22 or K-24 camera mounted in the bomber's camera well. The bombardier pre-set the ATF on the camera intervalometer, and when the bomber was at the simulated bomb release point the bombsight's automatic release mechanism started the camera intervalometer, which tripped the camera when the pre-set time expired.

Advanced and Operational Bombing Practice

After the Bombardier graduated from training he was given his orders and usually a short furlough before joining his crew. Once the bomber crews were assigned they trained as a unit and then remained as a unit in operations. This final phase of training simulated the various combat mission types and situations which utilized each of the crew's specialties to produce a successful mission. Advanced training in the Continental U.S. was conducted throughout America with emphasis on the southern and western tier of states with the best weather: Florida, Texas, New Mexico, Arizona, and California. The Bombardier carried out his assigned duties as will be described in the next section.

Early missions by the 8AF from England resulted in poor bombing, and increased practice bombing was required whenever the winter weather of 1942-43 permitted. The British Air Ministry provided bombing ranges, many of which were found to be too small to safely bomb from altitudes in excess of 20,000 feet. The radius of the danger at ranges used by medium bombers was from 500 to 650 yards, whereas the danger areas at ranges of high altitude heavy bombers were all in excess of 1,000 yards. To reach bombing ranges of suitable size round trip flights of 200 to 300 miles from 8AF bases were involved. The long flights, often in unfavorable weather, caused bombers to become lost or to have to land at scattered airfields throughout the north and west. In spring 1943 the Air Ministry made three ranges available, with 13 more available scheduled to be opened for use. In late 1943, because of the increased requirement for more bombing ranges and the ever-present danger of errant bombing, ranges were opened for use of non-explosive M38 practice bombs: Breast Sands was allotted to 1st Air Division; Stockyard Green and Button Walks to 2nd Air Division; and Tollesbury to the 3rd Air Division.

A B-25 practices mast-height bombing a large target warship built in the desert of Muroc Proving Ground, CA. (AAF)

The 1943 RKO film *Bombardier*, starring Pat O'Brien (center) and Randolph Scott (left), was the highly propagandized story of the rigorous training of Bombardier cadets and highlighted the fabled Norden Bombsight. (Author/RKO)

Hollywood and Bombardier Training

In 1943 RKO filmed *Bombardier*, the highly propagandized story of the rigorous training of Bombardier cadets, and highlighted the fabled Norden Bombsight. The movie starred Hollywood World War II stars Pat O'Brien as Maj. Chick Davis and Randolph Scott as Capt. Buck Oliver (Buck and Chick; the names say it all about the tone of the film). The movie was directed by Richard Wallace and produced by Robert Fellows from a screenplay and original story by John Twist. The movie had a strong supporting cast, including Eddie Albert, Robert Ryan, Walter Reed, and Anne Shirley as the love interest.

The storyline was based loosely on the actual formation of the first AAF Bombardier School. Maj. Chick Davis was the leading advocate of high altitude bombardment using the Norden Bombsight, while Capt. Buck Oliver was a believer in dive bombing. Davis manages to persuade his superiors of the value of the Norden and to establish a Bombardier's school. Of course, his foresight would prove to be invaluable, as after Pearl Harbor the first Bombardier class is trained and ready for combat. Davis leads a squadron to the South Pacific for a night bombing raid on Tokyo's largest aircraft factory. Capt. Oliver, his former rival, agrees to fly ahead and mark the target with incendiaries. Oliver is shot down over enemy territory before he can release the incendiary markers, jeopardizing the success of the mission. Oliver eludes capture and sets fire to the factory and, guided by the flames, the squadron finds its target and its accurately placed bombs destroy the factory.

Bombardier contained much authentic footage shot on location at the Bombardier Training School at Kirtland Field in Albuquerque. Director Richard Wallace and his crew spent six weeks at Kirtland filming the daily training routine of the bombardier students (many appeared as extras) and aggrandized the Norden Bombsights. The film was released in July 1943, and received generally favorable reviews from the critics and an Academy Award Nomination for Best Special Effects.

Bombardier's Duties

The bombardier's duties went beyond bombing, as he had to be able to take over the duties of the navigator in case he was disabled, and he also manned a gunsighting station and had to be proficient in its operation, as well as responsible as a photographer to take strike photos.

The bombardier carried out a number of pre-mission checks of the bombs, bomb racks, and bomb fuses, bomb formation lights, the electrical fuses and circuits, camera equipment, his nose gunsighting station. He checked the bombing instruments (altimeter, SCR-716 absolute altimeter) and pre-flighted the Norden Bombsight. He also helped the airplane commander in checking the C-1 Autopilot. The bombardier's kit contained a target folder that included aerial photographs of the target and approaches, target charts, the bombardier flimsy, weather data, and a sectional map of the area. Also included in the kit were bombing tables for the bombs to be carried, computers (E-6B, G-1, and C-2), stopwatch, tachometer, and Weems plotter. He was to "Dress warmly, but not tightly and to always use the oxygen mask microphone, making sure the connecting plugs fit firmly."

He was to use whatever de-icing facilities were available, such as heating pads, air blasts, ventilators, and heating fans, to remove ice from the inside of the Plexiglas nose. To minimize condensation and frosting on the bombsight eyepiece and telescope window he was to wipe them with a lint-free cloth or remove them and make use of the bombsight heating covers. At low temperatures, before reaching the IP, he was to check to see if the optics were fogging, and if they were he was to remove the telescope window and insert the heater tube.

Bombardier's duties after takeoff were to assist the airplane commander in looking for other bombers during turns and assembly and assist the navigator in his dead reckoning by taking drifts and determining ground speeds with the bombsight. He checked his guns, cameras, and bombsight, pulled the bomb pins at 5,000 feet, and watched for aircraft (friendly and enemy), shipping, and possible ditching survivors. In between he studied target area maps and photographs.

As the mission neared the target the bombardier became even busier. In selecting the proper axis of attack for a bombing run he had to consider the position of the sun; selection of a suitable IP; shape of target; wind direction and speed; and AA fire around the target. He had to recompute the bombing altitude and check it against the SCR-718 altimeter, and when the navigator gave him the wind, ground speed, and drift axis of attack these were entered into the bombsight computer. He turned on the Intervalometer and chose an IP. The C-1 Autopilot was set and several gentle turns were made with the course knob to check its operation. The level stabilizer was checked and the aircraft was to fly straight and level. When many groups attacked one target it would soon become obscured by smoke, and succeeding groups had to be prepared to do offset bombing. When the enemy released a smoke screen to obscure the target the bombardier had to attack down the ground wind if possible. Often he was able to see between the smoke furrows and locate check points which he could use for offset bombing.

An idealized publicity photo of a student bombardier entering an AT-11. (AAF)

The bombardier turned camera master switch ON at the IP and directed the radar operator to open the camera doors. After the bomber completed its turn and passed over the IP on the briefed bombing run, the lead bomber opened its bomb bay doors six minutes before the release point and the wing bombers opened their doors three minutes later. He rechecked the C-1 Autopilot and altimeter and then looked for as many checkpoints on the run in as possible to help locate the target. He turned ON all bomb switches, the bomb rack selector switches, and nose arming switch. With the advent of pattern bombing the navigator had little to do. Immediately after takeoff he had to pull the bomb pins, but thereafter he was the nose gunner. All the bombs were toggled when the lead bomber released its bombs, so the wing bombardiers did not have to use their bombsights.

Among the bombardier's duties was to go to the bomb bay and pull the bomb safety arming wires after takeoff. (AAF)

On a combined Radar-Bombsight bombing run the bombardier pre-set the latest drift reading from the navigator. The radar operator said, "ready on seven zero-degrees, be prepared for the 'Ready, Mark' signal." At the command "Mark" the bombardier turned ON the rate motor switch. The bombardier kept his hand on the displacement knob, and when the radar operator said, "ready on 68°" he prepared for "Ready, Mark." At the command "Mark" the bombardier turned the displacement knob to set the telescope index on 68°. When the radar operator said, "Ready on 65°prepared for 'Ready, Mark,'" at the command "Mark" the bombardier first turned the displacement knob to put the telescope index on 65° and quickly rotated the rate knob a slight amount in the same direction as the displacement knob. This procedure was repeated at sighting angle intervals of 5° until the value 5° before the dropping angle was reached. At this point only a displacement correction was made. If at any time during the bomb run the target could be seen visually the bombardier would say "I see it" and proceed with a normal visual bomb run. If the target again became obscured the bombardier would ask the radar operator to take over again and the radar synchronization would continue.

Usually bombers carried a single bomb camera mounted behind a flush door to record the bombing results. It was the responsibility of the bombardier to open the camera doors when the target was approached by means of a handle that remotely opened the camera doors by the means of the B-1 or B-2 Intervalometer mounted in the bombardier's compartment. The camera could be preset to automatically operate the shutter by electric remote control at specific intervals of time. After the bomb release the cameras were immediately started. The lead bomber in the formation continued on its bomb run for 45 seconds after its drop to get photos of the hits of the early bombers in the formation. Once the target was hit and began to burn it would disappear for hours and even days until the smoke and dust cleared away.

After the bombs were jettisoned the navigator LOCKED the bomb racks and the rack selector switches were turned OFF, the bomb bay doors were CLOSED, and the pilot was informed of these procedures. The bombsight was turned OFF, and as soon as the bombs impacted the cameras were turned OFF and a strike report was given to the radio operator for transmission.

Bombardier's CHECKLIST

The most carefully planned bombing mission can be ruined if the bombardier forgets an essential item of equipment or a vital step of procedure. A thorough check of equipment and steps is his only guarantee that he won't forget. This checklist is a valuable safeguard for his memory. It is not a guide to procedures.

BEFORE LOADING BOMBS

1. BOMB RACKS .... PREFLIGHTED
2. BOMBING INTERVALOMETER .... PREFLIGHTED
3. SWITCHES IN BOMBARDIER COMPARTMENT .... CHECKED
4. SWITCHES IN PILOT COMPARTMENT .... CHECKED
5. EMERGENCY RELEASE SYSTEM .... CHECKED
6. BOMB BAY SWITCHES .... OFF
7. NOSE COMPARTMENT .... CLEAR
8. WINDOWS .... CLEAN

BEFORE TAKEOFF

1. PERSONAL EQUIPMENT .... COMPLETE
2. BOMBARDIER'S KIT .... COMPLETE
3. TARGET FOLDER AND WEATHER DATA .... COMPLETE
4. OXYGEN AND MASK .... CHECKED
5. PARACHUTE AND LIFE VEST .... CHECKED
6. SPARE ELECTRICAL FUZES .... COMPLETE
7. BOMBS AND FUZES .... CHECKED
8. PINS (IF INACCESSIBLE IN FLIGHT) .... PULLED
9. BOMB BAY TANK SAFETY SWITCHES .... OFF
10. INTERPHONE SYSTEM .... CHECKED
11. BOMBSIGHT .... PREFLIGHTED
12. AUTOPILOT .... PREFLIGHTED
13. GUNS, TURRETS, AND GUNSIGHTS .... PREFLIGHTED
14. CAMERA AND CAMERA INTERVALOMETER .... PREFLIGHTED
15. ALTIMETER PRESSURE SCALE AT 29.92 .... SET
16. CLOCK .... SYNCHRONIZED
17. SWITCHES IN BOMBARDIER COMPARTMENT .... OFF

BEFORE IP

1. SWITCHES IN PILOT COMPARTMENT .... CHECKED
2. SWITCHES IN BOMBARDIER COMPARTMENT .... CHECKED
3. ALL BOMBSIGHT SWITCHES .... ON
4. BOMB BAY SWITCHES .... CHECKED
5. PINS .... PULLED
6. AUTOPILOT .... ADJUSTED
7. BOMBING ALTITUDE .... COMPUTED
8. DISC SPEED AND TRAIL IN BOMBSIGHT .... CHECKED
9. AB COMPUTER COMPLETELY SET UP .... CHECKED
10. BOMBING INTERVALOMETER SETTINGS .... CHECKED
11. CAMERA INTERVALOMETER SETTINGS .... CHECKED
12. CAMERA DOORS .... OPEN

BEFORE BOMBING RUN

1. BOMB BAY DOORS .... OPEN
2. BOMBSIGHT STABILIZER .... LEVEL
3. PROPER RACK SELECTOR SWITCHES .... ON
4. RELEASE HANDLE (OLD TYPE AIRCRAFT) .... SELECT
5. DRIFT AND DROPPING ANGLE .... PRE-SET

BEFORE LANDING

1. SWITCHES IN BOMBARDIER COMPARTMENT .... OFF
2. BOMBSIGHT .... POST-FLIGHTED
3. TURRETS AND GUNS .... STOWED
4. GUNS, TURRETS, AND GUNSIGHT SWITCHES .... OFF
5. BOMBING EQUIPMENT MALFUNCTION REPORT .... COMPLETE
6. INTELLIGENCE REPORT .... COMPLETE

It would be more than tragic to subject a bomber and its crew to the hazards of a mission, to consume irreplaceable time reaching the target, and then to discover that a malfunction prevents the successful accomplishment of that mission. You must avoid any such disastrous cancellation of a mission in the air that might have been prevented on the ground. The need for accurate preflighting of equipment, therefore, is only slightly less obvious than the need for accurate bombing procedure.

(BIF)

Bombardier's Compartment Gallery

B-18 Bombardier's Position (AAF)

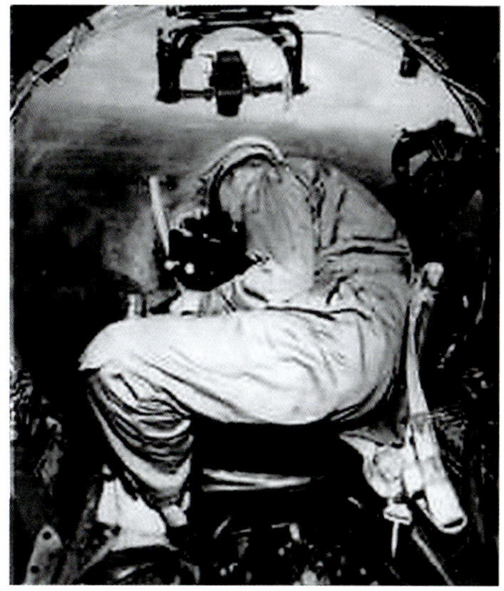

B-26 Bombardier's Position (AAF)

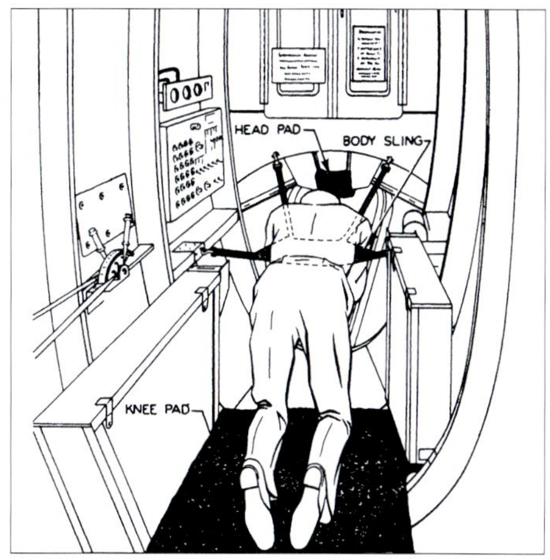

B-24 Bombardier's Position (Consolidated)

B-29 Bombardier's Position (Author/Pima)

B-17 Bombardier's Position (Author/CAFAZ)

B-25 Bombardier's Position (Author/CAFAZ)

6

Bombing Missions Described

ETO

Heavy Bomber Mission Procedure

In nearly two years and nine months of operations the 8th Air Force conducted its primary role of daylight high altitude precision bombing utilizing large formations of B-17s and B-24s. During this time basic bombing procedure and doctrine continued virtually unchanged from that established during the initial months of the war. Minor changes were made to improve aircraft, bombing, and defensive performance, and to contradict German fighter interceptor, radar, and flak countermeasures.

By the time VIII Bomber Command operations began in earnest its bombing operations were governed by the priority listing of objectives in the Combined Bomber Offensive (CBO) directives of the Casablanca Directive of January 1943, as discussed earlier. Until February 1944 Headquarters, 8th Air Force at Bushey Park was mainly involved with operational policy and administration. In February the 8AF Headquarters was reorganized and employed as an inclusive headquarters for the direction of both 8th and 15th Air Forces and redesignated HQ, United States Strategic Air Forces in Europe. The VIII Bomber Command at High Wycombe (*Pinetree*) became the new HQ, 8th Air Force, merging most of the functions of the former HQ 8th AF and the HQ VIII BC, which was discontinued. This restructuring had little or no effect on doctrine or operational procedures.

Compared to their contemporaries in other theaters, the England-based bomber pilot lived in relative comfort. A lucky few bomber groups inherited bases built in the 1930s by the RAF. They were equipped with permanent buildings, usually centrally heated, and definitely more comfortable than the accommodations of the newly-built airbases, which were of the Nissen-type or other temporary type buildings (e.g. Liang, Thorne, Janes). The Nissan hut was a generic term referring to a basic prefabricated building design: a long semi-circle of khaki-green double-corrugated steel sheet attached to a steel frame that was anchored to a concrete slab, whose ends were constructed of brick or wood. Two windows and a door stood at one or both ends, but larger Nissens had windows along their sides. The original design could be Nissen, Quonset, Iris, or Romney, and could house four to 40 men. A coke-burning stove stood at its center but did little against the

The **Quonset** and larger **Nissen Huts** were pre-fabricated semi-circular buildings that were the backbone of new USAAF bases in the UK. (AAF)

damp English weather, which pervaded everything and everywhere. The stove took forever to heat up and required constant and skillful attention to supply its inadequate output of heat. Forced by the North Sea winds blowing across the fens and moors, the dampness seeped into the quarters, making them cold and dank. Nonetheless, compared to the tent-lodging of the MTO and Pacific the English airbase was preferred. The comforts of these lodgings would be lost for many groups in the Winter of 1944-45, when they transferred to newly captured bases on the Continent and were billeted in cold tents. On base, the center of the pilot's social life was the Officer's Club, where he could have a warm English beer, play cards, cribbage, or darts, read, or write a letter home. A PX made available the pilot's weekly rations: cigarettes, candy bars, chewing gum, and soap and razor blades. Mail was more regular in the ETO, and R&R was closer at hand and more entertaining. Bicycle riding became a major diversion and local English villages were invaded daily.

The American air groups intruded and changed the way of life of many East Anglican villages, with these changes being both physical and psychological. While some new USAAF bases were former RAF bases, large tracts of local land were procured and cleared and quarters were requisitioned and occupied. The colorful new occupants of these bases displayed novel eccentricities and were often considered "over-sexed, overpaid, and over here." However, many villagers enjoyed the company of the Yanks. The Pub was the center of English social life, and often was the only local diversion available to the Americans, whom the English found to be friendly and generous. After a long mission, the Pub was a place for the pilot to lift a pint of ale or cider with his friends. Occasionally a local family would invite an airman to dinner, and "A Yank for Christmas" was often the start of a lifelong friendship. Each was a foreigner to the other and the best in the guest and host was brought to bear, cementing grassroots Allied alliances. In all, the English overlooked the inconvenience and the occasional unpleasant incident in exchange for the ultimate result.

Two-day passes, called "48s," were issued every two or three weeks. A cold, drafty train ride to London, standing; a foot-numbing three hours to a wartime soiree. Still, it was a good place to make female acquaintances, especially if one were lucky enough to get to sit in the snug compartments. Piccadilly was the destination, with its pubs, cafes, theaters, nude shows, and dance halls. Dance halls, the converted Covent Garden Opera House, and the most famous of all, Hammersmith Palais, featuring American-style swing bands, everyone dancing, English-style, in a large circle. There was

Two-day passes, called "48s," were issued every two or three weeks, and the favorite destination was London with its pubs, cafes, theaters, nude shows, and dance halls. (AAF)

American bases and flyers were located near English towns and villages, and the Yanks interacted with the locals both at the Pub and with the children. (AAF)

"the Vic" (Victoria Hall), dancing to the records of Glenn Miller, Artie Shaw, and Jimmy Dorsey. Pub crawling, many a splitting headache was bequeathed by the English boilermaker: Beefeaters and Guinness. Fish and chips, served in a newspaper, by a street vendor. Nightclubs, American Eagle Club, The Nuthouse. Visit the Mecca for the homesick American G.I., the Red Cross' Rainbow Corner, where dunking doughnuts in coffee became a tradition. Play tourist at Big Ben, Parliament. Friendships and romantic attachments were almost instantaneous. There were women, young and old, virtuous and not, available for drinks, dinner, dancing, and the "Piccadilly Lilies" available for romance. Forty-eight hours went by quickly.

In the ETO, the major factor influence on bombing operations was the weather, and each day at 1015, 1600, and 2200 hours weather briefings were held at High Wycombe, providing forecasts of weather conditions in potential target areas and for 8AF bases. However, once H2X (AN/APS-15) Bombing Through Overcast (BTO) radar was available the weather forecast for the target area was no longer the determining factor, and selected targets with distinctive topography could be bombed with a high degree of success. Prior to radar bombing, unfavorable weather forecasts for the next day issued at 1600 hours would usually cause missions to be scrubbed. Adverse weather predicted for the bomber bases would also scrub missions, as large bomber forces would be unable to safely rendezvous in conditions of limited visibility.

The Deputy Commander of Operations (Chief of Operations) or his subordinate was informed of a favorable forecast and selected suitable targets from the CBO priority list, then determined the size of the mission. If there was a continuing high pressure area with clear skies in the target area an important target on the priority list was selected for visual bombing in a concentrated attack. If some cloud was possible over the target the mission could be divided among two or three primary targets to insure the chances of success. In addition to suitable weather, the availability of crews and aircraft were determinates in the selection of targets.

The Deputy Commander of Operations held an operational conference in the early evening to review the most current weather forecast for the mission. This conference was followed at 2200 by another to evaluate an updated weather forecast and any additional relevant information, and if the weather had deteriorated the proposed operations would be cancelled. By this time all key decisions involving targets, the force required to destroy them, and a coordinated plan for the participating divisions had usually been made by VIII Bomber Command at High Wycombe and subordinate headquarters in the chain of command informed. This information was be incorporated in an official Field Order, guiding the mission into combat, but its final structure could not be formulated at that stage. To give the

Prior to the introduction of radar bombing the weather unit was vital, as unfavorable weather forecasts for the next day would usually cause missions to be scrubbed. (AAF)

participating units as much time as possible to prepare aircraft and brief personnel most of the Operational Directives were sent to the units as an advance to a Field Order.

The headquarters of the three 8AF Bomb Divisions would receive advanced notice of an imminent mission soon after the first decision was made at High Wycombe. The Divisions then notified the Combat Wings, who then advised their individual groups. Once Division received the target and ordnance requirements detailed plans could be made by Specialists, who considered target identifications, established Mean Points of Impact (MPI) for bomb strikes, calculated bomb tonnages, stipulated the types of bombs to be dropped, assessed the number of aircraft needed, plotted routes and times, specified altitudes, and organized fighter support after consultation with VIII Fighter Command. As this advanced information to the Field Order became available it was sent by teleprinter to Combat Wing headquarters, giving the vital details for both Combat Wing and Group to begin preparations to attack the target (referred in code), determine the order of attack by the Combat Wings, and the number of squadrons in each, together with a tentative route and times.

The Combat Wing headquarters was concerned almost completely with operational issues, its chief purpose being to create a coordinated plan for its Groups (usually three) for all phases of a combat mission, and to act as the controlling organization during its implementation. There was a series of addenda via teletype messages along the chain of command informing them of corrections and new information. These Division teleprinter messages to Combat Wings were also transmitted to combat Groups.

Usually in the late afternoon or early evening of a major mission that was scheduled for the following day the Group, which was the major combat unit, received a first alert of the mission via a telephone message on the secret "scrambler" line in Group Operations' Message Center. Short range or small unit missions could first be advised in the early hours of the morning of the operation. The Watch Officer in Group Operations directed his Duty Clerk to inform all units involved, beginning with the Group CO or his alternate, then the Air Executive, S-3 Group Operations Officer, S-2 Intelligence Section, Group Navigator and Bombardier Officers, Weather Office, Flying Control, ordnance and armament sections, engineering office, the signals and photographic units, mess hall, motor pool, and the Charge of Quarters (CQ) on each squadron bivouac. This telephone message was a simple "Mission Alert" message to prepare each section for the release

The **Operations Room** was located in the Group Operations building. Here Squadron Operations Officers were to make any final revisions to the crew and aircraft status boards located on the walls and draw up a provisional availability list. (AAF)

of a Field Order. If this message was sent in the afternoon or early evening it could be an hour or two before the first advance was teletyped to Group Operations. Meanwhile, the duty officer informed the guard room, told the base telephone exchange to restrict calls, and requested the Military Police detachment to post MPs at the Operations Office and the Intelligence Section. CQs restricted personnel to the base.

The Advance Information to a Field Order, which provided the number of aircraft the group was to load with bombs and fuel, was sent to the Squadron Operations Officers at the Group Operations building. These officers were to make any final revisions to crew and aircraft status boards located on the walls of the Operations Room and draw up a provisional availability list. It was SOP for one squadron to stand down on every fourth mission unless there was a unique situation, such as a maximum effort requirement or insufficient crews and aircraft available from the other three squadrons. Similarly, Lead Crew availability followed a stipulated rotation.

Once the Advance to the Field Order was delivered to Operations, the aircraft and crews selected for the mission were posted on a black board using a schematic formation plan. Each aircraft was represented by a T-shaped symbol with the pilot's name (identifying the crew) posted on the horizontal bar. The last three digits of the aircraft serial number, plus the squadron call letter were marked on the tail of the T. Duty Clerks from armament, equipment, engineering, etc. went to Operations to relay the pertinent information to their sections. The Group Operations staff duplicated formation plans and other pertinent information for distribution to pilots and briefing officers.

A copy of the initial teletype message from Operations gave the S-2 duty officer the name of the target by coded number. The center of the S-2 Intelligence Office was the War Room, which was the top secret area on the base with the locked cipher office adjoining it. The Duty Officer used the cipher book to decode the target reference and then found the correct target folder from the large number on file.

The target folder consisted of four sheets of heavy acetate measuring 14x16 inches. It was stitched together in the center and on two of the remaining three sides with heavy cloth material, leaving one end of each pair of sheets open to allow insertion of data sheets. The folder could be stood on its end for ready reference. The target folder contained an aeronautical chart of the target area, target charts and perspectives, and vertical and oblique photographs of the target area. The aeronautical charts were regional 1:1,000,000 and sectional 1:500,000, and were used to navigate to and from the target. The target charts and perspectives were large scale charts centered on a particular target area and were designed to identify the target quickly. The standard size vertical photograph of the target had a transparency with numbered grid lines that was to be placed over the photograph, and by reference to a numerical code in the teletype order the required Mean Point of Impact (MPI), which was the center of the desired bomb pattern on target, was determined. Target information from S-2 files was then distributed to Group Operations and the Bombardier and Navigator offices, which were usually in the same headquarters building. The main function of S-2 was to provide all required intelligence data for briefing office and combat personnel from the constantly updated target files concerning all types of German defenses.

Maps, photographs, and other relevant material for navigators and bombardiers were amassed while the photographic laboratory duplicated flak charts and mission flimsies that had been prepared in the war room. In Operations, the route to the target was plotted on a large wall map using different color cotton thread, or with a red grease pencil if the map had a transparent sheet covering it. The Group Navigator's office plotted courses and distances and times for assembly. Weather data, giving temperature and wind figures expected on route, the air speeds, ground speeds, and drift on various legs to be flown were calculated and checked against times given in the Division figures received. The Group bombardier's office obtained information from Intelligence, Navigators, and the Weather Officer to assess target conditions, and with speeds, drift, and heading data computed bombsight settings for the attack altitude.

The information contained in the Advance to the Field Order varied, and many sections of a group had to wait several hours before the required information arrived from Operations via teleprinter. The Field Order from Division could be delayed for up to seven or eight hours while particulars were completed and checked. Usually the lengthy FO would arrive sometime before midnight via teleprinter on a three or four foot long sheet of yellow paper. It contained the bomb load and sometimes the important Zero Hour, which was a reference point for planning for the start of the mission for all participating units. Often the actual time of Zero Hour would be specified in an Annex to the Field Order. In the interim it allowed a Group to establish a schedule based on intervals starting from the Zero Hour when it became known. The intervals were a half hour to awakened and get the crews ready for an hour breakfast, a minimum of an hour for main crews' briefings before going to the bombers, ten minutes for

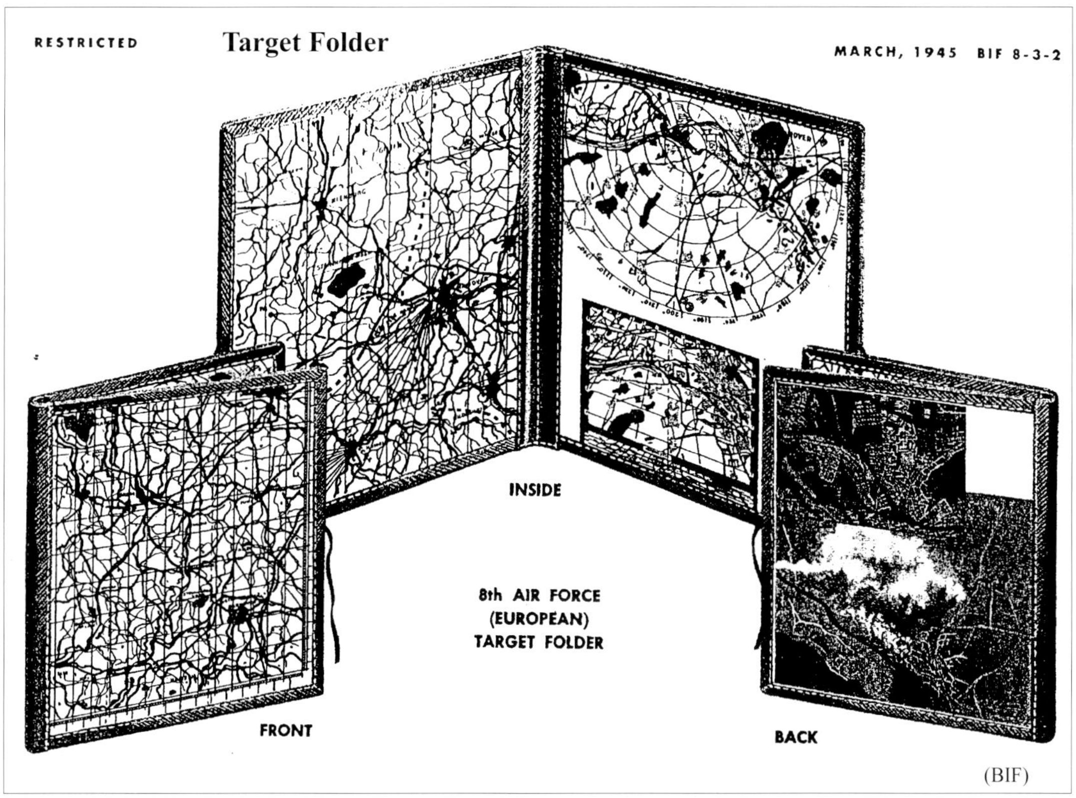

(BIF)

Maps, photographs, and other relevant material for navigators and bombardiers were amassed and studied by the **Photo Intelligence Unit**. (AAF)

Once the bomb load was established the information was sent to the Ordnance Unit, which previously had an inventory of the aircraft scheduled for the mission. A telephone message was sent to the armorers to begin to load the required bombs at the dump and transport them to the bombers. (AAF)

The Armament unit hoisted the bombs into bomb bays and then onto the vertical bomb racks, where the shackle was attached to the rack. The Ordnance man then screwed in the nose or tail fuses and safetied them with a pin and wire to prevent the arming vane from spinning and arming the bomb while the bomber was on the ground. (AAF)

"stations" (crew in aircraft), ten or 15 minutes for engine starting, ten or 15 minutes for assembly and taxiing, and a minimum of an hour for formation assembly from the time of first takeoff (more in unfavorable conditions). As Group Operations made out the schedule more Annexes to teletype messages would arrive, correcting or adding new information. A Field Order from the Combat Wing followed that from Division, usually within an hour, covering, in detail, the order and formations to be flown by Groups within the Combat Wing, assembly instructions, order of bombing at the target, and post target rally. Annexes could also be received to this Field Order.

Once the bomb load was established the information was sent to Ordnance, which previously had an inventory of the aircraft scheduled for the mission. Bomb loading crews had arrived at the bomb dump in the middle of the night, and many tried to catch some sleep until a telephone message came in to begin to load the required bombs onto the special bomb trailers at the dump and transport them to the bombers, where Armament hoisted the bombs into bomb bays.

Each bomber ground crew assigned an armorer to previously start the APU (Auxiliary Power Unit), called a "putt-putt," a two-stroke gasoline generator that augmented the bomber's electrical supply. He also checked that all the bomb rack release mechanisms were tested to ensure they were performing correctly prior to bomb loading. Each bomb loading vehicle crew, usually four Squadron Armament men, initially loaded the bombs by hand, but later loading was done by an electric cable hoist in the bomb bay. First stainless steel shackles were fitted to two lugs on the bomb and two cables elevated it into the proper position on the vertical rack, where the shackle was attached to the rack. As soon as all were in place an Ordnance man screwed in the nose or tail fuses and safetied them with a pin and wire to prevent the arming vane from spinning and arming the bomb while the bomber was on the ground. Sometimes the fuses were installed before loading, which was easier but considered more dangerous. Working in the cramped and poorly lit bomb bays was difficult and hazardous. Furthermore, if the mission was scrubbed the already tired Armament and Ordnance men would have to remove all bombs and move them back to the bomb dump.

Ordnance men transported previously belted ammunition stored in wooden boxes on flat surface trolleys from sheds near to the bomb dump to the bombers. The boxes were placed in the gunnery positions in the bomber for gunners to set up when they arrived. The .50 caliber machine guns were always removed from the bomber after each mission for cleaning and stored. An Armament vehicle picked up these guns from storage and placed them inside the aircraft or inside the ground crew's tent to protect then from the weather.

At many bases, ground crews lived a mile or two from the base and bicycles, jeeps, or trucks were the transport to the hardstand. To provide refuge from the fickle English weather, most crews set up tents or constructed more elaborate shelter from the wooden drop tank crates near their aircraft. The tour of duty of a ground crew was usually for the duration. They were assigned the responsibility for a single fighter during its service life.

The Lead Crew officers, who were specially trained to lead the Group formation, were awakened at least a half hour before the main body officers and four hours before takeoff to be present at a series of pre-briefings at Operations or the War Room. Lead Navigators and Bombardiers were given target and route details and identified check points, and numbered them on a 1:25,000 scale map. Command Pilots received similar relevant information. The Command Pilots and Lead Navigators and Bombardiers then received a general briefing to be certain that they were familiar with the mission.

Check points for all stages of the mission were to be a few of the best in each region. The Bombardier and Navigator collaborated in choosing these check points. In general, check points were selected for abrupt

Check Points

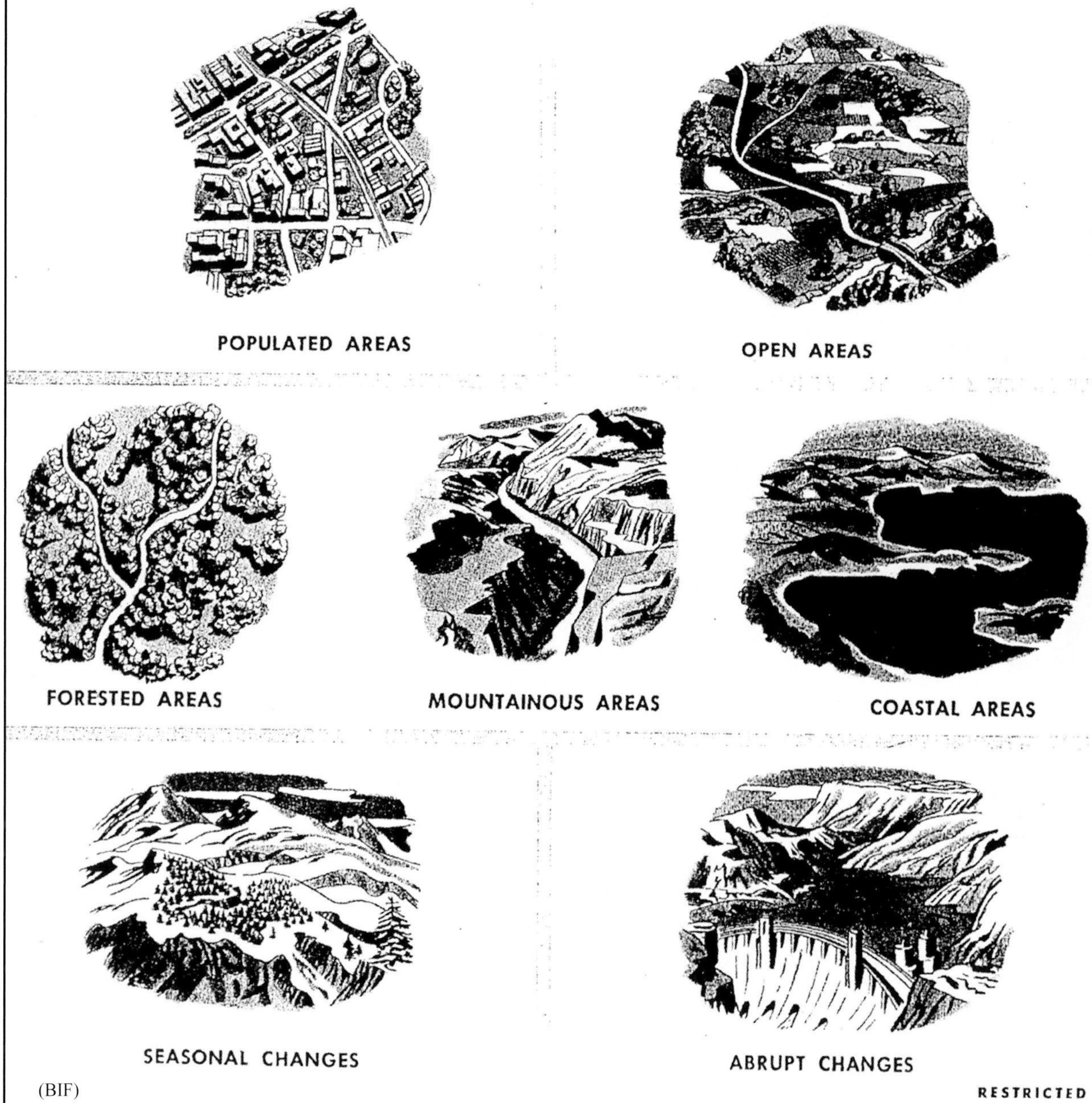

(BIF)

changes in physical appearance, such as mountains to flat areas or forests to farms. In choosing check points the following were considered (features that were distinct from their surrounding area and not duplicated nearby were chosen):

Easy to identify from high altitude.
Should be of a characteristic shape (e.g. round water tanks).
Combinations of features (e.g. water tank next to railroad tracks).
Patterns of designs.
In the target area note the position of the target in relation to each check point.

In Europe cultural check points were plentiful, while in the Pacific the Navigator and Bombardier had to rely on relief or distinct land and water combinations. Landmarks that made good check points:

Populated areas: Large cities with definite shapes. Small cities with some outstanding check point, such as a river, lake, or structure to identify them. Speedways, railroad yards, and underpasses, race tracks, stadiums, and grain elevators.
Open areas: Any town or village with identifying structures or terrain features adjacent. Paved highways, large railroads, race tracks, fair grounds, factories, bridges, and underpasses. Lakes, rivers, coastlines, mountains, and ridges when distinctive.
Forested areas: Transmission lines and railroad rights-of-way, roads and highways, forest lookout towers, farms, rivers, lakes, clearings, and open valleys.
Mountainous areas: General profile of ranges, prominent peaks, cuts, passes, and gorges, clearings, and grass valleys. Transmission lines, railroads, large bridges over gorges, highways, lookout stations, tunnel openings and mines.

Coastal areas: Unusual coastline features; inlets, river mouths, estuaries, and deltas. Lighthouses, marker buoys, breakwaters, jetties, towns and cities. Seasonal changes: Unusually shaped wooded areas in winter, or dry lakes and river beds if they contrasted with surrounding terrain.

Meanwhile, the remainder of the crews was awakened at 0200 or 0300 after trying to sleep knowing they were on "mission alert." Enlisted men and officers were quartered separately, but those on the same crew usually shared the same divided hut, so the CQ, the Duty Sergeant, had only to call the crew name denoted by the name of the first pilot. The men were permitted 30 minutes for dressing in OD pants and shirts, long underwear, silk scarf, leather jacket, and perhaps a knife secreted in the top of a boot. Then washing and shaving; a close shave was particularly important to prevent discomfort of whisker stubble rubbing in an oxygen mask. Finally, using the latrine for a last time and then to on to the Mess Hall. Some billets were a half a mile or more from the Mess Halls and transportation was made available. Men billeted nearby were expected to walk or use bicycles.

The Combat Mess consisted of a central cookhouse connected to two large dining halls, one each side: Officers and Enlisted Men. Cooks and kitchen staff arose an hour earlier to prepare breakfast for the Group's 200 to 400 men. The non-flatulent meal consisted of grapefruit juice, cereal, oatmeal, toast, and coffee, with either eggs (fresh, not the awful powdered type for combatants) or flapjacks as the main portion. Transport to convey the men from the Mess Halls to the Briefing Rooms was on hand a half-hour after breakfast began. Six-wheel 2x2 ton GMC covered trucks that could accommodate two or three bomber crews transported the men from the Mess Halls to Briefing.

The purpose of briefing was to present all crews, prior to takeoff, with the maximum amount of reliable information relevant to a mission so that the crews could fly along a designated route, correctly identify and bomb the target, and return safely by a prearranged plan. Briefing was usually scheduled an hour and a half after wake up. The large Nissen briefing room complexes were usually sited close to the field, and each consisted of two rooms that could seat 200 men that were joined by linking corridors. The officers and enlisted men could be briefed together or separately in different rooms or buildings. The briefing room, made famous in numerous Hollywood movies, contained rows of wooden folding chairs facing a raised wooden platform capped by a podium. There were maps, charts, and recognition posters on the walls. However, the room was both physically and psychologically dominated by a large curtain-covered wall map. The Briefing Room had a raised podium at one end with a large-scale map

The **Combat Mess** consisted of a central cookhouse connected to two large dining halls where the cooks and kitchen staff arose an hour earlier to prepare a non-flatulent breakfast for the Group's 200 to 400 men. (AAF)

The purpose of **Briefing**, which was usually scheduled an hour and a half after wake up, was to present all crews, prior to takeoff, with the maximum amount of reliable information relevant to a mission so that the crews could fly along a designated route, correctly identify and bomb the target, and return safely by a prearranged plan. (AAF)

of Western Europe suspended above it on the wall. Before the briefing a Duty Clerk from Operations used colored ribbons and pins to designate the mission route, target, and fighter rendezvous points on the map. He then covered the map by drawing a curtain.

After everyone was seated the Briefing Officer or Group Commander, along with the Duty Intelligence Officer (S-2) and the Weather Officer, entered the main briefing and marched down between the rows of seated airmen, anticipating the target, to the podium. The curtains were opened. High drama, just like the movies. A red string marked the route from the base to the rendezvous point and then to the bomber's target. The string zigzagged to avoid flak concentrations on route. The Briefing Officer had to be articulate, succinct, and precise, but also to be able to provide assurance and even levity to ease tensions. Once the curtains were withdrawn there was a predictable reaction depending on the target and depth of penetration involved. After whispers and nervous rustling, the Commanding Officer announced the target and discussed the importance of the target, then turned the briefing over to the Briefing Officer or S-2. The Briefing Officer outlined the route out and return; designated the units participating and types of formation to be flown; announced full time schedules; and issued landing instructions. He specified the rendezvous points and IP; axis, altitude, and airspeed of attack; and operational data about the target and aiming point. Information was also presented on bomb loadings, fusing, fuel, ammunition, supply, special tactics, weather, and communications.

The Intelligence Officer described the objective and covered details of the alternate target and target of last resort. He outlined the known enemy defenses and tactics, including AA batteries, fighter opposition, balloon barrages, dummies, and camouflage. All friendly information (convoys, balloon barrages, fighters, restricted areas, ground troops) was given. The Intelligence Officer then reminded the crews of things to look for en route, and gave warnings and reminders on procedures in the event of forced landings in enemy territory. The Mission Leader concluded the briefing by abstracting the Field Order (FO) and then used an epidiascope or projector to show target photos on a screen. The Weather Officer, usually the butt of light-hearted ribbing, took over next. Updated weather expectations were read; wind and cloud conditions on route, visibility, icing conditions, and the temperatures and altitudes, which caused revealing condensation trails, were discussed. Prior to closing questions were fielded. Times were repeated: engine start times, takeoff times, fighter rendezvous times, and target times. The Navigation Officer gave a time tick as all GI wristwatches were synchronized on a countdown to the exact time, marked by the word "Hack." Sometimes a Chaplain blessed the men, or short services or communion was offered directly after the briefing. The main briefing averaged about 40 minutes, following which bombardiers and navigators moved to an adjacent room or rooms to make their individual preparations with Operations and Intelligence staff on hand to help and advise.

Special Bombardier briefings were held by the staff bombardier to acquaint the Bombardiers with concise data covering all details of the mission from the IP to the target. Each bombardier was given a target folder, bombing tables, computers, stop watch, and other bombing aids.

The following information on the primary target was presented:

Target Identification: This covered the most prominent check points that aided in identifying the IP, those along the axis of attack, and those which bracketed the target. The officer in charge of the briefing used all available references to point out and emphasize landmarks and recognition features in the target area.

Approximate ETA over IP and Distance from IP to Target.

Type of Sighting: The lead bomber could sight for both course and range, while wing bombers released upon a signal from the leader or by visual recognition of lead bomber's release. Or the lead bomber could sight for both course and range and wing bombers for range only. Or bombers could make individual runs, as was the case in night operations.

Type of Release and Intervalometer Settings.

Plan for Evasive Action (if such action was to be used on the mission).

Altitude and Airspeed for Bombing Run.

Meteorological Report: This included the direction and speed of winds at flight level and aloft of the target, surface winds at the target, predicted target temperature and temperatures aloft, mean temperature, and the target pressure altitude.

Precomputed Data: This included DS, Trail, Tan Drop Angle, Sight Angle, BA, and TAS. These computations were not final, but served as a check on the actual air computations and made any large errors apparent.

Flimsy: The flimsy, special destructible information sheets were given to each bombardier participating in the mission. It included meteorological data, precomputed data, BA, and TAS, and any other facts pertinent to the bombing run.

General Information: Included the position of the sun with reference to the axis of attack, moon and tides, camera operation, and crew coordination.

The information for the primary target was repeated in the same detail for the secondary target.

Navigators picked up maps and flimsies and sat at tables to draft their flight plans. Although the Group would fly in a formation, each navigator had draft flight plans as if his bomber was making a single sortie. Pilots reviewed engine control data while waiting for any last minute instructions. After briefing, co-pilots went to the personal equipment store nearby to obtain the whole crew's evasion kits. The S-2 distributed maps and escape kits (consisting of money, francs or marks, waterproof maps printed on linen, candy bars, and concentrated foods). Every crewman was required to wear his dog tag ID, and the crew gave the S-2 or Sergeant their personal possessions, as orders stated that nothing could be taken into combat which might be helpful to the enemy in case of capture. Following the briefings the crew left for the ready room, and on the way there was the automatic last stop at the local "six-holer."

In the early smaller 8AF operations all crewmen had attended the same briefing, but by winter 1943-44 another Intelligence Officer usually conducted the separate gunner's briefing of about 20 minutes, which included mission details and focused on German defenses, particularly the latest known deployment of Luftwaffe fighters and the areas where interceptions were most likely. The Operations Officer followed, briefing on altitudes, weather, escort fighter types, and rendezvous. The Gunners then went to the Personal Equipment Store located near the briefing room to collect flight rations, electrical flying suits or heavy clothing, harness and parachutes, oxygen masks, and Mae West Life Vests at the same time they handed over their personal belongings. The Gunners dressed in the Flight Equipment Room and went out to join their officers in the waiting trucks. The co-pilot checked that all his gunners were present with correct equipment and distributed escape packs. Sometimes the Bombardiers or Navigators could be delayed because of last minute changes or corrections and the trucks would leave without them. The gunners usually arrived with the flight crew an hour before takeoff, but occasionally would be transported separately to arrive at the bomber early to check their weapons, clean them again if necessary, and remove surplus oil which might freeze at altitude, before installing each gun on its mount. When the turret guns were installed a ground crew armorer was needed. The guns were not charged with ammunition until after the bomber left the English coast to avoid accidental firing.

Radio Operators stayed behind after their briefing to receive signals information and any special radio and wireless procedures. Before getting their equipment and clothing they would each receive the day's wireless codes, radio call signs, and frequencies on a sheet of rice paper attached between two pieces of celluloid to prevent the valuable document from being sucked or blown out of the bomber. Once the electrically-heated flying suits were available crewmen were supplied with large carrying duffels in which all personal equipment could be carried from the Locker Room to the aircraft, where flying clothes were then changed into.

The Group aircraft mechanics pre-flighted their bombers at least three hours before takeoff. Those Ground Crew Chiefs whose aircraft were scheduled often went to their bombers soon after the mission alert was received and got what sleep they could in the hardstand tent. Each bomber had two ground mechanics assigned to it, a Crew Chief and an Assistant Crew Chief. Early in the war these two worked on the same aircraft, and it became "their plane." However, the policy of assigning a particular aircraft to a particular flight crew proved impractical and was generally discontinued during the later stages of the war. The Armorer was the third member of the ground crew team, usually assigned to one aircraft but sometimes serving two. The mechanics would begin by pulling through the props, the laborious job of pulling on each propeller blade to turn the engine and remove any fuel that had accumulated in the cylinders overnight. The Crew Chief then went to the cockpit and went through the engine priming procedure. After starting the APU to boost battery power his assistant, with fire extinguisher at hand, positioned himself where he could see hand signs given from the cockpit. The first engine that was started was the one which drove the electrical generators. Each engine was then run up and held at maximum revolutions to check oil pressure, turbo-supercharger, and magneto performance. The propeller feathering mechanism was also tested, along with all electrical and hydraulic functions that could be carried out safely while the bomber was parked.

If every check was satisfactory the engines were shut down to await the "gas wagon," which topped off the fuel tanks of every aircraft scheduled for the mission. Unless the mission was very short the tanks were topped off to allow a large fuel reserve in case of emergencies. A full load for both B-17 and B-24 was approximately 2,800 gallons, which was roughly one quarter of the bomber's gross weight at take-off. The fuel hose was manhandled up onto the wing, being careful not to damage any de-icing boots, to a man on the upper wing surface to insert the nozzle into the fillers, into which 100 octane gasoline was power-pumped from the tanker. The oxygen cart

A full fuel load for both B-17s and B-24s was approximately 2,800 gallons, and the fuel hose was manhandled up onto the upper wing surface to insert the nozzle into the fillers, into which 100 octane gasoline was power-pumped from the fuel tanker. (AAF)

The B-17 crew crowds onto a Jeep and arrives at the bomber hardstand. (AAF)

or truck crew conducted an oxygen check and replenished any bottles not registering full on each scheduled bomber.

The K-21 strike camera was installed on a number of bombers on every mission. These cameras operated automatically at pre-set intervals to record bomb strikes on the target. The camera well in a B-17 was located under the radio room floor and was accessible through a door in that compartment, while in the B-24 it was located to the rear of the fuselage floor hatch. After installing the camera the photo mechanic set the shutter speed, aperture opening, and the heater switch to prevent the mechanism freezing at altitude.

After arriving at the bomber hardstand, the pilot completed the Crew Loading List and the Form 1A for the Ground Crew Chief and went over the details with him. This form provided the current engineering state of the bomber and was used by the Crew Chief to record service and repair work. As a final visual check the Pilot and Crew Chief walked around the aircraft, inspecting tires, movable flying surfaces, filler vents, propellers, wing de-icing boots, and the undercarriage. Flak suits and steel helmets were delivered to the hardstand earlier and were placed into the aircraft with other personal gear. Often the pilots, and especially the navigators did not have time to dress in their flying suits before coming to the bomber, but there usually was time at the hardstand.

Ten minutes before "start engines" each member of the crew checked out one another's safety harness, parachute strap, and Mae West before entering the bomber. Most chose to enter a B-17 by the rear fuselage door and move forward through the bomb bay. Agile Bombardiers and Navigators pulled themselves up through the nose hatch door, but it was difficult in heavy flying clothes. On B-24s the rear fuselage could be reached via a ladder through the floor hatch, but most men chose to bend down under the open bomb bay and climb onto the narrow catwalk to go forward to the flight deck. The Navigator and Bombardier entered through the nose wheel hatch and assumed positions on the flight deck behind the pilots during take-off for safety precautions. The roll-up bomb doors on the Liberator were kept open while the bomber was parked or taxiing to vent any gasoline fumes that could have settled from the fuel transfer system at the forward end of the bomb bay.

The Pilot started the engines 25 minutes before scheduled takeoff and ten minutes before taxiing time. The start signal was a green flare fired by flying control and permitted the Pilots to run up engines, repeating those checks completed by the Crew Chief two or three hours earlier. The Flight Engineer, who doubled as the dorsal turret gunner, stood behind the pilot's shoulder to monitor the instruments. To conserve fuel it became the high squadron's routine to wait five minutes and the low squadron ten minutes after the lead before starting engines. When it was time to taxi the pilot signaled the ground crew to remove the wheel chocks. When there was a long distance on the taxiway from the hardstand to the perimeter taxiway the bomber taxied to a safe distance from the preceding bomber and the adjoining taxiway, as a miscalculation of distance could result in the nose or propeller striking the tail of the preceding bomber or a wingtip striking a nearby bomber. Pilots knew their takeoff order from the flight plan and watched for the tail call letter of the bomber that was to precede them to pass by before turning out onto the perimeter taxiway. Because it was not possible to see directly ahead over the nose taxiing in a B-17 required much more proficiency than in a B-24. The B-17 Pilot needed to taxi carefully, especially in the winter or in wet weather when if a wheel ran off the concrete the bomber could bog down, either blocking the taxiway or requiring the following bomber to detour.

The runway to be used was determined by the direction and force of the wind, but the long main runway was preferred and used when possible. The order of taxiing was lead, high, and low formation position squadrons. The lead bomber of the lead element moved onto the head of the runway, locking the tail or nose wheel leg. The following bombers held "cab rank" in line on the perimeter, spaced about a bomber's length apart. Usually squadron bombers approached the end of the runway from the side closest to their dispersal area. During the starting and stopping of taxiing each bomber would consume about 60 gallons of fuel.

The Group Operations Officer was in the control tower to oversee the takeoff and to assign another runway for use, or take whatever action was necessary to launch the mission if a problem occurred. He could contact pilots via their Command radios, but only in an absolute necessity, as use of the radio could alert the enemy of an approaching mission. After early 1944, with the great increase in air activity over southeast England the restrictions on tower-to-aircraft radio communication were decreased.

Takeoff began when the checker-painted flying control van parked off to the left of the head of the runway flashed a green Aldis light according to the take-off time schedule. The Pilot of the lead plane immediately released his brakes, heading the aircraft down the center of the runway, while the Co-pilot advanced all throttles for maximum power and the Flight Engineer monitored the instruments. Depending on the gross weight a B-17 or B-24 became airborne in about 3,000 feet, but it was SOP to keep the main wheels on the ground until near the end of the runway in order to gain the maximum airspeed possible for sustained lift off. At lift off the bomber would have a speed of 110-120 mph, and while the undercarriage retracted the bomber began a shallow climb away from base. After each bomber taxied onto the head of the runway and ran up its engines to full power against the brakes it would wait at 30 or 45 second intervals for the Aldis lamp in the control van to flash it off.

Pilots kept to a safe distance from the preceding bomber and the adjoining taxiway. Pilots knew their takeoff order from the flight plan and watched for the tail call-letter of the bomber that was to precede them to pass by before turning out onto the perimeter taxiway. (AAF)

B-17s and B-24s commonly carried a large bomb overload, the "war emergency load," to maximize their bombing capability. Both bombers had sufficient power to lift off and sustain a gross weight of 65,000 pounds. The failure of an outboard engine at the moment of lift off, or shortly after, could cause a wing to drop and cause a crash. The failure of an inboard engine did not affect directional stability as much, but could cause an emergency resulting in a crash.

After takeoff each bomber usually maintained a straight course for at least two minutes and then proceeded to the group assembly area, climbing at a predetermined rate, usually 300 feet per minute at 150 mph Indicated Air Speed (IAS). The assembly area originally comprised a five mile radius left hand orbit of the base. Later, when Groups increased to large numbers assembly areas needed to be more definitely specified both in location and altitude. The altitude at which assembly was made depended on cloud conditions. In clear weather assembly would generally occur from between 5,000 and 10,000 feet, but in extensive cloud assembly sometimes had to be made above the clouds as high as 20,000 feet, with climbs of up to 90 minutes through overcast. To minimize the risk of collision in bad weather Pilots flew exact headings, speeds, and timed legs. To minimize the risk when flying on instruments, each group was assigned a designated assembly area separated by at least five miles from the next.

Once the bombers reached their assembly altitude they first formed elements of three by the trailing aircraft turning inside the leader to catch up by cutting corners. In the same way each three-plane element turned inside the leading element to obtain its correct position and thus formed Squadron and Group formations. Squadron formations were separated by 400 to 500 feet, with the high Squadron 400 to 500 feet above the Lead Squadron and the Low Squadron 400 to 500 feet below the lead. A basic Squadron formation was two, three, or four three-plane elements, and the basic Group formation three squadrons flown as an inclined wedge, the High Squadron on the right and trailing the lead, the Low Squadron on the left and trailing the lead. During the war formations were changed many times to meet enemy countermeasures and improve formation bombing.

Initially, to help bombers join the correct formation, the Group Lead bomber periodically fired a specified color combination of two flares or flashed in Morse the Group identification letter by Aldis lamp from the tail position. An alternative method was to fly with the undercarriage lowered or trailing a cable flare. For assembly the 2nd Bomb Division used war-weary

"Assembly" aircraft were war-weary bombers (458BG B-24 shown) painted in vivid distinctive markings, with an array of lights installed in the fuselage sides to flash the group identification letter, and using special flare dispensing arrangements. (AAF)

B-24 "assembly" aircraft painted in vivid distinctive markings, with an array of lights installed in the fuselage sides to flash the group identification letter and using special flare dispensing arrangements.

During the summer of 1943 radio beacons were used for mission assembly and ultimately became a normal method of assembly, regardless of visibility. Initially RAF medium frequency beacons called "Splashers" were used until a system of special low-powered radio transmitters was developed specifically for group assembly. These transmitters, known as "Bunchers," were usually positioned close to the airfield in a hut or trailer and pulsed a distinctive Morse signal that could be picked up by a receiving set in a bomber over a range of 15 miles. The beacon was used as a fixed point in the assembly orbit, with the strength of the signal indicating when the receiving bomber was overhead. In poor weather Bunchers were particularly beneficial, as they aided in successful assembly in conditions which would have caused a mission to be cancelled.

Subject to the briefed altitude and weather conditions, between 30 and 60 minutes was allowed for Group assembly, with larger formations and higher altitudes requiring more time. Lead Navigators continued to check on their position by Gee navigational radio beacon fixes, or radio, or visual check points during assembly. A Pilot or Co-pilot in the lead bomber sat in the tail gun position to watch the formation and report to the Command Pilot or a senior member of Group staff who had taken his place in the cockpit. The Group CO, Air Executive, or a senior officer from the Combat Wing often flew in the lead bomber as Task Force Commander if he was also to be in the lead of the Combat Wing or Division formation, where he was responsible for decisions and control affecting his command during the mission.

At the specified time the Group departed on a course for the Combat Wing assembly point, flying directly across the Buncher transmitter. The route was usually planned as a dogleg, using a familiar English town as the turning point. In addition to allowing trailing elements or squadrons of the Group to catch up by shortening the turn at the dogleg, it enabled the Group to lose or make up time for the rendezvous with the other Groups of the Combat Wing at the precise time and location. Alternatively, Combat Wing assembly was affected by a large orbit of 12 minutes around one of the Group Bunchers. A firm schedule had to be followed because the entire Divisional bomber stream could become disorganized if a Group was a few minutes late or early at a control point.

A formation of heavy bombers could easily become scattered and disorganized by sudden changes of course and air speed. Groups of the Combat Wing were scheduled to arrive at the assembly point at precise times and altitudes so as to place them in their designated positions of lead, high, and low, forming an inclined wedge in the same fashion that Squadrons did within each individual Group. The Combat Wing then embarked on a dogleg course for the Division rendezvous, with the turning point again enabling Groups to improve their positions and the Wing leader to assemble the formations so that they would arrive at the Division rendezvous on time. The turn in the dogleg was again a prominent town or landmark, but if visibility was poor a Gee fix was taken to ensure the location of the turn.

Once the mission assembly reached 10,000 feet, the Navigator or Co-pilot alerted the crew on the interphone to go on oxygen, after which the crew checked their masks and oxygen flow regulator. At altitude the Bombardier or a Pilot called the crew every 15 minutes during the mission for an acknowledgement that they were on oxygen, as defective equipment or a disconnected line could cause unconsciousness in a few minutes and death in as little as 20 minutes. Before reaching oxygen altitude the Bombardier went to the bomb bay and removed the safety pins from the bombs. It was easier to move around the bomber without a portable oxygen bottle, and at higher altitudes the pins could ice up and be difficult to withdraw. If heated flying suits were worn these were plugged in and switched on and the rheostats set at the desired temperatures.

Division assembly was accomplished approximately 20 minutes after Wing assembly, usually over a visual coastal town or landmark, but near a Splasher beacon in case there was an undercast preventing the visual reference. Flares were fired by each Combat Wing as it reached the Divisional assembly line. The Division column would be formed at altitudes between 15,000 and 20,000 feet, depending on the distance to the point of penetration of enemy airspace, where it was desirable to be high enough to minimize the effects of AA fire.

Initially radio silence was strictly imposed, but by spring 1944 Group and Combat Wing leaders were allowed to call out positions over the "A" Channel for a time check. Radio silence was often broken for real or imagined emergencies and to confuse German monitoring stations as to the makeup and target of the bomber formations that had been picked up by enemy radar "spoof" information was broadcast by selected aircrews to deliberately mislead the enemy with subtle pieces of false information.

If all Divisions were headed for the same target or target area they were often massed into a single bomber stream upon crossing the Continental coastline to facilitate fighter escort rendezvous. At the coast the bombers were normally flying at altitudes of over 20,000 feet, and altitudes over enemy territory were typically maintained at between 24,000 and 27,000 feet for B-17s and 20,000 and 24,000 feet for B-24s, as the heavily loaded Liberators were more difficult to control at the greater altitudes. Missions were infrequently flown at lower altitudes when there was an occasion for improved bombing accuracy without compromising safety.

Until late April 1944 each Group sent out three or four extra bombers that assembled as a high element to the High Squadron and took the place of any bomber in the Group formation that aborted the mission. If any of these aircraft were not required they turned back at the English coast. After April 1944 all aircraft taking off for a mission were required to complete it and no extra bombers were needed. A few bomber crews did abort on nearly every mission, and crews were meticulously interrogated by an Operations Officer to make certain they had a legitimate reason to abort.

When the bomber was at least ten miles off the English coast the Navigator instructed the Radio Operator to turn off the IFF (Identification Friend or Foe), and when they were in the middle of the English Channel the Bombardier had the gunners test fire their guns with a short burst. Because body armor was heavy and uncomfortable most of the crew did not don their flak jackets and steel helmets until approaching flak areas or when beginning the bomb run. Any extra flak jackets were placed in areas to give additional protection.

During the entire mission all Radio Operators listened on Division Headquarters frequency on the hour and half hour for any recall, a diversion, or other coded Morse message that might be broadcast. To ensure his complete attention the Radio Operator of the lead bomber had no gun in his enclosed hatch. Verbal radio transmissions were received by the Pilot and Co-pilot of all bombers, and one or the other listened to the channels assigned for the mission.

The Liaison Set was used for W/T (Wireless Telegraphy in Morse signals) and had a range of up to 600 miles at combat altitude. The Command and VHF Sets were for R/T (Radio Telephone; verbal), having maximum ranges of 30 and 150 miles, respectively. Both could be used for bomber-to-bomber communication, but the more reliable and easily operated VHF set was employed for air-to-air communication and the Command Set for contact with the home base when over friendly territory. Radio silence was scrupulously maintained once enemy airspace was penetrated; the only urgent calls permitted were from the bomber leader for bombing changes or to alert the fighter escort if under attack. A practice was adopted whereby the lead aircraft of the Combat Wing or Division had two Navigators on board, one focused on pilotage (pin-pointing landmarks on his maps if conditions were favorable) and the other Navigator on Dead Reckoning (DR). Navigators could make use of enemy radio beacons for navigational purposes in addition to the Gee chain in England, which provided a fix for up to 200 miles. The prime source of navigation was DR based on calculations conducted before takeoff and amended to incorporate any changes necessary if wind direction and velocity differed from that given at briefing. Throughout the mission the

Scrupulous **formation flying** was important for mutual protection from *Luftwaffe* fighters and accurate bombing once over the target. (AAF)

Navigator called out times and headings to the Pilots over the interphone. Once H2X radar became standard on missions the Radar Navigator used this equipment to supplement the DR Navigator's plot.

The bomber formation routes were seldom direct to the Initial Point (IP), the point where the bomb run on target was to begin. Even though enemy fighter interception was a major threat, the mission routes were calculated to mislead the enemy as to the intended target by using a number of course changes. The range of Luftwaffe single-engine fighters, even fitted with an auxiliary fuel tank, was under two hours and these course changes often redirected fighter interceptions. Luftwaffe fighter tactics in attacking US heavy bombers varied greatly and depended on the type of fighter, its weapons, and the predilection of the fighter unit and pilot. Generally, because the bomber formations threw out massed defensive firepower, the Luftwaffe interceptions were distinguished by hit and run firing passes. Bomber crewmen made a practice of calling out fighter approaches over the interphone, using the clock position method. For example, a frontal attack would be "12 o'clock high, low or level" in relation to its relative altitude. This verbal call out of an approaching enemy enabled gunners who could not see it from their position to anticipate its flight path and be ready to fire when it came into view. Due to the danger of collisions within the formation, bombers were able to only take limited evasive action which was primarily an up and down oscillation but holding a steady course was thought to give the gunners a better possibility of hitting the enemy.

The Initial Point was a prominent landmark that also reflected a good radar image. A turn towards the target was made at the IP, ideally at 30° but at not more than 45° as this would cause the Groups to become scattered. The intent of the turn was to allow Combat Wing and Group formations to position for the run on the target in line astern. To achieve the required separation of formations so that they were spaced for individual runs on the target, the High Group could not make its turn until it was adequately separated from the Lead Group which turned directly over the IP. Likewise the Low Group did not turn until the High Group was clear. This placed each of the three Groups approximately two miles apart on slightly different courses which converged at the target. If the bombing was to be by Squadrons then they uncovered in similar fashion. This was the usual procedure at the IP until March 1944 when maneuvers were introduced that placed all three Groups directly in trail on the briefed target course. An analysis of bombing results during previous months definitely showed that the Lead Group achieved more accurate results than the following Groups. It was determined that the cause was the confusion with target identification through making approaches other than on the briefed line. The new procedure involved the High and Low Groups spreading out not less than five miles from the IP and assuming the required order and separation so that each should turn over the IP and follow in train to the target. The distance between Groups on a bomb run was planned to be two miles but on average was four to five miles.

Originally the turn at the IP was indicated by the lead bomber opening its bomb bay doors and then firing a signal flare: Red for attacking the primary target, and Red and Yellow for the secondary. Later, a change of target or bombing altitude was usually achieved by a coded radio message. Late in the war, B-24 units routinely opened their bomb doors five minutes before the scheduled drop.

During the bombing run the lead bomber of each formation was directed by the Lead Bombardier. If the bombing was to be by Groups or Squadrons, the Lead Bombardier sighted on the target for range and deflection while the lead bomber of elements in a Squadron or Squadrons in a Group sighted for range only. Range involved the distance between the bomber and target, deflection involved adjustments to ensure the bombs did not fall to one side or the other of the target. Operation of the bombsight controls actuated the Pilot's Directional Indicator (PDI), which showed the desired lateral flight attitudes which the Pilot was to fly. The PDI was used less after the spring of 1943 when successful Automatic Flight Control Equipment (AFCE) was introduced. The AFCE was an electrical transfer system which linked the bombsight to the automatic pilot, and allowed the Bombardier to operate the sight controls to actually fly the aircraft. (The AFCE is discussed in detail elsewhere.) The bomb release point was predetermined by a formula and data calculated prior to briefing and was inserted into the bombsight. When the Bombardier centered the target in the bombsight's telescope; it computed the precise moment to release the bombs and automatically released them.

During the bombing run the lead bomber of each formation was directed by the Lead Bombardier. In bombers without bombsights the Bombardier opened his bomb bay doors when the lead plane did, set up the desired release pattern, and watched the bomb bay of his Element or Squadron Leader. The instant the Leader's bombs began to leave their bomb bay the other Bombardiers on watch pressed and held the toggle switch that released their bombs. (AAF)

In bombers without bombsights the Bombardier opened his bomb bay doors when the lead plane did, set up the desired release pattern, and watched the bomb bay of his Element or Squadron Leader. The instant the Leader's bombs began to leave their bomb bay the other Bombardiers on watch pressed and held the toggle switch which released their bombs. The time lag between the Leader's and the other releases was compensated for in the data fed into the bombsight. In an emergency the bomb toggle switch could also be used to by-pass the automatic bombsight release and there was a manual release for jettisoning all bombs simultaneously. An Intervalometer which allowed the pre-selection of the desired number and time spacing of bombs was integrated into the electrical bomb release controls. Alternatively, a partial load or the whole load of bombs could be salvoed. A display panel at the Bombardier's position registered the release by switching off a red light for each released bomb. Bombers without a bombsight often had no bombardier on board and the bomb release was done by a Navigator or Gunner who watched for the lead plane to release and this "Togglier" pressed the toggle. In bombers with a bombsight the Bombardier directed the Radio Operator to switch on the strike camera which operated automatically, taking five or six pictures of the bomb strikes on the target at six to ten second intervals.

The selection of the bombing run was usually a compromise between avoiding the heaviest AA concentrations and the direction of wind and sunlight. Because downwind bombing reduced accuracy; the ideal wind direction was to carry smoke away from approach landmarks, from enemy smoke screens, and the first bomb strikes. Before the introduction of the AFCE, when AA fire was anticipated on the bomb run, the Lead Pilot took irregular evasive action, slight changes of course until a specified time from the bomb release line, generally 45 seconds. Once the AFCE was in use; straight bombing runs were necessary to improve bombing accuracy.

If the lead bomber was lost to enemy action on the bombing run, a Deputy flying on its wing in the Lead Element, or the Lead of the High Squadron, assumed command. When the bomb run was made on instruments the radar-guided Pathfinder bomber flew ahead of the Combat Wing and dropped Skymarker bombs that produced thick white smoke trails soon after release. The Pathfinder also discharged colored star shells and the use of smoke marker bombs was eventually adopted for all bombing.

After bombing the lead bomber flew straight ahead for ten seconds to allow trailing bombers of the formation to complete their drop and close bomb bay doors, and then turned and headed for the Rally Point. The Rally Point was the briefed location for Groups or Squadrons to reform into defensive Wing formations out of range of known AA batteries. At the Rally Point the High and Low Groups shortened the turn to regain their original positions relative to the Lead. Once away from the target the Combat Wing Leader instructed his Radio Operator to send a "Target Bombed" signal to headquarters. Once the bomber jettisoned its bombs and used half of its fuel; its air speed increased from 130-150 mph to 160-180 mph IAS. Once over the enemy coast radio communication was eased and damaged bombers could call direction finding stations for a course to the nearest airfield. Halfway across the English

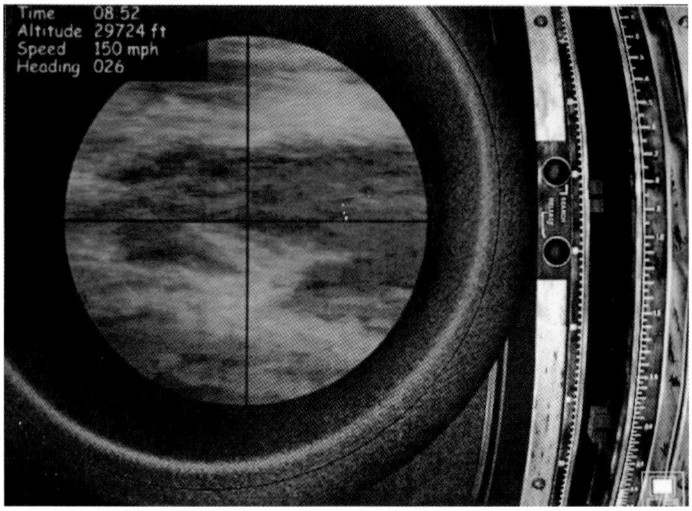

Actual view through the Norden bombsight. (AAF)

On reaching home base at 2,000 feet the Group formation turned to fly down wind by the runway in use and continued on this course for one minute after passing the airfield boundary, and the whole Group then made a 180° turn during which they into trail behind the Lead. (AAF)

Channel the IFF was switched on but during the entire mission after leaving England, bombers flying alone could identify themselves to fighters or other bombers as friendly by the colors of the day flares or flashing a code letter by Aldis lamp. In order to avoid use by the enemy, each set of two colors and letters was only in use for set periods.

After leaving hostile airspace the bomber stream separated into Divisions, each with its own briefed point of landfall. Altitude was decreased by 500 feet per minute at 170 to 175 mph IAS and at 10,000 feet the crew came off oxygen and was allowed to smoke. The Combat Wing Leader informed the Division home station of the anticipated time for landfall. When the English coast was reached, the bombers were flying at only a few thousand feet and each Division would separate and individual Groups flew to their bases.

Operations was immediately notified when Flying Control picked up radio talk on the VHF receiver and the delegated Operations Officer went to the tower to supervise Squadron formation and positioned on the High Right Element. In some Groups only the Lead Squadron Low Element changed position in this way. On reaching home base at 2,000 feet the Group formation turned to fly down wind by the runway in use and continued on this course for one minute after passing the airfield boundary. The whole Group then made a 180° turn during which the High Right and Low Left Squadrons went into trail behind the Lead with any changes in position of elements as previously described, made at this time. When the Lead Squadron reached the approach end of the runway the Leader dipped his left wing to signal a peel off which would be started by his left wing aircraft (No 3). The two left-most Elements were involved in this first peel-off, the remainder of the Squadron reducing height as it circled once more before a final approach. The other two Squadrons retained altitude, the second (high) orbiting once more over the original course and the third Squadron twice.

Bombers with wounded crewmen on board turned off the runway as soon as possible, stopping on the taxiway or in the nearest hardstand where an ambulance would be waiting. Other bombers taxied directly to their hardstands. If the bomber that led the mission was routed past the briefing room area it would sometimes be halted to let any Command Staff Officers get out. When the bomber reached its hardstand the ground crew assisted in parking the bomber. The bomber crew departed from the most convenient exits, bringing out personal equipment. Electrically heated flying suits and other flight garb were usually removed on the hardstand and put into carrying bags. Gunners removed and cleaned their guns and placed them for pick up by an Armament truck. Alternatively, guns were cleaned at the Squadron Armament hut after interrogation. The Flight Engineer and Pilot completed the Form 1A on which the Pilot reported any mechanical problems or known damage. Both air and ground crews inspected their bomber for battle damage while the former awaited transportation.

The combat crews boarded a truck that took them to the briefing room complex where each crew was first checked in by a clerk. The men entered the large locker room to return personal equipment (parachutes, flying suits, Mae Wests, escape kits, oxygen masks). Red Cross girls served coffee, hot chocolate, doughnuts and powdered egg and corned beef sandwiches. Also available from the flight surgeon was the traditional "mission whiskey." At another table an Operations Officer collected "Hot News," information considered essential for ASAP transmission. This information included enemy convoys, shipping or activity that might affect other operations, aircraft seen in distress, crashed, and ditched. Command Pilots reported to the Operations Officer in the briefing room, giving a brief rundown on the Group's performance during the mission which would form the basis of a "flash" report telephoned to Wing. On tactical missions (support of ground forces) flown during the last year and a half of the war, Interrogation Officers met crews on hardstands as they returned to carry out interrogations. Tactical missions usually involved only a brief incursion into enemy territory and if no opposition was encountered there was little point in interviewing all crewmen and sometimes only Lead Crews were interrogated after tactical missions.

After the crews deposited their equipment and had their refreshments, they went in specific groups, such as Bombardiers or Navigators, to the briefing room for interrogations by Interrogation Officers sitting at round tables. The Interrogation Officers used a standard set of questions covering target observations, flak and fighter opposition where encountered, tactics, fighter claims, weather, fighter support, aircraft in distress, plus other pertinent observations and suggestions. Following interrogation, flight crews were released to go to their

After returning to the briefing room the men entered the large locker room to return personal equipment, where Red Cross girls served coffee, hot chocolate, doughnuts, and powdered egg and corned beef sandwiches. (AAF)

barracks or the Mess Hall in trucks that ran a shuttle service. Most men were so exhausted after a mission and skipped the main meal, preferring to sleep but some, still on mission adrenalin, showered and dined before going to bed.

Gunner's claims were then reviewed by an Intelligence Officer with a special brief to compare the claims of various crews in an effort to eliminate duplication. Navigators and Bombardiers were required to give separate reports on their part, Navigators turning in their logs and Bombardiers completing bombing forms. Interrogation of Lead Crews was more intensive, particularly if there had been some errors made. This debriefing might take up to an hour and a half before all crews were processed.

Group Operations and Intelligence Offices were very active. The strike cameras were collected and their films removed and processed. When the prints were available they were examined by Intelligence Officers to plot the Group strike pattern on the target. A more comprehensive report of the Group's results, losses, and claims was prepared and sent immediately to both Wing and Division after interrogation (generally within an hour). Missing In Action (MIA) forms were completed for crews and individuals, aircraft damage reports compiled, and all major damage was photographed. Enemy opposition such as aircraft types encountered, destroyed, or damaged and the location and strength of flak were specified in other reports.

After the crews deposited their equipment and had their refreshments they went in batches, such as Bombardiers or Navigators, to the briefing room for **debriefing interrogations** by Interrogation Officers. (AAF)

When the bombers returned the ground crews work began again but most men had caught up on their sleep while the bombers were gone because battle damage or a major engineering problem could keep them working through the night. Routine maintenance as mandated by engineering requirements was performed on each bomber when it returned. If flak shrapnel or bullets had caused minor skin damage, the Metal Shop repair team riveted patches. However, repairing a bomber punctured in hundreds of places was a major enterprise and would put a bomber out of action. The Line Chief, who was responsible for supervising the mechanics and their work, would notify the Squadron Engineering Officer of any major problems and they would decide which bombers could not be ready for the next mission. Fuel tanks and oxygen were refilled and the bomber brought to serviceable standard as soon as possible.

Immediately after the mission the Intelligence Staff at Division Headquarters made a preliminary assessment of bombing results from the reports and strike photos received from the Groups. After this report was further detailed and refined it was teleprinted to VIII Bomber Command at High Wycombe and Annexes would follow as Division Staff had more time to examine the input from its Groups and Wings. At *Pinetree* analysts established the degree of target destruction, the resulting loss to the enemy, and, if necessary, a set a priority for future attacks on the same target. Information received on enemy flak and air defenses was also carefully examined and used to update intelligence data. This assessment would be augmented and supported by photographs of the target taken by reconnaissance aircraft after the mission. Assessment of the mission continued in the Intelligence Sections of High Command for some days following the operation by which time the Combat Groups had flown other missions.

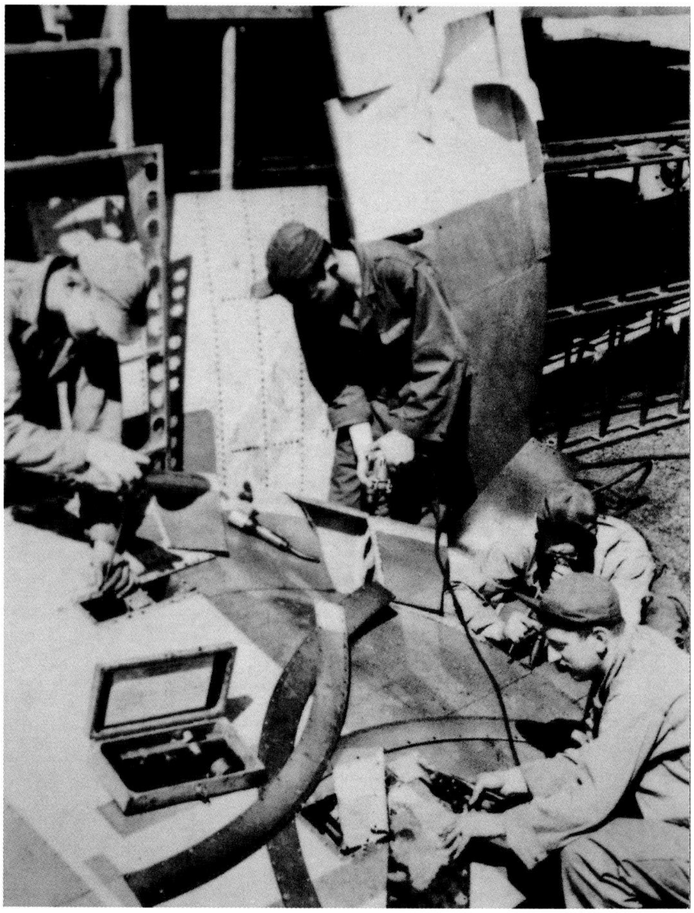

If flak, shrapnel, or bullets had caused minor skin damage to the bomber, the **Metal Shop repair** team clean cut out the damaged skin and riveted patches over it. (AAF)

PTO

After the missions flown from China and the initial missions flown from the bases in the Marianas it was apparent that bombing strategy and procedure to bomb Japan would follow much the same pattern as in bombing Germany.

Before any priority targets were selected, however, intelligence material was collected from every plausible source. In marked contrast to the ETO, where U.S. target specialists benefited from pre- and post-war British intelligence, facts on Japan were virtually non-existent. The Japanese had planned for war for many years and had been very secretive, and any information was pieced together from information gathered from business and vacationing travelers, missionaries, and former residents of Japan. The first 20th Air Force China-based photo reconnaissance missions by single B-29s were not flown until the spring of 1944. Using this information, the Committee of Operational Analysts (COA) and the Joint Target Committee (JTC) met in Washington and compiled a list of 1,000 precision objectives. From this list the Joint Chiefs of Staff chose Japanese aircraft production, the coke, steel, and oil industries, shipping, and Japanese industrial urban areas as major targets. The final priority list was drawn up by the COA in this order: 1) aircraft industry, 2) urban industrial areas, and 3) shipping.

The XXI Bomber Command target specialists of A-2 (Intelligence) collaborated closely with A-3 (Operations) in formulating missions. Their most critical need was for detailed current data about specific targets and the routes, which had to be obtained largely from aerial photos. Beginning in November 1944, the 3rd Photo Squadron operated from the Marianas and flew photo B-29s on almost daily missions to Japan. By August 1945 the Squadron had flown 433 photo missions and had photographed literally every square mile of Japan, and collected a mosaic of photos of target areas in Japan. PIs (photographic interpreters) closely examined each of thousands of prints, analyzing targets and defenses, and assembled and catalogued target data. Individual targets were analyzed for priority and then for structure, and so that the bomb experts could determine which type of bombs could do the most damage.

Target specialists of the XXI Bomber Command's Intelligence (A-2) and Operations (A-3) divisions met with veteran operations officers and experts in targets, navigation and weather, enemy AA and fighter defenses, armament, ordnance, and radar and radio. These planners devised a basic mission plan, called the "Fragmentary Plan," that included the number of bombers and required bomb load, the routes and altitudes to and from the target, navigational checkpoints, aiming points, and the axis and altitude of attack. This plan and others were sent to the Commanding General of the XXIBC for approval for future use. It was immediately sent to the A-2 at each Wing HQ as an advisory on probable missions in the three day to three week time frame. With this warning the Wing A-2s could study and gather the necessary mission data, such as maps, charts, route plans, etc. in a target file and file it until more specific orders were issued. In this way the Wings and aircrews would not have to depend on the pre-mission briefing alone. Also, XXI HQ was not committed to a specific mission at a specific time. If weather closed the scheduled target then an alternate target on file could be substituted and the bombers would not be grounded for lack of information.

The final orders from the CG of the XXIBC were issued in two stages. The "Intentions" stage was issued one or two days before the mission. It specified the target and authorized the wings to have their groups prepare all material for briefings and ready the bomb load. The "Firm Decision" stage was issued to the wings 12 to 24 hours before the mission, after the final weather forecast, and was passed to the groups. It included the date and hour of takeoff and authorized bomb loading.

Each Wing issued its own field orders, which included the order of takeoff for each Group. The Group A-3 prepared a schedule called the Signal Operation Instruction (SOI), also known as a "flimsy," which was given to each airplane commander, giving the exact time and order of take off for individual group bombers. With the flimsy and target file in hand the airplane commander attended the briefing. First to speak was the Group CO, who announced the target. The Operations Officer discussed the size of the mission. The Intelligence Officer, using the large wall map, described the target, the route to and from the target, checkpoints, assembly point, aiming points, and flak and enemy aircraft status. The Weather Officer gave a weather briefing. Then the Operations Officer spoke again and gave the assembly procedure, bombing altitude, types of bombs, bombing procedure, formation briefing, and AA and fighter avoidance, along with radar jamming. The Group briefing usually took half an hour. After the Group briefing there were more detailed specific mission briefings for each crewman. After these briefings the crew went back to their barracks to pick up some personal effects and visited the latrine. Before take off they ate a breakfast of scrambled powdered eggs, fried potatoes, toast and butter, canned fruit, canned tomato or orange juice, and the all important cup(s) of coffee.

Generally, B-29 mission taxiing, takeoff, and assembly were similar to the ETO. Flying at high altitudes in the large pressurized, temperature-controlled B-29, while much longer in duration, was infinitely more comfortable than flying in a cold and drafty B-17 or B-24. It was calculated that the mission time from briefing to debriefing was 20 to 24 hours. Japanese AA and fighter defenses did not begin to compare with Luftwaffe fighter and AA defenses. The relative unreliability and fuel consumption of the B-29's Wright R-3350 engines, especially the early models, and the weather were the main hazards facing the Superfortress crews.

The weather in the Marianas was better than that in Great Britain, but the weather over Japan was problematic. During the early high altitude daylight visual bombing missions over Japan weather was the most serious problem, and missions were frequently delayed for several days awaiting favorable forecasts. Good forecasts did not mean that the weather would be good over the target. Only 30% of the bombers sent out with favorable weather forecasts were able to bomb their primary targets, and of these many bombed through broken clouds. The remaining 70% arrived at the target area to find it obscured by clouds and were forced to bomb by radar or move on to secondary targets. The weather over the Japanese homeland was unreliable, and Long-Range forecasting was vital to mission planners. Neither the Russians nor Chinese had the means or ability to provide data from the Asian continent, from which the future weather over Japan would flow. To forecast the weather on the 1,300 mile route from the Marianas and over Japan the XXIBC sent out three daily weather strikes.

When the B-29s first flew over Japan at high altitudes they encountered previously unknown high winds of 120 mph, usually flowing from west to east. These winds, which could reach speeds of over 200 mph, are now known as the jet stream. Bombing runs with these high winds put the bomber's ground speeds at 400 to 500 mph, which made the Norden Bombsight ineffective. Bombing into the winds slowed the ground speeds so low as to put the bombers in jeopardy over areas heavily defended by antiaircraft guns. Bombing laterally to the winds was impossible due to the extreme drift. These winds also made second runs over a target difficult, as getting back to the target was a navigational problem and used too much fuel. On a mission to the Nakajima Musashino Engine Plant near Tokyo B-29s approached the target down wind in a 215 mph wind and, added to the bomber's airspeed, attempted to bomb the target at 535 mph!

During the long flight back from the target fuel consumption and engine troubles were a nagging problem. However, the bloody capture of Iwo Jima alleviated these fears. By the end of the war 2,395 of the 25,005 B-29 sorties flown (9.2%) had made emergency landings on Iwo Jima, saving 24,761 airmen. A summary of emergency landings showed that 1,872 (78.2%) of these landings were made for refueling or minor repairs and 524 (21.8%) were made for major maintenance, which included 311 (13%) for engine changes, 64 (2.6%) for battle damage, and 149 (6.2%) for other reasons.

7

Bombing Tactics

Development through Exercises and Maneuvers
Annual maneuvers were initiated by the U.S. Army Air Service in 1925 to bring aviation units together for training and operations, and to experiment with and to test organization, equipment, tactics, and logistics. Maneuvers furnished officers command and staff experience, and practice in managing large units in the field. Each of the maneuvers was assigned a different military problem. The 1927 maneuvers held in Texas were one-sided, as a field army and its aviation component faced a simulated enemy. In 1928 maneuvers were replaced with an Air Corps composite group that toured Army service schools demonstrating operations. In 1929 units were placed into a provisional wing for operations in California. The following year all available personnel and aircraft were formed into a large provisional air division to use as large a unit as possible for mass operations and to display the Air Corps to the American public. Lack of funding due to the Depression postponed maneuvers in 1932.

The use of exercises and maneuvers gave Gen. Andrews, the GHQ Air Force, and the Field Army the opportunity to test aviation organization, personnel, equipment, and methods during the mid-1930s, when the military buildup in Europe began to cause some alarm. The prospect of an enemy attacking the U.S. led to large coastal defense maneuvers in which Army aircraft searched for and attacked Navy ships approaching the coast, and protecting specific sites from attack by hostile aircraft. Air defense used civilian observers, the development of warning networks, and the testing of air raid blackout procedures. Air units also often took part in Army exercises and maneuvers, being responsible for direct support of ground forces and for independent operations.

In 1936 Gen. Delos Emmons, the CO of the First Wing at March Field, CA, tested bombardment formations (javelin-up and javelin-down, stagger, wedge, column, dispersed-column) and ways to release bombs (singly, by salvo, and in trail) to determine the bomb patterns produced under different conditions so the appropriate ones could be selected for each bombing mission. The 9BS dropped inert bombs from several altitudes flying different formations, varying distances and intervals between planes, and employing various combinations of altitude, speed, and wind direction. After a bomber formation completed its drop each bomb was located and its distance was measured from the target.

The highlight of the Second Army maneuvers of summer 1936 was a mission for which the 96BS won the Mackay Trophy. On 13 August 1936 Capt. Richard Nugent led three B-10Bs from Langley to fly 600 miles to attack ground forces in Michigan. Soon after takeoff the Martins ran into dense haze with solid overcast and Nugent led his unit flying on instruments in tight formation. When they encountered thunderstorms and heavy fog they separated, but once the weather improved Nugent regrouped and led them through the clouds towards their goal. On time over the target they released flares through the clouds and maneuvered as directed in the area before ending the flight at Selfridge Field.

The GHQ Air Force maneuvers of 10 to 23 May 1937 were held in California, and were among the most important and productive of the time. Brig.Gen. Delos Emmons, CO of the First Wing Commander (March Field), commanded the defense of Los Angeles and other ground targets outlined in lime at Muroc Dry Lake. Two P-26 and one PB-2 squadron from Muroc and the 63rd Coast Artillery (AA) were under Emmons' command. Brig.Gen. Gerald Brant, Second Wing Commander (Hamilton Field), commanded the attacking force of three B-10 squadrons from Fresno, Stockton, and Merced, and three A-17 squadrons from Bakersfield, Visalia, and Delano. The B-10s were to bomb LA with the A-17s using smokescreens and tear gas against the airdrome and antiaircraft positions. Pursuit aircraft were to intercept and attack bombers with camera guns, and would develop and hone their tactics against the somewhat slower but higher flying bombers. In the bombardment operations, it was found that close formations were desirable for bombing, and defense against enemy interceptor aircraft increased the odds of being hit by antiaircraft fire. This risk could be greatly reduced by flying in columns of single bombers separated by 10 to 15 seconds and staggered laterally and by at least 1,000 feet in altitude, by quickly losing altitude and turning 180° upon release of bombs, and by leaving in the direction from which they attacked. The time with the least AA hazard was during the 15 minutes just after dawn and the 15 minutes right before dark, when there was too much light for effective illumination by searchlight and too little light to render bombers visible to ground observers. The use of black paint on bombers made illumination by searchlight more difficult at night but gave the planes a clearer outline by day. A complete folder was needed for each intended target, as the success of the mission depended upon the identification of the objective. Night precision bombing was considered possible if flares or long-burning incendiary bombs could be developed and dropped to mark the aiming point. Extra bomb bay fuel tanks would be required for long cross-country deployments.

In 1938 the 19th Bombardment Group, commanded by Lt.Col. Harvey Burwell, tested mass bombing techniques at Muroc Dry Lake, CA. Nine B-18s, each carrying thirty-two 100 pound bombs, attacked a 900 foot wide x 2,400 foot long target from 12,000 feet in javelin-down formation (three elements of three planes each in column with the second and third elements stepped down). The lead bombardier signaled the other bombardiers to release their bombs in trail so that each bomb should fall 100 feet from the last in rows 100 feet apart. The bombs were dispersed over a large area, and mass bombing was determined to be an efficient method to neutralize or destroy airdromes, factories, harbors, and other large installations. The advantages of mass bombing were that all bombers did not require master bombardiers; it was simple and provided disciplined control; the mass of bombs did not require accuracy on large targets; and the formation gave the bombers mutual protection against enemy interceptors. The disadvantages were that at low to medium altitudes the formation was vulnerable to enemy AA gunners and bombs were wasted in mass bombing against a precision target.

The May maneuvers of 1938, consisting of 450 officers, 2,300 enlisted men, and 130 aircraft from three Wings, were held in the Northeast. The highlight of these maneuvers was the well-publicized interception of the Italian liner *Rex* and the first blackout on American soil. On 12 May 1938 Gen. Andrews commenced maneuvers that would give the B-17 an undeniable public boost over the B-18. With the cooperation of the Italian luxury liner *Rex* Andrews sent out three B-17s to intercept the liner as it was 725 miles off New York. Under intense newspaper and radio coverage orchestrated by Lt.Col. Ira Eaker, head of the AAC's Information Division, the three B-17s left Mitchel Field under the command of Maj. Vincent Meloy. On board were a radio announcer and sound engineers from NBC and a newsman and photographer representing the major news services. Ace navigator 1Lt. Curtis LeMay computed the expected position of the *Rex* and estimated the time of interception. After flying through heavy overcast and rain showers the B-17s arrived exactly on time and circled the liner while the passengers waved. The next day newspapers carried a dramatic front page photo of two B-17s flying over the *Rex* at smoke stack height.

In May 1939 Gen. Emmons, commanding the GHQ Air Force, asked his commanders to carry out as much training as possible under conditions of poor visibility or low overcast to uncover difficulties that would prevent successful bombing, and to discover what equipment and techniques would better chances of success.

High Altitude Bombing by Norden Bombsight

Bombing which was done from an altitude of 15,000 feet and above was generally called High Altitude Bombing (HAB), but did not denote bombing from the maximum or service ceiling of the bomber involved. The correct bombing altitude was to be selected to allow the successful destruction of the target within the limits of acceptable losses in men and equipment. However, bombing from higher and safer altitudes could reduce accuracy, causing less damage and necessitating bombing the target on a second mission. The Bombardier's Information File (BIF) stated:

"Effective bombing results demand your utmost in technical skill and accuracy. They also demand painstaking study of the target and target area. With the aid of maps, photos, and target guides, you must fix a picture of the target so firmly in your mind that you can bomb successfully even when only a part of the target area is visible."

Locating the Initial Point

The location of the target and the planned bombing route to the target were disclosed and discussed with the crews at a briefing just before the mission. The beginning of the planned bomb run was marked on the map as the Initial Point (IP), which was selected to be about 18 to 20 miles from the target. Although one consideration in selecting the IP was to avoid as much flak as possible, heavy flak could nevertheless be expected on the bomb run. Before trying to locate the Initial Point it was necessary that the bombardier identify the larger landmarks and terrain features near it. The IP was easier to find if the bombardier first located the area surrounding it by working with the navigator to locate it and then by pinpointing the most prominent features. A missed IP could mean a hurried bombing procedure that compromised bombing accuracy, but the bombardier was not to go

The **May 1938 Maneuvers** highlighted well-publicized interception of the Italian liner *Rex* and the first blackout on American soil. Pictured are Maj.Gen. Frank Andrews (left), Brig.Gen. Arnold Kronstad, and Brig.Gen. Delos Emmons. (AAF)

"fishtailing all over the sky trying to find a dot on the map from 15,000 feet or higher." If the Bombardier couldn't locate the IP with certainty but had identified several check points around it he was justified in making the turn on the briefed axis of attack.

Bomb Run

The bombing run from the Initial Point until the bombs were dropped lasted only a few minutes, but was the point of the entire U.S. bombing program and its mission. Once the IP was identified the bombardier began to enter numerical data into the bombsight: altitude, which determined the time of bombfall; forward speed, which determined the distance the bombs would travel forward from their initial point of release to their point of impact (the bombs would trail some distance behind the aircraft); wind strength and direction, which caused bomb deflection; and bomb ballistics, which affected dropping time and trajectory. The wind conditions were also checked at this time and drift was determined. In readying the sight for bombing, the bombardier would first set in the figures for drift and dropping angle, taking into account bomb ballistics, trail, altitude, and speed. This data had to be checked about five minutes before the bomb run.

Often in the vicinity of the IP the bombers began to experience antiaircraft fire. The bombardier tried to mislead the German AA gunners by taking gentle evasive action at the beginning of the bomb run. However, in the last four minutes or so of the bomb run evasive action was not compatible with accurate bombing and the bomber became vulnerable.

Once the bombsight data was entered, the bombardier was to be sure that he turned the bomber on the correct heading toward the target and held it until the check points had been identified to the left and right of the course, then to the left and right of the target. Then the bombardier was to narrow down his vision and course and not to look too far ahead for the target. The bombardier was to keep the check points oriented as well chosen check points helped the bombardier time his bombing run and establish an approximate course and range synchronization before the target itself was in sight. Because of the difficulty of using check points in determining how far the aircraft was from the target and how long it would take to get there, the bombardier was to use the sighting angle to make these estimates. The bombardier used a graph which had been prepared to give him the distance to the target at any sighting angle and at the bombing altitude. He was to use the predetermined ground speed to estimate the time it would take to fly that distance.

As soon as the target ahead was identified, the bombardier asked the pilot for control of the plane using the autopilot. When the bombsight was

The **bombing run from the Initial Point** until the bombs were dropped lasted only a few minutes, but was the point of the entire U.S. bombing program and its mission. (AAF)

connected to the autopilot, the bombardier was in control of the directional flight of the airplane by means of signals (right or left) through the bombsight. The bombardier's job was to pick up the target in the telescope of the bombsight and to align the cross hairs on the target. The vertical cross hair established course and the horizontal cross hair the rate of closure. By means of a control on the left of the sight, the bombardier centered the vertical cross hair on the Aiming Point (AP) and by means of a control on the right he brought the horizontal hair across the Aiming Point. The bombardier then checked the gyroscopic stabilization of the bombsight and clutched in the electrical drive motor. The sight then computed the time for the point of release of the bombs. On the right of the sight were two indices, one indicating the bombing angle set in by the bombardier, the other the factor established by alignment of the cross hair. The rate indicator synchronized with the forward speed of the aircraft and moved toward the other indicator. Thus, from the IP to the target, the pilot kept the plane at constant altitude and constant speed and the bombardier controlled the direction of the plane through the bombsight.

On a bombing run of average length, the gyro bubbles were leveled once and the gyro would maintain the established level (the gyro was caged). However, on a long bombing run, minor leveling adjustments could be necessary. After the gyro had been leveled the bubbles could shift erratically but this did not necessarily indicate that the gyro was tumbling. The gyro was not to be caged and uncaged on the bombing run as a substitute for good leveling as "the caging knob is for caging the gyro. It is not a leveling knob."

If the target was obscured by smoke from previous bombs or by a smoke screen, the bombardier placed the crosshairs on a check point along the axis of attack as close to the target as possible. He then moved the crosshairs to the approximate the location of the target. By using the computer grid or a similar device, the bombardier could accomplish offset aiming with reasonable accuracy.

When the bombs were jettisoned the bomber would pitch upwards and then it was the bombardier's job to go to the bomb bay, wearing his portable oxygen bottle, to make sure all the bombs were dropped and to take the appropriate action if they had not.

Virtually all Eighth Air Force bombing was formation bombing with the bombardier of the lead crew of the 36 bomber formation taking over for about eight minutes to aim a large pattern of 36 bomb loads at the target. His aiming point was chosen accordingly and would be different from the aiming point that would have been chosen had a single plane been bombing the target. The 35 other bombardiers of the individual bombers in the formation were watching the lead bomber so that each bombardier could toggle the bomb switch to drop his bombs when the leader did.

Crawfish

The method of releasing bombs visually, when bombardiers in a formation saw bombs falling from the lead ship, had several disadvantages: if the bombardier of an aircraft was engaging an enemy fighter he could miss the lead bombardier's drop; if a perfect formation was not flown then the lead bombardier's drop may not be seen for several seconds; or if a mechanical failure caused the lead bombardier's bombs not to drop, none of the formation's bombardiers would toggle their bombs. These possibilities were eliminated by *Crawfish*, by which, using a simple radio device, made it possible for the lead bombardier to simultaneously release all the bombs in his formation by merely pressing a button, dropping the loads of the other bombers on the target. *Crawfish* also eliminated the small but important delay which occurred when the formation's bombardiers waited until they saw the lead bombardier drop his bombs. Although these delays were only a few seconds, a three second delay in a bomber flying at 205 mph at 20,000 feet caused an error on the ground of 902 feet using a 500 pound GP bomb. These errors were magnified when bombardiers, because of their position in the formation, could not see the bombs of the lead plane until they had fallen some distance. Fewer bombardiers would be needed when using *Crawfish*, which meant that there could be more intensified training of fewer but better qualified students (if the war had continued). *Crawfish* was successfully tested operationally by the 96th Bomb Group/8AF near the end of the war and saw limited use in combat.

High Altitude H2X Radar Bombing

By 1944 the capabilities of H2X radar bombing under combat conditions had been ascertained, but it was not accurate enough for pinpoint bombing. However, the H2X radar scope was capable of presenting types of large isolated targets with sufficient clarity to be identified and bombed through the overcast. The H2X radar, in particular, was reasonably successful in the bombing of large isolated built-up areas such as large industrial complexes or factories in small cities, and thus was the American equivalent of British area bombing.

Throughout 1944 and until the end of the war in Europe most of the Eighth Air Force bombing was radar-assisted through the overcast; so-called blind bombing. The groups were led to their targets by Pathfinder (PFF) aircraft which were specially equipped B-17s or B-24s whose crews were intensively trained in the use of their H2X radar equipment. For the first PFF missions there were only enough Pathfinder aircraft available to direct the leading combat wings of each of the three bomb divisions. Succeeding wings had to bomb on smoke trails left by the groups ahead. These trails were often dissipated by wind and more smoke bombs were dropped by succeeding group leaders in an attempt to replenish the smoke at the marked spots but this was not accurate and resulted in widely scattered bombfalls. In August 1944, when more aircraft were available, a H2X Pathfinder led each combat wing but it was not until December 1944 that enough H2X Pathfinder airplanes were available so that each bomb group had its own Pathfinder planes.

High Altitude Bombing by LORAN/PPI Radar Sighting

As the B-29 approached Japan the radar navigator divided his attention between two radarscopes. On his left was the LORAN from which he obtained periodic fixes from powerful beacons located along his route. On his right was the Plan Position Indicator (PPI) scope that was an auxiliary "remote" scope that showed 360° scanned images of the earth's surface below. It operated in the same way as the parent scope on the radar operator's Bombing Through Overcast (BTO) unit located aft of the tunnel. Both the radar operator and navigator closely watched their respective PPI scopes looking for radar checkpoints (i.e. islands, coastlines, rivers, etc.) that were easily recognized on a radar screen. From these checkpoints the navigator could check and correct his position.

As the bomber approached the overcast target city it appeared as an irregular white patch at the edge of the PPI scope. The circular PPI scope was divided into compass headings with a "lubber line" extending from the center of the circle (the true heading of the aircraft) toward the target. The PPI could be adjusted in range to enlarge the image of the area below on the scope and to bring out the light and shadows on the scope that represented land and water, factories, docks and other landmarks. As the bomber drew nearer the target the blurred images on the scope slowly moved nearer the center of the scope that constantly represented the position of the bomber. The radar operator set his computers for the correct sighting angles and a "bombing circle" was turned on the scope in the exact slant-range setting.

Meanwhile, the bombardier adjusted his Norden Bombsight for the latest drift, speed and altitude. At this point the bombardier was unable to see the target through the overcast to obtain the sighting angle but the radar operator could see it electronically and informed the bombardier over the interphones. Through training, experience and the pre-mission briefing the radar operator was able to identify something in the irregular white patch on his scope as the target that was nearing the center of the scope. There was smaller circle inside the scope screen surrounding the scope center called the "bombing circle." The moment the outer edge of the white target touched the bombing circle the radar operator would inform the bombardier to insert the data. This procedure was continued through each new sighting angle as the bomber approached the target. When the target converged with the exact center of the scope the Norden Bombsight automatically released the bombs.

Radar bombing, while never as accurate as visual bombing, allowed the 20AF to continue its bombing campaign through the chronic poor weather over Japan. Radar allowed the bombers to find and bomb urban areas with sufficient accuracy and then through sheer quantity of aircraft and weight of bombs (25 times that required for visual bombing) cause heavy damage.

Offset Bombing

"Offset bombing" was a technique that was developed against specific targets such as buildings, refineries, marshalling yards that were often not easily made out on the PPI radarscope or when many groups attack one target it could become obscured by smoke. Like a golfer using the flag to aim at the cup, the radar operator would pick as his offset aiming point a nearby point that did show up clearly on the PPI. By predetermining the exact distance of this offset checkpoint from the unseen target, the radar operator was able to clock a time delay from the AP to the actual bomb release point.

Train Bombing

Train bombing gave the bombardier the best possible chance of partially or totally destroying the target. A series of bombs were dropped evenly spaced across the target. The Intervalometer controlled the spacing of bombs in the train. In releasing a train of bombs, the bombardier released the first bomb to hit short of the target a distance equal to half the length of the train; attempting to place the middle bomb of the train on the target's center. This technique made it likely that at least one or more bombs would hit the target in range.

The bombardier could place the first bomb of the train the proper distance short of the target by decreasing trail, decreasing Disc Speed (DS), or by selecting an aiming point the proper distance short of the target. The bombardier could easily decrease the trail setting but, unless the bombsight had a trail spotting device, this could result in an appreciable error in Crosstrail.

If a definite object, such as a road or building, was on the axis of attack and the proper distance short of the center of the target, it could be used as the aiming point. This would place the Mean Point of Impact (MPI) of the train of bombs on the target's center without requiring the decrease of trail or DS. When using the Intervalometer the bombardier would place the train select switch at TRAIN at least one minute prior to release and set counter knob pointer at number of bombs desired in train. If he were releasing all the bombs on the racks in train, he would set the pointer at a number greater than his entire load to be sure that all the bombs dropped. He would set the Ground Speed (GS) he expected to have over the target opposite desired bomb spacing on the Intervalometer. When the indices met, the bombardier checked to see if Intervalometer was working properly. If a malfunction occurred and all bombs had not been released, he was to salvo the remaining bombs or change train select switch to SELECT and toggle them as fast as possible.

Medium Altitude Bombing

The operation of the bombsight and the general bombing problem at medium altitudes were basically the same as at high altitudes. However, there were a few differences as medium bombardment was primarily utilized to neutralize enemy airfields and to cut lines of communication. Because of limited operational range, medium bombardment was used in strategic bombing only as a supplement to heavy bombardment.

The targets generally selected for medium bombardment were marshaling yards, railroad and highway bridges, and airfield installations. Troop concentrations and ammunition and supply dumps also become objectives when it was used in direct support of ground forces. In the bombing of bridges or other rectangular targets, it was determined that an axis of attack at an angle of 45° to 90° with the target's longitudinal axis presented the best prospect for a direct hit.

Examination of medium and heavy bombardment records disclosed that bombing accuracy increased as bombing formations decreased in size. For medium bombardment the most effective and accurate method of attack was by flights of six bombers spread to give the desired bombing pattern. In each flight of six bombers the lead bombardier sighted for range and deflection while the wing bombardiers dropped on the leader. Medium altitude missions are usually carried out with pre-set data subject only to minor corrections because the bombing runs were shorter and the objective was to get over the target and out again in the shortest possible time. Bombing accuracy was not to be sacrificed in the attempt to avoid flak. Teamwork was an overriding factor because many medium bombers were not equipped with autopilots. Evasive action with short bombing runs was almost indispensable at medium altitudes because of the intensity of AA fire by automatic weapons and the greater degree of accuracy obtained by heavy guns. The pilot had to be skilled in following the PDI. The pilot and bombardier needed a high degree of coordination to provide maximum help for the bombardier on the bombing run.

Formation Bombing
Flying in a prescribed pattern or formation increased defensive strength and bombing efficiency. The composition and configuration of a formation was usually was based on the strength, disposition, and employment of the individual combat unit. Generally, all bombers in a formation were of the same type in order to maintain the formation. There were no prescribed types of formations that had to be strictly followed but each formation had to meet the requirements of the specific mission and had to be flexible to adapt to changing situations during the mission. The components of a bomber formation were:

Element	2 to 4 aircraft
Flight	2 or more Elements
Combat Box (or Group)	2 or more Flights
Combat Wing	2 or more Groups

Early formation bombing consisted of bombing in elements of three bombers but as enemy opposition increased, formations enlarged to include 6, 12, 18, and 21 bombers. These larger formations were employed to provide heavier fire power when deep penetrations were made into areas which were heavily defended. Two methods of bombing were normally used by formations: individual range bombing and pattern bombing.

Individual Range Bombing
In individual range bombing, all airplanes in the formation carried bombsights. The leader sighted for range and deflection and the wing bombardiers sighted for range only. Because the bombing platform in a wing airplane was unstable while the airplane is trying to maintain formation, individual range bombing was not been especially effective and resulted in patterns being scattered and inaccurate with bombs falling before and behind the target.

Pattern Bombing
In pattern bombing, the lead bombardier sighted for both course and range and the wing bombardiers dropped their bombs on the leader, either when they sighted the lead bomber's bombs being released, or upon a prearranged signal. Pattern bombing with dependable lead bombardiers produced better results as by this method more bombs were placed in the target area in a more compact pattern. Best bombing patterns were made by groups which flew the best formations as good formation flying and quick release on the leader was the keys to effective pattern bombing. Good formation bombing gave the desired pattern in width while the Intervalometer in the bomber was designed to give you the desired pattern in length.

Typical Daylight Formation Mission
A typical daylight, six aircraft formation bombing mission proceeded as follows. A Norden Bombsight sight was carried in the lead ship of each element and D-8 sights were used in wing ships. Bombardiers in the lead ships sighted for both range and deflection. Bombardiers in wing ships dropped bombs on the lead ship drop.

Squadron Stagger Formation

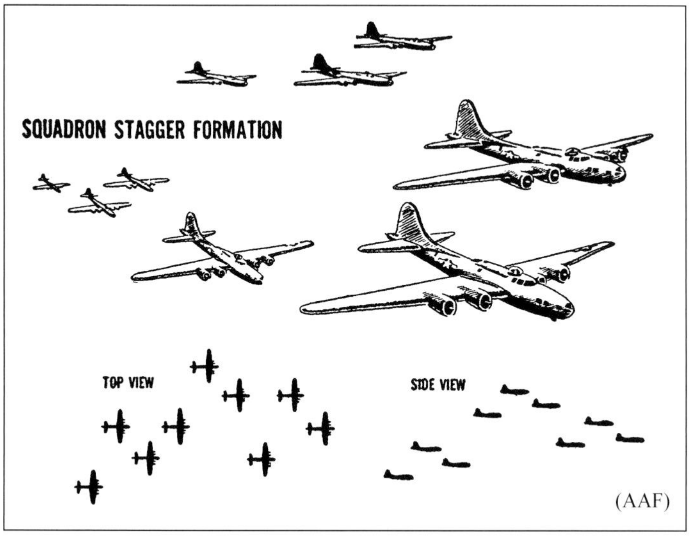

(AAF)

Squadron Javelin Down

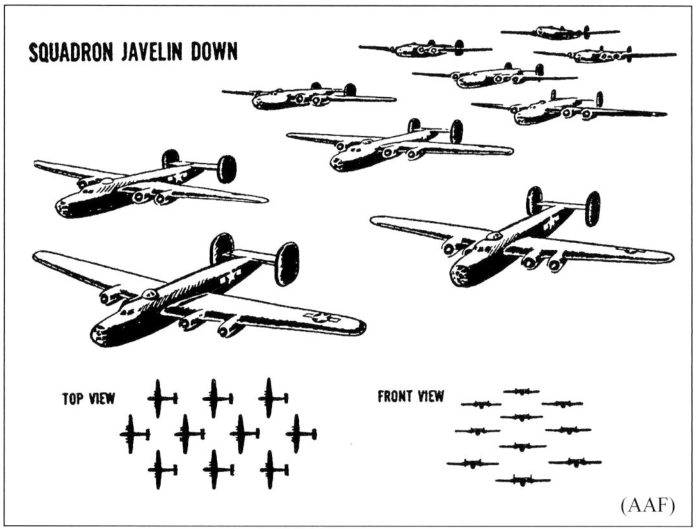

(AAF)

The flight leader took off at a predetermined time and the other aircraft tookoff at 30 second intervals and joined the formation. After formation had been joined, a climbing circle was made over the field at 170 mph. The flight leader was to have an approximate power setting of 32 inches Hg at 2,200 rpm with the wing aircraft at 2,400 rpm. The climb continued on course until an altitude of 10,000 feet was gained. Upon reaching the desired altitude, the leader assumed that AA fire would be encountered and took evasive action. Upon approaching the target, the lead aircraft went into a gentle left turn, diving at 1,000 feet per minute onto the target. This final turn required judgment and precision timing on the part of the lead ship. After diving to the desired bombing altitude of 8,000 feet the lead aircraft flew toward the target, to a position to allow approximately a 20 second straight and level at 230 mph bombing run. The wing aircraft opened their bomb bay doors immediately upon seeing doors of lead bomber open, and bombs were dropped on the lead ship. Each bombardier-navigator had to be alert in releasing his bombs as soon as he saw the first bomb leave the lead ship. Immediately upon closing the bomb bay doors, the leader again made a left turn, diving at 1,000 feet per minute with a bank not exceeding 15° and 250 mph. This dive was held until 7,000 feet altitude was reached and was followed by the wing aircraft. After bombing was completed, the flight returned to base and broke up into three elements for landing

Synchronous Bombing

Synchronous bombing attacks were used during daylight operations and required close cooperation between the pilot and bombardier with the pilot being aware of the problems of the bombardier while thoroughly comprehending his responsibilities as pilot. Prior to takeoff the pilot and bombardier conferred about the proposed bomb run so that the pilot was well informed with the approach, the target, and enemy opposition. The pilot had to be prepared to make the bomb run either by setting up the C-1 autopilot or by manually following the PDI (while making a bomb run by PDI, the pilot had to level the bombsight and open the bomb bay. He had to be able to make immediate PDI corrections while maintaining altitude and airspeed.

Night Bombing

Flying in formation at night was difficult so between 24 and 48 bombers carrying 250 or 500 pound GP bombs were deployed separately at five minute intervals. Each aircraft flew independently to within 50 miles of the target approaching at under 1,000 feet and never over 3,000 feet, trying to evade enemy radar for as long as possible. Immediately before beginning the bombing run the bombers climbed to 8,000 to 9,000 feet; signaled by the target which had just previously been lit by flares dropped by pathfinders. Each bomber was assigned set target times and a number of runs over target with each pilot briefed to release his bombs on the target within a specific time measured in seconds. After the first bombing run, the pilot was to fly from the target on a predetermined heading, for a predetermined length of time, and then return to bomb the target again within another specific time period. Meanwhile, between the two target runs of this first bomber, another bomber flew in, making its first run and then left the target area on another course. After the first bomber had finished its second attack, and at about the time the second bomber was turning to come back over the target for its second pass, a third bomber was making its first attack. After the third bomber had completed its initial bombing run, the second bomber proceeded with its second run. The attack continued accordingly and since a large number of bombers were involved over the target making several individual passes, timing was imperative. The pilots were permitted to approach the target at altitudes determined by the caliber and strength of enemy AA fire encountered which varied from target to target. The basic evasive practice against AA fire and searchlights were gradual turns right and left and gradual climbing and diving maneuvers. During the war in North Africa, the MTO, and the Pacific enemy night fighters were rarely reported but in the ETO Luftwaffe night fighters took a heavy toll on RAF bombers which operated principally at night.

Pattern (Carpet) Bombing

The type of attack most frequently used by US medium bombers and less frequently by heavy bombers during daylight was pattern bombing (called carpet bombing today). This technique was implemented because the target area contained many targets, dispersed from each other, all of which were equally vital to destroy and would not be susceptible to precision bombing. These targets included airfields, supply dispersal areas, troop concentrations, etc. that could be more easily destroyed by enveloping the area with a pattern (carpet) of bombs. Precise target analysis was important to ensure the destruction of the target and the plan for the formation bombing approach was made upon it.

During daylight, the bombers operated mainly in formations of 18 aircraft in three six bomber boxes, flying in a tight, shallow V formation. They flew in three flights of six aircraft, divided into two elements of three in each flight. The bombers in each element flew from only few feet to 25 feet apart with the rear element flying 25 to 50 feet above or below the lead element to stay out of their prop wash. Each flight flew no more than 50 yards apart and occasionally much closer or in a tight formation. It was routine for the lead flight to be lowest and the other two flights higher. Whether the left or right flight was highest was determined by the direction of the turn to be made away from the target area with the flight that had to make the greatest turn placed highest.

Like night bombing the approach to the target was made at low-level to evade enemy radar, with a gradual climb to the bombing approach was begun at between 6,500 and 8,500 feet, with the actual altitude subject to the weather conditions. Just before the approach, the formation (flight) leader signaled the formation to open up and position itself corresponding to an established plan based on the size and character of the target. The distances between the bombers in the element, between each element, and between the three flights were determined in order to envelop the target with a pattern of bombs hitting not more than 50 feet apart. The formation released their bombs when the formation leader dropped his bombs.

The bombing run was made at an angle of between 20° and 30°, so that the bombing pattern would form a parallelogram. The area bounded by the parallelogram was the area the bombers tried to cover with their formation pattern bombing because it gave the aircraft a longer dropping time over the target. The bomber crews observed that when toggling their bombs at approximately half second intervals, they could put an average of two more bombs per aircraft into the target than if they attacked the columns from an exact 90° angle.

Anti-shipping Bombing Procedure

Anti-shipping bombing was mainly conducted by medium bomber units, particularly B-25s. A frequently used tactic was for three formations or combinations of formations to be used to fly counter shipping missions with two three-ship elements at 200 feet or less; three three-ship elements at 8,000 to 10,000 feet; and three three-ship elements at from 8,000 feet to 10,000 feet with the two three-ship elements attacking twenty seconds after the high flight at 200 feet or less. While on search, the six-ship formation was flown at 100 feet above the surface of the water in either right or left echelon. The flight was made at an indicated air speed of 190 to 200 miles per hour. The total length of each mission ranged from three hours to four hours. The direction of attack was at the discretion of the flight leader so as to fit the proper approach to the different targets.

The factors which controlled the approach were: the size of the convoy; the type of merchant vessels and location in (the) convoy; size, number, and type of escort vessels and how located; size and disposition of enemy aerial escort; and position of convoy with reference to the sun. When the method of attack and the number of ships to be attacked was established prearranged signals were used and the attack commenced.

The controlling factor in regard to the number of bombs to be dropped was the type of target. The usual merchant ship required only a stick of three bombs per aircraft or nine bombs per element; large tankers being of greater importance necessitate the dropping of the entire bomb load. The accuracy of the altitude used was approximately 60% direct hits with another 15% of very near misses, giving 75% effective bomb load. The altitude used was from 150 feet to 200 feet with the air speed above 220 miles per hour. No bombsight was necessary if a combat crew was experienced and there was perfect coordination between bombardier and pilot. Some vessels, especially barges, threw up a heavy concentration of AA fire making it dangerous to bomb at low altitude and the converging attack was developed.

The formation was made up of three-ship elements flying in staggered formation at 300 feet until a target was sighted; when they climbed to an altitude of from 8,000 to 10,000 feet. The convoy was approached from the stern with the leader gave the attention signal for the two elements turn 45° to the basic course, and proceed on the new course for 45 seconds. Then, turning in on the target, the approach was made at 195 to 200 miles per hour until the peel off, when the leader decreased airspeed to 190 miles per hour.

Anti-shipping Attack

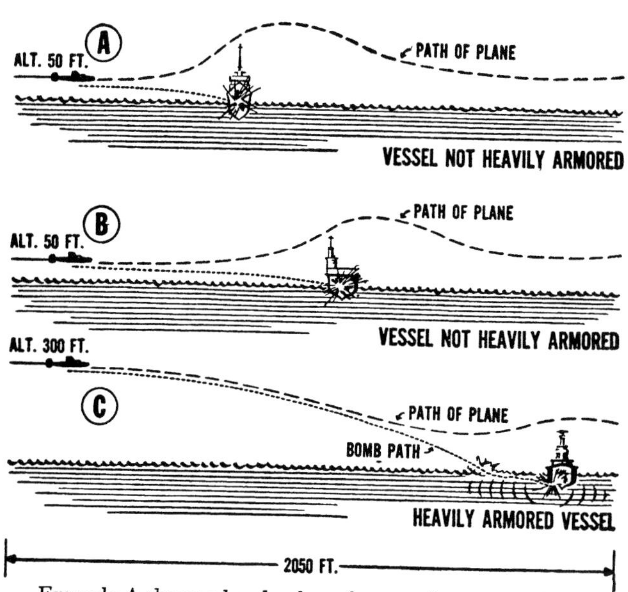

Example A shows a bomb release from 50 feet at a moderate speed. In Example B the airplane is traveling at a higher speed; here the bomb must be released farther from the ship. Example C shows how, when attacking a heavily armored vessel, the aircraft must be at a higher altitude so the bomb will submerge and detonate beneath the water.

(AAF)

The Number Two element descended to 500 feet and the Number Three element ascended 500 feet with a change in air speed due to the change in altitude giving ample spacing at the target. After leaving the target, the formation either turned right or left as prearranged in order to reform.

The combination of high and low-level attack was used only on a definite and important target. The low-level attack was the same as before, except it hit the target from 30 to 40 seconds after the high flight had released its bombs. Each element in the high flight calling "Bombs Away" when its bombs were released so that the low element would know when it was clear to start their run. Their run had to be as close as possible in order to take advantage of the confusion and the AA fire drawn by the high flight.

Minimum Altitude Bombing

Minimum altitude bombing was used in the Pacific with a high degree of success against both land and sea targets with the tactics employed varying with the target involved. Minimum altitude bombing against shipping or pinpoint targets usually used a single bomber or a coordinated attack of two or more aircraft, depending upon the expected opposition. The procedure was to drop three bombs, spaced to bracket the target with the second bomb intended to be a direct hit.

The enemy could be surprised by taking advantage of speed and the masking characteristics of weather and sun and terrain features such as hills, mountains, craters, and jungles. There were certain advantageous approaches to every defended area which, because they were best, the enemy also defended with the heaviest AA fire so surprise and safety could be achieved by avoiding these approaches and varying the axis of attack.

Minimum altitude bombing was often carried out by a line-abreast formation of as many bombers as were required to cover the target area and which also affording maximum simultaneous strafing power. Predetermined

Minimum Altitude Bombing

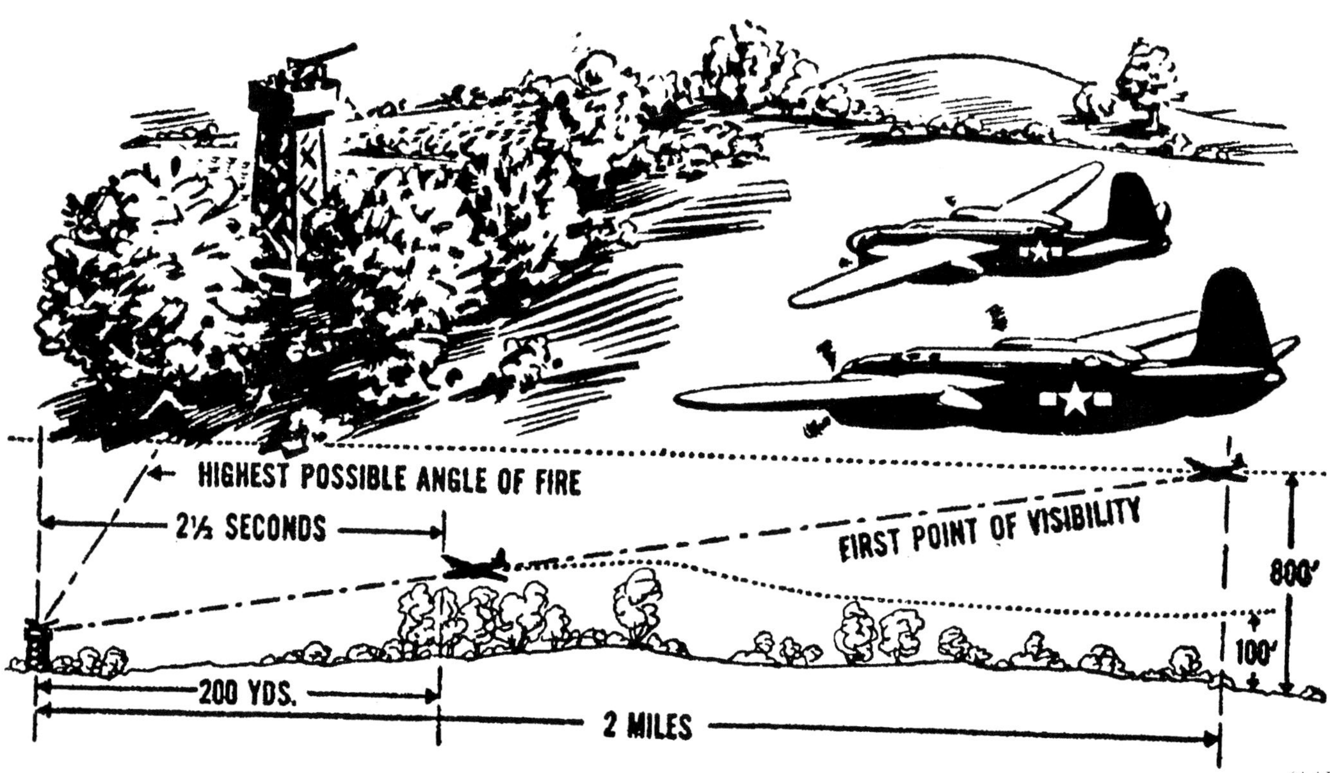

(AAF)

computations were pre-set into the bombsights. Bomb fusing had the explosion occurring after the bomber was a safe distance away. The bombs could be dropped in train or toggled out at suitable intervals, depending upon the size and type of target. With some types of bombs, it was often necessary for the bomber to increase altitude slightly before releasing them which made the bomber more vulnerable to enemy automatic weapon fire.

The advantages of minimum bombing were the element of surprise; good visibility of target at time of release; short approaches were possible and evasive tactics could be used until almost at the bomb release point; reduced exposure to heavy ground AA fire; the bomber could also strafe to suppress enemy ground fire and inflict further damage; and it allowed photographic possibilities,

The disadvantages minimum bombing were that the bombers flying in line abreast formation had to fly a given course and could not veer too much from course. The attackers were within range of automatic AA ground weapons and flak towers.

When encountering fire from AA automatic weapons the bombers were to fly straight through area as rapidly as possible; take advantage of terrain features to confuse AA gunners, making it difficult for them to distinguish between the aircraft and background; and to try to determine a course in advance, or at the last moment if necessary, which would give enemy AA gunners only a brief time to aim and fire.

Dive Bombing

Because of the angle of approach dive bombing afforded the pilot a longer and more stable view of the target but gave the same opportunity to enemy defenses. The gunsight was used for bomb targeting orientation but because a bomb's aerodynamics (i.e. lift properties) weren't the same as the aircraft's (i.e. it was to hit the ground) it "flew" on a different flight path from aircraft. Consequently, although the target was stationary, the pilot had to lead the target slightly beyond where it was to hit. The correct amount of lead necessary depended on the dive angle (the steeper the dive, the less lead was required) and the range at which the pilot released the bomb (the farther away the bomb was released, the more lead was required).

Dive bombing procedure was to approach the target slightly to one side at about 6,000-8,000 feet altitude with the pilot reducing his speed to 150 mph. When the target was about to pass under his wingtip, the pilot executed a wingover in the direction of the target rather than pushing the nose over into a dive. The wingover permitted the pilot to keep the target in sight. Excessive speed reduced accuracy and by dropping his flaps the pilot could keep his airspeed under control or he could use his dive brakes or spoilers if they were equipped on the aircraft. The pilot dove at a 45 to 60° angle with his throttle pulled all the way back to keep his speed down. He maneuvered the aircraft to line the gun sight on the target and to stabilize the aircraft. Once stabilized, the pilot judged the appropriate amount of lead and released the bomb at about 3,000 feet. After the release, he advanced the throttle and pulled out of the dive, recovering above 1,000 feet. (Note: Dive bombing will be discussed in more detail in Volume 3)

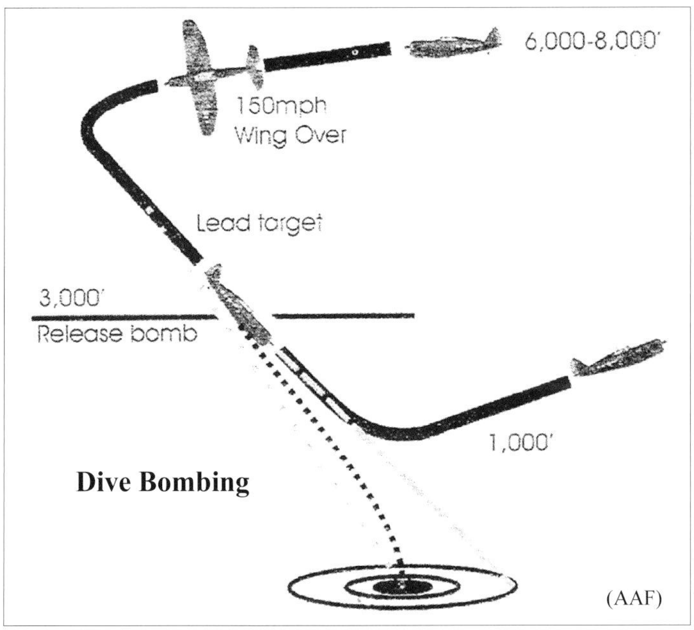

Dive Bombing

(AAF)

Low Altitude Bombing Methods

Glide Bombing

The difference between glide bombing and dive bombing was in the approach angle. Glide bombing was developed to allow bombing attacks by medium bombers not equipped with bombsights and those carrying bombs with fuses too dangerous for release at low altitudes. The glide bomb technique was particularly well suited to attack targets located in rough terrain which prevented the low-level attack and for attacking targets at night when a clear view of the terrain and target could be maintained at low-level. Glide bombing could be used successfully on any targets vulnerable to all standard General Purpose bombs up to and including the 1,000 pound GP bomb. Parachute-type bombs and VT fused bombs were to be released from level flight and consequently were adaptable for glide bombing.

The glide bombing attack began with an approach on the target at an altitude of 4,000 to 6,000 feet depending upon the height of the surrounding terrain. The pilot was to close on the target slightly to the right, allowing an unobstructed view of the target throughout his approach. After a dive angle of 25° to 35° was set up to the target, a diving turn to the left was made lining up on the target. The bomb bay doors were opened immediately upon rolling out of the turn and establishing an airspeed of 300 to 320 mph to maintain accuracy. The technique for determining the bomb release point in the round out could be acquired only through demonstration flights with an instructor and by constant practice. The bombs were to be released when the attitude of the airplane was 20° or less below horizontal in the round out. The pullout began when the aircraft reached the lowest part of the round out no lower than the minimum altitude specified for releasing the bomb type carried (usually 500 to 700 feet. Evasive action from the target was determined by the surrounding terrain and enemy fire, trying to remain above 200 feet. However, the minimum altitude limit was not to be disregarded and airspeed could be increased as required. It was critical that the pilot understood the limitations of his bomber and knew the minimum allowable altitude of the type bomb carried. The diving run was not to be too flat causing the bombs to land short or even ricochet. The dive was to be made at positive Gs to release the bombs accurately. As the bombs would fall in the direction of the flight path the pilot was to avoid using his rudder pedals when lining up the target (yawing would not significantly change the flight path).

Skip Bombing (Masthead-height Bombing)

The AAC's inter-war doctrine against enemy shipping was to use conventional bombing tactics at 20,000 feet to avoid enemy AA fire. However, bomber

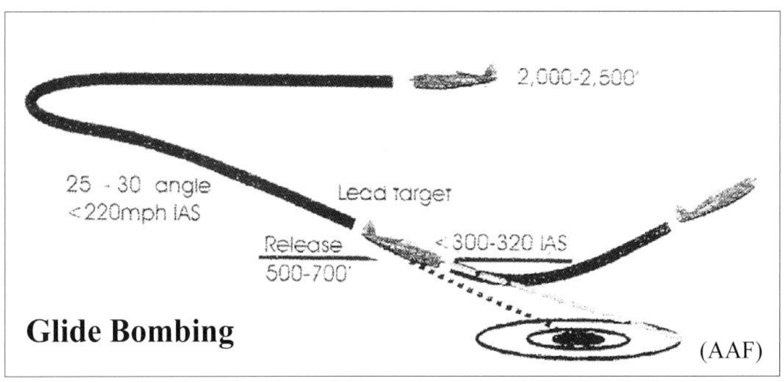

Glide Bombing

(AAF)

formations needed to be large enough to insure that pattern bombing would cover any movement of the target in the interval between release and impact of the bombs. Once the war broke out the RAF high altitude attack experience against enemy shipping demonstrated that another method was needed.

In April 1941, Gen. H.H. Arnold was in Great Britain to meet with Prime Minister Winston Churchill when he heard several senior RAF officers discuss the skip bombing technique that had been used by RAF Blenheim medium bombers against the German Pocket Battleship *Admiral Scheer*. When he returned to the US Arnold directed the Air Proving Ground Command (APGC) at Eglin Field, FL to "determine the practicability of effectively attacking water borne surface vessels from minimum altitudes with demolition bombs" and to "develop tactics and techniques for accomplishing such attacks."

The APCG final report issued on 7 December 1942 authorized the skip bombing concept and recommended that "training pilots in these techniques be initiated at the earliest possible moment." The tests concluded that skip bombing was better than torpedo bombing because it was less dangerous and more accurate. During a torpedo attack the attacking aircraft had to maintain a 20 to 30 second level approach at slower speeds; offering itself as a easy target for enemy AA gunners. During a skip bombing attack the approach could be at a lower altitude and at the maximum sea level speed of the attacking aircraft. The skip bomber required only two to three seconds of straight approach in which to sight and release its bombs; allowing the pilot to use evasive maneuvers to elude the fire from enemy AA gunners before and after bomb release. The aircraft itself aimed the bombs essentially at point blank range as the speed of the aircraft literally hurled the bomb at the side of the target.

The APGC investigation used heavy and medium bombers and fighter aircraft to determine which aircraft type was best suited to the requirements of the new technique. Heavy bombers were found to be too slow and not maneuverable enough while fighters did not have sufficient range and payload. The B-25 and B-26 were found to be most suited due to their enemy AA suppressing forward fire power, adequate range, high speeds, and maneuverability. The bombs used in these attacks were standard Armor Piercing types with delayed action fuses to allow the attackers to escape the debris of the exploding bombs and to ensure that the explosion occurred after the penetration of the bombs. When the bombs were dropped they were aimed through the machine gun sight.

Two methods of skip bombing attack were recommended. The first was the Quartering Frontal Attack on armored surface vessels with more than one inch of side armor plate at maximum level flight speed and 150 feet to 300 feet altitude, dropping 1,000 or 2,000 pound demolition bombs. The bombs were ideally aimed to hit the water short of the target and not skip, but travel under water; using a delayed action fuse to detonate under the keel of the vessel producing a greater explosive effect and possibly breaking the keel. The second was the Broadside Attack on unarmored or lightly armored surface vessels with less than one inch of side armor plate at maximum level flight speed and at the minimum altitude necessary to clear the target (below 50 feet was recommended), dropping bombs of the suitable size. On this type of attack the bombs were not to strike the water first but to crash directly into the side of the ship and then be exploded by a delayed action fuse. The delay in explosion gave the attacker time to cross over the target and escape the bomb's explosion. However, often the bomb would strike the water first and then either hit the target or skip over it.

In July 1942, Gen. George Kenney had been disappointed in the poor bombing record of his 5th Air Force bombers and had long considered the benefits of low-level bombing attack. During a long trans-Pacific flight, Kenney and his aid, Maj. William Benn, discussed the feasibility of skip bombing. During a layover at Nandi in the Fiji Islands they decided to conduct an impromptu test. In his book General Kenney Reports Kenney describes the test:

"It looked as though there might be something in dropping a bomb with a five second delay fuse from level flight at an altitude of 50 feet and a few hundred feet away from the vessel, with the idea of having the bomb skip along the water until it bumped into the side of the ship....The more we talked about the scheme, the more enthusiastic we got, so finally we borrowed a B-26 from the boys at Nandi, loaded with dummy bombs and tried the idea out against some coral knobs offshore."

Skip Bombing (Masthead-height Bombing)

(AAF)

When the two reached Australia Kenney appointed Benn to be the CO of the 63BS of the 43BG(H), a B-17 unit. In early October 1942, Benn initiated skip bombing tests using 100 pound bombs dropped from a B-17 to establish the correct combination of speed, altitude, and dropping distance to the target. The initial target was a small sand bar surrounded by shallow water chosen so that the skip of the bomb and its distance and height could be observed. The next tests were conducted against a wreck in the Port Moresby Harbor and on his second test run Benn scored a direct hit. The tests concluded that a three bomb string with a five second delay was optimal to get a hit. Benn realized that the B-17 heavy bomber was not suited to skip bombing because of its lack of speed, maneuverability, and lack of adequate forward firing armament to suppress enemy AA fire. Soon the 90BS, a B-25 unit, trained in the skip bombing technique and accurately test bombed the Port Moresby harbor wreck. The unit refined their technique to eliminate the need to calculate the ricochet distance but tried to time their release to hit the side of the target instead of skipping the bomb short into the target; naming the new technique "Masthead-height Bombing." In their practice attack runs against the wreck the B-25 pilots picked out a reference point on the nose of their aircraft to use as an improvised bombsight and made the high speed, mast-high attack and then broke off in low-level evasive turns. The results were so notable that the V Bomber Command asserted: "A well-trained pilot should be able to hit a ship nearly every time using the masthead technique." Because masthead bombing required the attacker to fly directly over the target, the correct fusing was vital. In the original skip bombing tests at Eglin, the APGC had examined fusing. A tail fuse with a minimum four second delay would "provide a probable minimum safety margin of approximately 700 feet from the detonation of a ricocheting 100 and 500 pound aerial bomb." The APGC approved the M106 fuse but after testing the 5AF paired this fuse with an Australian detonator set for five second delay. This combination had some initial problems when tested on the Port Moresby wreck. One aircraft was badly damaged and made a forced landing on a reef as a fuse instantaneously detonated; while another bomb hit the wreck and also exploded instantaneously but inside the wreck so that the B-25 suffered only minor damage; but soon the fuse combination was perfected.

The final development in the skip bombing procedure was to develop a tactic to insure that the B-25s could get near enough to the target to drop the bomb without being knocked down by Japanese light and medium AA fire. When a Japanese convoy had been sighted, four squadrons of six B-25s each were alerted. The Mitchells carrying four 500 pound bombs with 4-5 second delay fuses were divided into two waves of 12 bombers with the second wave taking off 15 to 20 minutes after the first wave. This allowed the first wave to search and locate the convoy, saving fuel for the second wave to give it more time over target.

The first wave leader, wanting to maintain the element of surprise attempted to put as many aircraft over the convoy as possible on the first run. He hoped to sink or damage enough ships to slow or stop the convoy making the remaining dispersed and damaged ships easy targets. A line abreast formation as wide as the convoy made the first run from the preferred stern to bow position. The sweep was made at high speed, mast-high thoroughly strafing the decks and neutralizing the AA. On the first pass bombs were to be dropped only when a specific target presented itself and not releasing more than two bombs.

For the follow up attacks the formation could then separate into pairs or single aircraft to methodically attack the stragglers, depending on the size of the vessel being attacked. The two plane attack was used in attacking individual warships destroyers or larger or very large merchant ships. The B-25 crews were trained to attack in pairs simultaneously with one attacker assigned as the strafer and the other as the bomber. The attack was made from just abeam of the stern with the pilots remaining in a slight turning dive, changing course and altitude and gaining airspeed to reduce exposure to AA fire. When the strafer was closing it would begin to fire from stern to stem, covering the other bomber as it made its bombing attack and at 200 to 300 feet from the vessel the bombing aircraft would release its bombs and then both would drop to the deck to make a violent evasive getaway. The single plane attack was made on vessels ranging in size from destroyer escorts and smaller. The attacks were made from directly astern to limit AA fire while the pilot fishtailed to increase the B-25's cone of strafing fire on the vessel. Given the convoy's location by radio the second wave arrived to attack the crippled convoy that had been reduced to easy targets with their AA defenses neutralized

Glip Bombing

Skip Bombing, successfully used by the 5AF against other targets, was tried against bridges in Burma in late 1944, by 10AF Mitchells. But the results were poor as it required 15.5 tons of bombs dropped and 30 tons of valuable gasoline consumed for each bridge finally destroyed. The results of the attacks showed that some of the bombs skipped under the bridge and exploded on the far bank, while other bombs skipped completely over the bridge, while others just ricocheted off course.

Unofficial credit for the accidental discovery of the Glip technique was given to Maj. Robert Erdin of the 490BS of the 341st Bomb Group while he was leading an attack on a bridge on the Mu River. While attacking at low-level Erdin suddenly was forced to pull up to avoid an approaching tall tree while dropping his bombs. Certain that the attack was another failure, the tail gunner observed two hits on the bridge, as it appeared that the pull up caused the bombs to strike at the correct angle, preventing them from ricocheting.

From Erdin's discovery a new bridge bombing technique was developed by Col. D.L. Clark, CO of the 341st Bomb Group and his Squadron Operations Officer, Maj. James Flanagan. The technique was a "double glide" approach at a steep glide angle, suddenly followed by a shallow glide. It was named "Glip" for the combination of **Gl**ide-Sk**ip** bombing techniques it employed. The new technique would reduce the average of tons of bombs dropped per bridge destroyed to just over six tons.

In using the Glip technique the pilot approached the long axis of the bridge at 1,000 to 1,500 feet, gliding at 30° to 35° at a speed of 260 to 280 mph. As the bridge was approached the Mitchell was put into a 15° to 20° angle and while the bomber was in the glide, the modified N-6 gunsight that was pre-set before takeoff was aimed at the bridge. The angle that was set into the sight was obtained from the skip bombing tables minus a correction to compensate for the glide angle. The bombs were released by the pilot from on deck (150 feet) at the time of the smooth, sharp pull out, and followed by evasive action. The bomber was protected from AA fire during the double glide approach as each phase, the steep glide and then the shallow glide, did not allow the enemy gunners time for accurate aiming; especially in the face of strafing machine gun fire from the diving B-25s. In the first 159 sorties only two bombers were seriously damaged.

Throughout the steep and shallow phases of the glide the bomber flew directly along the longitudinal axis of the bridge. Since bridges as targets were long the errors in range that were not excessive were negated by the length of the bridge. To prevent the low flying bomber from being hit by the blast or fragments of its own bombs, the bombs were fused for a specific delay. Using this fusing the bombs which often passed through the bridge deck exploded in the water below with enough force to lift the bridge spans off their piers and fall into the water. If the explosion occurred close to a pier the explosive force could destroy the pier or displace a span.

The first Glip mission was flown on 11 December 1944 but the results were inauspicious with 12 tons of bombs expended for no bridges destroyed; and the results of the next four missions were much worse with no bridges destroyed. But then the results improved on the sixth mission when 12 B-25s destroyed four bridges with an average of three tons of bombs per bridge. During the next two months, 19 bridges were destroyed at 6.25 tons of bombs per bridge. The results were so impressive that Maj.Gen. Howard Davidson, 10AF CG referred to the 490BS as "The Burma Bridge Busters" and the squadron tagged itself as the "Dental Clinic" for their bridge work.

8

Effects of Bombs

Strike Photos and Strike Reports

Strike Photos

In each combat box (squadron, group) several aircraft carried automatic cameras. These cameras began shooting shortly after the bombs were released and continued at short intervals until after the bombs hit the ground. On the face of the strike photographs were the name of the target, the date of the attack, the unit attacking, the number of the photograph in the series, and the altitude of attack. By assembling these photographs the bombfall of each attacking unit could be identified and plotted individually with respect to the aiming point. Circles of 500, 1,000, and 2,000 feet were drawn around the aiming point, and the bomb craters were marked within these circles. Also, the picture indicated the track of the bombing aircraft. The finished products were called bomb plots, and separate plots of the results of each unit's attacks were made whenever possible.

Strike Reports

A strike report was referred to as the "Bombs Away Message" and was to be sent by each bomber that had bombed individually or if it was done by a formation, by the Formation Leader only. The strike reports were to be made immediately after the bombs had been dropped on the primary and secondary targets. If the bombers had bombed the last resort target or target of opportunity, their strike reports were delayed for at least one hour to allow a clear radio channel for those bombers attacking primary or secondary targets. Normal radio procedures with codes were used. There were two types of Strike Reports, the Normal Strike Report #1 and the Incendiary Strike Report #2. The Normal Strike Report #1 included:

In each combat box several aircraft carried automatic cameras that would begin shooting **Strike Photographs** shortly after the bombs were released and continued at short intervals until after the bombs hit the ground. (AAF)

By assembling these **Strike Photographs** the bombfall of each attacking unit could be identified and plotted individually with respect to the aiming point. (AAF)

Target bombed:
- P = Primary Target
- S = Secondary Target
- L = Last Resort Target
- O = Target of Opportunity

Method of Bombing:
- V = Visual
- R = Radar Bombing
- N = Navigation

Bombing Results:
- 1 = Excellent; meaning pattern centered on aiming point
- 2 = Good; meaning few hits on aiming point
- 3 = Fair; meaning hits in target area
- 4 = Poor; meaning missed the target area
- 5 = Unobserved

Fighter Escort:
- A = Friendly fighter escort present
- B = No friendly fighter escort

Number of planes in Bomber Formation:
- 1 = One plane
- 2 = Two planes
- 3 = Three planes
- Etc. Etc.

The six-character message was repeated three times to insure reception and a sample message would be: PV3A11 PV3A11 PV3A11 which would mean:

"Primary target was bombed visually and the observed results were that hits were made in the target area but no hits were observed on the aiming point, friendly fighter escort was present and there were 11 bombers in the formation." The Incendiary Strike Report #2 included:

Target bombed:
- P = Primary Target
- S = Secondary Target
- L = Last Resort Target
- O = Target of Opportunity

Method of Bombing:
- V = Visual
- R = Radar Bombing
- N = Navigation

Cloud Coverage:
- 1 to 9 for tenths, x for 10/10ths

Situation to Target:
- A = General conflagration
- B = Several large fires
- C = Many fires
- D = Few scattered fires
- E = Unobserved

Fighter Opposition:
- 1 = Heavy
- 2 = Moderate
- 3 = Meager
- 4 = None

Flak:
- A = Heavy
- B= Moderate
- C = Meager
- D = Slight
- E = None

The six-character code message was repeated three times and a sample message would be: PR8E4D PR8E4D PR8E4D which would mean:

"Primary target was bombed by radar, 8/10th's cloud coverage over the target, the situation over the target was unobserved, there was no fighter opposition, and flak was slight."

Bomb Blast

A bomb depends on over-pressure, temperature, and fragmentation of the bomb casing (shrapnel) to damage or destroy a target. A cubic foot of TNT on explosion releases about 10,000 cubic feet of gas at a temperature of about 5,000°F. This gas expands at about 8,000 fps, achieving an over-pressure of 147,000 psi. This destructive force results in cratering when the bomb hits the earth and declines quickly because of the tamping effect of the soil. The fragmentation effect declines with distance.

Shock Front

Generation

The hot gases ejected by a detonating bomb swept out and compressed the surrounding air and threw that compressed body of air against adjacent layers of air forming a belt within which the air had high pressure and high outward velocity. This belt was limited by an extremely sharp front (less than one thousandth of an inch) called the "shock front or wave" in which the pressure suddenly increased.

Travel

The shock front traveled away from the point of detonation with an extremely high initial velocity; for example, it was 3,000 feet per second at 60 feet from a 4,000 pound Light Case bomb where the pressure jump was 100 pounds per square inch. As the shock front traveled on, its velocity then decreased rapidly towards the velocity of sound (1,100 feet per second) and the pressure jump decreased.

Duration

The excess pressure prevailing at a point in the air after the arrival of the shock front decreased and vanished in a short time (about 0.04 second at 400 feet from a 4,000 pound Light bomb; about 0.006 second at 50 feet from a 100 pound General Purpose bomb, and was followed by minor disturbances which often included a partial vacuum. The entire disturbance produced in air by detonation of a bomb was called "blast."

Peak Pressure

Definition

The peak pressure was the highest excess pressure (e.g. the pressure in excess of that directly in front of the shock front) which was attained directly at the shock front. It gave a measure of the maximum force exerted against a structure by the blast (pressure times area equals force).

Effect of Orientation

The orientation to the shock front of the surface on which blast pressure was measured had a great effect on the pressure recorded. The blast effect received by a surface which was parallel to the advancing shock front was greater by several times than that received by a surface which is edge-on to the exploding bomb. This ratio varied from eight at very short distances to two at very long distances from the point of detonation. The effect on oblique surfaces was intermediate.

Impulse

A blast cannot travel quickly around anything as large as the wall of a house; therefore the pressure difference established by the blast on the outer and inner faces of such a wall persisted until the blast had subsided. As a result of the great inertia (structural strength) of walls, the deformation produced by the blast seldom reached the point of the wall's collapse before the blast subsided. A wall that continued to deform further after that time could finally overcome its inertia and collapse. This eventual deformation leading to collapse depended on the velocity acquired by the wall under the impact of the blast. This velocity depended in turn not only on the blast pressure but also on its duration, specifically, on its measurable impulse which was the average pressure multiplied by the duration (that is, the integral of pressure with respect to time).

Radii and Areas of Effectiveness

The damage caused by various types of bombs on load bearing wall construction could be correlated with the blast impulse measured at various distances from the bomb. Therefore, the known relation of impulse to distance for any type of bomb could be used to estimate the distance at which the bomb would cause a certain degree of damage.

Effects of Confinement

The presence of obstacles that prevented the effect of blast in some direction could increase the effect of the blast in other directions. A blast wave traveling along a tunnel, a corridor; a trench, and in the case of large bombs, even along a street, was effectively confined, so that its intensity decreased much more slowly than in the open. When a bomb detonated inside a house, demolition of the walls could occur even if the distance to the walls exceeded the radius of demolition for the same wall and for the same type of bomb bursting in the open. This was due to a variety of effects, among which was the "multiple punch" effect created by the blast waves striking a wall in quick succession after having been reflected by other walls. If the effect of a blast was intensified on one side of a wall by its confining action, it was reduced by the same token on the opposite side of the wall by its screening action.

Protection from Blast

A wall effectively reduced blast pressure and impulse on objects close behind it, if it was about 10 feet by 10 feet or larger and was of sufficient strength to withstand the blast. Foxholes, slit trenches, or ditches reduced the blast pressure by about 50% in the range where serious injury to personnel would otherwise occur. A single right angle bend in a tunnel reduced the blast pressure about 50%. A system of four such bends reduced it to about 15%.

Effect of Charge Weight Ratio

The action of the explosive of a bomb detonating in the air imparted a great speed to the bomb casing which broke up into fragments and later produced an air blast. The lighter the casing, the less energy it required to accelerate it. Therefore, a high charge/weight ratio increased the effect of detonation in air in two ways. It would reduce the fraction of energy taken up by fragments, and it would increase the weight of the charge included in a bomb of given weight; thus Light Case bombs were the most effective from the standpoint of blast effectiveness.

Bomb Targets

Lethal Radius of Bomb Sizes

Bomb Size (lbs)	Lethal Radius (ft)
100	40-60
250	47-70
500	60-90
1,000	70-105
2,000	83-125

Effect of Blast on Industrial Structures

The demolition of industrial structures which generally were steel framed could not be analyzed in the same comparative simple terms as the demolition of buildings with load-bearing walls. It was estimated that the factory area whose structures were damaged effectively by a direct hit with a 500 pound GP bomb (AN-M64) with a .01 second delay fuse averaged about 400-450 square yards, A great reduction of damage occurred when the same bomb was fused for .025 second delay, because its detonation then occurred far below the roof structure. The area of damage by other GP bombs was similar when expressed in square yards per ton of bombs.

Bomb Fragment Damage

Choice of Bombs

The type of explosive charge in the bombs compared were:

20lb Frag/23lb Parafrag bomb	TNT
90lb Frag bomb	Comp B
100lb GP bomb	Amatol
260lb Frag bomb	Comp B
500lb GP bomb	Amatol

General Considerations

At low or medium; altitudes, the 20 pound Fragmentation Bomb, AN-M41 or AN-M41A1 was preferred for use against personnel or when only light damage was desired. For low altitude bombing, the parachute on the 23 pound Fragmentation Bomb, M40 or M40A1 greatly improved its effect over the nonparachute bomb AN-M41 which, except for having fins instead of a parachute, was identical with the M40 bomb. When released from high altitudes, the 20 pound Fragmentation Bomb AN-M41 or AN-M41A1 was reduced in effectiveness. These bombs were to be used in accordance with the type of damage required. The 90 pound Fragmentation Bomb M82 could be used in clusters of six and when so used were particularly effective if the required damage was at most equivalent to perforation of 0.25 inch mild steel. When this bomb was used in individual suspension, substitution of the 120 pound parafrag gave increased effect from low altitudes. For heavier damage the large Fragmentation Bombs or the 500 pound GP bomb could be used.

20 Pound Fragmentation Bomb Fragmentation and Damage

The fragmentation bomb was specifically designed for destruction of equipment and personnel. The outside of the 20 pound fragmentation

Typical Bomb Targets

Bomb	Fuze delay		Altitude of attack	Target	Radius effective within
	Nose	Tail			
Fragmentation, fin type	SQ	Non	High	Personnel. Light vehicles. Planes in open	25′
Fragmentation, parachute type	SQ	Non	Low	Personnel. Light vehicles. Planes in open	25′
100-lb. G.P	0.1	0.25	High	Planes in open	75′
	SQ	Non	High	Ammunition dump	dh
	0.1	Non	High	Hangars	dh
	0.1	Non	High	Vehicles, light	75′
	0.1	Non	High	Vehicles, heavy	dh
	0.1	Non	High	Oil tanks	25′
	0.1	Non	High	Railroad engines and cars	dh
	0.1	Non	High	Railroad trackage	7′
250-lb. G. P	0.1	0.025	High	Hangars	dh
	SQ	Non	High	Planes in open	100′
	SQ	Non	High	Ammunition dump	dh
	0.1	Non	High	Vehicles, light	100′
	0.1	Non	High	Vehicles, heavy	dh
	0.1	0.025	High	Light industrial building	dh
	0.1	0.025	High	Residential	dh
	0.1	Non	High	Oil tanks	50′
	0.1	Non	High	Railroad stock	10′
	0.1	Non	High	Railroad trackage	9′
	0.1	0.025	High	Unarmored ships less than 1,500 tons	25′
500-lb. G. P		4, 11, or 45 sec	Min., or low	Light railroad bridges	15′
	0.1	0.01	High	Light railroad bridges	15′
	0.1	0.025	High	Light industrial buildings	dh
	0.1	0.025	High	Heavy industrial buildings	dh
	0.1	0.025	High	Residential	dh
	0.1	0.025	High	Power plants and substations	dh
		4, 11, or 45 sec	Min	Railroad embankment	dh
	0.1	0.025	High	Destroyers, ships, larger than 1,500 tons	35′
	0.1	0.025	High	Wharves and docks	25′
		4, 11, or 45 sec	Min	Wharves and docks	dh
1,000-lb. G. P		4, 11, or 45 sec	Min., or low	Concrete pier bridges	15′
	0.1	0.10	High	Concrete pier bridges	15′
		4, 11, or 45 sec	Low	Heavy railroad steel bridge	15′
	0.1	0.01	High	Heavy railroad steel bridge	15′
	0.1	0.025	High	Bombproof buildings, 2 story	dh
	0.1	0.1	High	Bombproof buildings more than 2 story	dh
	0.1	0.025	High	Heavy industrial building	dh
	0.1	0.025	High	Residential	dh
	0.1	0.025	High	Aircraft carrier, cruisers	35′
	0.1	0.025	High	Battleships and battle cruisers	30′
		4, 11, or 45 sec	Min	All ships except battleships and battle cruisers	dh
	0.1	0.025	High	Wharf locks and gates	dh
		4, 11, or 45 sec	Min	Wharf locks and gates	dh
		4, 11, or 45 sec	Min	Submarine slips, open end	dh
1,000-lb. S.A.P		0.1	High	Battleship and cruiser	10′
		0.025	High	Heavy concrete buildings	dh
		4, 11 or 45 sec	Min	All ships except battleships and cruisers	dh
1,000-lb. A.P		0.1	High	All ships	dh
1,600-lb. A.P		0.1	High	All ships	dh
2,000-lb. G.P		4, 11, or 45 sec	Min	Heavy reinforced concrete bridges and buildings	15′
	0.1	0.01	High	Heavy reinforced concrete bridges and buildings	15′
	SQ	Non	High	Residential	100′
	0.1	0.025	High	Dams, light masonry	15′
	4	4	Min	Dams, heavy masonry	75′ upstream
	0.1	0.025	High	Battleship and cruiser	45′
		4, 11, or 45 sec	Min	All ships	Side of ship
		4, 11, or 45 sec	Min	Battleship and cruiser—at anchor	75′
4,000-lb. L.C	SQ	Non	High	Residential	900

Dh—Direct hit required. Min.—Minimum.

Kassel Fiesler Aircraft Plant (AAF)

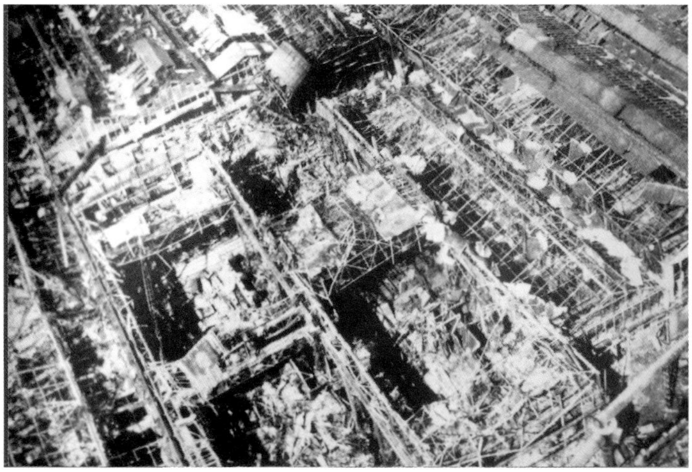

Essen Krupp Armament Works (AAF)

bomb was wrapped with a spiral spring which was 0.44 of an inch in cross section and broke into 500 to 800 pieces with an average weight of 0.2 to 0.3 ounces. When the bomb exploded in a vertical position the spray of pieces tended to rise 3° to 5°. About 85% of the fragments were projected in a band three feet high at a distance of 30 feet with density of one fragment per square foot of the vertical target. At 40 yards there was one fragment per square yard of the vertical target. The fragments were projected with an initial velocity of 4,000 to 5,000 feet per second to a distance of 500 to 600 yards. Penetration tests showed that at 165 feet 0.875inch plywood reinforced with 0.125 inch steel were penetrated by 60% of the fragments.

Types of Damage

The types of damage considered were casualties and normal perforation of mild steel of 0.125 inch, 0.25 inch, and 0.50 inch thickness. A casualty was defined as a hit by a fragment with at least 58 foot pounds of energy which caused incapacitation but not necessarily death. Normal perforation of mild steel occurred when a fragment, traveling perpendicular to the face of the plate, passed completely through the plate of the indicated thickness. Damage in which there was perforation of 0.125 inch mild steel was effective against aircraft on the ground. Damage in which there was perforation of 0.25 inch or 0.50 inch mild steel was effective against trucks, light armored vehicles, railway rolling stock, and targets of similar resistant nature.

Safety Limits

There were distances, as calculated by fragment damage tables, from a bomb burst at which a soldier had a given chance of being wounded by a fragment from different bomb types. Suppose, for example, that a soldier was required to take a 1-in-a-1,000 chance of being wounded by a fragment from a 20 pound bomb. Then suppose that the soldier was in open terrain in such a position that a two square foot area of his body was exposed to fragments coming directly from the bomb. According to a fragment damage table, the number of casualty producing fragments, per square foot, to which the soldier was exposed was 1/1,000 occurred at a distance of about 300 feet from the bomb. In the instance of a man in a bomber wearing the standard body armor, a fragment capable of piercing the plane fuselage, the body armor, and then wounding a man, would be capable of 0.125 inch mild steel.

Air Bursts

Against personnel in medium foxholes or on rough terrain, or against other moderately shielded targets, an air burst of the 500 pound GP

Mersberg-Launa Synthetic Oil Works (AAF)

bomb, AN-M64 or AN-M64A1, or the larger size Fragmentation Bomb (220 pound or more) was recommended. A burst height from 35 to 60 feet would be effective, with the higher burst counteracting the greater target shielding.

Optimal Burst Height
The optimum height of burst of a bomb depended upon the type of shielding of the targets to be attacked. In the complete lack of shielding by the terrain, by other targets, and on open, level ground, the optimum height of burst was just off the ground; to raise the height of the burst still higher would cause a loss of effect approximately:

Burst Height	% Loss*
50 feet	25-50%
30 feet	5-15%
100 feet	70-80%

* % loss in targets effectively damaged

Types of Shielding
Air bursts were recommended against men in foxholes or open trenches and against personnel shielded by rough terrain. The type of shielding known as the "10° foxhole" was the most common foxhole and was due to its definition as a foxhole in which an occupant will, on the average, be unharmed by fragments with an angle of fall less than 10°. Hastily dug in positions on level ground corresponded to "Zero degree foxholes," as did trenches in which the heads of men were even with the ground level.

Dispersion
When a fuse for regulating the height of burst was available and caused a known dispersion in the height of burst, it was possible to determine the mean height to which the burst was to be adjusted by tables. The mean optimum height in the case of dispersion was generally larger than the optimum heights read from the figures on the tables. As the type of shielding progressed from the weak 0° shielding to the strong 30° shielding, the optimum heights of burst were approximately:

Bomb Type	**Optimum Height of Burst***
20lb bomb AN-M41 or AN-M41A1	20-30 feet
90lb bomb M82	30-50 feet
100lb bomb AN-M30 or AN-M30A1	30-50 feet
260lb bomb AN-M81	35-70 feet
500lb bomb AN-M64 or AN-M64A1	30-60 feet

* No dispersion at 0° to 30° shielding

The greater the height of burst; the greater was the effect of the shielding. In the case of heavy shielding, low bomb angles of fall (approximately 45°) were superior to high bomb angles of fall (approximately 75°). For average shielding, the angles of fall (45°-75°) did not affect the result to any significant. Computations demonstrated that a tail initiation of the burst would more than double the effect in the case of low shielding and high angle of fall.

Earth Penetration, Crater Formation, and Earth Shock

Displacement and Depth Penetrated
Displacement and depth penetrated were measured from the center of the hole of entry at ground level to the center of gravity of the bomb at the time of detonation. Displacement was measured horizontally in the direction of aircraft travel while depth was measured perpendicular to the surface. Unintended factors such as the type of earth, differences in the constitution of the earth at the point of impact, stones, etc., had large influence on the behavior of penetrating bombs.

Shape of the Underground Trajectories
The underground trajectories of bombs were generally J-shaped. A bomb traveled straight as long as its yaw remained small but swerved after its instability had resulted in a significant yaw. Swerving generally occurred in a direction that brought the bomb nearer to the surface in an erratic path. Bombs frequently swerved to the right or left of their initial trajectory, resulting in significant lateral offset, sometimes even in a backward direction with respect to the motion of a bombing aircraft. It was reported that American bombs swerved to a considerably lesser extent than similar British or German bombs, that is, the J-shape of their path was less prominent. The underground trajectory was of importance in considering the attack on enemy fortifications.

Fuse Delay
The times of operation of the nose fuse with instantaneous setting and any of the standard tail fuses with non-delay detonators were estimated as: Instantaneous nose fuse at 0.0005 second and Non-delay tail fuse at 0.002 to 0.003 second (depending on the size of the bomb).

The time limits for delay elements of the American tail fuses, with the Primer-Detonator M14, were set by acceptance tests as:

0.01 second nominal delay: 0.007 to 0.014 second.
0.025 second nominal delay: 0.018 to 0.032 second.
0.1 second nominal delay: 0.10 to 0.15 second.

Variations within these limits affected the depth of the burst and thus the crater size to a significant degree.

Cratering Effect of Bombs with Delayed and Instant Fusing

Bomb Size (lbs)	**Fuse Type**	**Crater Depth (ft)**	**Crater Diameter (ft)**
500	Delayed	5	20
500	Instant	2	9
1,000	Delayed	13	45
1,000	Instant	6	20
2,000	Delayed	17	50
2,000	Instant	7	22

(In sandy loam)

Quality of the Soil
Different soils were arranged in a rough range with respect to their resistance to bomb penetration and detonation. Dry sand was extremely high in resistance because, it did not easily transmit and distribute the action of the bomb over a wide region; and because its successive layers had to be crushed with a substantial dissipation of energy. Conversely, wet clay was extremely low in resistance. Its water content tended to distribute the effects of penetration and detonation over wide ranges, so that wet clay could more easily give in to a bomb without being crushed. In general, the greater the water content and plasticity the soil possessed, the less resistance it offered to penetration and to the formation of large craters. Data for three types of soil appeared on tables: soft, corresponding to fairly wet clay; medium, corresponding to a sandy clay loam or to soft chalk; and hard, corresponding to sand or gravel or mixtures thereof. Some degree of interpolation between these types of soils was possible. From these tables it appeared that the maximum crater diameter did not depend on the quality of the soil to the same extent as did the depth of penetration.

Earth Shock Effect
A violent shock was transmitted earthquake-like through the earth from the point of a bomb explosion. The demolition of buildings by earth shock was somewhat unpredictable, since it depended, among other things, on whether the building vibrated in phase with the shock waves from the detonated bomb. Demolition did not appear to extend to buildings which were at a greater distance from the point of burst than the maximum crater

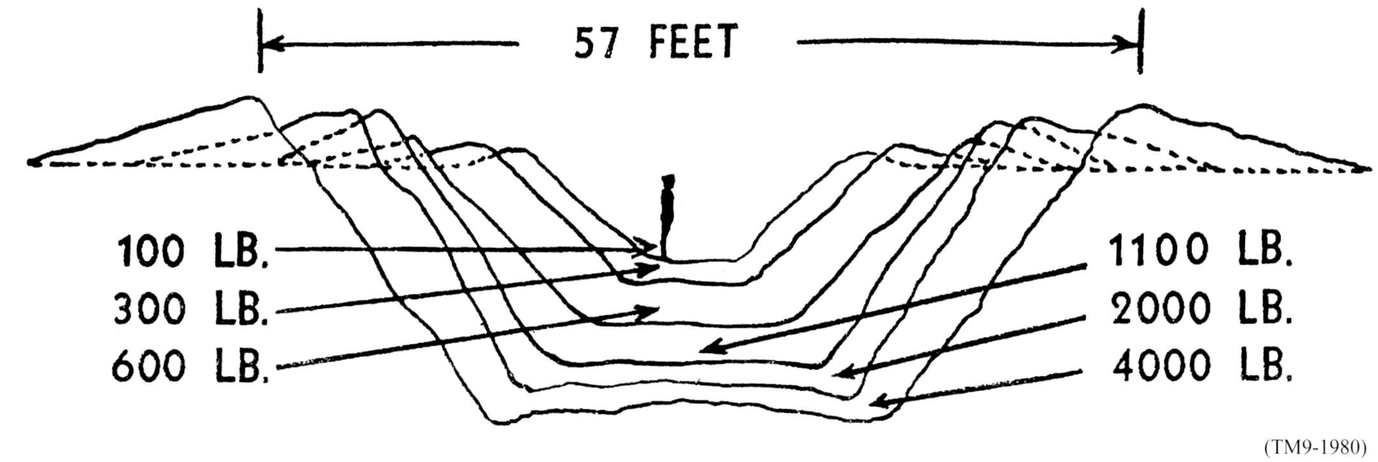

Size of craters caused by aerial bombs varies in direct proportion to bomb weight.

diameter produced by the bomb. Damage to fixed gun emplacements by the bomb action tilting them effectively seemed to be confined to a distance of about the maximum crater diameter. Damage to ceramic utility pipes of earthenware, brick, or tile extended to pipes whose closest approach to the point of detonation was equal to or slightly greater than the maximum crater diameter. Damage to cast iron pipes was likely to occur up to distances from the point of burst of about 0.6 of the maximum crater diameter. Any trench or duct tended to absorb a ground shock, even though its walls could be damaged. In particular, utility pipes laid in ducts were effectively protected, unless included the crater. Adjacent structures or earthworks shifted the center of the crater from the point of detonation. The presence of a trench relieved the earth pressure, so that craters were shifted in that direction. On the other craters were shifted away from embankments or strong structures that withstand the earth shock.

Crater Refill on Airfield Runways

The amount of material that had to be trucked to refill a bomb crater considerably affected the amount of effort that had to be spent in repairing it. The amount of material required excluded the loose material that was already available in the bottom or on the lip of the crater. Crude estimates of the volume of loose soil that had to be trucked in for repair was based on the assumption that all the available and trucked in soil had to be packed hard. It was estimated that the manpower requirement for repair required about 1.5 man-hours per cubic yard of material needed.

Bombing from Minimum Altitude

Bombs generally ricocheted when dropped on level or gently sloping soil from bombers flying at minimum altitude. Such bombs did penetrate steep embankments. For example, if the releasing bomber flying at nearly 400 miles per hour, and the embankment had a 45° inclination, the penetration path followed was similar to that of a bomb dropped from 5,000 feet on level ground. Less penetration was achieved if the bomber was slower or the embankment was not as steep.

Underfooting, Columns and Stanchions

The cratering action of bombs was used to remove the ground support from columns or stanchions in industrial structures, cranes, chimneys, or bridges. This form of attack was usually successful whenever the foot of a structural element was included within the crater limits so a large enough bomb was required to create a large enough crater to include the foot of the particular target.

Armor Penetration by Bombs

General

The relatively large dispersion and low striking velocity of bombs prevented the direct attack of armored targets for perforation from being generally beneficial, except for targets of unusual importance or size. However, large Armor Piercing bombs dropped from high altitudes could perforate the armored decks of battleships and steel roofed fortifications.

Deformation, Rupture, and Low Order Detonation

General Purpose and Semi-Armor Piercing bombs with delay fuses did not withstand the impact of striking heavy armor. This impact led to deformation and breakage of the bomb body which generally was accompanied or preceded by a low-order detonation of the explosive filling (Amatol, TNT, or Comp B). However, when a GP or SAP bomb struck sufficiently thin armor plate, the plate rather than the bomb was deformed and ruptured so that a perforation resulted without effective damage to the bomb.

Armor Penetration by GP and SAP Bombs

BOMB TYPE		Max. thickness of plate perforated without breakup or low order detonation	Max. thickness of plate punched through by quick fusing detonation
100 lb	GP AN-M30 and AN-M30A1	1.0	1.8
250 lb	GP AN-M57 and AN-M57A1	1.3	2.3
500 lb	GP AN-M64 and AN-M64A1	1.5	3.0
1,000 lb	GP AN-M6S and AN-M6SA1	1.7	3.8
2,000 lb	GP, AM-M66, AN-M66A1 and AN-M66A2.	2.0	4.8
500 lb	SAP, AN-MS8, AN-MS8A1 and AN-MS8A2.	2.0	2.0 (est.)
1,000 lb	SAP, AN-MS9 and AM-MS9A1	2.5	2.5 (est.)

Munster *Luftwaffe* **Airdrome** (AAF)

Armor Penetration by GP and SAP Bombs

See chart on previous page.

SAP bombs performed better than GP bombs of equal weight. Armor Piercing Bombs with standard Explosive D filling withstood impact on all but the heaviest armor without appreciable deformation or danger of low-order detonation. The use of the 1,000 pound and 1,600 pound bombs against armor thicker than seven and eight inches respectively was not recommended, because of the danger of deformation.

Effects of Detonation on Armor

General Purpose and, to some extent, Semi-Armor Piercing Bombs provided with a quick fuse achieved considerable effect when hitting armor plate of moderate thickness which would withstand the impact of the same bombs with delay fuse. These bombs punched through the armor, letting fragments and some of the detonation gases pass through the plate. However, no substantial demolition could be thus caused on heavy structures behind the plate punched by detonation in contrast to the effect of a delay-fused bomb which perforated and burst behind the plate.

Bombing of Concrete

General

The relatively large dispersion and low striking velocities of bombs prevented the bombing of strongly built concrete fortifications from being generally advantageous. Large Armor Piercing Bombs dropped from high altitude were effective in perforating all but the thicker roofs of fortifications, but the general area effect of the many unavoidable misses was negligible. On the other hand, General Purpose Bombs, which were effective for area bombing of defensive positions, were generally ineffective against thick concrete because of the rupture of the bomb case and its low penetrative power. Finally, Semi-Armor Piercing Bombs were specially designed to contain the largest possible charge consistent with sufficient structural strength to withstand impact stresses and so SAP bombs possessed optimum characteristics against concrete.

Effect of Impact

GB Bombs

General Purpose Bombs with a delay fuse did not withstand impact on thick concrete slabs as the impact led to deformation or breakage of the casing which was generally accompanied by a low order detonation of the explosive filling (Amatol, TNT, of Comp B). Breakage also was expected when a delay fused GP bomb struck a strong fortification covered with a layer of earth that was somewhat thinner than the maximum earth penetration. However, when a GP bomb hit a sufficiently thin concrete slab, the slab rather than the bomb was ruptured so that a perforation resulted without effective damage to the bomb.

SAP and AP Bombs

Semi-Armor Piercing and Armor Piercing Bombs withstood impact on strong concrete without damage that could weaken their effective detonation. However, AP bombs dropped from high altitude (over

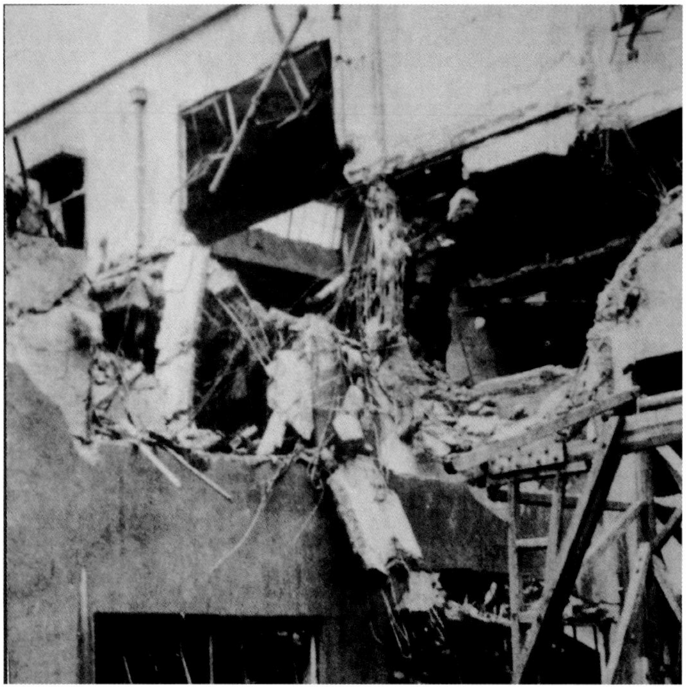

Duren Armament Works (AAF)

15,000 feet) are known to deform appreciably and this reduced their penetrative ability to some extent. Hits against heavy concrete columns or beams resulted in damage impairing the effectiveness of GP but not of SAP or AP bombs.

Effects of Detonation on Concrete

The destructive effect achieved by the detonation of AP or SAP bombs that did not perforate a concrete slab was small to moderate. General Purpose Bombs fitted with instantaneous nose fuses or better, with non-delay tail fuses, achieved a substantial effect.

Cratering in Concrete

The shallow penetration of GP and SAP bombs that did perforate concrete slabs resulted in wide cracking and spalling of the front face of the slab with the formation of a crater which was quite variable in size. As a guide to the expected diameter of the crater, it was assumed that it would be about four times the depth. When AP bombs succeeded in penetrating deeper than two to 2.5 feet there was no further increase of the crater depth, but rather a bore hole slightly larger than the diameter of the bomb was formed at the bottom of the crater.

Back Face Effects: Scabbing

A shock wave traveled across a concrete slab ahead of a penetrating bomb or the expanding gases that resulted from its detonation. As this shock wave reflected from the back face of the slab, this face tended to crack with violent ejection of loose pieces of concrete and formation of a back crater. This phenomenon, called "scabbing," occurred when the bomb or its detonation products came sufficiently close to the back face and to cause serious damage to personnel or light material behind the slab. Complete penetration was achieved when the front face crater and the scab crater merged. The thickness of concrete slab that could be perforated was greater than the depth of penetration in a very thick slab. Heavily scabbed roofs showed significant sag even not blown through. Special forms of surface steel reinforcement were sometimes used to prevent scabbing.

Rebound

A bomb that did not perforate a slab tended to rebound. It was not known how long it took under various conditions for a bomb to penetrate and rebound the small amount necessary to render detonation ineffective against the slab. It was probable that it took longer than 0.025 second for a medium or large bomb to rebound this amount, but probably less than 0.1 second. It was almost certain that whenever a fuse delay in excess of 0.1 second was used, the bomb rebound was sufficient to cause ineffective detonation.

Attack on a Vertical Wall

Minimum altitude attack on vertical concrete walls generally was impracticable because of the necessity of using long delay fusing for the safety of the attacking aircraft. Also the penetrating effect would be no better than that attained from 5,000 feet on horizontal roof slabs.

Effect of Dirt Covering Upon Concrete

Dirt covering on the roof or wall of a concrete fortification cushioned the impact of the bomb so as to reduce its penetrating power. A thickness of earth of 20% of the maximum underground trajectory of a bomb was expected to reduce its penetrating power in underlying concrete by less than 20%. Newly piled dirt was likely to cushion the impact of a bomb even less than wet clay.

Effect of Underground Detonation

The underground detonation of bombs was comparatively effective against the underground portion of concrete fortifications because of the confining effect of the earth. The difficulty in this type of attack was that the bomb had to be made to detonate within a comparatively narrow area around the target at a sufficient depth. If the concrete target was hit by a GP bomb before its velocity was greatly reduced, there was a rupture of the bomb and consequent failure to detonate.

Comparative Effects of US and European Bombs

See chart on following page.

Ju-87 Stuka D-3 in propaganda photo with an array of *Luftwaffe* bombs. (Author)

Comparative properties and effects of European and American high-explosive bombs.

Weight of bomb (pounds)	Caliber of bomb (inches)	Weight of bomb filling (pounds)	Sectional density of bomb (lbs./sq. in.)	Depth of penetration (feet)		Crater dimensions in earth (feet)		Crater dimensions in concrete (feet)		Radius of destruction in earth (feet)		Hori-zontal radius of rup-ture in earth (feet)	Hori-zontal radius of rup-ture in concrete (feet)	Danger zone from frag-ments (feet)
				Natural earth	Re-en-forced concrete	Diam-eter	Depth	Diam-eter	Depth	Hori-zontal	Depth			
European Bombs														
	a	a	a	a	d	e	e	e	e	f	f	g	g	h
110	7.1	57	2.78	13.7	1.1	27.4	3.4	3.8	0.9	11.0	23.7	25.5	12.6	200
220	9.8	120	2.92	14.4	1.3	28.8	4.8	5.2	1.3	14.0	27.4	32.9	16.3	300
660	14.2	360	4.20	20.7	1.8	41.4	6.9	10.1	2.8	20.2	38.9	47.4	23.5	400
1,100	16.6	600	5.00	24.6	2.1	49.2	8.3	13.4	3.8	23.9	46.5	56.2	27.8	600
2,200	21.6	1,200	6.00	29.5	2.6	59.0	9.8	18.2	5.2	30.2	55.2	70.9	35.1	1,200
4,000	25.6	2,200	7.80	38.0	3.3	76.0	12.7	26.4	7.7	41.8	72.8	86.7	42.9	2,400
American Bombs														
b	b	b	b	c	c	b	b	e	e	f	f	g	g	
100 (120)*	7.9	67	2.13	10.5	0.9	20.0	5.0	3.2	0.7	11.5	22.0	27.0	13.4	200
300 (285)*	12.2	148	2.43	12.0	1.0	27.0	7.0	4.4	1.1	15.0	25.5	35.4	17.5	300
600 (625)*	16.5	349	2.90	14.3	1.2	37.0	10.0	6.7	1.8	20.0	32.4	46.9	23.2	400
1,100 (1,130)*	20.8	632	3.32	16.3	1.4	45.0	13.0	9.0	2.5	24.4	38.4	57.2	28.3	600
2,000 (2,030)*	18.5	1,060	7.55	37.1	3.2	53.0	16.0	22.4	6.4	28.9	61.7	68.0	33.7	1,200

a FromM. Bazant, ' The Use of Re-enforced Concrete for Fortifications and Air Raid Shelters," in *Travaux*, Nos. 52 and 53, April and May 1937, Tables 2 and 3, for impact velocity of 820 ft./sec., corresponding to a bombing altitude of 13,350 ft. at 200 m.p.h.
b From Technical Regulations 1370-G, War Department, Washington, D.C.
c Computed in accordance with formula on p. 30, 'Civil Air Defense" (New York: McGraw-Hill Book Co., 1941), for impact velocity of 820 ft./sec.
d From Bazant, (*loc. cit.*), Table 2, for concrete slab supported over whole of its surface.
e Computed from depths of penetration, in accordance with formulas on p. 39, "Civil Air Defense," for "normal" bomb ($n=1.0$).
f Computed from formulas on p. 42, "Civil Air Defense."
g Computed from formula on p. 43, "Civil Air Defense."
h From "War on Great Cities," by Frank Morison (Albert Henry Ross); London: Faber & Faber.

* Actual weight of bomb.

(Chart from Army Ordnance Magazine, July-August, 1942.)

9

Miscellaneous Ordnance

Chemical Bombs (Incendiary, Gas, Smoke)

General

Chemical Bombs were those which have, as their main charge, a chemical agent which produces a toxic or irritating physiological effect, a screening smoke, an incendiary action, or a combination of any or all of these. Chemical Bombs were produced in two designs; bombs released in clusters for area bombing, and bombs released individually for point bombing. In some Chemical Bombs such as magnesium alloy incendiaries, the metal case served as the main charge of the bomb; in others, the charge was contained in the bomb body, and required an explosive burster to open the body and distribute the charge.

Bombs Released in Clusters

Generally, bombs designed for assembly in clusters had the following characteristics in common:

1) They were small, ranging from four to 10 pounds.
2) They were hexagonal, rather than round, to provide for solid packing in the cluster.
3) They were equipped with an integral, inertia-type fuse which was armed by the release of the bomb from the cluster. The arming mechanism of the fuse consisted of a safety plunger which was held depressed against spring action by the adjacent bomb in the cluster. When in this position the inner end of the plunger prevented the firing pin from firing the primer.

If a cluster should break up in handling or otherwise accidentally release its bombs, the fuses of such bombs were armed and dropping a bomb several feet onto its nose could cause the fuse to ignite the bomb.

Bombs Released Individually

Bombs released individually for bombing of point targets were 100 pounds and larger and had better flight characteristics than cluster bombs. These bombs were cylindrical with a rounded or ogival nose. Small bombs were adapted for nose fusing only while larger bombs were adapted for both nose and tail fuses. The fins could be installed to the bomb body (100 pound bombs) or issued separately. Each bomb contained a burster well, which was a tube opening into the fuse seat and extending the length of the bomb body.

Complete round-small bombs

The complete round of small Chemical Bombs consisted of:

1) Bomb body, including adapter, adapter sleeve, burster well, and chemical charge.
2) Fin assembly (included in body for 100 pound bombs).
3) Burster and igniter,
4) Nose fuse.
5) Arming wire assembly.

Complete round-large bombs

The complete rounds for larger Chemical Bombs will be described for the particular bomb.

Packing

One hundred pound Chemical Bombs with fin attached were packed and shipped in a wooden box. Larger bombs, without fin assembly, were shipped with lug protectors or shipping bands. Fin assembly, arming wire, fuses, and bursters were each packed separately.

Assembly

To assemble the complete round of the 100 and 115 pound bombs:

1) Remove bomb from packing and inspect it to be sure there were no leaks or other evidence of unserviceability.
2) If the fin was shipped separately, assemble to the bomb by removing fin lock nut, placing the assembly over tail of bomb with one fin in line with suspension lugs, replace the fin lock nut, and tightening it.
3) Remove the fuse hole plug and adapter sleeve. Inspect the fuse seat and burster well to be sure that the threads were not damaged and that there was no foreign matter present.
4) Insert the burster and press it in until the shoulder on the top of the burster was seated against the shoulder of the adapter without forcing it. If the burster would not enter or seat freely, the bomb was to be turned in for disposal.
5) Replace the adapter sleeve, seating it firmly against the burster.
6) Assemble nose fuse. .
7) If the bomb was not dropped, the above steps were to be reversed and each component returned to its original condition and packing.

Assembly (Large bombs)

Assembly of larger bombs will be described for the particular bomb.

Bomb, Chemical, 100 Pound, M47A2 (AAF)

Function
The Chemical Bomb was fused for instantaneous action on impact in order to prevent waste of the chemical agent. If the bomb body was light sheet metal, impact on a hard surface could rupture the case and scatter the chemical agent even when the bomb was dropped SAFE.

Precautions
In addition to the precautions for handling a conventional bomb, chemical ammunition required extra precautions as given in Technical Manual TM9-1900. CC, AC, and CG bombs were not to be stored in poorly ventilated locations. Chemical-detecting test papers were placed near these stored bombs and all personnel working in these magazines were to carry gas masks. Each bomb was to be weighed before being placed in storage and again before shipment or use. Any bomb showing a loss of weight of 10 pounds was considered as leaking seriously and was to be destroyed. Extreme care was employed in these magazines as AC was not only poisonous but also explosive. Gas masks were worn by all personnel when surveillance or inspection required the withdrawal of AC from the bomb, or when a leaking bomb was found.

Types of Chemical Bombs
Bomb, Chemical, 100 Pound, M47A2 (Metal Parts)
The M47A2 (Metal Parts) was the designation of the bomb case before it was loaded with gas, smoke, or incendiary filler. It was a round-nose, cylindrical-type with fins attached, measuring 48.92 inches maximum length and 8.125 inches diameter, and unloaded, it weighed 26 pounds. The body was constructed of sheet steel and was coated on the inside with oil.

Other models
Bomb, Chemical, 100 Pound, M47A differed only from the M47A2 in that the interior was coated with acid-proof black paint.

Bomb, Chemical, 500 Pound, M78
The M78 was a non-persistent gas bomb which weighed approximately 450 pounds as released with the chemical charge consisting of about 170 pounds of CC filler. The bomb body was similar to that of the 500 pound GP bomb except that the base was welded to the case and burster well extended the length of the bomb. The needle valve was installed in the base of the bomb for surveillance purposes. The burster well was closed by a nose and a tail plug.

Components
The complete round consisted of:

1) Bomb, chemical, 500 pound, M78, unfused, without the fin assembly, fuse seat liner, adapter-booster, or burster.
2) Fin, assembly for 500 pound GP bombs AN-M64 and AN-M64A1, incendiary, AN-M76 and chemical, M78.
3) Nose and tail fuses.
4) Adapter-booster, M115 or M115A1.
5) Burster, AN-M15.
6) Liner, fuse seat.
7) Wire, arming, assembly.

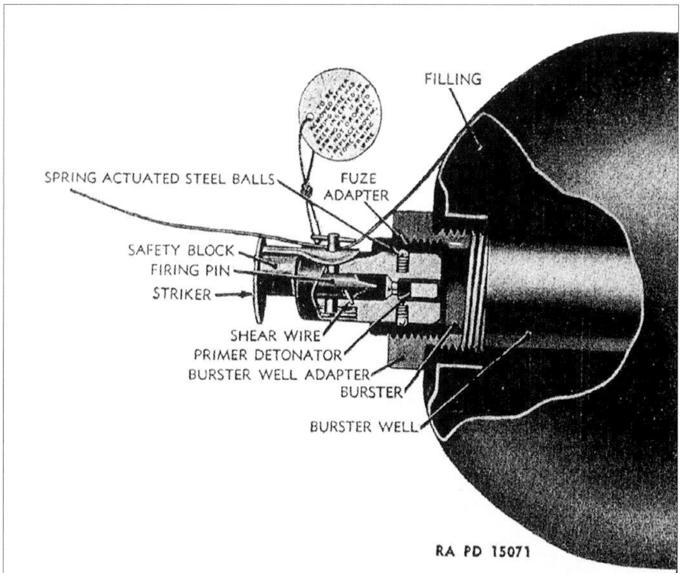

Figure 110. BOMB, chemical, 100-lb., section of nose.

Bomb, Chemical, 100 Pound, M47A2 Nose Mechanism (TM9-1980)

Bomb, Chemical, 1,000 Pound, AN-M79
The AN-M79 resembled the 500 pound, Chemical Bomb M78 except in size. The body was a 1,000 pound, GP bomb body modified in the same manner as the 500 pound GP was modified for the 500 pound bomb. The chemical charge consisted of about 200 pounds of AC filler of the 722 pounds of the complete round.

Components
1) Bomb, Chemical, 1,000 pound, AN-M79, unfused without fin assembly, fuse seat liner, adapter-booster, or burster.
2) Fin assembly for 1,000 pound GP bomb, AN-M65 and AN-M65A1 and chemical AN-M79.
3) Fuse, Bomb, AN-M103 or M103; or Fuse, Bomb, Mechanical Time, M127 with adapter-booster, M117.
4) Fuse, Bomb, AN-M102A2 or AN-M102A1, with primer detonator M14, non-delay.
5) AN-M16 Burster.
6) Adapter-booster, Ml 15 or M115A1.
7) Fuse seat liner.
8) Arming wire assembly.

Bomb, Chemical 1,000 Pound, AN-M79
This bomb was similar to the AC bomb described above except for the differences in filler and corresponding difference in weight. The chemical charge consisted of approximately 340 pounds of CC filler, and the complete round weighed about 860 pounds.
(Note: Chemical bombs used in poison gas dispersal are discussed in Volume 3.)

Flare, Aircraft, Parachute, M26AI (AN-M26)
The M26AI was a flare which was discharged from its case and ignited when the fuse functioned. It was supported by a parachute and burned for three to 3.5 minutes with a yellowish light of 300,000 candle power. The complete round was 50 inches long, eight inches in diameter, and weighed 52.5 pounds of which 14 pounds was flare charge.

Photoflash Bombs
Development
In the prewar, Maj. George Goddard was the head of Army Air Materiel Command Photographic Research Unit at Wright Field. Goddard was active in general camera and lens development, particularly the K- and T- series of cameras and high resolution metrogon lenses. After refining the film, lenses, and techniques used in daytime recon photography Goddard made major contributions in the development of night aerial photoreconnaissance. He took the first night aerial photo on 24 November 1925, using the K-1 camera using flash bombs he developed. Continuing his nocturnal photographic tests in the late 1930s Goddard used a B-18A flown by 1Lt. Marcus Cooper to circle his hometown of Rochester, NY, dropping his newly developed magnesium photographic "flash bombs." The 45 pound cylindrical bombs identified by two black bands were developed with the cooperation of the Eastman Co. of Rochester, NY. The flash bombs exploded with millions of candlepower flashes lasting but one-sixth second and culminating in a thunderclap on the ground. By using a photo cell and an electric synchronization device, the flash was coordinated to the shutter of an automatic 8x10 negative camera that was mounted to shoot through the bomber's floor. At 5,000 feet the bomb illuminated an area of about five square miles below and was so blinding that it concealed the position of the bomber from AA batteries. The flash bomb allowed accurate observation of enemy movements at night and as Goddard stated, "(they) marked the end of day that military leaders prayed for darkness or for a few extra hours of daylight."

Flare, Aircraft, Parachute, M26AI (AAF)

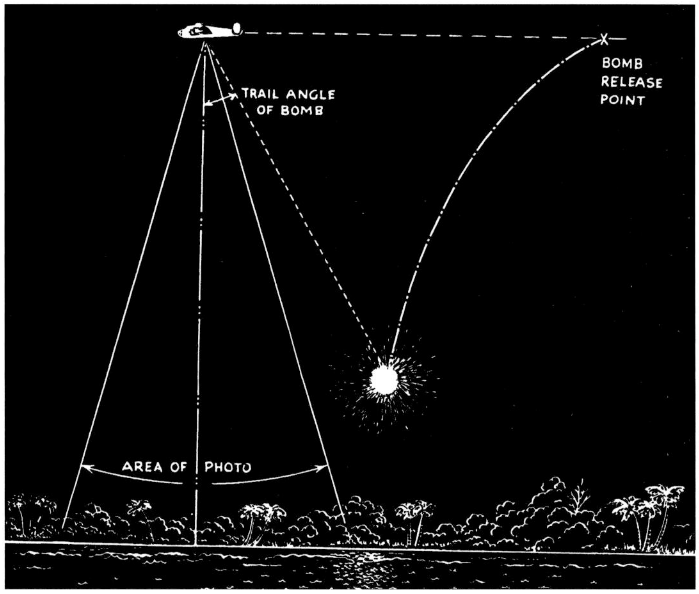

Photo Flash Bomb: The bomb's fuse was set so that the photo bomb would explode and its flash powder would ignite at a point behind the aircraft, causing a photo-electric cell to operate the camera shutter. (AAF) (Note: Size to read)

Bomb, Photoflash, 100 Pound, AN-M46 (AAF)

Bomb, Photoflash, 100 Pound, AN-M46

The AN-M46 used a cylindrical bomb case with a round nose. The complete round was 48.6 inches long and 7.8 inches in diameter and weighed 61.9 pounds and contained a charge of 25 pounds of photoflash powder in a fiber container. When the fuse functioned the charge exploded producing a flash 500 million candlepower, maximum, burning for 0.20 second.

In a typical photo run one M46 Photoflash bomb was used for each picture and a number were dropped in train by use of the intervalometer to obtain a sequence of pictures from which the mosaic of linked photos could be created. Each bomb furnished about a half billion candle power at the peak of the flash at which time a camera with predetermined lens, exposure and diaphragm settings took the photo.

Smoke Screens and Smoke Bombs

There were two tactical reasons, offensive and defensive, for laying a smoke screen. When used to support attacking ground troops it concealed their advance against enemy positions, blinded enemy observation, and deceived the enemy as to the area of the main attack. It could be used defensively to shroud large areas of vital installations in the event of an enemy air or ground attack or to cover a retreat.

There were three types of smoke screens: a blinding smoke, a smoke blanket, and smoke curtain. A blinding smoke was spread over enemy AA positions or their attacking tanks and infantry by aircraft flying only a few hundred feet overhead. This smoke was so thick that movement was almost impossible. The smoke blanket was much like the blinding smoke except that the smoke was laid upwind from the enemy and the wind was used to carry the huge smoke blanket over the enemy. The advantage of this method is that the aircraft laying the smoke was not as exposed to enemy ground and AA fire. A smoke curtain acted as a screen to enemy observation during the advance of troops especially during amphibious and airborne operations. Smoke screens could be laid by either spraying with smoke dispensers of by dropping smoke bombs which depended upon the surface winds to disperse them in the proper direction.

The smoke-laying aircraft carrying one to four dispensers would fly in two or three formations of two aircraft at an altitude of 250 feet and at 200-250 mph. In each formation the lead pilot partially discharged two tanks, waited four seconds and then discharged smoke from the remaining two. Staggered about 100 feet to the rear and about 100 to 150 feet apart to insure continuity of the screen the second pilot performed the same procedure. The smoke settled quickly to the ground and then rose to an average height of 400 feet along each of the 4,500 foot smoke screens. Each of the initial screens lasted about two to three minutes depending on the wind and remained effective for five to seven minutes before the smoke rose, bunched, and dispersed after ten more minutes. After an interval of several minutes another formation or the original formation would reinforce the screen by laying smoke over the existing layers at 75 to 100 feet. Often a third smoke-laying run would be made which could result in a dense screen that could be effective for an hour which was the necessary time to screen falling paratroopers during airborne operations. In the Pacific smoke dispensers were used to conceal paratroopers in airborne operations which were all successful due to the lack of enemy opposition.

Smoke Dispensers

The existing smoke screens (called "smokes") in the early part of the war were mostly chemical but were insufficient for the conditions as they were either poisonous, or corrosive, or liable to explosion during manufacture, or contained critical materials. Oil smokes were consisting basically of a vertical oil furnace into which water was injected near the top to quench the flame to produce a brownish smoke cloud. The M-1 oil-smoke pot, developed by the Chemical Warfare Service (CWS), resembled the orange grove smudge pot and was too large, cumbersome, and produced a thick black smoke cutting off light. However, white smoke was found to be preferable to a colored smoke as it was not necessary to cut off all of the light and less smoke would be necessary.

To produce a more efficient and compact smoke generator Irving Langmuir, a former Nobel Prize winner at the General Electric Company, and Victor LaMer at Columbia University, were granted independent contracts by the NDRC in the fall of 1940. The two men investigated aerosols, which is the suspension of particles of liquids or solids in air. The theory of light scattering, developed by Nobel Prize winner, Lord Rayleigh (John William Strutt) at the turn of the century, stated that light is scattered more if its wave length is short than if its wave length is long and showed how this scattering

A **smoke curtain** acted as a screen to enemy observation during the advance of troops, especially during amphibious and airborne operations, as seen here during the first successful air drop in the Pacific at Nadzab, New Guinea, in September 1943 by the 503rd Parachute Infantry. (AAF)

M-2 Smoke Generator (AAF)

M-2 Smoke Generator and **M-10 Tank** (AAF)

M10 Smoke Tanks filled to a 30 gallon capacity of the FS smoke agent, giving it a total weight of 550 pounds. (AAF)

is related to the size of the smoke particles. At Columbia University and GE, LaMer and Langmuir independently developed smokes which had particles of uniform diameter that scattered light very effectively.

When light struck the smoke particles some of it was reflected from each small smoke particle and this scattered light traveled in all possible directions and reflected from other particles; increasing the effectiveness of the screen. If the scattered light is much more intense than the surrounding light an observer's eyes would be confused and unable to focus. If the smoke was made of colored particles, instead of scattering the light, the smoke absorbed much of it.

Once the particle size and the advantage of white smoke were determined, the next stage was to develop a smoke generator. Langmuir determined that it was essential to produce countless small droplets and blow them apart quickly enough so that they would not bump into each other and coalesce. Langmuir heated high-boiling fractions of petroleum and the vapor condensed to form droplets that when they reached cool air; much like steam from a tea kettle. When the cooling was rapid the droplets were small and when a jet sucked air into the stream of droplets and produced rapid dilution, the droplets remained small for long periods.

By the late fall 1941 Langmuir had developed a generator which led to a number of rather large land-based generators which required a truck bed for transport; culminating in the M-1 Mechanical Smoke Generator was manufactured by the Heil Company, Milwaukee. The Besler Corporation completed the development of a lightweight generator weighing about 165 pounds, called M-2 Mechanical Smoke Generator which was adapted for aircraft use.

B-25 or A-20 medium bombers or C-47s carried two to four underwing units while single engine fighter aircraft carried one on each underwing pylon or one under the fuselage midline. M10 smoke tanks had a 30 gallon capacity of the FS smoke agent giving it a total weight of 550 pounds. FS was a solution of sulfur trioxide in chlorosulfonic acid which when atomized reacted with water vapor to for a dense cloud of sulfuric and hydrochloric acid.

All crew members were equipped with gas masks that were to be donned beginning 30 seconds before release of chemical until the aircraft landed and was stopped. Laying a smoke screen could be problematic as, of course, the wind had to be taken into consideration. Chemical missions were not to be flown when the wind velocity was greater than 20 mph. The direction of wind was to be determined as the chemicals were to be dropped from a flight path perpendicular to the wind and about 600 feet above the ground. Towns and inhabited areas along route were to be avoided. The FS was more effective in humid conditions as it was dependent on moisture in the air.

Smoke Bombs

USN Smoke Bombs

The Navy was the primary user of smoke bombs employing them to support amphibious landings in the Pacific where it was too dangerous for water craft to approach a heavily-defended beaches to disperse smoke.

Navy Aircraft Floating Smoke Bombs

The Navy smoke bombs were floating bombs designed for dropping from aircraft for the purpose of creating a smoke screen, primarily on the surface of a body of water (by using a fuse adapter these bombs could also function on land impact). The aircraft floating smoke bombs for Naval use were filled with HC smoke mix (Type A, composed of hexachlorethane, zinc dust, ammonium perchlorate, ammonium chloride, and magnesium carbonate), which produced a dense white smoke when burning. The 100 Pound Smoke Bomb Mark three Mod 0 produced smoke for six to 10 minutes, the 50 Pound Smoke Bomb Mark one Mod1 produced smoke for three to five minutes, and the 50 Pound Smoke Bomb Mark one Mod two produced

Modified smoke generator installed on the wing pylon of a P-47. (AAF)

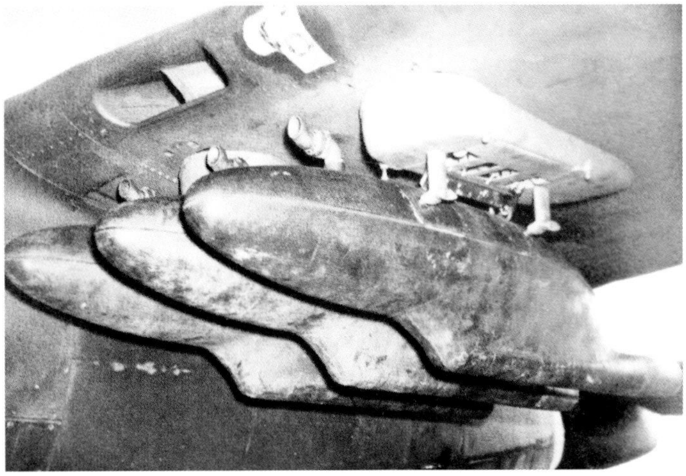

Modified smoke generator installed on wing racks of a B-25. (AAF)

smoke for six to seven and a half minutes. All floating smoke bombs were deemed safe for takeoff and landings everywhere, including carriers. The Grumman TBF was equipped to carry 10 Bombs Mark 1 Mod1 or Mark one Mod 2, or four bombs Mark 3 Mod 0. When their bomb bays were equipped with bombs only, the capacity was 12 bombs Mark 1 Mod1 or Mark 1Mod 2, or six bombs Mark 3 Mod 0.

Types of Navy Smoke Bombs

10 Pound HC Smoke Bomb M77

This bomb consisted of a sheet steel leak-proof hexagonal case 2.87 inches across the flats and 19.5 inches long, weighing approximately 13 pounds when filled. It had no device for stabilization in flight, and therefore used the "all-ways" type Fuse M150 housed in the tail cup dome. The bomb was filled with 9.5 pounds of Type C HC smoke mixture (Hexachlorethane-zinc oxide-aluminum mix). The M77 was used mainly in cluster configuration.

100 Pound Aircraft Smoke Bomb Mark 3 Mod 0

This bomb consisted of an aluminum nose casting which carried the smoke charge, a hollow wooden float to provide buoyancy, and four tail fins to provide good flight characteristics. The bomb was shipped with a water-impact Fuse Mark Mod1 in the nose. At the tail of the float was a valve cap with a valve to prevent water from leaking into the interior of the bomb and to act as a baffle giving lateral distribution to the smoke. The bomb weighed 102 pounds, loaded and fused, and contained 59 pounds of HC smoke mixture. The outside dimensions of the bomb were 48.5 inches long by 10.25 inches in diameter. It had a ballistic coefficient of 0.882 and an approximate maximum striking velocity of 795 feet per second. The bomb had two movable suspension bands and could be suspended from any bomb rack or shackle subject. The normal position of the suspension bands for external racks requiring two lug suspension was for the nose baffle and suspension lugs were in line with the carrying aircraft bisecting two adjacent tail fins.

50 Pound Aircraft Smoke Bombs Mark one Mod1 and Mark one Mod 2

These bombs were similar to the 100 Pound Smoke Bomb Mark 3 Mod 0 but were smaller at 38.3 inches long and 8.85 inches in diameter and weighed 54 pounds, loaded and fused, and contained 28 pounds of HC smoke mixture. This bomb had a ballistic coefficient of 0.627 and an approximate maximum striking velocity of 694 feet per second. These bombs could have either one or suspension bands and either a single or two lug suspension could be used. The only difference between the characteristics of the Smoke Bomb Mark one Mod1 and the Smoke Bomb Mark 1 Mod 2 was the burning time; the Mark 1 Mod1 emitting smoke for three to six minutes and the Mark 1 Mod 2 for six to seven and a half minutes. This bomb had either one or two movable suspension bands or a movable band with an additional attached lug and could be used with either single or double suspension.

The Smoke Bombs were all equipped with the water impact nose fuse Mark 3 Mod1 and when installed in the bomb and the bomb released over water, functioned upon impact as follows: The firing pin, which was held in place by a creep spring, was driven into a primer by fluid pressure. The spit of the primer ignited a length of time fuse which gave an 18 second delay. The time fuse ignited a quick match which ignited the starting mixture, and this initiated the burning of the smoke mixture. Gas pressure formed by the burning smoke mixture broke the vent discs and opened the valve cap at the tail of the bomb, permitting the smoke to be released.

100 Pound Quick-Opening Cluster E44 of 14 Ten Pound HC Smoke Bombs M77

This bomb, for use over land only, was designed to provide frontal or flank cover for amphibious operations or troop movements and to blanket large areas of enemy positions with smoke. Each cluster opened a few feet below the releasing plane and when dropped from 500 feet altitude dispersed its bombs over a somewhat elliptical area about 50 yards across. The bombs required two to four minutes after hitting the ground to build up an effective screen and would produce smoke from eight to 20 minutes.

A retaining pin was removed from the fuse when the fused bombs were assembled in the cluster. While the bombs were in the cluster, the closeness of their casings held a release clip to the body of the fuse. When the bombs were released, the arming pin and release clip were forced out by the arming pin spring, permitting the safety pin to enter the cavity in the striker. Impact forced the striker and sleeve together, piercing the primer, which in turn ignited the first fire mixture, which ignited the HC smoke mix. The heat generated by the burning of the first fire mixture and the HC smoke mix melted the zinc alloy fuse body. The smoke was then emitted through the fuse hole in the tail cup.

100 Pound Smoke Bomb Cluster E44 of 14 10 Pound HC Smoke Bombs M77

This smoke bomb cluster consisted primarily of an M4 cluster adapter, in which fourteen 10 Pound HC Smoke Bombs M77 were installed. The complete cluster, weighing 193 pounds, was issued fully assembled and ready for loading.

100 Pound Smoke AN-M47 Cutaway

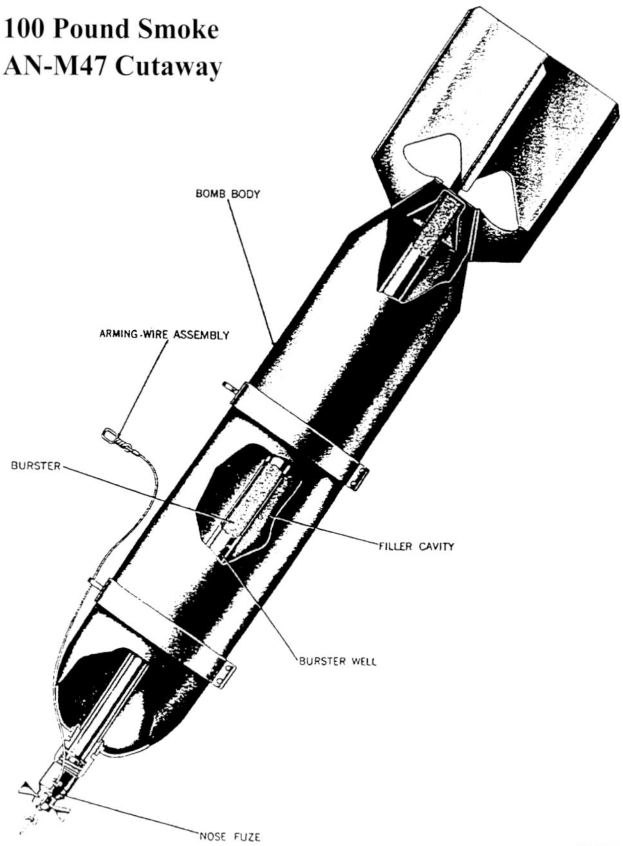

(USN)

100 Pound Smoke Bomb M47A2 and AN-M47AS
This smoke bomb consisted of a 100 pound bomb body M47A2 filled with either 100 pounds of WP (white phosphorus) or 72 pounds of PWP (plasticized white phosphorus: a mixture of white phosphorus and synthetic rubber in xylene). This bomb was equipped with a Tetryl burster M4 (1.56 pounds of Tetryl) for high altitude bombing; or black powder burster M18 (260 grams of Black Powder and 260 grams Sand) for low altitude bombing; and an instantaneous functioning, air-arming nose Fuse AN-M126A1. The only difference between the M47A2 and the AN-M47A3 was in the length of the tail fins. The tail fins of the AN-M47A3 are three inches longer for increased flight stability.

When the bomb was released from the aircraft, the arming wire was withdrawn and the arming vanes of the fuse were free to rotate. After 725 feet of air travel the fuse was fully armed. Upon impact the striker over-powered the creep spring and struck the detonator, exploding the burster, which scattered the white phosphorus over a circular area of approximately 60 to 100 yards in diameter. An effective white smoke screen was produced for one to two minutes with WP and three in five minutes PWP.

The Smoke Bomb Bodies M47A2 and AN-M47A3 were 46 inches long (49 inches long including spacer, sleeve, shipping plug and tail) and eight inches in diameter. The body was made of 1/16 inch lap-welded steel and was threaded at the nose to take an axial burster well, which extended to the tail of the bomb body. A sheet steel box-type tail assembly was welded to the bomb body. With the burster well installed, the empty bomb weighed approximately 26 pounds. Two suspension bands of sheet steel, each equipped with a suspension lug, circumscribed the bomb body. The bomb ready for dropping weighed approximately 126 pounds when loaded with WP and 98 pounds when loaded with PWP. The Smoke Bombs M47A2 and AN-M47A3 could be suspended from any two hook or single hook racks or shackles. For suspension from single hook racks or shackles, one suspension band was removed and the remaining band loosened, slid up to approximately the center of gravity of the bomb and then retightened.

Target Identification (TI) Bombs
The TI also was a pyrotechnic device consisting of a modified GP case with a nose fuse and expelling charge, and a number of pyrotechnic candles which were ignited by the expelling charge and burned with characteristic color and pattern. These bombs were used by Pathfinder aircraft that preceded the main bombing formations to designate or identify the target; facilitating sighting and reducing the probability of error.

Bomb, TI, 100 Pound, Smoke, Red, M84
The 100 Pound TI did not contain pyrotechnic candles. It was used to indicate a bomb release point when bombing was performed above an overcast and on ground targets which could not be distinguished. The bomb was set for air burst releasing a large cloud of red smoke which lingered for a considerable time. The bomb consisted of a round nose, cylindrical sheet steel body fitted with a box fin. The complete round was 53.1 inches long and 8.1 inches in diameter; weighed 103 pounds of which 72 pounds was red iron oxide (hematite) filler. An AN-M4 burster ruptured the case to eject the red filler. The 250 pound TI was fused with a mechanical time nose fuse.

Bomb, T1, Smoke, Red, 100 Pound, M84AI
The M84AI was an AAF smoke bomb that differed from both the conventional smoke bomb and target identification bombs in that it was

Filling a 250 pound "Skymaster" Target Identification Bomb. (AAF)

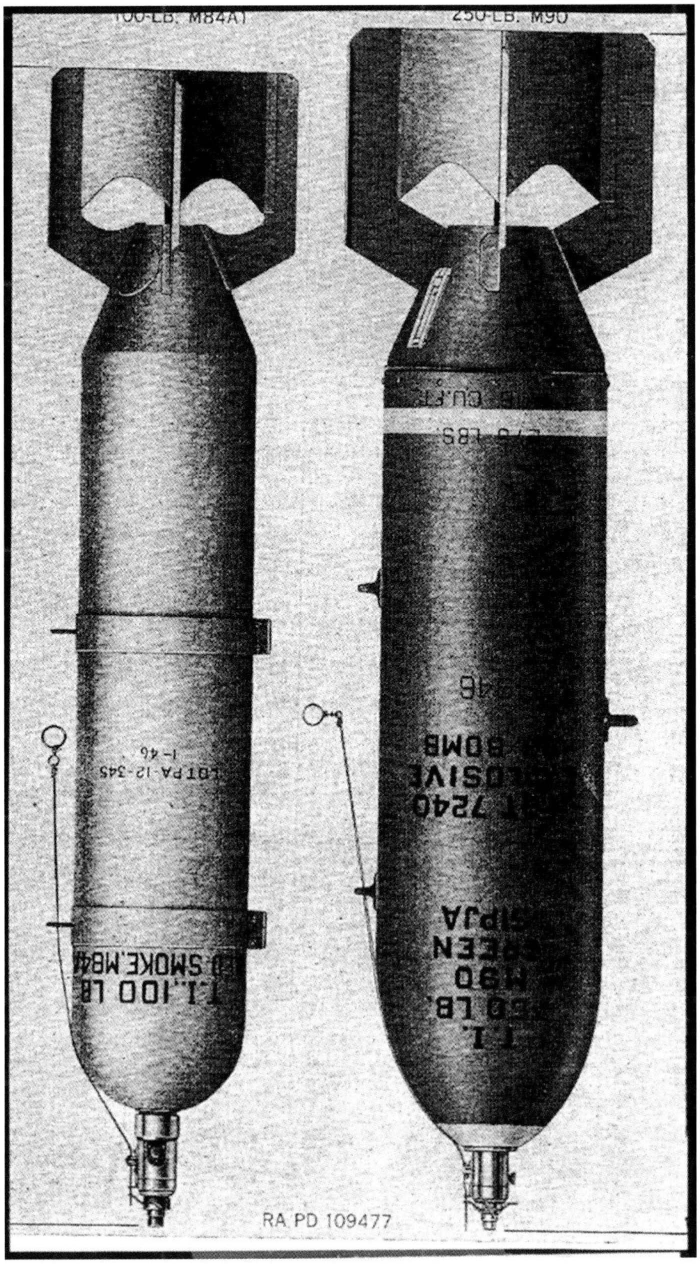

100 Pound M84 and 250 Pound M90 (TM9-1980)

used to indicate a bomb release point when bombing operations were carried out above overcast and the ground targets were not discernible. The bomb was usually set for an air burst and when the bomb burst, a large cloud of red smoke was produced which hung in the air for a considerable time.

This bomb consisted of a round nose, cylindrical sheet steel body fitted with a box fin. The complete round, containing 72 pounds of red iron oxide (hematite) filler, weighed 103 pounds, was 63.1 inches long, and 8.1 inches in diameter. The Burster, AN-M4 was used with this bomb to rupture the case and expel the filler.

Other Models

An earlier modification, the Bomb, T1, Smoke, Red, 100 Pound, M84 was the same as the M84AI except that it is fitted with a shorter fin assembly; making the complete round length only 50.1 inches.

Bomb, TI, 250 Pound, All Models (M89, 90, 91, 98, and, 100)

All models of the 250 pound Target Identification bombs contained a filler of 61 pyrotechnic candles of various types. This TI bomb was a modified 250 pound GP bomb body which when fused was 56.8 inches long and 10.84 inches in diameter. The 250 pound TI was fused with a mechanical time nose fuse. The weight of the different models varied depending on the type of candles used and ranged from 241 to 265 pounds. Model designations were assigned to these bombs on the basis of the various combinations of color and non-delay, delay of various lengths of time, or explosive. There were various designs of candle employed, red, green, yellow, or combinations; red-green, red-yellow, and yellow-green. M103 candles were non-delay; M104 were delay (2.75, 4.0, and 5.25 minutes); M105 were explosive; and M107 were a combination with a three minute burning time. The model M89 250 TI contained 61 M103 candles; the M90 contained 57 M103 and 4 M105 candles; the M91 contained 16 M103, 15 M104 (2.75 minute delay), 15 M104 (4 minute delay); and 15 M104 (5.25 minute delay) candles; the M98 contained 31 M103 and 31 M105 candles; and the M100 contained 61 M107 candles.

AA Bombs

Background

British Long Aerial Mine (LAM)

The British designed the Long Aerial Mine (LAM) for dispersing Luftwaffe bomber formations and was used for a short time only against night bombers during the Blitz of 1940/1941. The LAM was a 14 pound cylindrical container measuring 14 inches long and seven inches in diameter which opened at both ends after release. A support parachute, attached by a line, was deployed from one end of the container. The towing parachute attached by 2,000 feet of piano wire fell out of the other end of the container. A one pound bomb was attached to the container by a weak link and line to which was attached a small stabilizer parachute. When a bomber hit the piano wire a shock wave traveled up the wire causing the weak link to break away from the container and open the stabilizing parachute. The shock wave also traveled down the wire; opening the towing parachute. As the bomber continued flying on; the towing parachute dragged the bomb down into it and exploded.

In tests a twin-engine Hanley Page Harrow transport could carry a 120 LAMs and when laid at 200 foot intervals it could lay an aerial minefield approximately four and a half miles long. Because Luftwaffe night bombers didn't fly in formation they were difficult to locate by radar vectoring and only one LAM success was ever claimed during the Blitz; after which they were never a threat over England.

Luftwaffe SD-2 "Butterfly" Aerial Bomb

The Luftwaffe also developed the SD-2 "Butterfly" bomb which was a 4.4 pound, 3.5 inch long by three inch diameter cylindrical cast iron casing containing 7.5 ounces of TNT. The Butterfly bomb was encased in thin four piece sheet steel container with two hinged end flaps and two pieces that were hinged together covering the sides of the bomb. The inner bomb and the outer container were attached by a six inch arming cable that was connected to the bomb's airburst fuse. All four outer casing parts were hinged together with torsion springs that forced these parts away from the inner bomb body but were prevented from opening until a safety pin was pulled when container opened. After release, the sides of the outer casing opened upward resembling butterfly wings and the end pieces also opened and because of the air drag, rose to the upper end of the six inch wire cable connected to the fuse. The rotation of the wings relative to the bomb body armed the fuse. The deployment of the wings slowed the fall of the bombs in the path of the approaching bombers. There were four types of containers: AB 23 SD-2 container holding 23 bombs; the AB 250-3 container holding

250 pound TI igniting among mixed conventional and incendiary cluster bomb load. (AAF)

108 bombs; the Mark 500 Roden container holding six bombs; and the AB 24 container holding 24 bombs. By the time the Luftwaffe was ready to deploy the SD-2 types in large numbers American escorts fighters ruled the skies and Luftwaffe single and twin-engined fighters were prevented from approaching close enough to drop their bombs.

U.S. Navy Anti-aircraft Bomb Mark 34

The Navy Bureau of Ordnance became interested in developing an air-to-air bomb against enemy bomber formations and investigated both the British LAM and German SD-2 bombs. The LAM concept was discarded as too complicated with its multiple parachutes. The German winged SD-2 bomb was also too complicated but its container concept was thought to be feasible.

The AA Bomb Mark 34 anti-aircraft, air-to-air bomb was developed as a small, light case bomb that carried a two pound TNT charge. To make a direct hit more likely BuOrd designed bomb containers that released 20 bombs at a time in an explosive pattern 450 feet long and 150 feet wide. The tactical use of the bomb was based on the assumption that fighters were able to fly above bomber formations and drop large numbers of small bombs on them. While the two pound TNT charge was small it was capable of punching a lethal four to five foot hole in an aircraft wing or fuselage with a direct hit.

While anti-aircraft bombs were strongly advocated at the higher planning levels of the Navy; combat echelons did not embrace it. Since a direct hit was required, Navy fighter pilots much preferred to attack the lightly-armed Japanese bombers with guns as they were able to fire many more accurate bullets than they could have dropped bombs. Also, the attacker using guns had much greater speed and maneuverability to evade any enemy fighters escorting the bombers than flying straight and level to drop the AA bombs. Nonetheless, the weapon saw little use in this intended role as large enemy bomber formations in the Pacific were non-existent by the time the bombs were ready. Over 200,000 AA bombs were produced and were mainly used to supplement strafing attacks against enemy personnel and parked aircraft.

Practice Bombs

General

Practice bombs of various sizes and weights to simulate service bombs were provided for target practice. Practice bombs had a fuse and spotting charge, others were completely inert, and one type of practice bomb was used to provide a colored target on snow-covered bombing ranges. Some were loaded with sand mimic the desired weight while others were manufactured to weight. The practice bomb signal was a cylindrical container filled with black powder or a fluorescent dye. The purpose of the signal was to indicate the point of impact of a practice bomb when dropped either on land or water targets. Black powder signals, upon impact, produced a flash and a puff of smoke. Fluorescent dye signal were actuated by water and produced a slick for spotting purposes.

Bomb, Practice, Miniature, 3 Pound, MK23 MOD1 (AN-Mk23 Mod1)

The Mk23 Mod1 was a streamlined miniature practice bomb 8.25 inches long and 2.18 inches in diameter. It was made of cast iron and its weight without the signal but with firing pin assembly was approximately 2.87 pounds and three pounds with the signal. In order to assemble the spotting charge, it is only necessary to remove the cotter pin in the nose of the bomb, remove the firing pin, insert the signal, and replace the firing pin and cotter pin.

Other Models

Signal, Bomb, Practice, Miniature, Mk4 or Mk6 (fluoresce dye) over water.

Bomb, Practice, Miniature, 4.5 Pound, Mk43 Mod1

Was the same as the Mk 23 type except that it was made of lead and consequently weighed approximately 4.5 pounds.

Bomb, Practice, Miniature, 3 Pound, Mk23 Mod0 and 4.5 Pound, Mk 43 Mod 0

Was the same as the Mk23 Mod1 except that they lacked the sheet metal stabilizing shrouds across the tail vanes.

Types of Practice Bombs: A) 3# M23, B) 23# M73 with parachute, C) 100# M38

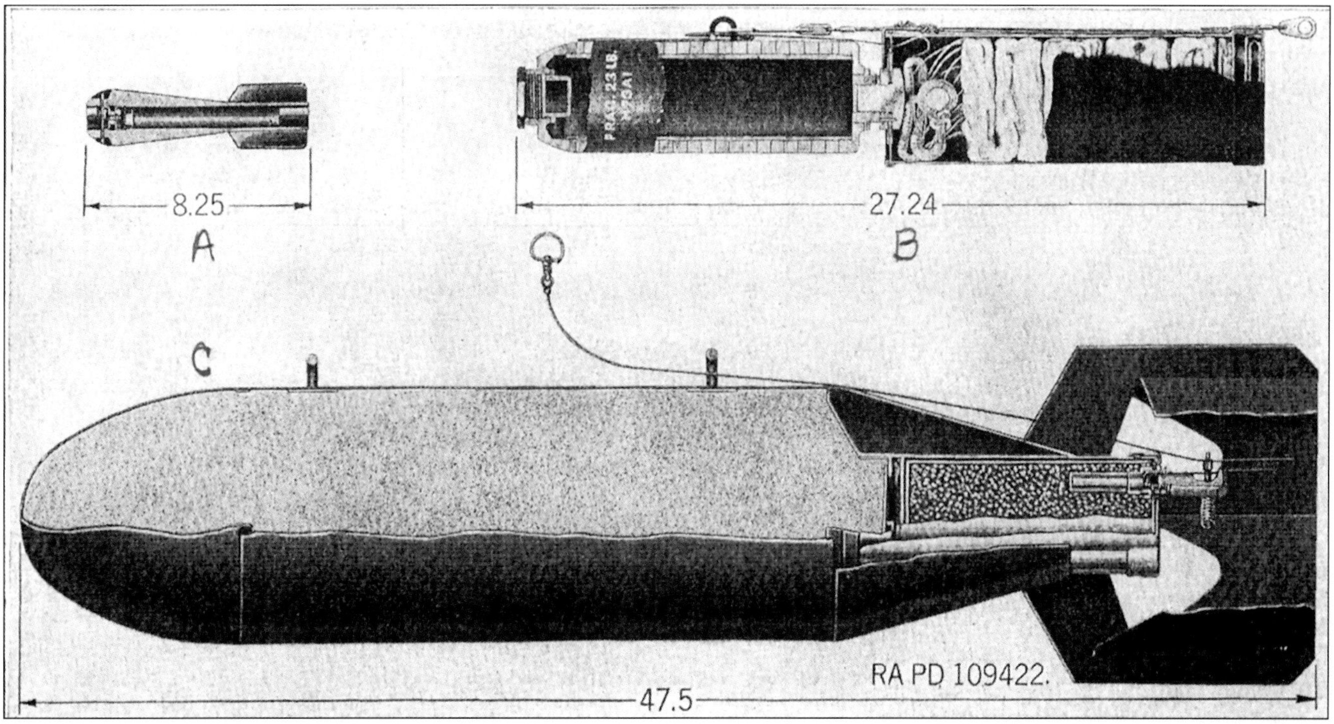

(TM9-1980)

Bomb, Practice, 20 Pound, M48

The M48 was a fin stabilized fragmentation bomb 21.8 inches long and contained two ounces of black powder. It was intended to simulate the M41 20 pound fragmentation bomb.

Bombs, Practice, 23 Pound Size, M71 and M73

These bombs simulated parachute-type Fragmentation Bombs for assembly in clusters or for individual suspension dependent upon the model. There were four models of 23 pound practice bombs: M71, M71A1, M73, and M73A1. They consisted of an empty Fragmentation Bomb body fitted with either the M3 or M4 parachute unit. These bombs did not require fuse or spotting charge since the parachute was ample for spotting purposes. The 23 pound bombs ranged from 26.8 (M71 models) to 28.5 (M73 models) inches long. Both the M71A1 and M73A1 differed from their respective basic models by the addition of a cylindrical shoulder, 0.25 inch long, to the nose of the bomb body. There was no spotting charge installed as the parachute was ample for spotting purposes.

20 pound M48 Practice Bomb being loaded in a A-15. (AAF)

Bomb, Practice 100 Pound, M38A2

The M38A2 was a round-nosed cylindrical bomb designed to simulate GP bombs. It was 47.5 inches long and 8.12 inches in diameter and the fin and body assembly weighed 15 pounds. As issued, the fin was assembled to the body which was empty. At the point of use, 80 pounds of sand were poured in the bomb case, and the spotting charge added to create the complete round which weighed 100 pounds. To fill the bomb with sand the bomb was place upright and filled completely with a uniform sand mixture. The sand load was shaken well so that there was no room for shifting, If a lighter loading was desired dry sawdust or dry sifted ashes were mixed with the with the sand. The spotting charge, Charge, Spotting, Assembly, M1A1, for Practice Bomb, 100-M38A2 (black powder), was installed in a sleeve at the base of the bomb within the fin box. These assemblies consisted of a three pound charge and an integral fuse consisting of an inertia type firing pin and a blank loaded shotgun shell as the primer. The M3 produced a large cloud of black smoke and was authorized over snow-covered ranges. The M4 was authorized for use on range equipped with sonic spotting devices. The M1A1 was used for all other purposes.

Other Models

Bomb, Target, Practice, 100 Pound, M75A1

The M75AI was designed to provide a target reference for practice bombing over snow- covered ranges. The bomb resembled the 100 pound TI red

100 pound Practice Bombs being loaded through doors into an AT-11. (AAF)

smoke bomb M84A1 and consisted of a light sheet metal case, a charge of red iron oxide (hematite), a burster, and a fuse. The bomb was 61.62 inches long and 8.125 inches in diameter, and weighed 101.22 pounds of which 72 pounds was hematite. Upon impact, the burster distributed the charge over an area 35 feet in diameter.

Bomb, Target, Practice, 100 Pound, M7
Was an earlier design of the M76A1. The fin assembly of the M75 was three inches shorter than that assembled to the M75A1 and thus the complete round length of the M75 was only 48.62 inches. The suspension lugs of the M76A1 were designed for greater strength than those installed on the M75. In all other respects the M75 was the same as the M75A1 including component.

Bomb, Practice, 100 Pound, M85 (Concrete)
The M85 was a round nosed cylindrical type bomb constructed completely (except for fin assembly and spotting charge) of reinforced concrete. It simulated the M38A2 in general shape and used the same spotting charges as the M38A2. The M85 (complete) was 38.26 inches long and weighed 103.5 pounds.

Drill Bombs
Drill bombs were provided for the training of ground crews in assembling, fusing, unfusing, and other handling of bombs. Each bomb in service was represented by a corresponding drill bomb which carried the same model designation. The complete round for a drill bomb corresponded exactly to the complete round of the service bomb it simulated except that the components were inert and were sand loaded when necessary. They differed from inert practice bombs in that practice bombs were expendable and drill bombs were not. When necessary to avoid confusion, the bomb type simulated would be indicated in the nomenclature, for example: Cluster, Drill (fragment bomb) was Cluster, Drill (practice bomb).

Gauge Bombs
Gauge bombs were completely inert bombs furnished to the Air Force by the Ordnance Corps for use in gauging and testing aircraft.

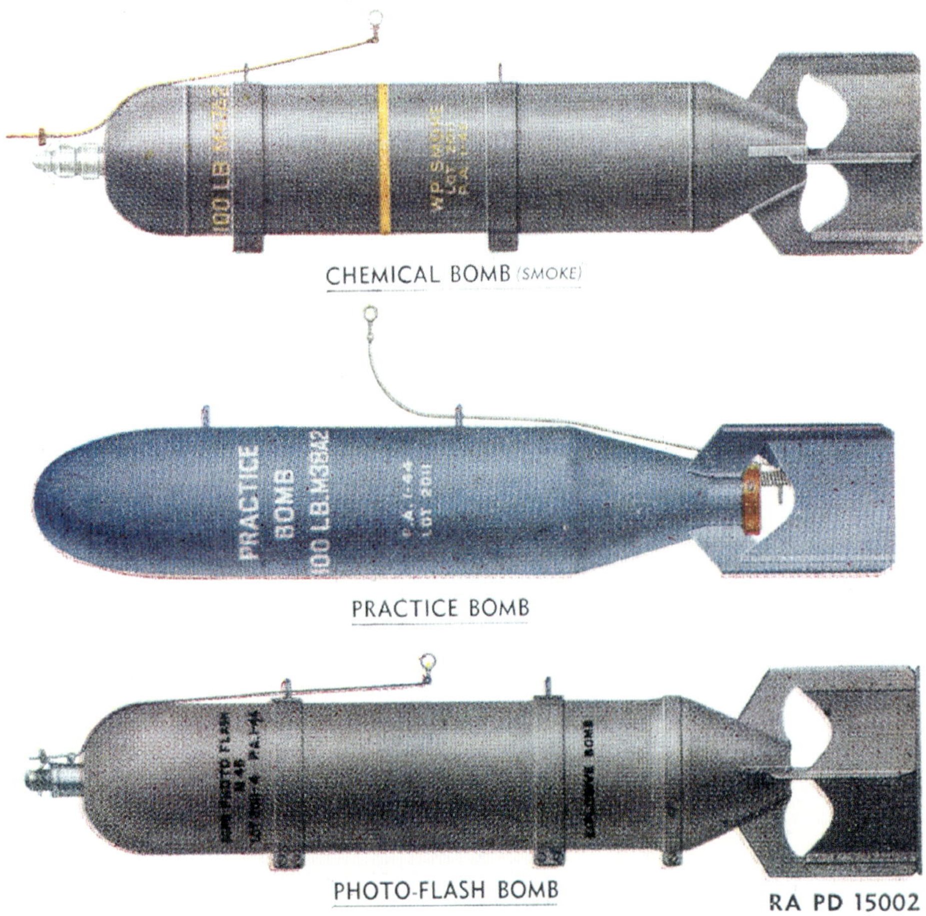

Painting and Marking of Bombs (TM9-1980)

Glossary

Acceleration: The rate of change of velocity.

Actual Range: The horizontal travel of a bomb, from release to impact measured on a level with the point of impact.

AES (Automatic Erection System): Modification of Norden Bombsight to allow for automatic leveling of bombsight without resorting to manual adjustment based on spirit levels.

AFCE (Automatic Flight Control Equipment): Air Corps term for gyroscopically stabilized automatic pilot designed to manipulate aircraft controls through the bombsight in order to maintain level flight during the bombing run. Different from Navy SBAE in serving as general aircraft automatic pilot in addition to bombing operations.

Altimeter Aircraft instrument used for determining vertical distance above sea level.

Altitude: In bombing altitude refers to the altitude or the actual distance of the aircraft above the target.

Area Target: In American usage, a precision target that required a distribution of bombs throughout the area of the target.

Automatic Pilot: Device designed to manipulate the control surfaces of an aircraft automatically to insure level flight free of yaw, pitch, or roll. Also called autopilot.

Automatic Release System: Device on Norden Bombsight allowing for automatic and instantaneous release of bombs when sighting angle and dropping angle indicators coincided.

Ballistic Coefficient: A number assigner to a bomb according to its size, shape, and weight which was a measure of its air resistance of streamlining. It was determined by proving ground testing. The number was based on an arbitrary standard of one.

Bomb Run: The brief part of a bombing mission immediately preceding bomb release. Also called bombing approach.

Calibrated Indicated Air Speed (CIAS): The indicated reading corrected for instrumental installation errors.

CEP (Circular Error Probable): Measure of accuracy and reliability of bombing. Expressed as radius of a circle within which at least 50% of bombs dropped will land.

Circular Error: Distance from a given point of impact, or from the mean point of impact of a pattern of bombs, to the center of the target, measured as the radius of a circle around the point of impact, or the mean point of impact of a pattern of bombs.

Cross Trail: The distance from the track, right or left that the bombfalls due to the fact that the trail was in the direction reverse to the heading and not in reverse to the track.

Dead Reckoning (DR): Estimating an aircraft's position at a given time by calculating heading, time, speed, and wind from a known position. Used in bombing from or through clouds or overcast.

Deflection: Distance measured on the ground from the point directly under an aircraft on a track parallel to the target to the target.

Deflection Error: The distance from a given point of impact or from the mean point of impact of a bombing pattern, to the center of the target measured perpendicular to the direction of approach (normal to the ground track).

Dive Bombing: Descending from high-altitude horizontal flight to low altitude at an angle of between 70° and 90° from the horizontal in Navy usage, or above 30° from the horizontal in Army usage, releasing the bomb or bombs just prior to recovery from the dive.

Drift Angle: The angle, measured in degrees, between the heading and the track.

Dropping Angle (Range Angle): That angle at the aircraft between the vertical and the target that subtended the actual range.

Fuse: Mechanical detonating device for setting off the bursting charge of a bomb. Delayed fuses allowed penetration of the bomb before explosion to produce a greater mining and tamping effect.

Glide Bombing Attachment (GBA): Modification of Norden Bombsight to allow bomb-aiming while in a glide or climb.

Glide Bombing: Descending from higher altitude horizontal flight to lower altitude at an angle between 40 and 50° from the horizontal in Navy usage and less than 30° from the horizontal in AAF usage, releasing the bomb or bombs just prior to recovery from the glide.

Gross Error: Bombing errors of greater than 3,000 feet, not considered in the AAF's accuracy calculations.

Ground Speed: Velocity of an aircraft relative to ground.

Ground Track: Track of an aircraft on the ground.

Gyroscope: Spinning flywheel revolving around an axis mounted to be free to rotate about one or both of two axes perpendicular to each other and to the axis of spin with a tendency to hold a fixed position in space.

Gyrostabilizer: Gyroscope-stabilized device for maintaining level flight.

Heading: The direction in which an aircraft was pointed regardless of its path over the ground.

Horizontal Bombing: Releasing bomb or bombs in level, horizontal flight.

Initial Point (IP): Geographic point located approximately five minutes from a target to provide an exact orientation for the bombing run.

Intervalometer: An electromechanical device for dropping two or more bombs in succession to achieve a predetermined pattern of explosions on the ground. Also see **Train Bombing.**

M-series Bombsights: Army designation for Norden synchronous bombsights, series M-l through M-9.

Mark XI Bombsights: Navy designation for Norden timing bombsights.

Mark XV Bombsights: Navy designation for Norden synchronous bombsights, Mod1 through Mod5, redesignated Mark 15 during World War II.

Mil: Navy method of measuring bombsight accuracy, in terms of angular measurement of errors, equal to a distance of one foot for each 1,000 feet of altitude.

Mining Effect: Increase in destructive power of a bomb by burying in the earth prior to detonation, estimated at approximately 4.5times the power of a bomb's high explosive charge. Effect is achieved through tamping.

Morale Bombing: Attempting to destroy the will of an enemy people by the terror of direct bombing on that people.

MPI (Mean Point of Impact): Center of impact of a pattern of bombs.

NOSMO (Norden Sight Modification): Norden optical bombsights combined with H2X radar.

Overcast: Covering of clouds. Expressed in tenths (1/10th, 2/10th etc.) to represent the degree of vision blockage.

Pattern Bombing: Dropping a number of bombs from a formation of bombers to achieve a relatively uniform distribution for the purpose of saturating a target to improve the probabilities of hitting the target. Also known as carpet bombing. See Saturation bombing.

Pitch: Movement of an airplane around its lateral axis (from wing tip to wing tip).

Precession: The motion of the axis of a spinning body when there is an external force acting on the axis (e.g. the slowing of the rotation of a gyro due to friction)

Precision Target: Targets that, to be destroyed, require either a direct hit by a bomb of the proper size or a hit within a limited distance from there.

Radial Error: Direct linear distance from the target to the point of bomb impact.

Range: Distance measured on the ground from the point directly under an aircraft to the target or point of bomb detonation along the proper deflection track.

Range Angle: Angle formed by line of sight to target and vertical line from aircraft to ground at the time of bomb release.

Range Component of Cross Trial: The distance that the bomb hit over the target due to the bombsight allowed for trail in reverse to the track and not in reverse to the heading as it occurred.

Range Error: The distance from a given point of impact, or from the mean point of impact of a pattern of bombs, to the center of the target, measured parallel to the direction of approach (along the ground track of the aircraft).

Roll: Movement of an airplane around its longitudinal axis (from nose to tail).

S-1 Bombsights: AAF designation for Sperry synchronous bombsights.

Salvo: At the time of release, dropping all bombs instantaneously from an airplane.

Saturation Bombing: Dropping a number of bombs from a formation of bombers to achieve a relatively uniform distribution for the purpose of saturating a target to improve the probabilities of achieving a hit. Also known as carpet bombing. See Pattern bombing.

SBAE (Stabilized Bombing Approach Equipment): Navy term for gyroscopically stabilized automatic pilot designed to manipulate aircraft controls through the bombsight in order to maintain level flight during the bombing run. See AFCE.

Sighting Angle: The angle between the line of sight and the vertical at any moment was the sighting angle at that moment. The sighting angle and dropping angle were the same only at the instant of release.

Slant Range: Straight-line distance from aircraft to target.

Speed of Closing: The velocity of approach of an aircraft relative to the target.

Synchronous Technique: Turning of a wheel or gear in a bombsight mechanism to match the movement of the aircraft over a fixed point on the ground. Measurement of the movement of an aircraft relative to a fixed point on the ground.

Tamping: Filling in above an explosive charge to increase its power. Achieved in mining effect when bombs are dropped from high altitude.

Terminal Velocity: That rate of fall at which the air resistance was equal to the bomb weight and beyond which no further increased in velocity can occur. Terminal velocity could not be used as an expression of the ballistic characteristics of a bomb.

Time of fall: Total time required for a bomb to travel from point of release to point of impact. (The Time of fall was a function of the ballistic coefficient and was set in the Norden Bombsight through a quantity known as disc speed)

Timing Technique: Use of stopwatch to measure the time required to fly over the same object on the ground, measured during the swing of a bombsight's telescope through a predetermined arc or from the movement of the object from the front cross hair to the back cross hair in a bombsight's telescope, in order to determine ground speed. Measurement of a fixed point's movement relative to the aircraft.

Track: The vertical projection the ground of the aircraft's path.

Trail: The horizontal distance in a direction reverse to the aircraft's heading between the point vertically under the aircraft at the instant of impact and the point of impact.

Trail Angle: The angle at which the impact was observed back of the vertical under the aircraft, or angle back of the aircraft which subtended the trail.

Train Bombing: Dropping two or more bombs in succession at predetermined intervals (using an intervalometer) from the same airplane to achieve dispersal across an area target.

Trajectory: The parabolic curved path traced by a bomb from the point of release to the point of impact.

True Air Speed (TAS): The actual speed of an aircraft relative to the air. It was determined using standard navigation computers, by correcting the calibrated air speed for density, using temperature and pressure altitude corrections. It was used for finding the velocity of the wind, the ground speed, and the correct trail setting.

Undercast: Referring more directly to a cloud layer below aircraft.

Velocity: The rate of change of place or position.

Yaw: Movement of an airplane around its vertical axis (from ventral to dorsal).

Bibliography

Magazine Articles and Press Releases

Aeroplane, "Skip Bombing," *Aeroplane*, November 26, 1943.

Churchill, Edward, "What We Learned from the B-19," *Flying*, August 1942

Craig, Gary, "Norden Bombsight," *War Monthly*, No.23, February 1976

Daniels, George (ed), "Know Your Bombs," *Flying Manual*, No.9, 1942.

Department of the Navy, "Radio Proximity (VT) Fuses," *Naval Historical Center*, 2000.

Erdmann, James, "Monroe Leaflet Bomb," *Naval Institute Proceedings.*

Flying, "Radar in Air Combat," *Flying*, October 1945.

Flying, "Spider Silk for Bomb Sights," *Flying*, July 1942.

Gordon, Wayne, "Skip Bombing Pioneer," *Flying*, September 1943.

Hare, Paul, "US Aircraft Production: Success or Scandal?," *Relevance*, Summer 1996.

Impact, "B-29 Strikes," *Impact,* June 1945.

Impact, "Bombing Through Overcast," *Impact*, January 1944.

Impact, "Bombing Through Smoke," *Impact*, September 1944.

Impact, "Fire is Result of Fragmentation,' *Impact*, June 1943.

Impact, "First Hand Accounts Make Minimum Altitude Bombing Lessons More Specific," *Impact*, Vol.1 No.3, June 1943.

Impact, "For Better Bombing, Try Crawfish," *Impact*, June 1945.

Impact, "Kennedy Cocktails," *Impact*, January, 1944.

Impact, "Low Level Attack Rights and Wrongs," *Impact*, November, 1943.

Impact, "Photo Bomb's Night View of Jap Island," *Impact*, August 1943.

Impact, "SHORAN: New Bombing Technique," *Impact*, March 1945.

Impact, "Spike-Bombing Japanese Rails," *Impact*, July 1944.

Johnson, Wray, "Airpower and Restraint in Small Wars," *Aerospace Journal*, Fall 2001.

Kent, John, "Cover Up Combat," *Air News*, January 1945.

Knight, Charlotte, *"Radar Bombing," Air Force*, October 1945.

LeMay, Curtis, "The AAF's War of Research" *Flying*, June, 1946.

McDowell, George, "Bombs Aboard," *Flying*, November 1942.

Morton, Harold, "The VT Fuse," *Army Ordnance*, January-February 1946.

Moye, William, "Developing the Proximity Fuse, and Its Legacy," US Army Materiel Command, February, 2003.

Peck, James, "Radar: Magic Eye that Sees the Invisible," *Popular Science,* January 1945.

Rilling, Frank, "School for Bombardiers," *Flying*, March, 1942.

Salisbury, Winfield, "SCR-584 Jamming," *SMEC Vintage Electrics*, Vol. 2, 1990.

Sharpe, Edward, "Optical and Magnetic Fuses," *SMEC Vintage Electrics*, Vol.2, No.1.

Sharpe, Edward, "Radio Proximity Fuse," *SMEC Vintage Electrics*, Vol.2, No.1.

Stribling, S.R., "The Aerial Bomb," *Flying*, January 1943.

Taylor, George, "Glip Bombing," *Air Force Magazine*, June 1945.

Time, "A Bomb on Norden," *Time*, 1 January 1945.

Wilmore, Cleland, "Practicing Glip Bombing," from History of the 22BS in the CBI, 1997.

Books

Althof, William, *Sky Ships*, Orion, NY, 1990.

Anderton, David, *B-29 Superfortress at War*, Scribner, NY, 1978.

Ayling, Keith, *Bombardment Aviation*, Military Service, PA, 1944.

Birdsall, Steve, *Superfortress*, Squadron/Signal. TX. 1980.

Bowman, Martin, *The B-24 Liberator: 1939-1945*, Wensum, UK, 1979.

Boyce, Joseph, *New Weapons for Air Warfare*, Little Brown, Boston. 1947

Bridgeman, Leonard (Ed.), *Jane's All the World's Aircraft, 1945-46*, Arco, NY, 1970 (reprint).

Brown, Ezra, *Knights of the Air*, Time-Life, NY, 1980.

Budiansky, Stephen, *Airpower*, Viking, NY, 2004.

Campbell, John & Donna, *Consolidated B-24 Liberator*, Schiffer, PA, 1993.

Clark, Ronald, *The Role of the Bomber*, Crowell, NY, 1977.

Clarke, R.M., *Fortress and Superfortress Portfolio*, Brooklands, UK, n.d.

Cooper, Brian, *Story of the Bomber 1914-1945*, Octopus, UK, 1975.

Crane, Conrad, *Bombs, Cities, and Civilians*, U. of Kansas, KS, 1993.

Craven, W.F. & Cate, J.L., *Army Air Forces in World War II, Vol. 1-VII,* University of Chicago, IL, 1953.

Creed, Roscoe, *PBY: The Catalina Flying Boat*, NIP, MD, 198.

Cross, Robin, *The Bombers*, MacMillan, NY, 1987.

Douhet, Giulio, *Command of the Air*, Arno, NY, 1972 (reprint).

Drake, Francis, *Vertical Warfare*, Doubleday, NJ, 1943.

Dubuque, Jean and Gleckner, Robert, *Development of the Heavy Bomber, 1918-1944,* Maxwell AFB, AL, 1951.

Dunlap, Orrin, *Radar: What Radar Is and How It Works,* Harper, NY, 1946.

Erdmann, James, *Leaflet Operations in the Second World War*, Pvt. Printing, CO, 1969.

Finney, Robert, *History of the Air Corps Tactical School, 1920-1940*, Air University, AL, 1955.

Fleischer, Wolfgang, *German Air-Dropped Weapons to 1945*, Midland, UK , 2004.

Gaston, James, *Planning the American Air War*, National Defense U., Wash, DC, 1982.

Gray, C.G. and Bridgman, Leonard, *Jane's All the World's Aircraft 1938*, Arco, NY, n.d. (reprint edition).

Green, William, *Famous Bombers of the Second World War,* Doubleday, NY, 1964.

Greer, Thomas, *Development of Air Doctrine in the Army Air Arm*, 1917-1941, Office of air Force History, Wash DC, 1955.

Hall, R. Cargill, *Case Studies in Strategic Bombing*, University Press of the Pacific. HI, 2005.

Hallion, Richard, *Taking Flight*, Oxford, NY, 2003.

Hansell, Haywood, *Strategic Air War against Germany and Japan*, Office of Air Force History, Wash, DC, 1986.

Hansell, Haywood, *Air Plan That Defeated Hitler*, Higgins-MacArthur, GA, 1972.

Henry, Chris, *Depth Charge*, Pen & Sword, UK , 2005.

Holder, Bill, *B-24 Liberator*, Squadron/Signal, TX, 2005.

Jablonski, Edward, *America in the Air War*, Time-Life Books, NY, 1982.

Jackson, Donald, *The Aeronauts,* Time-Life Books, NY, 1981.

Johnsen, Frederick, *Consolidated B-24 Liberator, Warbird Tech Vol.1,* Specialty, MN, 1996.

Johnson, Edward, *Marine Corps Aviation: The Early Years, 1917-1940*, USMC, Wash. DC, 1977.

Johnson, Herbert, *Wingless Eagle*, UNC, NC, 2004.

Jones, Lloyd, US *Bombers: B-1 to 1980s*, Aero, CA, 1974.

Kemp, Paul, *U-Boats Destroyed*, Arms & Armour, UK , 1999.

Kennett, Lee, *History of Strategic Bombing*, Scribners, NY, 1982.

Lent, Henry, *Bombardier*, MacMillan, NY, 1944.

Ley, Willi, *Bombs and Bombing*, Modern Age Books, NY, 1941.

Lloyd, Alwyn, *B-17 Flying Fortress in Scale & Detail*, Aero, PA, 1986.

Lindqvist, Sven, *A History of Bombing*, New Press, NY, 2000.

Lloyd, Alwyn, Liberator: *America's Global Bomber*, Pictorial Histories, MT, 1993.

Lovell, Bernard, *Echoes of War: Story of H2S Radar*, Hilger, UK, 1991.

Lundstrom, John, *The First Team*, NIP, MD, 1984.

MacBean, John, and Hogben, Arthur, *Bombs Gone*, PSL, UK , 1990.

Maurer, Maurer, *Aviation in the US Army 1919-1939*, Office of Air Force History, Wash DC, 1987.

McArthur, Charles, *Operations Analysis in the US Army Eighth Air Force in World War II*, American Mathematical Society, RI, 1990.

McFarland, Stephen, *America's Pursuit of Precision Bombing 1910-1945*, Smithsonian, Wash., DC, 1995.

Moolman, Valerie, *Road to Kittyhawk*, Time-Life Books, NY, 1981.

Nevin, David, *Architects of Airpower*, Time-Life Books, NY, 1981.

Orriss, Bruce, *When Hollywood Ruled the Skies*, Aero, CA, 1984.

Pace, Steve, *Warbird History: B-25 Mitchell*, Motor Books, WI, 1994.

Pape, Gary & Harrison, Ronald, *Queen of the Midnight Skies*, Schiffer, PA, 1992.

Pardini, Albert, *The Legendary Norden Bombsight*, Schiffer, PA, 1999.

Prendergast, Curtis, *First Aviators*, Time-Life, NY, 1980.

Price, Alfred, *Aircraft vs. Submarine*, Kimber, UK , 1973.

Reynolds, Clark, *Carrier War*, Time-Life Books, NY, 1982.

Rosendahl, Charles, *United States Navy in World War II*, Atlantis, FL, 2007.

Saundby, Robert, *Air Bombardment: The Story of Its Development*, Harper, NY, 1961.

Savage, Mark, *How Planes Fight and Bomb*, Watts, NY, 1943.

Saward, Dudley, *Bomber's Eye,* Cassell, NY, UK, 1959.

Saward, Dudley, *Victory Denied,* Watts, NY, 1987.

Scutts, Jerry, *B-25 Mitchell at War*, Motorbooks, WI, 1983.

Scutts, Jerry, *Marine Mitchells in World War 2*, Phalanx, MN, 1993.

Scutts, Jerry, *North American B-25 Mitchell*, Crowood, UK, 2001.

Seagrave, Sterling, *Soldiers of Fortune*, Time-Life Books, NY, 1981.

Sherry, Michael, *Rise of American Airpower*, Yale, CT, 1987.

Sloan, John, *Route as Briefed*, Argus, OH, 1946.

Spaight, James, *Bombing Vindicated*, Bles, UK, 1944.

Tannehill, Victor, *Boomerang! Story of the 320th Bomb Group*, Pvt. Printing, WI, 1981.

Tannehill, Victor, *Saga of the 320th*, Boomerang, CO, 1984.

Taylor, Blaine, *Fascist Eagle*, Pictorial Histories, MT, 1996.

Thom, Walter, *Brotherhood of Courage*, 305 BGMA, NY, 1986.

Thixton, Marshall, et al, *Bombs Away*, FNP, CT. 1998.

Thompson, Scott, *Douglas A-26 and B-26 Invader*, Crowood, UK, 2002.

Thompson, Scott, *Douglas Havoc and Boston*, Crowood, UK, 2004.

Verrier, Anthony, Bomber Offensive, MacMillan, NY, 1968.

Wolf, William, *The Boeing B-29 Superfortress The Ultimate Look From Drawing Board to VJ-Day*, Schiffer, PA, 2005.

Wolf, William, *The Consolidated B-32 Dominator: The Ultimate Look From Drawing Board to Scrapyard*, Schiffer, PA, 2006.

Wolf, William, *The Douglas B-18 Bolo: The Ultimate Look From Drawing Board to U-Boat Hunter*, Schiffer, PA, 2006.

Wolf, William, *The North American B-25 Mitchell: The Ultimate Look From Drawing Board to Flying Arsenal*, Schiffer, PA, 2008.

Technical Manuals and Reports

AAFAC: *Anti-submarine Manual SOP*, 29 July 1943.

AAFAC: "Anti-submarine Monthly Intelligence Report," August 1943.

AAFSAT, *Handbook for Bombardiers*, Orlando, FL, 19 November 1943.

AAFTC, *Student's Manual Bombing*, Wash. DC, c. 1945.

AAF/ATSC, *Case History of the Norden Bombsight and C-1 Autopilot*, ATSC, Historical Office, OH, 1945.

American Expeditionary Forces, "High Altitude Bombsights," 20 August 1918.

British Bombing Survey Unit, *Strategic Air War against Germany, 1939-45, HMSO*, UK, n.d reprint.

Consolidated Aircraft Corp., *Service and Instruction Manual, Airplane General, B-24D*, 1 October 1942.

Consolidated-Vultee Aircraft Company, *Model B-32: Erection & Maintenance Manual*, Ft. Worth, TX, 1945.

Fifth Air Force HQ, *Report on Skip Bombing*, APP, 14 March 1943.

MacIsaac, David, (ed.), *United States Strategic Bombing Survey*, (10 volumes), Garland, NY, 1976.

Roberts, Lt.Col. Jack, "Radar Performance Report," March 1943.

20th Air Force, *A Statistical Summary of Its Operations Against Japan, June 44-August 45*, 20th AF HQ, October 1945.

20th Air Force, *Problem of the Radar Operator, B-29 Aircraft*, 20AF HQ, 6 October, 1944

US Army, *Ballistic Data Performance of Ammunition*, TM9-1907, July 1948.

US Army, *Ballistic Data Performance of Ammunition*, TM9-1907, 23 September 1944.

USAAC, *Handbook of Service Instructions for the Model B-18 Bombardment Airplanes; TO No. 01-40EA-1*, Air Materiel Command, March 1938.

USAAC, *Handbook of Operation and Flight Instructions for the Model B-18A Bombardment Airplanes; TO No. 01-40EB-1*, Air Materiel Command, November 1940.

USAAC, *Handbook of Operation and Flight Instructions for the Model B-23 Bombardment Airplanes*, Air Materiel Division, OH, 20 July, 1940.

USAAF, *AAF Statistical Digest*, Office of Statistical Control, December 1945.

USAAF, *Anti-submarine Command*, AAFRH No. 7, April, 1945.

USAAF, *B-29 Maintenance and Familiarization Manual*, AAF, 1945

USAAF, *B-29 Parts Catalog, AN 01-20EJ-4*, AAF, 1945

USAAF, *B-29 Structural Repair, AN 01 20EJ-3*, AAF, 1945

USAAF, "Bomber and Fighter Tactics in Combat," Office of the Assistant Chief of Staff, Wash. DC, c. 1943.

USAAF, *Bombs for Aircraft*, TM9-1980. Wash. DC, November 1944.

USAAF, *Erection and Maintenance Instructions for the Army Model B-17G*, TO-01-120EF-2, 1 December 1942.

USAAF, *Erection and Maintenance Instructions for the Army Model B-17G*, AN-01-120EG-2, September 1944.

USAAF, *Erection and Maintenance Instructions for the Army Model B-29, TO, No. 01-20 EJ-2*, 1943

USAAF, *Familiarization Manual for the Operation of the Model B-17F Bombardment Airplane*, 1 February 1943.

USAAF, "Final Report on Minimum Altitude Attack of Water-Borne Surface Vessels with Aircraft Bombs," No.1-42-12, Eglin AFB, FL, 7 December 1942.

USAAF, *Official World War II Guide to the AAF*, Simon Schuster, NY, 1944.

USAAF, *Parts Breakdown: B-26H/J and PBJ-1H/J Aircraft, TO 1B-25J-4*, 15 March 1945.

USAAF, *Pilot's Flight Operating Instructions for the Army Models G, H, J, L, & M,* AN-01-5EE-1, 30 November 1944.

USAAF Training Command, *Student's Manual: Bombing*, 1945.

USAF, *Bombs for Aircraft*, TM9-1980. Wash. DC, 1950.

USN, *Aircraft Smoke Bombs*, OP1050, 28 November, 1945.

War Department, *Bombardier's Information File (BIF)*, March, 1945.

War Department, *Radar Observers' Bombardment Information File (ROBIF),* July, 1945.

XXI Bomber Command, *Combat Crew Manual*, May 1945.

Websites

www.nps,gov/history; "Second Generation Norden Bombsight Vault"

www.geocities.com; "Conditioning"

www.historynet.com; "Lawrence Sperry: Autopilot Inventor and Aviation Innovator"

www.lancaster-archive.com; Major Bombsights used in WW2 by RAF Bomber Command, Henry Black.

www.//341stbombgroup.com; "Method of Glip Bombing"

www.//twinbeech.com; Gates, Robert, "The Norden Bombsight and the US Naval Proving Ground."

www.twinbeech.com/norden_bombsight, Norden Bombsight

www.vo67.org; "The Last Combat Use of the Norden Bombsight"

Videos/DVDs

Norden Bombsight Training Film, Shoestring Educational Productions, CA, 2006.

Sperry S-1 Training Film, Shoestring Educational Productions, CA, 2006.

Index

(Note: Bold type page numbers have photos of subject)

Other Books by William Wolf

Death Rattlers: Marine Squadron VMF-323 over Okinawa

Victory Roll: The American Fighter Pilot and Aircraft in World War II

American Fighter-Bombers in World War II: USAAF Jabos in the MTO and ETO

13th Fighter Command in World War II: Air Combat over Guadalcanal and the Solomons

Boeing B-29 Superfortress: The Ultimate Look: From Drawing Board to VJ-Day

Consolidated B-32 Dominator: The Ultimate Look: from Drawing Board to Scrapyard.

Douglas B-18 Bolo: The Ultimate Look: from Drawing Board to U-Boat Hunter

North American B-25 Mitchell: The Ultimate Look: from Drawing Board to Flying Arsenal

U.S. Aerial Armament in World War II The Ultimate Look: Vol.1: Guns, Ammunition, and Turrets